11th Edition

Higher Education Law in America

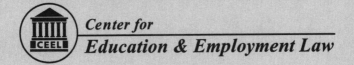

Center for
Education & Employment Law

Center for Education & Employment Law
P.O. Box 3008
Malvern, PA 19355

Copyright © 2010 by Center for Education & Employment Law.
All rights reserved. No part of this publication may be reproduced by any means, electronic
or mechanical, including photocopying, without prior written permission from the publisher.
First edition 2000
Printed in the United States of America

> "This publication is designed to provide accurate and authoritative information in regard
> to the subject matter covered. It is sold with the understanding that the publisher is not
> engaged in rendering legal, accounting or other professional services. If legal advice or
> other expert assistance is required, the service of a competent professional person
> should be sought." *-from a Declaration of Principles jointly adopted by a Committee of
> the American Bar Association and a Committee of Publishers and associations.*

Library of Congress Cataloging-in Publication Data

Higher Education Law in America.

     p. cm.

Includes index.

ISBN 978-1-933043-50-0 (pbk.)

1. Universities and colleges--Law and legislation--United States. I. Center for Education &
Employment Law.

KF4225 .H54 2000

378.73--dc21

                                       00-055074

ISBN 978-1-933043-50-0

Cover Design by Tammi Coxe

Other Titles Published
By Center for Education & Employment Law:

Deskbook Encyclopedia of American School Law
Deskbook Encyclopedia of Employment Law
Deskbook Encyclopedia of Public Employment Law
Federal Laws Prohibiting Employment Discrimination
Legal Update for Teachers: The Complete Principal's Guide
Private School Law in America
Statutes, Regulations and Case Law Protecting Individuals with Disabilities
Students with Disabilities and Special Education
U.S. Supreme Court Education Cases
U.S. Supreme Court Employment Cases

378.73
Ce

TABLE OF CONTENTS

TABLE OF CONTENTS

CHAPTER TWO
Discrimination Against Students

CHAPTER THREE
Athletics and Student Activities

CHAPTER FOUR
Freedom of Speech and Religion

TABLE OF CONTENTS

CHAPTER FIVE
Employment

TABLE OF CONTENTS

TABLE OF CONTENTS

TABLE OF CONTENTS

INTRODUCTION

Higher Education Law in America provides an encyclopedic compilation of federal and state court decisions in the area of college and university law. We have reviewed hundreds of federal and state court decisions involving higher education law and have included the most important ones in this deskbook. The chapters have been arranged topically, and the cases have been presented in an easy-to-use manner.

Each chapter contains explanatory passages at the beginning of each section to help you develop an overall understanding of the legal issues in that particular area. The case summaries have been written in everyday language, and at the start of each case is a brief note highlighting the holding or the significant issues discussed within. Further, the case summaries themselves contain boldface type to emphasize important facts, issues and holdings.

We feel that *Higher Education Law in America* will help you understand your rights and responsibilities under state and federal law. It has been designed with professional educators in mind, but also has tremendous value for lawyers. We hope you will use this book to protect yourself and to gain greater wisdom and understanding. Hopefully, we have succeeded in making the law accessible to you regardless of your level of understanding of the legal system.

Jim Roth, Esq.
Senior Legal Editor
Center for Education & Employment Law

ABOUT THE EDITORS

James A. Roth is editor of *Legal Notes for Education* and *Special Education Law Update,* and a co-editor of *Students with Disabilities and Special Education Law.* He is a graduate of the University of Minnesotaand William Mitchell College of Law, and is admitted to the Minnesota Bar. Mr. Roth is an adjunct faculty member at Hamline University, St. Paul, Minnesota, and an adjunct program assistant professor at St. Mary's University of Minnesota, Twin Cities Campus.

Steve McEllistrem is the Senior Legal Editor at the Center for Education & Employment Law. He is a co-author of Students with Disabilities and Special Education Law and Higher Education Law in America, and is the former managing editor of the monthly newsletter Special Education Law Update. He graduated cum laude from William Mitchell College of Law and received his undergraduate degree from the University of Minnesota. Mr. McEllistrem is admitted to the Minnesota Bar.

Thomas D'Agostino is a managing editor at the Center for Education & Employment Law and is the editor of *Higher Education Legal Alert.* He is a co-author of *Keeping Your School Safe & Secure: A Practical Guide.* He graduated from the Duquesne University School of Law and received his undergraduate degree from Ramapo College of New Jersey. He is a past member of the American Bar Association's Section of Individual Rights and Responsibilities as well as the Pennsylvania Bar Association's Legal Services to Persons with Disabilities Committee. Mr. D'Agostino is admitted to the Pennsylvania Bar.

Curt J. Brown is the Group Publisher of the Center for Education & Employment Law. Prior to assuming his present position, he gained extensive experience in business-to-business publishing, including management of well-known publications such as *What's Working in Human Resources, What's New in Benefits & Compensation, Keep Up to Date with Payroll, Supervisors Legal Update,* and *Facility Manager's Alert.* Mr. Brown graduated from Villanova University School of Law and graduated magna cum laude from Bloomsburg University with a B.S. in Business Administration. He is admitted to the Pennsylvania Bar.

Carol Warner is the editor *EducationTechNews.com* and two monthly newsletters: *School Safety & Security Alert* and *Legal Update for Teachers.* She is also a contributing editor for *HigherEdMorning.com* and *Higher Education Legal Alert.* Before joining the Center for Education & Employment Law, she was an editor for two employment law newsletters: *What's Working in Human*

Resources and *What's New in Benefits & Compensation*. Carol is a graduate of The New York Institute of Technology and holds a Bachelor of Arts in English with an emphasis in professional writing.

Elizabeth A. Wheeler is editor of the monthly newsletter *Private Education Law Report* and the *Private School Law in America* deskbook. She's also a contributing editor for the newsletters *Higher Education Legal Alert* and *School Safety & Security Alert*. A graduate of Macalester College and Capital University Law School, she's a member of the Massachusetts bar. Before joining the Center for Education & Employment Law, she was a legal editor for a South Boston publisher, where she edited employment law and education law newsletters.

How to Use Your Deskbook

We have designed *Higher Education Law in America* in an accessible format for both professional educators and attorneys to use as a research and reference tool toward prevention of legal problems.

Research Tool

As a research tool, our deskbook allows you to conduct your research on two different levels – by topics or cases.

Topic Research

◆ If you have a general interest in a particular **topic** area, our **table of contents** provides descriptive chapter headings containing detailed subheadings from each chapter.

> ➤ For your convenience, we also include the chapter table of contents at the beginning of each chapter.

Example:
For more information on liability, the table of contents indicates that a discussion of instructor misconduct takes place in Chapter Nine, under Intentional Conduct, on page 398:

CHAPTER NINE
School Liability

◆ If you have a specific interest in a particular **issue**, our comprehensive **index** collects all of the relevant page references to particular issues.

> **Example:**
> For more information on student activities, the index provides references to all of the cases dealing with student activities instead of only those cases dealing with fraternities and sororities:
>
> Statewide testing, 46-47, 355-356
> **→** Student activities
>   Fraternities and sororities, 130-132
>   Hazing, 135-138
>   Injuries, 134-135
>   Operation and school supervision, 129-130
>   Organizational liability, 130-132
> · Student activity fees, 171-173

Case Research

◆ If you know the **name** of a particular case, our **table of cases** will allow you to quickly reference the location of the case.

> **Example:**
> If someone mentioned a case named *Godinez v. Siena College,* looking in the table of cases, which has been arranged alphabetically, the case would be listed under section "G" and would be found on p. 406 of the text.
>
> **G**
>
> Glenn v. Univ. of Southern California, 409
> Glover v. Jackson State Univ., 376
> **→** Godinez v. Siena College, 406
> Gonzaga Univ. v. Doe, 43, 44, 45
> Gonzales v. North Carolina State Univ., 84
> Gordon v. Purdue Univ., 9

How to Use Your Deskbook

✓ Each of the cases summarized in the deskbook also contains the case citation, which will allow you to access the full text of the case if you would like to learn more about it. See *How to Read a Case Citation,* p. 499.

◆ If your interest lies in cases from a **particular state**, our **table of cases by state** will identify the cases from your state and direct you to their page numbers.

Example:
    If cases from California are of interest, the table of cases by state, arranged alphabetically, lists all of the case summaries contained in the deskbook from that state.

CALIFORNIA

Barnhart v. Cabrillo Community College, 391
Bessard v. California Community
    Colleges, 154
Brown v. Li, 166

✓ Remember, the judicial system has two court systems — state and federal court — which generally function independently from each other. See *The Judicial System,* p. 495. We have included the federal court cases in the table of cases by state according to the state in which the court resides. However, federal court decisions often impact other federal courts within that particular circuit. Therefore, it may be helpful to review cases from all of the states contained in a particular circuit.

Reference Tool

As a reference tool, we have highlighted important resources which provide the framework for many legal issues.

◆ If you would like to see specific wording of the **U.S. Constitution**, refer to **Appendix A**, which includes relevant provisions of the U.S. Constitution such as the First Amendment (freedom of speech and religion) and the Fourteenth Amendment (which contains the Equal Protection Clause and the Due Process Clause).

How to Use Your Deskbook

◆ If you would like to review **U.S. Supreme Court decisions** in a particular subject matter area, our topical list of U.S. Supreme Court case citations located in **Appendix B** will be helpful.

The book also contains a glossary, which provides definitions of legal terms and certain statutes. The glossary can be found on p. 501.

We hope you benefit from the use of *Higher Education Law in America.* If you have any questions about how to use the deskbook, please contact James Roth at jroth@pbp.com.

TABLE OF CASES

TABLE OF CASES

TABLE OF CASES

TABLE OF CASES

TABLE OF CASES

TABLE OF CASES

TABLE OF CASES BY STATE

COLORADO

CONNECTICUT

MINNESOTA

MISSISSIPPI

MISSOURI

TABLE OF CASES BY STATE

TABLE OF CASES BY STATE

WYOMING

CHAPTER ONE

Student Rights

I. THE CONTRACTUAL RELATIONSHIP

Public institutions are government entities which have constitutional due process obligations to provide students notice and an opportunity to be heard. By contrast, private institutions have a contractual relationship with students, and need only provide the procedures they specifically promise to provide.

A. Breach of Contract

◆ *A Pennsylvania public university had certain due process obligations to its students, but its student handbook did not constitute a binding contract.*

The student claimed she was unfairly dismissed from a clinical practicum for violating safety rules. She had to withdraw from another practicum and, instead of waiting a year to retake them, she completed the requirements at a private university. The student sued the State System of Higher Education for breach of contract, alleging the university did not follow the procedures set out in its handbook when it dismissed her from the practicum. After deciding the handbook constituted a binding contract between the parties, the state Board of Claims held it had no authority over state contracts to provide education.

On appeal, the Commonwealth Court of Pennsylvania held the claim was properly dismissed because the board lacked jurisdiction (authority) to hear the dispute. **But the board incorrectly found a public institution's handbook forms a binding contract with a student.** Instead, the court held the board lacked jurisdiction over the claim because the handbook was not a contract. While private institutions have a contractual relationship with students, Pennsylvania public institutions have a due process obligation to provide students notice and an opportunity to be heard. **The court held a public university handbook did not constitute a contract** and affirmed the decision. *Tran v. State System of Higher Educ.*, 986 A.2d 179 (Pa. Commw. Ct. 2009).

◆ *An expelled graduate student had no constitutional right to stay in the Indiana University School of Optometry.*

The student received two D+ grades and an incomplete grade. He claimed two professors assigned him poor grades for purely arbitrary reasons and that a third professor refused to let him take an exam. As a result, the university did not allow him to take clinical rotations that were degree requirements. The student failed a clinical rotation and was dismissed from the program. He sued the university board and several employees in a federal district court, which dismissed the case. On appeal, the U.S. Court of Appeals, Seventh Circuit, found **students generally have no federal constitutional right to remain in a graduate institution**. An exception applies if the student can show an implied contract. But to claim an implied contract was formed, the student must identify some promise from the university that was not honored. This promise could be made in a catalogue or some other written material.

The student said the promises he was relying on had been posted around campus in university bulletins and flyers. But he did not specify what they were, instead claiming the specific promises would be unearthed during the pretrial investigation and information-sharing procedure called "discovery." As a result, the court held the case had been properly dismissed. Repeating language from the lower court decision, the court held that allowing the case to proceed without specific facts would "sanction a fishing expedition costing both parties, and the court, valuable time and resources." *Bissessur v. Indiana Univ. Board of Trustees*, 581 F.3d 599 (7th Cir. 2009).

◆ *A dental school student who was "de-enrolled" due to a billing error could pursue a breach of contract claim against New York University (NYU).*

After enrolling in NYU's dental school in 1993, the student took a break. He was granted readmission as a part-time student in 2002-03. When NYU granted readmission, it advised the student he would be assessed tuition fees based on the number of credits he took. Due to a billing error that NYU later admitted was its own fault, the student was overcharged tuition. Although staff members assured him the mistake would be corrected, NYU mailed him delinquency notices and informed him he was de-enrolled for failure to meet financial obligations. Despite being de-enrolled, the student continued to attend his classes and passed his final exams. But when he asked a professor for his final grade, she told him she was not allowed to release it due to his failure to pay tuition. The student then paid the allegedly outstanding amount and learned for the first time that he had been de-enrolled. After his request to be re-enrolled was denied, he sued NYU in a state court for breach of contract.

Although the trial court ruled against the student, the New York Supreme Court, Appellate Division, reversed the decision. It held a lawsuit for breach of contract was the appropriate recourse. When NYU readmitted the student, it promised him he would be billed for tuition on a per-credit basis. **Despite this representation, NYU failed to bill the student as promised and to promptly correct the overcharge.** Moreover, NYU did not notify the student that he had been de-enrolled, even though its own handbook said he should have been so advised. NYU failed to grant him a degree after he had fully paid the correct tuition amount. The trial court's ruling was reversed. *Eidlisz v. New York Univ.*, 61 A.2d 473, 876 N.Y.S.2d 400 (N.Y. App. Div. 2009).

◆   *Virginia's highest court rejected a claim by female students that a college for women that transitioned to a coeducational facility breached a contract.*

The college was established in 1891. It remained a predominantly female institution until 2006, when its trustees decided to make it coeducational. A group of students sued the college in a state court, claiming the college breached a contract that included a promise of a four-year education at a women's college. They relied on an academic catalogue which stated that the college offered "an education fully and completely directed toward women." The students claimed they chose the school specifically because it provided a single-sex environment. The college filed a motion seeking documentation on the existence of a contract to keep the school from going coed. The students produced letters of offers of admission, e-mails and other correspondence.

The trial court dismissed the complaint, and the students appealed to the Supreme Court of Virginia. On appeal, the students repeated their claim that a contract was formed when they accepted offers of admission, paid tuition and registered for classes. The court rejected the claims, explaining that **to be a legally binding contract, an agreement must be definite as to all terms, identify the subject matter involved, and state essential commitments and agreements relating to the subject matter**. In addition, contract terms must be "clear, definite and explicit." None of the evidence demonstrated the existence of a contract that would require the college to remain all-female while the students were enrolled. There was no language in any document indicating a clear promise by the college to remain predominantly female for the duration of their studies. As the students failed to prove the existence of contract, the court affirmed the judgment for the college. *Dodge v. Trustees of Randolph-Macon Woman's College*, 276 Va. 1, 661 S.E.2d 801 (Va. 2008).

◆   *A Florida university could change its academic requirements without being in breach of contract, as long as it did not act arbitrarily or capriciously.*

When the student began his osteopathic medical program at the university, he received a student handbook describing the program requirements. Students had to complete two years of course work and clinical rotations, and pass the Comlex Level I exam. The handbook specified that all graduation requirements were to be completed within six years, but it stated the university reserved the right to change its rules, policies and procedures. The student failed five required courses in his first year. During the next academic year, the university changed the handbook to require all students to pass both the Comlex Level II and Comlex Level I exams. The student did not pass the Level II exam, and he was dismissed from the program for failing to meet the six-year deadline.

The student sued the university in a state court for breaching an implied contract created by the handbook. The court denied the university's pretrial motion for a directed verdict, and a jury found he should get $819,000. Appeal reached a Florida district court of appeal, which held that the trial court should have granted the university's motion for a directed verdict. The relationship between the university and student was contractual, and there was an implied condition that students would conform to university rules and regulations. **The handbook gave the dean discretion to revise or modify policies at any time. Courts give great deference to decisions of colleges and universities regarding their degree requirements.** The university could change its academic requirements, as long as it did not act arbitrarily or capriciously. The denial of the motion for a directed verdict was reversed. *Jallali v. Nova Southeastern Univ.*, 992 So.2d 338 (Fla. Dist. Ct. App. 2008).

♦ *A New Jersey university did not breach a contract by dismissing a nursing student for failing to meet academic requirements.*

The student was part of a group assigned to write a paper and deliver an oral presentation. But when the group gave the presentation, the instructor decided his contribution did not relate to the topic. Other members of the group complained to the instructor, who assigned him a zero for the oral presentation. As a result, the student failed the class. He appealed to a student affairs committee, which found he should have received an incomplete grade and been allowed to complete an alternative assignment. When the student submitted this assignment, it did not meet applicable specifications, and his zero grade stood.

At a meeting with a dean and professor, the student refused to retake the course and was later dismissed from the nursing program. He sued the university and officials in a state court for breach of contract, intentional infliction of emotional distress and violation of his due process rights. Among other things, **he claimed the course syllabus distributed by the class instructor constituted an enforceable contract**. The court held for the university, and the student appealed. A New Jersey Appellate Division Court upheld the finding of no breach of contract. As the emotional distress claim lacked merit and there was no violation of due process, the judgment for the university was affirmed. *Yarcheski v. Univ. of Medicine and Dentistry of New Jersey*, No. C-358-06, 2008 WL 5133687 (N.J. Super. Ct. App. Div. 12/9/08)

♦ *The District Court of Appeal of Florida held a university did not exercise its discretion arbitrarily by dismissing a student.*

The student attended a master's program in social work. After he received a failing grade in a field practicum course, the university dismissed him. The student was granted two administrative appeals. Both times, his failing grade and dismissal were affirmed. The student sued the university, alleging it denied him due process because the university acted in bad faith when it dismissed him. He claimed the dean of the school of social work and a member of the student review and termination committee were biased against him.

The state court of appeal found no evidence to support the student's claims. **The court held university authorities have wide discretion in determining whether a student has met academic requirements. Courts will not interfere unless school authorities acted in bad faith or exercised their discretion arbitrarily.** The court of appeal found the student's field instructor indicated the student needed improvement in 10 out of 38 areas evaluated. The field director also noted his difficulties with staff and clients at the agency where he performed his field practicum. The student's clients were unhappy with his performance and demeanor and did not want to participate in any more sessions with him. For all these reasons, the court of appeal held the university did not act in bad faith or exercise its discretion arbitrarily when it dismissed the student. It affirmed the judgment. *Karlan v. Florida Int'l Univ. Board of Trustees*, 927 So.2d 91 (Fla. Dist. Ct. App. 2006).

◆ *The Supreme Judicial Court of Maine held a handbook reservation clause, which allowed a college to unilaterally change the terms of its handbook without notice to students, defeated a student's breach of contract claim.*

A college appeals board found a male student guilty of sexual assault. The board prohibited him from living in campus housing, eating in college dining halls, and being on campus after 11:00 p.m. It placed him on permanent disciplinary probation. The student sued the college in a state court for breach of contract. The court found the college did not breach any contractual obligation to the student and held for the school. The student appealed, arguing the college breached its contract because the decision by the college to allow the female student to appeal did not meet his reasonable expectations. He said the disciplinary process described in the student handbook did not authorize the female student's appeal to the dean's hearing board.

On appeal, the Supreme Judicial Court of Maine held the handbook was not a contract *per se*. **A reservation clause in the handbook allowed the college to unilaterally change handbook terms without notice to the students.** As a result, the court affirmed the judgment for the college. *Millien v. Colby College*, 874 A.2d 397 (Me. 2005).

◆ *The U.S. Supreme Court held that the doctrine of substantial performance applied to contracts in an academic setting.*

An overweight Rhode Island student joined a college's nursing program in her sophomore year. During her junior year, the college began pressuring her to lose weight. She received a failing grade in a clinical nursing course, for reasons related to her weight rather than her performance. By school rules, the failing grade should have resulted in expulsion from the program. However, the school offered her a contract that allowed her to stay in the program if she lost at least two pounds per week. She failed to lose the weight, was asked to withdraw from the program, and transferred to another nursing program. She sued the college in a federal district court, alleging that it had violated the Rehabilitation Act and that it had breached an implied contract to educate her. She was awarded damages for breach of contract. The jury determined that the student had substantially performed her obligations under the contract so as to enable her to prevail on her claim against the school. Appeal reached the U.S. Supreme Court. The Supreme Court held that the court of appeals should have reviewed the case *de novo* (as if hearing it for the first time). The appellate court should not have deferred to the district court's determination of what state law would be. Instead, **it should have examined the doctrine of substantial performance to ascertain whether it ought to be applied to a contract in an academic setting**. The Court reversed and remanded the case. *Salve Regina College v. Russell*, 499 U.S. 225, 111 S.Ct. 1217, 113 L.Ed.2d 190 (1991).

B. Fraudulent Misrepresentation

In Alabama, a party can be held liable for fraud even where a misrepresentation is "made by mistake and innocently," if another party acted on the misrepresentation and suffered harm. See Craig v. Forest Institute of Professional Psychology, *713 So.2d 967 (Ala. Civ. App. 1997).*

◆ *The Court of Appeals of Ohio upheld a decision to reject fraud claims by two students in a surgical technician program who claimed their college denied them externships during their last term of study.*

At the time the students completed their classroom work, the college told them that no externship sites were available. When the students were finally placed in externships, both of them were asked to consider transferring into different programs. They both left the college and later filed a state court action against it for breach of contract, fraud and violation of a state consumer sales practices act. To support their claims for fraud, the students claimed the college knew it was enrolling more students than it could place in hospital externships.

After the court awarded pretrial judgment to the college, the students appealed to the state court of appeals. According to the court, **the placement delay may have reflected poor planning by the college, but it did not support a claim based on knowing or false representation**. On the other hand, the court reversed the trial court's decision to reject claims raised under the state consumer sales practices act. To constitute a violation of the act, conduct does not need to rise to the level of fraud, negligence or breach of contract. In this case, a fact issue was present as to whether the college unfairly or deceptively represented that externships would be available during the final term of the program. The judgment was reversed in part, and the case was returned to the trial court for further proceedings. *Hacker v. National College of Business and Technology*, 186 Ohio App.3d 203, 927 N.E.2d 38 (Ohio Ct. App. 2010).

◆ *A Texas chiropractic student failed to convince a court that a college made misrepresentations about its graduation requirements.*

Among other requirements, the college required students to complete 10 trimesters of work. The student completed her 10 trimesters, but the college refused to award her a degree because she failed a clinical exit examination.

According to the student, the college told her before she took the examination that her application for graduation had already been approved. She also said a college official told her before she took that examination that she should not worry about passing it. The student sued the college in a state court, raising a claim under a state consumer protection statute. She added claims for fraud, negligent misrepresentation and equitable estoppel. The court ruled for the college, and the student appealed. The Court of Appeals of Texas held all four of the claims had a common element of reliance, meaning she could not prevail unless she showed she relied on misrepresentations by the college. However, **the student did not show she relied on any alleged misrepresentation made by college officials and could not prevail on any of her claims**. As a result, the trial court judgment was affirmed. *Wood v. Texas Chiropractic College*, No. 01-07-00952-CV, 2008 WL 2854268 (Tex. Ct. App. 7/24/08).

◆   *A federal district court held a Colorado student was required to arbitrate his claim that a school falsely represented the nature of one of its programs.*

The student claimed the college made false representations about its surgical technologist program. When he enrolled, he signed an agreement indicating that any dispute arising from his enrollment was to be resolved through arbitration. Relying on the agreement, the college filed a motion to compel arbitration. **The Federal Arbitration Act states that contractual arbitration provisions are generally "valid, irrevocable, and enforceable."** Parties can go to court to seek an order requiring enforcement of a contractual arbitration provision. Since the student showed no unusual circumstances justifying removal of the arbitration requirement, the college's motion to compel arbitration was granted. *Rodriguez v. Corinthian Colleges*, No. 07-cv-02648-EWN-MJW, 2008 WL 2979505 (D. Colo. 8/1/08).

◆   *Students who claimed they were fraudulently induced to enroll in a Texas vocational college had to pursue their claims via arbitration.*

Students enrolled at the San Antonio College of Medical and Dental Assistants agreed in writing to use arbitration to resolve any dispute relating to enrollment. Without pursuing arbitration, 45 students sued the college in state court, claiming it falsely told them they would be eligible for licenses as journeymen or master electricians upon graduation. They sought refunds of their tuition and other costs. A state trial court refused to compel arbitration, and the Court of Appeals of Texas affirmed the judgment.

The case reached the Supreme Court of Texas, which held that the students were required to arbitrate their claims. State law required vocational schools to provide refunds to students who were fraudulently induced to enroll by the school's owner or representatives. **The court held that fraudulent inducement claims arise from general obligations imposed by law, not the contract.** A party cannot avoid an agreement to arbitrate merely by recasting a contractual dispute as a tortious interference claim against a company's owner, officer, agent or affiliate. Allowing such a practice would make it too easy to avoid arbitration agreements. Parties who clearly agree to arbitration are bound to use it. *In re Kaplan Higher Educ. Corp.*, 235 S.W.3d 206 (Tex. 2007).

◆ *A student did not show breach of contract or fraudulent misrepresentation by a college that accused him of selling copies of an upcoming examination.*

After an investigation and hearing, the college concluded the student had engaged in academic misconduct and dismissed him from the program. He sued the college for breach of contract, fraudulent misrepresentation, and fraudulent nondisclosure. The student filed a separate breach of contract claim against the teacher of the class in which he was accused of cheating. A jury ruled in his favor on the fraudulent misrepresentation claim against the college and awarded him $20,000 in damages. It also ruled for the student on his breach of contract claim against the teacher and awarded him $10,000 on that claim. The court set aside the verdict against the college on the fraudulent misrepresentation claim. On the breach of contract and fraudulent nondisclosure claims against the college, the jury found against the student.

The Supreme Court of Missouri reversed the judgment on the breach of contract claim against the teacher. The claim was based on the employment contract between the teacher and the college, and the student was not entitled to third-party beneficiary status under it. The court upheld the trial court's decision to set aside the fraudulent misrepresentation verdict. Any alleged misrepresentation regarding the disciplinary hearings did not harm the student because he did almost nothing to prepare for them. **Because the student did not present evidence showing he relied on representations that the college would follow certain due process procedures at his appeal hearing, he could not prove fraudulent misrepresentation.** *Verni v. Cleveland Chiropractic College,* 212 S.W.2d 150 (Mo. 2007).

◆ *The Indiana Court of Appeals held a student had to show a university acted with a dishonest purpose in order to prove bad faith.*

An Indiana student who was pursuing a doctorate in economics received an "Unsatisfactory" grade in a thesis research course. An economics policy committee met and told the student he would be dismissed from the doctoral program if he did not find a new faculty advisor and submit a plan and timetable for completing his thesis. Despite receiving an extension, the student did not complete these tasks. The economics policy committee dismissed him from the doctoral program. After exhausting internal appeals with the university, the student sued the university and the professor who had assigned an unsatisfactory grade for breach of contract, negligence and defamation. A state trial court held the university's actions constituted academic judgment that it would not disturb, absent bad faith. The court later held the contractual relationship between the parties and the question of bad faith required further consideration. The student received permission to file an amended complaint. He responded by filing an amended complaint alleging a claim of bad faith.

The court dismissed the amended complaint. On appeal, the state court of appeals upheld the dismissal of the amended complaint. **Courts do not rigidly apply contract law principles to education disputes, even though the relationship between students and educational institutions is contractual in nature.** Courts recognize that implied contracts exist between students and universities, and the nature of contractual terms varies. **To prove bad faith, the student had to show more than bad judgment or negligence. Instead, he**

needed to show the university acted with a dishonest purpose. The amended complaint did not support a claim of bad faith. It simply alleged that the university failed to comply with obligations set forth in the policies and procedures manual and the university bulletin. As the complaint did not support a claim for bad-faith breach of contract, the court upheld the lower court's decision. *Gordon v. Purdue Univ.*, 862 N.E.2d 1244 (Ind. Ct. App. 2007).

◆ *A federal district court in New York refused to dismiss students' claims that a university engaged in deceptive business practices and breached a contract when it made changes to its drama program, including a change in its name.*

Current and former students sued the university, claiming the changes were deceptive business practices and in breach of contract. To address the contract claim, the court referred to a catalogue the university published every other year to promote the drama program. The catalogue included a policy relating to changes, which said course offerings, academic requirements, degree programs, tuition, fees and faculty were subject to change at any time.

The court held "the relationship between a university and its students is contractual." It would be inappropriate to grant judgment to the students on the claim that the change in the name of the program was a breach of contract. Although the catalogue clearly stated that degree programs were subject to change, it also emphasized the prestige and uniqueness of the program and promised students they would receive diplomas bearing the previous name. Under these circumstances, a factual issue existed as to whether the university breached its contract with the students when it changed the name of the program. The court found a factual question as to whether the catalogue was likely to mislead a reasonable consumer and as to whether it fully disclosed the university's right to change the program name. *Deen v. New School Univ.*, No. 05 Civ. 7174 KMW, 2007 WL 1032295 (S.D.N.Y. 3/27/07).

◆ *Two university employees could be sued for fraud where they allegedly misled a student about a music media program.*

A student enrolled at an Alabama university because its catalogue indicated it had a music media major and "state of the art" equipment. However, the student encountered problems when he tried to take classes in music media. His academic advisor first required him to take the university's core-requirement courses, then told him the university was seeking an instructor to teach music media classes. When the student was finally placed in a "basic recording" course, the instructor missed the first four classes. Another instructor later showed him the university's outdated recording studio, in which some of the equipment did not work. He informed the student that he was not qualified to teach basic recording. The student withdrew from school and sued the university, its board, a number of officials and his advisor for breach of contract and fraud. A state court dismissed his claims, but the Supreme Court of Alabama reinstated fraud claims against the advisor and a vice president of academic affairs. **There was evidence that they made misrepresentations to the student with the intent to deceive him, and that he relied on those misrepresentations.** *Byrd v. Lamar*, 846 So.2d 334 (Ala. 2002).

C. Tuition Issues

State laws creating favorable in-state tuition rates are valid insofar as they create a presumption of residency based on reliable indicators. However, an inflexible or improperly applied presumption is open to challenge.

For tuition cases involving undocumented alien students, please see Chapter 10, Section I.B of this volume.

◆   *A state court upheld a determination by Florida Atlantic University (FAU) that a student did not qualify for resident tuition rates.*

After graduating from a Michigan high school, the student went to Florida to attend a community college. Three years later, she transferred to FAU. After a year at FAU, the student took steps to qualify as a resident of the state for in-state tuition rates. She obtained a Florida driver's license and executed a declaration of domicile. FAU denied the student's application to reclassify her as a Florida resident for tuition purposes, and she commenced a state court action against FAU. A Florida district court of appeal explained that a student seeking to qualify for resident tuition rates must show Florida residency for the previous 12 months, and that Florida is the student's permanent domicile. In this case, there was sufficient evidence to support FAU's conclusion that residency in Florida was merely incident to the student's school enrollment.

Although the student had been in the state for the previous 12 months, she did not produce enough evidence to show she intended to reside in Florida permanently. **She did not own real property in the state or have a vehicle registered there, and she did not work there on a full-time basis.** In addition, the student did not get her Florida driver's license or execute a declaration of domicile until just a month before she applied for residency reclassification. When she initially applied to FAU in 2007, she said she was not a Florida resident. This statement contradicted the student's later claim that she intended to become a resident in 2005. There was enough evidence to support FAU's decision, and the court affirmed it. *Hallendy v. Florida Atlantic Univ.*, 16 So.3d 1057 (Fla. Dist. Ct. App. 2009).

◆   *A student seeking in-state tuition rates for her program at Mississippi State University (MSU) was unable to pursue federal claims due to immunity.*

After gaining admission to MSU's College of Veterinary Medicine, the student signed a contract to pay in-state or out-of-state tuition as determined by the school's admissions committee. Soon after her marriage to an active-duty member of the United States Air Force, her husband was permanently transferred to a military base in Mississippi. The student asked the school to change her residency status from out-of-state to in-state. Her request was denied several times. MSU finally changed the rate for the student's final year of school. By then, she had paid about $85,000 more in tuition than she would have paid otherwise. The student sued MSU in a federal district court for violating her federal due process and equal protection rights.

MSU moved to dismiss the case based on Eleventh Amendment immunity. According to the court, the Eleventh Amendment bars suits against non-consenting states by private individuals in federal court. This immunity extends to state departments and agencies that can properly be deemed to be "arms of the state." The court concluded that **Mississippi State University is an arm of the state for purposes of Eleventh Amendment immunity** analysis. As a result, the university was immune to the federal claims. As MSU never consented to a state law claim against it in federal court, the court had no authority to consider the state law claims. The federal claims were dismissed, and the state law claims were dismissed without prejudice. *Yoder v. Mississippi State Univ.*, No. 1:09CV7-D-D, 2010 WL 364466 (N.D. Miss. 2/1/10).

◆ *The Virginia Supreme Court held a student did not present sufficient evidence of residence to overcome a presumption that he was in the state just to attend law school.*

The student completed a graduate degree program in Indiana, then moved to Virginia. During his first year at a Virginia law school, he paid an out-of-state tuition rate while taking steps to establish residency in Virginia. He registered his car in Virginia, obtained a state driver's license, and registered as a voter. Before the start of his second year, the student asked the school to reclassify him as a state resident. While over a year had passed since he moved to the state, the law school said he failed to prove he had established and maintained a Virginia domicile for a year before the start of his second year of study.

The student's appeals to the school failed, but a state circuit court reversed its decision. The case reached the Virginia Supreme Court. The court held that to qualify for in-state tuition in Virginia, students must prove they have been domiciled in the state for at least a year and have abandoned any previous domicile. Importantly, **the law specifies that an out-of-state student who attends school in Virginia is presumed to be in the state for the purpose of attending school and not a resident of the state**. Students cannot prove they have become Virginia residents simply by "performing acts which are auxiliary to fulfilling educational purposes" or acts that are "required or routinely performed by temporary residents." State law sets out a number of factors to be considered in determining whether a student has established residency for tuition purposes, including income taxes, driver's license, motor vehicle registration, voter registration, employment, property ownership, sources of financial support, military records and employment offers following graduation. After reciting these factors, the court found the university had reasonably concluded the student was in Virginia primarily to attend law school. The school's nonresidency determination was reinstated. *George Mason Univ. v. Floyd*, 654 S.E.2d 556 (Va. 2008).

◆ *A New Jersey university wrongly denied its in-state tuition rate to an applicant based solely on the residence of her out-of-state parents.*

Rutgers University denied a student's request for the in-state tuition rate because she was financially dependent on her parents and they resided outside the state. The student provided information detailing her ties with the state and her intention to stay there. She also noted that under state law, any individual who has lived in the state for 12 months is presumed to be entitled to the in-state rate. The university rejected her arguments. The student appealed to a state court, which held for Rutgers.

Appeal reached the Supreme Court of New Jersey, which held that state law established a presumption of residency for anyone who lived in the state for 12 months. Because the student had lived in the state for over four years when she enrolled at Rutgers, she was entitled to the presumption. While Rutgers argued that its interpretation established a counter-presumption of non-domicile when an individual is financially supported by out-of-state parents, this was plainly at odds with the statute. **The court said the regulation merely neutralized the presumption of domicile when a student is financially dependent on out-of-state parents.** Instead of tipping the presumption against residency, financial dependence on out-of-state parents eliminated the presumption of residency. It did not create a contrary presumption of nonresidency. The case was remanded so that Rutgers could more fully consider the evidence relating to whether the student was entitled to the in-state tuition rate. *Shim v. Rutgers*, 191 N.J. 374, 924 A.2d 465 (N.J. 2007).

◆   *Arizona's highest court refused to address a constitutional challenge to the state's decision to substantially raise tuition rates at state universities.*

The Arizona Constitution requires state universities to provide instruction "as nearly free as possible," and provides for the state board of regents to set tuition and fees. The board approved a request from state universities to increase tuition rates by over 39% for the 2003-2004 academic year. Four students at the University of Arizona sued the board and the state legislature to challenge the increase, saying it violated the "as nearly free as possible" constitutional provision. A state court dismissed the claims, finding the board and legislature had state law immunity. The case reached the Arizona Supreme Court, which held the case presented a nonjusticiable political question that was not suited for resolution by the judicial branch. **Decisions about setting university tuition were entrusted by the state's constitution to other government branches, and there were no manageable standards a state court could apply to determine whether tuition was being provided "as nearly free as possible."** As neither case law nor statutes provided adequate guidance, the supreme court held the case had been properly dismissed. *Kromko v. Arizona Board of Regents*, 216 Ariz. 190 165 P.3d 168 (Ariz. 2007).

◆   *A federal district court found a Montana student had no constitutional right to his school transcripts and or continued enrollment at a state university.*

A sophomore at Montana State University (MSU) enrolled in a program that would enable him to study in England. After leaving his studies in England early, officials at the school in England informed officials at MSU that he had left without completing his exams and that he owed rent at his residence hall. MSU responded by suspending the student for the remainder of the summer term, terminating his financial aid, and placing a hold on all of his academic records. After his grievance was denied, he sued university officials in federal court, claiming they unconstitutionally deprived him of his property interest in continued enrollment and transcripts without due process. A federal magistrate judge recommended dismissing the case. The court adopted the recommendation. **Legal precedent established that a student has no**

property interest in a transcript, which is owned by the school and not the student. As to the other claim, there is no clearly established right to continued enrollment. Summary judgment was granted to the university officials. *Comer v. Meyers*, No. CV-06-65 BURFC, 2007 WL 1810684 (D. Mont. 6/20/07).

◆ *The Court of Appeals of Maryland held state universities were not liable to students who claimed unreasonable mid-year tuition increases.*

When the state board of university regents learned it was about to lose funding, it approved tuition increases of up to 5% during a semester. Several students sued the board in a state circuit court for breach of contract and related claims. The court granted the board's motion for summary judgment and dismissed the case. The students appealed the contract issue to the Court of Appeals of Maryland. It held **the board was protected by sovereign immunity against the contract claim because the students did not establish they had a written contract**. The legal relationship between the students and universities was characterized as a "quasi-contract." Under a quasi-contract theory, the board could make unilateral changes within the parties' reasonable expectations. The court held the board qualified for sovereign immunity as an arm of the state government. Since the state code provided for a sovereign immunity waiver only in tuition cases that involve a refund, waiver did not apply. The court affirmed the judgment for the board. *Stern v. Board of Regents, Univ. System of Maryland*, 836 A.2d 996 (Md. 2004).

D. Educational Malpractice

Courts have been reluctant to recognize educational malpractice claims. In Leiby v. Univ. of Akron, *below, an Ohio court rejected a student's educational malpractice claim based on his contention that his diplomas were "worthless." It held Ohio does not recognize claims for educational malpractice, as they lack readily acceptable standards of care, cause or injury.*

Educational malpractice claims are further disfavored due to public policy considerations, such as increased litigation and appropriate deference by the courts to academic decisions. In Ross v. Creighton Univ., *957 F.2d 410 (7th Cir. 1992), the U.S. Court of Appeals, Seventh Circuit, found courts in at least 11 states have considered and rejected educational malpractice claims. The main reasons for doing so included: 1) the **lack of a satisfactory standard of care** by which to evaluate an educator, 2) the inherent **uncertainties about the cause and nature of damages**, 3) the **potential for a flood of litigation**, and 4) the threat of **embroiling courts in the day-to-day operations of schools**.*

◆ *An Ohio university did not breach a contract by using exams from one semester for the following semester.*

A student earned bachelor's and master's degrees from an Ohio university. He later sued the university in the state court system, alleging it breached a contract with him by permitting several instructors to reuse exams from one semester to the next. Relying on *Elliott v. Univ. of Cincinnati*, 134 Ohio App.3d 203, 730 N.E.2d 996 (Ohio 1999), the court said **the relationship between a university and a student who enrolls, pays tuition, and attends class is**

contractual. A court looks to university guidelines for the terms of the contractual relationship. The court said the terms of the contract between the student and the university were contained in the university's undergraduate and graduate bulletins. No specific passage in the bulletins disallowed reusing exams. Instead, the student relied on language in bulletins that read, "Faculty must not tolerate academic dishonesty nor discrimination or harassment from students to other students." As the handbook did not prohibit instructors from using old exams, the court found no breach of contract. Ohio courts do not recognize a cause of action for educational malpractice, and the court awarded summary judgment to the university. *Leiby v. Univ. of Akron*, No. 2004-10094, 2005 WL 3163943 (Ohio Ct. Cl. 11/9/05).

The student appealed to the Court of Appeals of Ohio, which agreed with the trial court's findings that university undergraduate and graduate bulletins were contracts that created no direct or implied prohibition against the re-use of exams or exam questions by professors. The student was unable to show he had suffered economic harm from any alleged breach of contract. While he claimed his diplomas were "worthless," **Ohio law does not recognize educational malpractice**. Accordingly, the court affirmed the judgment. *Leiby v. Univ. of Akron*, No. 2004-10094, 2006 WL 1530152 (Ohio Ct. App. 6/6/06).

◆ *Connecticut courts have resisted claims of "educational malpractice" and generally defer to educational institutions in their academic decisions. But the Supreme Court of Connecticut recognized at least two situations where courts will entertain a claim for breach of a contract for educational services in* Gupta v. New Britain General Hospital, *239 Conn. 574 (Conn. 1996).*

A Yale University School of Medicine handbook granted students three opportunities to pass the U.S. Medical Licensing Examination before dismissal. **That was a distinct contractual promise independent of the medical school's obligation to offer a reasonable educational program.** As a result, a student who was dismissed after two unsuccessful attempts at passing Step 1 of the USMLE would receive a trial to consider his breach of contract claim. Breach of contract may be found if the educational program failed in some fundamental respect, like not offering any of the courses necessary to become certified in a particular field. *Morris v. Yale Univ. School of Medicine*, No. 05CV848 (JBA), 2006 WL 908155 (D. Conn. 4/4/06).

◆ *Although educational malpractice claims cannot succeed in most states, including Minnesota, claims alleging consumer fraud or deceptive trade practices can be used where a school fails to perform specific promises.*

A group of students filed a lawsuit against a for-profit, proprietary trade school, claiming fraud, misrepresentation, breach of contract and violation of the Minnesota consumer fraud and deceptive trade practices statutes in connection with a computer program offered by the school. A trial court characterized the students' claims as educational malpractice claims and granted the school's motion for pretrial judgment. The trial court further determined that neither the consumer fraud nor the deceptive trade practices statutes applied, and that neither of these statutes allowed damages.

The state court of appeals noted that **while educational malpractice**

claims were barred by public policy, claims for breach of contract, fraud or other intentional torts alleging the failure to provide promised educational services were actionable. Under this analysis, the trial court correctly granted pretrial judgment to the school on the claims challenging the instructors and quality of education provided. The claims arising from the alleged failure to fulfill certain representations and promises were actionable; therefore, the trial court erred in granting pretrial judgment to the school on those claims. They were remanded to the trial court along with the claims based on the state consumer fraud statute (which allowed the recovery of money damages) and the state deceptive trade practices statute (which did not allow the recovery of money damages, but did allow for injunctive relief). *Alsides v. Brown Institute, Ltd.*, 592 N.W.2d 468 (Minn. Ct. App. 1999).

II. DISCIPLINARY ACTIONS

A. Due Process

1. Hearings and Procedural Safeguards

The Due Process Clause of the Fourteenth Amendment requires state entities to provide notice and an opportunity to be heard when individual liberty or property interests are at stake. Due process includes the notion of fundamental fairness and notice and an opportunity to be heard at some point during disciplinary procedures. A federal district court explained that informal procedures may minimize the risk of lawsuits in higher education disciplinary cases. These include: 1) use of an impartial decisionmaker; 2) providing notice of the charges and the evidence against the student; 3) an opportunity for the student to appear before the decisionmaker; 4) an opportunity for the student to suggest witnesses; 5) avoiding the imposition of sanctions against witnesses; and 6) permitting the student to either voluntarily accept discipline or the ruling of the decisionmaker. A. v. C. College, 863 F.Supp. 156 (S.D.N.Y. 1994).

As noted in Tran v. State System of Higher Educ., *986 A.2d 179 (Pa. Commw. Ct. 2009), this chapter, public institutions are government entities with a due process obligation to provide notice and an opportunity to be heard. All public and private institutions must comply with any due process procedures communicated to students in their rules and regulations.*

◆ *A Florida state law school student was entitled to appropriate notice and a hearing prior to expulsion based on falsified admission records.*

A Florida law school learned that two employees in its admissions office fabricated documents and registration records to help an applicant get into law school. One was close friends with the applicant's family. Administrators met twice with the applicant, but they did not offer him a formal hearing before expelling him based on "fabricated admission and registration records." A state district court of appeal reviewed the expulsion decision, where the applicant claimed a right to a notice and a hearing prior to the action. The court agreed. Under the state's administrative procedure act, agency decisions that are based on disputed facts must be reversed if the aggrieved party was not given a hearing.

State universities such as the law school were subject to the provisions of the administrative procedure act. In addition, **Florida universities and colleges must adopt rules to ensure due process and fairness for student discipline.** In this case, the meetings did not satisfy the hearing requirement because the applicant did not receive notice of the charges against him before they were held. As the school improperly denied his statutory right to notice and a hearing under the state administrative code, the court reversed the order of expulsion and ordered a hearing. *Morris v. Florida Agricultural and Mechanical Univ.*, 23 So.2d 167 (Fla. Dist. Ct. App. 2009).

◆ *Students at public institutions have a protected property interest in due process under the Fourteenth Amendment to the Constitution.*

In a Michigan case, the Constitution required less than the student code called for, and the university was not obligated to strictly abide by the code's provisions. A student was accused of stalking and harassing a professor. She received a hearing before a disciplinary board that found she violated the university statement of student rights and code of student conduct.

At the hearing, the student was not allowed to cross-examine the professor. A hearing board then ordered her expulsion. Appeal reached the Court of Appeals of Michigan, which held the student received notice of the hearing and a written statement outlining the charges against her. She was allowed to call witnesses, state her version of the facts and record the hearing. The university offered an appeal process, and the student was allowed to continue her studies. Even if the university did not technically comply with all the requirements of its student code, it provided due process in this case. **Nothing about the university's decision would have been made any more accurate or fair by adding the further procedural protections insisted upon by the student.** Since the steps the university took to provide due process were adequate, the court affirmed the decision for the university. *Lee v. Univ. of Michigan-Dearborn*, No. 284541, 2009 WL 1362617 (Mich. Ct. App. 5/12/09).

◆ *University of Nevada officials did not violate the due process rights of a student when it noted disciplinary violations and placed a hold on his records.*

The university placed a hold on the student's transcripts after he refused to submit to sanctions imposed by a disciplinary panel for violations of the student code. Discipline was based on fighting his roommate and possession of alcohol his dorm room. The student failed to appear for a meeting about one of the incidents and left the university. He then sued the university in a federal district court, claiming it was wrongful to place a hold on his records and add notations to them about his disciplinary incidents. The student claimed due process violations, breach of contract, negligence, negligent hiring, and infliction of emotional distress. After the court dismissed due process claims relating to the first incident and the claims for infliction of emotional distress, the university sought judgment on claims arising from the second incident.

With respect to the second incident, the court rejected the student's claims that the university violated his due process rights by placing a hold and making remarks on his transcript without giving him adequate notice and a chance to be heard. **The university sent him a letter describing the violations and telling him to contact the student conduct office promptly.** It notified the student of the charges and gave him an opportunity to discuss them. The court rejected the student's contract claim because the university did not act arbitrarily, capriciously, or in bad faith. All the remaining claims for negligence, retaliation and harassment were also rejected. *Lucey v. State of Nevada*, No. 2:07-cv-00658-RLH-RJJ, 2009 WL 971667 (D. Nev. 4/9/09).

◆ *A Michigan student could proceed with her claims that she was dismissed from a university's dental school without due process.*

A University of Michigan Dental School student began having trouble concentrating in class and was later diagnosed as having Attention Deficit Disorder. Despite testing accommodations, she failed a course and was placed on academic probation. The student later failed a course taken to remediate the initial failure, and an academic review board voted to dismiss her. However, she filed a successful appeal and remediated both courses. After the student failed two more classes and took two incompletes, the school returned her to academic probation. Later, the academic review board voted to dismiss her and her appeal was dismissed. The student sued the university in a federal district court for breach of contract and violation of her due process rights.

Although most of the claims were dismissed, the court held the due process claim could proceed. As continued enrollment in a public university is a property interest, the student could not be dismissed without due process. **To prove a violation, the student had to show she was not adequately informed about her academic situation.** She also had to show that the decision to dismiss her was not "careful and deliberate." Factual issues were present as to both of these questions. The academic review board never sent a letter advising her of her pending dismissal, raising an issue of adequate notice. There was also a question as to whether the review board's dismissal decision was reached after adequate deliberation. While the remaining claims were dismissed, the due process claim survived pretrial dismissal. *Zwick v. Regents of the Univ. of Michigan*, No. 06-12639, 2008 WL 1902031 (E.D. Mich. 4/28/08).

◆ *A New York Appellate Division Court reversed a lower court's decision to modify discipline imposed on a university student for marijuana possession.*

Authorities discovered marijuana, drug paraphernalia and a large amount of cash in the student's dorm room. The university suspended him and instructed him to contact a university official to begin the disciplinary process. Meanwhile, he was criminally charged with marijuana possession and accepted a plea bargain. At the university hearing, the student said he did not know the contraband was in his room and suggested it belonged to a roommate. He also said he used some of the items to collect pollen and grind flowers. The university discredited this testimony and suspended the student until a date after he had completed 500 community service hours. The student filed a state court action to block the university from enforcing its decision.

The court upheld the finding of a university rules violation, but held he should be reinstated after completing only 100 hours of community service. On appeal, **the New York Supreme Court, Appellate Division, held that judicial**

review of university nonacademic disciplinary decisions is limited. A university's decision with respect to these matters will be upheld unless it failed to follow its own guidelines and acted in an arbitrary and capricious manner. In this case, the university followed its published policy when it disciplined the student. He was provided with notice and a hearing, and the findings were supported by the record. As the sanction was proportionate to the offense, the university's discipline was reinstated. *Quercia v. New York Univ.*, 41 A.D.3d 295, 838 N.Y.S.2d 538 (N.Y. App. Div. 2007).

◆ *A Connecticut college did not violate a student's due process rights as he received notice and a chance to be heard regarding the charges against him.*

The student contacted a female classmate in a chat room. He made several attempts to date her, but she rejected his advances. The student continued to pursue the classmate, appearing uninvited at her dormitory room and giving her gifts. The student e-mailed a professor about his "excessive interest" in the classmate. The professor was disturbed by the e-mail, in which the student asked him to protect the classmate from other males. After an investigation, the student was told to have no further contact with the classmate. About a month later, he offered to pay a person to spy on her. The university held a disciplinary hearing, after which a hearing officer found the student had stalked the classmate. The student was suspended for 15 months, barred from student activities and prevented from earning credits. After an unsuccessful internal appeal, the student filed an action in state court, seeking an order that would require the university to reinstate him as a full-time student in good standing.

The court found the student was entitled to the requested order only if he could show the suspension proceeding did not meet due process requirements. He failed to make this showing as **he could not prove a violation of any due process rights. There is no fundamental right to attend college. The student received notice of the charges against him, and neither the form nor content of the notice prejudiced his ability to defend the charges.** As he was not denied due process with respect to the university's procedures, the court denied his request for a preliminary injunction. *Danso v. Univ. of Connecticut*, 50 Conn.Supp. 256, 919 A.2d 1100 (Conn. Super. Ct. 2007).

◆ *A New York college violated a student's right to due process by not complying with its own procedures.*

The student applied for admission to a master's degree program while he was an undergraduate at the college. The program sent him a conditional acceptance letter stating he would be accepted if he earned at least a B in his first four program courses and completed all admission requirements. Later, the director of the graduate program sent the student a letter stating she had reviewed his grades and discussed them with his professors. She did not believe he should continue in the program because his personal beliefs about teaching and learning were too different from the goals of the program. The college did not allow the student to register for additional courses and withdrew his registration for the upcoming semester. The student sued the college in a state court, alleging due process violations for failure to provide the procedures for dismissal expressed in the college's own rules and regulations. The court dismissed the case, and the student appealed to a state appellate division court.

The court rejected the college's argument that he was not fully matriculated because he had only been "conditionally accepted" by the graduate program. The student satisfied admission requirements and the conditions of the acceptance letter. The college said nothing in the letter about a later review and did not mention in its handbook or catalogue that it would review a student's personal goals before making a decision. **The court found the college could not dismiss the student without following the due process procedures stated in its rules and regulations.** The judgment was modified with directions to reinstate the student. *Matter of McConnell v. Le Moyne College*, 25 A.D.3d 1066, 808 N.Y.S.2d 860 (N.Y. App. Div. 2006).

◆ *A Pennsylvania university did not deprive a student of due process when it suspended him for sexually assaulting another student.*

A Pennsylvania university dean received an e-mail from a female student alleging a male student had pulled her shirt up and fondled her breasts at a campus party. The university scheduled a discipline hearing before the judicial board to determine if the student violated the student code of conduct. The university informed him in writing of the date and time of the hearing and of the charges against him. During the hearing, the female student testified to the authenticity of the e-mail she wrote and answered the student's questions.

The dean informed the student in writing of the board's decision to suspend him for two years. The student appealed to the Commonwealth Court of Pennsylvania. He claimed the evidence was insufficient to support the board's finding and that the hearing violated his due process rights by failing to provide sufficient time to prepare a response and secure witnesses. The court stated **the student was entitled to due process, which includes basic principles of fundamental fairness. At a minimum, the university had to provide him notice of the charges and an opportunity for a hearing.** However, the university did not have to provide a "full-dress judicial hearing," subject to the rules of evidence or representation by an attorney. Pennsylvania state universities must comply with 22 Pa. Code § 505.3. The court held the university did so by providing the student with the date, time and place of the hearing, an opportunity to submit written, physical or testimonial evidence, allowing him to question witnesses, and affording him sufficient time to prepare a defense. **The university adhered to its procedures and applied the correct standard of review, affording the student adequate due process.** *Ruane v. Shippensburg Univ.*, 871 A.2d 859 (Pa. Commw. Ct. 2005).

◆ *The U.S. Court of Appeals, Sixth Circuit, held an Ohio medical college did not violate a student's due process rights during his disciplinary hearing.*

The student was arrested for a felony drug crime. The college notified him by letter that it was suspending him until investigations and hearings on his drug charge were completed, and advised him of his right to an investigation. The student decided not to schedule an investigation until the pending criminal charges were resolved. The student was not permitted on campus until the completion of a disciplinary hearing. A few months later, the student pled guilty to a felony drug charge, then asked for a hearing. The college sent him a written notice to appear before its student conduct and ethics committee to answer questions about his arrest. The student was not entitled to be represented by an attorney at the hearing because the criminal proceedings had ended. However, the college allowed his attorney to be present. At the hearing, the officer who had arrested the student testified. The committee questioned the officer, but denied the student's attorney an opportunity to do so.

The college expelled the student for violating its zero-tolerance drug policy. The student sued the college in a federal district court for due process violations. The court dismissed the case. On appeal, the Sixth Circuit stated **the Due Process Clause of the Fourteenth Amendment protects individual liberty and property interests. The student's interest in pursuing an education was a protected property interest. Due process is flexible, and its basic requirements are notice and an opportunity to be heard. Additional procedures vary based on the circumstances of each case.** The student argued the college fell short of the process his circumstances demanded, because he had a significant interest in continuing his medical education. The court held the college provided him sufficient notice of the disciplinary charges against him and the procedures that would follow. While the college did not permit the student's attorney to cross-examine the officer, the procedures it used were fundamentally fair. The judgment for the college was affirmed. *Flaim v. Medical College of Ohio*, 418 F.3d 629 (6th Cir. 2005).

◆ *A South Carolina student who was recently dismissed from his academic program was still a "student" when he received an on-campus parking ticket.*

The University of South Carolina dismissed the student for academic reasons. While his dismissal was on appeal, he agreed to be placed on conduct probation for 15 months in settlement of an earlier nonacademic incident. The student signed a form acknowledging the board had explained his rights to him. He later argued with a university police officer over a parking citation. The officer issued him a notice of policy violation for harassment. The university then denied the student's academic dismissal appeal. He failed to attend a campus judicial board hearing on the parking citation and the board expelled him. The student appealed his expulsion, arguing he was not a student at the time of the citation incident and did not have to adhere to university policies.

The university denied the student's appeal and he sued it in a state court. The court granted the university's motion for summary judgment, and the student appealed to the Court of Appeals of South Carolina. The court noted the student had settled his disciplinary appeal by agreeing to conduct probation for 15 months. He clearly considered he would be a student in the future. The court found no change in his student status between the date he signed the agreement and the parking violation. **The court rejected the student's contention that the university handbook definition of "continuing student relationship" was vague. The academic appellate process was still taking place at the time of the parking violation and the dismissal became final long after the incident.** The student held himself out to be a student and continued his student relationship with the school. The court affirmed the decision for the university. *Carter v. Univ. of South Carolina*, 360 S.C.App. 428, 602 S.E.2d 59 (S.C. Ct. App. 2004).

2. Private Schools

Private entities are not bound by the Constitution and have broad discretion to establish disciplinary rules and procedures through their contractual relationships with students. Private school students are generally entitled to receive only those procedural safeguards which are specifically promised by the private institution.

◆ *A Tennessee court found evidence to support a jury verdict against an optometry college for dismissing a student in breach of their contract.*

In the student's third year of his optometry program, college faculty recommended he avoid dismissal for poor grades by voluntarily withdrawing and then reapplying. He did and was conditionally re-admitted with the requirement that he earn at least a C in every course. After receiving a D in one class and failures in two classes he was auditing, the student was dismissed. After some negotiations, the college president offered to revise his transcript to reflect withdrawal instead of a dismissal, and to write a letter of good standing. The student agreed, and the college sent the letter and revised transcript to other optometry schools at his request. However, the student was unable to transfer and sued the college in a state court for breach of contract and negligence.

A jury found that even though the college violated its own policies, it did not violate the withdrawal agreement with the student. On appeal, **the state court of appeals found the evidence supported the jury's finding that the college violated its policy when it dismissed the student for failing audited classes**. While the student argued there should be a new trial so he could further pursue his claims, the court found the verdict for the college was not inconsistent and was supported by the evidence. As a result, the court refused to disturb the verdict. *Rutherford v. Southern College of Optometry*, No. W2008-02268-COA-R3-CV, 2009 WL 5064972 (Tenn. Ct. App. 12/28/09).

◆ *A registered sex offender could not bring federal claims against a private Kentucky university and its staff because they were not state actors.*

In a federal district court lawsuit asserting violations of the U.S. and Kentucky Constitutions, the offender claimed the university and staff members wrongfully banned him from attending classes on campus. He acknowledged that he was subject to a state sex offender registration act, but he said he was in compliance with it. The offender claimed that in barring him from campus, the university failed to follow its own guidelines for student conduct and discipline.

The court explained that federal claims filed under 42 U.S.C. § 1983 may survive only against persons who acted with the authority of the state, or "under color of state law." **Private actors can be sued for constitutional violations only if their actions are "fairly attributable to the state."** The university was a private, for-profit corporation, and there was no indication it was publicly funded or that the state controlled its operations. The court held that as the offender failed to state a claim for violation of his rights under the Constitution, he could not proceed with his Section 1983 claims. *McGlothin v. Strayer Univ.*, No. 09-231-JMH, 2009 WL 1956463 (E.D. Ky. 7/6/09).

◆ *A federal court restated the rule that private school students are entitled only to those procedural safeguards which the school specifically provides.*

A Pennsylvania nursing assistant student was dismissed from a joint program between two institutions for posing a threat to patients. An assistant program administrator stated he gave medication to patients after being told not to, and was insubordinate. She also declared the student was "dangerous," and that "this is life and death." In a federal district court action against both institutions, the student claimed breach of the covenant of good faith and fair dealing, denial of due process and tortious interference with contract.

After initially refusing to dismiss the student's breach of contract claim, the court awarded judgment to the institutions. There was no evidence that he was dismissed for any reason but patient safety. While the student asserted due process violations because he did not have a full hearing, the Pennsylvania state court system has held that fundamental fairness is met in public school cases even if there is no "full-dress judicial hearing." If fundamental fairness was met in a public school case where a student was not represented by counsel, the court found it was surely met in a private school case. In any event, this was a breach of contract action. No contract provision entitled the student to representation by counsel. **"Students who are being disciplined are entitled only to those procedural safeguards which the school specifically provides."** As a result, the institutions were entitled to judgment. *Kimberg v. Univ. of Scranton*, No. 3:06cv1209, 2009 WL 222658 (M.D. Pa. 1/29/09).

◆ *A federal district court held a Maryland university did not breach a contract by interfering with a student's ability to complete a thesis.*

The student pursued a doctorate degree at a private university. He fulfilled the requirements for his degree except his thesis. Under a university policy, students were allowed a maximum of seven years from the date they enrolled to obtain a degree. The university extended the deadline for the student several times. After the last extension, the university denied the student further access to the office space. The student sued the university in a federal district court, alleging it breached a contract by sabotaging his ability to complete the thesis, among other things. He contended his enrollment in the university established an implied contract. **The court agreed that the relationship between a student and a private university is largely contractual in nature. Such a contract requires a university to act in good faith, and to act fairly.**

There was evidence that the university reasonably accommodated the student above and beyond any reasonably imagined contractual requirement. **Courts intervene into academic decisions only if a student completes all academic requirements and the school's refusal to grant a degree is "arbitrary and capricious."** Many of the events the student complained about were academic judgments. As nothing suggested the university acted in an arbitrary or capricious manner, there was no breach of contract. The court also dismissed the student's race and national origin discrimination claims. *Onawola v. Johns Hopkins Univ.*, 412 F.Supp.2d 529 (D. Md. 2006).

The Fourth Circuit later affirmed the decision in a brief memorandum. *Onawola v. Johns Hopkins Univ.*, 221 Fed.Appx. 211 (4th Cir. 2007).

◆ *A federal district court refused to dismiss an action by a Florida law school student who was expelled without the use of school academic procedures.*

The student allegedly threatened to blow up an office at the school and frightened three students with intimidating behavior. A school counselor called him "the most volatile and frightening student she had encountered." The school dean issued the student an expulsion letter based on "serious threats" and "physically intimidating conduct." The student claimed he did not receive any notice of the charges and was not provided with a hearing. He sued the school and several officials in a federal district court for negligence, defamation and breach of contract. The school and officials moved for dismissal.

The court agreed to dismiss the negligence claim. Under Florida law, a student may be suspended or expelled for breaching a university's code of conduct. Even if school officials were mistaken in issuing the notice, they were not liable unless they acted with malice. The dean's statements were privileged as they were based on the school's interest or duty to investigate and resolve the case. As there was no finding of malice, the negligence and defamation claims were dismissed. The court held a contract existed between the student and school, which was governed by the student handbook. **The law school's code of academic integrity specified that students would receive procedural protections before any expulsion decision.** The court denied the motion to dismiss this claim, as the school may have breached contract terms. The court dismissed the remaining claims. *Jarzynka v. St. Thomas Univ. School of Law*, 310 F.Supp.2d 1256 (S.D. Fla. 2004). The U.S. Court of Appeals, Eleventh Circuit, affirmed the judgment without an opinion. *Jarzynka v. St. Thomas Univ. School of Law*, 210 Fed.Appx. 8955 (11th Cir. 2006).

◆ *The Supreme Court of Kentucky held a state licensing statute did not create a duty for a private college to provide due process procedures.*

College officials searched the student's dorm room after others reported he threatened to harm a classmate. The search yielded three pocket knives and a large Army survival knife. An official handed him a dismissal letter, but told him he could be readmitted if he agreed to psychiatric treatment and evaluation. The student did not deny the threats and admitted he owned the knives, but he later sued the college in a state court for due process violations. The court noted the college's student handbook prohibited dangerous weapons and included dismissal as a sanction. As the handbook clearly warned students that weapons possession could result in dismissal, the court held for the college. On appeal, the Supreme Court of Kentucky found the licensing statute was intended to protect citizens from fraudulent or substandard educational institutions.

The statute did not impose due process obligations on private colleges. A **private college "does not necessarily subject itself to the entire panoply of due process requirements that would be applicable at a state-sponsored education institution."** While a contract had been formed, the court found the handbook did not guarantee due process rights. The handbook stated that under unusual circumstances, due process procedures would not be followed. As the student admitted misconduct, an immediate dismissal was justified and there was no need for a hearing. *Centre College v. Trzop*, 127 S.W.3d 562 (Ky. 2003).

◆ *An Illinois private university had a rational basis for expelling a student who failed to earn credits for two consecutive semesters.*

The student failed two required field work assignments for her master's in social work program. The student accused the university of failing to offer her a remediation plan as described in the university handbook. The university claimed she did not qualify for remediation and expelled her from the program under a handbook policy requiring dismissal of any student failing to earn credit in consecutive semesters. She sued the university in a state court for breach of contract and other claims. The court held the university handbook created a contract and found the university breached the contract by not creating a remediation plan. It ordered the university to refund her tuition.

The university appealed to the Appellate Court of Illinois, which found the university adequately documented the student's problems. It held the relationship between a student and private university is not purely contractual. Courts are generally unwilling to interfere with private university student regulations. **A student may prevail on a contract claim against a private university only if an adverse academic decision is arbitrary, capricious or in bad faith.** A student must show a dismissal was without any discernable rational basis. As there was no such showing in this case, the court reversed the judgment. *Raethz v. Aurora Univ.*, 805 N.E.2d 696 (Ill. App. Ct. 2004).

B. Academic Dismissals

Courts have traditionally left grading policies to the special expertise of educators, but may review a grading policy that is arbitrary and capricious, irrational, made in bad faith or contrary to federal or state law.

In Susan M. v. New York Law School, *556 N.E.2d 1104 (N.Y. 1990), New York's highest court restated the general rule that **courts do not substitute their judgment for that of university faculty on matters such as degree requirements and academic dismissals**.*

1. Poor Performance

◆ *The dismissal of a student who failed to timely complete a thesis did not violate his due process or contract rights.*

The student received an unsatisfactory grade on a Ph.D. candidacy exam and did not timely complete his thesis. He continued to take classes for two years, after which he was "retroactively removed" from the program. The student sued the university and a committee chair in a federal district court for due process violations. The court held the claims against the university and the chair in his official capacity were barred by the Eleventh Amendment. **In a disciplinary context, due process requires that a student receive notice and an opportunity to be heard.** However, less is required for academic dismissals, where no formal hearing is required. The university easily met this standard when it notified the student he had failed the exam, told him he had violated rules regarding students who failed the exam, and met with him to tell him he had not timely completed his thesis. These actions more than satisfied due process requirements. The court also rejected a breach of contract claim.

On appeal, the U.S. Court of Appeals, Fourth Circuit, found no error in the district court's finding that the student was dismissed for academic, rather than disciplinary reasons. Removal from the program had been based on his failure to timely complete his thesis after he failed a candidacy exam. The graduate studies committee interpreted its rules governing academic standards for timely completion of graduate program requirements, and not disciplinary rules governing student conduct. As a result, the court found the student ineligible to remain in the program. **Since he was removed for academic, rather than for disciplinary reasons, the district court properly found the decision was due a heightened level of deference and "subject to greatly reduced procedural requirements."** Also affirmed were the district court findings that the head of the graduate studies committee was entitled to qualified immunity, and that the university's graduate student handbook did not create a contract between the parties. *Brown v. Rector and Visitors of the Univ. of Virginia*, 361 Fed.Appx. 531 (4th Cir. 2010).

◆ *A federal court refused to order an Ohio law school to reinstate an expelled student until his lawsuit over the dismissal was decided.*

During his first semester of law school, the student was placed on academic probation due to his 1.4 GPA. To continue to his second year, he needed a cumulative 2.0 GPA by the end of the year. The student was referred to a doctor for testing, and he was diagnosed with Attention Deficit Hyperactivity Disorder. While the law school granted requests for some accommodations he sought, it denied others. As it turned out, the student earned higher grades on exams he took without accommodations. His spring semester GPA was 2.0 – but as his cumulative GPA was 1.82, the school dismissed him.

In a federal district court action, the student claimed the law school failed to reasonably accommodate him by giving him only half the extra exam time his doctor recommended, denying him another semester to pull up his GPA, and imposing an arbitrary cumulative 2.0 GPA requirement. He asked the court to order the school to reinstate him pending the resolution of his lawsuit. It refused. To receive a preliminary injunction, the student had to show he was likely to win his case. **The court found the expulsion decision was entitled to deference. It appeared the cause behind the student's dismissal was his lack of effort – not any failure to provide him reasonable accommodations.** The court found this conclusion was backed up by the fact that he got higher grades on the exams he took without accommodations. *Oser v. Capital Univ. Law School*, No. 2:09-cv-709, 2009 WL 2913919 (S.D. Ohio 9/8/09).

◆ *An Indiana university did not violate the Constitution by dismissing a graduate student for poor academic performance.*

The student claimed a faculty member prevented him from taking a final exam, causing him to receive an incomplete grade. He later received Ds in two courses. According to the student, the grades were arbitrary, and a professor threatened him when he said he was appealing the grades to an academic fairness committee. He later failed a clinical rotation and was dismissed for poor academic performance. The student complained that he received little feedback from faculty, and that the university acted arbitrarily and in bad faith.

In a federal lawsuit against the university and officials, the student claimed violation of his Due Process and Equal Protection rights and breach of contract. The court held the claims against the university were barred by the Eleventh Amendment. It rejected the claim that the university violated a constitutional right to continued graduate education. Any such entitlement is a matter of contract, and **dismissal of a student based on poor academic performance is not a constitutional violation.** The court rejected a procedural due process claim, because the student did not show he was deprived of a constitutionally protected interest. **The process required by educational institutions "is no more than an informal 'give and take'"** that gives a student a chance to state his case. The student appealed to the U.S. Court of Appeals, Seventh Circuit, which held he did not show the university made any promises to him or show how a contract was formed. It held the district court had properly dismissed the case, noting that a **"graduate student does not have a federal constitutional right to a continued graduate education."** *Bissessur v. Indiana Univ. Board of Trustees*, 581 F.3d 599 (7th Cir. 2009).

◆ *Courts reviewing academic decisions show great deference to the judgment of academic professionals, as the following Alabama case demonstrates.*

A nursing school student said her dismissal from a community college violated her due process rights and resulted from a conspiracy among academic officials to oust her. She was dismissed under a school policy barring any student with two D grades from continuing. In a federal district court lawsuit, the student claimed the college violated her due process rights by failing to expunge a D grade after she received an A in a follow-up class. She also alleged a civil conspiracy, an unlawful deprivation of rights to make and enforce contracts under federal law, and a state law claim for the tort of outrage.

First, the court held the federal claims against the college were barred by the Eleventh Amendment. Federal damage claims against individual college officials in their official capacities were barred by the Eleventh Amendment as essentially claims against the state. The court rejected the due process claims, since the student could not establish that the decision to exclude her was "arbitrary and capricious." **There was no showing that officials acted with an improper motive in connection with the decision to remove her from the program.** The student did not produce any evidence showing the reason for her dismissal was unrelated to her academic performance. The court also rejected her conspiracy and outrage claims. *Wright v. Chattahoochee Valley Community College*, No. 3:06-CV-1087-WKW, 2008 WL 4877948 (M.D. Ala. 11/12/08).

◆ *The decision to dismiss a graduate student from a master's program was not a retaliatory response to a prior lawsuit he filed against the university.*

While enrolled in the program, the student filed an administrative charge of unlawful discrimination against the university. About a year later, he filed a discrimination lawsuit. The student abandoned his work on a research project associated with his graduate program to focus on his case. He refused to follow guidance offered by advisors, and for two-and-a-half years he had no contact with his faculty advisors about his project. During that time, the student failed to provide a proposal that complied with program guidelines. He asked for an extension to complete his final research paper, but he did not include an academic plan and indicated he was "undecided" about when he would complete his work. The extension request was denied, and he was dismissed.

The student filed a second suit against the university, claiming he was dismissed in retaliation for the earlier suit. A state court ruled against him, and he appealed to the Court of Appeals of Massachusetts. It noted the lapse of more than two years between the time the first suit was filed and the time the student was dismissed. This gap indicated there was no causal connection between the two events. The retaliation claim also failed because the student failed to show the university's reasons for dismissing him were pretextual. There was no evidence that he was making progress toward completion of his degree. Other students whose requests were granted showed they were working to overcome the obstacles that led to the extension request. In contrast, the student did not indicate he was interested in finishing the program. For these reasons, the judgment was affirmed. *Nguyen v. Univ. of Massachusetts at Boston*, 72 Mass.App.Ct. 1107, 889 N.E.2d 981 (Table) (Mass. App. Ct. 2008).

◆   *The Supreme Court of Alaska held a university did not violate a student's due process rights by dismissing him and denying him readmission.*

The student did not get along with a field instructor who supervised his field course work toward a social work degree. Although the field instructor did not recommend a failing grade, a faculty liaison professor assigned him an incomplete grade that was later changed to failure. An academic review panel upheld the grade, and the university later denied his reapplication. The student sued the university in the state court system, alleging due process violations for allegedly not following its own rules and failing to provide him with proper notice and an opportunity to be heard. The student added discrimination claims based on his gender and a disability. The court held the professor gave the student adequate notice of his academic deficiencies. She warned him several times about ongoing lateness and inferior work. The state supreme court affirmed the decision, agreeing that the university had provided the student with due process. **A person has no due process interest in admission to a professional school in the absence of dishonesty or publication of the reason for denying admission.** *Hermosillo v. Univ. of Alaska, Anchorage*, No. S-10563, 2004 WL 362384 (Alaska 2004).

◆   *The Court of Appeals of Tennessee held in favor of a college that refused to reinstate a student who was dismissed after he failed a course twice.*

The student attended a school of dentistry at a college in Tennessee. He repeated his freshman year because he had previously failed courses in gross anatomy and microscopic anatomy. The college had an academic policy of dismissing students who failed the same course twice. During the fall semester, the student failed the same two courses. The college notified the student it was dismissing him. The student evaluation and promotion committee dismissed the student for poor academic performance. The dean of the school of dentistry rejected the student's appeal and dismissed him from the college.

The student's appeal was denied, and he sued the college in a state court for breach of contract. He based his claim on breach of the terms of the college academic policies and procedures, and the student affairs handbook. The court dismissed the case, and the student appealed to the Court of Appeals of Tennessee. The student argued the college violated its policies by not providing him an opportunity to have his grades recalculated or giving him supportive assistance to appeal. **The court stated it was not equipped to review a university's academic policies. Courts do not substitute their judgment for that of university faculty on matters such as degree requirements and academic dismissals. The court rejected the student's breach of contract claim because college policies did not form a contract.** It affirmed the judgment for the college. *Lord v. Meharry Medical College School of Dentistry*, No. M2004-00264-COA-R3-CV, 2005 WL 1950119 (Tenn. Ct. App. 8/12/05).

◆ *A federal district court denied a District of Columbia student's request for an order to require a university to allow him to graduate.*

The student intended to graduate from the university with a degree in Computer Science in May 2005. He missed two required classes in computer science because of a medical condition, and received incomplete grades, making him unable to graduate in May. The student and his professors agreed he could complete the courses if he complied with certain conditions. The student failed to meet the conditions, and the university refused to let him graduate. He sued the university in a federal district court for breach of contract and race discrimination. The court considered his motion for a temporary restraining order. Even though the student admitted breaching the terms of the agreement with his professors, he asked the court to direct the university to let him graduate as if he received incomplete grades in the courses. **The court held the student failed to establish a strong likelihood of prevailing on his pending claims for breach of contract, race discrimination and equal protection against the school. It denied the request for a temporary restraining order.** The court believed the university and the other students who did meet their requirements could be harmed by allowing the student to receive his degree without meeting university requirements. *Habte v. George Washington Univ.*, No. Civ. 050962JGP, 2005 WL 1204882 (D.D.C. 5/19/05).

◆ *Schools and universities are generally given a great deal of latitude by courts in making academic decisions. Their choices, however, must have some rational basis and not be arbitrary. The Supreme Court upheld a university's decision to dismiss a student from an advanced academic program based on poor performance.*

A student was enrolled in the University of Michigan's "Inteflex" program, which is a special six-year course of study leading to both an undergraduate and medical degree. The student struggled with the curriculum for six years, completing only four years' worth of study and barely achieving minimal competence. Because he was given a grade of "incomplete" in several important classes and was forced to delay taking his examinations, he was placed on an irregular program. Finally, he completed the four years of basic study necessary to take the NBME Part I, a test administered by the National Board of Medical Examiners which is a prerequisite to the final two years of study under the Inteflex program. Unfortunately, the student failed the exam, receiving the lowest score ever in the brief history of the Inteflex program. The university's medical school executive board reviewed the student's academic career, decided to drop him from registration in the program, and denied his request to retake NBME Part I. The executive board was not swayed by arguments that his failure on the exam was due to his mother's heart attack 18 months previously, the excessive amount of time he had spent on an essay contest that he had entered, and his breakup with his girlfriend. The student brought suit in federal court claiming breach of contract under state law and also alleging a violation of his due process rights under the U.S. Constitution.

Evidence showed the university had a practice of allowing students who had failed the NBME Part I to retake the test one, two, three, or even four times. The student here was the only person ever refused permission to retake the test. The district court ruled against him on the contract claim and further held that his dismissal was not violative of the Due Process Clause. The U.S. Court of Appeals, Sixth Circuit, held the student had possessed a property interest in his continued participation in the Inteflex program, and that the university had arbitrarily deprived him of that property interest. The U.S. Supreme Court unanimously reversed the court of appeals' decision and reinstated the district court's ruling against the student. **The Due Process Clause was not offended because the university's liberal retesting custom gave rise to no state law entitlement to retake NBME Part I.** Furthermore, the university had based its decision to dismiss the student upon careful, clear and conscientious deliberation, which took his entire academic career into account. The university had acted in good faith. The Supreme Court further observed that the discretion to determine, on academic grounds, who may be admitted to study is one of the "four essential freedoms" of a university. The Court thus held that the Due Process Clause was not violated by the student's dismissal. *Regents of Univ. of Michigan v. Ewing*, 474 U.S. 214, 106 S.Ct. 507, 88 L.Ed.2d 523 (1985).

◆ *Unlike dismissals for disciplinary reasons, dismissals for academic reasons do not require the procedural requirements of* Goss v. Lopez, *419 U.S. 565 (1975), a public high school case involving suspensions of students for misconduct. In disciplinary cases, school officials must give a student notice of the charges and an opportunity to respond to them. School officials have broader discretion in dealing with academic expulsions and suspensions than in disciplinary actions involving misconduct.*

The academic performance of students at the University of Missouri-Kansas City Medical School was assessed periodically by the Council of Evaluation, a faculty-student body with the power to recommend probation or dismissal subject to approval by a faculty committee and the dean. Several faculty members expressed dissatisfaction with the performance of a medical student. As a result, the Council of Evaluation recommended that she be advanced to her final year on a probationary status. Faculty complaints continued, and the council warned the student that absent "radical improvement," she would be dismissed. She was allowed to take a set of oral and practical examinations as an "appeal" from the council's decision.

The student spent a substantial portion of time with seven practicing physicians who supervised the examinations. Two recommended that she be allowed to graduate. Two recommended that she be dropped immediately from the school. The remaining three recommended that she not be allowed to graduate in June and be continued on probation pending further reports of her progress. Subsequent reports regarding the student were negative, and she was dropped from the program following the council's recommendation. The student sued, alleging that she had not been accorded due process prior to her dismissal. The district court determined that the student had been afforded due process. The U.S. Court of Appeals, Eighth Circuit, reversed.

On appeal, the U.S. Supreme Court held that **the student had been given due process as guaranteed by the Fourteenth Amendment**. The procedures leading to the student's dismissal, under which the student was fully informed of faculty dissatisfaction with her progress, and the consequent threat to the student's graduation and continued enrollment did not violate the Fourteenth Amendment. **Dismissals for academic reasons do not necessitate a hearing before the school's decision-making body.** *Board of Curators v. Horowitz,* 435 U.S. 78, 98 S.Ct. 948, 55 L.Ed.2d 124 (1978).

◆ *A Tennessee state university did not have to provide a medical student a formal hearing to suspend him for academic reasons.*

The student was informed of his academic deficiencies and unprofessional conduct by a dean toward the end of his second year. Although he eventually passed all his second-year courses, he failed the USMLE Step 1 the following summer. Early in his third year, after a negative report to the student promotion committee, a recommendation was made that the student be suspended, and the suspension was upheld. The student appealed internally without success, then sued the state under 42 U.S.C. § 1983 for violating his Fourteenth Amendment due process rights. A federal district court ruled in his favor, but the Sixth Circuit reversed, noting that academic decisions, unlike disciplinary decisions, do not require a formal hearing to satisfy the Fourteenth Amendment's procedural due process requirements. **The medical school reached a careful and deliberate decision** based on an evaluation of the student's medical knowledge, ethical conduct and interpersonal skills. This adhered to its internal procedures and provided the student with sufficient procedural due process. *Ku v. State of Tennessee,* 322 F.3d 431 (6th Cir. 2003).

2. Cheating and Plagiarism

◆ *A former Columbia University student who committed plagiarism did not show the resulting decision to expel him was unlawfully motivated.*

The plagiarism charge was referred to a disciplinary committee, which voted to expel the student. Although he admitted to plagiarism, he claimed he was expelled because of his race and because he had refused to submit to an administrator's sexual advances and filed a complaint about them. In a federal district court lawsuit against the university, the student alleged retaliation under Title IX, race discrimination and breach of contract. After the court held for the university, appeal went before the U.S. Court of Appeals, Second Circuit.

On appeal, the court explained that to prove a retaliation claim, the student had to show he engaged in a protected activity of which the university was aware. Even if he could make this showing, the school could defeat the claim by offering a legitimate, nondiscriminatory reason for its decision. There was no evidence to support the conclusion that the student was really expelled for a reason other than plagiarism. Since he could not show the university gave a pretextual reason for dismissing him, the race discrimination claim failed. **As for a breach of contract, the student did not have hard evidence that the university was in breach or that he performed his contractual duties.** The decision for the university was affirmed. *Shelton v. Trustees of Columbia Univ.*, No. 09-2301-cv, 2010 WL 807810 (2d Cir. 3/10/10).

◆ *A New York court held a university did not act arbitrarily or otherwise improperly when it decided to expel a student for plagiarism.*

The student was repeatedly told to remove plagiarized portions of her master's thesis from drafts she prepared. Eventually, she was expelled for plagiarism. After the expulsion, the university notified the student of the charges against her, and she received a chance to present her side of the story at an appeals committee hearing. She later filed a state court action challenging the expulsion, claiming she was expelled on the basis of national origin. It was also claimed that the expulsion decision was arbitrary, capricious and irrational.

After a lower court denied the student's request to set aside the expulsion, the student appealed. A New York Appellate Division Court upheld the expulsion decision. **The record showed the school substantially complied with applicable procedures for dealing with students accused of plagiarism.** It was acceptable for the professor who reported the plagiarism to serve on a committee that considered the charges. It was also acceptable for an associate dean of academic services to serve on two committees that were involved in the expulsion decision. *Dequito v. The New School for General Studies*, 68 A.D.3d 559, 890 N.Y.S.2d 56 (N.Y. App. Div. 2009).

◆ *A student's lawsuit alleging wrongful expulsion by the University of Kansas was barred by Eleventh Amendment immunity.*

According to the student, a program director and two professors conspired to falsely accuse him of plagiarism. He initially challenged his expulsion in a federal district court in Pennsylvania, but the case was dismissed for lack of jurisdiction. The student then filed a new action against the university, program director and professors in a federal district court in Kansas. The university argued that the case should be dismissed because it was an arm of the state and enjoyed Eleventh Amendment immunity. The court rejected the student's claim that the university waived its immunity by subjecting itself to the Pennsylvania action. **An intent to waive immunity must be expressed by affirmative activity, not by "mere inaction."** As the university never took any affirmative step to waive its Eleventh Amendment immunity, the case was dismissed. *Marten v. Godwin*, No. 08-4031-EFM, 2009 WL 2475257 (D. Kan. 8/12/09).

◆ *The Supreme Court of Vermont rejected a medical student's claim that a university violated state law by dismissing him for falsifying documents.*

In the student's fourth year of the medical program, a faculty member discovered he had falsely reported completing a rotation at another medical school. At a hearing of the committee on fitness, the student admitted lying about the rotation. The university later discovered he had engaged in other misconduct and had falsely reported at his hearing that he graduated *magna cum laude* from an undergraduate institution. It was further learned he had falsified reports of completing rotations at other schools and had impersonated an employee of his undergraduate institution. Based on this information, the college held a second hearing, where the student admitted his misconduct. But he said it was caused by his Tourette's Syndrome and a related obsessive behavior disorder.

The university dismissed the student, and he sued the university in a state court under the Vermont Public Accommodations Act. He claimed the medical school failed to accommodate his condition. The court held for the university, finding the student did not meet the medical school's essential eligibility requirements. It also found the accommodation he sought was not reasonable, and that he posed a risk of harm to patients. On appeal, the state supreme court explained that decisions about academic standards are entitled to deference. The university had legitimate interests in enforcing its standards, protecting patients and producing students who could successfully practice medicine. As the student did not meet the medical school's essential eligibility requirements, his disability discrimination claims failed. His dishonesty and fraud were unacceptable, regardless of their cause. **It would fundamentally alter the nature of the medical school to require the school to accept dishonest behavior. Nor did the student timely meet his duty to seek an accommodation.** Accordingly, the decision for the university was affirmed. *Bhatt v. Univ. of Vermont*, 958 A.2d 637 (Vt. 2008).

◆ *A Georgia university did not breach a contract with a medical student by expelling him for dishonesty and plagiarism.*

A medical student at Emory University was referred to a conduct code committee on three charges of dishonesty, and an honor council on a plagiarism charge. Prior to the conduct code hearing, he received information about the charges against him. After concerns arose regarding the hearing procedures, the process was restarted and a second conduct code committee hearing was held. The honor council denied the student's request to record its hearing, and a student participant searched him to make sure he did not bring recording devices into the room. Following the hearings, the school expelled him.

In a state court lawsuit against the university, the student claimed he was expelled because he had criticized Emory employees, and he further alleged the school breached its contract with him by failing to follow university hearing procedures. A state trial court held for the school, its dean and an associate dean. The Court of Appeals of Georgia rejected the student's arguments regarding hearing procedures, **noting he received information about the charges before the first hearing**. Although he complained that the hearing was not transcribed, the student handbook did not require this. The student received proper notice regarding the honor council hearing. A faculty member tried to talk to him about the hearing and sent him a letter notifying him of the investigation. Although the hearing did not take place within 21 days of the charge, this was not an absolute requirement. The school followed all applicable handbook guidelines, and the court affirmed the decision on the breach of contract claim. There was no merit to the student's assault and battery claims, because he did not show an attempt "to commit a violent injury" and did not show the person who conducted the search acted with the school's authorization. *Kuritzky v. Emory Univ.*, 294 Ga.App. 370, 669 S.E.2d 179 (Ga. Ct. App. 2008).

◆ *A Texas student who cheated on a paper was not denied due process when he was dismissed for failing to maintain a 2.0 grade point average.*

A course instructor concluded the student and a classmate had violated a rule against collaborating on a paper and assigned both students zero grades. The student's final grade for the course slipped to failing. He pursued an honor court complaint against the classmate and asked for a time extension to file a request for a grade change. After the semester ended, the university notified the student of his dismissal for failure to meet school academic requirements. After an unsuccessful appeal within the university, he sued the university and others in a state court for defamation, breach of contract, fraud and violation of due process. The court granted summary judgment against him. On appeal, the Court of Appeals of Texas rejected the student's claim that he had a property interest in university rules and regulations. **Under Supreme Court precedents, students lack a substantive interest in specific academic procedures. The student lacked a "right" to have his paper graded fairly.** This claim had merit only if the university acted irrationally in assigning the grade. Assigning a zero grade for cheating was logical punishment that did not violate due process rights, and the court affirmed the judgment. *Jackson v. Texas Southern Univ.*, 213 S.W.3d 437 (Tex. Ct. App. 2007).

◆ *An engineering student failed to convince a Florida court that a university failed to follow appropriate disciplinary procedures before expelling him.*

The student failed a required engineering class three times. While enrolled in the class for a fourth time, the course professor determined that his paper was missing after an open-book examination. The professor partially graded all the returned examinations and placed them in an envelope in his office. When he returned to his office later in the same day, he found the student's had been placed with all the others. The paper indicated an expected time of return but did not show the time it was actually handed in. Still, the professor left part of his examination ungraded, hoping the student would contact him to discuss the discrepancy. The student never contacted the professor about the examination.

As the professor's suspicions were elevated, he arranged for the final examination to be videotaped. The tape showed the student receiving a note from another student during the examination. After the final examination, the professor met with the student and later filed a formal complaint of academic misconduct against him. The university expelled the student, and he brought a state court action for due process violations. The court rejected the claims. **The evidence showed the university provided adequate due process and followed appropriate disciplinary procedures before it expelled the student.** Since there was substantial evidence to support the charges of academic misconduct, the court affirmed the expulsion. *Colorado v. Florida Int'l Univ.*, 967 So.2d 372 (Fla. Dist. Ct. App. 2007).

◆ *A federal district court denied an Ohio law school student's request to stop an investigation into allegations that he cheated on a test.*

All students at the law school were required to read and agree to the terms of the honor code. Among other things, the code called a three-member team to investigate misconduct charges. It also called for notice to accused students of the charges and a hearing before a seven-member panel. Accused students could choose one of the investigators. The honor council president rejected the student's proposed investigator because she may have been a witness to the misconduct. When the school commenced its investigation, the student filed a court action to prevent the council from proceeding with its investigation.

Noting that the honor council proceeding was not criminal in nature and that the law school was not a state actor, **the court concluded the school was not bound by the Due Process Clause**. The code was drafted by students, and like others, the student took an oath to abide by it. Honor code procedures were not unfair, as they provided for an investigation and gave students notice of prohibited conduct. The council president had a good reason to deny the student's request to appoint an investigator, and he was given adequate time to prepare his case. The student would not suffer irreparable harm if the motion was denied. As the requested order would "interfere seriously with law student self-governance" and would hurt efforts to protect the public from misconduct by attorneys, the court denied the motion for an injunction. *Valente v. Univ. of Dayton School of Law*, No. 3:07-cv-473, 2008 WL 343112 (S.D. Ohio 2/6/08).

◆ *A Pennsylvania court upheld a college's decision to sanction a student who was found guilty of plagiarizing a paper for a biology course.*

A student enrolled in an investigative laboratory biology course in which the professor assigned her to work with two classmates on a lab experiment. Parts of the student's paper were identical to a classmate's, and the professor suspected plagiarism. The school investigated, and an honors committee panel found a "reasonable likelihood" that she had violated the honor code. A college judicial board held a hearing and found the student guilty of plagiarism. The board imposed a failing grade for the course and stripped her of an honor she had won in another course. It also ordered her to perform community service and placed her on academic probation for the rest of her time at the school. The student sued the classmates, college and professor in state court for breach of contract, defamation, infliction of emotional distress and negligence.

The court dismissed her complaint. On appeal, the Superior Court of Pennsylvania found the parties had a contractual relationship governed by a student handbook. Although the student claimed the college breached the contract by failing to follow its procedures for misconduct claims, **the record showed she was provided all the procedural protections of the handbook**. The court rejected the breach of contract claim against the professor. The student's vague assertions that he was biased were insufficient. The court rejected the defamation claims against all the defendants, as their statements were opinion, fact, or lacked defamatory intent. As the negligence and emotional distress claims were properly dismissed, the court affirmed the judgment. *Reardon v. Allegheny College*, 926 A.2d 477 (Pa. Super. Ct. 2007).

◆ *Due process requires that an individual with a constitutionally protected interest receive notice and a meaningful opportunity to be heard.*

A student enrolled in the University of Michigan school of dentistry. Like all students, she signed an acknowledgement to abide by the school honor code. The student was accused of violating the code in a class. When the university notified her of the violation, she waived her right to an honor council hearing. Instead, the student chose to have a three-member *ad hoc* faculty committee hear her case. After a hearing, the faculty committee members unanimously agreed that she committed a violation and recommended the school expel her. The student appealed to an executive committee which held another hearing where she admitted the violation. The committee suspended her until the next semester and placed her on probation. After the student returned to school, she was again accused of code violations. The committee formally expelled her, and she sought a state court order to prevent the action.

The court denied the request, and the student appealed. The Court of Appeals of Michigan **held due process requires that an individual receive notice and a meaningful opportunity to be heard. To prove a constitutional risk of bias, an individual must show the risk or probability of unfairness was too high to be tolerated.** The court held the student did not prove an unacceptable risk of bias. Members of the honor council and *ad hoc* committee only submitted recommendations to the executive committee. The court rejected the student's contention that two honor council members who were classmates could not be impartial. As familiarity with a case does not disqualify a decision-maker, the judgment was affirmed. *Imitiaz v. Board of Regents of Univ. of Michigan*, No. 253107, 2006 WL 510057 (Mich. Ct. App. 3/2/06).

◆ *A Florida university followed its code and did not violate any due process rights pertaining to the waiver of a student hearing.*

The student enrolled in "Senior Project," a required course for a degree in construction management. He dropped the class after two weeks, but reenrolled in it the next year. As part of the course, students were required to develop a hypothetical construction company. When the student submitted documentation for his company, the course instructor believed parts of it were identical to those submitted by others in the previous semester. At a hearing, the instructor presented evidence and testified about the student's cheating, plagiarism and academic dishonesty. The student admitted hiring an architect to design part of his project and using part of the classmates' work from the previous semester. He claimed he had continued working with the group after dropping the course. A university vice provost upheld plagiarism, cheating and collusion charges, and expelled the student. After unsuccessful appeals within the university, the student sought review by a Florida district court of appeal.

The court found the university had followed the procedures specified in its code and did not violate any due process rights pertaining to the waiver of a review board hearing. A letter from the vice provost in advance of the hearing directed the student to read handbook provisions on academic misconduct, grievance procedures and student rights. The court held the university's failure to strictly comply with state administrative code requirements was harmless error and did not violate the student's due process rights. The hearing transcript revealed that he never tried to cross-examine the instructor, who identified 27 items in his work that were identical to work submitted by other students. As sufficient grounds for expulsion existed, the court affirmed the decision. *Matar v. Florida Int'l Univ.*, 944 So.2d 1153 (Fla. Dist. Ct. App. 2006).

◆   *The Appeals Court of Massachusetts held a university fully complied with its disciplinary procedures in finding a student guilty of plagiarism.*

A Brandeis University professor noticed a second-term senior student did not properly attribute four secondary sources in a paper. She filed a student judicial system referral report, accusing him of verbatim plagiarism. The university's board of student conduct unanimously found the student guilty of plagiarism, and he unsuccessfully challenged the finding through the university appeal process. The student sued Brandeis in a Massachusetts trial court for breach of contract and breach of fiduciary duty. The court granted Brandeis' motion for summary judgment, and the student appealed. **The state court of appeals explained the university was expected to conduct hearings with basic fairness.** In reviewing the record, the court found Brandeis satisfied that expectation by providing the student all of the process he was due under the terms of the handbook, from notification of the charge through the hearing process. **The handbook clearly warned him that violation of academic honesty policies could lead to serious penalties.** Moreover, the sanction was consistent with those imposed on other upperclassmen for similar infractions. The trial court did not err in granting summary judgment to the university. *Morris v. Brandeis Univ.*, 804 N.E.2d 961 (Mass. App. Ct. 2004).

C. Nonacademic Dismissals

In Schulman v. Franklin & Marshall College, *538 A.2d 49 (Pa. Super. Ct. 1988), the court held courts should not interfere with internal disciplinary matters unless they are biased, prejudicial or lacking in due process.*

◆   *No constitutional violation or other legal violation occurred when an Ohio medical student was dismissed from a university.*

After the student failed four exams in his second year, a medical school committee placed him on academic leave and required him to complete a program that focused on counseling and communication skills. He took a paid research position at the university while on leave, but he later claimed that he was not paid for all the hours that he worked. While repeating his second year at the medical school, the student was again referred to the committee, based on a female student's harassment claim, other unspecified complaints about his behavior in a lab, and his failure to remediate an exam. This time, the committee required him to remediate the exam and submit to a fitness-for-duty exam. After the latter exam showed he had "strong narcissistic traits and an inability to perceive or admit to his own mistakes," the committee decided he should be dismissed from the school. When the committee's decision was upheld in an internal appeal, the student withdrew from the medical school and then filed a state court action for breach of contract and unpaid wages.

After the court held for the university, the student appealed to the Court of Appeals of Ohio. **There was no evidence that the medical school owed him written notice of the grounds for dismissal, or a hearing and record of committee proceedings, as he claimed.** Nor was the school required to make sure the student was present when the reasons for the proceedings against him were explained. As for his claim for unpaid wages, he conceded he was never told in clear terms what work he would be paid for, or how or when he would be paid. As a result, he did not show he had a contract of employment with the university, and the judgment for the university was affirmed. *Obukhoff v. Case Western Reserve Univ.*, No. 93381, 2010 WL 1254589 (Ohio Ct. App. 4/1/10).

◆ *A nursing student's crude blog depiction of a patient's birthing experience did not violate the University of Louisville's honor code.*

As a nursing student at the university, the student was assigned to follow an obstetric patient through the birthing process. She made a blog post on her MySpace page stating that babies "are demons sent to us from hell to torture us for the whole eternity." It commented that having children is "like being ripped apart by rabid monkeys," and "pregnancy makes an ok-looking woman ugly." The post referred to the patient's newborn as "the new Creep." The student was soon dismissed from the program for breach of the honor code and a patient confidentiality agreement. She filed a federal district court action against the university, associate dean and dean, claiming speech rights and due process violations. Declining to address the constitutional claims, the court found the student did not violate the honor code or her confidentiality agreement.

Although the post stated the number of the patient's children and the date she was in labor, the court noted it did not disclose her name, address, financial or employment-related information. As the post did not include information that could lead to the discovery of the patient's identity, it did not violate the confidentiality provision of the honor code or the confidentiality agreement. **Nor did the post violate a "professionalism" provision of the honor code, since the student did not post it as a representative of the school of nursing.** Because the post did not violate the honor code or confidentiality agreement, the court ordered the immediate reinstatement of the student. *Yoder v. Univ. of Louisville*, No. 3:09-CV-205-S, 2009 WL 2406235 (W.D. Ky. 8/3/09).

◆ *Because she did not show a likelihood of irreparable injury, a California paralegal student was not entitled to reinstatement after being suspended.*

A student at West Valley College (California), was suspended after she was involved in several confrontations with teachers, administration and staff. She sued the college in a federal district court and requested a temporary restraining order (TRO) that would require the college to reinstate her immediately. According to the student, she was arrested in violation of her civil rights and suspended without due process. She claimed violation of her equal protection and speech rights. After dismissing the student's request for a TRO because of lack of notice to the college, the court denied a request for a preliminary order that would cancel her suspension and immediately reinstate her to classes.

The court noted evidence that the student habitually failed to a leave a campus restroom when asked by a custodian. She was charged with becoming belligerent, yelling obscenities at the custodian, and harassing and threatening other staff members. There was further evidence that she resisted arrest when police were called to remove her from campus. **Since the semester had ended, the court found no immediate reason to issue an order that would reinstate the student.** Even if she could prevail on the merits of her claims, she could pursue her program at another institution. As the hardship of reinstating a "repeatedly disruptive student" to the college was greater than the hardship to the student, the court denied her application for preliminary relief. *Mou v. West Valley College*, No. C 09-1910 JF (RS), 2009 WL 1858049 (N.D. Cal. 6/29/09).

◆ *A Pennsylvania university could deny a degree to a student who did not complete a student teaching placement, communicated with students on MySpace and posted a picture on the Internet of herself drinking alcohol.*

Despite being told not to refer students or teachers to personal Web pages, the student communicated with high school students on her MySpace page. Her page included a picture captioned "drunken pirate," which showed her wearing a pirate hat and holding a plastic cup. The page had a message that appeared to be critical of a teacher at the high school. The university assigned the student negative evaluations as a student teacher. The high school refused to let her complete her student teaching assignment, and the university refused to award her an education degree. Instead, the student earned an English degree. After unsuccessfully appealing the school's decision not to award her a teaching degree, she sued the university in a federal court.

First, the court denied the student's request for an order requiring the university to award her an education degree. Under state law, students seeking a teaching degree must complete a student teaching placement. The court also denied the student's request for an order requiring the university to recommend her to the state education department for certification. Ordering officials to do so would be pointless, because her **failure to complete her student teaching assignment made her ineligible for certification and would conceal her failure to complete the assignment**. There was no merit to the student's First Amendment claim based on the university's response to her MySpace postings. At the time of the postings, she was acting as a public employee, not a student. To prevail on a First Amendment claim, the student needed to show the posting related to a matter of public concern. As she admitted the postings related to personal matters only, her First Amendment claim failed. *Snyder v. Millersville Univ.*, No. 07-1660, 2008 WL 5093140 (E.D. Pa. 12/3/08).

◆ *A federal court denied an expelled student's Second Amendment claims against the University of Nebraska.*

The university expelled the student for carrying a concealed weapon on campus. He was told to complete anger management courses before he would be allowed to re-enroll. Instead, the student sued the university and state in a federal district court for violating his due process rights and a right to bear arms under the Second Amendment. **The court held college students are entitled to procedural due process in the form of adequate notice, specific charges, and a hearing.** However, the student did not claim he was denied adequate notice, and so failed to allege a due process violation. Instead of dismissing the claim, the court granted him 30 days to amend his complaint in a way that clearly stated a due process claim under the Fourteenth Amendment.

The court found that the right to bear arms under the Second Amendment is limited, and that states can ban the carrying of a concealed weapon. As the student's simple allegation of a Second Amendment violation was insufficient, the court gave him 30 days to either make a clearer statement or face dismissal of the case. *Swait v. Univ. of Nebraska at Omaha*, No. 8:08CV404, 2008 WL 5083245 (D. Neb. 11/25/08).

◆ *A Pennsylvania university permissibly dismissed a student from its medical program following an extended leave of absence.*

A medical student asked for a leave of absence based on his belief that his telephone conversations were being monitored. He also said someone at the school was intercepting his electronic conversations and posting them on a listserve. The request was granted, but when he extended it by filing three additional requests, the school told him he would not be allowed to return without documentation showing fitness to continue his studies. After the student failed to provide the documentation, a school committee voted to dismiss him. He sued the school and several officials for defamation and invasion of privacy. The student also said the school breached a contract by failing to follow procedures outlined in the school's code of ethics. The court ruled against him, and he appealed to the U.S. Court of Appeals, Third Circuit.

The court held the invasion of privacy and defamation claims were barred by a one-year statute of limitations. The student failed to establish his contract claims, as they were limited to actions that took place during his dismissal hearings. In addition, the student could not pursue a claim of tortious interference with contract because the school was not a party to a contract. **There was insufficient evidence that he was improperly dismissed from school or that anyone had intercepted his electronic conversations and posted them on a listserve.** As the court found no evidence showing the school had violated its code of ethics, the judgment for the school was affirmed. *Motise v. Parrish*, 297 Fed.Appx. 149 (3d Cir. 2008).

◆ *The suspension of a New York business school student was not disproportionate to the offense of harassing other students.*

A New York Appellate Division Court dismissed a student's petition to annul his suspension by Columbia University's business school for one year. The court refused to annul the decision to ban him for life from using the university's Career Services and Alumni Affairs and from certain recruiting-related student activities. The student had sent harassing communications to and about several other students at the business school. The student received an opportunity to present his side of the story and to appeal internally. **The court found the school fulfilled all the required process due the student for a disciplinary proceeding on a nonacademic matter. It said the university's actions were not disproportionate to the student's conduct,** and it dismissed the student's petition. *Fernandez v. Columbia Univ.*, 790 N.Y.S.2d 603 (N.Y. App. Div. 2005).

◆   *A federal appeals court found no merit to a student's claim that a Texas university maintained a "zero tolerance" drug policy.*

A Southwest Texas State University student claimed the university's drug policy, as written in the student handbook, mandated automatic dismissal if a student was found guilty of the possession, use or distribution of illegal drugs. In protest of what he deemed a "zero tolerance drug policy," he lit a marijuana cigarette at an on-campus rally. The university suspended him for two semesters. He sued the university and various officials in a federal district court, alleging the policy violated his Equal Protection rights. The court granted summary judgment to the university, and the student appealed.

The U.S. Court of Appeals, Fifth Circuit, found that although the handbook had some conflicting language, there was no evidence it contained a "zero tolerance" drug policy. **The court found the policy provided disciplinary options to impose suspensions or dismissals, undermining the "zero tolerance" policy argument. Student code penalty provisions were not automatic.** Moreover, students were entitled to a hearing before a disciplinary committee with the discretion to consider mitigating factors and reduce suspensions to probation. The court held the student's Equal Protection claim lacked merit, and it affirmed the judgment. *Anderson v. Southwest Texas State Univ.*, 73 Fed.Appx. 775 (5th Cir. 2003).

III. STUDENT PRIVACY RIGHTS

A. The Family Educational Rights and Privacy Act

The Family Educational Rights and Privacy Act (FERPA), 20 U.S.C. § 1232g, was enacted in 1974 to grant eligible students access to their education records and to protect records from access by unauthorized persons.

FERPA applies to any educational institution receiving federal funds. It contains detailed requirements regarding the maintenance and disclosure of student records. These requirements become applicable only upon a student's attendance at the school. FERPA, at 20 U.S.C. § 1232g(d), requires institutions to allow students to inspect and review their education records.

When students request access to their education records, schools must grant that access within a reasonable time, not to exceed 45 days. Students also must be given the opportunity for a hearing to challenge the content of their education records, or to ensure that the records are not inaccurate, misleading, or otherwise in violation of their privacy or other rights.

FERPA applies only to "education records," which are "records related to a student that are maintained by an educational agency or a party acting for the agency." Records that originate from a school, or are created by non-school entities, may become education records if they are "maintained" by a school.

Records maintained by a law enforcement agency of an institution (for the purpose of law enforcement) do not constitute education records for purposes of FERPA. Schools cannot release, or provide access to, any personally identifiable information on students other than directory information without written consent. Violating FERPA results in a loss of federal funds.

FERPA regulations, codified at 34 C.F.R. Part 99, describe when personally identifiable information may be disclosed without consent by a parent or eligible student. "Personal identifiers" may indirectly identify a student. These include date and place of birth, mother's maiden name, or "information that, alone or in combination," may allow identification by a reasonable person in the school community. A student's social security number or student identification number is personally identifiable information that may not be disclosed as directory information under 34 C.F.R. Part 99.3.

Under 34 C.F.R. Part 99.31(a)(1), **educational institutions "must use reasonable methods to ensure that officials obtain access to only those education records in which they have legitimate educational interests."**

Part 99.31(a)(2) permits educational agencies to disclose education records without consent to another institution, even after a student has enrolled or transferred, for reasons related to enrollment or transfer.

A 2008 amendment to 34 C.F.R. Part 99.36 lent guidance to a FERPA provision permitting disclosures in "health and safety emergencies." *An agency or institution may make a disclosure to any person, including parents, whose knowledge of the information is necessary to protect the health or safety of the student or other individual. A college or university can include in the education records of any student "appropriate information … concerning disciplinary action taken against such student for conduct that posed a significant risk to the safety or well-being of that student, other students, or other members of the school community." 20 U.S.C. § 1232g(h).*

FERPA excludes notes used only as a personal memory aid and kept in the sole possession of the maker. These "desk drawer" notes cannot be revealed to any other person, except a temporary substitute for the maker of the record.

◆   *FERPA did not prevent an Ohio community college from disclosing prior complaints against an instructor accused of sexually harassing a student.*

In the student's federal district court action against the college, it was claimed that the instructor's supervisor knew of similar conduct in the past and that the college and supervisor failed to take adequate steps to eliminate the risk he posed. During pretrial activity, the student sought class rosters from classes taught by the instructor for the four years prior to the harassment she claimed. She also sought "every document relevant to any student complaint/concern" about the instructor. The college denied the requested information, arguing it could not be disclosed under FERPA. The court found some prior student complaints could be relevant to the present claims. Complaints similar in nature to the student's would support charges that the college and supervisor were aware of prior misconduct. However, not all potential complaints against the instructor would be relevant. For example, a complaint relating to a grade dispute would not be relevant. The court concluded that the request should be limited to prior complaints of alleged sexual harassment. There was insufficient evidence to show that class rosters were relevant to the student's claims.

FERPA did not bar the request for prior student complaints relating to alleged sexual harassment. **Any such student complaints were records that related directly to school employees and only indirectly to students**, and they were not "student records" within the meaning of FERPA. FERPA's limitations on disclosure did not apply to the request for student complaints of sexual harassment. *Briggs v. Board of Trustees Columbus State Community College*, No. 2:08-CV-644, 2009 WL 2047899 (S.D. Ohio 7/8/09).

◆ *A federal district court refused to dismiss a newspaper's open records act claims relating to a University of Oklahoma investigation of student-athletes.*

The *Dallas Morning News* asked the University of Oklahoma to provide employment records relating to some student-athletes by a particular employer. The university responded by providing documents with some information blocked from them. The university claimed the blocking was required by FERPA. The newspaper sued the university in a federal district court for open records act violations. The court refused to dismiss the claims, finding the newspaper had adequately alleged wrongful denial of access to additional records. **The newspaper also claimed that even if FERPA applied, the university withheld more information than the statute authorized.** Because the newspaper had stated a valid claim, the court denied the university's dismissal motion. *Dallas Morning News v. State of Oklahoma*, No. CIV-06-1104-M, 2007 WL 1237771 (W.D. Okla. 4/27/07).

◆ *As FERPA creates no individually enforceable rights, a disabled student could not pursue an action for wrongful disclosure of his condition.*

A Massachusetts university baseball coach told the team that the student had bipolar disorder. The student sued the university in a federal district court for violations of FERPA. The court determined it was unclear as to whether the coach's statement violated the nondisclosure rules of FERPA. **Even if it did, the student had no right of action in court to redress such a violation, because FERPA does not create any individually enforceable rights.** Violations of FERPA are redressed by the Secretary of Education, who may direct in certain circumstances that funds be withheld from the educational institution. Accordingly, the court dismissed the FERPA claim. *Zona v. Clark Univ.*, 436 F.Supp.2d 287 (D. Mass. 2006).

◆ *A North Carolina University obtained a court order to seal depositions and a student's academic transcript in a sexual harassment lawsuit.*

The university, a coach and employee sought depositions from students and their parents. The university, coach and employee also filed the affidavit of the university's registrar with the student's final official transcript attached. The university moved to seal the depositions and affidavit. Because the First Amendment gives the public a right to see and hear all evidence in a civil trial, courts may seal documents filed with a motion for summary judgment only if the government has a compelling interest to do so. Because the depositions contained private information on other students, the university argued they should be sealed to protect their privacy interests. The court disagreed.

The court found no violation of the other students' privacy rights because they had no reasonable expectation of privacy in information exchanged with team members. **The depositions were not protected by FERPA, as they were not "education records."** FERPA was only one consideration in deciding if the student's interest was compelling. She previously took no position on her privacy interests, leaving the court to assume she had no significant interest in having her academic records sealed. A FERPA exception allows the disclosure of relevant educational records on a student who initiates legal action against a university. Because the student had ample opportunity to respond to the motion to seal the record, the court concluded she effectively consented to the release of her academic records. *Jennings v. Univ. of North Carolina*, 340 F. Supp.2d 679 (M.D.N.C. 2004).

◆ *An Illinois student's defamation and invasion of privacy claims were barred because they arose from remarks made by a professor that were deemed to be within the scope of his employment.*

An Illinois political science professor suspected a colleague of having a sexual relationship with a graduate student. He informed the department chair about their behavior and discussed the matter with four other professors. He also informed the student's boyfriend of his suspicions. During this time, other students complained that the colleague was generally unavailable and did not keep his office hours. The student filed a grievance against the professor, charging him with sexual harassment and violating her privacy, and made a charge against him with the Illinois Department of Human Rights. The professor sued the student in a federal district court, alleging deprivation of his First Amendment speech rights and retaliation. The student counterclaimed for defamation, intentional infliction of emotional distress and invasion of her privacy rights. The court awarded summary judgment to the professor.

The Seventh Circuit held the professor showed his comments were made within the scope of his employment. Evidence indicated the university was concerned about inappropriate professor-student relationships and encouraged professors to report suspicious relationships. The professor communicated his concerns during the academic year within normal office hours. The court rejected the student's characterization of his remarks as gossip. The professor spoke to other professors about the colleague's lack of professionalism and his observations were motivated, at least in part, by an intent to serve the university. **The court rejected the FERPA claim based on *Gonzaga Univ. v. Doe*, below, in which the Supreme Court held there is no private cause of action for FERPA violations under 42 U.S.C. § 1983.** *Shockley v. Svoboda*, 342 F.3d 736 (7th Cir. 2003).

◆ *A student who claimed that a university violated FERPA could not sue under 42 U.S.C. § 1983 to enforce individual "rights" under the act.*

A student attended a private university in Washington, intending to teach in the state's public school system after his graduation. At the time, the state required new teachers to obtain an affidavit of good moral character from the dean of their college or university. When the university's teacher certification specialist overheard a conversation implicating the student in sexual misconduct with a classmate, she commenced an investigation of the student and reported the allegations against him to the state teacher certification agency. She later informed the student that the university would not provide him with the affidavit of good moral character required for certification as a Washington teacher. The student sued the university and the specialist under state law and under 42 U.S.C. § 1983, alleging a violation of FERPA. A jury awarded the student over $1 million in damages. The case reached the U.S. Supreme Court, which ruled that **FERPA creates no personal rights that can be enforced under Section 1983**. Congress enacted FERPA to force schools to respect students' privacy with respect to educational records. It did not confer upon students enforceable rights. As a result, the Court reversed and remanded the case for further proceedings. *Gonzaga Univ. v. Doe*, 536 U.S. 273, 122 S.Ct. 2268, 153 L.Ed.2d 309 (2002).

◆   *Using students to correct other students' work and call out the grades in class did not violate FERPA.*

An Oklahoma parent sued a school district and various administrators under FERPA after learning that students sometimes graded other students' assignments and called out the results in class. A federal court held this practice did not violate FERPA because calling out grades did not involve "education records" within the meaning of the statute. The Tenth Circuit reversed, but the U.S. Supreme Court noted that **student papers are not "maintained" within the meaning of FERPA when students correct them and call out grades**. Moreover, correcting a student's work can be as much a part of the assignment as taking the test itself. The momentary handling of assignments by students was not equivalent to the storing of information in a records room or a school's permanent secure database. *Owasso Independent School Dist. No. I-011 v. Falvo*, 534 U.S. 426, 122 S.Ct. 934, 151 L.Ed.2d 896 (2002).

◆   *University disciplinary records were held to be "education records" under FERPA and thus could not be disclosed to the press.*

A student newspaper at an Ohio university sought student disciplinary records from the University Disciplinary Board for an article about crime trends on campus. After a lawsuit, the Ohio Supreme Court held that student disciplinary records were not "education records" under FERPA. As a result, the university had to hand over the records, without name, Social Security number and student identification number. Another newspaper then requested disciplinary records from two Ohio universities. The U.S. Department of Education (DOE) asked a federal district court for an order to prevent the universities from disclosing the disciplinary records. The court agreed with the DOE that disciplinary records are "education records" under FERPA, and issued an injunction to prevent the release of the information.

The Sixth Circuit Court of Appeals affirmed, noting that **because the disciplinary records related to students and were kept by the universities, they were education records under FERPA**. Since university disciplinary proceedings are not like criminal trials, which have been traditionally open to the press and the public, an order preventing release of the information was appropriate. *U.S. v. Miami Univ.*, 294 F.3d 797 (6th Cir. 2002).

◆   *Student applicant information was not protected by FERPA where it was not personally identifiable.*

The University of Wisconsin System received a request for records of applicants applying for admission to the system's 11 undergraduate campuses, its law school and its medical school over a six-year period. The system partially complied with the request, but withheld information on standardized test scores, race and gender because it believed the information was protected by FERPA and because it believed the release of such information would require it to create new records. The case reached the Supreme Court of Wisconsin, which held that **FERPA did not prevent disclosure of the requested data because it was not personally identifiable information**.

Even though it might be possible for the data to create a list of identifying characteristics, the court concluded that the information was not personally identifiable. Also, the court noted that the system would not have to create new records to comply with the request. It merely would have to redact personally identifiable information from records it already maintained. Doing so would be burdensome; however, the system could charge a fee for photocopying records to alleviate its costs. The system had to provide the requested information. *Osborn v. Board of Regents of Univ. of Wisconsin System*, 647 N.W.2d 158 (Wis. 2002).

◆ *FERPA does not create students right to learn how grades are assigned.*

A federal district court held that **neither FERPA nor a Texas school policy provided a means for a student to obtain information on how a grade was assigned. At most, the student in this case was only entitled to know whether the assigned grade was recorded accurately** in the records. *Tarka v. Cunningham*, 741 F.Supp. 1281 (W.D. Tex. 1990).

B. State Law Privacy Rights

While there is no private right of action under FERPA for damages under Gonzaga Univ. v. Doe, this chapter, state laws modeled on FERPA may create enforceable privacy rights for students. Students may also bring common law claims based on enrollment contracts or other agreements with educational institutions.

◆ *A California university did not violate a state privacy statute by failing to safeguard the privacy of student exams.*

California's Information Practices Act (CIPA) limits the disclosure of personal information about individuals by state agencies and requires them to maintain complete and accurate records. A University of California student accused university officials of failing to safeguard student exams by leaving them unguarded and in plain view in hallways. He sought to inspect and copy his personal records and exams, and to correct information contained in his personal records. The student further claimed the university violated the CIPA by destroying some of his personal records, including his exams. A state superior court found the student was not damaged by the alleged CIPA violations. Moreover, the court upheld university policies and procedures and held the exams could be discarded.

On appeal, **the Court of Appeal of California held student exams were not covered by the CIPA because they were not stored or maintained by the university**. The CIPA applied only to "records" containing "personal information." In turn, CIPA defined "records" as "any file or grouping of information about an individual that is maintained by an agency." Student exams were typically returned to students or held by individual instructors, and they did not contain personal information. CIPA defined "personal information" as information that "identifies or describes an individual," such as by physical description, Social Security number or home address. Since exams containing only a name or student number did not constitute "personal information" under the CIPA, the court affirmed the judgment. *Moghadam v. Regents of Univ. of California*, 169 Cal.App.4th 466, 86 Cal.Rptr.3d 739 (Cal. Ct. App. 2008).

◆ *A private Georgia university did not violate the state's Open Records Act by refusing to grant a student's request to see the records of other students.*

The student stated she had been sexually assaulted on campus. She asked the university for records of other students who were victims of rapes and sexual assaults on campus. The university refused the request, and the student sued the university in a Georgia trial court, alleging it violated the state's Open Records Act. The court found the school's police force performed public functions in the enforcement of state laws. It held the records sought by the student were subject to the act and allowed her to view them. The university appealed to the Court of Appeals of Georgia.

The court explained the state Open Records Act generally required that all "public records" be open to inspection by the general public. It held the act was intended to encourage public access to information and promote public confidence in government through access to public records. The university was a nonprofit corporation, not a government agency. Campus officers were not public officials based on the state's decision to authorize them to perform certain duties. The court found the records were not "public records" because they were not prepared, maintained or received in the course of the operation of a public office or agency. The court reversed the judgment, as the documents maintained by the school police were not covered by the Act. *Mercer Univ. v. Barrett and Farahany, LLP*, 610 S.E.2d 138 (Ga. Ct. App. 2005).

◆ *Parts of a statewide test that were owned by the state were public records and had to be disclosed to a student.*

The Ohio Department of Education (ODE) administers the Ohio Proficiency Test to high school seniors to ensure that they have requisite knowledge in selected academic areas. Ohio State University also administered a statewide test to high school students that was developed to accelerate the modernization of vocational education in the state. Part of that test was developed and owned by a private entity. Both tests used a new format each time a test was administered and the tests were owned in part by the state agencies that administered them. An Ohio student who had taken both examinations requested access to the tests after they had been administered.

The Supreme Court of Ohio ruled **the state-owned parts of both tests were public records within the meaning of state law**. Further, none of the exceptions to the state law presumption in favor of public disclosure applied. The student sought release of the information for educational purposes and did not seek to use it for a commercial purpose. A state law that prohibits assisting a student in cheating on proficiency tests was not applicable to this case. The student was entitled to an order for disclosure of the requested information. However, the portion of the test devised by the private entity was not a public record and was not subject to release. *State ex rel. Rea v. Ohio Dep't of Educ.*, 81 Ohio St.3d 527, 692 N.E.2d 596 (Ohio 1998).

◆ *A Colorado student could sue a college for ordering an HIV test without his permission.*

A student in a medical assistant training program told his instructor that he had tested positive for HIV and asked him to keep that information confidential. The instructor informed the class that all students were required to be tested for rubella. The student consented to the test with the understanding that his sample would be tested for rubella only. However, the instructor contacted the lab and asked that the student's sample be tested for HIV. She did not request such testing for any other student. After the sample tested positive, the lab reported the student's name, address and HIV status to the state of health (as required by law) and informed the college of the results. The student sued the college for invasion of privacy, asserting it unreasonably disclosed private facts and intruded upon his seclusion. The court dismissed the intrusion upon seclusion claim, but a jury found the student was entitled to damages for the college's unreasonable disclosure of private facts.

On appeal, the Colorado Court of Appeals held in his favor. **The claim for intrusion upon seclusion involved the college's authorization of a test that the student had not authorized, which was the improper appropriation of confidential information. The claim for unreasonable disclosure of private facts involved the dissemination of that information.** That the student suffered harm because of the disclosure of information did not mean he could not have suffered harm because of the improper appropriation of the information. The court reversed and remanded the case. *Doe v. High-Tech Institute, Inc.*, 972 P.2d 1060 (Colo. Ct. App. 1998).

C. Computer Privacy

◆ *The remote search of a dormitory computer did not violate a Wisconsin student hacker's reasonable expectation of privacy in the computer.*

A California-based Qualcomm computer system administrator informed the University of Wisconsin – Madison that someone had hacked Qualcomm's network through a computer connected to the university's network. A university investigator confirmed the report and discovered the hacker had also gained access to the university network. Concerned that the university's 60,000-account e-mail system was in immediate jeopardy, the investigator accessed the computer from a remote location. After viewing the computer's temporary directory, the investigator confirmed the unauthorized activity and took the computer off line to protect the university's e-mail system. He contacted university police and a federal agent who was working on the case. The investigator and university went to the hacker's dorm room and unplugged the computer from the network. The hacker arrived and gave the investigator permission to run a few commands. The test confirmed that the computer had been used to hack the networks. Federal agents obtained a warrant and seized the computer. The hacker was indicted on multiple offenses. A federal district court denied his motions to suppress evidence gathered via the remote search.

On appeal, **the U.S. Court of Appeals, Ninth Circuit, held the student hacker had a reasonable privacy expectation in his personal computer, which was not eliminated by attaching it to the university's network. The investigator's actions were not taken for law enforcement purposes, and a search warrant was not needed because he was acting in his role as a system administrator.** University policy authorized the investigator to rectify emergency situations that threatened the integrity of campus computers or communication systems. His actions were justified because he needed to act at once to protect the system. Under the circumstances, the court found the remote search of the computer was "remarkably limited." The investigator was logged in to the computer for just 15 minutes, and did not view, delete or modify any files. As the investigator's actions were taken to secure the university's e-mail server, the court held the evidence obtained during the searches was admissible. *U.S. v. Heckencamp*, 482 F.3d 1142 (9th Cir. 2007).

◆ *A student who allegedly saved child pornography on university computer-lab computers was not entitled to privacy under the Fourth Amendment.*

A Maine student left an image on a university computer screen that a university employee considered pedophilic. University authorities investigated the incident and discovered similar images on the hard drives of other computer-lab computers. The university contacted the police, and the student was indicted for receiving child pornography in violation of 18 U.S.C. § 2252A(a)(2). The prosecution obtained two hard drives from the university that allegedly contained illegal images, as well as the university's computer usage logs, which indicated when the student used the computers. The student filed a motion to have the hard drives and logs suppressed as the product of searches that violated his Fourth Amendment right against unreasonable searches and seizures. A federal court judge ruled the student had no right to privacy in this matter and denied the motion to suppress. **To assert a right under the Fourth Amendment, a defendant must show that he believes he had a right to privacy and that society would find his expectation objectively reasonable.**

Because the usage logs were maintained for the benefit of the university, they could not be suppressed. The judge cited *Smith v. Maryland*, 442 U.S. 735 (1970), in which the U.S. Supreme Court held that a telephone customer had no legitimate expectation of privacy in telephone numbers he had dialed because, in dialing, he voluntarily conveyed the information to the telephone company and assumed the risk that the information could be disclosed. As for the hard drives, the judge found the student pointed to no computer privacy policies at the university, no statements made to him about the use of the computer lab, no practices concerning access to and retention of the contents of the hard drives or even password requirements. **The student was simply using university computers under circumstances where images on the monitor were visible to others.** *U.S. v. Butler*, 151 F.Supp.2d 82 (D. Me. 2001).

IV. GRADING AND CURRICULUM

Courts typically use restraint when considering academic matters. In Univ. of Pennsylvania v. EEOC, *493 U.S. 182 (1990), the U.S. Supreme Court stated that courts should avoid second-guessing legitimate academic judgments.*

◆ *New York Law School did not breach an implied contract with a student by assigning him a grade of "C" for a particular course.*

After transferring to New York Law School, the student claimed he was disadvantaged by being placed in a Legal Writing II course instead of Legal Writing I. After being assigned a C grade, he said the law school breached an implied contract with him by arbitrarily assigning the grade. To support his breach of contract claim, the student relied on statements on a law school website. He said the statements, such as one indicating the school offered "the right program for every student," created a contract and required the school to act in good faith. In the student's state court action, the trial court held **New York courts generally do not intervene in grading disputes because doing so would "inappropriately involve the courts in the very core of academic and educational decision making."** Through its student handbook, the law school clearly informed all students that it used a letter grading system, not a pass-fail system. The court granted the law school's motion to dismiss the case.

On appeal, the New York Supreme Court, Appellate Division, held "only specific promises set forth in a school's bulletins, circulars and handbooks which are material to the student's relationship with the school, can establish the existence of an implied contract." While academic judgments are not beyond all judicial review, "that review is limited to the question of whether the challenged determination was arbitrary and capricious, irrational, made in bad faith or contrary to Constitution or statute." As the lower court found no promise to the student that a pass/fail grading system would be used, the court affirmed the judgment for the law school. *Keefe v. New York Law School*, 71 A.D.3d 569, 897 N.Y.S.2d 94 (N.Y. App. Div. 2010).

◆ *Columbia University alumni failed to force the elimination of a women's studies program or the addition of a corresponding "men's studies" program.*

In a federal class action lawsuit, two male alumni accused the U.S. Department of Education and Columbia officials of violating the Establishment Clause by "aiding the establishment of the religion of feminism" at the university. They also claimed a violation of their due process rights, their equal protection rights and Title IX of the Education Amendments of 1972. The alumni requested declaratory relief, injunctive relief and nominal damages.

To support their claims, the alumni asserted the women's studies program harmed them by propagating negative information about males. They also said they were harmed by the absence of a men's studies program. According to the court, they did not assert any injury in fact. Neither of the males enrolled in the women's studies program, and they had no firsthand exposure to it. At most, the injury they suffered was subjective and not an objective, concrete harm. **Because they did not suffer an injury in fact, the alumni did not have**

standing to raise their claims relating to the women's studies program. Similarly, they did not suffer concrete and particularized injury from the absence of a men's studies program at the university. As a result, they could not pursue the case. *Den Hollander v. Institute for Research on Women & Gender at Columbia Univ.*, No. 08 Civ. 7286, 2009 WL 1025960 (S.D.N.Y. 4/15/09).

◆   *A graduate student could not proceed with a federal case claiming Illinois university officials wrongfully failed to acknowledge her doctorate degree.*

Four years after the student completed course work for a doctoral degree in educational psychology and defended her thesis, she learned the university had never properly posted the degree. A university dean assured the student's prospective employer that this was a clerical error. But when the student took another job, her new employer was unable to verify completion of her doctorate work. As a result, she lost the job, and later sued university officials in a federal district court. After the case was dismissed, the student appealed to the U.S. Court of Appeals, Seventh Circuit. The appeals court explained that under state law, a claim arising from a state employee's breach of a duty must be filed in a state court, if the duty is imposed by virtue of his employment with the state.

In this case, university officials had the chance to block the degree only because they worked for a state university. Their obligation to be truthful and fair with respect to doctorate candidates existed because of where they worked. Similarly, the duty to process degrees and accurately report graduate status was held by the officials because of where they worked. Although the student argued she should be allowed to keep her case in federal court because her suit was really against the officials and not the state, the court disagreed. **She did not allege any violation of a state law or constitutional provision.** Since the student could not file her suit in federal court, the court affirmed the decision. *Turpin v. Koropchak*, 567 F.3d 880 (7th Cir. 2009).

◆   *A federal court refused to dismiss an Arizona student's claim that a university refused to grant him incomplete grades based on his back ailment.*

After being withdrawn from three classes, the student appealed and was allowed to re-enroll in two of them. He e-mailed a complaint to an administrator about the university's previous refusal to give him incomplete grades, and he later claimed retaliation for sending the e-mail. The student sued the university in a federal district court for disability discrimination, retaliation, breach of contract and infliction of emotional distress. With respect to the disability bias claims under the Americans with Disabilities Act and the Rehabilitation Act, the court decided a factual issue was present as to whether the student had a disability within the meaning of the law. **There was also a factual issue regarding whether the law required the university to accommodate the student's back condition by granting his request for incomplete grades.**

While the court refused to dismiss the disability bias claims, the university was entitled to judgment on the student's retaliation claim. This was because the university provided legitimate reasons for its actions. For example, the university threatened to dismiss the student because he behaved abusively toward administrators, and it restricted him from taking a course because it was not designed for doctoral students. The court also granted dismissal of the emotional distress claim because the facts did not indicate "extreme and outrageous conduct." Finally, the court denied pretrial judgment for a breach of contract claim. *Yount v. Regent Univ.*, No. CV-08-8011-PCT-DGC, 2009 WL 995596 (D. Ariz. 4/14/09).

◆ *A federal appeals court rejected several claims raised by a California university student who was dissatisfied with a grade.*

After expressing dissatisfaction with a grade he received, the student was given an opportunity to appear before a faculty panel. After the panel issued a decision against him, he sued the university in a federal district court for violation of his constitutional rights under 42 U.S.C. § 1983. The student claimed due process and equal protection violations and added a conspiracy claim under 42 U.S.C. § 1985. The court held for the university. On appeal, the U.S. Court of Appeals, Ninth Circuit, held the substantive due process claim failed because **the student did not show the university's academic assessment was arbitrary**. The procedural due process claim failed because he was given the chance to appear before the faculty panel. **The panel considered his concerns and made its decision after careful deliberation.** The equal protection claim also failed, because the student did not claim he was treated differently than similarly situated individuals. The conspiracy claim was based on conclusory allegations without factual support. Accordingly, the court affirmed the judgment for the university. *Negrete v. Trustees of the California State Univ.*, 260 Fed.Appx. 9 (9th Cir. 2007).

◆ *The U.S. Court of Appeals, Sixth Circuit, held a Vanderbilt University student deserved a chance to convince a jury that his professor was negligent in his method of returning graded papers.*

The student was enrolled in an organic chemistry class. The professor placed graded answer sheets for the class in a stack on a table outside the classroom. Students had to go through the stack to find their answer sheets. The professor allowed students to resubmit their answer sheets for a "re-grade" if they believed he incorrectly marked them. The student found one of his correct answers was marked incorrect and returned the paper for re-grading. The professor believed the student had changed the answer and reported the student to Vanderbilt's honor council. The honor council conducted a hearing, and found the student guilty of cheating. He received a failing grade for the organic chemistry class and was suspended for the summer session. After an unsuccessful appeal, the student sued Vanderbilt in a federal district court for negligence, among other claims. The court held criteria to determine a standard of care for a teacher returning graded exams has never been established. Consequently, the student could not prove negligence.

On appeal, the Sixth Circuit found **Vanderbilt owed its students a duty not to engage in conduct that posed an unreasonable and foreseeable risk of harm**. Vanderbilt argued it could not have foreseen that a student would sabotage another student's test to improve his own position in the curve. The Sixth Circuit disagreed, in view of the competitive environment in academic institutions. The court found it unclear whether the manner in which the professor distributed graded answer sheets posed an unreasonable risk of harm. **A jury could conclude the burden on the professor to use another method**

for returning tests was minimal and find the harm to students was foreseeable. The gravity of harm created by the professor's method was severe. A wrongful conviction by a disciplinary committee could ruin a student's chances of getting into graduate school. The professor breached the university's duty of care by acting in a way that posed an unreasonable and foreseeable risk of harm. A jury would have to decide whether Vanderbilt injured the student. The court reversed and remanded the judgment. *Atria v. Vanderbilt Univ.*, 142 Fed.Appx. 246 (6th Cir 2005).

◆ *A New York student, who was homeschooled through high school, lost his equal protection claim in a federal district court against a state college.*

After the college admitted the student, it notified him by letter that college records showed he had not provided any papers to prove he had graduated from a high school or received a GED. The letter also informed the student that the state education department required students to have a high school diploma or equivalent before they could graduate from a New York state college. The college told the student to obtain a GED. The student deliberately did not try to get a GED, asserting it carried the stigma of being a substitute for a high school diploma used primarily for high school dropouts. He then sued the college in a federal district court, alleging it violated his equal protection rights by treating him differently from similarly situated public school graduates. He argued that because his homeschool education was substantially equivalent to a public school education, the college had no rational basis to treat him differently.

The court stated **the college did not have to take the word of the student that he received the equivalent of a public high school education.** In *Univ. of Pennsylvania v. EEOC*, 493 U.S. 182 (1990), the U.S. Supreme Court stated that **courts should avoid second-guessing legitimate academic judgments and respect a faculty's professional judgment.** The court held the actions of the college were rationally related to its legitimate interests in maintaining academic standards and the integrity of its degree-granting programs. It granted the request of the college to dismiss the equal protection claim. A year after the student filed the lawsuit, New York amended its regulations governing homeschooling. The new regulations stated that as long as students who were homeschooled met certain instructional requirements, they could graduate from a New York college. The college later issued the student an associate degree. *Owens v. Parrinello*, 365 F. Supp.2d 353 (W.D.N.Y. 2005).

◆ *The U.S. Court of Appeals, Ninth Circuit, rejected an appeal by a former student who claimed the University of California violated the First Amendment and state law by offering a curriculum that included religious studies classes.*

The court held the former student alleged no facts supporting a conclusion that the course offerings advanced a non-secular purpose, had a primary effect of advancing or inhibiting religion and fostered an excessive entanglement with religion. The former student had filed multiple lawsuits against the university in federal courts, many of them alleging race discrimination. The university expelled him in 1999 for misconduct after he unsuccessfully challenged a C grade in a rhetoric class. *LaFreniere v. Regents of Univ. of California*, 207 Fed.Appx. 783 (9th Cir. 2006).

V. CAMPUS SAFETY AND SECURITY

A. Search and Seizure

The Fourth Amendment to the U.S. Constitution prohibits unreasonable searches and seizures by states, including state institutions of higher education. A "seizure" does not occur every time police stop and question a person. Officers may rely on reliable reports from staff to make investigatory stops.

◆   *In* New Jersey v. T.L.O., *the U.S. Supreme Court held a school search need only be reasonable at its inception, and not overly intrusive under the circumstances. Courts have applied T.L.O. to public colleges and university cases, based on the strong state interest in protecting student safety.*

A New Jersey high school teacher found two girls smoking in the lavatory in violation of school rules. She brought them to the assistant vice principal's office where one of the girls admitted smoking in the lavatory. The other denied even being a smoker. The assistant vice principal then asked the latter girl to come to his private office, where he opened her purse and found a pack of cigarettes. As he reached for them he noticed rolling papers and decided to thoroughly search the entire purse. He found marijuana, a pipe, empty plastic bags, a substantial number of one dollar bills and a list of "people who owe me money." He then turned her over to the police. After a juvenile court hearing, the girl was found delinquent. Appeal reached the U.S. Supreme Court.

The Supreme Court held the search did not violate the Fourth Amendment. **When police conduct a search, they have to meet the probable cause standard. However, school officials are held to a lower standard: reasonable suspicion.** Two considerations are relevant in determining the reasonableness of a search. First, the search must be justified initially by reasonable suspicion. Second, the scope and conduct of the search must be reasonably related to the circumstances that gave rise to the search, and school officials must take into account the student's age, sex and the nature of the offense. **The Court upheld the search of the student in this case because the initial search for cigarettes was supported by reasonable suspicion.** The discovery of the rolling papers then justified the further searching of the purse since such papers are commonly used to roll marijuana cigarettes. The "reasonableness" standard was met by school officials in these circumstances. *New Jersey v. T.L.O.*, 469 U.S. 325, 105 S.Ct. 733, 83 L.Ed.2d 720 (1985).

◆   *Massachusetts roommates who consented to the search of their dorm room by a campus police officer could not later claim to have been illegally searched.*

After a report that one of the roommates had been bullying other students and "waving a knife around," campus police went to his dorm room. An officer told the roommates he was there because of a report of a gun in the room. He found a plastic gun under the bed. Upon further searching, two knives and a spiked martial arts weapon were found. The roommates signed *Miranda* waiver forms and forms consenting to further searching of the room, which yielded cocaine, psilocybin and marijuana. The roommates were arrested and charged with various drug crimes. A trial judge granted their motion to suppress evidence retrieved during the search. The officer's initial entry into the dorm room was held unlawful because he did not wait for an invitation to enter.

On appeal, the Court of Appeals of Massachusetts found the officer's entry into the room was authorized under the college's conditions of residency. **The officer did not need a warrant or consent to enter the room, as he acted in reliance on a credible report from two students that one of the roommates had a knife.** Campus police did not act in a manner offensive to the dignity of the roommates. They voluntarily consented to the search of the room. As the request to conduct a search was not ambiguous, and they were old enough to know they could have refused to allow a search, the lower court's decision was reversed. *Comwlth. v. Carr*, 918 N.E.2d 847 (Mass. App. Ct. 2009).

◆ *A mentally disabled African-American woman did not prove she was unlawfully excluded from a Northwestern University library.*

Although not affiliated with the university, the woman used its law school library to research disability law. After the law school revoked her permission to use its facilities, she researched elsewhere. The woman accused a student in a computer lab of assaulting her, and she was escorted from the building. Later, she claimed campus security told her to leave another library. In a federal district court action against Northwestern, the woman claimed race and disability discrimination under federal laws. After the court dismissed her case, she appealed to the U.S. Court of Appeals, Seventh Circuit. It found the claims relied on laws requiring proof of differential treatment based on race or disability. **But as the woman did not allege any facts that could reasonably lead to the belief that the university excluded her on either basis, the district court was correct in dismissing the action.** *Gillard v. Northwestern Univ.*, 366 Fed.Appx. 686 (7th Cir. 2010).

◆ *Private security guards employed by a New York university did not have to follow the same rules as municipal police.*

University of Rochester security guards searched a man for weapons. A metal scanner registered positive and a guard removed three baggies filled with white powder from the man's pocket. When asked what the substance was, he replied "crack." A police officer field-tested the substance, determining that it was cocaine. The man was arrested for possession of a controlled substance. He sought to suppress the evidence, claiming the security officers had no reasonable basis to take him into custody or search him. He also claimed that any incriminating statements or identification of him had to be excluded.

A New York court held **university-employed private security guards did not have to follow the same rules as city police. They did not work for the state and thus were not bound by the Fourth Amendment.** As for the incriminating statements and the identification issues, the man was entitled to have that evidence precluded as to the police because he did not receive the notice he should have received under New York law. However, the statements he made to the private security guard were not precluded. The man was entitled to a hearing to determine whether these statements were made voluntarily. *People v. Capers*, 836 N.Y.S.2d 487 (Table) (N.Y. City Ct. 2007).

◆ *A "seizure" does not occur every time police stop and question a person. Officers may rely on trustworthy reports from staff to make investigatory stops.*

An African-American library patron was using a computer in a library at the New Jersey Institute of Technology. An assistant librarian called the security department to report him for taking a stapler. The patron agreed to answer questions by the police, then let them search his bag. After they did not find the stapler, the patron left the building. He sued the officers, institute and library staff in a federal district court for constitutional rights violations. He claimed the officers and staff falsely accused him of stealing computer software rather than a stapler and subjected him to an unreasonable search and seizure. The court awarded summary judgment to the institute and staff.

The patron appealed to the U.S. Court of Appeals, Third Circuit. While he admitted consenting to the questioning and the search of his bag, he claimed the consent was invalid because one officer failed to inform him that he had a right to refuse the search. The court found there was no such requirement. The patron's consent was valid, as the investigation lasted only seven minutes, took place in public, and was not threatening or intimidating. The district court had properly held that no jury could have found a Fourth Amendment violation. **The U.S. Supreme Court has held a seizure does not occur every time police officers approach someone to ask a few questions. The court found the patron obviously did not feel coerced or threatened into remaining in the library or responding to questions.** After the brief search of his bag, he walked out of the library without responding to the officer's request for his name. In any event, **officers may rely on a trustworthy secondhand report and need not base an investigatory stop on personal observation**. The court rejected the patron's additional arguments and affirmed the judgment. *Only v. Cyr*, 205 Fed.Appx. 947 (3d Cir. 2006).

B. Other Police Matters

To help assure campus security, some of the states have empowered state universities and their campus police to exercise their authority off campus.

◆ *A non-student offender found guilty of receiving computers stolen from an Ohio university was unable to overcome his state court conviction.*

Nine computers disappeared from the library at Central State University. A number of university students observed suspicious activity that helped lead to the conviction of the offender on two counts of receiving stolen property. A judge sentenced him to two years in prison, and he appealed to the Court of Appeals of Ohio. Affirming the judgment, the court found trial court testimony clearly linked the offender to the theft. There was also evidence of the resale of the school's computers. University staff testified that computers were missing, and students testified about seeing the offender in the computer lab. The court affirmed the conviction, noting that **circumstantial and direct evidence have the same weight under Ohio law**. Also, the jury was free to believe who had the most convincing version of events – and they decided it was the prosecutor. *State v. Brown*, No. 08CA87, 2009 WL 3527465 (Ohio Ct. App. 10/30/09).

◆ *A California court reversed a criminal conviction over an online threat by a student who was disgruntled by his expulsion from a community college.*

After being diagnosed with paranoid schizophrenia in the U.S. Navy, the student attended a California community college. As he neared graduation, he e-mailed his counselor that "I am the actual leader of Al Qaeda and others the USA labels as terrorists." He asked for permission to "set up a recruitment station on campus to recruit assassins for the job of killing Bush and fighting the evil american government." After a hearing, the college expelled him. Six months later, the college was locked down due to an Internet posting by the student. Police searched his home and found marijuana and several threatening writings, one listing the college as a bombing target. The student pleaded guilty to a criminal threat charge. Appeal reached the state court of appeal, which held **prosecutors did not establish he used an electronic device to communicate a threat or obscenity to another person.** Instead, the student uploaded a general Internet posting without making a specific threat to the person who discovered it. While a misdemeanor conviction for annoyance was reversed, his guilty plea to a different charge based on the same conduct stood. *People v. Sssotlohiefmjn*, No. E047144, 2010 WL 219336 (Cal. Ct. App. 1/22/10).

◆ *A federal district court rejected a man's claim that Marquette University safety officers violated his rights when arresting him for aggravated battery.*

Marquette University Department of Public Safety (DPS) officers assisted the Milwaukee police in arresting the man for aggravated battery. He claimed a DPS employee and Milwaukee police officers held him "hostage" for about two hours and placed him in a "bogus" lineup. After the man was convicted for aggravated battery, he sued the DPS in a federal district court for false imprisonment and violation of his due process rights. **The court explained that to prevail, the man had to show an intentional deprivation of a constitutionally protected right "under color of state law."** He further had to show any constitutional deprivation was caused by an official DPS policy, ordinance, or regulation. A single employee who was not named as a party was the only person from DPS who had anything to do with the arrest. As the claims were insufficient to hold the DPS or any employees liable, DPS received pretrial judgment. *Scott v. Marquette Univ. Dep't of Public Safety*, No. 06-C-0384, 2009 WL 2240234 (E.D. Wis. 7/27/09).

◆ *A Florida university did not violate a student's due process rights when it relied on an unsworn police report as a basis for imposing discipline on him.*

The student asserted the use of the police report in his disciplinary hearing violated his due process rights. He said the police report was unsworn hearsay evidence and that its use violated the university's code of student conduct. The court held the use of an unsworn report did not violate this code provision, which applied only to witnesses who testified at disciplinary hearings. Since the challenged evidence related to a report and not to witness testimony, there was no violation of the code provision. Even though hearsay evidence was used, the court held the student was given all the process he was due. **He was confronted with the report and had a chance to rebut the charges against him.** Also, the student made no attempt to call witnesses or present evidence.

He refused to answer questions and relied on his right not to incriminate himself. Under the circumstances, there was no due process violation. *Heiken v. Univ. of Cent. Florida*, 995 So.2d 1145 (Fla. Dist. Ct. App. 2008).

◆ *University of Virginia campus police had authority to act within a statutorily prescribed distance from the jurisdictional limits of Charlottesville.*

A University of Virginia campus police officer observed a vehicle being driven erratically. The officer pulled over the vehicle, and the driver failed a series of field sobriety tests. The driver was arrested and later convicted of driving while intoxicated. By statute, University of Virginia police have concurrent jurisdiction with the City of Charlottesville police department. When the campus officer pulled over the vehicle, he was 200 yards outside the city limits. The driver challenged his conviction on this basis, saying the officer was outside of his jurisdiction when he pulled him over and arrested him. A Virginia trial court rejected this claim and upheld the conviction.

The relevant statute gave both the Charlottesville police and University of Virginia campus police the authority to act "within a statutorily prescribed distance from the jurisdictional limits" of the city. On appeal, the Court of Appeals of Virginia upheld the conviction. *Boatwright v. Comwlth. of Virginia*, 50 Va.App. 169, 647 S.E.2d 515 (Va. Ct. App. 2007).

◆ *The use of deadly force by police was justified based on probable cause to believe an intruder threatened serious bodily harm.*

A security guard at a Minnesota college noticed a car driving on a sidewalk near campus. Local police were called and the driver attempted to get away. Police eventually shot the driver to death. The college security guard did not fire shots. The driver's widow alleged that her husband had bipolar disorder. She sued the police department, officers, security guard and college in a federal district court for violating his constitutional right to be free from unreasonable searches and seizures. The case reached the U.S. Court of Appeals, Eighth Circuit, which found **the use of deadly force was justified. Officers had probable cause to believe the driver posed a threat of serious harm.**

Constitutional claims against private actors, such as the college and security guard, were viable "only if they are willing participants in a joint action with public servants acting under color of state law." In this case, the security guard did nothing more than follow the suspect into an alley. **His level of involvement was insufficient to subject him or the college to liability for constitutional violations.** The court rejected the widow's claim that a shooting could have been avoided if the officers had been trained how to approach people with mental illness. Threatening behavior, not a lack of training, caused the shooting. *Sanders v. City of Minneapolis*, 474 F.3d 523 (8th Cir. 2007).

◆ *The U.S. Court of Appeals, Fifth Circuit, held private religious university campus police had probable cause to arrest a student who tried to register for classes after he was suspended from school.*

The school suspended the student for violating the student code of conduct by stalking two female students. When the student appeared at school to register for a summer session, campus police arrested him for criminal trespass and turned him over to county police. Although the student was charged with criminal trespass, the district attorney's office later dropped the charges. The student sued the university, campus police and a university dean in a federal district court for false arrest, false imprisonment and malicious prosecution, among other claims. The school, campus police, and dean requested summary judgment and dismissal of the charges, as the student did not offer facts to show they acted with malice. The district court agreed and dismissed the action. The student appealed to the Fifth Circuit, which found the university and its officials had probable cause to arrest and prosecute the student. It affirmed the district court judgment. *Barnes v. Johnson*, 99 Fed.Appx. 534 (5th Cir. 2004).

C. Liability

◆ *A student who involuntarily withdrew from a Texas college based on his juvenile criminal history was not allowed to further pursue a federal case.*

In his federal lawsuit, the student sued the college, its parent organization and two college officials. He claimed due process violations, breach of contract, intentional infliction of emotional distress, and negligent hiring, training and supervision. A federal magistrate judge issued a report and recommendation to dismiss the case. Claims for punitive damages were not authorized against a Texas governmental unit. **The college and its parent were immune to claims for negligent hiring, negligent training, negligent supervision and intentional infliction of emotional distress.** Similarly, the claims of intentional infliction of emotional distress against the individual defendants in their official capacities were barred by immunity. In addition, the magistrate found expulsion from the program was not extreme or outrageous. There was no cause of action allowing the student to pursue monetary damages under the due process clause of the state constitution. *Kimbrough v. Alamo Colleges*, No. SA-09-CV-0738 XR (NN), 2010 WL 841368 (W.D. Tex. 3/8/10).

◆ *A New York federal court dismissed a student's federal claims against New York University (NYU) for making a false police report about him.*

A university security employee accused the student of stealing a wallet in a locker room. Although the student denied this, the employee called NYU's public safety administrator, who in turn called municipal police. A municipal police officer arrested and jailed the student. After the student was acquitted of all charges, he accused NYU of refusing to let him return as a student. He sued NYU and New York City in a federal district court for federal civil rights violations, race discrimination, and conspiracy. He added state law claims for false arrest and malicious prosecution. The court found the federal claims were all based on conclusory allegations and did not state necessary facts. The race discrimination claim failed because the student did not claim he was mistreated because of his race. There was no evidence that NYU conspired with the police to frame him, defeating the conspiracy claim. **The court dismissed all the federal claims against NYU as they were based on conclusory allegations.** But the federal claims against the city remained viable. *Johnson v. City of New York*, 669 F.Supp.2d 444 (S.D.N.Y. 2009).

◆ *An Arkansas federal judge refused to dismiss a private security contractor and an employee from a lawsuit brought by a university chief of police.*

According to the chief, the security contractor was volatile and dangerous. The chief stated that the contractor and some of his private security guards were involved in "several instances of disturbing and abusive conduct." This culminated when the contractor fought with university police officers and the chief unsuccessfully tried to arrest him. The chief stated the contractor resisted so violently that the chief suffered arm and shoulder injuries requiring surgery and rehabilitation, stress bad enough to trigger a heart condition, and severe and persistent emotional distress. When the contractor sought to dismiss the case, the court refused. Arkansas law requires "substantial evidence" that a contract was intended to benefit a person before a judge can determine if there is a third party beneficiary. The judge decided it was too early in the proceedings to make this determination. **He also refused to dismiss the excessive force claim, since enough facts were presented to support it at this stage of the lawsuit.** *Weatherspoon v. Univ. of Arkansas Board of Trustees*, No. 4:08CV00635 JLH, 2009 WL 3765916 (E.D. Ark. 11/10/09).

◆ *A Florida court held that in an emergency, a university can exclude a student and provide a hearing afterward to protect the campus.*

A graduate of Florida Atlantic University (FAU) returned to FAU for a graduate program but was dismissed for receiving a failing grade. She then enrolled in continuing education classes. Faculty members became fearful of the student after she appealed her dismissal, saying she made veiled threats. FAU issued a "no trespass warning" that barred her from campus and classes.

The student was arrested three times for violating the warning and was convicted of trespassing charges. After several more incidents, the student returned to the FAU library and was banned from FAU campuses indefinitely. She sued FAU in a state court, claiming it violated her due process rights by issuing her a trespass warning and banning her from campus without a hearing. The court granted FAU's motion for pretrial judgment, and the student appealed. A Florida District Court of Appeal found that due process protection can extend to interests in specific benefits that have been created by state laws or state university rules and policies. It was a mistake for the trial court to rule the student lacked any interest in continued enrollment. Since FAU could not permanently deprive her of access to its campus without notice and an opportunity for a hearing, the court reversed the judgment. **However, the court recognized that in emergencies, a university can exclude a student and provide a hearing afterward.** *Lankheim v. Florida Atlantic Univ.*, 992 So.2d 828 (Fla. Dist. Ct. App. 2008).

◆ *A federal district court held in favor of a Pennsylvania university that expelled a male student for bizarre behavior and threats against others.*

The student was accused of bizarre behavior by several female students who feared he might harm them. They complained to the university that he graphically described how he would kill people. After two hearings, the university found the student guilty of threatening the safety of others and suspended him for the rest of the school year. When he reapplied for admission, the university denied his application and permanently expelled him. The student appealed the denial of his application in a letter that was splattered with blood. He then sued the university in a federal district court. The court found no basis for the lawsuit. The university committed no constitutional violation by disciplining him. The student argued that the university treated his case differently from the way it handled a claim against a student stalker. **According to the court, at the very most, the university may have treated the student more harshly than the student stalker. However, that was not enough to prove the university violated his constitutional rights.** The court granted the university's motion for dismissal. *Hubler v. Widener Univ.*, No. Civ.A. 05-01785-JF, Civ.A. 05-01920-JF, 2006 WL 437542 (E.D. Pa. 2/22/06).

◆ *An Oregon public university did not violate the First Amendment by expelling a student who threatened a university administrator.*

The student kept guns and ammunition in his dorm room and told acquaintances that he wanted to kill or hurt an assistant director of residence life. University officials told the assistant director about the comments and recommended that he and his family move off campus for a few days. The assistant director followed the recommendation and also obtained a restraining order against the student. The school then held a hearing at which a committee recommended expulsion for violating the student conduct code and standards relating to residence housing. The university adopted the recommendation, and the student sought court review, claiming the expulsion violated his free speech rights. **The court held that it was reasonable for school officials to expel him since the threats disrupted university activities.** *Hagel v. Portland State Univ.*, 228 Or.App. 239 (Or. Ct. App. 2009).

◆ *A New York court reinstated a student's claim for wrongful expulsion for drug possession because a field test may not have been conducted properly.*

Elmira College officials received an anonymous tip that a student had cocaine in her dorm room. Based on the tip, school staff searched her room and found white powder under a desk. The college director of campus security conducted a field test, and the powder appeared to test positive for cocaine. A hearing was held, at which the student said a positive cocaine test involves three steps, including a step that produces a pink color and a step that produces a pink-over-blue color sequence. She noted that the testing form submitted by the school claimed the test was positive for cocaine, even though it listed the color of the substance as pink. Despite this evidence, the student was expelled from the school. After an administrative appeal failed, she filed a state court case to annul the expulsion. A state appellate division court said it was unclear whether the security director who performed the field test properly completed the form or incorrectly believed pink indicated a conclusive positive result. **It was arbitrary and capricious for the college to rely on an ambiguous test result.** The field test was the only evidence relied on by the college to support its decision to expel the student. Because the test results were not conclusive, the university could not base its expulsion decision solely on them. *Warner v. Elmira College*, 59 A.D.3d 909, 873 N.Y.S.2d 381 (N.Y. App. Div. 2009).

◆ *A student identified as a safety threat was properly dismissed from a Pennsylvania nurse anesthesia program.*

The university said the student constantly needed assistance, and nurse anesthetists who supervised him said he had clinical performance issues. The university placed the student on probation and later dismissed him from the program for jeopardizing the health or safety of patients. He sued the university in a federal district court for breach of contract and related claims. The court rejected the student's claim that his contract called for progressive discipline prior to dismissal from the program. **A university handbook separately provided that it could dismiss any student who jeopardized the safety or welfare of a patient.** There was no evidence that the student was dismissed for any reason other than patient safety. The court upheld the action. *Kimberg v. Univ. of Scranton*, No. 3:06cv1209, 2009 WL 222658 (M.D. Pa. 1/29/09).

◆ *The criminal prosecution of a temporary instructor charged with making e-mail and phone threats to college personnel was allowed to proceed.*

Based on his poor job performance during a one-year appointment, the college decided not to renew the temporary instructor's contract. Shortly thereafter, the college began receiving reports that he was making threatening statements to college faculty and administrators. The college responded by barring him from campus. However, the threats did not stop. The instructor sent several e-mails and made phone calls in which he threatened to kill faculty and administrators, as well as members of their families. Threats were made to professors, a department chairman, the vice president of the college, and the dean of the college. After the FBI executed a search warrant at the instructor's residence and seized evidence relating to the case, a grand jury indicted him on nine counts of transmitting an interstate e-mail threat to kill or injure another person. It also indicted him on three counts of interstate threats via telephone.

The instructor sought dismissal, claiming the indictment did not sufficiently allege that he transmitted a "true threat," as the applicable statute required. **The court found a "true threat" exists if the recipient is familiar with the context of the communication and would interpret it as a true threat.** In this case, it was clear that each count of the indictment met this test. Therefore, the motion to dismiss the indictment on that ground was denied. The court also denied the instructor's motion to suppress evidence seized when the warrant was executed. *United States v. Li*, 537 F.Supp.2d 431 (N.D. N.Y. 2008).

◆ *A federal district court refused to grant pretrial judgment to a university accused of negligently allowing a student to stab another student to death.*

The deceased student's estate sued the university in a federal district court for premises liability, fraudulent misrepresentation and negligence. In denying the university's motion for pretrial dismissal, the court found the fraudulent misrepresentation claim was based on university recruitment materials and a Web site claiming its campus was a "safe, peaceful environment." Advertising claimed campus security personnel worked closely with state and local police agencies, and that campus security promptly reported all criminal activity. While the university argued that these statements were opinion rather than fact, the court held reasonable jurors might disagree on this. Fact issues existed as to whether the student relied on university representations about campus safety, and **the estate raised a question about notice to the university of the slayer's mental health history during his admission process.** *Estate of Butler v. Maharishi Univ. of Management*, 589 F.Supp.2d 1150 (S.D. Iowa 2008).

◆ *A Missouri appeals court upheld the criminal conviction of a campus intruder who told a police officer he had explosives and "was taking over."*

The intruder entered university offices, saying he wanted to take classes there. He acted strangely when he met with a professor. The next day, the intruder returned to the office. When the university president's assistant asked him to leave, he slammed the door to the office. The assistant hit a panic button to summon security, and the intruder ran out of the building. He went to the office of the psychology professor, apologized to her and left a written marriage proposal on her desk. When security personnel found the intruder, he told them he was from Homeland Security and said the university had failed a test because he was able to drive onto the campus. As he became more and more agitated, his comments became increasingly bizarre, and police arrested him for trespassing. The intruder told police he had explosives in his truck, which was parked on university property. The campus was evacuated, and a bomb squad was called. After a thorough search that included the use of a robot, no explosives were found. The intruder was charged with making a terroristic threat, and a jury found him guilty. He received a three-year jail sentence.

The intruder appealed to the Court of Appeals of Missouri, claiming the evidence was insufficient to support the conviction. **The court rejected the argument that a false report of explosives was not encompassed by the statute. The threat involved a "condition involving danger to life,"** which is an element of the offense of the crime. It would defy logic to hold that a failure to specify the type or amount of explosives made the situation less dangerous. As the evidence was sufficient to show the intruder consciously disregarded a substantial risk of causing the evacuation of the university, his conviction was affirmed. *State v. Tanis*, 247 S.W.3d 610 (Mo. Ct. App. 2008).

CHAPTER TWO

Discrimination Against Students

I. DISABILITY DISCRIMINATION

A. Eligibility for Disability Law Protection

The Americans with Disabilities Act (ADA), 42 U.S.C. Sections 12101, et. seq., and Section 504 of the Rehabilitation Act, 29 U.S.C. § 794, are federal laws protecting the rights of disabled individuals. Section 504 states the general rule that "no otherwise qualified individual with a disability" shall, "solely by reason of her or his disability, be excluded from the participation in, be denied the benefits of, or be subjected to discrimination under any program or activity receiving Federal financial assistance."

The ADA is based on the anti-discrimination principles of Rehabilitation Act Section 504. While Section 504 applies only to recipients of federal funding, the ADA applies to a broader class of employers, public accommodations and facilities, including institutions of higher education. In 2008, Congress broadened certain ADA provisions to correct Supreme Court decisions that interpreted the Act differently than Section 504 of the Rehabilitation Act. Congress found that the ADA was enacted with the intent to "provide a clear and comprehensive national mandate for the elimination of discrimination against individuals with disabilities," and to provide broad coverage.

While Congress expected the ADA's definition of "disability" would be interpreted consistently with how courts were interpreting the definition of "handicapped individual" under Rehabilitation Act Section 504, it declared "that expectation has not been fulfilled." Sutton v. United Air Lines, Inc., *527 U.S. 471 (1999) and* Toyota Motor Mfg., Kentucky, Inc. v. Williams, *534 U.S. 184 (2002) were singled out as cases in which the Supreme Court interpreted the term "substantially limits" more restrictively than Congress intended.*

The 2008 Amendments addressed the term "disability," which is defined as "a physical or mental impairment that substantially limits one or more major life activities" of an individual. At the time of the Amendments, ADA regulations defined "substantially limits" as "significantly restricted." This required "a greater degree of limitation" than Congress intended.

"Disability" in the amended ADA is to be construed in favor of broad coverage of individuals, "to the maximum extent permitted by the terms of this Act." Congress specified that "substantially limits" is to be interpreted consistently with its findings and purposes. U.S. Public Laws 110-325 (S. 3406), 110th Congress, Second Session. "ADA Amendments Act of 2008." 29 U.S.C. Section 705, 42 U.S.C. Sections 12101-03, 12106-14, 12201, 12205a.

◆ *Arizona State University (ASU) did not violate a blind student's rights by using electronic textbooks without audio controls in a pilot textbook program.*

As part of the pilot program, students used a Kindle DX, an electronic device that simulates the experience of reading a book. While the device had a text-to-speech function, there was no audio option for menus and controls, and was inaccessible to blind users. The pilot program was limited to one year, and only three classes of honors college students were eligible to participate in it.

A blind ASU student who was not enrolled in the honors college sued ASU and its board of regents in a federal district court for disability discrimination, claiming use of the inaccessible technology offended him and made him feel unwelcome. ASU moved to dismiss the case for lack of standing, and the court granted the motion. It noted that to have standing, the student had to show ASU caused an injury that could be redressed by a favorable court ruling. He failed to do so, as he did not identify any ASU policy that would negatively impact him. He was not affected by the pilot program because he was ineligible for honors college classes. Nor could the student establish standing by alleging he was offended and felt unwelcome due to ASU's use of the program. **He could not challenge the pilot program simply because he disagreed with it.** *National Federation of the Blind v. Arizona Board of Regents*, No. CV-09-1359-PHX-GMS, 2009 WL 3352332 (D. Ariz. 10/16/09).

◆ *A student's claims under the Americans with Disabilities Act (ADA) and Rehabilitation Act failed because she did not allege the existence of a disability.*

The student accused the university of preventing her from timely completing her doctorate degree, wrongfully recording grades and not following proper grievance procedures. She complained that the university required her to repeat courses that she failed and to pay additional fees before continuing toward degree completion. According to the student, the university denied her disability-related accommodations in 13 of her 15 courses and for her residency workshops. She sought grade adjustments, an order protecting her from retaliation and $33 million in punitive damages. The university sought dismissal, which the court granted. It did so because **the student failed to**

assert the existence of a covered disability under the ADA or Rehabilitation Act. She only claimed to have an unspecified health disability, and she did not state the nature of any alleged physical or mental impairment. The student did not say how any alleged physical or mental impairment limited her. The court granted the university's dismissal motion, although it did allow the student to amend her complaint by a stated deadline. *Ernest v. Univ. of Phoenix*, No. 08-CV-2363-H (POR), 2009 WL 4282006 (S.D. Calif. 11/25/09).

◆ *In one of the first cases to interpret the 2008 ADA Amendments Act, the Sixth Circuit noted Congress' expansion of the term "substantially limits."*

A Kentucky medical student with a reading disorder had obtained testing accommodations throughout his educational career. However, when it was time for him to take the United States Medical Licensing Examination, the National Board of Medical Examiners (NBME) denied his request for accommodations.

The student sued the NBME in a federal district court, claiming ADA violations and seeking an order that would require the NBME to grant the accommodations. The court denied the request, finding his reading disorder was not a "disability" under the ADA. After the court's decision, the ADA Amendments Act of 2008 took effect. The student sought review by the U.S. Court of Appeals, Sixth Circuit. The court first agreed that the amended ADA applied to the case, as the student sought prospective relief. **To prove he had a disability under the ADA, the student had to show he was substantially limited in a major life activity.** The evidence showed he read "in a slow and labored fashion when compared to the general public." Reading is a major life activity under the ADA. Congress specifically found in the 2008 amendments that courts have interpreted the phrase "substantially limits" too narrowly. In finding the student was not disabled, the district court had relied on one of the Supreme Court decisions that was invalidated by the ADA Amendments Act. As the amended act applied, the district court would have to reconsider the case, which was returned to it for this purpose. *Jenkins v. National Board of Medical Examiners*, No. 08-5371, 2009 WL 331638 (6th Cir. 2/11/09).

◆ *A federal appeals court rejected a student's claim that he was entitled to sanctions in a discrimination case against a Florida university.*

The student failed four courses in his first two semesters of college and was placed on academic probation. He was then diagnosed with Attention Deficit Hyperactivity Disorder. A university Student Advancement Committee (SAC) allowed the student to retake his examinations, but he failed one of them and was required to repeat his first year of study. After failing two more courses, the university dismissed the student, and he sued the university in a federal district court for disability discrimination. In pretrial activity, the court ordered the university to provide information relating to students who failed courses and appeared before the SAC. It also ordered disclosure of information relating to action taken against these students. In response, the university compiled a chart identifying students by year of enrollment, enrollment status, courses failed, the SAC's recommendation and the action taken.

After a jury found the student did not have a disability, he asked the court to find the university had compiled misleading data. The court denied his request, and he appealed to the U.S. Court of Appeals, Eleventh Circuit. It held the absence of the requested information did not hurt the student's case. **To prevail in a discrimination case, he needed a meaningful comparison between himself and others who had to retake exams.** He did not seek this information, and the university could not be faulted for failing to provide it. A jury had rejected his claims for unrelated reasons. Since the lack of more detailed information did not prevent the student from pursuing his case, the court affirmed the judgment for the university. *Hirsch v. Nova Southeastern Univ.*, 289 Fed.Appx. 364 (11th Cir. 2008).

◆   *A federal district court rejected a medical school applicant's request for an order forcing a medical association to certify his medical school applications.*

The American Association of Medical Colleges (AAMC) denied a visually impaired student's request for accommodations on the Medical College Admission Test (MCAT). He sought a court order requiring the AAMC to certify his medical school applications and to send his MCAT scores to medical schools with his applications. At the time he sought the order, the student had not yet taken the MCAT, but had taken two practice MCATs. The court explained that the AAMC does not certify medical school applications. Instead, the certification process is performed by the American Medical College Admission Service (AMCAS). The student's application to AMCAS was not verified because it included information that did not match information on his transcripts. **Because the student had not yet taken the MCAT, and because the AAMC does not certify medical school applications, the court denied his request for relief.** *Rumbin v. Ass'n of American Medical Colleges*, No. 3:08CV983JBA, 2008 WL 5115282 (D. Conn. 12/2/08).

◆   *A South Carolina university did not violate the ADA by dismissing a student with a closed head injury who was incompetent to practice medicine.*

The student suffered a severe closed head injury when he fell down an embankment while attending an Illinois health sciences university. The injury caused visual problems and dyslexia. Within a year of the injury, the student returned to school and eventually graduated with the help of accommodations. Following his graduation, the student began a residency program at the Medical University of South Carolina (MUSC). His performance during a second rotation was evaluated as unsatisfactory. MUSC denied his request to use a hand-held scanning device, but it allowed him to carry a reduced patient load and increased its level of supervision over him. Despite these accommodations, the student's performance continued to decline. He was unable to retain basic medical knowledge, and a senior resident reported he could not make decisions. A neuropsychological evaluation of the student found his reading rate was four to five times slower than an average person. The evaluation verified that he could not make quick decisions. MUSC placed the student in a remedial program where his performance continued to deteriorate.

After MUSC dismissed the student from the program, he filed an ADA lawsuit in a federal court. **The court found he was not a qualified individual with a disability under the ADA, because he was unable to perform the essential function of caring for patients.** Despite the provision of several accommodations, he was unable to perform the work of a resident. The court also rejected the student's claim that MUSC violated the ADA by not providing him with a scanning device. That accommodation was not required, because it would not have significantly reduced the amount of time the student spent reading. The court also rejected his claims of retaliation and breach of contract, and it awarded judgment to MUSC. *Stopka v. Medical Univ. of South Carolina*, No. 2:05-1728-CWH, 2007 WL 2022188 (D.S.C. 7/11/07).

◆ *Finding that a university met its duty to accommodate a student with a visual impairment, a federal district court rejected a student's ADA claims.*

The University of Washington (UW) accommodated the student's visual impairment by providing him with large type or electronic formats, copies of classroom overheads, lighting modifications, extra time for assignments, and permission to tape-record lectures. Despite these accommodations, the student's grade point average (GPA) dropped to 1.89. After being placed on probation, he left the university and enrolled at another college. He later returned to UW, but his GPA dipped to 1.90, and UW dismissed him for poor academic performance. The student sued UW under the ADA for disability discrimination in a federal district court. **The court granted UW's pretrial motion for judgment because he was not qualified to remain a student at the university.** The student was dismissed under established university guidelines based on his poor academic performance, and he did not produce any evidence showing additional reasonable accommodations would have enabled him to meet minimum academic requirements. **Courts typically defer to the academic decisions of higher education administrators.** *Chen v. Univ. of Washington*, No. C07-055RSM, 2008 WL 628926 (W.D. Wash. 3/5/08).

◆ *The non-disabled parent of a disabled student could sue a university under Section 504 to vindicate her rights.*

A job applicant unsuccessfully applied for a position with the University of Missouri. She sued the university in a federal district court, alleging it did not hire her because of her son's disability. The university argued Section 504 did not allow the applicant to claim discrimination on the basis of another person's disability. The court disagreed, finding Section 504 extends to "any persons aggrieved by" violations. **Courts have held that individuals and entities who are injured by discrimination on the basis of a disability may sue under Section 504 even though they are not themselves disabled.** Congress intended to prohibit discrimination against any disabled individual who would benefit from a federally funded program or activity. *Feurer v. Curators of Univ. of Missouri*, No. 4:06CV750 HEA, 2006 WL 2385260 (E.D. Mo. 9/17/06).

◆ *A Virginia university did not discriminate against a student by dismissing him from a program and revoking an offer to medical school.*

A student applied to a university's school of medicine. As an alternative to placing the applicant on a waiting list, the university offered him a spot in its Medical Academic Advancement Post-baccalaureate (Postbacc) program. The medical school would accept the student after a year if he completed the Postbacc program's requirements, which included maintaining a 2.75

grade-point average, with no grade lower than C. He did not meet program requirements, but was allowed to remain on a probationary basis. The student's cumulative GPA fell under 2.75, and he was dropped from the program. After an unsuccessful appeal, he sued the university in a federal district court for violating the ADA. **The court held the student was not disabled, and that his perceived disability did not lead to his dismissal. It said the university dismissed him solely because his grades fell below the GPA requirements.** The Fourth Circuit agreed. It held the university did not violate the ADA because it dismissed the student for reasons unrelated to a perceived disability and provided him reasonable accommodations for any perceived disability. *Betts v. The Rector and Visitors of the Univ. of Virginia*, 145 Fed.Appx. 7 (4th Cir. 2005).

♦   *The University of Connecticut did not violate federal disability law by dismissing a student after multiple failures on part of a medical licensing exam.*

The student failed her first- and second-year course requirements, then Step I of the medical licensing exam twice. A university neuropsychologist reported the student's academic problems were caused by dyslexia, attention deficit disorder, anxiety and depression. The National Board of Medical Examiners declined the student's request for accommodations on Step I, stating she was not disabled. The student sued the board and university in a federal district court for refusing to meet her requests for accommodation. The case reached the Second Circuit, which explained that qualified disabled individuals are entitled to reasonable accommodations under the ADA and Section 504 for access to and participation in public services and accommodations.

To establish a violation, the student had to show she was a "qualified individual" with a disability. The court held she never proved she was a qualified individual with a disability or was otherwise eligible to continue her medical studies. School records showed she was an average student throughout her academic career. The court found the school in no way discriminated against the student and actually went the extra mile to support her. The board did not discriminate against her by refusing to accommodate her, as she did not show she was disabled. The judgment was affirmed. *Powell v. National Board of Medical Examiners*, 364 F.3d 79 (2d Cir. 2004).

♦   *A Kentucky university did not discriminate against a law school student on the basis of disability by refusing to readmit him to the program.*

During his first semester of law school, the student became depressed. A few of his professors suggested he take a leave and return the next fall. The student withdrew before taking his final exams. The university denied his application for readmission, which was submitted one day late. After the university refused to reconsider the reapplication, the student sued the university in a state court for disability discrimination in violation of the Kentucky Civil Rights Act, which mirrors the language of the ADA and the Rehabilitation Act. The court awarded summary judgment to the university, and the student appealed to the Court of Appeals of Kentucky.

The student argued he was qualified for readmission because his test scores and undergraduate grade point average remained the same as in his original application. The court rejected this argument, stating that only his second application was under review. **To prevail, the student had to show he was otherwise qualified apart from his disability. The court explained that an "otherwise qualified" person under Section 504 is one who is able to meet all program requirements in spite of a disability.** Educational institutions are not required to disregard the disabilities of an applicant, provided the disability is relevant to reasonable qualifications for admittance. Institutions need not make substantial modifications in reasonable standards or programs to accommodate individuals with disabilities. The court held the university had considered the student's disability and other valid factors in reaching its decision and found he was not a qualified applicant. The court affirmed the judgment for the university. *Hash v. Univ. of Kentucky*, 138 S.W.3d 123 (Ky. Ct. App. 2004).

B. Reasonable Accommodation

The ADA and Section 504 of the Rehabilitation Act require colleges and universities to provide persons with disabilities "reasonable accommodations" that do not eliminate or substantially modify program requirements.

An accommodation is "reasonable" if it is necessary to provide a disabled person the opportunity to obtain program benefits that would be available if not for a disability. If an accommodation would fundamentally alter the nature of an education program, it is not "reasonable" and federal law does not require the institution to offer it. Higher education institutions are not required to provide accommodations that would undercut their academic integrity.

◆ *Since a Maryland college had a legitimate reason to dismiss a doctoral candidate, it did not violate the Americans with Disabilities Act.*

Although the student's grades were excellent, faculty members were concerned that he lacked "awareness of [his] impact on others" and did not recognize "power differentials." He was accepted for a teaching internship at Montana State University. In his first semester there, he asked an undergraduate in his class out, in violation of a college handbook. The undergraduate later told her professor she was afraid to come to class because of the student. Loyola dismissed the student, expressing deep concern about his inability to recognize and respect power differentials. He sued Loyola in a federal district court for disability discrimination. **The court held that even if the student had a disability, there was no evidence that his ability to learn was substantially limited as compared to the average person.** He performed well academically both before and after he was diagnosed with Attention Deficit Hyperactivity Disorder. The student did not seem to rely on his medication and had twice denied in writing that he was disabled. The court dismissed the case. *Herzog v. Loyola College in Maryland, Inc.*, No. RDB-07-02416, 2009 WL 3271246 (D. Md. 10/9/09).

◆ *By allowing a disabled student a chance to substitute courses, Purdue University met its duty to reasonably accommodate him under federal law.*

After earning bad grades in his first semester, the student sought assistance from a university office for students with disabilities. To obtain a degree, he had to complete a number of foreign language courses. A foreign language committee proposed that he complete two lower-level courses in a different language rather than attempt a higher-level Spanish course he had dropped. Following this recommendation, the student enrolled in a lower-level French course. He was then caught cheating on his mid-term examination in the lower-level French class, and he withdrew from it to avoid being expelled. The student transferred to another Purdue campus, where he was allowed to take Latin and an East Asian studies course to fulfill his foreign language requirement. He graduated a year later than planned and then sued the university in a federal district court, alleging that failure to accommodate his disability forced him to attend school an extra year. **The court held the university met its duty to reasonably accommodate the student when it allowed him to substitute the French course for the advanced Spanish course.** *Strahl v. Trustees of Purdue Univ.*, No. 4:07-cv-61-AS, 2009 WL 1085736 (N.D. Ind. 4/22/09).

◆ *A Virginia federal court dismissed a disability discrimination lawsuit filed by an unsuccessful medical school applicant.*

The student's undergraduate grades and MCAT test score were far below the median grades and scores for students accepted by Virginia Commonwealth University (VCU) School of Medicine. He unsuccessfully applied to the medical school four times. VCU declined his request for accommodations such as adjustment of his grades and test scores, and he sued VCU in a federal district court for disability discrimination. The court found the student could not show he was "otherwise qualified" as defined by federal law. VCU did not violate its legal duty to grant the student reasonable accommodations. His requests were unreasonable. **VCU was not required to lower its academic standards by adjusting his GPA or disregarding his MCAT scores.** The court held for VCU because there was no disability discrimination and VCU had no duty to grant the accommodations sought. *Manickavasagar v. Virginia Comwlth. Univ. School of Medicine*, 667 F.Supp.2d 635 (E.D. Va. 2010).

◆ *The U.S. Supreme Court held that schools do not have to make accommodations that fundamentally alter the nature of the programs offered.*

A nursing school applicant with severe hearing impairments claimed the school's denial of her admission violated Section 504, which states that an "otherwise qualified individual with a disability" may not be excluded from a federally funded program "solely by reason of her or his disability." The school explained the hearing disability made it unsafe for the applicant to practice as a registered nurse. The school pointed out that even with a hearing aid, she had to rely on her lip-reading skills, and that patient safety demanded the ability to understand speech without reliance on lip-reading.

Agreeing with the school, **the Supreme Court held the term "otherwise qualified individual with a disability" meant an individual who is qualified in spite of his or her disability.** The applicant's contention that her disability should be disregarded for purposes of determining whether she was otherwise qualified was rejected, as was her contention that Section 504 imposed an obligation on the school to undertake affirmative action to modify its curriculum to accommodate her disability. While a school may be required in certain cases to make minor curricular modifications to accommodate a disability, the applicant here was physically able to take only academic courses. **No accommodations were required since clinical study would be foreclosed due to patient safety concerns.** The Court held that Section 504 did not require a major curricular modification such as allowing the applicant to bypass clinical study. The denial of admission was upheld. *Southeastern Community College v. Davis*, 442 U.S. 397, 99 S.Ct. 2361, 60 L.Ed.2d 980 (1979).

◆ *California law did not entitle people with learning and reading disabilities to accommodations on standardized tests.*

The Association of American Medical Colleges (AAMC) administers the Medical College Admission Test (MCAT), which is used to evaluate whether applicants should be admitted to medical school. The AAMC evaluates requests for accommodations under ADA standards. Four individuals with reading-related disabilities and/or Attention Deficit Hyperactivity Disorder asked the AAMC for testing accommodations. When their requests were denied, they sued the AAMC for disability discrimination under state laws defining the term "disability" more broadly than the ADA does.

The AAMC argued it would be wrong to apply the more generous state standard to these accommodation requests because the MCAT is a national test that requires consistent standards. A state superior court disagreed and ordered the AAMC to apply state law to the requests. But on appeal, the Court of Appeal of California held **the state's Unruh Civil Rights Act does not apply to practices that apply equally to all. AAMC test time limits were neutral and applied to all test-takers.** The students did not claim the AAMC applied its policy in an intentionally discriminatory way. Accommodations were also not required by the state Disabled Persons Act, which focuses on ensuring physical access to public places. **There was no allegation that the AAMC denied any person with a disability access to its facilities.** As neither act required performance-related accommodations for MCAT applicants, the court reversed the judgment. *Turner v. Ass'n of American Medical Colleges*, 167 Cal.App.4th 1401, 85 Cal.Rptr.3d 94 (Cal. Ct. App. 2008).

◆ *A disabled Michigan student who was not enrolled in a degree-granting program lacked any right under federal law to live in university housing.*

The student attended a nondegree program established to provide a post-secondary educational experience for students with mild cognitive disabilities. Participants had to take at least 12 credits per semester and paid regular tuition rates. However, they did not take exams, receive grades or use the regular application procedure. After participating in the program for some time while living with his parents, the student applied for university housing. His application was denied because he was enrolled in a nondegree program.

When the university denied a waiver request, the student sued the university in a federal district court for violating the federal Fair Housing Act and Rehabilitation Act Section 504. The university argued it was not required to grant a waiver from its housing policy because all students not enrolled in degree-granting programs lacked rights to on-campus housing. The court denied the student's request for relief, finding the university was immune to Fair Housing Act claims under the Eleventh Amendment. In addition, **waiver**

of the housing policy was not an accommodation addressing a disability-related limitation. Instead, the housing policy applied equally to non-disabled students and students with disabilities. *Fialka-Feldman v. Oakland Univ. Board of Trustees*, No. 08-14922, 2009 WL 275652 (E.D. Mich. 2/5/09).

◆ *A Louisiana court held a state university violated the ADA by failing to provide adequate restroom access in the student union.*

A student had difficulty entering a restroom in the student union because the doorway was too narrow for her wheelchair. After a struggle, she was able to enter, but she urinated on herself and was hurt while trying to exit. The student sued the university in a state court for violating Title II of the ADA and state law. Denying the university's claim to Eleventh Amendment immunity, the court held the student was entitled to ADA protection and found the university discriminated against her based on her disability. On appeal, the Court of Appeal of Louisiana held the university's claim to immunity was waived when it accepted federal funds. It held the student had a disability under the ADA, since a neurologist said her wheelchair was medically necessary.

As her ability to walk was substantially limited, the student was "disabled" under the ADA. Finally, the court held the university illegally discriminated against her based on her disability. **The university admitted the restroom door was too narrow and did not comply with applicable access requirements. There was not a single accessible restroom in the building where the incident took place**, and the university did not show that providing wheelchair access would have created an undue financial burden. *Covington v. McNeese State Univ.*, 996 So.2d 667 (La. Ct. App. 2008).

The Supreme Court of Louisiana denied further review in *Covington v. McNeese State Univ.*, 3 So.3d 491 (La. 2008).

◆ *A student obtained a federal court order requiring a California community college district to improve its campus wheelchair access.*

According to the student, he was encountering multiple barriers to the use of his wheelchair every day on campus. He sought a court order to require the district to comply with ADA Title II access requirements. The court entered a permanent order requiring the community college district to make several improvements, including accessible desks and workstations in all classrooms. It ordered the district to hire an access expert, approved by the student, to oversee placement of accessible desks and workstations. **The district was banned from charging students with disabilities fees for accommodations such as parking spaces or elevator keys.** It was further required to establish a schedule for a wheelchair-accessible shuttle to take students with disabilities to areas of the campus that lacked accessible paths of travel. An access expert was to oversee the removal of physical access barriers and submit status reports on barrier removal every three months. The district was also required to publicize its modified policies relating to access in written materials, and to make those materials available to students with disabilities at student orientations. *Huezo v. Los Angeles Community College Dist.*, No. CV 04-09772 MMM (JWJx), 2008 WL 4184659 (C.D. Cal. 9/9/08).

◆ *A federal court rejected a student's claim that Temple University unlawfully denied her requests for accommodations and dismissed her.*

The student attended Temple University as a dental student. She missed many classes and failed exams, and she was placed on academic probation. The student fell on a stairway and injured her shoulder and neck. She missed a mid-term, and did not show up for a make-up exam. Temple granted the student's request for more time to complete work, freedom to move about in class, and to rearrange seats. Even with the accommodations, her grades were poor. Temple extended additional accommodations, but the student continued to fail examinations and sometimes did not show up for make-ups. After failing most of her courses, she took a leave. Temple provided some accommodations upon her return, but denied her request to significantly reduce her schedule. The student continued to miss classes and fail exams, and she was finally dismissed.

The student sued Temple in a federal court for ADA and Rehabilitation Act violations. She claimed to have medical conditions including migraine headaches, hearing loss, neck sprain and irritable bowel syndrome. However, she failed to document these problems. The court ruled against her, and she appealed. The U.S. Court of Appeals, Third Circuit, held the student did not produce enough evidence regarding the nature and severity of her impairments to proceed with her case. Even if the student could show she had a disability, she was not qualified to continue in the program. She struggled academically at Temple from the beginning, and was on academic probation even before she first requested accommodations. **Temple showed that some of the requested accommodations would have fundamentally altered its program, and they were thus not required.** *Millington v. Temple Univ. School of Dentistry*, 261 Fed.Appx. 363 (3d Cir. 2008).

◆ *A medical school did not violate a Michigan anti-discrimination law when it dismissed a student with learning and visual disabilities.*

The student had a long history of academic difficulties at the University of Michigan Medical School. When the school learned she might have cognitive learning difficulties, it offered to allow her to defer examinations. She was granted a leave of absence to address a visual impairment, and was diagnosed with a condition that makes it difficult to focus and refocus her eyes. The student's academic difficulties continued despite the provision of multiple disability-related accommodations. Because she failed to meet academic requirements, she was dismissed from the program. The student sued the university board of regents, claiming the school failed to provide reasonable accommodations in violation of the state law against disability discrimination.

A state trial court granted the board's motion for summary judgment, and the student appealed. The Court of Appeals of Michigan found the school accommodated her by providing double time to complete her examinations and allowing her breaks during them. The school also allowed the student to retake classes, view videotapes of lectures, switch clinical rotations, and take multiple leaves of absence. **She did not present evidence showing deferral of examinations was a medically required accommodation. In addition, the record clearly showed the student was not qualified to remain at the school.** She was dismissed from the program because of poor academic performance and not because of her disability. *Fernandez v. Univ. of Michigan Board of Regents*, No. 275296, 2007 WL 3357348 (Mich. Ct. App. 11/13/07).

◆   *A federal district court denied a school's motion for pretrial judgment on a former student's claims that it failed to accommodate his mental disability.*

After the student was admitted to the University of Puerto Rico's architecture program, his psychiatrist informed a professor that the student was under his care for a schizoaffective disorder. When the student later asked the professor for extra time to complete class work, the professor reportedly refused, ridiculing him in front of the class and suggesting that he reconsider a career in architecture. The student said he met with an academic counselor who failed to offer any accommodations and suggested that he drop the course.

The student failed the course and he claimed his professors, advisor and the school's dean all failed to provide him reasonable accommodations for his disability. He sued the university in a federal district court for violating the ADA and the Rehabilitation Act. **The court held that to defeat the ADA claims, the university had to show it used neutral criteria or that granting the requested accommodations would require it to lower its academic standards.** The university did not make this showing. Factual issues existed regarding the accommodations offered and whether they were reasonable. As a result, the court refused to grant pretrial judgment to the university. *Toledo v. Univ. of Puerto Rico*, No. 01-1980(SEC), 2008 WL 189561 (D.P.R. 1/18/08).

◆   *A deaf California student was entitled to input in choosing an interpreter, despite evidence that this accommodation would be costly.*

The student sued her college under the ADA and Rehabilitation Act for failing to provide her with adequate sign-language interpreter services. She also claimed the college forced her to "sign away her rights" by completing an application for the services. **A federal district court explained that federal disability laws required the college to provide "meaningful access" to its programs through reasonable modifications. Modifications that could be classified as "fundamental" or "substantial" are not required.**

Under Title II of the ADA, the college had the discretion to offer other aids aside from interpreter services. The college had the burden of showing another alternative was equally effective. The court was unable to determine from the record whether any alternatives were equally effective. This question could not be decided on a pretrial motion. The college presented evidence showing that providing the student a personal interpreter would constitute almost 7% of its annual budget. However, the college did not conclusively show that allowing her to choose an interpreter would create an undue administrative burden. Instead, it suggested the student's input in selecting an interpreter was required. The pretrial motions were denied. *Hayden v. Redwoods Community College Dist.*, No. C-05-01785 NJV, 2007 WL 61886 (N.D. Cal. 1/8/07).

◆   *The U.S. Court of Appeals, Eighth Circuit, held a Missouri student failed to prove a university violated the ADA by refusing requested accommodations.*

The student was wheelchair-bound and sight impaired due to cerebral palsy. The chair of the Department of American Studies refused to allow the student to enroll in a graduate-level American studies course until he completed his graduate school application, eliminated some incomplete undergraduate grades, and was admitted to the graduate school. The graduate school allowed the student to attend as an unclassified graduate student in the American Studies Department. However, he attempted 12 credit hours the next semester and earned none. The student was disqualified from federal financial aid and complained of disability discrimination. The university barred him from entering its campus after learning he had threatened a professor.

The student sued the university in a federal district court for violating the ADA. The court granted the university's motion for dismissal, and the student appealed to the Eighth Circuit. The court found the university offered him many accommodations, such as changes in his academic status and classes. On the list of accommodations he stated he did not receive, he failed to specify which ones had been rejected. Also, he did not explain why he needed each requested accommodation. **An accommodation is reasonable only if it is related to a disability.** As the student failed to substantiate with sufficient evidence that the university did not provide certain requested accommodations, and that reasonable accommodations would have qualified him for admission into the graduate school, the court affirmed the judgment. *Mershon v. St. Louis Univ.*, 442 F.3d 1069 (8th Cir. 2006).

◆ *A New York graduate institute did not make reasonable attempts to accommodate a student with lupus in a Ph.D. distance learning program.*

The program in clinical psychology had a 300-hour residency requirement. The institute denied the student's request to transfer to a different residency group because it was oversubscribed. It also denied her permission to fulfill her residency requirement by video-conferencing. The student sued the institute under the ADA and Rehabilitation Act. A federal district court held for the institute, and the student appealed. The U.S. Court of Appeals, Second Circuit, held the institute did not violate the ADA or Rehabilitation Act by denying the request for a different group. However, a jury might find that the institute failed to properly evaluate the student's request for a delay in the start of her program and to fulfill her residency requirement through video-conferencing. **The court found evidence that the institute had failed to engage in an interactive process of finding an accommodation for her.** The case was remanded to the district court for further proceedings. *Hartnett v. Fielding Graduate Institute*, 198 Fed.Appx. 89 (2d Cir. 2006).

C. Liability Issues

◆ *A Maryland student with disabilities could not bring a federal case against a university after a state court dismissed her nearly identical lawsuit.*

After the university expelled the student, she said she was harassed and verbally abused by administrators who questioned her use of a service dog. She also claimed the university retaliated against her for seeking disability-related accommodations by refusing to let her inspect her student records, denying her an extension for coursework, circulating rumors that she engaged in academic dishonesty, placing her on probation, and expelling her. A state court dismissed the student's action against the university and a dean for defamation, libel, intentional infliction of emotional distress, harassment and negligence. She filed a new case against the university in federal court, relying on the same facts, but asserting claims under Section 504 of the Rehabilitation Act, the Americans with Disabilities Act, and Title IX. Applying a legal doctrine known as *res judicata*, the court dismissed the case. Both cases involved the student and university as parties, and the state court judgment was a final decision on the merits. **Cases between identical parties that rely on the same facts must be dismissed even if they present different legal theories.** In a brief order, the U.S. Court of Appeals, Fourth Circuit, affirmed the judgment. *Hall v. St. Mary's Seminary & Univ.*, No. 09-1564, 2010 WL 2000998 (4th Cir. 5/20/10).

◆ *A Texas student who was dismissed from a community college paramedic program received a chance to amend her claim for wrongful dismissal.*

After being diagnosed with Attention Deficit Hyperactivity Disorder, the student took prescription drugs. According to the student, she was wrongfully expelled for failing a required drug test because she was taking prescription drugs. She filed an action in a federal district court. Although most of the claims were dismissed, the court allowed the student a chance to allege the university violated her right to equal protection and discriminated against her on the basis of sex. If the amended complaint provided enough facts to meet the standard needed to state a federal claim, the lawsuit could proceed. **While the college had immunity for any state law negligence claims, the court found it possible that the student could provide enough factual information to back up her federal claims.** *Davis v. Collin County Community College Dist.*, No. 4:09cv309, 2009 WL 3764135 (E.D. Tex. 11/9/09).

◆ *A Nevada community college and the University of Nevada, Las Vegas, failed to accommodate a student's hearing impairment.*

The student claimed the community college and university failed to provide her accommodations to ensure equal access in the classroom. She sued the institutions in a federal district court, asserting they acted with deliberate indifference to her rights. After the court ruled against her, she appealed to the U.S. Court of Appeals, Ninth Circuit. It found evidence that the student had complained about the quality of interpreter services several times. A jury should be presented with factual disputes about whether the student was provided a qualified interpreter and adequate note-taking services. Evidence indicated that officials had acknowledged a problem with the provision of note-taking services. The student also alleged she was wrongfully denied real-time captioning services for a global economics class.

Because the experts for the parties disagreed as to whether it would be proper to provide a combination of services, this question had to be decided by a jury. **A jury would also have to resolve the question of whether the student could show deliberate indifference by the institutions, which would determine her eligibility for an award of damages.** The case was returned to the district court for further proceedings. *Button v. Board of Regents of Univ. and Community College System of Nevada*, 289 Fed.Appx. 964 (9th Cir. 2008).

◆ *A federal court allowed a disabled student's failure-to-accommodate and retaliation claims to proceed against a District of Columbia law school.*

During orientation, the student told a law school official about her learning disability and need for accommodations. The school offered her double time to complete examinations, a separate testing room, and a notetaker. But it did not always provide a notetaker, and later provided her lecture transcripts instead. The student claimed the transcripts were often untimely and sometimes did not come. After the school suspended her for plagiarism, she sued it in a federal district court for disability discrimination, retaliation, defamation, breach of contract and violation of her due process rights. The court held many of the claims were barred because they were not filed within an applicable one-year limitations period. The student adequately set forth claims for retaliation and failure to provide reasonable accommodations. **But since the school was required by law to provide her with disability-related accommodations, any failure to do so could not serve as the basis of a breach of contract claim.** *DiLella v. Univ. of the District of Columbia David A. Clarke School of Law*, 570 F.Supp.2d 1 (D.D.C. 2008).

◆ *A wheelchair-bound student made out a valid federal law claim against Rutgers University for failing to make her graduation ceremony accessible.*

The student completed all her required courses and graduated in May 2006. In a federal district court lawsuit filed against the university in March 2008, she claimed she had access problems throughout her time at Rutgers. In particular, the student alleged she was not provided accessible housing and sometimes had to be carried down stairs from her second-story apartment. She was forced to miss class when sidewalks were not cleared of snow, did not receive accessible parking, and was denied proper transportation because bus drivers did not know how to operate bus chair lifts. The court found many claims were filed outside the applicable two-year limitations period. **The student established no link between her graduation ceremony and the other events.** While she was allowed to add claims based on her graduation, her remaining untimely claims were dismissed. *Muha v. Rutgers, the State Univ. of New Jersey*, No. 08-2142 (FLW), 2009 WL 689738 (D.N.J. 3/11/09).

◆ *A federal court in Nebraska restated the rule that employees and administrators are not individually liable for violations of federal laws protecting disabled individuals, since they do not "operate" an institution.*

The court noted that other federal courts have held **university employees and administrators do not "operate" a university in a way that exposes them to liability under the Americans with Disabilities Act and the Rehabilitation Act.** The court explained that to prevail on a breach of contract claim, the student first had to state there was a promise between himself and the university. As he was unable to show any promise, his breach of contract claim failed. The student did not allege facts to support his claim for intentional infliction of emotional distress. He did not show intentional or reckless conduct that was so outrageous and extreme as to go beyond all possible bounds of decency. *White v. Creighton Univ.*, No. 8:06 CV 536, 2006 WL 3419782 (D. Neb. 11/27/06). The university later moved the court for pretrial judgment. The student failed to respond to the motion. The court granted the university's motion, finding absolutely no evidence to counter the university's explanation that the student was dismissed due to his academic performance. *White v. Creighton Univ.*, No. 06CV536, 2008 WL 64692 (D. Neb. 1/3/08).

◆ *The U.S. Supreme Court held a university should receive a final ruling on whether it had to pay the costs of a deaf student's interpreter.*

A deaf graduate student at a Texas university requested a sign-language interpreter. The university refused to pay for an interpreter because he did not meet university financial assistance guidelines. The student sued the university in a federal district court under Section 504. He sought an order requiring the appointment of an interpreter at the university's expense for as long as he remained there. The court granted his request for a preliminary order requiring the university to pay for the interpreter. The university appealed to the U.S. Court of Appeals, Fifth Circuit, which affirmed the preliminary order but vacated the stay pending administrative action. The university complied with the order by paying for the interpreter. The student completed his graduate program. The U.S. Supreme Court granted review to address the university's argument that the lower courts should make a final ruling on who was to pay for the interpreter. The student argued that the case was now moot in view of his graduation. The Court vacated the appeals court's decision and remanded the case for a trial to allow the university a full opportunity to argue for recoupment of its payments for the interpreter. *Univ. of Texas v. Camenisch*, 451 U.S. 390, 101 S.Ct. 1830, 68 L.Ed.2d 175 (1981).

II. SEX DISCRIMINATION AND HARASSMENT

Title IX of the Education Amendments of 1972 prohibits recipients of federal funding from denying program participation or benefits based on gender. States have enacted their own laws prohibiting discrimination on the basis of gender to comply with federal law. If a public institution is involved, students may attach equal protection claims to discrimination complaints.

A. Discrimination

◆ *An applicant to a Pennsylvania university could proceed with a federal action claiming that she was denied admission based on her gender.*

Between 2002 and 2007, the applicant sought admission to the University of Pennsylvania School of Veterinary Medicine six times. Her grades and GRE scores were at the low end of the range accepted by the school, but she said that during her interviews there had been improper discussions relating to her status as a mother with young children and a husband in the military. During post-denial interviews, an associate dean of admissions allegedly encouraged her to continue to apply. The applicant sued the university in a federal court, claiming she was denied admission on the basis of her gender in violation of Title IX.

The court refused to dismiss the Title IX claim of gender bias based on direct evidence that admissions committee members had considered her status as a mother with young children and a husband in the military when they rejected her 2004 and 2006 applications. An interviewer allegedly asked her whether she would be able to handle the program if her husband was deployed. The court concluded that in light of this evidence, **there was a factual issue as to whether the applicant was rejected because she was a mother of young children with a husband in the military**. However, the court dismissed her claims for retaliation and fraudulent misrepresentation. *Tingley-Kelley v. Trustees of the Univ. of Pennsylvania*, 677 F.Supp.2d 763 (E.D. Pa. 2010).

◆   *State universities could validly refuse to recognize student groups that did not comply with university nondiscrimination policies.*

San Diego State University and Long Beach State University had nondiscrimination policies barring official recognition of student groups that discriminated on stated grounds, including religion and sexual orientation. Each student group had to indicate compliance with the policy. Four Christian student groups required their members to be Christians and frowned on homosexuality. They sued state university officials in a federal district court for First Amendment violations. The court found the student organization program was a limited public forum in which any restrictions on student speech had to be viewpoint-neutral and reasonable. The policies here furthered a legitimate state interest in providing all university students a chance to participate in a range of opportunities. Any restriction caused by the policy was reasonable and did not violate First Amendment association rights. **Agreeing with the universities, the court found the policy regulated conduct, not speech.**

The universities did not infringe on the groups' free speech rights by compelling speech or regulating their viewpoint. The court noted that the Free Exercise Clause is not violated by a neutral policy of general application. This is true even when a restriction bars conduct that is called for by a person's religion or burdens a religious practice. The universities had a rational basis for the policy. There was no equal protection violation, as the groups did not show they were singled out for different treatment from other groups. The court held for the universities on all the claims. *Every Nation Campus Ministries at San Diego State Univ. v. Achtenberg*, 597 F.Supp.2d 1075 (S.D. Cal. 2009).

◆   *A Massachusetts appeals court held that state law required the National Board of Medical Examiners (NBME) to provide extra time on a licensing examination to a student to pump breast milk.*

The student was the mother of a four-month-old, and was already granted double time and a separate testing room for her Attention Deficit Hyperactivity Disorder and dyslexia. But the NBME balked when she asked for an extra 60 minutes of break time per test day so she could pump breast milk. It offered alternative accommodations, including permission to pump breast milk in a private room during the allocated break time. The student rejected the alternatives and sued the board in state court, claiming that the board policy of granting extra time only to those with disabilities had an unlawful disparate impact on nursing mothers. The court denied her motion for a preliminary injunction, and she appealed to the Court of Appeals of Massachusetts. The court recited evidence that a nursing mother of a four-month-old infant should express breast milk at least every three hours and that the failure to do so can lead to medical problems such as blocked milk ducts and mastitis.

Nursing mothers also require regular trips to the restroom because they consume additional calories and liquids to maintain an adequate milk supply. Evidence showed the student needed an additional 60 minutes during the course of the examination to express breast milk. It said the 45 minutes offered by the board was "patently insufficient." Without the additional time, the student was placed at a significant disadvantage compared to her peers. **The NBME's test structure unfairly subjected breastfeeding women to greater hardships than other test-takers, and the court vacated the lower court's ruling.** It entered an order requiring the NBME to grant the student an additional 60 minutes of break time per test day. The state's highest court affirmed the judgment without opinion. *Currier v. National Board of Medical Examiners*, 450 Mass. 1102, 875 N.E. 863 (Table) (Mass. 2007).

♦   *Gender-based distinctions in academic fields generally will not withstand constitutional scrutiny. The Supreme Court held that a university for women could not justify a policy that denied men the opportunity to enroll for credit.*

The policy of the Mississippi University for Women, a state-supported university, was to limit its enrollment to women. The university denied otherwise qualified males the right to enroll for credit in its School of Nursing. One male, who was denied admission, sued in federal court claiming that the university's policy violated the Fourteenth Amendment's Equal Protection Clause. The lower federal courts agreed, and the school appealed to the U.S. Supreme Court. The Court held **the university's discriminatory admission policy against men was not substantially and directly related to an important governmental objective**. The school argued that women enrolled in its School of Nursing would be adversely affected by the presence of men. However, the record showed that the nursing school allowed men to attend classes in the school as auditors, thus fatally undermining the school's claim that admission of men would adversely affect women students. The Court held that the policy of the university, which limited enrollment to women, violated the Equal Protection Clause. *Mississippi Univ. for Women v. Hogan*, 458 U.S. 718, 102 S.Ct. 3331, 73 L.Ed.2d 1090 (1982).

♦   *The U.S. Supreme Court held the categorical exclusion of women from the Virginia Military Institute (VMI) denied equal protection to women.*

The U.S. Attorney General's office filed a complaint against the state of Virginia and VMI on behalf of a female high school student seeking admission to the state-affiliated, male-only college. A federal court found that because single-gender education conferred substantial benefits on students and preserved the unique military training offered at VMI, the exclusion of women did not violate the Equal Protection Clause. The U.S. Court of Appeals, Fourth Circuit, vacated the judgment, ruling that Virginia had failed to state an adequate policy justifying the male-only program. On remand, the district court found that the institution of coeducational methods at VMI would materially affect its program. It approved the state's plan for instituting a parallel program for women even though the program differed substantially from VMI's in its academic offerings, educational methods and financial resources. The court of appeals affirmed, and the U.S. Supreme Court agreed to review the case.

The Court stated that parties seeking to defend gender-based government action must demonstrate an exceedingly persuasive justification that is genuine and not invented as a response to litigation. Virginia had failed to show an exceedingly persuasive justification for excluding women from VMI. There was evidence that some women would be able to participate at VMI, and the lower courts had improperly found that most women would not gain from the adversarial method employed by the college. **The remedy proposed by Virginia left its exclusionary policy intact and afforded women no opportunity to experience the rigorous military training offered at VMI.** The parallel women's program was substantially limited in its course offerings, and participants would not gain the benefits of association with VMI's faculty, stature, funding, prestige and alumni support. The proposal did not remedy the constitutional violation, and the Court reversed and remanded the case. *U.S. v. Virginia*, 518 U.S. 515, 116 S.Ct. 2264, 135 L.Ed.2d 735 (1996).

B. Harassment

1. Sexual Harassment by Employees

Title IX liability standards were established by the U.S. Supreme Court in Franklin v. Gwinnett County Public Schools, *503 U.S. 60, 112 S.Ct. 1028, 117 L.Ed.2d 208 (1992),* Gebser v. Lago Vista Independent School Dist., *524 U.S. 274 (1998), and* Davis v. Monroe County Board of Educ., *526 U.S. 629 (1999).*

Title IX liability based on the conduct of an employee requires proof that an official with authority to take corrective action actually knew of the conduct, but remained deliberately indifferent to it. In addition, the student must show the harassment was so severe, pervasive and objectively offensive that it caused a deprivation of educational benefits. **Since Title IX applies only to federal funding recipients, there is no individual liability under the Act.**

◆ *A federal court found no merit to a South Carolina student's harassment lawsuit, as she had consented to a relationship with the alleged harasser.*

The student attended a Halloween party at her instructor's apartment. Over the next three days, she sent him over 100 text messages. Three days after the Halloween party, the two began a sexual relationship that lasted the rest of the semester. Three weeks after the instructor posted the student's course grade, she told the college for the first time that he had been sexually harassing her. She said that up until that time, she had pretended his conduct toward her was welcome because she feared he would otherwise sabotage her course grade.

The college discharged the instructor, and the student sued him and the college in a federal district court for civil rights violations, battery, harassment, stalking, intentional infliction of emotional distress and assault. After the court held for the college, it held **no reasonable jury could return a verdict for the student against the instructor**. It noted she had initiated the relationship and had sent him more than 950 text messages. The student had continued the relationship even after her grade was posted. Under the circumstances, no reasonable jury could find the instructor's conduct was unwelcome. Similarly, the student's claims of assault, battery and intentional infliction of emotional distress were barred because she consented to the conduct. *Ray v. Bowers*, No. 2:08-CV-3512-PMD, 2009 WL 4893209 (D.S.C. 12/17/09).

◆   *The suspension of a California college student was not a retaliatory response to her allegation that she was sexually assaulted by one of her teachers.*

The student filed a formal discrimination complaint with the college, claiming a math teacher sexually assaulted her. An outside investigator found insufficient evidence to support the claim. The student later made the statement "pray for me that the devil doesn't triumph over me." College officials interpreted this as a threat, placed her on probation and suspended her indefinitely. In a federal district court action against the college, the student claimed unlawful retaliation under Title IX and discrimination based on her post-traumatic stress disorder (PTSD) in violation of the Americans with Disabilities Act (ADA). **The court held the Title IX claim failed because the student did not establish a causal connection between her complaint and the discipline issued two years later.** She did not link her PTSD to any conduct by the college. As a result, the ADA claim failed. There was no merit to the student's claim that the college discriminated based on her religion when it interpreted her comment as a threat. As she waited too long to file a state law tort claim for assault, the court dismissed the case. *Thomsen v. City College of San Francisco*, No. C 08-3333-SBA, 2008 WL 5000221 (N.D. Cal. 11/21/08).

◆   *Because it responded reasonably to a student's complaints, an Illinois community college was not liable for sexual harassment by an instructor.*

A part-time cosmetology instructor at an Illinois community college had a consensual sexual relationship with a student. After the relationship ended, the instructor left the college, and the college hired the student as a part-time cosmetology teacher. The instructor returned to the college to complete her associate's degree requirements, and the two had several run-ins. The former student was told not to have contact with his former instructor. In addition, the college director of safety and security told the former instructor she would be suspended if she continued to contact faculty members about her problems. She then reported the former student was harassing her, but did not provide specifics. Later, the instructor made a similar, generalized report to a college vice president. The college removed the former student from campus during finals week and did not rehire him. The former instructor finished her coursework and obtained her degree. After she graduated, the college agreed to take steps to keep the two separate if they should return. But the former instructor later sued the college in a federal district court for violating Title IX.

The instructor also sued her former student, accusing him of using his position as a teacher to sexually harass her. He counterclaimed for malicious prosecution, abuse of process, assault, battery and intentional infliction of emotional distress. The court held for the college on the Title IX claim, as there was insufficient evidence that the former instructor was harassed. **Moreover, the college acted reasonably both before and after it received specific information relating to the former student's conduct.** Steps were taken to prevent the two from having contact with each other, and the fact that those steps did not succeed did not show the college acted unreasonably. The court rejected the remaining claims. *Seats v. Kaskaskia College Community College Dist. #501*, No. 07-cv-843-JPG, 2008 WL 5235980 (S.D. Ill. 12/15/08).

◆ *An Arizona student lacked evidence to support a sexual harassment claim.*

The student claimed an instructor sexually harassed her and created a hostile environment by telling sexual jokes to students. She said he suggested in front of a class that she should use oral sex for birth control and accused students who were late for class of "fooling around ... with their boyfriends." As the student was married, she interpreted the latter comment as an accusation of adultery. She withdrew from school and filed a federal lawsuit charging the college and instructor with sexual harassment in violation of Title IX and other federal laws. The court held that to prove sexual harassment, the student had to show she was subjected to sexual advances, requests for sexual favors, or other sexual conduct. She also had to show the conduct was unwelcome and was so severe or pervasive that it altered the conditions of her education and created an abusive educational environment. But aside from the student's allegations, no evidence supported these claims. **Even if her claims were true, she did not show misconduct so severe or pervasive that it created a sexually hostile or abusive educational environment.** As the college could not be held liable unless the instructor was acting pursuant to a policy or custom, the claims against the college failed. *Currie v. Maricopa County Community College Dist.*, No. CV-07-2093-PHX-FJM, 2008 WL 4905980 (D. Ariz. 11/13/08).

◆ *A North Carolina court affirmed a decision to award monetary damages to two students who successfully claimed that a professor sexually harassed them.*

A student research assistant claimed a professor sexually harassed her for almost 10 years. She then refused to take a class he taught, but because the class was required, she was forced to discontinue her studies. After the student reported the professor's misconduct to the university sexual harassment officer, she learned that he had harassed other employees and students in the past. The university then conducted an investigation which revealed that the professor had sexually harassed at least eight other women. There was evidence that the university did not take any corrective action despite being informed of at least one of the cases. The university allowed the professor to resign with a year's pay and a neutral letter of reference. Two students filed separate claims against the university, alleging negligent retention and supervision of the professor. They added claims for negligent infliction of mental and emotional distress.

An administrative commission found for the students and awarded them $150,000 each. The university appealed to the Court of Appeals of North Carolina, arguing that there was no evidence of negligence. The court held the university's failure to properly respond to the earlier harassment incidents caused injury to the students. It rejected the university's argument that it could not investigate one of the past cases because a student failed to file a formal complaint. Whether she had filed a formal complaint or not, the university knew about the allegations. **The university should have asked for**

a written complaint, documented the oral complaint, and investigated the charges. Doing so might have prevented the later harassment. The decision to award the students monetary damages was affirmed. *Gonzales v. North Carolina State Univ.*, 659 S.E.2d 9 (N.C. Ct. App. 2008); *Wood v. North Carolina State Univ.*, 189 N.C.App. 789, 661 S.E.2d 55 (Table) (N.C. Ct. App. 4/15/08).

◆ *An Arkansas student failed to show university officials were legally responsible for sexual harassment by a professor.*

The student visited the professor's home to prepare a grant proposal. She said they had dinner and that the professor kissed her, held her down on his bed, and told her he wanted to have sex with her. The student said he later tried to contact her, resulting in "emotionally distressing meetings." She complained to university officials, who forced the professor to resign within a week. The student sued the university and officials in a federal district court for Title IX and constitutional violations. The court refused to dismiss monetary damage claims against the officials, and they appealed to the U.S. Court of Appeals, Eighth Circuit. **The court noted the officials had no direct contact with the professor during the relevant time period.** The student did not present sufficient evidence that they did not respond to her complaints or act to prevent sexual harassment. The university had a strong, published policy against sexual harassment. **The student did not prove the officials were deliberately indifferent to sexual harassment. As a result, they could not be held liable for damages.** The court returned the case to the district court with directions to separate the claims against the professor and dismiss the remaining federal claims against the officials. *Cox v. Sugg*, 484 F.3d 1062 (8th Cir. 2007).

◆ *An Oklahoma college did not violate Title IX as it was not deliberately indifferent to a complaint about a professor's sexual behavior.*

A student was enrolled in two classes taught by a tenured professor. She claimed that the professor touched her inappropriately several times. The professor also made many sexual comments, she said, in front of her peers, and others while they were alone. The student sued the university in a federal district court, alleging it violated Title IX because it was deliberately indifferent to sexual harassment. She claimed the college knew the professor sexually harassed others before she enrolled at the college. The court found the college did not have actual knowledge of prior incidents. In addition, those incidents were too dissimilar, too infrequent, and too distant in time.

On appeal, the U.S. Court of Appeals, Tenth Circuit, applied the Supreme Court's reasoning in *Gebser v. Lago Vista Independent School Dist.*, 524 U.S. 274 (1998). The court stated that the courts have differed on whether notice sufficient to trigger liability may consist of prior complaints or must consist of notice regarding current harassment in the recipient's programs. There was evidence in this case that the professor had dated two students close to his age. The court held this did not provide the college with the knowledge that the professor posed a substantial risk of sexual harassment to college students. The other student complaints of inappropriate sexual behavior against the professor occurred almost 10 years earlier. Those complaints involved significantly different behavior, including inappropriate touching and name-calling. **The court rejected the student's contention that the college was deliberately indifferent to her allegations, and affirmed the judgment for the college.** *Escue v. Northern Oklahoma College*, 450 F.3d 1146 (10th Cir. 2006).

◆ *A Connecticut community college was required to further defend claims that it did not respond adequately to reported sexual harassment by a professor.*

The student claimed a professor sexually assaulted her. Three days later, the community college fired the professor. The student sued the college, its board of trustees and the professor under Title IX, asserting claims of hostile environment and sexual harassment. She said the college was aware of four prior complaints against the professor involving similar behavior.

The court explained that to prove her claims, **the student needed to show the college had actual notice of the professor's misconduct but failed to adequately respond to it in a manner that showed deliberate indifference.** There was evidence that college officials knew of the previous incidents, and there was a fact issue as to whether the college adequately responded to them. Although the college claimed it responded adequately by investigating and warning the professor that he was only to have academic relationships with students, a fact issue existed as to whether proper reporting procedures were followed. While the court refused to award pretrial judgment to the student on her Title IX claims, her state law claims of negligent infliction of emotional distress and negligent retention and supervision were dismissed, as they were barred by the Eleventh Amendment. *Doe v. Norwalk Community College*, No. 3:04-cv-1976(JCH), 2007 WL 2066496 (D. Conn. 7/16/07).

2. Sexual Harassment by Peers

In 2009, the Supreme Court issued Fitzgerald v. Barnstable School Committee, *its first opinion on student sexual harassment since 1998. In it, the Court held Title IX does not bar students from bringing "parallel and concurrent" gender discrimination claims against schools under the Equal Protection Clause via 42 U.S.C. Section 1983. Section 1983 is a federal statute that creates no rights itself, but enforces rights created by federal laws and the Constitution. For additional harassment cases involving student-athletes, please see Chapter Three, Section I.D. of this volume.*

◆ A Massachusetts kindergarten student was harassed by a third-grader on a school bus. Her parents reported this to the principal, but the third-grader repeatedly denied the report and the school could not corroborate the student's account. Police found insufficient evidence for criminal charges, and the principal decided there was not enough evidence for school discipline. The family sued the school committee in a federal district court under Title IX and related laws. The court held for the school committee, and the family appealed.

The U.S. Court of Appeals, First Circuit, found no Title IX violation and held Title IX's private remedy precluded using 42 U.S.C. § 1983 to advance Title IX claims. The U.S. Supreme Court agreed to hear the case and noted

Title IX's statutory remedy was limited to the withdrawal of federal funds. While Title IX claims could be brought against institutions that received federal funds, there was no individual liability for school officials or employees under Title IX. **The Court held that "parallel and concurrent Section 1983 claims will neither circumvent required procedures, nor allow access to new remedies."** Whereas Title IX reached only federal-funding recipients, Section 1983 claims could be brought against individuals and government entities. Where activities and defendants were subject to liability under both Title IX and Section 1983, the standards of liability were not the same. **Title IX's standard of liability required a student to show an official with authority to take corrective action against harassment responded with "deliberate indifference."** By contrast, a student trying to state a Section 1983 claim for an Equal Protection Clause violation had only to show harassment resulting from an official custom, policy or practice. Accordingly, Section 1983 was available to enforce equal protection claims for gender discrimination. *Fitzgerald v. Barnstable School Committee*, 129 S.Ct. 788 (U.S. 2009).

◆ *The estate of a New York student who killed herself seven months after she was raped on campus could advance several claims against the college.*

According to the student's mother, the college violated Title IX and was liable for negligence, infliction of emotional distress, fraud, deprivation of federally secured rights and wrongful death. She filed a federal district court action against the college, which considered a motion by the college for dismissal. The court found the complaint alleged that the college refused to take any action following the rape, instead deferring entirely to a criminal investigation. It held the mother raised a sufficient claim that the college was deliberately indifferent to the assault and her daughter's attempts to report it.

To prove a Title IX violation, "deliberate indifference" must be shown. A key is whether the defendant acted reasonably under the circumstances. In this case, the complaint alleged a valid equal protection claim based on collaboration by the college with a local police detective to conceal reports of sexual assault. The court also refused to dismiss a fraud claim that was based on the college's alleged misrepresentation of campus safety to help recruit students. The claim of intentional infliction of emotional distress survived pretrial dismissal, as the court found a jury should decide whether the college's reliance on a police investigation conducted by one of its own employees was outrageous enough to support the claim. *McGrath v. Dominican College of Blauvelt, New York*, 672 F.Supp.2d 477 (S.D.N.Y. 2009).

◆ *A student could not sue a Missouri university for intentional infliction of emotional distress based on its alleged mishandling of her rape allegations.*

The student was raped at a university fraternity party. She claimed the university suspended her from the field hockey team and failed to take adequate steps to make sure she would not have further contact with the assailant. The student and her parents filed a federal lawsuit against the university and 50 unnamed defendants, claiming negligence and violation of Title IX. They added a claim of intentional infliction of emotional distress based on the university's response to the report of a sexual assault and related claims.

First, the court determined the student's suit was not barred by her failure to indicate her real name. Pseudonyms were warranted because the interest in preserving her privacy outweighed the public interest in learning her true identity. However, the court agreed with the university that her claim for intentional infliction of emotional distress should be dismissed. This was because the student was unable to show she suffered bodily harm as a result of any emotional distress. **She also failed to show the conduct causing emotional distress was intended solely to cause such distress.** Finally, the court granted the motion to dismiss all the claims against the 50 unnamed defendants, as the student made only vague allegations about them. *Roe v. St. Louis Univ.*, No. 4:08CV1474 JCH, 2009 WL 910738 (E.D. Mo. 4/2/09).

◆ *A Vermont student was not relieved of a university sexual harassment reporting requirement that was mandated by state law.*

A University of Vermont student reported being drugged and raped at a fraternity party. A university victim's advocate understood she was reporting a rape and not harassment. Acting on the advocate's advice, the student reported the incident to the University Center for Student Ethics and Standards, and she and a male student soon agreed in writing not to have any contact with each other. At a disciplinary hearing, the university found the student did not prove her rape charge. After withdrawing from school, she sued the university in a state court for failing to promptly investigate sexual harassment.

The court held for the university, finding the student should have used the university's harassment policy before suing. The student appealed to the Supreme Court of Vermont. On appeal, the student argued the university did not give her a copy of its harassment policy when she reported the rape. Instead, the court held state law required institutions to conduct prompt investigations when they received actual notice of conduct that may constitute harassment. **The law specifies that complainants cannot sue before exhausting an available harassment policy.** Rejecting the student's claim that she gave notice of conduct that could be construed as harassment, the court held the university was not required to automatically treat the complaint as one for sexual harassment. She had the option of filing a sexual harassment complaint, but chose not to do so. The court affirmed the judgment for the university. *Allen v. Univ. of Vermont*, 973 A.2d 1183 (Vt. 2009).

◆ *A student who sued the University of Georgia for sexual assault by student-athletes in a dorm room presented enough evidence of harassment to advance to a trial.*

The student went to a student-athlete's dorm room, where she consented to sexual relations. She did not know one of his teammates was hiding in a closet. The teammate sexually assaulted the student and invited another teammate to sexually assault and rape her. The student filed criminal charges against the student-athlete and teammates. She withdrew from the university. The student-athletes were charged with disorderly conduct under the university's code of conduct and suspended from athletics. A university judiciary panel held hearings almost a year after the incident and decided not to punish the student-athletes. The student sued the university in a federal district court for violating Title IX. The court held for the university, and the student appealed.

The U.S. Court of Appeals, Eleventh Circuit, held **student-on-student harassment violates Title IX. A university may be held liable for Title IX violations if it acts with deliberate indifference to known acts of harassment that are so severe, pervasive and objectively offensive that they bar a victim's access to an educational opportunity or benefit.** The student claimed the university had accepted the student-athlete even though it knew of his history of similar misconduct at other schools. The court found the university did not sufficiently respond to the student's allegations. Within 48 hours of the incident, the university made a preliminary report of the incident. However, it exercised almost no control over the student-athlete and failed to enforce its harassment policies. As the student presented evidence of discrimination that effectively barred her access to an educational opportunity or benefit, the court reversed the judgment. *Williams v. Univ. of Georgia*, 441 F.3d 1287 (11th Cir. 2006).

III. RACE AND NATIONAL ORIGIN DISCRIMINATION

The Equal Protection Clause of the Fourteenth Amendment, Title VI of the Civil Rights Act of 1964, 42 U.S.C. § 1981 and state anti-discrimination laws all prohibit discrimination against individuals in educational settings. Title VI provides that no person shall on the ground of race or color be excluded from participating in any program receiving federal financial assistance.

A. Affirmative Action

◆ *A federal district court held the University of Texas (UT) could make "narrowly tailored" use of race in admissions decisions to encourage diversity.*

Two Caucasian females who were denied admission to UT filed a federal district court action, claiming that UT admissions policies were racially discriminatory. They asserted a violation of their equal protection rights under the Fourteenth Amendment, and they sought declaratory and injunctive relief. After the court denied the motion for a preliminary injunction, it considered motions by both parties for pretrial judgment on the Equal Protection Clause question.

The court explained that UT used two "indexes" to evaluate candidates. A Personal Achievement Index included race as a "special circumstance" which reviewers could consider. Other special circumstances were socio-economic status and whether the student lived in a single-parent household. In addition, Texas law required UT to admit any high school student in the top 10% of his or her class at the time of the application. **Diversity may be a compelling state interest that can justify the use of race in admissions decisions at public universities under *Grutter v. Bollinger*, this chapter.** According to the court, a diverse student body promoted cross-racial understanding and helped eliminate stereotypes. To be valid, use of race must be narrowly tailored to further the interest of attaining a diverse student body. UT's admissions policy was similar to the policy approved by the Supreme Court in *Grutter*, and the court held that UT had a compelling interest in attaining a diverse student body. This interest justified consideration of race as part of the admissions process. Race was considered only as part of a holistic review under which UT considered many factors. As a result, UT was awarded pretrial judgment. *Fisher v. Univ. of Texas at Austin*, 645 F.Supp.2d 587 (W.D. Tex. 2009).

◆   *While achieving a diverse student body may be a worthy goal, the means to achieve that goal must comply with the Equal Protection Clause. The U.S. Supreme Court allowed race to be used as a "plus" factor in admissions.*

The University of Michigan had an admissions policy for its law school that used race as a "plus" factor for underrepresented minorities. The policy was flexible, utilized an individualized assessment system, and did not create quotas. The policy was challenged as unconstitutional by white students who were not accepted for enrollment. The case reached the U.S. Supreme Court, which upheld the policy. **The Court first noted that the goal of achieving diversity in the student body was a compelling governmental interest.** As a result, the policy would not violate the Equal Protection Clause if it was narrowly tailored to achieving that goal. Since the law school's policy did not set impermissible quotas, and since **it utilized an individualized assessment system by using race/ethnicity as a "plus" factor when evaluating individual applicants for admission**, it was constitutional. The Court also noted that race-conscious admissions policies should be limited in time so that racial preferences can be ended as soon as practicable. *Grutter v. Bollinger*, 539 U.S. 306, 123 S.Ct. 2325, 156 L.E.2d 304 (2003).

◆   *The Supreme Court found unconstitutional the University of Michigan's undergraduate admissions policy, which awarded applicants in underrepresented minority groups 20 points out of 100 needed for admission.*

Applying the same strict scrutiny analysis it used in *Grutter*, above, the Court held the undergraduate policy was not narrowly tailored to achieve the compelling governmental interest in a diverse student body. **The undergraduate admissions policy did not assess points on an individualized basis**, but rather awarded them to all minority applicants. The failure to review each applicant individually doomed the policy under the Equal Protection Clause. *Gratz v. Bollinger*, 539 U.S. 244, 123 S.Ct. 2411, 156 L.Ed.2d 257 (2003).

◆   *A Michigan constitutional amendment barring racial preferences by state universities did not violate the First Amendment or Equal Protection Clause.*

In November 2006, Michigan voters approved Proposal 2, a ballot initiative to bar preferential treatment based on race or gender in public education. The proposal would amend the state's constitution and was set to take effect in December 2006. A day after the measure passed, individuals and groups who opposed it sued the governor and two state universities. They sought a declaratory judgment that the amendment was invalid, and a permanent injunction barring its enforcement. The universities filed a cross-claim for permission to continue using their existing admissions and financial aid policies. A white male who had applied for admission to the University of

Michigan Law School sought to intervene in the case, as did a public interest group. They wanted the amendment to take effect on schedule. The court issued an order barring the application of Proposal 2 to the universities' admissions and financial aid policies until July 1, 2007. It then allowed the student to intervene. On appeal, the Sixth Circuit held the preliminary order did not state a sufficient ground for blocking Proposal 2 under federal law.

The court rejected the argument that the amendment violated the Equal Protection Clause of the Fourteenth Amendment. It found a state constitutional amendment that eliminates racial distinctions "would seem to be an equal protection virtue, not an equal protection vice." The court also rejected the argument that Proposal 2 was preempted by Title VI of the Civil Rights Act of 1964. Nor did Title IX preempt the amendment. As the student showed a strong likelihood of reversing the district court's order, the Sixth Circuit granted his motion for a stay pending his appeal. *Coalition to Defend Affirmative Action v. Granholm*, 473 F.3d 237 (6th Cir. 2006).

◆   *The Supreme Court held that a university could avoid liability for a race-based admission policy if it could show that the applicant would have been denied admission absent the policy.*

An African immigrant of Caucasian descent applied for admission to the Ph.D. program in counseling psychology at a Texas public university. The university considered the race of its applicants at some stage of the review process and denied admission to the applicant. He sued for money damages and injunctive relief, asserting that the race-conscious admission policy violated the Equal Protection Clause. The university moved for summary judgment, arguing that even if it had not used race-based criteria, it would not have admitted the applicant because of his GPA and his GRE score.

A federal district court granted summary judgment to the university, but the Fifth Circuit Court of Appeals reversed. The case reached the U.S. Supreme Court, which noted that its decision in *Mt. Healthy City Board of Educ. v. Doyle*, 429 U.S. 274, 97 S.Ct. 568, 50 L.Ed.2d 471 (1977), made clear that **if the government has considered an impermissible criterion in making an adverse decision to the plaintiff, it can still avoid liability by demonstrating that it would have made the same decision absent the forbidden consideration**. Therefore, if the state could show that it would have made the decision to deny admission to the applicant absent the race-based policy, it would be entitled to summary judgment on the claim for damages. With respect to the claim for injunctive relief, it appeared that the university had stopped using a race-based admissions policy. However, that issue had to be decided on remand. *Texas v. Lesage*, 528 U.S. 18, 120 S.Ct. 467, 145 L.Ed.2d 347 (1999).

◆   *The University of Washington Law School's admission policy did not discriminate against applicants on the basis of race.*

The law school had no racial quotas, targets or goals for admission or enrollment, but considered race, ethnicity and other diversity factors as a "plus" in admission decisions. The school also relied on nonracial diversity factors. Several white applicants who were denied admission to the law school sued the university in a federal district court for race discrimination. The court denied summary judgment to the applicants, and they appealed. The Ninth Circuit Court of Appeals relied on *Grutter v. Bollinger*, above. It found the law school acted in good faith to implement its admissions process and satisfied the factors described in *Grutter*. **The school did not establish quotas, targets or goals for admission or enrollment of minorities, nor did it direct the admission of a certain number of minority applicants.** As the law school followed the guidelines in *Grutter* by conducting a "highly-individualized, holistic review of each applicant's file," the court affirmed the judgment. *Smith v. Univ. of Washington Law School*, 392 F.3d 367 (9th Cir. 2004).

◆   *The Florida Supreme Court held the NAACP had associational standing to challenge an executive order abolishing the use of race and gender preferences for admission to Florida state institutions of higher learning.*

The state board of regents amended three sections of the state administrative code in response to Executive Order 99-281, which asked the board to immediately prohibit racial or gender set-asides, preferences, or quotas in admissions to all Florida institutions of higher education. The NAACP and its members brought a rule challenge under state law. An administrative law judge denied a motion for dismissal by the board of regents and the state board of education, finding the NAACP had "associational standing" because its members included students in middle school, high school and college. The Florida District Court of Appeal reversed and remanded the case. It held the NAACP could not establish associational standing because it failed to show how its members would suffer a real and immediate injury. On appeal, the Supreme Court of Florida held an association that challenges a state rule must demonstrate a substantial number of its members are substantially affected by the rule. The rule's subject matter must be within the association's general scope of interest and activity, and the relief requested must be of the type appropriate for a trade association representing its members.

The record in this case indicated some NAACP members were prospective state university candidates who would be affected by the changes. The appellate decision required the NAACP to prove actual harm to gain associational standing. State law did not impose this requirement. **As the NAACP showed the amendments would have a sufficient impact on its membership, it satisfied the requirement of "substantial impact" for "associational standing."** The court quashed the decision and remanded the case. *NAACP v. Florida Board of Regents*, 863 So.2d 294 (Fla. 2003).

◆   *Although a university's use of racial preferences for admissions to law school was unconstitutional, four students failed to show that they would have been admitted to the school absent the discrimination.*

Four white students applied for admission to the University of Texas School of Law. After they were denied admission, they sued under Title VI of the Civil Rights Act of 1964 and 42 U.S.C. §§ 1981 and 1983, asserting that the law school's use of racial preferences for the purpose of achieving a diverse student body violated those laws. A federal district court held that although the government had a compelling interest in achieving a diverse student body, and a compelling interest in overcoming the present effects of past race discrimination, the school's use of separate admissions procedures for minority and nonminority students was not narrowly tailored to achieve those compelling interests. The students had the ultimate burden to prove that they would have been admitted to the law school absent the unconstitutional procedures used by the university. The court held they did not meet that burden.

On appeal, the Fifth Circuit held **the law school's use of racial preferences served no compelling state interests** and that the burden should have been on the law school to show that under a constitutional admissions procedure, the students would not have been admitted. On remand, the district court held **the university showed the students would not have been admitted even if its procedures had been constitutional**. *Hopwood v. Texas*, 999 F.Supp. 872 (W.D. Tex. 1998). On second appeal to the Fifth Circuit, the court upheld the district court's determination that the students would not have been admitted to the law school even if the admissions policy was constitutional. *Hopwood v. Texas*, 236 F.3d 256 (5th Cir. 2000).

♦ *In 1978, the Supreme Court held a special admissions program at a California medical school that reserved close to one-sixth of the school's openings each year for minority students violated the Equal Protection Clause.*

The Medical School of the University of California at Davis had two admission programs for its entering class of 100 students. Under the regular procedure, candidates whose overall undergraduate grade point averages fell below 2.5 on a scale of 4.0 were summarily rejected. The special admissions policy, designed to assist minority or other disadvantaged applicants, reserved 16 of the 100 openings each year for medical school admission based upon criteria other than that used in the general admissions program. Special admission applicants did not need to meet the 2.5 or better grade point average of the general admission group, and their Medical College Admission Test scores, measured against general admission candidates.

A white male brought suit to compel his admission to medical school after he was twice rejected for admission even though candidates with lower grade point averages and lower test score results were being admitted under the special admissions program. The plaintiff alleged that **the special admissions excluded him from medical school on the basis of his race** in violation of the Equal Protection Clause of the Fourteenth Amendment, the California Constitution, and Title VI of the 1964 Civil Rights Act. The California Supreme Court concluded that the special admissions program was not the least intrusive means of achieving the state's goals of integrating the medical profession under a strict scrutiny standard. On appeal, the U.S. Supreme Court held that **while the goal of achieving a diverse student body is sufficiently compelling to justify considerations of race in admissions decisions under some circumstances, the special admissions program, which foreclosed consideration to persons such as the plaintiff, was unnecessary to achieve this compelling goal and was therefore invalid under the Equal Protection Clause.** Since the school could not prove that the plaintiff would not have been admitted even if there had been no special admissions program, the Court ordered that he be admitted to the medical school. *Regents of the Univ. of California v. Bakke*, 438 U.S. 265, 98 S.Ct. 2733, 57 L.Ed.2d 750 (1978).

B. Discrimination and Equal Protection

◆ *A white student who was beaten by his African-American roommate failed to prove Tennessee State University (TSU) was responsible for his injuries.*

According to the student, the roommate called him a "cracker" and often used the word "nigger." While the student and his father met with a university director to discuss the roommate's conduct, they did not raise race as an issue, and they did not request a change in roommate assignments. Soon after one of the meetings, the roommate beat the student with a clothes iron in their dorm room. TSU police arrested the roommate, who promptly moved out of the dorm but finished the semester at TSU. According to the student, TSU did not officially suspend the roommate for several months, and he continued to appear on campus. When the student returned to TSU for his sophomore year, his grades slipped and he lost a scholarship. In the student's federal district court action against the university, he asserted race discrimination in violation of Title VI of the 1964 Civil Rights Act. **The court held TSU did not have knowledge of severe and pervasive harassment because the student did not inform TSU about any racial tensions.** Nor was TSU's conduct unreasonable under the circumstances. After the attack, the roommate was arrested and forced out of his dorm room. TSU's motion for pretrial judgment was granted. *Maislin v. Tennessee State Univ.*, 665 F.Supp.2d 922 (M.D. Tenn. 2009).

◆ *A student of Asian ancestry was unable to prove that a California community college librarian discriminated against her based on her race.*

According to the student, the librarian falsely accused her of using library computers for personal reasons and on some occasions forced her to leave the library. Although the student filed a complaint against the college asserting the librarian bullied and harassed her, she did not allege race discrimination. After an investigation, the community college declined to find bullying by the librarian. The student transferred to another college within the community college district, where she again encountered the librarian, who had been transferred to work at the same college. In a federal district court, the student sued the community college district and librarian for race discrimination. The court found insufficient evidence of discrimination based on race. **Undisputed evidence showed the librarian treated all students poorly.** The student did not counter this evidence, and one of her own witnesses stated that the librarian's behavior was not based on race. As a result, the court held for the librarian and community college district. *Santos v. Peralta Community College Dist.*, No. C-07-5227 EMC, 2009 WL 3809797 (N.D. Cal. 11/13/09).

◆ *Penn State University (PSU) did not violate an applicant's rights by conditioning his admission on an agreement to attend free counseling sessions.*

The applicant revealed he had been expelled from another university and had a criminal history involving violence and driving while intoxicated. The applicant was admitted on condition that he attend five free counseling sessions with PSU counselors under a policy relating to applicants with known behavior problems. He refused to attend the counseling sessions, and PSU cancelled his classes and placed his admission on hold. He then sued the university's senior director of student affairs and its chancellor in a federal district court, claiming racial discrimination and discrimination based on his criminal record.

The court dismissed the lawsuit, which alleged violations of the Eighth and Fourteenth Amendments. The Cruel and Unusual Punishment Clause of the Eighth Amendment does not apply in the civil context. According to the court, the applicant did not produce enough evidence to support an equal protection claim under the Fourteenth Amendment, as **he did not show he was treated differently than similarly situated individuals. He did not show he was treated differently because of his race.** The applicant could not proceed with a procedural due process claim because he did not appeal PSU's decision that he was required to attend counseling. The court awarded pretrial judgment to PSU. *Wright v. Speece*, No. 08-4784, 2009 WL 1383282 (E.D. Pa. 5/14/09).

◆   *A Florida university did not unlawfully discriminate against an unqualified intern by declining to hire him for a paid position.*

As a non-student and a volunteer, the intern received no pay or benefits, although he tried to secure paid positions. His applications were denied, since one was open only to students and the other was filled before he applied for it. In a federal district court action, the intern accused the university of race discrimination. The court agreed with the university, noting he was ineligible for the first position as a non-student. As for the other position, he did not show he was as well qualified for the job as the person chosen for it. **The university said the intern performed poorly, and this was a legitimate, nondiscriminatory reason for the decision not to hire him.** Because he did not show this reason was a pretext for unlawful bias, his claim of race discrimination failed, and the case was dismissed. *Cummings v. Univ. of Florida*, No. 1:04cv430-SPM/AK, 2008 WL 4534262 (N.D. Fla. 9/30/08).

◆   *A Georgia university properly suspended an African-American nursing student for selling stolen textbooks to the university's bookstore.*

A nursing student was accused of violating the university code of conduct by re-selling four stolen textbooks to a university bookstore. A disciplinary hearing was held, and she was suspended for two years. The student claimed race discrimination was present, as five white students who were accused of theft were not penalized as harshly as she was. The university argued the penalties differed because of individual circumstances, not race. The student sued the university in a federal district court, asserting due process and equal protection violations. She added race discrimination and breach of contract claims based on the university's undergraduate catalogue. The court held for the university, and the student appealed to the U.S. Court of Appeals, Eleventh Circuit. First, the court upheld the dismissal of the due process and equal protection claims. The student filed those claims under 42 U.S.C. § 1983, a federal law which permits claims for money damages against "persons" who act under color of state law in a way that violates an individual's federal rights.

The university board of regents was not a "person" within the meaning of Section 1983. The court also rejected the student's race discrimination claim, which was filed under Title VI of the Civil Rights Act of 1964. As the court explained, **Title VI bars recipients of federal funding from discriminating on the basis of race in any federally funded program**. Applying an equal protection analysis, the Eleventh Circuit rejected the claim that the suspension decision was motivated by an intent to discriminate on the basis of race. As white students disciplined by the university were not similarly situated to the student, the different punishment did not prove racial bias. Differences in individual circumstances justified the imposition of less severe punishments on white students. The court also rejected the breach of contract claim, as the catalogue stated it was for "informational purposes only and should not be construed as the basis of a contract." Since the lower court had properly rejected the contract claim, the judgment was affirmed. *Carr v. Board of Regents of the Univ. System of Georgia*, 249 Fed.Appx. 146 (11th Cir. 2007).

◆ *A federal appeals court held the University of Colorado did not violate a student's rights under federal disability and civil rights laws.*

The student, a native of Zaire, attended the university's pre-med program. She sued the university in a federal district court, alleging it discriminated against her because of a disability in violation of Rehabilitation Act Section 504. The student claimed she suffered from an unspecified disability due to injuries she sustained while working for the university. She claimed four professors failed to honor letters of accommodation issued by the university's office of disabilities services, and did not provide other accommodations. The university argued the student never gave one of her professors a letter of accommodation. Instead, she gave the professor a letter from the program coordinator seeking extra time on exams because English was her second language. The letter did not mention the student needed an accommodation due to a disability. **The court found the professor provided her extra time to sit for an exam. The student failed to present any evidence that the university denied her request for accommodation**, and the court granted the university's motion for summary judgment. *Buhendwa v. Univ. of Colorado at Boulder*, No. Civ. A03CV00485 REBOES, 2005 WL 2141581 (D. Colo. 8/22/05).

On appeal, the U.S. Court of Appeals, Tenth Circuit, held the student's disability bias claim failed. **The student later admitted that the professor refused to grant her extra time on the final examination because she fell asleep and not because she had test-taking anxiety.** Her race bias claim, filed under Title VI of the Civil Rights Act of 1964, also failed. Although the student claimed she was treated differently than similarly situated "blond students," the other students were not similarly situated because they did not fall asleep during the final examination. In addition, there was no evidence that any of the blond students had missed any quizzes. The court affirmed the district court's judgment for the university. *Buhendwa v. Univ. of Colorado at Boulder*, 214 Fed.Appx. 823 (10th Cir. 2007).

◆ *A federal district court rejected a Pennsylvania student's claim that he was dismissed from a university's nursing program based on his race.*

A LaSalle University nursing student received a D in one class and an F in another. He asked for permission to withdraw from one class, but he waited until the last day of class to do so. Because he missed the deadline for requesting withdrawal, the request was denied. It was LaSalle's policy to dismiss any nursing student who received two grades lower than C in the same semester. LaSalle applied the policy to the student and dismissed him from the program. He sued the university in a federal district court under 42 U.S.C. § 1981, claiming he was dismissed on the basis of his race.

The university filed a motion for pretrial judgment. The student responded by asking for permission to add claims of gender and disability discrimination. The court denied the request to add the new claims, ruling they were barred by a two-year statute of limitations. In addition, a disability claim would fail because the student's visual impairment was not serious enough to qualify as a "disability" under federal law. **The claim of race discrimination failed because the student had admitted in a deposition that he did not believe that race played a role in the two failing grades he received.** He did not show he was treated differently than similarly situated white or non-disabled students. In addition, there was no evidence showing that the reason LaSalle gave for the dismissal – poor academic performance – was a pretext for discrimination. The court granted the university's pretrial motion *Underwood v. LaSalle Univ.*, No. 07-1441, 2007 WL 4245737 (E.D. Pa. 12/3/07).

◆ *A Columbia University student raised valid claims that an advisor subjected him to discrimination based on his race and sex.*

The student claimed he was expelled for failing to submit to an advisor's advances. He also claimed the advisor told him he was expelled "for being a black [expletive] who thinks that he is too good." The student filed a federal district court lawsuit against Columbia, asserting race and sex discrimination. He also claimed the university breached written and implied contracts with him. The court dismissed the case, and the student appealed. The U.S. Court of Appeals, Second Circuit, held the district court should not have dismissed the complaint and denied his request to replead certain claims. When dismissal is based on the failure of an unrepresented party to meet court rules, a court should allow the party to replead the case at least once, unless it is very clear that he has no case. **The university conceded that the allegations relating to sex and race discrimination, if proven, could entitle the student to relief.** Similarly, it was not beyond doubt that the contract-based claims were meritless. The judgment was vacated in part, and the case was returned to the district court for further proceedings. *Shelton v. Trustees of Columbia Univ.*, 236 Fed.Appx. 648 (2d Cir. 2007).

◆ *The U.S. Supreme Court held individuals cannot sue colleges, schools and states for policies that unintentionally discriminate against minorities under Title VI. They may still sue entities for acts of intentional discrimination.*

Alabama amended its constitution in 1990 to declare English its official language. It began administering driver's license exams only in English, and a federal court agreed with a class of individuals that the state violated a Title VI regulation published by the U.S. Department of Justice. Title VI is one of the principal federal laws preventing discrimination on the basis of race, color or national origin. It prohibits recipients of federal funding, including states and educational institutions, from practicing discrimination in any covered program or activity and is commonly cited in education cases alleging discrimination on those grounds. The case reached the U.S. Supreme Court, which noted **Title VI prohibits only intentional discrimination** and cannot be used to enforce a disparate-impact action. **Because disparate-impact regulations of the kind at issue in this case did not apply to Title VI, the private right of action under Title VI Section 601 did not include a private right to enforce disparate-impact regulations.** The lower court judgments were reversed. *Alexander v. Sandoval*, 532 U.S. 275, 121 S.Ct. 1511, 149 L.Ed.2d 517 (2001).

◆ *A Pennsylvania university did not discriminate against a student based on her race when it dismissed her for academic failure.*

The student had to repeat her first year of college, then failed four courses in her repeat year. She met with a professor to talk about her study habits. The professor suggested that the student study from her notes instead of index cards and suggested that she visit the university's Recruitment, Admission and Retention Office (RAR) for extra help. RAR is a federally funded program that actively recruits minority students and offers them support services. All African-American students received an RAR invitation, regardless of their academic qualifications or background. A different professor later advised the student to study from old exams and expressed surprise that the other professor had not made the same suggestion. A Caucasian student told the student that the professor who had advised her to go to RAR had told the Caucasian student to study from past tests. At the end of her repeat year, a university committee dismissed the student because she received several failing grades while on probation. She sued the university in a federal district court.

The court held for the university, and the student appealed to the U.S. Court of Appeals, Third Circuit. The student argued the professor's suggestion that she go to the RAR program for help stereotyped her. She said the RAR program implied that African-American students were less qualified or capable of meeting the demands of the university. **The court found no evidence to show a connection between racial stereotyping and the academic dismissal. The student failed to prove the university dismissed her because of race.** The only evidence she offered to prove discrimination was that the professor gave her different advice than she gave to a Caucasian student. The court held that offering different students different advice did not mean the professor did so because of race. The judgment for the university was affirmed. *Manning v. Temple Univ.*, No. 05-1215, 157 Fed. Appx. 509 (3d Cir. 2005).

C. National Origin

◆ *An Iranian dental school student with D grades could not proceed with a national origin discrimination case against Marquette University.*

After compiling a D grade average, the university dental school dismissed the student. He filed a state circuit court action against Marquette, alleging national origin discrimination. To support his claim, he alleged that a Caucasian student was treated more favorably than he was. The court dismissed the complaint, finding he did not show he was similarly-situated to the other student. **On appeal, the Court of Appeals of Wisconsin held the student failed to show he was similarly-situated to the Caucasian student in all relevant respects.** The Caucasian student completed his first year of studies with no unsatisfactory grades, while the Iranian student did not. In addition, the Caucasian student offered a medical explanation when his grades began to slip. Marquette was not made aware of any medical problems suffered by the Iranian student at a relevant time. As he did not show he was similarly-situated to the other student, the judgment for Marquette was affirmed. *Amir v. Marquette Univ.*, 322 Wis.2d 572, 776 N.W.2d 287 (Table) (Wis. Ct. App. 2009).

◆ *A federal district court denied a trial for a student who did not provide enough information to support his race and national origin claims.*

According to the student, two architecture professors complained about his accent, criticized his proposal based on preconceived racial beliefs, and created a hostile learning environment. They eventually dropped him from the class. But when the student took the same class from a different professor, he again failed. After the university expelled the student, he sued the university and architecture professors in a federal district court. **It found the student "utterly fail[ed] to make the minimal showing necessary to avoid dismissal."** Under the rules for filing federal cases, legal papers are supposed to provide plain, short statements that give notice of the claims and grounds for asserting them. Since the student merely made "labels and conclusions" and not a factual basis sufficient to avoid dismissal, he was unable to proceed with the case. The court dismissed the action, saying it refused to "second-guess an educational institution's application of its own academic standards and procedures" without a valid allegation it had acted with an illegal motive. *Wanko v. Catholic Univ. of America*, No. 08-2115 (RJL), 2009 WL 3052477 (D.D.C. 9/22/09).

◆ *A student who was dismissed from Howard University for poor academic performance was unable to proceed with a federal action against the university.*

University rules specified that students who received over nine credit hours of grade C or below should be dropped from their courses of study. University rules allowed graduate faculty to recommend the dismissal of any student who was not performing satisfactorily. In four semesters of work, the student did not achieve any grade higher than C, and his academic advisor did not approve his thesis proposal. After he was dismissed for poor academic performance and unwillingness to listen to his academic advisor, he sued the university and several faculty members in a federal court for national origin and disability discrimination under Titles VI and VII of the Civil Rights Act, Title IX of the Education Amendments of 1972 and the Americans with Disabilities Act.

The court found many of the claims failed because they did not apply to the facts. **Claims asserted against the individual defendants could not proceed because none of the laws under which they were brought permitted claims against individuals.** The student alleged race and disability discrimination, which Title IX does not address. The Title VII claims were time-barred, and the remaining claims under Title VI and the Rehabilitation Act failed because the student did not show that the reason the school provided for the dismissal – poor academic performance – was really a pretext for unlawful discrimination. *Mwabira-Simera v. Howard Univ.*, 692 F.Supp.2d 65 (D.D.C. 2010).

◆ *A Mississippi university did not discriminate against a native African who abruptly left an orientation.*

The student was a native of Nigeria and an Illinois resident. He contacted Jackson State University in Mississippi to learn about a new doctorate program in higher education. He successfully applied, signed a "partnership agreement" and submitted a deposit of $2,000 to hold his place. But before the orientation had even begun and without telling anyone from Jackson State, the student returned to Illinois. Jackson State officials later learned he returned to Illinois because he was a candidate to become the president of the community college where he worked and had been asked to return by the board of trustees. However, he never told Jackson State officials of this. A Jackson State official informed the student he would not be allowed to participate in the program.

The student sued Jackson State and several officials for discrimination on the basis of his national origin and related federal claims under 42 U.S.C. § 1983. **The court held that under Section 1983, claims for monetary damages are not allowed against a state entity or state officials in their official capacities.** The student could not sue the individuals in their individual capacities, as they had qualified immunity. He had not completed the registration process, and it was reasonable for the officials to conclude he lacked a property interest in the program. The national origin discrimination claim failed because the student could not show officials intentionally discriminated against him based on national origin. *Senu-Oke v. Jackson State Univ.*, 521 F.Supp.2d 551 (S.D. Miss. 2007).

◆ *A citizen of the Dominican Republic was permitted to proceed with a Title VI complaint against a New York university.*

The student claimed he was harassed by peers and had to complete a group project by himself because no one would work with him. He claimed this caused feelings of inferiority and adversely affected his education. The student claimed he was "teased, insulted, mocked, degraded and ridiculed" in another class as a member of a minority group by a professor and other students. A female student brought harassment allegations against him. A student services panel held he would be permitted to complete his degree, but would be considered a "persona non grata" in university facilities.

The student sued the university in a federal district court for race discrimination. He included a claim under Title VI. **A federal magistrate judge found the student failed to show race had anything to do with the sexual harassment and disciplinary proceedings against him.** However, the judge permitted him to amend his Title VI claim against the university by alleging intentional discrimination. He recommended that this claim proceed. *Rodriguez v. New York Univ.*, No. 05 Civ. 7374 JSR, 2007 WL 117775 (S.D.N.Y. 1/16/07).

◆ *A Texas federal district court dismissed a Cameroon native's race and national origin discrimination claim against an associate professor.*

The University of Houston admitted the student to a doctoral degree program in the Department of English. She claimed an associate professor questioned her about her country of origin and academic profile. The professor allegedly threatened to ruin the student's transcript and delay her graduation. She brought grading and discrimination complaints against the professor under a university policy. The English department dismissed the accusations as unfounded. At about the same time, another professor in the English department accused the student of plagiarism. The university honesty panel, which included the associate professor, concluded the student had plagiarized and she received an F for that class. The student was later expelled after another charge of plagiarism by the same professor. The student sued the university, professor, and others in a federal district court for discrimination and retaliation under Title VI. The court held **Title VI claims may only be brought against entities that receive federal funding, not individuals, and dismissed the Title VI claim against the associate professor**. *Bisong v. Univ. of Houston*, Civil Action No. H-06-1815, 2006 WL 2414410 (S.D. Tex. 8/18/06).

IV. AGE DISCRIMINATION

In addition to state laws, the Age Discrimination Act of 1975 (42 U.S.C. § 6101, et seq.) provides the basis for claims of age discrimination by students. Similar to Title IX claims, however, the Age Discrimination Act applies only to programs or activities receiving federal funding. The Age Discrimination in Employment Act (ADEA) has broad coverage, but applies only in employment cases. The Age Discrimination Act was interpreted in the following Alabama case concerning age-based housing discrimination claims.

◆ *A federal district court rejected a student's claim that Alabama State University violated the federal Age Discrimination Act by removing him from campus housing.*

When the student was 41 years old, the university removed him from campus housing for unspecified reasons. He sued the university in a federal district court for violating the Age Discrimination Act, a federal law that bars discrimination on the basis of age in programs and activities that receive any form of federal financial assistance. **The court dismissed the case for failing to comply with Age Discrimination Act requirement that he first file an administrative complaint.** An Age Discrimination Act provision requires claimants to provide written notice to the Secretary of Health and Human Services, the Attorney General of the United States and the person against whom the action is directed before filing suit. As the student admitted that he did not file an administrative complaint, the court granted the university's motion to dismiss the case. *McGhee v. Alabama State Univ.*, No. 2:09-cv-0092-MEF, 2009 WL 1684604 (M.D. Ala. 6/12/09).

◆ *A 31-year-old Louisiana student raised a discrimination claim against a university after he was excluded from the varsity football team.*

According to the student, the head football coach would not let him try out for the team because he was too old. In response, he sued university officials in a federal district court for age discrimination. Following negotiations, the university signed a commitment to resolve the action. After six years, the student refiled the case in court. But the court dismissed the case as untimely. The Fifth Circuit Court of Appeals returned the case to the district court for more specific findings. The court against dismissed the case, and the student filed another appeal. The Fifth Circuit explained that two requirements had to be met in order to file an age bias claim. First, **the student was required to exhaust his administrative remedies before filing suit**. Second, he needed to provide written notice of his intention to sue to the Secretary of Health and Human Services, the United States Attorney General and the defendant. **Since the student was unable to show he met these requirements, the case had been properly dismissed.** *Parker v. Board of Supervisors Univ. of Louisiana-Lafayette*, 296 Fed.Appx. 414 (5th Cir. 2008).

◆ *The claim that a California college librarian subjected a student to harassing and discriminatory conduct was ordered to proceed.*

A Merritt College student claimed a college librarian harassed her at least five times. She said the librarian falsely accused her of using a library computer for personal use. After complaining to the dean of the library and other college employees, the student sued the college in a federal district court for violating the state's Fair Employment and Housing Act (FEHA). She added federal age and race discrimination claims against the college and librarian under 42 U.S.C. § 1981 along with state law claims of intentional infliction of emotional distress, breach of contract and negligent misrepresentation. The court first dismissed the FEHA claim against the college, as the statute covers only discrimination in employment. The Section 1981 claims were also dismissed, because they were based on age discrimination, which Section 1981 does not address. However, **the court refused to dismiss the Section 1981 claim of race discrimination against the librarian in her individual capacity**. The court dismissed the remaining state law claims so the student could re-file them in a state court. *Santos v. Merritt College*, No. C-07-5227 EMC, 2008 WL 131696 (N.D. Cal. 1/11/08).

◆ *The U.S. Court of Appeals, Second Circuit, held Cornell University had a valid reason to expel a student that was not based on her age or gender.*

The female student attended Cornell's veterinary program. She twice failed required exams, and the university expelled her. The student sued the university in a federal district court, alleging discrimination based on her gender and because of her age in violation of the Age Discrimination Act. The court held the student did not prove the motivation to expel her was based on gender or age discrimination and dismissed the claims. The student appealed to the Second Circuit. The court found she had failed to exhaust her administrative remedies before she filed suit. **The court agreed with the district court's finding that the student failed to prove the university had expelled male**

students who twice failed required exams. It affirmed the judgment. *Curto v. Edmundson*, 392 F.3d 502 (2d Cir. 2004).

◆   *An older student's claim of age discrimination failed where he could not show that he was qualified for entrance into a medical school's class.*

A 53-year-old psychologist applied to be a member of a first-year medical class at the Albert Einstein College of Medicine. The psychologist was called for an interview and was recommended for acceptance by the interviewer. However, the psychologist was not accepted. He alleged age discrimination in violation of New York Education Law and filed suit in a state court. The complaint alleged that faculty members indicated that the problem was not with the psychologist's qualifications, but with his age. The school contended that the psychologist's qualifications clearly precluded him, and that it had followed its established and published admittance regulations. The school was granted a dismissal, and the psychologist appealed to a state appellate court.

The issue in this case was whether the psychologist was otherwise qualified for admittance, ignoring his age. A court's review of a school's policies is limited to determining whether it acted in good faith or irrationally and arbitrarily. The school showed that the psychologist's grades, as reflected by his science classes and overall grade point average, were clearly unacceptable. It also alleged that his Medical College Aptitude Test score was lower than any student accepted. The psychologist pointed out that he was called for an interview and not summarily dismissed. He also noted his accomplishments in his current field, which included having hosted a weekly television show on mental health. The court ruled that **the psychologist was trying to create his own entrance standards, which the court had no power to allow**. The dismissal of claims was affirmed. *Brown v. Albert Einstein College of Medicine*, 568 N.Y.S.2d 61 (N.Y. App. Div. 1991).

CHAPTER THREE

Athletics and Student Activities

I. ATHLETIC PROGRAMS

A. Eligibility of Participants

◆ *No contract was breached when a Duke University golf coach dismissed a student from the golf team and revoked his access to university golf facilities.*

According to the student, Duke University head golf coach Rod Myers promised him lifetime access to Duke's state-of-the-art training facilities when he recruited him as a high school golfer. While the student accepted an offer to attend Duke and play on the golf team, he was not awarded a scholarship. After Myers died, his successor dismissed the student from the team and revoked his access to Duke's golf facilities. The student sued the successor coach and Duke in a federal district court for breach of contract and related claims. A federal magistrate judge rejected the contract claim, explaining that **student policy manuals are not binding contracts**. The manuals upon which the student relied to support his breach of contract claim could be unilaterally altered at any time. The magistrate judge rejected a claim that the university and the coach breached a covenant of good faith and fair dealing. **Without a contract, a covenant of good faith and fair dealing does not exist, and the student could not claim tortious interference with any contract.** *Giuliani v. Duke Univ.*, No. 1:08CV502, 2009 WL 1408869 (M.D.N.C. 5/19/09).

◆ *Central Michigan University (CMU) was entitled to immunity for a breach of contract claim by a student who lost her athletic scholarship.*

CMU offered a student an athletic scholarship to play basketball. She declined other scholarship offers and enrolled at CMU. She later claimed

CMU's first-year coach harassed her, said she was not her "type" of person and repeatedly tried to force her to transfer. After missing some practices, the coach told her she was dismissing her from the team and that she would lose her scholarship. The student sued CMU, the coach and other CMU officials in a federal district court for breach of contract and violation of her due process and equal protection rights. She added claims of defamation, interference with contract, intentional infliction of emotional distress, negligent hiring and negligent supervision. **The court dismissed the breach of contract claims against CMU and individual officials on the basis of sovereign immunity.** However, the court granted the student an opportunity to further develop her negligent hiring and supervision claims, explaining that she could not win on these claims unless she showed the athletic director's conduct was gross negligence. This claim was not dismissed at this stage of the case. The court further directed the parties to file supplemental briefs regarding the student's defamation claims. *Heike v. Guevara*, 654 F.Supp.2d 658 (E.D. Mich. 2009).

◆ *There is no recognized constitutional right to participate in interscholastic athletics or other extracurricular activities. The possibility of obtaining a college athletic scholarship is also not protected.*

A Kentucky high school student admitted to the school principal that he had been drinking alcohol before coming to a school dance. The school board excluded him from playing basketball and all other extracurricular activities. He sued the board and principal in state court, asserting the discipline was arbitrary and capricious. He further alleged discrimination and due process violations. The court dismissed the complaint, and the student appealed.

The Court of Appeals of Kentucky noted that students have no fundamental or vested property right to participate in interscholastic athletics. For that reason, the student's constitutional claims were not viable and had been properly dismissed. The court stated a school board may suspend or expel a student for violating lawful school regulations. However, the student stated a valid claim that the board acted arbitrarily and capriciously in denying his opportunity to participate in interscholastic athletics. The court returned this claim to the trial court, holding it should not have been dismissed on the basis of the summary pretrial record. *Critchelow v. Breckinridge County Board of Educ.*, No. 2005-CA-001194-MR, 2006 WL 3456658 (Ky. Ct. App. 2006).

◆ *A soccer player who was subject to an athletic conference transfer rule failed to demonstrate that the rule violated federal antitrust laws.*

The player decided to attend the University of Southern California (USC). USC athletic officials purportedly told her that she would be free to transfer to another school without penalty as long as she finished her freshman year at USC and met all academic requirements. After learning that USC athletes received fraudulent academic credit, the player transferred to the University of California, Los Angeles (UCLA). Both USC and UCLA are members of the Pacific 10 Athletic Association (PAC 10). USC opposed the transfer and sought sanctions against the player pursuant to the PAC 10's transfer rule, which would not allow her to play soccer for UCLA during her first year there. As a result, the player sued USC, the USC officials who recruited her and the PAC

10. She alleged that USC had enforced PAC 10 sanctions only against her and never against other transferring athletes because she participated in an investigation into possible academic fraud at USC. She asserted that the transfer rule conflicted with the federal Sherman Act, 15 U.S.C. § 1, which prohibits contracts or conspiracies that restrain trade or commerce.

A federal district court dismissed the complaint, and the player appealed to the U.S. Court of Appeals, Ninth Circuit. The student had to prove the transfer rule produced significant anti-competitive effects in relevant geographic and product markets. The player claimed the relevant geographic market in this case was the Los Angeles area, and the relevant product market was the UCLA women's soccer program. The Ninth Circuit rejected this interpretation. First, it noted that schools outside the Los Angeles area attempted to recruit the player for similar soccer programs, so the relevant geographic market should extend to the national market of women's collegiate soccer programs. Even if the player had correctly asserted that the relevant market was national in scope, her suit would have failed because she objected to a PAC 10 transfer rule, which only applies to member schools and not the entire national market of college soccer programs. **As the player admitted she was the only USC athlete to suffer sanctions under the transfer rule, she conceded that the rule did not affect all relevant consumers, thereby foiling her antitrust claim.** *Tanaka v. Univ. of Southern California*, 252 F.3d 1059 (9th Cir. 2001).

◆   *In the following case, the California Supreme Court held student-athletes have lower privacy expectations than the general student population.*

In 1986, the NCAA instituted a drug testing program for six categories of banned drugs including steroids and street drugs. In order to participate, all students had to sign a consent form at the start of each school year allowing the drug tests. Two Stanford athletes instituted an action in a California trial court, alleging that the drug testing program violated their right to privacy. The court granted a preliminary injunction prohibiting the NCAA from enforcing its drug testing program against Stanford or its students, except in football and men's basketball. After a trial, the court permanently enjoined the NCAA from enforcing its drug-testing program against Stanford or its student-athletes.

The case reached the Supreme Court of California, which held that student-athletes have a lower expectation of privacy than the general student population. Observation of urination obviously implicated privacy interests. However, by its nature, participation in highly competitive post-season championship events involved close regulation and scrutiny of the physical fitness and bodily condition of student-athletes. **Required physical examinations (including urinalysis) and the special regulation of sleep habits, diet, fitness and other activities that intrude significantly on privacy interests are routine aspects of a college athlete's life not shared by other students or the population at large.** Further, the court noted that drug testing programs involving student-athletes have routinely survived Fourth Amendment privacy challenges. The court concluded that the NCAA had an interest in protecting the health and safety of student-athletes involved in NCAA-regulated competition. *Hill v. NCAA*, 26 Cal.Rptr.2d 834 (Cal. 1994).

◆ *A drug testing program was struck down where it was not voluntary, and where the college athletes did not have a diminished expectation of privacy.*

The University of Colorado conducted a drug testing program for intercollegiate athletes that entailed a urine test at each annual physical with random tests thereafter. A program amendment substituted random rapid eye examinations for urinalysis, and the university prohibited any athlete refusing to consent to the testing from participating in intercollegiate athletics. The program called for progressive sanctions ranging from required participation in rehabilitation programs to permanent suspension from athletics. A group of athletes filed a class action suit against the university in a Colorado trial court seeking declaratory and injunctive relief. The court ruled for the athletes.

The Supreme Court of Colorado observed that the program did not ensure confidentiality and was mandatory. The university was unable to articulate an important governmental interest for the program. **Unlike cases involving high school athletes, college students did not have a diminished expectation of privacy under the Fourth Amendment that justified government searches in the absence of an important governmental interest.** Random, suspicionless urinalysis was unconstitutional. University student athletes did not consent to participation in the program because there could be no voluntary consent where the failure to consent resulted in denial of a governmental benefit. The court affirmed the decision for the athletes. *Univ. of Colorado v. Derdeyn*, 863 P.2d 929 (Colo. 1993).

B. NCAA Rules

The National Collegiate Athletic Association (NCAA) is a voluntary, nonprofit association which regulates college athletics, defines eligibility for players and imposes sanctions for violating its rules. NCAA rules limit student eligibility for interscholastic competition to a five-year period and prevent athletic participation for one year after a transfer between member institutions. The NCAA's core course requirement excludes from consideration for initial eligibility all courses taught below regular high school instructional levels.

◆ *The U.S. Supreme Court has held that the NCAA is not a recipient of federal funds and is therefore not subject to suit under Title IX.*

The case was filed by a college graduate who had played two years of intercollegiate volleyball at a private college before enrolling in postgraduate programs at two other colleges. Because she had exhausted only two years of her athletic eligibility, she sought a waiver from the NCAA's Postbaccalaureate Bylaw, which allows postgraduate student-athletes to compete in intercollegiate sports only at the institution where they received an undergraduate degree. The student sued the NCAA in a Pennsylvania federal court after it denied her requests for a waiver. She claimed that the NCAA discriminated against her on the basis of gender in violation of Title IX. The complaint asserted that the NCAA granted more waivers to male postgraduate students than it did to females. The case reached the U.S. Supreme Court, which noted that Title IX covers entities that receive federal financial assistance – whether direct or indirect – whereas those entities that only benefit economically from federal financial assistance are not covered. **Because the NCAA only benefited economically from institutions that received federal financial assistance, it could not be sued under Title IX.** *NCAA v. Smith*, 525 U.S. 459, 119 S.Ct. 924, 142 L.Ed.2d 929 (1999).

◆ *An assistant football coach who was forced to give up his job due to rules violations was unable to advance various claims against the NCAA.*

Officials at the University of Kentucky (UK) confronted the coach with evidence of NCAA rules violations. He agreed to step down and later claimed that he did so based on assurances that no further action would be taken against him. However, UK conducted an internal investigation and turned over its findings to the NCAA. In turn, the NCAA held a hearing to consider charges of improper recruiting practices, such as improperly inducing prospective athletes and high school coaches, and fraudulently assisting student-athletes in the form of preparation of their work. The NCAA sanctioned UK for the rules violations. It also imposed an eight-year restriction on the coach and any NCAA member seeking to hire him for an athletic-related position.

The coach sued the NCAA, UK and the Southeastern Conference in a federal district court for conspiracy to violate antitrust laws, fraud, civil conspiracy and interference with his employment contract. The court dismissed the action, and the coach appealed. The U.S. Court of Appeals, Sixth Circuit, held the antitrust claim was properly dismissed. Since the coach did not advance a commercial claim, he failed to allege an antitrust injury. Instead, **NCAA rules were anti-commercial and designed to promote and ensure competitiveness among member institutions.** The coach admitted his own misconduct had caused any injury he may have suffered, defeating his fraud claim. A breach of contract claim was disallowed as against public policy. The court noted that if not for the coach's own misconduct, he would still have his job. Accordingly, the judgment against him was affirmed. *Bassett v. NCAA*, 528 F.3d 426 (6th Cir. 2008).

◆ *A federal district court denied a Kansas student-athlete's request for an order to prevent the enforcement of an NCAA athletic eligibility rule.*

The student transferred to the University of Kansas (KU) in 2004 after beginning college at another school three years earlier. He earned a spot on the KU football team as a walk-on and eventually became an alternate starter on the defensive line. The NCAA denied KU's request for a waiver of the NCAA's five-year eligibility rule. After an unsuccessful appeal, the student sued KU and the NCAA in a federal district court for civil rights violations. He petitioned a federal district court for an order preventing the university from enforcing the NCAA's eligibility ruling. After a hearing, **the court found the five-year eligibility period begins to run when a student-athlete initially registers and attends the first day of classes in a regular term of an academic year for a minimum full-time program of studies.** The NCAA may grant a waiver of the eligibility rule for reasons beyond the control of the student or institution which deprive the student-athlete of the opportunity to participate for more than one season in his/her spot within the five-year period. **An NCAA member school may grant a one-year extension of the five-year period for a female**

student-athlete for reasons of pregnancy. The student contended that he missed the chance to participate in football when his girlfriend became pregnant some time before he enrolled at KU. He said he decided not to attend college so he could work and care for his daughter.

The student argued a female could have taken advantage of the pregnancy exception under NCAA bylaws. The court rejected the student's gender discrimination claim. It also found no merit to his claim that he would be unable to complete his education and lose any chance to be recruited by a professional football team. The student's financial aid package was not an athletic grant and the threat of losing a professional career was speculative. **The court denied the student's request for relief, finding it was in the public interest to allow the NCAA to enforce its own rules without court intervention.** *Butler v. NCAA*, Civ. Act. No. 06-2319 KHV, 2006 WL 2398683 (D. Kan. 8/15/06).

◆ *An Illinois court held a student's religious courses and computer classes were not "core courses" under the NCAA academic eligibility requirements.*

The NCAA sets eligibility requirements for Division I competition, which mandate that students take at least 13 high school "core courses" and that students achieve a specified minimum grade point average in those courses as well as a specified minimum score on either the SAT or ACT. The higher a student's test score, the lower the required GPA needed. An 18-year-old black student who excelled at basketball graduated from a private, Catholic high school. He was heavily recruited by colleges and universities, and selected a private Illinois university. The NCAA ruled the student was not qualified to compete in Division I play during his freshman season, and he sued the NCAA in a federal district court for an order allowing him to play in his freshman year.

The student asserted that the NCAA had improperly found him to be ineligible by excluding from the "core course" requirements two religion and two computer classes. The court determined the religion courses **were taught from a particular religious point of view – based on a Christian ideology**. The court also determined that, based on the syllabi **for the computer classes, at least 50% of the course instruction included keyboarding or word processing**, which took the classes outside core status. As a result, the student did not have even a negligible chance of success on the merits of his claim, and he was not entitled to injunctive relief. Further, the student's claims of breach of contract and misrepresentation likewise had a very slim chance of success. The court refused to overrule the NCAA's eligibility determination, and the student was not allowed to play basketball during his freshman season. *Hall v. NCAA*, 985 F.Supp. 782 (N.D. Ill. 1997).

◆ *A wrestler who transferred from a Rhode Island university had to sit out for one year because he was not in good academic standing.*

The student, a talented wrestler, failed a course during his first semester at Nebraska and did not repeat the course before transferring to Brown. The NCAA notified him he would be prohibited from wrestling the next academic year because he had not successfully repeated the course. The student sued the NCAA in a federal district court, seeking an injunction to restrain the NCAA from preventing him from wrestling. The court denied the injunction. **NCAA regulations prevent athletic participation for one year after transfer.** There is an exception to this rule for students in good academic standing who would have been eligible to participate had they remained at their previous institution. As the student had failed the course, he would have been ineligible at both Nebraska and Brown. He could not bring constitutional claims against the NCAA, as it is private entity. *Collier v. NCAA*, 783 F.Supp. 1576 (D.R.I. 1992).

C. Students with Disabilities

◆ *A deceased student-athlete's claims against several colleges that stopped recruiting him survived his death. His federal lawsuit also challenged the NCAA's core course requirement.*

A New Jersey student with learning disabilities was recruited for football by several NCAA Division I schools. The NCAA ruled that a number of his high school special education classes did not satisfy its core course requirement and declared him ineligible for interscholastic sports during his freshman season. The student claimed the universities then stopped recruiting him and that the NCAA's core course requirement violated Section 504 of the Rehabilitation Act and the ADA. He filed a federal district court action against the NCAA, universities and the ACT/Clearinghouse, which administers college entrance examinations. The court found that because of an intervening change in NCAA rules, the student had the potential of regaining a year of eligibility. While the ADA and Section 504 claims against the NCAA were dismissed, he could proceed against the universities under the ADA and Section 504.

The student died, but his estate continued the litigation. After several years of litigation, the student's mother revealed to the NCAA and universities for the first time that the student had been in and out of drug treatment and mental health programs from fall 1998 until 2001. He was hospitalized in 1999 after attempting to commit suicide. The mother revealed that the student's death resulted from an apparent drug overdose. His medical records indicated his pre-existing drug condition, which had never been disclosed to the NCAA or the universities. The district court sanctioned the mother and her attorneys. It held the failure to disclose the information was willful and in bad faith.

The U.S. Court of Appeals, Third Circuit, found the district court's ruling immunized the NCAA and universities from liability. The judgment was "fundamentally flawed" by failing to focus on the correct time frame. **The court held a determination of whether a person is a "qualified individual with a disability" under the ADA is not made from the time a lawsuit is filed, "but from the time at which the alleged discriminatory decision was made."** The discrimination being alleged took place during the 1995-96 school year, when the student was deemed ineligible for football under NCAA rules. The evidence of any substance abuse by the student in 1995-96 was minimal. His substance abuse was irrelevant for purposes of establishing liability. The district court's contrary ruling was reversed. The mother would not, however, be permitted to use posthumously revealed information to her own advantage. The court reversed a district court order sanctioning the mother's attorneys for failing to disclose the student's full medical history. While the action was "an ongoing saga," the case was returned to the district court for a determination of whether the NCAA and universities violated the ADA and Rehabilitation Act. *Bowers v. NCAA*, 475 F.3d 524 (3d Cir. 2007).

◆   *The University of North Carolina at Greensboro did not violate federal disability laws when it dismissed a disabled student from its golf team.*

The student earned a partial golf scholarship and was the fourth best player on the team in his freshman year. The next year, the student's father informed the golf coach of his diagnosis with Obsessive-Compulsive Disorder. The father explained that his son's condition caused him to repeat certain ritualistic behaviors and have negative thoughts. The coach responded by suggesting that the student red-shirt for the season and agreed to allow him to attend therapy sessions that sometimes conflicted with team practices. The coach began to emphasize procedures to be followed when a player was late or absent from practice. Throughout the season, the student was late to many practices and workouts, or absent. He did not play in any more tournaments. The coach did not excuse the absences as a disability-related accommodation because the student did not register with the university office of disability services. At the end of the season, the coach removed him from the team for misconduct and rules violations. As a result, the student lost his scholarship. He transferred to another college where he played on the golf team.

The student sued the university in federal court for violating the Americans with Disabilities Act and Section 504 of the Rehabilitation Act by dismissing him from the team and failing to renew his scholarship. The court granted the university's motion for pre-trial judgment, because the student failed to show he had a "disability" within the meaning of the Rehabilitation Act. **Although he had a mental impairment, he did not show it substantially limited his ability to perform any major life activity.** He was typically on time for appointments, completed course work and was able to follow school rules. The student's condition had improved significantly as a result of therapy and medication. The coach's red-shirt offer did not prove he regarded the student as disabled. University officials met to discuss his condition and consulted with its counseling and testing center. This conduct did not prove a perception of disability. *Costello v. Univ. of North Carolina Greensboro*, No. 1:03CV01050, 2006 WL 3694579 (M.D.N.C. 12/14/06).

◆   *A college football player with a disability could be prohibited from continuing to play without violating Section 504 of the Rehabilitation Act.*

A University of Kansas student who was on a football scholarship experienced an episode of transient quadriplegia during a scrimmage. The team physician discovered that the student had a congenital condition that put him at an extremely high risk for suffering severe and potentially permanent neurological injuries, including quadriplegia. **The university disqualified the student from participating in intercollegiate football.** Although he obtained opinions from three other doctors stating that his risk of injury was no greater than any other player's, the university denied his request to rejoin the football team. He filed a lawsuit against the university in a federal district court, claiming it had violated Section 504, which prohibits discrimination by recipients of federal funding against individuals on the basis of disability, if the individual is otherwise qualified to participate in the recipient's programs or activities. The court denied the university's motion to dismiss the lawsuit, and the student sought order to require his reinstatement to the football team.

Because Section 504's definition of a person with a disability involves a consideration of whether the individual is impaired in some major life activity, the court considered whether intercollegiate athletic participation was a major life activity. The university argued that it was not, because the general population cannot participate in college athletics. The student argued that his grades improved, and he gained many other opportunities for personal development by playing on the team. **The court agreed that playing football was related to the major life activity of learning, but held that his disqualification was not a substantial limitation on his continuing ability to learn.** The university had not revoked the student's athletic scholarship, and he retained the opportunity to participate in the football program in a role other than player. The court accepted the conclusion of the university's physicians that there was a reasonable basis for his exclusion from the team that did not violate Section 504. The court denied the student's motion. *Pahulu v. Univ. of Kansas*, 897 F.Supp. 1387 (D. Kan. 1995).

D. Discrimination and Harassment

1. Gender Equity in Athletics

Title IX of the Education Amendments of 1972 (20 U.S.C. § 1681, et seq.*) prohibits sex discrimination in education programs, including interscholastic, intercollegiate, club and intramural athletics. It applies only to programs that receive federal financial assistance. One of the most important Title IX implementing regulations is 34 C.F.R. § 106.41(c). It states that*:

A [federal funding] recipient which operates or sponsors interscholastic, intercollegiate, club or intramural athletics shall provide equal athletic opportunity for members of both sexes. In determining whether equal opportunities are available the Director will consider, among other factors:

(1) Whether the selection of sports and levels of competition effectively accommodate the interests and abilities of members of both sexes; (2) The provision of equipment and supplies; (3) Scheduling of games and practice time; (4) Travel and per diem allowance; (5) Opportunity to receive coaching and academic tutoring; (6) Assignment and compensation of coaches and tutors; (7) Provision of locker rooms, practice and competitive facilities; (8) Provision of medical and training facilities and services; (9) Provision of housing and dining facilities and services; (10) Publicity.

Unequal aggregate expenditures for members of each sex or unequal expenditures for male and female teams if a recipient operates or sponsors separate teams will not constitute noncompliance with this section, but the Assistant Secretary [for Civil Rights of the U.S. Department of Education] may consider the failure to provide necessary funds for teams for one sex in assessing equality of opportunity for members of each sex.

A "three-part test" approved by the Office for Civil Rights (OCR) affords educational institutions three ways to demonstrate Title IX compliance. Compliance with Title IX may be shown by demonstrating: (1) **substantial proportionality** (the number of men and women in intercollegiate athletics is proportionate to their enrollment at the institution); or (2) **the institution has a "history and continuing practice of program expansion" for the underrepresented sex. If a university cannot satisfy the first two options, a third method allows it to show it "fully and effectively accommodates"** the interests of women. See 44 Fed.Reg. 71,413, December 11, 1979.

◆ *Female wrestlers at the University of California, Davis (UCD) were not required to give the university prior notice before filing a Title IX lawsuit.*

At the time of their enrollment, a small number of females participated on UCD's mostly-male team, and females wrestled only against other women. But they enjoyed benefits associated with varsity status, such as training, coaching and access to facilities. UCD effectively ended female wrestling participation by requiring females to beat male wrestlers in their weight classes under men's rules. Three female wrestlers sued UCD and several university officials in a federal district court for Title IX and equal protection violations. The court held their equal protection claims were subsumed by Title IX. It then held for UCD on the Title IX claims for money damages, because the students failed to give UCD notice and a chance to cure any Title IX deficiencies before they filed suit. On review, the U.S. Court of Appeals, Ninth Circuit held the Title IX notice requirement was based on a misapplication of *Gebser v. Lago Independent School Dist.*, 534 U.S. 274 (1998), Chapter Two, Section B.I.

The Ninth Circuit held ***Gebser's* notice requirement applied only when an alleged Title IX violation was based on an institution's deliberate indifference.** No notice requirement applied to Title IX claims based on an affirmative institutional decision, such as cases alleging inequality of athletic opportunity. The Ninth Circuit also rejected UCD's alternative argument that it was entitled to judgment because it was in compliance with Title IX. Nor did UCD prove a continuing practice of program expansion. Finally, the court held that the students' equal protection claims should proceed. In *Fitzgerald v. Barnstable School Committee*, 129 S.Ct. 788 (U.S. 2009), the Supreme Court held Title IX does not bar parallel and concurrent equal protection claims. See Chapter Two, Section II.B.2. An equal protection claim was timely. As a result, the judgment was reversed, and the case was returned to the district court. *Mansourian v. Regents of the Univ. of California*, 602 F.3d 957 (9th Cir. 2010).

◆ *A federal district court in Virginia rejected a bid to invalidate a three-part test that has been used to measure Title IX compliance for more than 30 years.*

Officials at James Madison University voted to eliminate seven men's and three women's sports to bring the university's varsity athletic program into compliance with Title IX. A nonprofit corporation called Equity in Athletics (EIA) sued the U.S. Department of Education to block the cuts. EIA claimed a longstanding test to gauge compliance with Title IX violated the Equal Protection Clause, the First Amendment's associational provisions, the Spending Clause and Title IX itself. The court found the three-part test did not violate Title IX, as the test did not impose an affirmative action requirement.

The test did not require gender-based quotas or statistical balancing. Instead, institutions can comply with Title IX by offering athletic opportunities for males and females in numbers substantially proportionate to their enrollment.

Nor did the limited consideration of sex authorized by the test violate equal protection guarantees. After rejecting a Spending Clause claim, the court held the policy interpretation was a reasonable interpretation of Title IX regulations that was entitled to deference. The policy interpretation and later clarifications were not subject to notice-and-comment requirements because they did not "create new rights, impose new obligations, or change the existing law." The court dismissed the case. *Equity in Athletics, Inc. v. Dep't of Educ.*, 675 F.Supp.2d 660 (W.D. Va. 2009).

◆ *Quinnipiac University was prohibited from eliminating women's varsity volleyball on a preliminary basis as a potential Title IX violation.*

Quinnipiac cut men's golf, men's outdoor track and women's volleyball for budgetary reasons. It added a women's competitive cheer team to meet its Title IX obligations for equal athletic opportunity. Members of the volleyball team, their coach and a high school recruit sued the university under Title IX. The court explained that Title IX requires federal funding recipients to provide equal athletic opportunities for both sexes. **Universities can meet their Title IX obligations by providing participation opportunities that are "substantially proportionate" to their male/female enrollment ratios.**

Quinnipiac said it would provide athletic participation opportunities to its male and female students in proportion to its expected gender composition of 63% women and 37% men. But the court said the university was not likely to meet the proportionality test because its athletic department set the size of team rosters to create gender balance. In theory, this increased athletic opportunities for an underrepresented sex without having to add more sports. **But in practice at Quinnipiac, rosters were manipulated to show it was meeting its obligations as of a reporting date.** For example, a baseball coach "deleted" six players to reach a desired roster number, only to add them back a few weeks later. Under the circumstances, the court held Quinnipiac did not produce enough genuine participation opportunities for women. Because Quinnipiac did not show it was providing true athletic opportunities, the court preliminarily enjoined it from eliminating women's volleyball or any other women's teams. *Biediger v. Quinnipiac Univ.*, 616 F.Supp.2d 277 (D. Conn. 2009).

◆ *The University of Cincinnati did not violate federal law by ending its intercollegiate women's rowing program and adding a women's lacrosse team.*

Planners at the university responded to a $27 million shortfall for the 2007 fiscal year by proposing a reduction in force, consolidation of academic divisions, and eliminating some sections and courses. The university instituted a hiring freeze, cut research funding, and halted capital projects. The university athletic director recommended that the intercollegiate rowing team be discontinued and that a women's intercollegiate lacrosse team be substituted for it. A study indicated the annual cost of the women's rowing program was between $200,000 and $300,000, while lacrosse would cost between $100,000 and $200,000. The university could charge admission for lacrosse games, but not for rowing team events. The university board of trustees accepted the recommendation, and rowing was retained only as a non-varsity club team.

Rowing team members filed a class action lawsuit against the university in a federal district court, claiming Title IX violations and denial of equal opportunities for athletic scholarships. The court explained that **the university could show Title IX compliance by providing participation opportunities at rates "substantially proportionate" to enrollment rates, expanding its programs for women, or accommodating the athletic interests of women**. Statistics showed 49% of university student-athletes were female. Opportunities for participation by female students were thus "more than proportional" to the percentage of female students. As the school was in compliance with Title IX, the university was awarded pretrial judgment. *Miller v. Univ. of Cincinnati*, No. 1:05-cv-764, 2008 WL 203025 (S.D. Ohio 1/22/08).

◆ *A female place kicker who was dropped from the Duke University football team because of her sex was not entitled to punitive damages under Title IX.*

A female student who made the Duke University football team but was later dropped from it sued the university in a federal district court. She alleged discrimination in violation of Title IX when the football coach refused to allow her to participate in summer camps, games, and practices, and made offensive comments to her regarding her attempts to participate in the football program. After the case was initially dismissed, the Fourth Circuit concluded that once the student was allowed to try out for football, the university could not discriminate against her based on her sex. Although Title IX regulations made a distinction between contact and non-contact sports operated for members of one sex, the court concluded that this distinction vanished once a member of the opposite sex was allowed to try out for a single-sex contact sport team. Since the student was a member of the university's male football team at one point, her allegations of discrimination under Title IX stated a cause of action.

At trial, a jury awarded the student $2 million in punitive damages. Duke sought to set aside the punitive damages award, arguing that even if the evidence supported the judgment, there is no clear-cut legal authority stating that punitive damages are allowable under Title IX. The Fourth Circuit again heard the case and agreed that the student was not entitled to punitive damages under Title IX. **Since Title IX is modeled after Title VI, and since the Supreme Court has held that punitive damages are not available in private actions brought under Title VI** (see *Barnes v. Gorman*, 536 U.S. 181 (2002)), **the court concluded that they are not available under Title IX either.** The court remanded the case for a determination of whether the student was entitled to her attorneys' fees. *Mercer v. Duke Univ.*, 50 Fed. Appx. 643 (4th Cir. 2002).

◆ *An Ohio university could eliminate three men's teams to come into compliance with Title IX.*

An Ohio university with a history of disproportionately few women athletes determined that the best way to achieve gender equity under Title IX was to eliminate three men's teams. It eliminated men's soccer, tennis and wrestling. In the lawsuit that followed, men's team members asserted that the decision to cut their teams violated Title IX and the Equal Protection Clause. A federal district court ruled in favor of the university, and the U.S. Court of Appeals, Sixth Circuit, affirmed the judgment. It held a federal policy interpretation of Title IX allowed the elimination of men's sports to comply with the law, and the men's teams were not challenging the constitutionality of either Title IX or its regulations. Moreover, **participation in collegiate athletics is not a constitutional right. Nor does Title IX grant rights to male athletes.** The court determined that there was no equal protection violation in the elimination of the teams. *Miami Univ. Wrestling Club v. Miami Univ.*, 302 F.3d 608 (6th Cir. 2002).

2. Sexual Harassment

◆   *An Alabama community college was not liable for the rape of a student-athlete by one of her basketball coaches.*

In her state court lawsuit, the student claimed the community college hired her assailant to act as an assistant, even though he had been jailed "relating to the death of a child." A teammate claimed he touched her inappropriately on two occasions. The player stated she viewed the assistant as a father figure and spent time at his home. He also gave her rides. But the assistant raped the student in a motel room after an away basketball game. She sued the college in a state court for violating Title IX and other federal laws. The court held for the college and officials, and the student appealed to the state supreme court.

The court rejected claims that the college did not properly investigate the touching incidents or the inappropriate relationship between the student and assistant. Evidence showed the touching incident was promptly investigated. **While the head basketball coach's failure to strictly follow investigation procedures might have been negligent, it did not prove deliberate indifference.** The court also rejected the student's argument that the head coach should have seen the assistant was sexually harassing her and should have unilaterally initiated procedures under the college sexual harassment policy. This argument failed because she admitted she did not consider her relationship with him to be sexual. The judgment against the student was affirmed. *J.B. v. Lawson State Community College*, 29 So.3d 164 (Ala. 2009).

◆   *A federal appeals court reinstated claims that the University of Colorado (CU) violated Title IX by encouraging student-athletes to commit rape.*

Two female students claimed that a football player and a female tutor for the athletic department planned a football recruiting event to provide recruits an opportunity to have sex with intoxicated female students. They further claimed recruits and players sexually assaulted them, and they sued CU for violating Title IX. The students contended the university had control over recruits and players, but failed to control or eliminate the risk. The court held the university could not be deliberately indifferent to acts it knew nothing about. The students could not prove CU was liable without showing it had actual knowledge and was deliberately indifferent to the misconduct.

On appeal, the U.S. Court of Appeals, Tenth Circuit, explained that CU could not be liable under Title IX unless it showed the assaults resulted from its deliberate indifference. **Deliberate indifference could be established by**

proving a failure to train regarding obvious risks. In this case, there was evidence that CU and its head football coach were deliberately indifferent to the need to provide training and undermined efforts to prevent harassment. Evidence showed that player-hosts received little or no direction regarding proper behavior or level of responsibility. In addition, the coach prevented a female player from remaining on the team after she complained of harassment, and hired an assistant coach who had been accused of assaulting a woman. As a jury could find the coach knew of a serious risk of sexual harassment, the judgment was reversed. *Simpson v. Univ. of Colorado*, 500 F.3d 1170 (10th Cir. 2007). CU reportedly agreed to pay one of the students $2.5 million to settle the case. A settlement called for a payment of $385,000 to the other student.

◆   *The University of Washington (UW) may have inadequately responded to a sexual assault allegation against a key player for the UW football team.*

A female student claimed the player forced his way into her dorm room and raped her shortly after she broke off their relationship. The student made no report until months later. A UW associate athletic director (AAD) learned of the assault and suggested that the student leave her position as an assistant equipment manager. He also warned her that team members would probably harass her if they learned of her report. The student refused to give up her job, and UW officials including a Title IX compliance officer decided to conduct mediation. After the player denied the allegation, the AAD refused to suspend him. A UW ombudsman asked the student if she was "making everything up" and had her sign a form saying she considered the matter closed. The student suffered from anxiety and depression, and she underwent counseling. She then sued UW in a state court for Title IX violations. After the court ruled for UW, the Court of Appeals of Washington reversed the judgment, finding a jury should consider the evidence. UW officials had knowledge of the incident, and **UW could be held liable if it responded to the student's reports in a way that was "clearly unreasonable in light of all the known circumstances."** *S.S. v. Alexander*, 143 Wash.App. 75, 177 P.3d 724 (Wash. Ct. App. 2008).

◆   *The informal atmosphere of collegiate athletics includes profanity, slang, and sarcasm that does not always create a hostile educational environment.*

A student who played on a North Carolina university women's intercollegiate soccer team claimed a coach asked players about their sexual activities. She alleged the coach commented on players' legs and breasts and called one player a "slut." The coach met with the student in his hotel room while the rest of the team was at an out-of-town tournament. He asked her about her social life and who she was sleeping with. The student told him it was not his business, and he soon dismissed her from the team. After the university investigated the student's complaint against the coach, he apologized to her and promised to refrain from further discussing sexual matters with players.

However, the student sued the university in a federal district court, alleging he had created a hostile sexual environment. The held for the university, and the student appealed. A three-judge panel of the U.S. Court of Appeals, Fourth Circuit, held **a Title IX hostile environment claim requires proof of harassment that is so severe or pervasive that it creates an abusive**

educational environment. It found no reasonable jury could find the coach's remarks created a hostile environment, and it affirmed the judgment. *Jennings v. Univ. of North Carolina*, 444 F.3d 255 (4th Cir. 2006).

All the judges of the Fourth Circuit agreed to reconsider the appeal, and decided the student had stated a valid discrimination claim under Title IX based on a hostile environment. She made a sufficient showing that she was subjected to severe or pervasive sexual harassment. **The evidence indicated the coach's comments were not "of a joking and teasing nature," but were degrading and humiliating.** The student also showed the coach's conduct negatively affected her ability to participate in soccer. The fact that she was disappointed at being cut did not defeat her Title IX claim. There was enough evidence to show the university had actual notice of a hostile environment. *Jennings v. Univ. of North Carolina*, 482 F.3d 686 (4th Cir. 2007).

◆ *The Supreme Court recognized a retaliation claim under Title IX, finding coaches are often in the best position to vindicate the rights of student-athletes.*

An Alabama high school teacher discovered the girls' basketball team did not receive the same funding or access to equipment and facilities as boys' teams. The teacher claimed his job was made difficult by lack of adequate funding, equipment and facilities, and he began complaining to supervisors. He stated the district did not respond to his complaints and gave him negative evaluations before removing him as girls' coach. The teacher sued the school board in a federal district court, claiming the loss of his supplemental coaching contracts constituted unlawful retaliation in violation of Title IX. The court dismissed the case, and its decision was affirmed by the Eleventh Circuit.

The Supreme Court **held Title IX covers retaliation against a person for complaining about sex discrimination**. "Retaliation is, by definition an intentional act," and is a form of discrimination, since the person who complains is treated differently than others. **A program that retaliates against a person based on a sex discrimination complaint intentionally discriminates in violation of Title IX.** Without finding that actual discrimination had occurred, the Court held the teacher was entitled to bring his case before the district court and attempt to show the board was liable. A private right of action for retaliation was within the statute's prohibition of intentional sex discrimination. Title IX did not require the victim of retaliation to also be the victim of discrimination. The Court stated "if retaliation were not prohibited, Title IX's enforcement scheme would unravel." Teachers and coaches were often in the best position to vindicate the rights of students by identifying discrimination and notifying administrators. **The text of Title IX itself gave the board sufficient notice that it could not retaliate against the teacher after he complained of discrimination. Title IX regulations have been on the books for nearly 30 years.** The Court found a reasonable school board would realize it could not cover up violations of Title IX by retaliating against teachers. It reversed and remanded the case to allow the teacher to try to prove retaliation by the board. *Jackson v. Birmingham Board of Educ.*, 544 U.S. 167 (2005).

3. Race Discrimination

◆ *Former University of Arkansas basketball coach Nolan Richardson was unable to prove his discharge was based on race.*

Richardson became Arkansas' first African-American head coach in 1985 and his team won the NCAA men's basketball championship in 1994. In 2000, a sportswriter wrote an article in which he said Richardson had called Arkansas fans "redneck SOBs." Fans complained about the comment. A former board member contacted the athletic director (AD) and told him Richardson should be fired for the statement. Shortly after that, the AD allegedly asked the columnist if he would write a column equating Richardson's comment with a white person calling the coach a "nigger." The columnist said he wanted to avoid controversy and later told Richardson about the conversation. After losing a game against Kentucky in 2002, Richardson said "if they go ahead and pay me my money, they can take the job tomorrow." The university chancellor felt the statement was damaging to basketball recruiting and recommended firing Richardson. When he refused to retire, the university discharged him. Richardson sued the university in a federal district court for violating Title VII of the Civil Rights Act of 1964. The court found Richardson failed to prove the university fired him because of his race and held in favor of the university.

Richardson appealed to the U.S. Court of Appeals, Eighth Circuit. The court held he would have to show a specific link between the alleged discrimination and the decision to discharge him. **The court agreed with the district court's conclusion that when the university discharged Richardson – two years after his remark to the columnist – Richardson and the AD had already made amends, and Richardson had signed a new contract. The court found this evidence severed any possible link between the remark and the discharge.** *Richardson v. Sugg*, 448 F.3d 1046 (8th Cir. 2006).

◆ *Two African-American student-athletes could pursue their race discrimination lawsuit against the NCAA under Proposition 16.*

The NCAA used Proposition 16 to determine which first-year college students could play Division I and II sports. The rule used a combination of high school grades in NCAA-approved "core courses" and scores on such standardized tests as the SAT and the ACT to determine eligibility. Two African-American students who signed national letters of intent to play sports at Division I schools failed to meet the NCAA's test score requirements. They were not allowed to play intercollegiate athletics their freshman year.

The students sued the NCAA in a federal district court, alleging the NCAA intentionally discriminated against them on the basis of race in violation of Title VI of the Civil Rights Act of 1964 and 42 U.S.C. § 1981, and violated the Americans with Disabilities Act (ADA) and Section 504 regarding one of the athletes. The court noted one athlete had proved causation by claiming the design of Proposition 16 discriminated against her because of a disability. However, these claims failed because an NCAA rule change allows student-athletes who do not qualify for their initial year of eligibility to recoup that lost year with good grades. As a result, **the athlete was not denied a year of**

eligibility by failing to meet the qualifying requirements, and lacked standing to bring ADA and Section 504 claims. The court dismissed the race discrimination claims brought under Title VI and Section 1981. On appeal, the Third Circuit reversed in part, noting **the students sufficiently alleged race discrimination** under Section 1981 to survive pretrial dismissal. Their claim that the NCAA considered race when it adopted Proposition 16 could proceed. However, the Title VI, ADA, and Section 504 claims were properly dismissed. *Pryor v. NCAA*, 288 F.3d 548 (3d Cir. 2002).

◆ *The NCAA was not liable for Title VI claims alleging Proposition 16 had a disparate impact on African-American students.*

A number of African-American high school student-athletes graduated from high school with GPAs exceeding NCAA requirements. However, they all scored lower than the minimum SAT score required for participation in Division I collegiate athletics as freshmen. They sued the NCAA, asserting that the minimum SAT score requirement of Proposition 16 had a disparate impact on African-American athletes in violation of Title VI. A Pennsylvania federal district court held the NCAA could be sued under Title VI, and that Proposition 16 had a disparate impact on African-Americans. The NCAA appealed to the Third Circuit, which assumed the NCAA received indirect federal financial assistance through its member institutions. It stated **Title VI was intended to be program specific. In other words, it only prohibited discrimination in programs or activities that received federal funds.** Even though Congress had enacted the Civil Rights Restoration Act to broaden the protections of Title VI and Title IX, the Department of Education had not yet enacted regulations to implement that statute. It was unclear if those regulations could prohibit neutral actions that had a discriminatory effect. As a result, **the NCAA did not come under the umbrella of Title VI. It was not a direct recipient of federal funds and did not exert sufficient authority over its member institutions to make it liable under Title VI.** *Cureton v. NCAA*, 198 F.3d 107 (3d Cir. 1999).

The students moved the district court to amend their complaint to allege intentional discrimination. The judge denied the motion, finding they had waited too long, and that allowing the amendment would result in impermissible prejudice to the NCAA. The Third Circuit upheld the district court's decision. *Cureton v. NCAA*, 252 F.3d 267 (3d Cir. 2001).

E. Injuries

Collegiate athletic participants assume the risks inherent in sports competition. The Supreme Judicial Court of Massachusetts explained that to hold a university liable for injuries to a student-athlete during a competitive athletic event, there must be a showing of willful, wanton or reckless conduct by participants. In Gauvin v. Clark, *404 Mass. 450, 537 N.E.2d 94 (Mass. 1989), the court said players engaging in sports agree to undergo some physical contacts which could amount to assault and battery without their consent. For that reason, college hockey participants only had a duty to refrain from reckless misconduct. This standard applies to non-contact sports, but may not apply to cheerleading injuries, as seen in* Torres v. Univ. of Massachusetts, *below.*

◆   *A spectator assumed the risk of injury at a Syracuse University hockey game and could not recover damages from the university for his injuries.*

Near the end of the game, the spectator was in an area of the rink where the players would exit the ice. Some players stopped to talk to him, and one of them got into a fight with another fan. The spectator tried to pull them apart, but fell over a barricade and broke his ankle. He later sued both universities and the individuals involved in the fight in a New York supreme court. He claimed Syracuse failed to provide enough supervision at the game. **The court found the spectator had voluntarily involved himself in the fight. In so doing, he assumed the risk of getting hurt.** The court granted a motion for pretrial judgment against the spectator and he appealed to a state appellate division court. It held the university owed spectators a duty of reasonable care to maintain safe conditions. **However, there was no duty to protect spectators from unexpected and unforeseeable assaults.** There had never been a fight between a spectator and a hockey player at the facility before, and the fight was not preceded by escalating hostilities. The sudden confrontation was not reasonably foreseeable, and it was quickly stopped by university staff. As the university acted reasonably, the judgment in its favor was affirmed. A different result was reached with respect to the claims against the other participants.

The court agreed with the fight participants that **the spectator could not recover damages from them because he assumed the risk of injury by intervening**. Under a rule called the "danger invites rescue" doctrine, a person is not barred from recovery for attempting a rescue based on a reasonable belief that the party in need of rescue was about to suffer a serious injury. A jury would have to decide whether the spectator acted reasonably and could rely on the "danger invites rescue" doctrine. The judgment for the university was affirmed, but the judgment regarding the participants was reversed. *O'Connor v. Syracuse Univ.*, 66 A.D.3d 1187, 887 N.Y.S.2d 353 (N.Y. App. Div. 2009).

The Court of Appeals of New York denied a motion for appeal. *O'Connor v. Syracuse Univ.*, 14 N.Y.3d 766, 898 N.Y.S.2d 92 (N.Y. 2010).

◆   *New Hampshire parents may proceed with an action against Dartmouth College for the wrongful death of a student who was injured in a ski class.*

The student took an introductory ski class at a college-owned and operated facility. Instructors knew she was inexperienced, but told her to ski down a trail alone while they accompanied other students. She followed their directions but veered off course and hit a tree, fracturing her skull. The student became paraplegic and later died. Her parents sued the college in a federal district court for negligence and wrongful death. Dartmouth filed a motion to dismiss the case, relying on the state's "Ski Statute," which barred claims for injuries occurring due to risks inherent in skiing. The court found the negligence **claim was essentially one for "negligent instruction." There was no reason to categorize negligent instruction as an inherent risk of skiing.** New Hampshire's highest court had held in an earlier case that the Ski Statute did not bar a claim of negligent instruction. As a result, the statute's provisions regarding inherent risks did not bar the action. The court also rejected Dartmouth's argument that the action was time-barred. *Porter v. Dartmouth College*, Civil No. 07-cv-28-PB, 2007 WL 3124623 (D.N.H. 10/24/07).

Over two years after the case was filed, attorneys realized the parents had never sought appointment as their child's administrators. Dartmouth filed a motion to dismiss the case. Two weeks later, the parents obtained letters of administration from a state probate court. The federal district court allowed them to proceed despite their delay in securing the letters of administration. The parents had cured their mistake, and the college was not harmed by the delay. *Porter v. Dartmouth College*, 678 F.Supp.2d 15 (D.N.H. 2010).

◆ *A New York Appellate Division court preserved negligence claims raised by a student who injured her back while swimming for a university team.*

The student said her injury was caused by the training methods used by her coach, and that he continued to use the same methods even after she complained of back pain. She sued the university and the coach in a state court for negligent hiring and supervision. The university and coach argued that the student was an experienced swimmer who assumed the risk of hurting her back. The court denied them pretrial judgment, and appeal went to the state appellate division. On appeal, the appellate court held the lower court should have awarded pretrial judgment to the university on the negligent hiring and supervision claims. It explained that **when an injured plaintiff seeks to recover damages based on actions taken by an employee within the scope of employment, the doctrines of negligent hiring and negligent supervision do not apply**. However, the court upheld the ruling in favor of the student on her claim that the coach negligently continued to employ particular training methods even after she complained of back pain. A question of fact was also present as to whether she had assumed the risk of injury. *Segal v. St. John's Univ.*, 69 A.D.3d 702, 893 N.Y.S.2d 221 (N.Y. App. Div. 2010).

◆ *An Ohio cheerleading coach was not liable for catastrophic injuries to a cheerleader who fell while participating in a human pyramid maneuver.*

Not all the cheerleaders had performed the maneuver on the day of the fall and some had never seen it. A substitute spotter failed to catch the cheerleader, and she fell to the ground from about 15 feet. She suffered catastrophic injuries, including paraplegia. In a state court lawsuit against the university, the cheerleader claimed her injuries were caused by her coach's negligence. The case reached the Court of Appeals of Ohio, which held **an injury from a fall was an inherent risk of cheerleading and that the cheerleader voluntarily assumed that risk**. The risk of injury could be managed but not eliminated. Further, the court found the coach did not act intentionally or recklessly in causing the student's injuries. *Crace v. Kent State Univ.*, 185 Ohio App.3d 534, 924 N.E.3d 906 (Ohio Ct. App. 2009).

◆ *A New York court allowed a student-athlete to proceed with a claim that Iona College failed to keep MRSA bacteria out of its athletic facilities.*

The student-athlete claimed he contracted an MRSA infection at Iona's athletic facilities. He filed a state court action against Iona asserting the college had a duty to keep its facilities free of MRSA bacteria and to routinely screen for the presence of MRSA bacteria. The student asserted Iona had a duty to provide medical care and to instruct him regarding precautionary measures to help him avoid infection, and that the college had actual or constructive notice of MRSA bacteria in its facilities but negligently failed to remove it.

After the court dismissed the claims, the student appealed to the New York Supreme Court, Appellate Division. **The court held the trial court properly dismissed the claim that Iona had a duty to maintain MRSA-free facilities.** Such an obligation exceeded any recognized duty under law. However, the court held the lower court should not have dismissed the claim that Iona knew that its athletic facilities were not MRSA-free but failed to properly address the situation. The claim could proceed in further court activity. *Zaffarese v. Iona College*, 879 N.Y.S.2d 348 (N.Y. App. Div. 2009).

◆ *Texas law barred a spectator's lawsuit against a state university based on his fall from bleachers at a baseball game.*

The spectator fell about six feet to the ground from the top row of the bleachers. In his state court lawsuit against the host institution, he claimed the seat backing gave way as a result of metal fatigue. State law immunized governmental entities from liability for injuries resulting from the recreational use of their premises, unless the injury resulted from gross negligence or from willful or wanton conduct. The court denied the university's motion for dismissal, and an appeal followed. The Court of Appeals of Texas stated that under the state recreational use statute, the university could not be held liable unless it was grossly negligent or acted willfully or wantonly. The statute applied to "recreational activity," which included any activity associated with enjoying the outdoors. This **broad language justified the conclusion that the statute applied to the conduct of sitting on bleachers and watching a game**. Because the recreational use statute applied, and the spectator did not allege or prove gross negligence, willful conduct or wanton conduct by the university, the court dismissed the action. *Sam Houston State Univ. v. Anderson*, No. 10-07-00403-CV, 2008 WL 4901233 (Tex. Ct. App. 11/12/08).

◆ *An Illinois court upheld a lower court's decision to approve a $16 million payment to relatives of a college football player who died during a practice.*

A Northwestern University varsity football player died after completing a preseason football conditioning drill. His parents sued the university in the Illinois court system for wrongful death and related claims. After four years of pretrial activity, the case was mediated by a judge. The parties agreed to settle the case if Northwestern offered a payment of $16 million. After the student's mother rejected the settlement, Northwestern asked the court to direct that the money not be paid until all appeals had been exhausted. The court denied Northwestern's motion and ordered it to pay the settlement into an interest-bearing account. It also allocated settlement proceeds to members of the student's estate, and it determined that the mother's law firm was entitled to its fee. The mother, a brother, and a half-brother appealed, arguing that the trial court lacked the authority to force the settlement over their objections.

The Appellate Court of Illinois held that the mother, brother and half-brother lacked standing to pursue appeals in their individual capacities. None of them were parties of record in their individual capacities in the underlying case. The mother had appeal rights in her capacity as a co-administrator of the estate. However, her appeal failed because the trial court had the power to accept and execute the settlement on her behalf. **The mother had a duty to act in the best interest of the estate, and she was an agent of the court who was subject to its control and direction.** This was not her case, the court noted. Because the trial court made a reasoned determination that the settlement was in the best interest of the minors involved in the proceedings, the trial court had the power to accept the settlement. *Will v. Northwestern Univ.*, 378 Ill.App.2d 280, 881 N.E.2d 481 (Ill. App. Ct. 2007).

◆   *A Georgia court held an insurer was required to provide a defense to an athletic association sued by a college athlete for failing to provide disability insurance.*

An assistant athletic director (AAD) at the University of Georgia coordinated a disability insurance program for student-athletes. He obtained a coverage quote for a student from an insurance broker, but he failed to send the broker a coverage request form with the student's signature. The student was seriously hurt while playing for the football team and became disabled for life from playing any contact sports. The insurer refused to backdate coverage, and the student was denied $500,000 that would have been payable under the policy. He sued the university athletic association and AAD in a state court for breach of fiduciary duties, breach of contract, and negligence. The association notified its liability carrier of the lawsuit and asked for defense and indemnity.

The carrier refused to provide a defense, claiming that two policy exceptions relieved it of any duty to defend the action. The association then sued the carrier in the state court system. The court ruled for the association, and the carrier appealed. The Court of Appeals of Georgia affirmed the determination that the policy required the carrier to provide a defense to the suit. Moreover, **the connection between the student's injury and his claims was too attenuated to apply a bodily injury exclusion.** The conduct of the insured parties was not causally related to the injury, and the conduct that gave rise to the student's claims occurred before he was injured. Therefore, the exception did not apply. The court affirmed the judgment for the university association, noting a question remained as to whether the carrier was required to cover the loss. *Fireman's Fund Insurance Co. v. Univ. of Georgia Athletic Ass'n*, 288 Ga.App. 355, 654 S.E.2d 207 (Ga. Ct. App. 2007).

◆   *A Connecticut student-athlete's signed waiver of liability did not protect a university from liability for negligence.*

The student was a pitcher on the university baseball team. During a batting practice he was behind an L-screen, which is a safety device placed in front of pitchers. The screen has an opening so the pitcher can throw the ball to the batter. A batter hit a ball that struck the student on the head. He sued the university in a state court for negligence. The student claimed the screen was defective, damaged, worn and improperly repaired. The university contended the student had voluntarily and knowingly signed a waiver releasing it from liability caused by or arising out of his athletic participation.

The court found the university's release form did not expressly refer to negligence. In *Wagenblast v. Odessa School Dist.*, 110 Wash.2d 845, 758 P.2d 968 (Wash. 1988) – a case involving minors – the court found **"exculpatory**

releases from any future university district negligence are invalid because they violate university policy." The superior court found that waiver agreements that do not explicitly refer to negligent conduct should not bar negligence claims by students – adults or minors – who engage in sports activities that present a risk of injury. The court denied the university's motion for dismissal on the student's negligence claim against the university. *Zides v. Quinnipiac Univ.*, 40 Conn.L.Rptr. 745 (Conn. Super. Ct. 2006).

◆ *The Supreme Court of California held a community college was not liable for injuries to a student who was hit by a pitch during a baseball game.*

During a preseason road game against another community college, the host team's pitcher hit the student in the head with a pitch, cracking his batting helmet. The student said he was intentionally hit in retaliation for an earlier pitch thrown by a pitcher for his team that hit an opposing batter. The student staggered, felt dizzy, and was in pain, but his manager and first base coach told him to stay in the game. He was later told to sit on the bench, but his injuries were not immediately treated. The student sued the host community college in a state superior court. The case was dismissed, but the Court of Appeal of California reversed the judgment, finding the college owed the student a duty of supervision. The Supreme Court of California agreed to review the case.

The court held the college players were co-participants, and its coaches and managers had supervisory authority over the game. **Co-participants had a duty not to act recklessly, outside the bounds of the sport. Coaches and instructors had a duty not to increase the risks inherent in sports participation.** Colleges derive economic and marketing benefits from a major sports program. These benefits justified finding that a host school owed a duty to home and visiting players to not increase the risk inherent in the sport. The court found the host college did not fail in its duty to supervise and control the pitcher. **Being hit by a pitch was an inherent risk of baseball. The failure to provide umpires did not increase the inherent risk.** The host college had no duty to provide medical care, as the student did not submit evidence of injury. Colleges are not vicariously liable for the actions of their student-athletes during competition. The court reversed the judgment. *Avila v. Citrus Community College Dist.*, 38 Cal.4th 148, 131 P.3d 383 (Cal. 2006).

◆ *A Massachusetts cheerleader was allowed to proceed with a negligence action against her university after being severely injured at practice.*

The cheerleader was injured when she fell during a pyramid stunt called "the flying squirrel." The maneuver required two cheerleaders to stand on the shoulders of two others, who launched her about 10 feet up to the shoulders of cheerleaders on the upper tier. Although she was experienced, the cheerleader had never tried this maneuver before. The coach talked her through the exercise and placed spotters at the front and sides of the pyramid, but none in the rear. He spent about five minutes instructing the spotters. The squad attempted the stunt when the coach was not there. The cheerleader fell from the top of the pyramid and landed in the rear, suffering serious neck fractures that caused her to become disabled and unable to cheerlead or run again. She sued the university in a Massachusetts superior court, alleging negligence by the coach.

The university argued it could not be held liable for negligence under

Gauvin v. Clark, 404 Mass. 450, 537 N.E.2d 94 (Mass. 1989), unless there was evidence of willful or reckless conduct in the context of a sporting event. **The court disagreed and denied a summary judgment motion by the university. It held the university owed the student a duty to exercise reasonable care. The failure to do so in this case caused her injuries.** *Torres v. Univ. of Massachusetts*, 20 Mass.L.Rptr. 310 (Mass. Super. 2005).

◆ *A federal district court held a Vermont student waived any claims against his school for injuries suffered during an intercollegiate hockey game.*

The student signed a "Student Athlete Agreement to Participate in Intercollegiate Sports" before his first season on the team. The agreement stated in part: "I understand the dangers and risks of trying out for and playing and practicing in the above sports." It also indicated "I hereby voluntarily assume all risks associated with participation and agree to hold harmless [the university and coaches] . . . except in the event of their gross negligence."

An opposing player checked the student during a game, causing him to fall backward and strike his head on the ice. He continued to play on the team, but two years later, he suffered a concussion. The student was diagnosed with mild but permanent neuropsychological deficits from the checking incident two years earlier. The university required the student to sign an additional release, but he failed to do so. He left the university the next year to play professional hockey. The student sued the university in a federal district court for negligence. The university contended the participation agreement barred the action and that the student assumed the risk of injury. The student argued the "hold harmless" language of the agreement was ambiguous and unenforceable. **The court held the words "hold harmless" did not make the agreement ambiguous. The agreement clearly demonstrated the intent to relieve the university from liability except in cases of gross negligence.** The court granted the university's motion for summary judgment and dismissed the negligence claim. *Sanders v. Univ. of Vermont*, No. 2:00-CV-424 (D. Vt. 2004).

◆ *An Indiana university was not liable to a varsity baseball player for injuries he suffered while practicing with the team. Student-athletes assume the risk of foreseeable and inherent dangers in collegiate athletics.*

The injury occurred during a baseball team practice inside a university gym. During a practice drill, the student was struck in the eye by a ball thrown by a teammate, causing severe and permanent injury. The student sued the university, coaching staff and teammate in a state court for negligence.

The court dismissed the case, and the student appealed. The Court of Appeals of Indiana stated that while the state supreme court has held secondary schools owe their students a duty to exercise ordinary and reasonable care, it has never imposed this duty on colleges or universities. The student argued the trend is for courts to find a "special" relationship between colleges or universities and their student-athletes. The court disagreed, stating the reasonable care standard was created to guide people in their everyday lives, not for athletes who choose to participate in sports. The court found being hit by a ball during team practice is an inherent and foreseeable danger of athletic participation. **Athletes assume the risk of a certain amount of foreseeable**

and inherent danger. The court held that avoiding reckless or malicious behavior or intentional injury was the standard of care for sporting events and practices. **Athletes should not recover in negligence cases unless they prove malicious, reckless or intentional conduct.** As the university, coaches and teammate owed no duty of care to the student, the judgment was affirmed. *Geiersbach v. Frieje*, 807 N.E. 2d 114 (Ind. Ct. App. 2004).

◆   *The Court of Appeals of Massachusetts dismissed a Boston College season ticket holder's challenge to the loss of his season tickets, finding Boston College had the right to revoke his ticket privileges due to his disorderly conduct.*

A group of spectators who were tailgating during a Boston College football game got into a fight with college police. The college revoked one spectator's season tickets for disorderly conduct and barred him from entering the campus. The spectator sued the college in a state court for "unlawful trespass warning," revocation of his season tickets, and intentional infliction of emotional distress. The court granted Boston College's motion for summary judgment and the spectator appealed to the Court of Appeals of Massachusetts.

The court noted each season ticket issued by Boston College clearly indicated it was a "revocable license." Consequently, **the college had the right to revoke the ticket privileges at any time and for any nondiscriminatory reason. With regard to his trespass claim, the court stated that as a private college, Boston College could bar the spectator from its campus, regardless of his guilt or innocence.** The evidence did not support the intentional infliction of emotional distress claim. The actions of the college police were not "so extreme and outrageous as to be beyond all bounds of decency." The court upheld the trial court's decision to dismiss the case. *Dischino v. Boston College*, 60 Mass.App.Ct. 1105, 799 N.E.2d 605 (Table) (Mass. App. Ct. 2003).

◆   *Universities may assume an affirmative duty of care toward student-athletes if there is evidence of a "special relationship" with the university.*

A University of North Carolina (UNC) cheerleader was injured in 1985 while the JV cheerleading squad was warming up before a women's basketball game. The squad did not use mats during the warm-up. While practicing a pyramid, the cheerleader fell off the top, and spotters were unable to prevent her head and shoulders from hitting the hardwood floor. The cheerleader suffered permanent brain damage. UNC did not provide a coach for the JV cheerleading squad during the 1984–1985 school year, instead providing a part-time "administrative supervisor." The supervisor did not supervise the team's stunts, training or safety during games and practice. The JV cheerleaders essentially coached themselves, deciding how and when to perform stunts.

The case reached the North Carolina Court of Appeals, which found UNC owed the cheerleader a duty of care because she had a "special relationship" with the university. UNC depended on the JV cheerleading team to act as its representatives. The university provided the squad with uniforms and transportation, as well as the use of school facilities for practice. Cheerleading satisfied one credit hour of UNC's physical education requirement. Additional evidence of a special relationship included the fact that UNC exerts a considerable degree of control over its cheerleaders. **UNC not only had an**

affirmative duty of care, but voluntarily undertook a separate duty of care by assuming responsibilities to teach cheerleaders about safety. The court reversed and remanded the decision, leaving the commission to determine whether UNC breached its duty to the cheerleader. *Davidson v. Univ. of North Carolina at Chapel Hill*, 543 S.E.2d 920 (N.C. Ct. App. 2001).

II. STUDENT ACTIVITIES

In Beach v. Univ. of Utah, *726 P.2d 413 (Utah 1986), the Supreme Court of Utah explained that "colleges and universities are educational institutions, not custodial." It held imposing liability on higher educational institutions for injuries arising from illegally drinking alcohol would require them to "baby-sit" each student. Colleges and universities may limit official recognition of particular organizations and impose restrictions on them.*

A. Operation and School Supervision

◆ *Washington State University (WSU) was allowed to revoke official recognition of a fraternity for five years for drug and alcohol violations.*

WSU said fraternity members used, possessed, manufactured and/or distributed illegal drugs on fraternity property and at a rental house occupied by fraternity members. WSU cited the fraternity for a number of violations, including supplying alcohol to minors at fraternity-sponsored events. A student conduct board held a hearing, where the fraternity's national executive director admitted underage drinking issues. The board found the fraternity responsible for each charge and withdrew official recognition for five years. In a state court action, the fraternity alleged that WSU failed to follow proper procedures and violated the fraternity's constitutional rights to freedom of association.

After the court rejected all the fraternity's claims, appeal reached the Court of Appeals of Washington. The court found sufficient evidence to support the university's decision. **Evidence showed illegal activity was "actively condoned" by fraternity officers.** The fraternity's risk manager, live-in advisor and social chair had all bought illegal drugs, and the fraternity failed to take reasonable steps to stop illegal activity. Fraternities at WSU were expected to follow the law and university policies and to respond promptly if officers, members or guests engaged in illegal behavior. As the evidence supported WSU's decision and the sanction imposed was not arbitrary and capricious, the court affirmed the discipline. *Alpha Kappa Lambda Fraternity v. Washington State Univ.*, 152 Wash.App. 401, 216 P.3d 451 (Wash. Ct. App. 2009).

◆ *A challenge to the University of Florida's refusal to recognize a fraternity as a registered student organization (RSO) was mooted by new university rules.*

In a federal district court case, the fraternity said it was unconstitutionally denied the benefits of RSO status. The university had concerns regarding sex bias by the fraternity. After the case was filed, the fraternity entered into an affiliation with a sorority. While the affiliation satisfied the university's sex bias concerns, it denied RSO status because the fraternity discriminated on the basis of religion. The fraternity amended its complaint to include new First Amendment and Fourteenth Amendment claims. It asked the court to order the university to award it RSO status. After further proceedings, the university modified a handbook policy relating to the registration of student organizations.

The new policy stated that religious student organizations would not be denied registration as RSOs just because they limited their membership or leadership positions to students with the same religious beliefs as the organization. The university registered the fraternity as an RSO and stated its intention to follow the new policy. Following these changes, the court granted the university's motion to dismiss the case on the ground that there was no longer a live controversy and the case was moot. **As the relief sought by the fraternity had been obtained, there was no live controversy for the court to consider**, and the case had to be dismissed. On appeal, the U.S. Court of Appeals, Eleventh Circuit, affirmed the judgment. *Beta Upsilon Chi Upsilon Chapter at the Univ. of Florida v. Machen*, 586 F.3d 908 (11th Cir. 2009).

◆   *A Florida court ordered a university to reinstate a fraternity that was suspended for violating regulations governing alcohol and reckless behavior.*

The evidence of the fraternity misconduct consisted entirely of videotaped interviews and the testimony of two investigating police officers. A Florida District Court of Appeal found all the evidence consisted of inadmissible hearsay. The university's own rules gave the fraternity the right to question adverse witnesses at a hearing, and it was clearly denied this right. **Without the improperly admitted evidence, nothing supported the decision to suspend the fraternity.** The court reversed the university's decision and ordered it to reinstate the fraternity. *Alpha Eta Chapter of Pi Kappa Alpha Fraternity v. Univ. of Florida*, 982 So.2d 55 (Fla. Dist. Ct. App. 2008).

◆   *A federal district court rejected a fraternity's claim that a New York university violated federal antitrust law by requiring all students to live in university housing.*

Four people died in a car crash on the campus of Colgate University in 2000. One was an underage member of Delta Kappa Epsilon (DKE). Colgate responded by announcing it would require all its students to live in university-owned housing. Colgate took steps to buy and operate all fraternity and sorority housing and residential services on its campus. Many chapters negotiated for purchase prices in excess of their market values. Colgate offered DKE $725,000 for its fraternity house, but DKE chose not to sell. In response, Colgate withdrew its recognition of the local DKE chapter. DKE sued Colgate in a federal district court for violating the federal Sherman Antitrust Act.

The court held that to prevail, DKE needed to show Colgate had engaged in improper conduct that had the effect of controlling prices or excluding competition, resulting in a high degree of market power. The court determined that the relevant market for purposes of an antitrust claim was the student housing market for all selective colleges nationwide. **Once a student decided to enroll at a particular college, the student agreed to submit to college policies to protect the welfare of its students.** In this case, Colgate created a residential policy that was part of the education it provided. The court held that

Colgate's residential policy, which required all students to live in housing it owned, was an exercise of its lawful rights. *Delta Kappa Epsilon (DKE) Alumni Corp. v. Colgate Univ.*, 492 F.Supp.2d 106 (N.D.N.Y. 2007).

◆   *Texas A&M University officials could not be held liable for the collapse of a bonfire stack that killed 12 students and injured 27 others.*

After the tragic collapse of a bonfire stack that killed or injured several students, the students' representatives sued the university and its officials for violating student constitutional rights to bodily integrity. The representatives claimed the university encouraged unqualified students to build the bonfire and failed to provide adequate supervision. A federal district court dismissed the claims against university officials, finding them barred by sovereign immunity.

The U.S. Court of Appeals, Fifth Circuit, found the representatives stated a claim under the "state-created danger" theory, and the case was returned to the district court for more proceedings. The district court again held for the officials, this time on the basis of qualified immunity. The representatives filed another appeal to the Fifth Circuit, which found the officials were entitled to immunity as long as their conduct was objectively reasonable in light of clearly established law. **Although the state-created danger theory was a valid theory, it was not clearly established as a basis for recovery at the time of the accident. Because the theory was not clearly established when the bonfire stack collapsed, the university officials did not have fair notice that their conduct may have violated the students' constitutional rights.** As a result, the officials were entitled to qualified immunity. *Breen v. Texas A&M Univ.*, 485 F.3d 325 (5th Cir. 2007).

◆   *A college could use money from a fund-raising campaign to eliminate single-sex fraternities and sororities.*

A New Hampshire college initiated a five-year fund-raising campaign that raised about $568 million from alumni. Several years later, the board of trustees announced that it was going to use some of the money raised to eliminate single-sex fraternities and sororities. A group of alumni who had contributed to the campaign sued the college to prevent it from using the funds for that purpose. They asserted that the college had engaged in misrepresentation in violation of the state Consumer Protection Act, and that the board of trustees had withheld information about its intent to eliminate traditional fraternities and sororities. They also alleged that the board was in a fiduciary relationship to the alumni because there were alums on the board.

A state court dismissed their lawsuit, and the Supreme Court of New Hampshire affirmed the judgment. First, the board of trustees did not owe a fiduciary duty to the alumni despite the existence of alums on the board. Second, **the alumni failed to show that the board engaged in intentional, fraudulent nondisclosure**. And third, since the fund-raising campaign was not commerce (the transactions were in the nature of a gift), there was no violation of the Consumer Protection Act. *Brzica v. Trustees of Dartmouth College*, 791 A.2d 990 (N.H. 2002).

B. Organizational Liability

◆   *The Phi Kappa Tau fraternity chapter at the University of Mississippi was not liable in negligence for a woman's injuries.*

A fraternity brother provided beer to an underage fraternity member at the fraternity house during the summer of 2001, when school was not in session. The woman was riding on the back of a four-wheeler on the grounds of the house. The fraternity member confronted the driver and threw a bottle that struck the woman in the face, injuring her. She sued the local and national chapters of the fraternity for negligence in a federal district court. The court held for the fraternity chapters, finding they did not owe the woman any legal duty under state law. She appealed to the U.S. Court of Appeals, Fifth Circuit.

The court affirmed the district court judgment. **As unincorporated associations, the chapters were not liable for the wrongful acts of their members unless they "encouraged, promoted, or subsequently ratified them." There was no evidence that the chapters encouraged or ratified the member's behavior.** There was no duty on the part of the national chapter to supervise the local chapter more closely, as no special relationship existed in this case. *Lewis v. Univ. of Southern Mississippi*, No. 06-60375, 2007 WL 1112660 (5th Cir. 4/12/07).

◆   *The family of a Louisiana student who killed herself after an alleged rape was allowed to proceed with claims that local police and a fraternity caused her death by threatening and harassing her after the attack.*

The student was raped by a member of a fraternity at an off-campus residence. Her family claimed the fraternity and a local police officer continually harassed her in an attempt to dissuade her from reporting the rape. The officer, who was a fraternity alumnus, allegedly told the student the authorities would do nothing if she reported the incident. The family said the officer also told her she would be sued for defamation or slander if she insisted on pressing charges. The student then hanged herself. A trial court threw out the family's negligence claims against the officer and police department, but the Court of Appeal of Louisiana reversed the judgment. **Although state law generally immunizes the government from liability for discretionary actions, an exception applies to acts that constitute malicious, intentional or willful misconduct.** If the allegations about the police officer's actions were true, this exception might apply. *Garza v. Delta Tau Delta Fraternity National*, No. 2006 CA 0698, 2007 WL 914875 (La. Ct. App. 3/28/07).

◆   *An Ohio student lacked evidence to show who might have injured her at a campus event, defeating her negligence claim against a fraternity.*

The student rode on a fraternity float in a homecoming parade. Those riding floats tossed candy to parade watchers. The parade passed by a fraternity house. A group of people gathered in front of the house to watch the parade. Intoxicated fraternity members threw candy at people on the floats. The student was struck in the eye and injured by a thrown piece of candy in front of the house. Believing a fraternity member was responsible, she sued the fraternity in a state court for negligence and loss of consortium, seeking $1.5 million. The court held the fraternity owed the student no duty of care, and she did not prove who caused her injury. On appeal, **the Court of Appeals of Ohio held that to prove negligence, the student needed to show that the fraternity's actions directly and proximately caused her injury.** She failed to make this showing, admitting she did not know who threw the candy that hit her. In fact, the student could not identify anyone standing near the house at the time of the incident. Evidence showed the group in front of the house included non-members of the fraternity who were also throwing candy at floats. As no evidence indicated a fraternity member threw the candy that struck the student, her case failed. *Muir v. Phi Mu Delta*, No. 6-07-09, 2007 WL 2983152 (Ohio Ct. App. 10/15/07).

◆ *A Texas fraternity and its members were not liable to a student for statements resulting in the withdrawal of his pledge invitation.*

A student who had pledged to join the Phi Gamma Delta Fraternity was accused of sexual misconduct. He denied the allegations, claiming they were part of an extortion scheme to gain money. Phi Gamma withdrew its pledge invitation. A year later, the student pledged to join a chapter of the same fraternity at a different Texas university campus. He was denied admittance based on information communicated between fraternity members at different chapters. The student sued the fraternity and various fraternity members in the state court system for damaging his reputation and subjecting him to increased hazing based on the allegations of sexual misconduct. The court held for the fraternities and their members. The student appealed, arguing that Phi Gamma owed him a duty of care because its members made statements in the course and scope of their fraternity membership. The Court of Appeals of Texas found no evidence indicating the fraternity was incorporated in the state.

As an unincorporated entity, the fraternity did not owe the student any duty of care. Moreover, he was unable to show a member's remarks were made in the course of his official duties as a fraternity historian. **There was no evidence that these comments were communicated to other fraternities at the University of Texas.** The court agreed with the trial court that the hazing claim was untimely filed under a two-year state statute of limitation. The judgment was affirmed. *Waddill v. Phi Gamma Delta Fraternity Lambda Tau Chapter, Texas Tech Univ.*, 114 S.W.3d 136 (Tex. Ct. App. 2003).

◆ *A Kansas fraternity pledge could not sue the fraternity or its members when he passed out after drinking too much.*

A student attended a Pledge Dad night at a fraternity at the University of Kansas. While there, he consumed a large amount of alcoholic beverages. At 2:00 a.m., his pledge dad found him passed out in the living room of the fraternity house and took him to a local hospital emergency room, where his blood alcohol level was measured at .294. The student later sued the national fraternity, the local chapter and five individual members for negligence, and the company that owned the property for premises liability. The court ruled in favor of all the defendants, and the Kansas Supreme Court affirmed. **The local chapter was not a legal entity and therefore could not be sued.** Further, the individual members could not be liable because **they did not breach any duty they owed him; he voluntarily drank alcohol** that night. As far as the national fraternity was concerned, there was no special relationship between the student and the fraternity so as to give rise to liability. Finally, the company that owned the property could not be held liable for conditions on the premises at a fraternity party. *Prime v. Beta Gamma Chapter of Pi Kappa Alpha*, 47 P.3d 402 (Kan. 2002).

◆ *A national fraternity could not be held liable for a student's injuries because it was not in a position to control the actions of its chapters on a day-to-day basis and had no knowledge of any hazing activity.*

A student at a private university in Louisiana was accepted into a fraternity. During the intake process, he was physically beaten and abused by several members of the fraternity while they were conducting hazing activities. The student and his parents sued the national fraternity in a state court to recover damages for the injuries sustained as a result of the hazing. The court held for the national fraternity, and the student and his parents appealed. They argued the national fraternity should be liable for the actions of its chapter members because it had a duty to prevent injury to new members. They also asserted that the national fraternity's action in forbidding hazing activities showed a clear knowledge and formal approval of those activities.

The Court of Appeal of Louisiana noted that the national executive director of the fraternity had stated by affidavit that he had no knowledge of any hazing activity at the local chapter and that the **national fraternity took numerous steps to inform local chapters and members that hazing activities were clearly prohibited**. Further, deposition testimony by several local chapter members indicated that **any hazing activity that occurred was purposely hidden from the national fraternity**. Because the national fraternity was not in a position to control the actions of its chapters on a day-to-day basis, and because it had no knowledge of any hazing activity, it could not be held liable for the student's injuries. The trial court decision was affirmed. *Walker v. Phi Beta Sigma Fraternity (RHO Chapter)*, 706 So.2d 525 (La. Ct. App. 1997).

C. Injuries

◆ *A New Jersey court held a university was not liable for the death of a student who died when he fell from his fourth-floor dorm window after a party.*

A county prosecutor investigated and found that the student had leaned out the window and accidentally fallen. The student's family filed a negligence action against the university in a state court, asserting its alcohol policy was not appropriate and was negligently enforced. A jury found the death was caused by negligence, and it assessed damages of $520,000. As the parties were equally negligent, the court entered a judgment against the university in the amount of $260,000. The university appealed to a state appellate court, where it argued any negligence claim was barred by a state charitable immunity act.

Under the act, the university was immune from negligence claims raised by a person injured while benefiting from the university. But no immunity was available if injury resulted from "willful, wanton or grossly negligent" conduct. The court said providing student housing "falls within the broad range of reasonable educational goals" the university sought to achieve. Students living in dormitories received the benefit of the university's educational works. The student's violation of a university alcohol policy did not alter his status as a beneficiary of the university's works while he lived in the dormitory. **As he was a beneficiary of the university's works, the immunity statute was applicable** and the judgment for the family was reversed. *Orzech v. Fairleigh Dickinson Univ.*, 985 A.2d 189 (N.J. Super. App. Div. 2009).

◆ *A Delaware trial court refused to suppress evidence of underage drinking uncovered by police in an "informal frat house."*

At the time of the search, a college freshman had just died of suspected alcohol poisoning following a party. Police went to the house with a search warrant for evidence of alcohol consumption. They forced their way into a student's room and seized a can of beer, an empty bottle of vodka and a cup of beer. Based on this evidence, the police charged the student with underage possession and/or consumption of alcohol. He argued the police exceeded the scope of the search warrant by forcing the locked door to his room when he was not a named tenant of the house. But the court found the warrant was valid and the search was legal. **As the search warrant followed the state's requirement to specifically describe "the place to be searched and the persons or things to be seized," the court found the police conducted a legal search.** *State v. Ciccarelli*, No. 0812018008, 2009 WL 3340113 (Del. Ct. Com. Pl. 10/13/09).

◆ *A Maine university officer was unable to prove a fraternity intentionally inflicted emotional distress on him by publicizing his past legal troubles.*

As the director of the University of Maine at Orono office of community standards, the officer reviewed student misconduct charges and oversaw the student discipline process. He sometimes adjudicated cases himself. In 2002, the officer investigated misconduct charges against a fraternity. In response to his investigation, a group of current and former fraternity members hired a private investigator to determine whether he might be biased against their fraternity or against fraternities in general. The investigator discovered the officer had been convicted of "driving while ability impaired," and that a former girlfriend had gotten a temporary restraining order against him. The fraternity assembled court documents and newspaper articles relating to these proceedings and sent them to university officials, the board of trustees and two local newspapers. The officer claimed the disclosure caused him emotional distress, and he sued the fraternity in a district court.

The court found that **as a public official, the officer was required to show the memo contained a false statement that was made with actual malice.** As he did not meet this test, the court ruled for the fraternity. On appeal, the U.S. Court of Appeals, First Circuit, affirmed the judgment. It agreed with the lower court that the officer was properly classified as a public official for purposes of his emotional distress claim. He failed to show the fraternity made a false statement of fact. The officer's legal difficulties relating to domestic violence were documented by the restraining order, and he did not show the fraternity made a false statement about him. As a result, the judgment was affirmed. *Fiacco v. Sigma Epsilon Fraternity*, 528 F.3d 94 (1st Cir. 2008).

◆ *A court upheld a $10,000 jury verdict for a bar patron who said a University of Minnesota police officer performed a "knee-drop" on his head.*

The patron got in a fight at a bar near the University of Minnesota campus. After being ejected from the bar, he accused bar security of starting another fight with him in a parking lot. University police arrived and pinned the patron to the ground. He said that while he was down, an officer violently smashed his knee onto his head. Witnesses later confirmed that the officer had used a "knee-drop" maneuver. The patron avoided criminal conviction for disorderly conduct, then filed a civil case in a federal court against the officer for excessive force. A jury awarded the patron $10,000 plus nearly $220,000 in attorneys' fees. The officer appealed to the U.S. Court of Appeals, Eighth Circuit.

The court rejected the officer's claim that the lower court should have allowed evidence of the patron's prior criminal history. The lower court had properly excluded a statement made by the patron's lawyer during the criminal trial. The statement indicated no one had accepted responsibility for the knee-drop maneuver. The lower court did not abuse its discretion when it told the jury that a criminal defendant does not have to call witnesses. It was not obligated to tell the jury that the officer could have been called as a witness. **Even though it dwarfed the $10,000 damage award, the appeals court upheld the award of $219,648.50 attorneys' fees.** Rejecting the officer's other arguments, the court affirmed the judgment for the patron. *Gill v. Maciejewski,* 546 F.3d 577 (8th Cir. 2008).

◆ *A fraternity could not be held responsible for the deaths of six Texas students who were struck by a pickup truck on their way to a fraternity party.*

After a football game, a fraternity threw a party. Nine students drove to the party and parked on the road, after which they walked to the fraternity. Three of the students walked on the grass; the other six walked on the paved shoulder with their backs to oncoming traffic. Another student was driving a pickup truck along the road at that time and fell asleep at the wheel. The truck collided with some of the vehicles parked on the road and fatally injured the six students walking on the shoulder. **Their estates sued the fraternity for negligence, alleging that it engaged in "dangerous conduct" and that it created a foreseeable risk of harm.** A trial court ruled for the fraternity, and the Texas Court of Appeals affirmed. The appeals court noted there were two causes of the accident: the student driver falling asleep, and the six students walking on the shoulder with their backs to oncoming traffic. As a result, the fraternity could not be held liable for negligence. *Calp v. Tau Kappa Epsilon Fraternity,* 75 S.W.3d 641 (Tex. Ct. App. 2002).

◆ *A Missouri student could pursue his claims against a college and a fraternity after he was shot.*

A student enrolled in a college and moved into a fraternity house. During a party, he got into a heated telephone conversation with a man who was not a student at the college. He then tried to lock the front door of the fraternity but was unable to do so because the lock was broken. When the man appeared later and shot him, he sued the college and the fraternity for negligently failing to maintain the premises. A state court granted pretrial judgment to the defendants, but the Supreme Court of Missouri reversed and remanded the case. Here, there were material issues of fact concerning who was a landlord and who was a tenant such that a trial had to be conducted. **Without knowing the status of the parties, the court could not determine the respective duties of the college, the fraternity and the student.** *Letsinger v. Drury College,* 68 S.W.3d 408 (Mo. 2002).

D. Hazing

◆ *A Virginia university did not violate the speech or due process rights of a fraternity by suspending a fraternity chapter for disciplinary reasons.*

The Iota Xi Chapter of the Sigma Chi Fraternity was officially recognized at George Mason University. A university student judicial board met and found the chapter responsible for hazing, providing alcohol to minors and sponsoring a party under conditions that led to sexual assault. As a result, the chapter was suspended for 10 years. The university barred chapter members from associating with fraternal organizations recognized by the university, and it withdrew official recognition of the chapter. The chapter and two members sued university officials in a federal district court for constitutional violations.

The court rejected the chapter's claims, finding **the university provided due process before imposing sanctions. The fraternity had notice of the charges and a meaningful opportunity to be heard.** Withdrawal of official recognition did not stop chapter members from associating with one another, defeating their speech rights claim. On appeal, the U.S. Court of Appeals, Fourth Circuit, held the university did not deprive fraternity members of any liberty interest in free association, as it did not bar anyone from joining other fraternities. Nor did the publication of the hearing outcome in a university newspaper deprive the fraternity or its members of any protected property interest. **There is no constitutional right to be free from stigma such as that allegedly created by the article, and the chapter did not identify any injury from the publication.** The court affirmed the decision to reject the speech claims. Even if marching and singing near the library was protected speech, the university had other adequate reasons to impose sanctions. *Iota Xi Chapter of Sigma Chi Fraternity v. Patterson,* 566 F.3d 138 (4th Cir. 2009).

◆ *A federal appeals court held a decision to suspend three Illinois students for hazing a sorority pledge was not based on their African-American race.*

The university suspended the students for beating a pledge repeatedly over a four-day period. The university suspended them under its student conduct code provision on hazing. One student was suspended for two years, and the others were suspended for three years. They sued the university in a federal district court, claiming race discrimination under Title VI of the Civil Rights Act of 1964 and the Equal Protection Clause. They said the university punished them more severely than it would have punished them if they had been white.

The court held for the university, and the students appealed. The U.S. Court of Appeals, Seventh Circuit, found insufficient evidence of race discrimination to pursue the claims. **The university did not distinguish by race when punishing the hazers.** The court rejected the contention that the university systematically punished hazing more harshly when it was carried out by African-Americans. Other examples of student misconduct could not meaningfully be compared to the students' situation. The court rejected the students' due process claims, which were based on the charge that the university's disciplinary procedures were a sham. The claims failed because the students did not adequately allege deprivation of a protected constitutional property right. As a result, the district court's decision was affirmed. *Williams v. Wendler*, 530 F.3d. 584 (7th Cir. 2008).

◆   *Although a fraternity had a duty to a Pennsylvania student, it did not breach that duty when local chapter members hazed him.*

A University of Pittsburgh student applied to the Beta Epsilon chapter of the Kappa Alpha Psi fraternity after Kappa lifted a restriction on inducting new members that had been imposed when a Kappa pledge died in Missouri. The student attended a fraternity gathering and was paddled more than 200 times by four fraternity brothers. He went to the hospital the next day and remained there for three weeks with renal failure, seizures and hypertension.

He later sued Kappa, the local chapter, the chapter advisor and a number of others for negligence. A Pennsylvania trial court ruled in favor of the defendants, and an appellate court largely affirmed. Here, even though Kappa owed a duty of care to the student, the student failed to show that it breached that duty. For example, he failed to show that the two-year moratorium on new members was merely a symbolic gesture and not a sincere attempt to curb hazing. However, **he was allowed to proceed with his lawsuit against the chapter advisor**. The evidence indicated that the chapter advisor failed to discuss hazing with local chapter members and did not advise them to read the executive orders that imposed sanctions for hazing. *Kenner v. Kappa Alpha Psi Fraternity*, 808 A.2d 178 (Pa. Super. Ct. 2002).

◆   *Corps of Cadets officials at Texas A&M were entitled to immunity in the following hazing case.*

The Texas A&M Corps of Cadets is a voluntary student military training organization consisting of approximately 2,000 students (about 5% of the student population). Members of the Corps live together, drill together, stand for inspections and physically train on a daily basis. A freshman student enrolled as a member of the Corps and joined a precision rifle drill team. **During "hell week," he was allegedly subjected to numerous hazing incidents by the drill team advisors, including having his head taped like a mummy, and endured several beatings.** He also was allegedly beaten after the drill team lost a competition to another university's team. He never reported the incidents to school authorities; however, he did tell his parents, who then informed school authorities that hazing was occurring. When asked about hazing by the faculty advisor, the student downplayed the seriousness of it. Near the end of his first year, he went to a "hound interview" (seeking to become an advisor to the drill team) where he was beaten and forced to cut himself with a knife. He and his parents then met with the Commandant of the Corps, who took them to the university police to file criminal charges. All the drill team advisors were then expelled or suspended for hazing.

The U.S. District Court for the Southern District of Texas held that **the actions of the Corps officials in educating students about the illegality of hazing were reasonable**. They disseminated brochures and other materials to students what hazing was and how to prevent it. They met with students and their parents to discuss hazing and to encourage parents to report it if they saw evidence of it, and they reasonably believed that their efforts were sufficient to prevent constitutional violations. **As a result, the court found that the officials were entitled to qualified immunity from suit.** On appeal, the Fifth Circuit Court of Appeals affirmed the grant of immunity to the officials. The student failed to show that the officials were deliberately indifferent to his constitutional rights. *Alton v. Hopgood*, 168 F.3d 196 (5th Cir. 1999).

◆ *A university that knew about prior instances of hazing had a duty to protect a student from such behavior.*

Members of a Nebraska fraternity kidnapped a pledge, handcuffed him to a radiator and gave him a large quantity of alcohol. After the pledge became ill from his intoxication, he was taken to a third-floor restroom where he was handcuffed to a toilet pipe. The pledge attempted to escape by exiting a restroom window and sliding down a drainpipe. However, he fell and suffered severe injuries. He sued the university, claiming that it had acted negligently in failing to enforce prohibitions against acts of hazing, the consumption of alcohol, and acts of physical abuse, when it knew or should have known that the fraternity was in violation of those prohibitions. The university moved for a pretrial judgment, asserting that it owed the pledge no duty to supervise the fraternity and protect him from harm. The court granted the university's motion, and appeal was taken to the Supreme Court of Nebraska. It held **the university could be liable to the pledge as an invitee on its property**. Because the university knew of two prior instances of hazing at fraternities on campus, and because it was aware of several incidents involving members of that fraternity, the acts taken against the pledge were reasonably foreseeable.

The university had a duty to protect the pledge. Whether it breached that duty was a question of fact that had to be decided at trial. The court reversed the pretrial judgment in favor of the university. *Knoll v. Board of Regents of the Univ. of Nebraska*, 601 N.W.2d 757 (Neb. 1999).

◆ *A university could not be held liable for a student's hazing where it had no reason to know that hazing was going on.*

A student transferred to Cornell University after spending his first two years at other institutions. He was accepted to pledge a fraternity, the national organization of which prohibited hazing, as did Cornell. After allegedly enduring beatings and torture, psychological coercion, and embarrassment, the student sued Cornell for negligent supervision, premises liability and breach of an implied contract to protect him. The U.S. District Court for the Northern District of New York dismissed the action, finding that there was no special relationship between the university and the student, and that the university published information about the dangers of hazing and its prohibition on campus. **Further, the university did not have sufficient reason to believe that hazing activities were going on; and once it became aware of the**

hazing, it took disciplinary action against the perpetrators. Finally, the court could find no evidence of any specific promises by the university that could be deemed part of an implied contract. The university was not liable for the hazing of the student. *Lloyd v. Alpha Phi Alpha Fraternity*, 1999 U.S. Dist. LEXIS 906 (N.D.N.Y. 1/26/99).

◆ *Fraternity members could be sued for negligence and for violating an anti-hazing statute in the following case.*

A 17-year-old college freshman was invited to pledge a fraternity and died after consuming excessive amounts of alcohol during a hazing ritual. His parents sued several members of the fraternity for negligence and also asserted claims under two New York statutes. The fraternity members sought to have two of the causes of action against them dismissed, and the case reached the Supreme Court, Appellate Division. The court held the fraternity members were not entitled to dismissal. **The parents alleged their son's intoxication was not entirely voluntary and that careless acts by the fraternity members went beyond the mere furnishing of intoxicants.** The action against the fraternity members could proceed. *Oja v. Grand Chapter of Theta Chi Fraternity*, 684 N.Y.S.2d 344 (N.Y. App. Div. 1999).

◆ *Where the consumption of alcohol is coerced by social pressure or otherwise, it may not be voluntary, and liability may result.*

A Missouri university student was invited to become a member of a campus organization that was responsible for organizing the annual St. Pat's festivities. To gain membership to the organization, the student had to undergo an initiation that allegedly consisted of the coerced chugging and excessive consumption of alcohol, as well as other physical and verbal abuse. Members of the organization allegedly forced the student to consume a heated preparation of grain alcohol and green peas until he became unconscious, then left him unattended despite knowing that a participant in the initiation had died three years earlier. The student died two days later, and his parents filed a wrongful death lawsuit against the organization and the individual members who had conducted the initiation, as well as the fraternities on whose property the initiation took place. The trial court dismissed the action, and the parents appealed to the Court of Appeals of Missouri.

The court of appeals reversed and remanded the case. **Here, despite the apparently voluntary consumption of alcohol by the student, there may have been great social pressure to drink.** That coercion may have overcome any decision the student might have made about whether he should consume alcohol and, if so, how much he should consume. The case should not have been dismissed. *Nisbet v. Bucher*, 949 S.W.2d 111 (Mo. Ct. App. 1997).

CHAPTER FOUR

Freedom of Speech and Religion

I. EMPLOYEES

A. Protected Speech

1. Retaliation

To prove retaliation based on the exercise of First Amendment speech rights, public employees must demonstrate that their speech resulted in some adverse employment action. Like any other speech rights claim against a public employer, the employee must show that the speech involved a matter of public concern, and that the exercise of protected speech outweighed the employer's interest in efficient workplace operations.

◆   *A tenured Mississippi business professor, who was removed from teaching duties due to his behavior, failed to convince a federal appeals court that the discipline came in retaliation for his criticism of the university.*

According to the dean of the college of business, the professor's behavior created an environment where students and faculty members in his department felt unsafe. In a letter to the university president, the dean described the professor's "negative and disruptive behavior" and charged him with failing to engage in scholarly or professional activities. The president removed the professor from teaching duties but directed him to continue research activities.

The professor stopped doing his research and sued the university and several officials in a federal district court for speech rights and due process violations. He claimed the discipline came in retaliation for creating a website critical of the university and for filing a complaint with an accrediting agency. A university ombudsman recommended a mental health assessment to determine the professor's fitness to teach. The court held for the university and officials, and the professor appealed to the U.S. Court of Appeals, Fifth Circuit. It held **he could not establish retaliation since he had not suffered any "adverse employment action."** All the "tangible accoutrements of his position – except teaching duties – remained stable." Any protected speech was not a substantial or motivating factor leading to the discipline. No due process violation or breach of any contract was shown. Since the president did not violate any clearly established constitutional rights, she was entitled to immunity. Immunity also barred the professor's retaliation claims against other university officials, as well as his state law claims. Due to the lateness of the ombudsman's report, the lower court had to consider the professor's claim for injunctive relief. *DePree v. Saunders*, 588 F.3d 282 (5th Cir. 2009). The U.S. Supreme Court denied review in *DePree v. Saunders*, 2010 WL 1004526 (U.S. 6/16/10).

◆   *A Delaware State University professor and department chair was unable to show he was dismissed in retaliation for engaging in protected conduct.*

After discovering a grade irregularity in the transcript of a student-athlete, the university registrar found the professor had changed incomplete and failing grades to passing grades for 48 students. He was not the professor of record for many grades he changed, but he claimed the authority to do so as department chair. The university president instituted dismissal proceedings against the professor, and after a hearing, a disciplinary committee recommended suspending him for misrepresented and unauthorized grade changes. The president pursued dismissal instead of suspension, and university trustees later voted to dismiss the professor. He claimed the action was in retaliation for his opposition to the university's selection of the president and other incidents.

In a civil rights action filed by the professor, a federal district court held for the board of trustees and president. On appeal, the U.S. Court of Appeals, Third Circuit, explained that as a public employee, the professor could only claim First Amendment protection if he was speaking as a citizen on a matter of public concern. However, he was not speaking as a citizen when he rescinded a speaking invitation and when acting as an advisor to student-athletes. Any speech he engaged in during these activities was unprotected because it related to his official duties. In addition, **the professor failed to show the president's**

decision to pursue his discharge was motivated by his speech. And even if the president was aware of these actions, there was evidence that he still would have pursued dismissal of the professor. As a result, the judgment was affirmed. *Gorum v. Sessoms*, 561 F.3d 179 (3d Cir. 2009).

◆ *No illegal retaliation occurred when a university terminated an employee and refused to rehire her after she reported problems with clinical trials.*

A Georgia medical college hired the employee as a coordinator/research associate to work with a particular doctor as he conducted trials. She soon reported his failure to get informed consent paperwork from patients and his failure to report adverse reactions. Relations between the two became strained, and the employee began applying for other positions within the college and a hospital. She again reported problems with the doctor's trials and filed reports with federal agencies. The employee later sued medical college officials in a federal district court, claiming they retaliated against her by discharging her and failing to hire her for another job. **The court found her complaints were unprotected by the First Amendment, because they were made pursuant to her official duties.** Her retaliation claim relating to her post-termination complaints failed, mainly because she did not file them until after she had stopped applying for other jobs at the hospital. *Abreu-Velez v. Board of Regents of the Univ. System of Georgia*, No. CV 105-186, 2009 WL 362926 (S.D. Ga. 2/12/09). In a brief memorandum, the U.S. Court of Appeals, Eleventh Circuit, affirmed the judgment. *Abreu-Velez v. Board of Regents of the Univ. System of Georgia*, 328 Fed.Appx. 611 (11th Cir. 2009).

◆ *A department manager was entitled to go before a jury with his claim that a New Mexico university retaliated against him for speaking out about financial dealings between the university and a state agency.*

The employee was the program manager of a university subdivision. An employee from the state health department told him the department would extend a grant to the school, but insisted the bulk of the funds flow through a nonprofit organization headed by a recent department retiree and the girlfriend of the program manager's supervisor. The manager suspected the employee was trying to avoid a state procurement law requiring the department to use a competitive bidding process. He declined the grant offer. The supervisor told the manager to resign or be fired. The manager resigned and sued the university in a state court. The case was removed to a federal district court, which granted the university's summary judgment motion.

The manager appealed to the U.S. Court of Appeals, Tenth Circuit. It held the statements about the grant were a matter of public concern because it alleged official wrongdoing. **The form and content of the manager's speech indicated he intended to vindicate the public interest, not to benefit himself. The manager's interest in speaking outweighed the university's interest in regulating him.** Since he was entitled to go before a jury to determine whether the university would have reached the same decision regardless of his speech, the court remanded the case. *Baca v. Sklar and the Board of Regents of the Univ. of New Mexico*, 398 F.3d 1210 (10th Cir. 2005).

2. Speech Pursuant to Official Duties

In Garcetti v. Ceballos, *547 U.S. 410 (2006), below, the U.S. Supreme Court restated the general rule that public employees have limited First Amendment rights to speak as private citizens on matters of public concern.*

Garcetti *clarified that a public employee's speech made pursuant to official duties is not protected by the First Amendment. The Court held "when public employees make statements pursuant to their official duties, the employees are not speaking as citizens for First Amendment purposes."*

◆ *Garcetti v. Ceballos* involved a California deputy district attorney who questioned a search warrant affidavit presented by a defense attorney. He determined that it contained serious misrepresentations by a sheriff and recommended dismissing the case. At a subsequent meeting, a heated discussion ensued. The DA's office decided to proceed with the prosecution, and the deputy district attorney was reassigned, then transferred to another courthouse and denied a promotion. He claimed the transfer was retaliatory, and sued county officials under 42 U.S.C. Section 1983 for First Amendment violations. The case reached the U.S. Supreme Court, which held that **public employees who make statements pursuant to their official duties are not speaking as citizens for First Amendment purposes, and are not insulated from employer discipline when they do so.** It was part of the deputy district attorney's job to advise his supervisors about the affidavit, and if his supervisors thought his speech was inflammatory or misguided, they had the authority to take corrective action against him. *Garcetti v. Ceballos*, 547 U.S. 410, 126 S.Ct. 1951, 164 L.Ed.2d 689 (2006).

◆ *The First Amendment does not protect speech that a public employee makes as part of his or her official job duties.*

A Florida community college vice president for external affairs was responsible for supervising grants, legal affairs, government affairs and cultural affairs. She also provided strategic planning and reported directly to the college president. During her tenure, the vice president objected to the president's behavior. She complained to the college provost that the school had apparently entered into an advertising contract without allowing for competitive bidding, as required by state law. Following her expression of this and other objections, the college notified her it was not renewing her contract.

The vice president sued the president and college in a federal district court, asserting retaliation for exercising her First Amendment rights. The court held for the president and college, and she appealed. The Eleventh Circuit found the First Amendment claim failed because the vice president's complaints were made pursuant to her job duties. **Although a state employee cannot be discharged in retaliation for engaging in protected speech, the First Amendment does not protect speech a public employee engages in as part of his official job duties.** The vice president was directly responsible for the legal affairs of the college, and it was her job to make sure the college followed applicable laws. She raised her concerns internally and did not present them to any government agency or media outlet until after she was informed her contract was not being renewed. Her statements "fell squarely within her job duties" and therefore were not protected by the First Amendment. The court affirmed the judgment. *Vila v. Padrón*, 484 F.3d 1334 (11th Cir. 2007).

3. Speech About the Public Concern

In Pickering v. Board of Educ., *below, the Supreme Court held a public employee may not be disciplined for speaking on matters of public concern unless there is proof that the communication was made in reckless disregard for the truth. In* Connick v. Myers, *461 U.S. 138 (1983), the Court held **a public employee's speech upon matters of purely personal interest has no constitutional protection**. In* Rankin v. McPherson, *483 U.S. 378 (1987), the Court held that whether an employee's speech addresses the public concern is determined by the content, form, and context of the speech.*

◆ *A University of Arkansas public safety officer was unable to show the denial of a promotion was based upon his speech.*

The officer reported to university officials that the chief of the university's department of public safety was misusing resources. Three years later, state police investigated the chief for misappropriating university resources, resulting in the chief's resignation. Although the officer sought to replace the chief, another candidate was selected for the position, and the officer sued the university board in a federal district court for First Amendment violations.

The court held for the board, and the officer appealed. The U.S. Court of Appeals, Eighth Circuit, explained that **public employee speech is protected only if the employee speaks as a citizen on a matter of public concern**. The speech must also outweigh the government interest in efficient services. While the officer's internal complaints about the chief were protected by the First Amendment, his statement to state police investigators was made pursuant to his job duties and was unprotected. To prevail on his First Amendment claim, the officer needed to show a connection between his internal complaints and the decision not to promote him. **The court found no evidence showing his internal complaints about the chief were a substantial or motivating factor in the decision to deny him the job as chief many years later.** As a result, the district court had proper grounds to deny the First Amendment claim. The district court correctly rejected a claim that the university violated the officer's due process rights, since he presented no evidence of any legitimate claim to a promotion. The judgment against the officer was affirmed. *Davenport v. Univ. of Arkansas Board of Trustees*, 553 F.3d 1110 (8th Cir. 2009).

◆ *A California university did not violate employee speech rights by using a form with a confidentiality provision for reporting violations.*

A nurse reported unsafe and unsanitary practices at a university hospital. She then claimed the university retaliated and discriminated against her, and she sued university regents in a state superior court. But the nurse did not first file an administrative complaint. She claimed she was excused from this requirement because the form the university used for filing complaints violated her First Amendment rights by requiring employees to keep subject matter confidential. The court denied relief, and the nurse appealed. **The Court of Appeal of California explained that the form required confidentiality only until a matter was resolved, and did not prevent any additional reporting.** Because the nurse was not required to submit to the confidentiality provision in order to file a retaliation complaint, she did not prove a speech violation. The court affirmed the judgment. *Jones v. Regents of the Univ. of California*, 164 Cal.App.4th 1072, 79 Cal.Rptr.3d 817 (Cal. Ct. App. 2008).

◆ *A South Dakota university did not violate an untenured physics professor's speech rights by not renewing his contract.*

The professor claimed the department director declined to address his concerns. He then accused the director of lying and badmouthing him. The university informed him by letter his contract might not be renewed, and it scheduled a meeting with the department chair and others. In the meeting, the professor admitted calling his department director "a lying, backstabbing sneak." The university did not renew his contract based on his lack of civility.

The professor sued the university in a federal district court, alleging First Amendment violations and seeking an order to prevent the university from not rehiring him. The university asserted the professor's remarks were complaints that were not of public concern and therefore not protected by the First Amendment. The court agreed, because **the professor's speech was personal, and not a matter of public concern**. It also rejected his claim that he required a preliminary injunction because having to pursue a career outside the university would cause him irreparable harm. The court balanced the damage to the professor against the harm the university would suffer if it was forced to reemploy him. Because forced reemployment would be disruptive to the university, the court dismissed the case. *Keating v. Univ. of South Dakota*, 386 F.Supp.2d 1096 (D.S.D. 2005).

◆ *When an employee speaks on a matter of public concern, and is then disciplined, courts use a balancing test to determine whether the employee's right to speak outweighs the employer's right to promote workplace efficiency.*

An Illinois school district fired a high school teacher for sending a letter to the editor of a local newspaper criticizing the board and district superintendent for their handling of school funding methods. The letter particularly criticized the board's handling of a bond issue and allocation of funding between school educational and athletic programs. The teacher also charged the superintendent with attempting to stifle opposing views on the subject. The board held a hearing at which it charged the teacher with publishing a defamatory letter. It then fired the teacher for making false statements. An Illinois court affirmed the board's action, as did the Illinois Supreme Court, which held the teacher's speech was unprotected by the First Amendment because his teaching position required him to refrain from statements about school operations.

The U.S. Supreme Court disagreed that public employment subjected the teacher to deprivation of his constitutional rights. **The state interest in regulating employee speech must be balanced with individual rights. The Court outlined a general analysis for evaluating public employee speech, ruling that employees are entitled to constitutional protection to comment**

on matters of public concern. The public interest in free speech and debate on matters of public concern was so great that it barred public officials from recovering damages for defamatory statements unless they were made with reckless disregard for their truth. Because there was no evidence presented that the letter damaged any board member's professional reputation, **the teacher's comments were not detrimental to the school system, but only constituted a difference of opinion.** Since there was no proof of reckless disregard for the truth by the teacher and the matter concerned the public interest, the board could not constitutionally terminate his employment. *Pickering v. Board of Educ.*, 391 U.S. 563, 88 S.Ct. 1731, 20 L.Ed.2d 811 (1968).

◆ *Where employees can be disciplined or discharged for legitimate reasons, the First Amendment will not protect them from the adverse action.*

An untenured Ohio teacher was not rehired after a number of incidents that led the school board to conclude he lacked tactfulness in handling professional matters. After the board decided not to reemploy the teacher, he asked for and received a list of the board's reasons. The board gave general reasons and noted that he had made an obscene gesture and had given an on-air opinion about school dress codes at a local radio station. The teacher sued for reinstatement on the grounds that his discussion with the radio station was protected by the First Amendment and that to refuse reemployment was a violation of his speech rights. A federal district court agreed, and ordered reinstatement with back pay. The Sixth Circuit affirmed the decision and the board appealed.

The U.S. Supreme Court first rejected the school board's argument that the Eleventh Amendment barred private lawsuits against a school district. But the Court overturned the lower court decisions, holding that apart from the actions for which the teacher might claim First Amendment protection, the board could have chosen not to rehire him on the basis of several other incidents. The radio station incident, while clearly implicating a protected right, was not the substantial reason for non-renewal. The board could have reached the same decision had the teacher not engaged in constitutionally protected conduct. **A marginal employee should not be able to prevent dismissal by engaging in constitutionally protected activity and then hiding under a constitutional shield as protection from all other actions that were not constitutionally protected.** The lower courts were instructed to determine whether the board's decision could have been reached absent the constitutionally protected activity of phoning the radio station, and, if such a decision could have been reached, whether remedial action to correct the violation would be necessary. *Mt. Healthy City School Dist. v. Doyle*, 429 U.S. 274 (1977).

◆ *The U.S. Supreme Court held a reasonable belief of workplace disruption can be enough to outweigh a speaker's rights under the First Amendment.*

In *Waters v. Churchill*, the Supreme Court held public employee termination is permitted where only a likelihood of disruption existed. **It was unnecessary to demonstrate an actual disruption if termination was based on the employer's reasonable belief that a disruption could occur.** *Waters v. Churchill*, 511 U.S. 661, 114 S.Ct. 1878, 128 L.Ed.2d 686 (1994).

B. Religion and Free Speech

The First Amendment's Establishment Clause prohibits Congress from making any law respecting the establishment of a religion. The Free Exercise Clause of the First Amendment bars Congress from making any law that prohibits the free exercise of religion.

Like the free speech provision of the First Amendment, the religion clauses apply only to governmental action and do not bind private institutions and their employees.

◆ *A New York university supervisor did not violate the Establishment Clause by allowing employees to decorate their cubicles with religious items.*

An accountant in the university bursar's office began to complain to the bursar about religious displays in the office. In particular, he objected to small angel figurines that his supervisor kept in his cubicle, religious posters hung outside the bursar's office, and an annual office party with a Christmas tree and Menorah display. Prior to filing these complaints, the accountant had a history of poor relationships with supervisors and co-workers. A performance review indicated he needed to improve his attitude and manner. He became involved in conflicts with five co-workers, and was reassigned to the accounting department. His performance problems continued there, and some co-workers asked not to work with him, as they could get things done faster without him.

The accountant complained that he was reassigned in retaliation for his complaints about the religious articles in the workplace. He sued the university in a federal district court for Establishment Clause violations and retaliation. He also claimed he was denied a reasonable accommodation for a mental disability. The court explained that **government action does not violate the Establishment Clause when it has a secular purpose, has a principal or primary effect that neither advances nor inhibits religion, and does not foster excessive entanglement with religion**. The accountant did not show the college acted with a religious purpose when it allowed employees to display religious items. There was no evidence that officials knew about or approved of much of the conduct he cited. The court also rejected the retaliation claim, ruling that neither a job transfer nor a negative job evaluation could be considered an "adverse employment action." The accountant's disability discrimination claim was rejected because he did not provide evidence of a disability. The court awarded pretrial judgment to the university. *Menes v. City Univ. of New York Hunter College*, 578 F.Supp.2d 598 (S.D.N.Y. 2008).

◆ *The Supreme Court held the act of certifying a union by the National Labor Relations Board (NLRB) infringed on a Catholic school's rights.*

The right of employees of a Catholic school system to join together and be recognized as a bargaining unit was successfully challenged in a case decided by the U.S. Supreme Court. In this case, the unions were certified by the NLRB as bargaining units, but the diocese refused to bargain.

The Court said that the religion clauses of the U.S. Constitution, which require religious organizations to finance their educational systems without governmental aid, also free the religious organizations of the obviously inhibiting effect and impact of unionization of their teachers. The court agreed with the employer's contention that **the very threshold act of certification of the union by the NLRB would necessarily alter and infringe upon the religious character of parochial schools**, since this would mean that the bishop would no longer be the sole repository of authority as required by church law. Instead, he would have to share some decision making with the union. This, said the Court, violated the religion clauses of the U.S. Constitution. *NLRB v. Catholic Bishop of Chicago*, 440 U.S. 490, 99 S.Ct. 1313, 59 L.Ed.2d 533 (1979).

C. Electronic Communications

◆ *A University of Virginia employee's e-mail to a member of a local NAACP chapter regarding the university pay scale was not protected speech.*

The employee and a co-worker were both NAACP members. The employee e-mailed the local NAACP chapter regarding a university pay scale restructuring. The chapter met to discuss this. The co-worker asked the employee to send her copies of documents distributed at the meeting. She used her university e-mail account to send the documents, and these were later forwarded to hundreds of other recipients. University officials investigated the action. The employee refused to answer questions involving her NAACP membership. Supervisors notified her "she was facing termination." According to the employee, she was not informed of the nature of the claims and a "hearing" amounted to being handed pink slips. She sued the university in a federal district court for First Amendment, due process and state law violations. After issuing a favorable initial ruling to the employee on her federal claims, the court awarded pretrial judgment to the university.

On appeal, **the U.S. Court of Appeals, Fourth Circuit, rejected the claim that the e-mail and attachments from the employee's work computer were protected speech**. Instead, the university's interest in providing effective and efficient services to the public strongly outweighed her interest in expression. The employee violated a state policy limiting personal e-mails from state computers and accounts. This policy supported the university's efforts to disseminate its own message. Even though the employee had an interest in her own communication, it did not outweigh that of the university. Questions by the university regarding her NAACP affiliation did not violate her association rights, as there was a legitimate state interest in ascertaining the source of potentially false and harmful data about the university pay structure. Since the employee admitted attending two meetings with officials to discuss her e-mail, due process was satisfied, and the lower court judgment for the university was affirmed. *Bowers v. Scurry*, 276 Fed.Appx. 278 (4th Cir. 2008).

◆ *An Internet user who viewed a university Web site page about evolution and religion lacked any constitutional right to have the site taken down.*

Two University of California employees obtained a National Science Foundation grant for a Web site to teach the science and history of evolutionary biology. Although information on the site indicated evolution and religion are compatible, a parent claimed the site exposed her to government-endorsed religious messages and "made her feel like an outsider." She noted that the site included links to a Web page containing statements by religious organizations. The parent asked a federal district court to block the site and sought an order that its content was unconstitutional. The court dismissed the case, finding she lacked standing to raise the claims and did not show she was injured by the content. On appeal, the U.S. Court of Appeals, Ninth Circuit, held a claim against the National Science Foundation was moot. The grant had expired, and there was no showing it would offer more funding. According to the parent, she was inhibited from using the Web site without running into religious symbols and statements. Like the district court, **the court held she had only an indirect connection with the site and thus lacked standing to challenge its content**. As her claims amounted only to an "abstract objection," the case had been properly dismissed. *Caldwell v. Caldwell*, 545 F.3d 1126 (9th Cir. 2008).

◆ *University of Houston Downtown (UHD) officials did not violate an adjunct professor's constitutional rights by limiting e-mail access for all adjuncts to times when they had actual course loads.*

The adjunct professor complained about a number of UHD policies, including compensation and treatment of adjunct professors. He claimed UHD denied access to his e-mail account after he attempted to use the system to distribute his complaints. The adjunct sued UHD and several administrators in a federal district court, asserting constitutional rights violations. He claimed UHD cut his course load from three courses to two in order to deprive him of benefits, terminate his retirement system status and cut his pay. The adjunct claimed Texas law violated the Constitution by prohibiting the unionization of state employees and the ability of non-citizens to become labor officials.

The court held for UHD, and the adjunct appealed to the Fifth Circuit. It **noted the U.S. Supreme Court has held a public school system's internal mail system is not a "state-created forum" for unlimited expression**. States may reserve forums for their intended purposes, as long as regulations are reasonable and not intended to suppress expression. **The court found no First Amendment violation. Restrictions created by a spam filter and the adjunct e-mail access policy were uniformly applied and were not based on content.** The policies were reasonable in view of UHD's goal of controlling the amount of data on its computer system. Any reduction in the adjunct's course load was not retaliatory. He was not treated differently than other UHD adjuncts, most of whom also taught only two courses. Adjunct faculty members are not similarly situated to full-time faculty members. They typically teach fewer classes than tenured or tenure-track professors and are not held to the same publishing expectations. As the adjunct could not compare himself to full-time faculty members, his Equal Protection Clause claim failed. The adjunct lacked standing to challenge Texas Labor Code Section 101.109. He could still file his own individual grievances, and he did not even claim he had tried to become a union officer or organizer. The court affirmed the judgment. *Faculty Rights Coalition v. Shahrokhi*, 204 Fed.Appx. 416 (5th Cir. 2006).

◆ *A federal court rejected a Georgia university police officer's claim that he was fired for complaining about pornography on a co-worker's computer.*

The officer complained to a university official that the co-worker was accessing and viewing pornography on his work computer. He told the official he did not want the people in his department to know he was the one who made the complaint. An investigation showed the co-worker had pornography on his computer, and he retired after being told he would be fired. Another department employee then noted his computer was running slowly. When a professional investigated, he discovered that someone had accessed the computer without authorization. Upon further investigation, a supervisor concluded it was the officer who had accessed the computer. The officer was discharged but was later reinstated to his position. He then asked the department of human resources to investigate the question of unauthorized access to the slow computer. Following this request, the university discharged the officer for insubordination, accessing a computer without authorization, and reporting an ongoing investigation.

The officer sued university officials in a federal district court, claiming he was fired for filing a complaint. The court rejected his claim against university regents. The claim was filed under 42 U.S.C. § 1983, which only permits claims against "persons." Since the board of regents was not a person, no Section 1983 claims against it could succeed. The university's chief of public safety could be liable for damages in his individual capacity only if he violated the officer's clearly established rights. The chief was performing a discretionary function when he disciplined the officer, who did not show he was discharged because of his speech. **Evidence showed the officer violated internal policies and was insubordinate.** Even if there was a violation of the First Amendment, the chief would enjoy immunity. *Dixon v. Board of Regents of the Univ. System of Georgia*, No. 1:06-CV-1696-TWT, 2007 WL 3476926 (N.D. Ga. 11/1/07).

D. Academic Freedom

Universities have the right to determine "who may teach, what may be taught, how it may be taught, and who may be admitted to study." **The right to academic freedom belongs to universities, not to individual professors.** *Hence, the courts have held that public university professors lack First Amendment rights to determine what will be taught.*

1. Classroom Speech

◆ *Virginia State University (VSU) administrators did not violate a professor's rights by changing a student's grade.*

For a physics course, the professor calculated each student's final grade by averaging the three highest scores on five quizzes. This calculation resulted in an average of 59 for one student. He said the student achieved quiz scores of 16, 66, 89, 21 and 22. Although the score of 59 merited a grade of F, the professor assigned the student a D. The student protested, believing he had earned higher scores on two quizzes, which would have entitled him to an A.

The student handed in faxed copies of the quizzes showing scores of 95, but the professor believed they were doctored and refused to change the grade. The department chairman sided with the student and changed the grade to an

A. The professor sued VSU in a federal district court for violating an asserted right to academic freedom. He also said administrators changed the grade to retaliate against him for testifying on behalf of a colleague who had filed a lawsuit against VSU. The professor asked the court to order VSU to change the grade to a D. He also sought monetary damages. The court explained that the U.S. Supreme Court has recognized that the Constitution gives "some measure of academic freedom to academic institutions." Universities have the right to determine "who may teach, what may be taught, how it may be taught, and who may be admitted to study." **The right to academic freedom belongs to universities and not to individual professors.** While professors at public institutions do not forfeit their First Amendment rights when they accept their jobs, decisions addressing academic freedom focus on the rights of academic institutions. VSU officials exercised their authority to change the grade without requiring the professor to do so personally. He lacked a constitutional right to academic freedom that would prevent VSU officials from changing the grade. The court granted VSU's motion to dismiss the claim. *Stronach v. Virginia State Univ.*, No. 3:07CV646-HEH, 2008 WL 161304 (E.D. Va. 1/15/08).

◆   *Institutions are entitled to direct their instructors to keep personal discussions about sexual orientation or religion out of their classes.*

An Illinois college instructor gave a gay student religious pamphlets on the sinfulness of homosexuality. One was entitled "Sin City" and told the story of a man who was beaten when he tried to stop a gay pride parade and was arrested by police. It also said a demon urged on a minister who preached that "God loves even gay people." The student complained to college officials and urged them to fire the instructor. In a follow-up letter, the student reported that the instructor had accused him of trying to get her fired. The college investigated and the Affirmative Action Office (AAO) and Equal Employment Opportunity Commission (EEOC) concluded that the instructor had sexually harassed the student based on sexual orientation. The college did not offer the instructor a position the following semester, and she sued the college in a federal district court for speech rights violations. The court held for the college and the instructor appealed to the U.S. Court of Appeals, Seventh Circuit.

The court relied on *Garcetti v. Ceballos*, this chapter, noting the case signalled the Court's concern that the courts give appropriate weight to a public employer's interests in First Amendment cases. In this case, **the college had an interest in ensuring that instructors stayed on the subject matter of their clinics and classrooms. The court affirmed the judgment for the college, as it could lawfully direct instructors to keep personal discussions about sexual orientation or religion out of a class or clinic.** *Piggee v. Carl Sandburg College*, 464 F.3d 667 (7th Cir. 2006).

◆   *An Ohio university did not violate a lecturer's First Amendment rights by telling her to communicate grading requirements more clearly to her students.*

The lecturer gave incomplete grades to 13 of 17 students in a writing class for improper formatting, improper citations, and/or textual changes to their work. She left it up to each student to determine which reason applied in his or her own case. The lecturer's listserv postings did not specify particular reasons for which students received incomplete grades, and at least one student complained. A supervisor told the lecturer her listserv postings were not sufficiently clear to inform students how to complete the course. She asked her to send each student in the class a letter with individualized instructions for earning a final grade. Five weeks later, several students complained that the lecturer did not provide this information. The supervisor again asked the lecturer to draft letters to each student and emphasized that incomplete grades were a serious problem affecting student academic and financial aid status. The lecturer never responded and did not prepare the letters. She later sued the director of the English department and the supervisor for violating her rights to speech and academic freedom. A federal district court dismissed the case.

On appeal, the U.S. Court of Appeals, Sixth Circuit, rejected the lecturer's claim that an instruction by a supervisor to communicate with students violated the First Amendment. **Any right to academic freedom recognized by the First Amendment applied to the university, not the lecturer. A university is entitled to determine who may teach, what may be taught, how it is taught, and who may be admitted.** These freedoms give a university the right to decide how classes are taught and how grades are assigned. **Professors have certain protections under the First Amendment, like making decisions about instruction and grading that differ from those of the university. They do not have to agree with the views of the university when it comes to a grade or a way to teach.** In this case, the university did not make the lecturer adopt the ideas of others as if they were her own. It simply asked her to explain to students exactly what was required to obtain a final grade. As the university did not violate the lecturer's rights, the court affirmed the judgment in its favor. *Johnson-Kurek v. Abu-Absi*, 423 F.3d 590 (6th Cir. 2005).

◆ *An Indiana university did not violate a professor's academic freedom by terminating his employment for poor job performance.*

Indiana State University hired an African history professor under a contract specifying a seven-year probationary period. A personnel committee recommended against reappointing him after two years, based on its finding that his performance was mediocre. The professor claimed a department chairperson advised him not to associate with other African professors and to become more involved with African-American activities. After exhausting his university appeals, the professor sued the university in a state court for due process and First Amendment violations. The university removed the case to a federal district court, which held his constitutional claims were meritless.

The professor appealed to the U.S. Court of Appeals, Seventh Circuit. It held that to succeed on a due process claim, the professor had to show the existence of a mutually explicit understanding of continued employment. A review of the contract showed the university had broad discretion to decide whether to reappoint him. As the professor did not establish a property interest in continued employment, his due process claim failed. His liberty interest claim failed because he could not show the university publicly communicated its denial of his reappointment and that the communication damaged his good name. **The professor's academic freedom claim was meritless. The**

statements by the department chairperson resembled employment advice. They were not connected with the performance of employment duties, and did not suppress the professor's First Amendment rights. Moreover, he was never sanctioned for having spoken about any issue. Accordingly, the court affirmed the judgment. *Omosegbon v. Wells*, 335 F.3d 668 (7th Cir. 2003).

2. Loyalty Oaths

In Sweezy v. New Hampshire, *354 U.S. 234 (1957), the U.S. Supreme Court declared unconstitutional a university policy aimed at prohibiting the employment of communist party members.*

◆ *A Washington statute aimed at prohibiting subversives from becoming teachers was too vague to be constitutional.*

Faculty members at the University of Washington brought a class action suit to declare two state statutes unconstitutional. One statute required all state employees to take loyalty oaths, and the other required all teachers to take an oath as a condition of employment. Both oaths dealt with employee loyalty to the U.S. Constitution and to the government. The public employee statute applied to all public employees and defined a "subversive person" as one who conspired to overthrow the government. The Communist Party also was named as a subversive organization. Persons designated as subversives or Communist Party members were ineligible for public employment.

The U.S. Supreme Court held that the statutes were vague and overbroad, and violated the Fourteenth Amendment's Due Process Clause. The statutes were too unspecific to provide sufficient notice of what conduct was prohibited. This constituted a denial of the teachers' due process rights. **The university could not require its teachers to take an oath that applied to some vague behavior in the future**, especially since there were First Amendment freedom of speech and association claims at stake. *Baggett v. Bullitt,* 377 U.S. 360, 84 S.Ct. 1316, 12 L.Ed.2d 377 (1963).

◆ *An Arizona statute that prohibited even associating with the Communist Party was struck down by the U.S. Supreme Court.*

An Arizona teacher who was a Quaker refused to take an oath required of all public employees under Arizona law. The oath swore that the employees would support both the Arizona and the U.S. Constitutions as well as state laws. The legislation also stated that anyone who took the oath and supported the Communist party or the violent overthrow of government would be discharged from employment and charged with perjury. The teacher sued for declaratory relief in the Arizona courts, having decided she could not take the oath in good conscience because she did not know what it meant.

The case eventually reached the U.S. Supreme Court, which held that political groups may have both legal and illegal aims and that there should not be a blanket prohibition on all groups that might have both legal and illegal goals. Such a prohibition would threaten legitimate political expression and association. The Court held that mere association with a group cannot be prohibited without a showing of "specific intent" to carry out the group's illegal purpose. It went on to say that **the Arizona statute was constitutionally deficient because it was not confined to those employees with a "specific intent" to do something illegal**. The statute infringed upon employee rights to free association by not punishing specific behavior that yielded a clear and present danger to government. The statute was struck down as unconstitutional. *Elfbrandt v. Russell,* 384 U.S. 11, 86 S.Ct. 1238, 16 L.Ed.2d 321 (1965).

◆ *A state could not require teachers to file annual affidavits listing every organization they belonged to in the past five years.*

The Arkansas Legislature established **a statute that required every teacher employed by a state-supported school or college to file an annual affidavit listing every organization to which he or she had belonged in the past five years**. A teacher who had worked for an Arkansas school system for 25 years and who was a member of the NAACP was told he would have to file such an affidavit before the start of the next school year. After he failed to do so, his contract for the next year was not renewed. He filed a class action lawsuit against the school district in a federal district court.

The court found that the teacher was not a member of the Communist Party, or any organization advocating the violent overthrow of the government. It upheld the statute, finding that the information requested by the school district was relevant. The Supreme Court of Arkansas had previously upheld the statute's constitutionality in a case brought by other teachers. The U.S. Supreme Court agreed to hear both cases and consolidated them for a hearing. The Court noted that the state certainly had a right to investigate teachers, since education of youth was a vital public interest. It stated that the requirement of the affidavit was reasonably related to the state's interest. However, the Court held that **requiring teachers to name all their associations interfered with teacher free speech and association rights**. The Court ruled that because fundamental rights were involved, governmental screening of teachers was required to be narrowly tailored to the state's ends. Because the statute went beyond what was necessary to meet the state's inquiry into the fitness of its teachers, the Court ruled it unconstitutional. *Shelton v. Tucker,* 364 U.S. 479, 81 S.Ct. 247, 5 L.Ed.2d 231 (1960).

◆ *A loyalty oath could not be administered to two applicants who objected to it on religious grounds.*

Two Jehovah's Witnesses applied for positions with the California Community College District. As part of state-mandated preemployment procedures, the district required the applicants to sign an oath swearing "true faith and allegiance" and to "support and defend" the United States and California Constitutions. The applicants refused to take the oath due to their religious beliefs, and the district rejected their applications.

The applicants sued the district under the Religious Freedom Restoration Act of 1993 (RFRA), challenging the validity of the loyalty oath as a condition precedent for employment. A California federal court held that **requiring the applicants to take an oath that violated their religious tenets placed an undue burden on their right to free exercise of religion**. The district failed to assert that the loyalty oath furthered a compelling government interest or was the least restrictive means of achieving that interest. Although employee loyalty was a compelling interest, the evidence failed to establish that a loyalty oath effectively achieved this goal. An alternative oath directed to an applicant's actions rather than his or her beliefs would be equally effective and less restrictive. Because the loyalty oath could not be justified under the compelling interest test articulated in the RFRA, the court enjoined the district from administering the loyalty oath to the applicants. *Bessard v. California Community Colleges*, 867 F.Supp. 1454 (E.D. Cal. 1994).

[*Editor's Note*: The U.S. Supreme Court held that the RFRA was unconstitutional as applied to state actions in *City of Boerne, Texas v. Flores*, 521 U.S. 507, 117 S.Ct. 2157, 138 L.Ed.2d 624 (1997).]

II. DEFAMATION

To pursue a defamation claim, a defamed party must allege that false material was "published" to a third party who understands it refers to the defamed party. The defamed party must suffer a loss of reputation and a "tangible injury," which is usually some harm to an economic interest.

Defenses to defamation include truth, privilege consent and opinion. The defense of privilege defeats many otherwise valid defamation claims in employment cases. In Fink v. California State Univ. Northridge, *No. B183977, 2006 WL 465947 (Cal. Ct. App. 2/28/06), the Court of Appeal of California held that statements reporting suspected criminal activity to law enforcement officers are privileged and cannot form the basis of a defamation claim.*

A judicial privilege applies to proceedings before government bodies and pursuant to a statute or administrative regulation. The U.S. Court of Appeals, Third Circuit, has limited an absolute privilege to judicial proceedings. Applying Pennsylvania law, the court held internal grievance proceedings are not entitled to the same absolute immunity as regular judicial proceedings. Overall v. Univ. of Pennsylvania, *412 F.3d 492 (3d Cir. 2005).*

◆ *A tenured Illinois professor was allowed to proceed with a defamation case against a university and its vice president in the federal court system.*

At a faculty council meeting, the professor complained that the arrest of student demonstrators on campus was part of a pattern of harassment against students who opposed the war in Iraq. A vice president who oversaw the campus police and student affairs said the professor and students were responsible for the incident. He also claimed the professor had been charged with stalking a student. Although she had been elected to be the chair by members of her department, the university declined to appoint her, and it did not give her a faculty excellence award for which she claimed to be eligible.

In a federal district court action against the vice president and university for defamation and retaliation, the court explained that **as a government official, the vice president had immunity if the defamatory statement was reasonably related to his public duties**. In making this determination, the relevant factors included whether the statements were made in his role as a supervisor, as part of an official duty to speak on behalf of his department, and to defend against allegations of wrongdoing. Based on the papers filed so far in the case, there was little information regarding the vice president's duties. However, the alleged statement regarding stalking did not appear to be reasonably related to any of his identified duties. For this reason, the court refused to dismiss the defamation and state law retaliation claims and denied the vice president's dismissal motion. *Capeheart v. Northern Illinois Univ.*, No. 08 CV 1423, 2010 WL 894052 (N.D. Ill. 3/9/10).

◆ *Pennsylvania law protects state employees from defamation lawsuits, barring a student's claim that she was falsely accused of plagiarism.*

After an instructor assigned the student an F on a paper for plagiarism, her course grade went to a C. Although she denied committing plagiarism, a university judicial board disagreed. Her course grade became an F, and she was dismissed from her doctoral program. Twelve years after being expelled, the student applied for readmission to the program but was rejected. She sued the instructor and university in a federal district court, alleging she was denied readmission due to bias and animosity. She also alleged that the instructor should have been fired for falsely accusing her of plagiarism. The court found the student's constitutional claims were untimely. Her defamation and negligence claims failed, because Pennsylvania's Sovereign Immunity Act protected a public university and faculty from claims based on civil wrongs committed when employees acted within the scope of their employment. **Since the instructor was acting within the scope of his employment at the university when he accused the student of plagiarism, the immunity act applied to any defamation and negligence claims**, requiring dismissal of the case. *Shuqin v. Rafoth*, No. 08-1343, 2009 WL 3834009 (W.D. Pa. 11/16/09).

◆ *A Louisiana university coach who submitted a false resume could not claim defamation or breach of contract based on his subsequent discharge.*

The coach was hired as head basketball coach after he submitted a resume indicating he had earned a degree from the University of Texas at San Antonio (UTSA). In fact, he had attended UTSA but did not graduate. After being hired, the coach filled out forms correctly indicating he had graduated from another university that was not accredited by the Southern Association of Colleges and Schools. After the hiring, a newspaper article mentioned his failure to graduate from UTSA and the university fired him for lying on his resume. The coach sued the university in a state court for defamation and breach of contract, claiming the resume had been sent by mistake and that he later submitted correct information. A trial court held for the university, and he appealed.

The Supreme Court of Louisiana held the defamation claim failed because the statements indicating the coach had misrepresented his qualifications on his resume were true. **A party cannot recover for defamation based on a true statement.** The breach of contract claim also failed, because the university had a valid reason to rescind the contract. Evidence showed the coach would not have been hired if the university had known he did not have a degree from an accredited school. *Cyprien v. Board of Supervisors for the Univ. of Louisiana System*, 5 So.3d 862 (La. 2009).

◆   *A Kentucky community college did not defame a teacher or retaliate against her in response to her complaints about her work environment.*

During her first year under a tenure-track contract, the teacher repeatedly refused to administer an opinion poll to her students as requested by another professor. Discussion about whether the poll should be included spread to other faculty members, and the teacher complained to a college dean and the college president about the behavior of some of her male co-workers. She alleged harassment and a hostile work environment. When the teacher learned her contract would not be renewed, she posted a cartoon outside her office depicting two hooded figures. One figure was labeled as the college president. The college maintained that the figures represented Ku Klux Klan members, and the dean removed them. After being placed on a paid leave of absence, the teacher sued the college and five employees for wrongful termination, breach of contract, infliction of emotional distress, and retaliation for exercising her speech rights. A state court dismissed the case, and she appealed.

On appeal, the Court of Appeals of Kentucky noted that the college did not terminate the teacher's contract but had instead placed her on paid leave. She did not allege any harassment until after the decision not to renew her contract had been made. **The court held that the Constitution does not protect defamatory statements. A suggestion that someone is a member of the Ku Klux Klan is defamatory.** In this case, the teacher failed to show she was treated more harshly than similarly situated males. While she presented evidence relating to another male professor who was asked to remove an offensive cartoon, his cartoon was discovered during a work week, when he was available for questioning. By contrast, the teacher's cartoon was removed during a weekend. The judgment for the community college was affirmed. *McBrearty v. Kentucky Community and Technical College System*, 262 S.W.3d 205 (Ky. Ct. App. 2008).

◆   *The Supreme Court of Indiana rejected a professor's defamation claims against two students who filed complaints of sexual harassment against him.*

Two female students filed formal complaints of sexual harassment against an Indiana education professor. Pursuant to its anti-harassment policy, the university affirmative action office investigated. After a series of interviews, the investigator found the professor had created a hostile educational environment. The investigator specifically found harassment in one of the complaints, but the second complaint was not timely reported. A three-person panel and a senior executive officer accepted the investigator's recommendation that the professor should not have teaching responsibilities or student contact. He was assigned to a research position for the remainder of his contract. The professor sued the university in a state court for defamation and malicious interference with his employment contract. The court held for the students on the malicious interference with contract claim, as the non-renewal decision was made before the complaints were filed. But it held further proceedings were required to determine if the students were entitled to a privilege for the defamation claim.

The Court of Appeals of Indiana held the students' complaints were protected by an absolute privilege, and the professor appealed. **The Supreme Court of Indiana explained that there is an absolute privilege for**

statements made during judicial proceedings, regardless of their truth or the motive behind them. The rule is intended to allow people to participate in judicial proceedings without fear of being sued for defamation. At least three other states – Maryland, California and New York – have extended the privilege to complaints to school authorities against educators. It was appropriate to extend the privilege in this way so students could raise complaints without fear of retaliatory litigation. *Hartman v. Keri*, 883 N.E.2d 774 (Ind. 2008).

◆ *A Rhode Island university did not defame a student when its security office posted a "crime alert" to inform the campus community about him.*

The student became involved in a late-night fight with another student. He punched the other student and knocked him to the ground, where he hit his head. A witness told the police that the student had a knife during the fight. Police filed criminal charges against the student, and the incident was reported to the university campus safety and security office. The office investigated and filed an incident report stating that the student was the likely aggressor in the fight. The security office then posted a crime alert at various campus locations, naming the student as the party responsible for the crime.

After being dismissed from the university, the student filed a federal district court action against the university for defamation and breach of contract. The court held the university had a qualified privilege to publish the alert. On appeal, the U.S. Court of Appeals, First Circuit, held the university enjoyed a qualified privilege with respect to the defamation claim. **The university reasonably believed it had a duty to report the crime to the campus community under the federal Clery Act.** The student did not show the university published the alert with spite, ill will or malice. The court also rejected the breach of contract claim, which was based on the university's alleged mishandling of his appeal. The university complied with student handbook terms relating to the appeal process. The judgment was affirmed in all respects. *Havlik v. Johnson & Wales Univ.*, 509 F.3d 25 (1st Cir. 2007).

◆ *Connecticut's highest court held that employers enjoy a qualified privilege to provide employment references with an employee's consent.*

A police officer for the University of New Haven Police Department applied for two other jobs while still working for New Haven. With her consent, two police departments contacted her New Haven supervisors. They suggested to one department that the officer had missed too much time from work and that her police skills were "marginal at best." The supervisors said the officer had poor leadership skills and had been "negative or uncaring" at times. In addition, other comments reflected negatively on her job performance. The officer's application was rejected, but she was hired by another department. After just three months, she was discharged for inferior job performance.

The officer sued the New Haven department and two supervisors for defamation, tortious interference with a business expectancy and intentional infliction of emotional distress. A jury returned a verdict against her, and she appealed. The Supreme Court of Connecticut held that a qualified privilege applies to employment references made with employee consent. It rejected the officer's argument that extending a qualified privilege would be inconsistent with state laws relating to the maintenance of personnel files and blacklisting. A "culture of silence" would be encouraged if a qualified privilege was not extended to employment references made in good faith and without improper motive. **Employers enjoy a qualified privilege from liability for defamation for employment references that are solicited from other employers with the employee's consent.** The judgment was affirmed. *Miron v. Univ. of New Haven Police Dep't*, 284 Conn. 35, 931 A.2d 847 (Conn. 2007).

◆ *An Indiana university did not defame a former professor when it published an account of the incident that led to his firing in a book.*

In the professor's lawsuit over the allegedly defamatory book passage, **the Indiana Court of Appeals held that to prove defamation, he had to show defamatory imputation, malice, publication, and damages.** A defamation claim cannot be based on a true statement. In a pretrial statement, the professor had admitted he did not take issue with the book's account of the classroom incident that led to his discharge. As he failed to establish three of the four elements needed to prove defamation, the action failed. *Felsher v. Univ. of Evansville*, 880 N.E.2d 335 (Table) (Ind. Ct. App. 2008).

◆ *A Texas appeals court threw out a $40,000 jury verdict on a university administrator's defamation claim based on improper jury instructions.*

A provost/vice president at Prairie View A&M University questioned the dean of arts and science about his recommendation for an applicant for chair of the chemistry department. A secretary overheard the provost/vice president make a comment to the effect that the dean of arts and science and the applicant were lovers. The applicant, who was a married man with children, sued the provost/vice president in the state court system for slander. A jury returned a verdict of $40,000 for the applicant, and the court entered judgment on the verdict. The provost/vice president appealed to the Court of Appeals of Texas, arguing that her comment was "rhetorical hyperbole," not a statement of fact.

The court found it unclear whether the provost/vice president made the comment sarcastically or sincerely. Because it had been appropriate for the jury to resolve this ambiguity, the court rejected her argument that the verdict could not stand. The evidence showed that both the dean and secretary understood the comment to assert that the dean and applicant had a romantic relationship. The court rejected the provost/vice president's argument that the jury should have had instructions relating to whether she enjoyed official immunity on the defamation claim. However, **the jury should have received instructions relating to whether the provost/vice president was entitled to claim a qualified privilege**. Because it did not, the judgment was reversed. *Thomas-Smith v. Mackin*, 238 S.W.3d 503 (Tex. Ct. App. 2007).

◆ *A federal appeals court held two faculty members did not defame a New York instructor during a closed faculty meeting.*

A tenure-track instructor learned she would not be reappointed, and she contended that faculty members who voted against her reappointment did so because she was pregnant. The president of the institute overturned the vote and reappointed her for a semester, making her eligible for tenure the following spring. The department again met to discuss the instructor's reappointment. She claimed two faculty members made inaccurate statements about her that resulted in the loss of her reappointment and her claim to tenure. The instructor sued the faculty members in a federal district court for defamation.

The court held a statement is defamatory if "it tends to expose the plaintiff to public contempt, ridicule, aversion, or disgrace, or induce an evil opinion of him in the minds of right-thinking persons." Under New York law, individuals are given absolute immunity for statements of opinion. The court dismissed the case, as the remarks were not shown to be false. On appeal, the U.S. Court of Appeals, Second Circuit, held that under New York law, **statements made as a part of a tenure review have qualified immunity from defamation**. To "pierce this immunity," the instructor had to show malice. As he did not show the alleged defamation was motivated by spite, the court affirmed the judgment against him. *Donofrio-Ferrezza v. Nier*, 178 Fed.Appx. 74 (2d Cir. 2006).

III. STUDENTS

A. Protected Speech

The Establishment Clause of the First Amendment to the U.S. Constitution requires government neutrality with respect to religion and non-religion. The Free Exercise Clause of the First Amendment prohibits government interference with the reasonable exercise of religious rights. Public institutions must refrain from content-based restrictions on speech.

1. Religious Speech

◆ *A federal appeals court rejected claims that a University of California (UC) policy for evaluating high school religion courses was unconstitutional.*

UC's policy for recognizing high school religion and ethics courses required that they "treat the study of religion or ethics from the standpoint of scholarly inquiry, rather than in a manner limited to one denomination or viewpoint." UC justified the policy to assure a multidisciplinary study of religion. An association representing Christian schools and students sued UC officials in a federal district court, asserting speech, free exercise, Establishment Clause and equal protection violations. After the court held for UC, appeal reached the U.S. Court of Appeals, Ninth Circuit, which said the association showed no risk that the policy would suppress protected speech.

The court held the policy did not stop high schools from teaching what they wanted, or prevent high school students from taking the courses they wanted. UC did not punish high schools or students, and the court found no unlawful viewpoint discrimination. Evidence indicated UC approved courses with religious content and viewpoints, even those using religious textbooks as primary texts. UC's refusal to accept four courses offered by a Christian school was reasonable because the courses were not college preparatory, lacked necessary course information or materials, or had other procedural defects. The court rejected an equal protection challenge because the policy applied equally to all in-state applicants. The judgment for UC was affirmed. *Ass'n of Christian Schools Int'l v. Stearns*, 362 Fed.Appx. 640 (9th Cir. 2010).

◆   *A federal district court allowed two California community college students to proceed with claims asserting violation of their religious speech rights.*

While the students were praying together in a faculty office, an instructor interrupted them and said they could not pray there. The two continued talking in a hallway, and the community college informed them that it intended to suspend them for disruptive behavior. After hearings, both students were given disciplinary letters warning them not to engage in disruptive behavior. They sued the community college in a federal district court for punishing them for engaging in private, non-disruptive prayer.

The court held that prayer is protected expression under the First Amendment. **It rejected the community college's argument that faculty participation in student-initiated, private prayer in an office violated the Establishment Clause.** It was not likely that an objective observer would view such prayer as state endorsement of a religious practice. The college had improperly imposed restrictions on religious expression. Restrictions on speech were not justified unless they were "narrowly tailored to serve a compelling government interest." Since the community college did not make this showing, the court declined to dismiss the free exercise, free expression and free association claims. However, the court dismissed the claim that the anti-prayer policy was an impermissible prior restraint on expression. There were also no equal protection or due process violations. *Kyriacou v. Peralta Community College Dist.*, No. C 08-4630 SI, 2009 WL 890887 (N.D. Cal. 3/31/09).

◆   *A federal court refused to dismiss a lawsuit against Eastern Michigan University (EMU) by a graduate student who claimed to be dismissed in violation of her religious rights for refusing to counsel a homosexual client.*

As part of a graduate counseling program, the student was supposed to counsel persons who paid a small fee. Before she was to meet a new client, she read his case file and saw he wanted help with a homosexual relationship. The student asked that the client be assigned to another student, because she would not "affirm any behavior that goes against what the Bible says." The professor charged the student with violating EMU's Counseling Student Handbook. After an informal review, a hearing was held where her strong religious beliefs were questioned in view of her entry into a profession with a code of ethics that opposes therapies which try to change a client's "perceived sexual orientation" from homosexual to heterosexual. A panel decided to dismiss the student from the program, and she sued EMU and several officials in a federal district court for speech rights violations. After denying a request for immunity, the court permitted the claims against individual defendants to proceed. **A trial was needed to determine if EMU retaliated against the student for expressing her religious beliefs and if EMU sought to compel her to act contrary to her faith.** *Ward v. Members of Board of Control of Eastern Michigan Univ.*, No. 09-CV-11237, 2010 WL 1141605 (E.D. Mich. 3/24/10).

◆ *Temple University's sexual harassment policy was worded so broadly that it violated a student's First Amendment rights.*

A Temple policy prohibited "expressive, visual, or physical conduct of a sexual or gender-motivated nature," if the conduct had the "purpose or effect" of unreasonably interfering with another person's "work, educational performance, or status." The policy also barred "sexual or gender-motivated" conduct intended to create "an intimidating, hostile or offensive environment" for others. A graduate student who served in the National Guard claimed the policy inhibited him from expressing his views about women in the military. He sued Temple, its president and two professors in a federal district court for First Amendment violations. While the case was pending, Temple modified the policy. The court considered the old policy and held it was unconstitutional.

On appeal, the U.S. Court of Appeals, Third Circuit, rejected Temple's claim that the case was moot since the old policy had been revised. The court found Temple might reinstitute the old policy without court intervention. There is no "harassment exception" to the First Amendment. The policy violated a general rule that **student speech cannot be barred unless it creates a real threat of disruption.** Under the policy, students could be punished even if their actions had no effect on others. Terms such as "hostile," "offensive," and "gender-motivated" were broad enough to ban some protected speech. The policy lacked a requirement that conduct or speech actually create a hostile environment or interfere with the work of others. The phrase "gender-motivated" required inquiry into the motivation of the speaker. It was also unclear whether it was the speaker's gender or the listener's that served as the motivation. A policy prohibition of conduct that "unreasonably interfere[d] with an individual's work" was suspect as well. The court affirmed the judgment. *DeJohn v. Temple Univ.*, 537 F.3d 301 (3d Cir. 2008).

◆ *A Pennsylvania student who opposed a Temple University play depicting Jesus Christ as a homosexual was not entitled to relief in federal court.*

Temple University put on a play depicting Jesus Christ and his disciples as homosexuals who engaged in sexual acts with one another. The student asked the university to prohibit the production on campus and planned an alternative event to portray Jesus according to his beliefs. However, university trustees met and decided not to provide a stage or any assistance for the student's planned event. The student became upset at the meeting and had to be restrained.

The vice president ordered campus police to handcuff the student and take him to a hospital for a psychiatric evaluation. A university official applied for a warrant to involuntarily commit him for an emergency psychiatric evaluation, but doctors released him. The student sued the university and officials in a federal district court for First Amendment and related claims. A jury held for the university, and the student appealed to the U.S. Court of Appeals, Third Circuit. It rejected the student's argument that the district court judge should have recused herself from the case. **The district court had permissibly allowed a university counselor to provide expert testimony,** and the court affirmed the judgment. *Marcavage v. Board of Trustees of Temple Univ. of the Comwlth. System of Higher Educ.*, 232 Fed.Appx. 79 (3d Cir. 2007).

◆ *A Virginia law school graduate could not force a college to display a brass cross on the altar of a chapel.*

The president of the College of William & Mary decided to store a cross that had been displayed in an on-campus chapel for years. A graduate of the college's school of law sued college officials in a federal district court, seeking an order to have the cross returned to the chapel's altar. He claimed that the removal of the cross violated his speech and religious free exercise rights. The court held the removal of the cross did not cause any legal injury to the student. Although he claimed he became emotionally upset when the cross was removed, this was not enough to show a violation of a legal right. **The student did not identify any action on the part of the college president that violated his right to free speech or free exercise of religion.** The chapel remained open, and the cross could be displayed at the request of chapel users. *Leach v. Nichol*, No. 4:07cv12, 2007 WL 1574409 (E.D. Va. 5/29/07).

On appeal, the U.S. Court of Appeals, Fourth Circuit, found no reason to reverse the decision. *Leach v. Nichol*, 256 Fed.Appx. 612 (4th Cir. 2007).

◆ *A federal district court dismissed claims that an assignment to read a religious-related book violated student free exercise rights.*

An orientation program held by the University of North Carolina, Chapel Hill (UNC) required incoming freshmen to read a book that explored Islam. UNC stated it was highly relevant in light of the then-recent terrorist attacks. Although the program had an exception for students with religious objections, several incoming students sued UNC in a federal district court for Free Exercise Clause violations. **The court considered UNC's motion for dismissal, and noted the book was not a religious reading.** It found the orientation program was an academic exercise.The court stated UNC had attempted to engage students in a scholarly debate about a religious subject, and encourage them to express their opinions. Students who objected to reading the book could refrain from doing so. **UNC did not compel the affirmation of any particular religious belief, favor any religious dogma, or punish the expression of any particular religion.** As UNC did not ask students to compromise or give up their religious beliefs, the court granted its motion to dismiss the action. While the court dismissed the claims against the university, it permitted the students to file a second amended complaint to add new factual allegations. *Yacovelli v. Moeser*, 324 F.Supp.2d 760 (M.D.N.C. 2004).

◆ *A Seventh Circuit panel allowed a theater student to continue with his production of a play that was alleged to be anti-Christian.*

The dispute arose after a theater student at an Indiana university chose to produce a play depicting a homosexual Christ-like character who engaged in sex with his apostles. A group of taxpayers, members of the state General Assembly, and Purdue University board members alleged that the publicly funded university would be violating the Establishment Clause by allowing the performance. A federal district court denied a request to stop the production. **Because the theater was a limited public forum, the university could not discriminate against the viewpoint of performers.** On appeal, the U.S. Court of Appeals, Seventh Circuit, upheld the decision. It found "absurd" the assertion that the First Amendment prevents state universities from providing venues for un-Christian ideas. There was no evidence that the university was hostile to Christianity because it did not tell the student to produce the play. *Linnemeir v. Board of Trustees of Purdue Univ.*, 260 F.3d 757 (7th Cir. 2001).

◆ *Graduation prayers were allowed at Indiana University.*

In a case involving graduation prayers at Indiana University, the Seventh Circuit distinguished the ceremonies from public school ceremonies involving younger students. **There was no element of coercion requiring students to participate in the large, impersonal university commencement exercises**, and many students and family members remained in their seats during the prayer. Adult students were unlikely to succumb to peer pressure and could choose not to attend the ceremony without suffering any severe consequences. The court agreed with the university that the prayers solemnized the ceremony, did not endorse any particular religion and allowed the university to continue a 155-year-old tradition. *Tanford v. Brand*, 104 F.3d 982 (7th Cir. 1997).

2. Academic Practices

◆ *A federal district court rejected a Texas student's claim that her professor violated her speech rights by banning abortion as a topic for an assignment.*

When the student chose abortion as the topic for her public speaking assignment in a speech communication class, the instructor told her it was off limits. She sued the instructor in a federal district court for violating her First Amendment rights. After rejecting the student's non-speech claims, the court explained that **the instructor could defeat any speech claim by showing he had a legitimate pedagogical reason for restricting her speech**. This was shown based on his statement that the topic of abortion was potentially disruptive and could shift the focus away from the topic of communication skills. Since the instructor had a valid pedagogical reason for banning the topic of abortion in his class, he was entitled to judgment on the speech claim. The student also failed to show his criticism of her was retaliatory. **The decision to grant a specific grade to a student is within the discretion of education professionals and not the judiciary.** All the remaining claims in the case were dismissed. *O'Neal v. Falcon*, 668 F.Supp.2d 979 (W.D. Tex. 2009).

◆ *A Virgin Islands student who was charged with raping another student obtained a court order preventing enforcement of a student code provision.*

University officials found the student guilty of violating its policy relating to hazing and harassment. As punishment, he was ordered to pay a fine of $200 and write a letter of apology to the other student. Instead, the student sued the university and officials in a federal district court for violating his speech and association rights. The court held the claims against the university were barred by sovereign immunity. However, the student could seek injunctive relief against university officials in their official capacities. The court rejected his challenge to a student code provision requiring students to report others who inflict or threaten bodily harm. The student failed to show how it violated his right to free speech. A code provision barring students from displaying "obscene, offensive or obstructive" signs at sports events, concerts and social-cultural events was reasonably related to legitimate pedagogical concerns.

A code provision barring "verbal assault, lewd, indecent or obscene conduct or expressions on university owned or controlled property or at university sponsored or supervised functions" did not infringe on student speech rights. Neither did a provision that banned "conduct which causes emotional distress," including "conduct which results in physical manifestations, significant restraints on normal behavior or conduct" and/or conduct which "compels the victim to seek assistance in dealing with distress." This provision encompassed only speech that significantly interfered with others. **But the court held a code provision barring speech that "frightens, demeans, degrades or disgraces any person" was unconstitutional.** It found the provision covered more speech than could reasonably be found to cause a threat of disruption. While the university could not enforce that part of its code, judgment for the university was awarded on the rest of the claims. *McCauley v. Univ. of Virgin Islands*, No. 2005-188, 2009 WL 2634368 (D.V.I. 8/21/09).

◆ *The University of Tennessee (UT) did not violate the Constitution by suspending a student for displaying anti-war banners in violation of its policy.*

The student hung anti-war banners from UT buildings and painted the words "NO WAR" on them. He was arrested for vandalism, public intoxication and evading arrest. The student admitted what he had done. UT's student handbook barred vandalism and acts violating any law. A UT facilities guide allowed notices only on designated bulletin boards and barred political signs. Relying in part on the fact that other graffiti was present on campus, the student insisted he did not know that painting on university buildings or hanging banners on them violated UT policy or state law. He sued UT officials in a federal district court for violating the First Amendment. He also claimed that he was arrested without probable cause in violation of the Fourth Amendment.

After the court held for UT, the student appealed to the U.S. Court of Appeals, Sixth Circuit. As to the First Amendment claim, the court explained that campus grounds were not public forums. As such, the university could reasonably restrict speech. **The evidence showed the messages were removed because they were "unusually noticeable and intrusive," not because they expressed a particular viewpoint.** Moreover, it would be reasonable for UT to bar political messages while allowing others, such as those relating to student activities. The court rejected the student's Fourth Amendment claim, as well as his claim that UT's policy on vandalism was unconstitutionally vague. The meaning of the term "vandalism" could be readily determined, and UT was not required to make sure all students had specific notice of its policies. *Wilson v. Johnson*, 247 Fed.Appx. 620 (6th Cir. 2007).

◆ *Because it was overbroad, a California state university's requirement that students "be civil to one another" violated the First Amendment.*

College Republicans at San Francisco State University (USF) displayed Hamas and Hezbollah flags that included the word "Allah" in Arabic during an anti-terrorism rally. Group members placed the flags on the ground and stepped on them. Several observers strongly objected, but the rally closed peacefully. A student later submitted a formal complaint to USF. A student organization hearing panel refused to impose discipline on group members for conduct inconsistent with USF goals, principles and policies. Nonetheless, the group and two members sued USF and others in a federal district court, challenging student code provisions requiring students to be "civil," punishing behavior that was "inconsistent" with USF "goals, principles and policies," and barring "intimidation" and "harassment." The court agreed with the students that the code provision requiring students to be "civil" was unconstitutionally overbroad. **There was a substantial likelihood that the civility requirement would "chill" expressive activity protected by the First Amendment.**

However, the court upheld the code provision prohibiting intimidation and harassment, finding it was not overbroad in the context of the handbook. The court invalidated the student handbook provision authorizing discipline based on behavior that was inconsistent with USF goals, principles, and policies. This provision was preceded by a section that vaguely required students to "engage in responsible behaviors that reflect well upon the university." There was substantial uncertainty about what was meant by "goals, principles, and policies," as well as "inconsistent." As the provision might chill the exercise of protected speech, the handbook provision was held unconstitutional. USF was halted from basing disciplinary proceedings on conduct that was not "civil" or was "inconsistent with its goals, principles, and policies." *College Republicans at San Francisco State Univ. v. Reed*, 523 F.Supp.2d 1005 (N.D. Cal. 2007).

◆ *A federal district court upheld the U.S. government's decision to tighten restrictions on American higher education programs offered in Cuba.*

Since 1963, the U.S. government has restricted travel to Cuba as part of a broad trade embargo. In 1999, federal regulations known as the Cuban Assets Control Regulations (CACR) allowed American colleges and universities to participate in structured educational programs in Cuba. The initial regulations had no minimum durational requirements, and students could enroll in Cuban educational institutions even if they were not enrolled in an undergraduate or degree program. In 2004, the government added a requirement that educational programs conducted by American schools in Cuba last at least 10 weeks. It also required any student using an institution's license for educational travel to Cuba to be enrolled at that school. Finally, it required teachers of educational programs in Cuba to be full-time, permanent faculty members. A group of students, professors and others challenged the regulations in a federal court.

The court held **the regulations did not violate the First Amendment because they were neutral with respect to content** and supported by the government interest in denying hard currency to Cuba. The court rejected the claim that the amendments violated an asserted Fifth Amendment right to international travel. Individuals have less freedom to travel abroad, and denying U.S. currency to the Castro government was an important government interest. Courts afford deference to the political branches of government with respect to foreign affairs. The regulations were not arbitrary and capricious and did not contravene the will of Congress. *Emergency Coalition to Defend Educational Travel v. U.S. Dep't of Treasury*, 498 F.Supp.2d 150 (D.D.C. 2007).

◆ *An Illinois university did not violate a graduate student's speech rights by dismissing her for a fraudulent scientific presentation.*

The student submitted research to a scientific journal and presented it at a conference. The university suspected her of academic misconduct. After a hearing, a university investigatory panel concluded the student fabricated scientific data she knew were invalid when she presented them at the conference. The university dismissed the student, and she sued the university in a federal district court for speech rights violations. The court held the university's interest in academic integrity outweighed her speech interests.

On appeal, the U.S. Court of Appeals, Seventh Circuit, found the university had a strong interest in its reputation in the academic and scientific community. **Public presentation of false data by a graduate-level student affiliated with the university significantly compromised that reputation. The First Amendment protects the marketplace of ideas but does not protect students from the consequences of their own fraudulence.** *Pugel v. Board of Trustees of Univ. of Illinois*, 378 F.3d 659 (7th Cir. 2004).

◆ *A student had no First Amendment right to have his master's thesis kept in a university library after he failed to comply with professional guidelines.*

A graduate student at a California university attempted to file his thesis in the university library after adding two new pages in which he criticized administrators with profanity. The thesis committee and a dean refused to allow the thesis to be filed because the extra pages did not meet professional standards for publication. Even though the university never filed a copy of the thesis, the student received a master's degree. He then sued the university in a federal district court. After losing there, the student appealed to the Ninth Circuit. It held **the thesis was a curriculum assignment with pedagogical objectives that required him to comply with professional guidelines. Because he failed to do so, he could not claim a First Amendment right** to have his thesis filed. He also failed on his due process claim because the decision to defer granting his degree was an academic one that was careful and deliberate. *Brown v. Li*, 308 F.3d 939 (9th Cir. 2002).

3. Retaliation

◆ *A federal court dismissed a graduate student's lawsuit asserting that the University of Houston (UH) trumped up discipline against him for activism.*

The student opposed department policies and faculty appointments. He founded two student activist groups and interrupted a faculty senate meeting with a fair trade protest. UH twice referred the student for discipline for "obstructing or interfering with university functions or activities." Meanwhile, supervising professors said he was insensitive and derogatory to students in his role as a teaching assistant. After several other students complained about the student, a professor had to regrade much of his teaching assistant work. Disciplinary referrals were made for violations of the UH disciplinary code.

The professor recommended banning the student from departmental positions, and UH followed the recommendation. The student sued UH in a federal district court for retaliation for exercising his speech rights. Claims against UH's former president failed, as he had nothing to do with denying any teaching assistant positions. **The court held UH had immunity under federal law unless the state consented to be sued or Congress validly abrogated its immunity.** As neither was true, the case was dismissed. *O'Brien v. Univ. of Houston*, No. H-08-2337, 2010 WL 890979 (S.D. Tex. 3/8/10).

◆ *A Pennsylvania student unsuccessfully claimed he was arrested in retaliation for accusing an instructor of discrimination.*

A white Jewish student argued with an African-American computer lab instructor over his use of computer lab facilities. A college policy permitted computer use by students enrolled in active, ongoing classes, but prohibited access for personal use. At the time, the student was not enrolled in an active, ongoing class and was using computers for his own use. He wrote a letter to the college president complaining about the denial of lab use. The dispute continued for eight months and resulted in the student's forcible removal from the computer lab by Pittsburgh police officers. He was arrested for trespass, but charges were later withdrawn. The student sued the college and officials including the instructor in a federal district court for speech rights violations and breach of contract. He claimed violation of his First Amendment rights. A federal district court held for the college and officials, and the student appealed.

The U.S. Court of Appeals, Third Circuit, said that **to prevail on a speech rights retaliation claim, the student had to show he engaged in protected speech and the college retaliated against him for making the speech.** The court found his letter was not a matter of public concern and was thus not protected activity. The student's contract claim failed because he had no contract with the college. The college was not required to provide written notice of every regulation governing the use of its facilities to enforce its regulations. The court affirmed the judgment for the college and officials. *Feldman v. Community College of Allegheny*, 85 Fed.Appx. 821 (3d Cir. 2004).

◆ *An expelled student could proceed with his First Amendment retaliation claim against Connecticut university officials.*

A Connecticut university student criticized the university administration and filed an ethics complaint against the university president. After the interim vice president and dean of student affairs accused him and two other students of making unauthorized changes to over 30 grades in violation of the university handbook, a hearing was conducted and the student was expelled. The university upheld the student's expulsion, but dropped proceedings against the two others. The student sued the university in a federal district court for speech and due process violations. The university sought dismissal on Eleventh Amendment immunity grounds, and a federal court granted the motion in part.

As an arm of the state, the university could not be liable for negligence. Also, the student received appropriate due process in the hearing and expulsion procedures used by the university. However, **there was a fact issue as to whether he had been expelled in retaliation for his speech against the administration.** The court refused to dismiss that claim and ordered a trial. *Brown v. Western Connecticut State Univ.*, 204 F.Supp.2d 355 (D. Conn. 2002).

B. Electronic Communications

Use of electronic media does not enhance or detract from speech rights. The same principles apply to cyberspace speech as for other media.

◆   *Like a traditional classroom, an online university discussion board is not a public forum where students have an absolute right to say what they want.*

A Southern Oregon University (SOU) online class was delivered entirely over the Internet. A student was disrespectful to classmates and the instructor in an online forum. After being warned about his conduct, the student enrolled in another online class and was charged with classroom defiance and disrespect. After a disciplinary hearing, SOU placed the student on probation. He sued SOU in a federal district court for civil rights violations. The court said a university conduct policy which prohibited the display of defiance or disrespect of others was not unconstitutionally vague or overbroad. Some regulation of speech is permissible. In the educational context, it is reasonable to limit speech rights to maintain order and discipline on university property. **The student was not barred from expressing his views. He was only barred from insulting others.** As the SOU policy furthered the important government interest in maintaining decorum and order in an online classroom environment, and students were put on notice of what conduct was prohibited, the policy was upheld as constitutional. **A classroom is not a public forum where students have an absolute right to say whatever they want.** The court denied the student's request for an order and held SOU could limit speech that might lead to disruption of its activities. *Harrell v. Southern Oregon Univ.*, No. 08-3037-CL, 2009 WL 3562732 (D. Ore. 10/30/09).

◆   *A student had no constitutional right to use an unflattering picture of Regent University President Pat Robertson as his Facebook profile picture.*

The student used a YouTube clip of Robertson scratching his face with his middle finger on his Facebook profile. At a certain point, it appeared as though Robertson was "flipping the bird." When school administrators learned of the picture, they told the student it violated a prohibition on profane or obscene behavior in the university's standards of personal conduct. The student removed the picture, but he posted a discussion on a public e-mail list declaring "[t]he value the picture serves is to show that Pat Robertson is a very bad man."

A short time later, the university received reports that the student was acting in an "unstable" and "erratic" manner and possibly kept a gun in his car. After he was barred from classes, he sued the university for speech and due process violations. He also raised Title IX and defamation claims. The court rejected the speech and due process claims because Regent is a private entity that is not obligated to comply with the Constitution. The Title IX claim failed because the student was not similarly situated to a female student who was allegedly permitted to have a stun gun on campus. She later agreed to surrender her gun. **The court rejected the student's defamation claim, as he deliberately manipulated television images, and there was no actual malice by university officials.** *Key v. Robertson*, 626 F.Supp.2d 566 (E.D. Va. 2009).

◆ *A California community college policy violated student speech rights by improperly restricting use of its library Internet service.*

A student viewed MySpace.com member profiles on a computer in the college library. A campus police officer accused him of viewing pornography and told him he could not access the site at the library. Although the student was not disciplined, he sued the community college district in a state superior court for violating a state law that gives students the same speech rights on campus they have when not on campus. The court held that the district's policy, which limited library Internet use to "appropriate academic, professional or institutional purposes," violated the state law because it was overbroad. The court ordered the district to revise its Internet use policy. The district revised the policy, and the court entered judgment in the case. Both sides appealed.

The Court of Appeal of California held that the revised policy complied with state law. While the student claimed the law gave students the same speech rights on campus that they enjoyed in their homes, the court held the law guaranteed only the speech rights they enjoyed "off campus." **Speech rights varied, depending on where the speech took place. In this case, the activities took place in a college library, which was like a public library.** For that reason, whether the revised policy met free speech requirements depended on whether it would be permissible if applied to public library users. Relying on a U.S. Supreme Court decision addressing Internet access in public libraries, the court held the revised policy was reasonable and not an effort to suppress expression based on viewpoint. As a result, the trial court had properly limited relief to declaring the old policy invalid and requiring the district to adopt a new one. *Crosby v. South Orange County Community College Dist.*, 172 Cal.4th 433, 91 Cal.Rptr.3d 161 (Cal. Ct. App. 2009).

◆ *A Delaware university could discipline a student whose Web site included a guide to skinning a cat and statements about rape, kidnap and murder.*

A university computer policy required students to comply with publishing and communication laws, but it did not directly address offensive content. After the student posted violent and sexual content on a Web site, an associate vice president attempted to remove the student from campus and barred him from his classes and his dormitory pending a psychiatric assessment. He charged the student with violating the computer use policy. The student obtained a health care provider letter declaring he was not a threat. But the university learned the student's dormitory access card had been used four times after his permission was revoked. A hearing was held to consider charges of disruptive conduct, failure to comply with an order to stay out of his dormitory, and violating the computer policy. A university hearing officer found the student did not violate the computer policy, but was guilty of the other two charges. He was suspended, banned from campus and placed on "deferred expulsion."

After an internal appeal failed, the student sued the university in a federal district court for due process and First Amendment violations. The court noted that the university did not have to provide procedural protections similar to those in criminal cases. **While students must be treated fairly, institutions "are not required to convert [their] classrooms into courtrooms."** The student received notice of the charges, actively participated in the hearing, and had a chance to present his side of the story. As a result, there was no violation of his due process rights. However, the court found the postings did not reflect a serious expression of an intent to inflict harm. In addition, the university did not show the content disrupted classwork or unreasonably interfered with others. *Murakowski v. Univ. of Delaware*, 575 F.Supp.2d 571 (D. Del. 2008).

C. Newspapers and Yearbooks

◆ *The U.S. Supreme Court has held that, at the collegiate level, the conduct of students and the dissemination of ideas – no matter how offensive could not be curtailed based solely on the "conventions of decency."*

A graduate student at the University of Missouri was expelled for distributing on campus a newspaper that violated university bylaws since it contained forms of "indecent speech." The newspaper was found objectionable for two reasons. First, on the front cover was a political cartoon of policemen raping the Statue of Liberty and the Goddess of Justice with a caption that read "… with Liberty and Justice for All." Secondly, the issue contained an article entitled "Mother Fucker Acquitted," which discussed the trial and acquittal on an assault charge of a New York youth. The student sued the university in a federal district court, for First Amendment violations. The court denied relief, but the U.S. Supreme Court held the student should be reinstated. It stated that **while a university has an undoubted prerogative to enforce reasonable rules governing student conduct, it is not immune from the sweep of the First Amendment**. The Court noted that *Healy v. James*, 408 U.S. 169 (1972), made it clear that the mere dissemination of ideas – no matter how offensive to good taste – may not be shut off in the name of "conventions of decency" alone. *Papish v. Univ. of Missouri*, 410 U.S. 667 (1973).

◆ *The U.S. Court of Appeals, Seventh Circuit, held a university dean was entitled to immunity for prior restraint of the content of a student newspaper.*

Students at an Illinois state university held positions on the student newspaper and student communications media board. According to board policy, only students determined newspaper content. No censorship or prior approval by university officials was allowed. The university became interested in the school paper, the *Innovator*, after it printed articles attacking the integrity of the dean of the college of arts and sciences. The dean and university president issued statements accusing the *Innovator* of irresponsible and defamatory journalism. The newspaper refused to retract comments that officials insisted were false, or even to print their responses. When the dean of student affairs notified the newspaper's printing company that a university official had to review and approve the newspaper's content before each issue was printed, the students sued the university for speech rights violations.

A federal district court refused to dismiss the claims against the dean. The Seventh Circuit held in 2003 that she was not entitled to qualified immunity because the prohibition against censorship within the university setting was clearly established at the time she acted. **The Supreme Court held that high school officials have broad powers to censor school-sponsored newspapers if their actions are supported by valid educational purposes in**

Hazelwood School Dist. v. Kuhlmeier, **484 U.S. 260 (1988).** The Court allowed prior restraint in *Hazelwood* because the student newspaper was prepared as part of a high school journalism curriculum. In this case, the Seventh Circuit found the greater maturity of college students made censorship of college newspapers untenable. *Hosty v. Carter*, 325 F.3d 945 (7th Cir. 2003).

The dean petitioned the Seventh Circuit for reconsideration. The petition was granted, and the court reversed its 2003 decision. The court held the *Hazelwood* standard could apply to a public university. Since public officials need not predict constitutional uncertainties, the dean was entitled to qualified immunity. *Hosty v. Carter*, 412 F.3d 731 (7th Cir. 2005).

◆ *A university violated the First and Fourteenth Amendment rights of a yearbook editor when it confiscated yearbooks for being "inappropriate."*

The editor of Kentucky State University's (KSU's) yearbook during the 1993–1994 school year decided to be innovative and, for the first time, gave the yearbook a theme: "Destination Unknown." The theme reflected the students' uncertainty about life after college and the pending question of whether the university was to become a community college. The yearbook included pictures from KSU events as well as current national and world events. KSU's vice president for student affairs objected to the final product. She opposed the yearbook's cover, theme, the lack of captions under many photos and the inclusion of current events unrelated to KSU. **The vice president and other university officials prohibited the yearbooks from being distributed and confiscated them.** The editor and another student sued the school on behalf of all KSU students in federal court, claiming their First and Fourteenth Amendment rights were violated. The court dismissed the suit, finding that the yearbook was a nonpublic forum because it was not intended to be a journal of expression, but rather a record of the events at KSU for its students. The students appealed to the U.S. Court of Appeals, Sixth Circuit.

The court noted it is well established that a high school yearbook is not a public forum and is subject to strict control by school officials. It held **a college yearbook was a limited public forum**. KSU's written policy toward the yearbook gave the student editors control over the publication because it did not allow a faculty/staff advisor to change the yearbook in order to alter the content. In addition, **the language of the university's student publication policy indicated that such publications were intended to be limited public forums**. The policy begins by saying, "The Board of Regents respects the integrity of student publications and the press, and the rights to exist in an atmosphere of free and responsible discussion and of intellectual exploration." The Sixth Circuit remanded the matter to the district court for further proceedings. *Kincaid v. Gibson*, 236 F.3d 342 (6th Cir. 2000).

D. Student Activity Fees

◆ *A federal district court held it permissible under the Establishment Clause for a state university to grant religious groups equal access to a public forum.*

The University of Wisconsin-Madison collects about $400 per semester from each student and allocates it toward segregated fees, which go toward a variety of non-instructional student services, programs and facilities. Of that $400, about $33 goes into a General Student Services Fund (GSSF), which funds the activities of student organizations. The stated purpose of the GSSF is to give students a way to "engage in dynamic discussions" relating to a number of enumerated topics – including religion – in extracurricular activities. The Roman Catholic Foundation (RCF) received funding from segregated fees, but the university denied reimbursement for some expenditures that supported worship, proselytizing, or religious instruction. The RCF and two student members sued the university in a federal district court, asserting discrimination on the basis of viewpoint and other First Amendment violations.

The court issued a preliminary order barring the university from enforcing any policy that prevented RCF from being reimbursed for activities on the basis of prayer, worship or proselytizing. In later proceedings, the court rejected the university's argument that it could not constitutionally fund worship, proselytizing or religious instruction out of segregated fees. **States can afford religious groups the same access to a public forum that they grant to secular groups.** As a result, the university could grant religious groups access to the segregated fee forum on the same basis that it provided access to non-religious groups. The university was free to enact viewpoint-neutral restrictions with respect to use of the funds. University officials had qualified immunity on the claims for money damages, and punitive damages were unavailable. The court did not enter a permanent order against the university as RCF sought. *Roman Catholic Foundation, UW-Madison v. Regents of the Univ. of Wisconsin System*, 578 F.Supp.2d 1121 (W.D. Wis. 2008).

The court later issued an order denying the group's request for permanent relief, limiting its relief to a declaratory judgment and denying monetary damages. It declined to characterize the university's conduct as "content based discrimination." *Roman Catholic Foundation, UW-Madison v. Regents of the Univ. of Wisconsin System*, 590 F.Supp.2d 1083 (W.D. Wis. 2008).

◆ *The U.S. Supreme Court held that the University of Wisconsin could assess a mandatory activity fee to fund student extracurricular programs.*

The University of Wisconsin required all students to pay the university a nonrefundable activity fee to support registered student groups. Students who objected to the collection and use of their student fees to support objectionable political and ideological expression sued university regents in a federal district court, asserting that the program violated their speech rights. The court held that the fee program compelled students to support political and ideological activity with which they disagreed in violation of the First Amendment. It prohibited the university from using student fees to fund registered student organizations engaged in such activity. The U.S. Court of Appeals, Seventh Circuit, affirmed in part, finding that the student activity fee program was not germane to the university's mission and burdened student speech.

The U.S. Supreme Court found that the university assessed the fee to facilitate the free and open exchange of ideas among students. Objecting students could insist upon certain safeguards regarding the compelled support of expressive activities. To insist upon germaneness to the university's mission would contravene the purpose of the program, which was to encourage a wide range of speech. The Court found it inevitable that the fees would subsidize some speech that students would find objectionable, and it declined to impose a constitutional requirement upon the university compelling it to refund fees to students. Viewpoint neutrality was the proper standard for the protection of the First Amendment rights of the objecting students. **The university could require students to support extracurricular speech of other students in a viewpoint-neutral manner**, and the parties had stipulated in this case that the program was viewpoint neutral. The university had wide latitude to adjust its extracurricular speech programs to accommodate students. The Court reversed and remanded the case for further proceedings. *Board of Regents of Univ. of Wisconsin System v. Southworth*, 529 U.S. 217 (2000).

On remand, the district court determined the university's updated fee system, which set forth the criteria groups had to meet before obtaining funding and required the student government to determine which groups received funding, was unconstitutional because it was not viewpoint neutral. Under the new system, the university's student government made funding decisions with little or no oversight. The court further held the criteria used to determine whether a group received funding was too subjective. The university was ordered to establish a viewpoint-neutral funding system. *Fry v. Board of Regents of Univ. of Wisconsin System*, 132 F.Supp.2d 744 (W.D. Wis. 2000).

◆ *The University of California did not violate the First Amendment by barring the use of student fees to campaign against a state ballot initiative.*

The Associated Students of the University of California at Santa Barbara (ASUCSB) opposed a state ballot initiative called Proposition 76. The proposition would have given the governor the power to limit or cut certain appropriations. ASUCSB passed a resolution allocating $1,000 in student funds to print flyers opposing the proposition. The university refused to disburse the funds from the student fee accounts. ASUCSB sued university officials in a federal district court for First Amendment violations.

The court held the organization had no constitutional right to spend student fees on ballot initiative campaigning. **Student fees were public money which belonged to university regents**, and therefore the government. **The decision to withhold the funds did not violate the First Amendment.** A written agreement between student organizations and the university specifically indicated the university's chancellor was empowered to impose and collect student activity fees. In addition, students paying the fees made their checks out to the regents and not to the organizations. University regents, not student organizations, had the power to raise, collect and control the fees. *Associated Students of the Univ. of California at Santa Barbara v. Regents of the Univ. of California*, No. C 05-04352 SI, 2007 WL 196747 (N.D. Cal. 1/23/07).

◆ *The U.S. Supreme Court held a university could not withhold authorization for payments to a printer on behalf of a Christian student organization.*

The University of Virginia collected a mandatory $14 student activity fee from full-time students each semester. The fees supported extracurricular activities that were related to the educational purposes of the university. University-recognized student groups could apply for funding by the activities fund, although not all groups requested funds. University guidelines excluded religious groups from student funding as well as activities that could jeopardize the university's tax-exempt status. A university-recognized student group published a Christian newspaper for which it sought $5,862 from the activities fund for printing costs. The student council denied funding because the group's activities were deemed religious under university guidelines. After exhausting appeals within the university, group members filed a lawsuit in a federal district court, claiming constitutional violations. The court held for the university, and its decision was affirmed by the U.S. Court of Appeals, Fourth Circuit.

The students appealed to the U.S. Supreme Court. The Court observed that **government entities must abstain from regulating speech on the basis of the speaker's opinion**. Upon establishing a limited public forum, state entities must respect the forum by refraining from the exclusion of speech based upon content. **Because the university had opened a limited public forum by paying other third-party contractors on behalf of student groups, it could not deny the religious group's claim for funds on the basis of its viewpoint.** Allowing the payment of the group's printing costs amounted to a policy of government neutrality for different viewpoints. The Court distinguished the student fee from a general tax and placed emphasis on the indirect nature of the benefit. The Court reversed the lower court decisions, ruling that access to public school facilities on a neutral basis does not violate the Establishment Clause of the First Amendment. *Rosenberger v. Rector and Visitors of Univ. of Virginia*, 515 U.S. 819, 115 S.Ct. 2510, 132 L.Ed.2d 700 (1995).

E. Student Elections

◆ *A college president improperly nullified student election results based on a school newspaper's support of a particular slate of candidates.*

The College of Staten Island had two student newspapers, the College Voice and the Banner. Both were funded by student activity fees, and there was no rule barring either from endorsing candidates in student elections. The College Voice published an election issue that actively encouraged voters to choose a particular slate of candidates. The Banner published a more balanced election issue. The election resulted in a victory for candidates endorsed by the College Voice. A student elections committee nullified the results based on the Voice's election issue, saying the electoral process had been compromised. The college president affirmed the decision in a memorandum that called the paper's election issue a "piece of campaign literature." College Voice staff and editors sued college officials in a federal district court for speech rights violations. The court identified a First Amendment violation, but held the president enjoyed qualified immunity from the claims.

On appeal, the U.S. Court of Appeals, Second Circuit, held that student journalists at public colleges operate in limited public forums. **Once a limited public forum is created, an institution cannot take action on the basis of viewpoint without a compelling reason.** In this case, the president had nullified the election based on the paper's viewpoint. As a result, her decision to nullify the election violated the First Amendment. Despite the violation, a question existed as to whether the president had immunity. Even though her conduct violated the law, she could have immunity if it was objectively reasonable for her to believe her actions were lawful. As the lower court had prematurely held the president was entitled to immunity, the case was returned for more proceedings. *Husain v. Springer*, 494 F.3d 108 (2d Cir. 2007).

◆ *A Montana student's constitutional challenge to a university rule limiting campaign spending in student elections failed.*

The student was elected president of the Associated Students of the University of Montana (ASUM). However, he violated an ASUM bylaw that limited candidates from spending more than $100 on their campaigns by spending about $300 on the campaign with his running mate. Although the two were censured, they were allowed to retain their offices. The student exceeded the limit again when he ran for the student senate the next year. This time, he was denied permission to assume office. The student sued university officials in a federal district court, claiming the spending cap violated the Speech Clause of the First Amendment. The district court upheld the cap and ruled against him, finding the spending limitation was reasonable. The student appealed.

The U.S. Court of Appeals, Ninth Circuit, noted that the student had now graduated, but was seeking an order requiring the university to clear all records of disciplinary sanctions based on the spending limit. Therefore, his graduation did not moot the case. **The court held the election was a limited public forum, created by the university to allow students to gain the educational experience of campaigning for a student government position.** Because the election was a limited public forum, the spending limitation was constitutional as long as it was viewpoint neutral and reasonable. The limitation met these requirements, because it did not favor one speaker's message over another's. It was reasonable, as it served the goal of teaching students responsible leadership and behavior. The district court's ruling in favor of university officials was affirmed. *Flint v. Dennison*, 488 F.3d 816 (9th Cir. 2007).

IV. USE OF CAMPUS FACILITIES

A. Students and Student Groups

In a long line of cases, the Supreme Court has devised a "forum analysis" to analyze student speech rights. While public institutions cannot restrict speech in traditional public forums, they may designate areas for expression and limit their use, so long as there is no viewpoint discrimination.

◆ *The U.S. Supreme Court held a California law college could deny official recognition to a Christian student organization that only accepted members who shared the organization's beliefs about religion and sexual orientation.*

Hastings College of Law, a part of the University of California, allowed Registered Student Organizations (RSOs) to use its communication channels, office space and email accounts. To obtain RSO status, student groups had to be non-commercial and comply with a nondiscrimination policy based on state laws prohibiting discrimination on characteristics such as religion and sexual orientation. The Christian Legal Society (CLS) believed that sexual activity should not occur outside marriage between a man and a woman. The CLS excluded students whose religious convictions differed from its Statement of Faith, which espoused Christian tenets. Finding the CLS excluded students from membership based on religion and sexual orientation, Hastings denied the CLS recognition as an RSO. In a federal district court action against Hastings, the CLS asserted speech, religious free exercise and due process violations.

The court found Hastings' policy was reasonable and viewpoint neutral, as did the U.S. Court of Appeals, Ninth Circuit. Appeal reached the U.S. Supreme Court, which rejected the argument that the nondiscrimination policy targeted "groups whose beliefs are based on religion or that disapprove of a particular kind of sexual behavior." Prior Supreme Court decisions permitted some restrictions on limited public forums such as the RSO program. The Court found **the CLS faced only indirect pressure to modify its policies. It could still exclude any person for any reason if it decided to forgo the benefits of RSO recognition.** There was a distinction between policies requiring action and those withholding benefits. While a university may not withhold benefits on the basis of a religious outlook, the policy in this case applied to "all comers." An all-comers requirement helped Hastings "police" its policy without inquiring into an RSO's motivation for membership restrictions. Hastings reasonably adhered to the view that the all-comers policy encouraged tolerance, cooperation and learning among students. Although the CLS could not take advantage of the benefits of RSO status, the Court found that electronic media and social networking sites reduced the importance of RSO channels. As for the CLS's claim that Hastings had no legitimate interest in regulating its membership, the Court found the law school was "caught in the crossfire between a group's desire to exclude and students' demand for equal access." **It was permissible for Hastings to "reasonably draw a line in the sand permitting all organizations to express what they wish but no group to discriminate in membership."** As the Hastings policy did not make distinctions based on a message or perspective, the judgment was affirmed. The Court held the all-comers condition on access to RSO was "textbook viewpoint neutral." *Christian Legal Society Chapter of the Univ. of California, Hastings College of Law v. Martinez*, 130 S.Ct. 2971 (U.S. 2010).

◆ *A Texas college could not halt students from participating in a demonstration staged by "Students for Concealed Carry on Campus" (SCCC).*

The SCCC promoted "empty-holster protests" to prompt changes in laws and college rules to allow concealed handguns on campuses. Tarrant County College District (TCC) limited student protests to a "free speech zone." To hold a protest there, students had to ask for permission at least 24 hours in advance. Two SCCC student leaders sued TCC in a federal district court for speech rights violations. The court held TCC interfered with their rights to speak in public by requiring a permit and limiting protests to the free speech zone. TCC could not enforce those rules. TCC removed the permit requirement from its manual and eliminated the free speech zone. It added new rules banning disruptive activities and on-campus speech that was "co-sponsored" by off-campus organizations. The court struck down these rules and held TCC must let students wear empty holsters in classrooms. **Student speech – which includes wearing something to symbolically communicate a message – can be restricted in classrooms only if the restriction is viewpoint neutral, furthers a substantial governmental interest, is unrelated to suppressing student speech, and does not overly restrict protective activities.**

While TCC could ban speech-making and leafleting in classes and halls, it could not show that the wearing of empty holsters was "inherently" disruptive. The court struck TCC's co-sponsorship rule, finding it could not prohibit speech for being affiliated with an off-campus group. *Smith v. Tarrant County College Dist.*, 694 F.Supp.2d 610 (N.D. Tex. 2010).

◆ *California state universities could validly refuse to recognize student groups that did not comply with their nondiscrimination policies.*

San Diego State University and Long Beach State University have nondiscrimination policies barring official recognition of student groups that discriminate on stated grounds, including religion and sexual orientation. Each student group must sign paperwork indicating that it will abide by the policy. Four Christian student groups required their members to be Christians and frowned on homosexuality. They sued state university officials in a federal district court for First Amendment violations. The court found the student organization program was a limited public forum in which any restrictions on speech had to be viewpoint-neutral and reasonable. The policies furthered a legitimate state interest in providing students a chance to participate in a range of opportunities. Any restriction caused by the policy was reasonable and did not violate First Amendment association rights. **Agreeing with the universities, the court found the policy regulated conduct, not speech.** The universities did not compel speech or regulate a viewpoint. The court noted that the Free Exercise Clause is not violated by a neutral policy of general application. This is true even when a restriction bars conduct that is called for by a person's religion or burdens a religious practice. The universities had a rational basis for the policy. There was no equal protection violation, as the groups did not show they were singled out for different treatment from other groups. The court held for the universities. *Every Nation Campus Ministries at San Diego State Univ. v. Achtenberg*, 597 F.Supp.2d 1075 (S.D. Cal. 2009).

◆ *Arizona State University (ASU) did not violate the Constitution by strictly limiting the amount of space student groups could use for events.*

ASU Students for Life is a pro-life student organization. It sought ASU's permission to display pro-life messages on panels measuring eight feet by 16 feet. Student groups could reserve one of 40 available outdoor zones, but ASU policy barred any one group from reserving more than one zone at a time. Because of the size of the exhibit, ASU Students for Life asked for permission to reserve 16 zones. The request was denied due to the one-zone policy. ASU told the group that a $300 fee and proof of insurance was necessary because the panels were obtained from an off-campus entity. The group sued ASU officials in a federal district court, claiming ASU policies violated its speech and equal protection rights. The court held that the restrictions placed on the group did not violate any speech or equal protection rights. **ASU's outdoor zones were** a limited public forum where ASU could impose restrictions that were reasonable and content-neutral. The insurance and one-zone requirements were content-neutral, since they were not applied to the group based on the message they sought to convey. ASU was awarded pretrial judgment. *ASU Students for Life v. Crow*, No. CV 06-1824-PHX-MHM, 2008 WL 686946 (D. Ariz. 3/10/08).

◆ *A New York university did not violate a fraternity's association rights by declining to recognize it as a student group because it refused to admit females.*

Chi Iota Colony is a fraternity devoted to community service and the expression of Jewish culture. It does not admit women, claiming that to do so would make it impossible to achieve and maintain the congeniality, cohesion and stability that enabled it to function. This conflicted with the university's nondiscrimination policy, which provided that student groups could not gain recognition unless they refrained from discriminating on the basis of gender.

The university rejected the fraternity's application to become an officially recognized student group. The fraternity sued the university in a federal district court for violating its First Amendment association rights. The court held the fraternity qualified as an "intimate association." Forcing it to admit females would burden its associational rights. The university appealed to the U.S. Court of Appeals, Second Circuit, which held the fraternity's interest in intimacy did not merit strict scrutiny. It placed no limit on membership size, and many Jewish men who expressed an interest in the fraternity were invited to join. The fraternity's purposes were inclusive, and it allowed non-members to attend some functions. **The college had a strong interest in assuring its resources were available to all students.** As the district court applied the wrong standard, its order was vacated. *Chi Iota Colony of Alpha Epsilon Pi Fraternity v. City Univ. of New York*, 502 F.3d 136 (2d Cir. 2007).

◆ *A student Christian organization obtained a preliminary order preventing a law school from revoking its official status.*

The dean of an Illinois law school revoked the official student organization status of the Christian Legal Society (CLS) because the organization excluded those who engaged in or affirmed homosexual conduct. The dean found the tenets of the national CLS violated the university's affirmative action/equal opportunity (EEO) policy. That policy said that the university would provide equal employment and education opportunities for all qualified people without regard to sexual orientation. All recognized student organizations had to comply with federal or state nondiscrimination laws. The CLS sued the university in a federal district court for First Amendment violations. The court denied its request for an order requiring the university to restore its official status. The CLS appealed to the U.S. Court of Appeals, Seventh Circuit.

The court found it unclear whether the CLS had violated any university policy. **It was likely that the university impermissibly infringed on the CLS's right of expressive association, and its speech rights.** The university failed to identify which federal or state law it believed the CLS had violated. CLS membership requirements did not exclude members on the basis of sexual orientation. Rather, the organization required members to adhere to certain standards of sexual conduct. **The university's affirmative action/EEO policy**

did not apply to CLS because the organization did not employ anyone. The court reversed the judgment and granted the CLS its requested order. *Christian Legal Society v. Walker*, 453 F.3d 853 (7th Cir. 2006).

◆ *A Texas state university policy that was used to prohibit students from distributing pro-life leaflets was held unconstitutional.*

The university policy required each organization handing out leaflets to include the organization's name on the leaflets. A student anti-abortion group distributed leaflets on campus without stating its name. The university attempted to prohibit members from passing out the leaflets. They sued the university in a federal district court, alleging the policy unconstitutionally restricted anonymous speech in a designated public forum. The court held the policy was unconstitutional, and the university appealed.

The U.S. Court of Appeals, Fifth Circuit, noted the Supreme Court has held anonymous pamphleteering is a form of advocacy that exemplifies the purpose behind the First Amendment. However, the right to anonymous speech on a public street differs from that of a student on the campus of a public university. Public universities can and typically do restrict access to campus facilities. Students often must identify themselves to university officials before they can use campus facilities. The Fifth Circuit held that on-campus speech is almost never totally anonymous. The university contended the policy served a significant state interest by preserving the campus for speech by students, faculty and staff. The students argued the university permitted non-affiliated people to speak anonymously on campus and hold anonymous signs. **The court agreed, and held the policy was too far-reaching, as it required the speaker to identify him or herself to every person receiving literature.** As the policy required speakers to sacrifice more anonymity than needed, the court affirmed the judgment. *Justice for All v. Faulkner*, 410 F.3d 760 (5th Cir. 2005).

◆ *Where a Washington college allowed secular demonstrations, it could not place restrictions on a demonstration based on religion.*

The dean of a community college allowed an anti-abortion demonstration on campus. His office received a number of complaints, leading him to ask campus security to remove the demonstrators. When they refused to leave, police were called, and a demonstrator was arrested. He later sued the dean and the head of campus security under 42 U.S.C. § 1983 for violating his First Amendment rights. A federal court granted pretrial judgment to the defendants, but the Ninth Circuit Court of Appeals reversed the judgment. The court held a **"no religious instruction or worship" condition imposed by the college dean violated the First Amendment as a content-based restriction on speech**. Only if that restriction was necessary to achieve a compelling state interest, and was narrowly designed to accomplish that interest, would it be constitutional. The court also held that the dean was not entitled to immunity under Section 1983 because he should have known that placing the "no religion" restriction on the demonstration violated the First Amendment. There also was a question of fact, requiring a trial, as to whether the security head was entitled to immunity. *Orin v. Barclay*, 272 F.3d 1207 (9th Cir. 2001).

◆   *Student rights to association may not be disregarded or limited.*

A group of students desired to form a local chapter of Students for a Democratic Society (SDS) at a state-supported college. They were, however, denied recognition as a campus organization. The students sued for declaratory and injunctive relief. A federal district court held the college's refusal to recognize the group, in light of the disruptive and violent nature of the national organization, was justifiable. The U.S. Court of Appeals for the Second Circuit affirmed, stating that the students had failed to avail themselves of the due process of law accorded to them and had failed to meet their burden of complying with the prevailing standards for recognition.

The U.S. Supreme Court held that **the lower courts erred in disregarding the First Amendment interest in freedom of association that the students had in furthering their personal beliefs**. It also held that putting the burden on the students (to show entitlement to recognition) rather than on the president (to justify nonrecognition) was also in error. The Court stated that insofar as the denial of recognition was based on the group's affiliation with the national SDS, or as a result of disagreement with the group's philosophy, the president's decision violated the students' First Amendment rights. A proper basis for nonrecognition might have been that the group refused to comply with a rule requiring them to abide by reasonable campus regulations. Since it was not clear that the college had such a rule, and whether the students intended to observe it, the case was remanded to the district court for resolution. *Healy v. James*, 408 U.S. 169, 92 S.Ct. 2338, 33 L.Ed.2d 266 (1972).

◆   *The Establishment Clause does not prevent private citizens from using public facilities for religious purposes.*

The University of Missouri at Kansas City, a state university, made its facilities available for the general use of registered student groups. A registered student religious group that had previously received permission to conduct its meetings in university facilities was informed that it could no longer do so because of a university regulation that prohibited use of its facilities for the purposes of religious worship or teaching. Members of the group sued in federal court, alleging that the regulation violated their First Amendment rights to free exercise of religion and freedom of speech. The court upheld the school's regulation, but the U.S. Court of Appeals, Eighth Circuit, reversed, stating that the regulation was discriminatory against religious speech and that the Establishment Clause does not bar a policy of equal access.

The Supreme Court agreed with the court of appeals' assessment, stating **that the university policy violated the fundamental principle that state regulation of speech must be content-neutral**. It is obligatory upon the state to show that the regulation is necessary to serve a compelling state interest and that it is narrowly drawn to achieve that end. The state was unable to do that here. The state's interest in achieving greater separation of church and state than is already ensured under the Establishment Clause was not sufficiently "compelling" to justify content-based discrimination against religious speech of the student group in question. *Widmar v. Vincent*, 454 U.S. 263, 102 S.Ct. 269, 70 L.Ed.2d 400 (1981).

B. Commercial Speech

◆   *The Supreme Court has held that restrictions on commercial free speech need not be subjected to as rigorous an analysis to determine the restrictions' reasonableness. As long as the restriction is reasonable, it will be upheld.*

The State University of New York (SUNY) prohibited private commercial enterprises from operating in SUNY facilities. Campus police prevented a housewares manufacturer from demonstrating and selling its products at a party hosted in a student dormitory. The manufacturer and a group of students sued SUNY in a federal district court, stating that the policy violated the First Amendment. The court held for SUNY, stating that the student dormitories did not constitute a public forum for purposes of commercial activity, and the restrictions were reasonable in light of the dormitories' purpose. The Second Circuit Court of Appeals reversed, stating that it was unclear whether the policy directly advanced SUNY's interest and whether it was the least restrictive means of achieving that interest. The U.S. Supreme Court granted review and stated that the court of appeals erred in requiring the district court to apply a least restrictive means test. The Court stated that **regulations on commercial speech require only a reasonable "fit" between the government's ends and the means chosen to accomplish those ends**. The Court reversed and remanded the case. *Board of Trustees of the State Univ. of New York v. Fox*, 492 U.S. 469, 109 S.Ct. 3028, 106 L.Ed.2d 388 (1989).

◆   *A student newspaper lost its First Amendment challenge to a Pennsylvania statute sanctioning businesses that advertise alcohol in any school publication.*

The Pitt News filed suit seeking to prevent the enforcement of "Act 199," a 1996 amendment to the state's liquor code that sanctioned advertisers of alcohol products in school newspapers. The U.S. Court of Appeals, Third Circuit, ruled that the newspaper could not sue because it could not demonstrate that its constitutional rights were being violated, and it could not sue on behalf of third parties. **The paper's loss of advertising revenue and subsequent decrease in the length of the publication did not demonstrate that its First Amendment rights were violated.** *The Pitt News v. Fisher*, 215 F.3d 354 (3d Cir. 2000), *cert. denied*, 121 S.Ct. 857 (U.S. 2001).

◆   *A university did not have to allow the KKK to underwrite a radio program.*

A not-for-profit public broadcast radio station operated by the University of Missouri (and a member of National Public Radio) received a request from the state coordinator for the Ku Klux Klan to underwrite a number of 15-second spots on the station's "All Things Considered" program. This would require the station to acknowledge the gift by reading a message from the Klan stating that it was a white Christian organization standing up for the rights and values of white Christians and leaving contact information.

The university's chancellor decided that allowing the underwriting would result in a loss of revenue to the station of at least $5 million, and rejected the offer. The state coordinator and the Klan sued the station manager, asserting that the station could not reject the offer because it was a public forum, and could not discriminate by viewpoint. The U.S. District Court for the Eastern

District of Missouri held that **the station did not have to accept the Klan's offer to underwrite "All Things Considered." The station's employees had the discretion to choose which underwriting offers to accept, and the underwriting program could not be deemed a public forum.** Further, the decision to reject the offer was not based on viewpoint but on business considerations. The court granted pretrial judgment to the station manager. The Eighth Circuit Court of Appeals affirmed. It noted that the underwriting spots constituted governmental speech and that the government could exercise discretion over what it chose to say. Since the station had the right to reject the proposed spots, the Klan's lawsuit could not succeed. *KKK v. Bennett*, 203 F.3d 1085 (8th Cir. 2000).

C. Non-Student Groups

◆   *The University of North Dakota (UND) did not violate speech rights by placing restrictions on how individuals can solicit petition signatures.*

UND's code of student life required completing a "special events form" for on-campus events and before soliciting petition signatures in student housing. Petitioners had to sit at designated tables and wait for students to come to them. UND policy prohibited signature collectors from harassing, embarrassing or intimidating people. A group of solicitors obtained UND's permission to collect signatures on campus sidewalks and lawns and inside campus buildings. But a student manager told the group that it could not seek signatures in the building unless the solicitors agreed to stay behind designated tables. One of the solicitors sued UND in a state court for First Amendment violations.

The court held for UND, and the solicitor appealed to the Supreme Court of North Dakota. It rejected the solicitor's claim that he should not have been required to gain UND permission before seeking signatures on UND property. **The First Amendment did not guarantee the solicitor an unrestricted right to use campus property to gather signatures.** Expressive activity on government property is subject to time, place and manner restrictions. UND's policy was content neutral and narrowly tailored to serve the goals of aiding in event planning, protecting the safety of UND property and people on campus, and making sure facilities were used appropriately. UND's ban on harassing, embarrassing or intimidating people asked to sign a petition did not violate the First Amendment. *Riemers v. State*, 767 N.W.2d 832 (N.D. 2009).

◆   *The U.S. Supreme Court held a federal law requiring higher education institutions to provide equal access to military recruiters or forfeit certain federal funding did not violate school speech or association rights.*

Congress enacted the Solomon Amendment to address restrictions put on military recruiting by law schools that disagreed with the U.S. government's policy on homosexuals in the military. The amendment disqualified institutions of higher learning from receiving certain federal funds, if any part of an institution denied access to military recruiters that was equal to that provided other recruiters. An association of law schools and faculties sued the U.S. government in a federal district court, asserting the Solomon Amendment violated the schools' First Amendment speech and association rights. The association claimed the amendment unconstitutionally required law schools to choose between federal funding and their speech and association rights. The court denied the association's request for a preliminary order against enforcement of the Amendment. Congress took note of the court's finding that the law could be interpreted as allowing schools to promote nondiscrimination policies by limiting military recruiting to undergraduate campuses. It amended the law to require "equal access" for military recruiters. Meanwhile, the association appealed to the U.S. Court of Appeals, Third Circuit. The court held the Solomon Amendment regulated speech, and it reversed the decision.

On appeal, the U.S. Supreme Court explained that the First Amendment protects rights of association, as well as free speech. The law schools "associated" with military recruiters only in the sense of their interactions with them. The Solomon Amendment forbade higher education institutions from applying their general nondiscrimination policies to military recruiters. Law schools had to provide the military the same access they provided to all other employment recruiters. The broad power of Congress to provide for defense included the authority to require campus access for military recruiters. Congress was free to attach reasonable conditions to federal funding. The Solomon Amendment regulated conduct, not speech. Law schools remained free to express their views on government policy while remaining eligible for federal funds. As there was no restriction on speech, the Amendment did not place unconstitutional conditions on receiving federal funds. The Court held the Solomon Amendment did not force the schools to associate with the military by granting it equal access. Students and faculty remained free to associate and voice their disapproval of the military's message, and the Court reversed the judgment. *Rumsfeld v. Forum for Academic and Institutional Rights*, 547 U.S. 47 (2006).

◆ *A California college policy requiring individuals to receive permission before distributing literature on campus violated the First Amendment.*

A member of Jews for Jesus distributed flyers at a San Francisco college campus. On several occasions, he left the campus after employees told him he could not distribute materials on campus because he did not have a permit. After the member was arrested for again distributing literature on campus, his group sued the college in a federal district court for speech rights violations.

The court noted college regulations governing on-campus solicitations required outside organizations and individuals to get prior permission before distributing literature on campus. They also required prior submission of the literature to the college for review, and they limited distribution to a designated campus plaza. After the lawsuit was filed, the college amended its regulations by omitting the prior approval requirement and requiring only that outsiders sign in to notify the college dean of their presence on campus. **The court explained that a requirement that an individual get advance permission to engage in expressive activities is an unconstitutional prior restraint on speech.** The old regulations wrongfully allowed college officials to review literature before it was distributed and gave them full discretion to deny permission to distribute it. Reasonable time, place and manner restrictions are valid, but the evidence in this case did not show whether the designation of a particular location was permissible. Under the new regulations, outside organizations and individuals could not be denied access to distribute literature or engage in other expressive activities in the designated location due to failure to obtain a permit. The new regulations removed the permit requirement, making the request for preliminary relief moot. *Jews for Jesus v. City College of San Francisco*, No. C 08-03876 MHP, 2009 WL 86703 (N.D. Cal. 1/12/09).

◆ *A New York community college lacked a right to regulate the use of its premises by outsiders because it failed to have a policy on facilities use.*

An ordained Baptist minister videotaped himself preaching and handing out religious leaflets on the campus of a New York community college. He was in an outdoor area where students often congregate. A student complained to the assistant dean for administrative services, who asked the minister to stop the videotaping. He refused. The dean then called police, who arrested the minister and charged him with criminal trespass. The charge was later dismissed, but he was cited for simple trespass. The minister sued the college and dean in a federal court for First Amendment violations. **The court explained that the right of a college to limit access depends on the nature of the forum.** If an area is designated as a place for public expression, then speech regulation needs to be "narrowly tailored to serve a significant government interest."

In this case, the college had no regulation authorizing the minister's removal. He had a First Amendment right to preach, hand out leaflets and videotape himself. His conduct did not obstruct the flow of people or vehicles in the area and did not create a disruption. Despite the violation, the Eleventh Amendment barred the minister's claims against the college, which was a state government unit. However, the dean could be sued in his official capacity for equitable relief. *Davis v. Stratton*, 575 F.Supp.2d 410 (N.D.N.Y. 2008).

◆ *An Indiana university did not violate the First Amendment when it prohibited a traveling evangelist from preaching on its campus.*

Traveling preacher James Gilles appeared in public places and preached for many years. His confrontational style led to disturbances, and he was arrested many times. In 2001, Gilles began preaching at Vincennes University without an invitation to be on the campus. His preaching led to a disturbance, and campus police asked him to leave. Following that incident, the university adopted a new policy requiring prior approval by the dean of students for all sales and solicitations on campus. Approved solicitors could solicit only on a walkway in front of the student union. Gilles sued university officials in a federal district court, claiming the policy violated his right to free speech. The court granted summary judgment against him, and he appealed.

The U.S. Court of Appeals, Seventh Circuit, held **public universities are not required to make all their facilities equally available to students and non-students. As owners of public property, public universities have the right to ensure the property is used only for lawfully dedicated purposes.** The university had the right to bar access to any outsider, as long as the exclusion was not based on the content of the speaker's message. In this case, the university had placed the area where Gilles sought to speak completely off limits to those who were not invited by a faculty member or student group.

Confining solicitors to the walkway in front of the student union was reasonable. Because the university could lawfully bar uninvited guests from using a particular area to speak, the district court's ruling was affirmed. *Gilles v. Blanchard*, 477 F.3d 466 (7th Cir. 2007).

◆ *A federal appeals court reinstated a traveling preacher's claim that a university violated his due process and speech rights.*

James Gilles, the evangelist described in the case above, spoke on the campus of Miami University for about 45 minutes before being interrupted by a security guard who threatened to arrest him if he did not obtain permission to speak on campus. A university policy stated that anyone with "legitimate business" had "the privilege of free access" to public areas of the university's buildings and grounds during times when they were open. The university informed Gilles his speech was not "legitimate business" and that its policy was to permit formal speeches only when the speaker was invited by the school or a recognized student organization. After trying without success to get an invitation to speak, Gilles sued the university in a federal district court for speech and due process violations. The court dismissed his complaint.

On appeal, the U.S. Court of Appeals, Sixth Circuit, noted that the university did not maintain a written policy requiring an invitation to speak. Nor was the policy well understood by the university officials who had the duty to enforce it. **In addition, the policy had no standards by which requests for permission to speak were to be evaluated.** The policy was vulnerable to a due process claim. Because the policy was so ill-defined, the court held it was improper to dismiss the speech claim at this stage. Although the speech claim was "improbable" and recovery was unlikely, the court found dismissal of the claim was premature. The case was remanded for further proceedings. *Gilles v. Garland*, 281 Fed.Appx. 501 (6th Cir. 2008).

◆ *Faculty members at Yale Law School failed to show their rights were violated by the Solomon Amendment.*

Yale Law School faculty members claimed the Solomon Amendment conflicted with Yale's nondiscrimination policy. Accordingly, the school prohibited military interview programs. When the military warned Yale that it could lose federal funding by denying access, Yale exempted military recruiters from its nondiscrimination policy. Members of the law school faculty then sued the Secretary of Defense, claiming the Solomon Amendment violated their First Amendment rights of freedom of speech and freedom of association. After the district court agreed, the U.S. Supreme Court held the Solomon Amendment does not violate the First Amendment in *Rumsfeld v. Forum for Academic and Institutional Rights*, above. With the benefit of that ruling, the Second Circuit Court of Appeals then considered an appeal in the Yale case.

The court held the Supreme Court most likely intended its ruling to include rejection of an academic freedom claim. Even if it did not, **the Solomon Amendment did not restrict the content of teaching or membership of teachers in organizations**. The claim that the amendment violated a right to academic freedom was indirect and speculative. The Second Circuit rejected the claim that the Solomon Amendment violated First Amendment rights to boycott recruiters, noting that the faculty members remained free to disassociate themselves from the recruiters in other ways. The Second Circuit reversed the district court's decision and ordered that judgment be entered in favor of the Secretary of Defense. *Burt v. Gates*, 502 F.3d 183 (2d Cir. 2007).

♦ *A federal district court dismissed a lawsuit filed against a Pennsylvania university by a traveling preacher.*

The preacher came to the university to preach and hand out literature regarding his beliefs on religion and abortion. He was not invited or sponsored, and he failed to comply with a written university policy that required him to register with the university at least two hours in advance. A university official and police chief warned the preacher he could not continue with his activities, but he refused to leave campus. As a result, he was issued a citation for criminal trespass. The preacher sued the university and university officials in a federal district court for violation of his First Amendment rights and his rights to due process and equal protection.

The university then instituted a new, more permissive policy regarding expressive activities on campus. The new policy removed the two-hour registration requirement and allowed non-sponsored presentations and demonstrations as long as they did not "disrupt the normal operation of the university or infringe on the rights of other members of the university community." The court noted the preacher's claims for injunctive and declaratory relief were based on a policy that had been replaced. **Because the new policy provided the preacher all the relief he sought, the court dismissed the case.** *Marcavage v. West Chester Univ.*, No. 06-CV-910, 2007 WL 789430 (E.D. Pa. 3/15/07).

CHAPTER FIVE

Employment

I. BREACH OF CONTRACT

Breach of contract claims arise from written contracts, academic custom and usage, faculty handbooks and reliance on written and oral statements implying or modifying an employment contract.

A. Written Contracts

◆ *A New Hampshire community college did not violate the constitutional rights of an adjunct professor when it declined to hire him on a full-time basis.*

According to the professor, the community college retaliated against him for accusing it of not providing sufficient services to students with disabilities. After he made this charge, he said the college violated his due process and equal protection rights by failing to renew his contract. He asserted that the college wrongly refused to hire him as a full-time faculty member. The professor added state law fraud and whistleblowers' protection act claims.

A federal magistrate recommended dismissal of the complaint. **The due process claims failed because the professor did not show he had any property interest in the renewal of his contract.** There was no "promise, policy, rule or practice" entitling him to contract renewal. The equal protection claim failed because the professor did not claim he was treated differently than

187

any similarly situated person. And the retaliation claim failed because he did not present any facts linking his complaints to the nonrenewal of his contract and refusals to hire him for a full-time job. Having rejected the federal claims, the court declined to exercise jurisdiction over the remaining state law claims. *Coleman v. Great Bay Community College*, No. 09-cv-161-SM, 2009 WL 3698398 (D.N.H. 10/30/09).

◆ *A librarian failed to show a Texas university breached its employment contract with her or constructively discharged her from employment.*

The university hired the librarian in 1972 and granted her tenure on the faculty of the library in 1981. Things went smoothly until the university hired a new library director in 1987. The director was not satisfied with the librarian's work performance, and he reassigned some of her duties. In 1993, the director and another official documented the librarian's alleged history of "low quality and quantity of work," rude behavior toward staff and the public, and excessive absenteeism. The director changed the librarian's title, and she complained that he had demoted her. The librarian requested retirement, then sued the university, director and another official in the state court system for breaching her employment contract and constructive discharge. The court held a trial. It refused to instruct the jury to consider the question of breach. Instead, it focused the jury on constructive discharge. The jury found for the university.

On appeal, the state court of appeals found the jury had received improper instructions and reversed the judgment. The university appealed to the Supreme Court of Texas, which reinstated the verdict. Although the librarian claimed she was demoted in breach of her contract, there was no evidence that she ever held any job other than as a tenured librarian. Her contract with the university did not specify any particular job functions. Nor did the librarian show she was constructively discharged from employment. **Constructive discharge does not take place merely because job assignments have changed. Instead, an employee must show she was subjected to unendurable working conditions.** As the librarian did not show this, the court reversed the judgment. *Baylor Univ. v. Coley*, 221 S.W.3d 599 (Tex. 2007).

◆ *Ohio State University (OSU) failed to negate a multi-million dollar verdict for a former basketball coach who was fired for loaning money to a recruit.*

The coach was a former national coach of the year. He began recruiting a seven-foot, three-inch player from the Republic of Serbia who was playing at a community college. The coach learned the recruit had played professionally in Europe. Although the coach knew this made the recruit ineligible to play for OSU, he continued to recruit him in hopes that the NCAA would allow him a waiver. The coach had an assistant deliver $6,000 to the recruit's family.

The recruit never enrolled at OSU, but when the coach disclosed the loan, he was fired for violating NCAA rules and a contract term requiring him to "run a clean and compliant program." The coach sued OSU in a state court for breach of contract. At the time of trial, the NCAA had opened an investigation but had not yet reached any conclusion. The court held the coach breached his contract by making the loan but found the breach was not "material" and did not justify discharge. It rendered a verdict for the coach and entered a judgment for nearly $2.5 million. On appeal, **the Court of Appeals of Ohio held the contract could be terminated only under specific conditions, none of which had occurred at the time OSU acted**. Although the loan could have constituted a material breach of contract if the NCAA determined it was a major infraction of its rules, OSU reached its own conclusion before the NCAA had finished its investigation. The trial court's finding that the loan did not substantially harm OSU was supported by the evidence, and the court affirmed the judgment. *O'Brien v. Ohio State Univ.*, No. 06AP-946, 2007 WL 2729077 (Ohio Ct. App. 9/20/07). The state supreme court denied review in *O'Brien v. Ohio State Univ.*, 117 Ohio St.3d 1406, 881 N.E.2d 274 (Ohio 2008).

◆   *The U.S. Court of Appeals, Third Circuit, held a Pennsylvania college did not breach a professor's employment contract by discharging her.*

The college hired the professor to be its Director of Athletics and Professor and Head of Physical Education and Athletics. She continued to work after her initial 2.5 year term and received salary letters advising her of annual increases. The college faculty handbook provided further guidance as to the terms and conditions of employment for faculty members. The college later discharged the professor, stating it believed the athletic department needed new leadership. It notified her a year and a half before the termination was to be effective. Assuming she was tenured, the professor tried to appeal the decision. The college president refused to accept the professor's claim she was tenured. He explained that she had never been tenured, but instead the professor served at the pleasure of the president as stated in her appointment letter.

The professor wrote to the president again and requested a hearing before a faculty tenure review appeals committee. The president denied the request, and the professor sued the college in a federal district court for breach of contract. **The court noted the professor's appointment letter clearly provided that the term of her position is "at the pleasure of the President of the College." This language expressly negated any possibility of tenured status as a faculty member.** The professor argued the words "at the pleasure of the president" referred only to her role as athletics director and department head. The court disagreed. It said the professor's attempt to interpret her letter as stating she was entitled to tenure was an attempt to create ambiguity where there was none. The court found the language was unambiguous and dismissed the case. *Atkinson v. Lafayette College*, 460 F.3d 447 (3d Cir. 2006).

◆   *A South Carolina faculty member could not sue a university for missing office items after he signed a release agreeing not to file further claims.*

The university suspended the faculty member after a student filed a sexual harassment complaint against him. The faculty member was instructed to leave the campus immediately and was not allowed to return pending a criminal investigation. He left behind several volumes of his private library in his locked office, along with teaching materials, maps, and personal mementos. After the faculty member was acquitted of the criminal charge he sued the university, alleging it wrongfully suspended him. The parties settled the case through mediation. Under the terms of the agreement, the faculty member released the university of any claims arising out of his employment and retained tenure.

The faculty member returned to the university and discovered his property was gone. The university never located the missing items, and he sued it in a state court for negligence. The court determined the release was comprehensive and dismissed the action. The faculty member appealed to the state court of appeals. It held **a valid release barred subsequent claims arising from the same circumstances, even if the parties may not have intended to release a specific claim**. The court held the release in this case clearly precluded future claims arising out the faculty member's employment. *Abu-Shawareb v. South Carolina State Univ.*, 613 S.E.2d 757 (S.C. Ct. App. 2004).

◆ *A Colorado state college followed appropriate procedures in terminating an employee's position when it became unable to fund it.*

A certified employee held a classified position under the state personnel system. His position did not receive regular state funding, and when special funding and interim funds were exhausted, the college eliminated it and dismissed him. An administrative law judge held the decision was not arbitrary or an abuse of discretion, and the state personnel board agreed. The employee appealed to the Court of Appeals of Colorado, which stated reorganizations and layoffs involve practical and financial concerns.

There are no credibility determinations to be made in terminating an employee based on a lack of funds. In contrast, disciplinary terminations do require credibility determinations and require the employer to act on the basis of "merit and fairness." The court held the employee lacked a property interest in his abolished position. **Although a public employee has a continued interest in employment, there can be no reasonable expectation that a position will never be abolished.** The human resources manager who processed the layoff complied with a statutory layoff matrix based on classification structure, employment history, performance evaluations, and veteran status. As there was no error in the board's order, the court affirmed it. *Velasquez v. Dep't of Higher Educ.*, 93 P.3d 540 (Colo. Ct. App. 2003). The Supreme Court of Colorado refused to consider an appeal. *Velasquez v. Dep't of Higher Educ.*, 2004 WL 1375406 (Colo. 2004).

◆ *Despite some procedural irregularities, a board of trustees could vote not to renew a college president's contract.*

A Texas college hired a president under a three-year contract, which contained an option for a three-year extension. Toward the end of the initial term, the board of trustees met by teleconference and voted not to renew the president's contract. He was given notice of the non-renewal in compliance with the terms of his contract. He then sued the college for breach of contract, asserting that the termination notice was invalid because the vote against renewing his contract occurred at a meeting that was not called in compliance with the college's bylaws. A state court granted pretrial judgment to the college, and the Texas Court of Appeals affirmed. Even though the teleconference was called in an irregular manner, that was insufficient to void the board's decision not to renew the president's contract. **Although the board's actions at that meeting were voidable, they could be ratified (and**

were) at a later meeting. Further, the president lacked standing to challenge the procedural violations. The president was not able to regain his job. *Swain v. Wiley College*, 74 S.W.3d 143 (Tex. Ct. App. 2002).

◆ *A doctor who signed a non-compete agreement could violate it where he was not harming the university's legitimate business interests.*

A Florida university hospital employed a doctor who signed a noncompete agreement stating that he would not engage in a "community-based clinical practice within a radius of 50 miles" of the university hospital for a two-year period following his employment. After leaving the university, the doctor began working in a community-based clinical practice within 50 miles of the university hospital. The university sued, seeking to enforce the noncompete agreement. The doctor argued that he was not causing irreparable injury to the university hospital's "legitimate business interests," because no former patients of the university hospital followed him to his current practice. A Florida court found that the doctor violated the terms of the non-compete agreement but that his new practice did not interfere with the university hospital's legitimate business interests.

On appeal, the Florida District Court of Appeal affirmed the judgment. Since **none of the doctor's former patients were receiving treatment from him,** and since his current practice was not attempting to recruit prospective university patients, the court refused to enforce the agreement. *Univ. of Florida, Board of Trustees v. Sanal*, 837 So.2d 512 (Fla. Dist. Ct. App. 2003).

◆ *In the absence of approval by University of Louisiana trustees, a coach who sought a promotion to athletic director had no claim against the system.*

The men's basketball coach for Northwestern State University (NSU) also sought the athletic director (AD) position when the AD announced his retirement. The coach was informed of a plan to name him athletic director/head basketball coach. The university president sent a letter to the coach outlining the plan, but noting that it would not be official until approved by the Board of Trustees for the University of Louisiana System. The board never approved the appointment of the coach to the AD position. When the president retired and an acting president was appointed, the acting president initiated a nationwide search for a new AD and invited the coach to apply. The coach instead sued the board for breach of contract and detrimental reliance.

A Louisiana trial court ruled in favor of the board, finding no contract existed. The court determined that since the board of trustees never approved the change in positions, no contract was ever formed. It also rejected the coach's contention that he turned down a job offer to be athletic director at the University of South Alabama because he had been promised the same position at NSU. The only evidence offered in support of this position was a letter from Southern Alabama's AD stating what the contract terms would be if the coach were offered a position. This letter was not a job offer. **Because the coach could not establish a contract or that he relied on a promise made by NSU to his detriment, he failed to establish a case** under state law, and the university was entitled to a judgment in its favor. The trial court decision was affirmed. *Barnett v. Board of Trustees*, 809 So.2d 184 (La. Ct. App. 2001).

B. Handbooks

◆ *A state court vacated Western Washington University's decision to suspend a professor because it should not have held a closed disciplinary hearing.*

Soon after the university awarded tenure to the professor, he began to accumulate complaints about verbally abusive behavior toward students, staff members and faculty members. He was repeatedly admonished for making demeaning, inappropriate comments about women, gay students and minorities, and for misconduct including carrying a knife in class. This conduct was tolerated for years, but the university eventually suspended the professor pending a hearing to consider charges that he violated the faculty code of ethics. At a closed hearing, the university suspended him for two quarters.

After a state court rejected his request for review, the professor appealed. The Court of Appeals of Washington held the faculty code of ethics was not unconstitutionally vague. Officials described the kind of conduct considered to be unacceptable, but the professor ignored their warnings. University discipline did not unduly restrict academic freedom. Most of the conduct for which discipline was imposed had nothing to do with instruction. However, the university violated the state administrative procedure act (APA) by closing the disciplinary hearing to the public. Under the APA, hearings must be open unless a provision of law authorizes secrecy. The court held a university handbook provision governing hearings was not a "provision of law" under the APA. Instead, it was a private contract between professors and the university. **Internal policies and directives generally do not create law.** Because the university violated the APA by closing the hearing, the court vacated the board's decision and returned the matter to the university for a new hearing. *Mills v. Western Washington Univ.*, 150 Wash.App. 260, 208 P.3d 13 (Wash. Ct. App. 2009). Review was denied in *Mills v. Western Washington Univ.*, 167 Wash.2d 1020, 225 P.3d 1011 (Wash. 2010).

◆ *Two California professors were entitled to a trial to consider if a Christian college discharged them based on marital status.*

The professors taught in the marriage and family counseling department of the college, which was affiliated with the Church of Christ. The church looked to the Bible as its ultimate constitution and required professors to accept the Bible as the word of God. The professors' teaching contracts indicated they were to comply with the faculty handbook. The handbook also stated that faculty members should conduct their on- and off-campus activities and relationships in a Christ-like manner. One of the professors filed for divorce, and a rumor circulated that he was having an affair with the other professor. The dean asked the divorcing professor to step down from his chair position but allowed him to keep teaching. When the professors announced their wedding, the college refused to renew their teaching contracts.

Both professors sued the college in a state court, alleging discrimination on the basis of marital status and breach of their continuing contracts. The court denied the college's request for summary judgment. **The college appealed to the California Court of Appeal, arguing it was entitled to the "ministerial exception," which allows religious institutions to enjoy immunity from**

examination into religious doctrine. The college argued it fired the professors for violating a rule prohibiting married co-workers from making up one department, not because of their marital status. The court found no evidence that the college cared about the professors' marital status. It showed concern only for whether the professors were perceived to be committing adultery. The court said the claim was based on a contract, not marital status discrimination. It held the trial court had to further consider whether the professors fell within the ministerial exception. *Hope Univ. v. Superior Court,* 119 Cal.App.4th 719, 14 Cal.Rptr.3d 643 (Cal. Ct. App. 2004).

◆ *A college that failed to provide a professor with written evaluations as required by the faculty handbook did not have to renew his contract.*

A private college in New York employed an untenured probationary assistant professor in its accounting department under a series of one-year contracts. The faculty handbook called for written evaluations to be provided each teacher, but the college failed to provide them. After the professor organized and participated in a student protest aimed at the accounting department's curriculum, the college sent him a letter along with his proposed contract notifying him that upon expiration of the contract, it would not be renewed. The letter indicated that **the basis for non-renewal was the impaired collegiality and confidence between the professor and the accounting department**. He signed the one-year, non-renewable contract that accompanied the letter and became unemployed at the end of the year.

The professor sued the college for breach of contract in a state trial court where pretrial judgment was granted to the college. The New York Supreme Court, Appellate Division, affirmed the lower court decision in favor of the college. It noted that the non-renewal of the professor's contract was solely related to his failure to get along with his colleagues and was not related to his teaching skills, which the college conceded were excellent. Also, even though the college failed to provide written evaluations as called for in the faculty handbook, **there was no duty to automatically renew the professor's contract if he was found to be an excellent teacher**. The college's decision not to renew the professor's contract did not amount to breach of contract. *DeSimone v. Siena College,* 663 N.Y.S.2d 701 (N.Y. App. Div. 1997).

C. AAUP Guidelines

Language from the American Association of University Professors (AAUP) "1940 Statement of Principles on Academic Freedom and Tenure with 1970 Interpretive Comments" has been included in the conditions of employment in some contracts for college faculty members. The AAUP Statement on Tenure provides: "[I]f the decision [on tenure] is negative, the appointment for the following year becomes a terminal one." Accordingly, a federal court held the **general rule in academia is that if a faculty member is denied tenure, he or she completes a terminal year of employment and then leaves the institution.** *See* McMahon v. Carroll College, 2007 WL 804149 (E.D. Wis. 3/9/07).

A 1925 AAUP Conference Statement on Academic Freedom and Tenure provides that the termination of a permanent or long-term appointment due to financial exigencies "should be sought only as a last resort, after every effort has been made to meet the need in other ways and to find for the teacher other employment in the institution. Situations which make drastic retrenchment of this sort necessary should preclude expansions of the staff at other points at the same time, except in extraordinary circumstances." Saxe v. Board of Trustees of Metropolitan State College of Denver, *179 P.3d 67 (Col. App. 2007).*

◆ *A university followed the proper procedures when it fired a professor for sexual harassment.*

A tenured anthropology professor at Baylor University took several students on a university-sponsored academic field trip to Guatemala. While there, he engaged in inappropriate sexual contact with female students and made crude sexual remarks to them. A student reported his conduct to university officials upon returning, and an investigation found the student's accusations to be true. When the professor refused to accept a demotion and mandated counseling, a hearing was conducted, after which the tenure committee recommended the professor's termination.

The president fired the professor, who sued for breach of contract and defamation. A jury found the university breached its contract with the professor, but the Texas Court of Appeals reversed. The inclusion of an American Association of University Professors (AAUP) statement in the employment manual did not mean that the manual incorporated the AAUP's termination procedures. **The university had clearly set forth its termination procedures and followed them in this case.** The professor received written notice of the charges against him and had an opportunity to challenge the evidence and confront witnesses at the hearing. The termination was upheld. *Fox v. Parker*, 98 S.W.3d 713 (Tex. Ct. App. 2003).

◆ *A professor could not use the American Association of University Professors (AAUP) guidelines, which had been incorporated into his contract, to modify the intent of the contract.*

A professor and a New Jersey private university entered into five separate employment contracts, each of which incorporated the terms of the university's collective bargaining agreement with the AAUP guidelines. However, the professor's applications for tenure were denied due to his lack of a doctorate degree and his failure to publish. His contract for a sixth academic year stated that his associate professor position was a "non-tenured position." In the following year, he was appointed as an associate dean but continued to teach three credits per semester without additional compensation. He was fired several years later because his overall performance was found to be "significantly below expectations." The professor filed a lawsuit in a New Jersey superior court, alleging that he had acquired *de facto* tenure under the provisions of the AAUP contract. The AAUP contract required that faculty members who had taught for 14 continuous academic semesters be granted tenure. The superior court held for the university, and the professor appealed.

A state appellate division court noted that **the provision requiring tenure for faculty members teaching 14 continuous semesters was a subsidiary provision that should not be interpreted so as to conflict with the principal**

purpose of the contract. The court rejected the professor's disproportionate emphasis on the provision to support his tenure claim. The interpretation of the probationary appointments provision urged by the professor unlawfully conflicted with the principal purpose of the university's formal tenure policy, which placed substantive and procedural prerequisites on the acquisition of tenure. The superior court ruling was affirmed. *Healy v. Fairleigh Dickinson Univ.*, 671 A.2d 182 (N.J. Super. Ct. App. Div. 1996).

◆ *Where a part of the AAUP guidelines was excluded from an employment contract, the university did not have to follow the procedures listed in that part.*

A private Louisiana university dismissed a tenured professor for alleged professional incompetence. She sued the university for reinstatement of tenure and employment. She argued that the university, after agreeing to modify her existing employment contract, failed to apply Paragraph Seven of the AAUP guidelines, which provide procedures for the termination of a tenured professor. The trial court held that the college had no obligation to comply with Paragraph Seven, and the professor appealed to the state court of appeal.

On appeal, the professor argued Paragraph Seven of the AAUP guidelines was an implied provision in her employment contract. Her contract incorporated the provisions listed in the university's faculty handbook, which provided procedures for the termination of faculty appointments. The appellate court held that **the faculty handbook and the contract clearly excluded Paragraph Seven of the AAUP guidelines. As a result, the paragraph did not apply to any procedures established by the university for the termination of tenured professors.** The court further stated that there was no merit to the professor's argument that the college agreed to modify her original employment contract. The court affirmed the trial court's decision. *Olivier v. Xavier Univ.*, 553 So.2d 1004 (La. Ct. App. 1989).

D. Implied Contracts

◆ *A Texas coach did not show Baylor University breached his contract by failing to rehire him. The Supreme Court of Texas also rejected his fraud claim.*

Baylor hired the coach to lead its women's volleyball team in 1989 without a written contract, as was its practice. In 1995, Baylor told its coaches that it planned to begin the practice of entering into written contracts. The volleyball coach said Baylor's general counsel announced it would enter into two-year contracts with its head coaches beginning in 1995-96. However, he never received a written contract. The coach sued Baylor in a state court, claiming it breached an oral promise to enter into a two-year written contract. He added a fraud claim based on a promise. The court held for Baylor, but the state court of appeals reversed the judgment. On appeal, the state supreme court noted the coach had admitted a written contract was never delivered. **Any contract for a period of more than one year must be evidenced by writing.** The court rejected the fraud claim, which was based on benefits the coach would have gained if a contract had been enforced. The court reversed the judgment and held for Baylor. *Baylor Univ. v. Sonnichsen*, 221 S.W.3d 632 (Tex. 2007).

♦ *The Court of Appeals of Wisconsin held Ripon College did not misrepresent information to an applicant for an assistant professor position.*

A college vice-president interviewed the applicant, who asked him about the college's financial condition. The vice-president described the college's endowment, and discussed past and present student enrollment numbers. He told the applicant that the college intended to raise faculty salaries so it could better compete with comparable institutions. The applicant turned down a higher-paying offer from another institution and accepted the job at the college.

The college eliminated the applicant's position at the end of an academic year, and she sued the college in a Wisconsin trial court for misrepresentation. The court awarded judgment to the college and the applicant appealed. The state court of appeals found the information disclosed to the applicant during her interview, including its intention to increase salaries, was true. **The court found she was asking the court to impose a duty on the college to provide her with predictions, not facts. Failure to offer predictions is not a misrepresentation.** As the college had no duty to predict future economic events, the court affirmed the judgment. *Bellon v. Ripon College*, 278 Wis.2d 790, 693 N.W.2d 330 (Wis. Ct. App. 2005).

♦ *The U.S. Court of Appeals, Ninth Circuit, held against an instructor who sued an Oregon community college for misrepresentation.*

The instructor was offered a contract and was assured his position was "as official as it gets." Based on these assurances, he resigned from a prior tenured teaching position. Because of budget shortfalls, the college president refused to recommend the approval of his contract and the board declined to do so. The college then claimed the contract was not binding without board approval and denied the instructor the secure position he originally had been offered.

The instructor sued the college in a federal district court. **The case reached the Ninth Circuit, which held he could not show the type of justifiable reliance required to establish a claim for misrepresentation.** It then granted a petition for a rehearing. After the rehearing, the Ninth Circuit found the instructor again did not show he justifiably relied on representations. Without the board's approval, no offer was within the community college's powers. *Oja v. Blue Mountain Community College*, 184 Fed.Appx. 597 (9th Cir. 2006).

♦ *A private New Jersey college did not breach its employment contract with an employee by firing her without a hearing for not revealing a criminal embezzlement matter.*

The college hired the employee as its director of graduate programs. She did not reveal that she and her husband were defending federal criminal charges of embezzling over $1 million in employee pension and profit-sharing funds from a previous venture. The college learned of the employee's indictment and guilty plea and suggested she resign. The employee agreed to resign but then changed her mind. The college stated it could discharge her without a hearing or other due process protections because she was an at-will employee. The employee sued the university in a federal district court for breach of contract.

The court dismissed the case, finding the employee was not a full-time faculty member and that there was no employment contract. The professor appealed to the U.S. Court of Appeals, Third Circuit. **Under New Jersey law, the professor was an employee at-will unless she presented evidence to show the parties intended to renew a fixed term contract. As she did not submit such evidence, the court held she was an employee at-will.** The college was not obligated to offer the professor due process when it terminated her employment. Since there was no employment contract at the time of the alleged breach, the court affirmed the judgment. *Fanelli v. Centenary College*, 112 Fed.Appx. 210 (3d Cir. 2004).

◆ *The Supreme Court of New Hampshire upheld a jury verdict which found that reappointment letters created an employment contract.*

A New Hampshire college audio-visual director worked for 11 years under annual reappointment letters describing terms such as his salary, employment period and duties. The college discharged the director prior to the end of the term of a reappointment letter. He sued the college for breach of contract in the state court system, alleging termination without good cause. The case went to trial, which resulted in a verdict for the director. The court denied the college's motion for a directed verdict. The college appealed to the state supreme court. It reviewed the terms of the reappointment letters and held a reasonable jury could find they constituted an employment contract. The fact that they stated 12-month terms was persuasive evidence that the director was not an "at-will" employee. The reappointment rights section of the College Handbook stated employees could be disciplined for just cause. The court held a reasonable jury could find the college was obligated to follow this provision. Since there was sufficient evidence for a jury to find an employment contract existed, the denial of a directed verdict was not an abuse of discretion. The jury verdict was upheld. *Dillman v. New Hampshire College*, 838 A.2d 1274 (N.H. 2003).

II. EMPLOYEE MISCONDUCT

Employee misconduct includes a variety of actions such as inappropriate, unethical, or criminal behavior. In addressing such actions, educational institutions may be bound by faculty handbooks or requirements for hearings.

◆ *A New York university did not commit constitutional violations when it discharged an ethics professor who pled guilty to embezzlement charges.*

The professor had taught at the university for more than 25 years when he pled guilty to third-degree robbery charges based on the embezzlement of almost $80,000 from a church where he served as an accountant. After the plea, he took a leave of absence from the university, but he later sought reinstatement with a full course load. The university instead informed the professor he would be discharged, and an arbitrator upheld the decision. A state court dismissed his petition for review, and an appeals court affirmed. It held that state law allowed employers to discriminate against felons in cases involving a direct relationship between the criminal offense and the felon's employment position. The professor sued the university in a federal court for equal protection and due process violations. The court held that the state court had decided all the relevant issues. It also rejected the professor's claim that he was not provided adequate due process in connection with his removal. He pled guilty to felony charges before being suspended, and criminal proceedings may take the place of pre-suspension hearings for due process purposes.

On appeal, the U.S. Court of Appeals, Second Circuit, held that the applicable collective bargaining agreement provided disciplinary procedures for faculty members who were convicted of felonies. The professor identified no fundamental right with which this provision interfered. He also identified no suspect class under which he could claim any discrimination. While a hearing is normally provided for tenured faculty, there was no need for one where the professor was suspended without pay after having been convicted of a felony. Such a conviction "demonstrates that the deprivation is not arbitrary and serves to assure that the employer's decision is not baseless or unwarranted." As none of the professor's arguments had any merit, the court affirmed the judgment against him. *Rosa v. City Univ. of New York*, 306 Fed.Appx. 655 (2d Cir. 2007).

◆   *The University of Minnesota could suspend a tenured professor who was found to have submitted false student evaluations for a class.*

Student evaluations were used to determine whether merit-based salary increases should be granted. Faculty members could collect student evaluations online or on paper. The university accepted one of the professor's two courses for an online evaluation system, but never communicated its decision to him. Even though he had opted for the online system, five paper student evaluations were found in a secretary's inbox. A department chairperson who reviewed the evaluations became suspicious because they all assigned abnormally high ratings. The chairperson was also suspicious because the forms were turned in after the semester was over and because in a prior semester, the professor had asked a secretary to make changes to forms that were already submitted. An investigation showed students in the course did not submit the evaluations.

When confronted, the professor denied knowing of the false evaluations. After a hearing, the faculty found he had engaged in misconduct, and suggested a suspension. A university committee found the professor had engaged in serious misconduct, and the president suspended him for one year without salary or benefits. A state trial court affirmed the university's decision, and the professor appealed to the Court of Appeals of Minnesota. While the court found that evidence regarding the charge of misconduct was circumstantial, it was sufficient to support the suspension. **The professor was the only person who would benefit from the false evaluations, and he had been in the office on the day the secretary found them.** He was not a credible witness and had engaged in questionable behavior in the past with respect to evaluations. The professor claimed the suspension statement was too vague. But the court said the order clearly meant he was to receive neither salary nor benefits for one year. As a result, the court upheld the decision. *Tennyson v. Univ. of Minnesota*, No. A07-1095, 2008 WL 2344257 (Minn. Ct. App. 6/10/08).

◆   *An Ohio university had good reason to discharge an employee who disclosed private information about a student to a newspaper reporter.*

The employee was a program assistant in a research and graduate studies program. When she started work there, she received a letter from the university explaining she must ensure the confidentiality of sensitive and protected record information. The assistant also received a copy of the university's policy for retaining and disseminating student information. She signed an agreement acknowledging she was familiar with the university's policies on student education records. The agreement stated employees who violated its terms might be reprimanded, suspended, dismissed or subjected to other disciplinary action. A student who was a candidate for student government participated in the program. The campus newspaper published a story listing grade averages of student candidates. It reported the student's GPA as 2.92. The assistant contacted the newspaper to tell them this was incorrect, and revealed that the student's correct GPA was 2.68. The newspaper printed a story with the headline "KSU staff member claims candidate lied about GPA." The student sued the university for disclosing her GPA. After providing a full hearing procedure, the university discharged the assistant for violating the agreement.

The assistant sued the university in the state court system. The case reached the Court of Appeals of Ohio. The court held that **the assistant's good reputation did not outweigh the harm she caused by knowingly disclosing confidential student information.** A good reputation could not mitigate intentional acts and their consequences. The assistant argued that as a secretarial staff member, she could not be expected to comply with a federal law – which is "at best confusing for lawyers." The court of appeals disagreed. The order of removal stated she was removed for violating her agreement, not for violating federal law. As the assistant knew she was violating her agreement, the court affirmed the judgment. *Swigart v. Kent State Univ.*, No. 2004-P-0037, 2005 WL 1077176 (Ohio Ct. App. 5/6/05).

◆   *A North Dakota instructor failed to counter a college's evidence that there was adequate cause to fire her for neglect of duties and incompetence.*

Bismarck State College (BSC) notified a tenured commercial art instructor it intended to dismiss her for disclosing a student's confidential information to a classroom of students. BSC alleged the disclosure violated state higher education board policy and federal law and demanded she apologize to the student. BSC later found the instructor's apology inappropriate and told her it considered her behavior to be a neglect of duty. She challenged the sufficiency of this notice. BSC amended the notice to include charges of neglecting teaching responsibilities by ending a class a month early and failing to clean up her classrooms. It also alleged incompetent teaching, an inappropriate pattern of behavior and incompetence. BSC then fired the instructor for cause. An administrative law judge upheld the dismissal and a state district court affirmed the decision, granting BSC's motion for summary judgment.

The Supreme Court of North Dakota found the trial court had properly ordered summary judgment on the instructor's breach of employment contract claim. She failed to present any facts to show why a jury would not have found adequate cause to fire her. **The instructor presented no facts to support her wrongful termination and conspiracy charges**, and the order for summary judgment was affirmed. *Peterson v. North Dakota Univ. System*, 678 N.W.2d (N.D. 2004).

♦ *An Idaho State University accountant was properly fired for misconduct that amounted to insubordination.*

The accountant received satisfactory performance reviews until she got a new boss, who became more critical. After an argument with her supervisor, she was given a written reprimand for refusing to accept a reasonable assignment (insubordination and conduct unbecoming a state employee). While on a medical leave, she made a threatening phone call to a university medical clinic and was issued a second written reprimand. She later raised a commotion in the financial services office and exhibited contumacious behavior at a grievance meeting, which led her supervisor to recommend termination. She challenged the dismissal, and the case made its way to the Idaho Supreme Court, which upheld it. Here, **the record established four incidents of misconduct that supported the decision to let her go.** *Horne v. Idaho State Univ.*, 69 P.3d 120 (Idaho 2003).

♦ *A professor's good-faith refusal to turn over student grades to her supervisor was not insubordination.*

A tenured associate professor refused to comply with her supervisor's request to turn over student grades to evaluate the professor's program. She asserted the student handbook's privacy policy permitted only the registrar to release grades and that no other department could release them without written student consent. The supervisor then issued the professor a written reprimand. An administrative law judge (ALJ) upheld the reprimand, finding her refusal to comply with the request amounted to insubordination because compliance would not threaten her health or safety. A state court affirmed the ALJ's decision. The West Virginia Supreme Court of Appeals held **the professor was not insubordinate because the privacy policy was ambiguous, and she reasonably believed the request was invalid.** As a result, she had a good-faith belief that she should not comply. The court ordered the reprimand to be expunged from her personnel file. *Butts v. Higher Educ. Interim Governing Board/Shepard College*, 569 S.E.2d 456 (W.Va. 2002).

III. TENURE AND PROMOTION DENIALS

A. Tenure and Promotion Cases

Tenured employees are entitled to any employment protections promised by their institutions. A public institution must comply with constitutional requirements for due process. At minimum, this amounts to notice and an opportunity to respond to any charges. Private institutions are not bound by the Constitution, but must afford employees any procedures that they have been promised. If an institution's policy (or a state law or regulation) requires it, an employee may also be entitled to a hearing with the right to confront and cross-examine witnesses, and the right to be represented by counsel.

♦ *Board of Regents v. Roth*, 408 U.S. 564 (1972) and *Perry v. Sindermann*, 408 U.S. 593 (1972), help define employee due process rights. *Roth* and *Sindermann* emphasize, first, that there must be an independent source for a liberty or property interest to exist. Such interests are not created by the Constitution, but arise by employment contract or by operation of state tenure laws. Second, if a liberty or property interest is not established, no requirement of due process exists under the Fourteenth Amendment. Third, **if a teacher possesses a liberty or property interest in employment, then due process is required and the teacher may not be dismissed without a hearing**.

A tenured teacher, or an untenured teacher during the term of his or her contract, possesses a property interest in continued employment. An untenured teacher who is not rehired after expiration of his or her contract is entitled to a due process hearing if the decision not to rehire is accompanied by a finding of incompetence or immorality, because the teacher's liberty of employment would be impaired by such a finding. However, probationary employees or at-will employees generally do not enjoy due process protections.

The *Roth* case explained that **for a teacher to be entitled to due process, there must be a "liberty" or "property" interest at stake**. The teacher in *Roth* was hired at a Wisconsin university for a fixed contract term of one year. At the end of the year, he was informed that he would not be rehired. No hearing was provided and no reason was given for the decision. In dismissing the teacher's due process claims, the Supreme Court stated that no liberty interest was implicated. In declining to rehire the teacher, the university made no charge against him such as incompetence or immorality. Such a charge would have made it difficult for the teacher to gain employment elsewhere and thus would have deprived him of liberty. As no reason was given for the non-renewal of his contract, the teacher's liberty interest in future employment was not impaired and he was not entitled to a hearing on these grounds.

The Court declared that because the teacher had not acquired tenure he possessed no property interest in continued employment at the university. To be sure, the teacher had a property interest in employment during the term of his one-year contract, but upon its expiration the teacher's property interest ceased to exist. The Court stated: **"To have a property interest in a benefit, a person clearly must have more than an abstract need or desire for it. He must have more than a unilateral expectation of it. He must, instead, have a legitimate claim of entitlement to it."** *Board of Regents v. Roth*, 408 U.S. 564, 92 S.Ct. 2701, 33 L.Ed.2d 548 (1972).

◆   The *Sindermann* case involved a teacher employed at a Texas university for four years under a series of one-year contracts. When he was not rehired for a fifth year, he brought suit contending that due process required a dismissal hearing. The Supreme Court held that "a person's interest in a benefit is a 'property' interest for due process purposes if there are such rules and mutually explicit understandings that support his claim of entitlement to the benefit that he may invoke at a hearing." Because the teacher had been employed at the university for four years, the Court felt that he may have acquired a protectable property interest in continued employment. The case was remanded to the trial court to determine whether there was an unwritten "common law" of tenure at the university. If so, the teacher would be entitled to a dismissal hearing. *Perry v. Sindermann*, 408 U.S. 593, 92 S.Ct. 2694, 33 L.Ed.2d 570 (1972).

♦ *A Pennsylvania university's decision to deny tenure to an associate professor did not violate any university handbook, policies or procedures.*

The professor accepted a position under a letter of acceptance by which he agreed to abide by university policies and procedures. These policies specified annual performance reviews, a third-year review, and eligibility for tenure in the sixth year. In the event tenure was denied, the seventh year would be the final year of employment. After satisfactory annual performance reviews during the early years of his employment, the professor applied for tenure. A five-member tenure committee made an inconclusive report, and tenure was denied. An appeal to a reconstituted four-member committee resulted in two committee members finding the professor marginally met tenure criteria while the others found he easily met the criteria. After being discharged, the professor sued the university in a state court for breach of contract. He also claimed the five-point scale used for his evaluations violated university policy.

The court rejected his claim that the university had a contractual duty to follow its policies and procedures, and that it failed to do so when it allowed a four-member committee to reconsider the application after a five-member committee did so. On appeal, the Superior Court of Pennsylvania held **it was within the prerogative of the university president to reconstitute the committee with four members**. This decision did not breach any contract with the professor. The same was true of the use of a five-point evaluation scale. The president was not required to agree with the initial committee's conclusion and the court affirmed the judgment for the university. *Robertson v. Drexel Univ.*, 991 A.2d 315 (Pa. Super. Ct. 2010).

♦ *A federal court upheld a decision to revoke the tenure of a faculty member based on charges that he neglected his professional responsibilities.*

University administrators filed a complaint seeking the revocation of the professor's tenure. The complaint referenced a suspension eight years earlier and a letter allegedly written by a university vice president on October 30, 1997. The complaint was supplemented by a statement of misconduct, which did not mention a letter of October 30, 1997. A faculty panel agreed with the charge of neglect for professional responsibilities and noted its decision was based on the professor's conduct after April 1999. During the revocation proceedings, the university did not release any letter dated October 30, 1997 to him. The professor sued the university in a federal court for breach of contract.

After dismissing most of his claims, the court held that even if a letter dated October 30, 1997 did exist, it was not relevant to the tenure revocation. The letter was not mentioned in the statement of misconduct that supported the complaint. **In addition, the panel clearly indicated its decision was based on actions after April 1999.** Therefore, whether or not the letter existed was immaterial, and the university was entitled to judgment. On appeal, the U.S. Court of Appeals, District of Columbia Circuit, affirmed the judgment. It found no binding contract, as the professor did not identify a relevant faculty code provision that was violated. Despite 28 alleged contractual breaches, there was no plausible claim for relief. The judgment was affirmed. *Saha v. George Washington Univ.*, 358 Fed.Appx. 205 (D.C. Cir. 2009).

◆ *A North Carolina university employee was not entitled to priority consideration for a vacant position based on her 10 years of work there.*

The employee worked in the university's Animal Science Department. She left for three years and returned as an administrative billing assistant in the Communication Technologies Department. The university promoted the employee to the position of Telecom Project Manager/Telecom Analyst II. A few months later, she was laid off, but a Telecom Analyst I position soon became vacant. The employee applied for the job, but the university hired a less experienced former employee who had also been let go. The employee filed a complaint with the state office of administrative hearings, alleging she was entitled to priority consideration for the job under North Carolina General Statutes Section 126-7.1. This law provides state employees with more than 10 years of service priority consideration over state employees with less than 10 years of service in the same or a related job classification. A state trial court held the employee was entitled to priority consideration for the job.

The university appealed. The Court of Appeals of North Carolina held the trial court misinterpreted the law. Under the trial court's reading, a state employee with over 10 years of service, regardless of the position, should receive priority consideration over another person with less than 10 years of service in the same or a related position classification. **As the employee did not have more than 10 years in the same or a related classification as the position for which she applied, she was not entitled to priority consideration** for the job. The court reversed the judgment. *Wilkins v. North Carolina State Univ.*, 178 N.C.App. 377, 631 S.E.2d 221 (N.C. Ct. App. 2006).

◆ *A District of Columbia professor did not prove a university interfered with her bid for tenure in a way that breached its duty of good faith and fair dealing.*

The professor worked in a tenure track position for five years, then applied for a tenured associate professor position. The tenure committee voted against tenure because it considered her research weak. A scholarly journal notified the professor that it had rejected a paper she authored due to serious criticism by reviewers. The university again denied the professor's request for tenure based on lack of progress in publishing. The professor sued the university in a District of Columbia court for breach of contract and breach of the covenant of good faith and fair dealing. The court held for the university, and she appealed.

On appeal to the District of Columbia Court of Appeals, the professor stated that she was denied sufficient lab space and that her research grant was arbitrarily cancelled. This made her unable to perform contractual publishing obligations, breaching both her contract and the covenant of good faith and fair dealing. **The court noted all contracts contain an implied duty of good faith and fair dealing. This means neither party may do anything which has the effect of destroying or injuring the rights of the other party under the contract.** The university took steps to make lab space available to the professor, but she failed to progress in her scholarly productivity. The court agreed with the university that courts are reluctant to interfere with tenure decisions. As the professor failed to satisfy the tenure requirements of the faculty handbook, the judgment was affirmed. *Allworth v. Howard Univ.*, 890 A.2d 194 (D.C. 2006).

◆ *A Kentucky tax professor will receive a trial in an action against a university for negligence and fraudulent representation.*

The university hired the professor for an academic year and agreed to pay him a $25,000 supplement funded by an endowment fund. The professor believed his appointment to the endowed professorship was permanent. After he accepted the position, the professor learned his appointment to the endowed professorship was temporary and his future supplemental salary was determined at the discretion of the dean. He left the university and sued it in a Kentucky trial court for negligently or fraudulently misrepresenting the terms of his contract verbally and through e-mails.

The court found no bad faith and dismissed the case. The professor appealed to the Court of Appeals of Kentucky. The court noted that the professor introduced oral communications, e-mails, and other correspondence that created doubt about the university's good faith. The dean would be entitled to official immunity for negligently performing discretionary acts as long as he acted in good faith. However, the hiring process included the non-discretionary aspect of representing or communicating the compensation package. **If the dean negligently represented the compensation package to the professor, a court could find the university liable.** The court held the trial court's finding that no facts supported a finding of bad faith was premature. It reversed and remanded the judgment to the trial court for further action. *Westin v. Shipley*, No. 2003-CA-001548-MR, 2004 WL 2260299 (Ky. Ct. App. 2004). State Supreme Court review was denied in 2005.

◆ *Kentucky university trustees were entitled to official immunity for their discretionary acts in denying a professor's application for tenure.*

A University of Louisville assistant professor applied for tenure after 11 years with the university. The university board of trustees denied the application and discharged him. The professor sued the university and trustees in a state court, which dismissed his claims for tortious interference with contractual relationships and breach of contract. The professor appealed to the Court of Appeals of Kentucky, where the trustees claimed official immunity. **The court held qualified official immunity applies to the negligent performance by an officer or employee of discretionary acts or functions performed in good faith within the scope of the employee's authority.** The court found the trustees' evaluations were based on personal deliberations and were discretionary. Because the professor offered no evidence of bad faith on the part of the board members, the court correctly dismissed the tortious interference claim. His contract expired at the end of its present term, and the court affirmed the judgment. *Haeberle v. Univ. of Louisville*, No. 2003-CA-000433-MR, 2004 WL 595257 (Ky. Ct. App. 2004).

◆ *The Ohio State University did not breach a contract with an instructor by refusing to increase her responsibilities or reappoint her.*

The instructor rejected a job offer outside the university, then changed her mind. After she decided to stay with the university, she talked with a vice provost about a new job title, salary and increased responsibilities. The university's office of academic affairs approved a new restructuring plan. The instructor alleged that she and the vice provost signed a position description confirming her duties and responsibilities in the restructuring process. The vice provost resigned and an interim provost changed the restructuring plan.

Dissatisfied with the changes, the instructor sued the university in a state court for breach of contract. The instructor claimed her agreement with the vice provost created both an oral and written contract. She said the vice provost promised her a new job title, increased management and supervisory responsibilities, and a salary adjustment. **The court held nothing in the position description or the vice provost's words or conduct constituted a binding obligation. The evidence showed instead that the position description was subject to change and depended on the vice provost.** The court found no contract guaranteeing the instructor the position of business manager or a particular salary range. The court held for the university. *White v. Ohio State Univ.*, 815 N.E.2d 1160 (Ohio Ct. Cl. 2004).

◆ *A California court held a temporary community college instructor was not a regular employee under the college system's academic classification system.*

The instructor taught less than 60% of the hours required for a full-time assignment and was deemed a temporary employee. He submitted three grant requests and worked on them during the intercession so as to not exceed the 60% rule. The college later rescinded one of the grant awards because it believed his work during the intercession might count toward the 60% rule. The college denied a request by the instructor's union for reclassification as a permanent employee and he petitioned a state court for relief. The court held his projects constituted "teaching" and that he exceeded the 60% rule. It ordered the college to reclassify the instructor as a permanent employee, and the university appealed to the Court of Appeal of California.

The court noted the California Code established three classifications for community college instructors including probationary contract employees, tenured regular employees, and temporary employees, who could be terminated at the discretion of the governing board. **Pursuant to the code, a temporary employee who teaches full time for a complete school year and is rehired for the next school year will automatically be reclassified as a contract employee.** The court held an instructor teaching adult or community college classes less than 60% of a full-time assignment must be classified as a temporary employee. It distinguished statutory teaching requirements from the research and grant projects, which it characterized as "faculty work." Since these projects could not be considered "teaching" under the statute, the instructor did not exceed the 60% rule and should not be reclassified. The trial court's judgment was reversed. *Kamler v. Marin Community College Dist.*, No. A098114, 2003 WL 21493662 (Cal. Ct. App. 2003).

◆ *A professor's position as associate dean was not a protected property interest preserved by her tenured faculty position.*

The University of North Dakota hired a professor in the School of Communication. She was also given administrative duties as the director of the School of Communication and as the associate dean of the College of Fine Arts and Communication. In 1995, she was told by her senior administrators to improve her administrative performance. Eventually, she was dismissed from her administrative duties, but remained a faculty member. She sued in federal court, alleging that her discharge from the administrative positions violated her protected property interests under tenure. The court dismissed her claim that she had a protected property interest in her administrative positions. Citing the North Dakota State Board of Higher Education Policy Manual, which was included in her employment contract, the district court noted that tenure does not extend to administrative positions.

The Eighth Circuit Court of Appeals agreed, noting that the professor's administrative position was at will, and thus did not evoke a protected property interest. In fact, the letter of understanding supplementing her employment contract stated, "Associate Deans have no specific term, but rather serve at the pleasure of the Dean." The circuit court found that the professor's position as director of the School of Communication included a three-year contract, but **her protected property interest had been satisfied because the university had fully compensated her for the salary associated with the position even though she did not serve out the full term**. *Rakow v. State of North Dakota*, 208 F.3d 218 (8th Cir. 2000).

B. Claims of Discrimination

◆ *A New York physics professor failed to present enough evidence to show he was denied tenure on the basis of his sex or national origin.*

Although the Equal Employment Opportunity Commission found probable cause of discrimination by the university based on certain staffing decisions, it did not link the staffing decisions to the denial of tenure for the professor. A federal district court then found sufficient evidence that tenure had been denied on the basis of permissible factors. The circumstances surrounding other decisions with which the professor sought comparison were sufficiently distinct to bar any inference of sex or national origin discrimination. **The court found there was no evidence that the university's admitted goal of increasing female student enrollment corresponded with an effort to change the gender mix of its faculty.** On appeal, the U.S. Court of Appeals, Second Circuit, found that the professor's claims against university officials were untimely. As there was no merit to his remaining arguments, the judgment for the university officials was affirmed. *Syrkin v. State Univ. of New York*, No. 09-3130, 2010 WL 986561 (2d Cir. 2010).

◆ *A Michigan professor who was denied tenure and discharged failed to show the university's actions breached a contract or were discriminatory.*

Kettering University terminated the professor's faculty appointment after an investigating committee found he misrepresented grant information, falsely stated he was the primary author of an article and keynote speaker at a conference from which he wrongfully withheld money, failed to accurately list dates on his employment application and made other misrepresentations. He sued the university in a federal court for breach of contract, retaliation and national origin discrimination. The court found insufficient evidence of bias. None of the comments he relied on to support his national origin discrimination claim mentioned his Iranian descent. The professor was unable to show the performance-related reasons for discharge were pretextual. Since the same faculty members who filed the complaint against him were part of the committee that helped hire him, a presumption against discrimination existed.

The retaliation claim failed because the university showed the discharge was related to his performance. **The professor's breach of contract claim failed because university policies permitted discharge for just cause and a faculty handbook gave the university the right to define the term "just cause."** As the deficiencies in the professor's work performance established just cause for discharge, the court dismissed the action. *Sanders v. Kettering Univ.*, No. 07-11905, 2009 WL 3010849 (E.D. Mich. 9/17/09).

◆ *A Tennessee professor who was a Hindu and a native of India failed to prove he was denied a promotion based on his religion or national origin.*

The professor joined Tennessee State University as an assistant professor in 1990. He was granted tenure and promoted to associate professor in 1997. But the university denied the professor's application for full professor, telling him he needed more substantial achievements in research and public service to be promoted. After he was again denied a promotion, the professor sued the university in a state court, claiming he was denied the promotions based on his national origin and religion. He also accused the university of violating its faculty handbook policies by allowing a professor to serve on two committees that considered his application and failing to provide him timely access to committee recommendations. The court granted a pretrial order for judgment.

On appeal, the state appeals court noted that the university faculty handbook confirmed its claim that research and public service activities were important considerations in the promotions process. **The university had consistently maintained that the professor was denied promotion due to his deficiencies in these areas.** He failed to submit evidence of public service or research activities, and the record showed he was not qualified for promotion. As a result, the judgment was affirmed. *Marpaka v. Hefner*, 289 S.W.3d 308 (Tenn. Ct. App. 2008). The Supreme Court of Tennessee denied an appeal in 2009.

◆ *Evidence did not support a court order for a North Carolina professor who claimed she was denied reappointment and tenure based on her race.*

The professor was the only African-American junior faculty member on the tenure track in her department. In 2007, the university received funding for a grant from the National Institutes of Health and designated the professor as project grant administrator. The grant required the project administrator to hold a faculty or scholar position at an academic or research organization. The university was authorized to release the grant to another qualifying institution. The university soon denied the professor reappointment and promotion to a tenured position based on her failure to timely submit an application package and failure to produce an adequate number of peer-reviewed publications.

The professor sued the university in a federal district court, claiming senior faculty members created a hostile work environment. She claimed the decision to deny her tenure was racially motivated, and she filed a motion for a preliminary order to stop the university from ending her employment as scheduled. The court explained that preliminary injunctions are extraordinary remedies that are granted only in limited circumstances. Neither potential loss of earnings nor potential damage to reputation would constitute irreparable harm. The professor was unlikely to prevail on the merits of her claim. **She presented little evidence that she was qualified for reappointment or promotion. The university's evidence corroborated its assertion that the professor's research productivity was not up to par.** Also, it was clear that she failed to submit her complete application for reappointment by the applicable deadline. Her motion was denied. *Weathers v. Univ. of North Carolina at Chapel Hill*, No. 1:08CV847, 2008 WL 5110952 (M.D.N.C. 12/4/08).

◆ *The Supreme Court of Rhode Island refused to overturn a $455,000 jury verdict for a professor who was denied tenure for unlawful reasons.*

After serving in the engineering division for three years, the professor had a falling out with the division's director of undergraduate programs over a grading controversy. The professor eventually changed the grades under protest, but his relationship with the director remained sour. The director asked the professor to interview a minority candidate for a vacant position. The professor claimed the director's secretary told him the interview was being conducted for "some affirmative action considerations." The professor refused to conduct the interview, saying he was concerned it might be illegal to interview a candidate for a job that had already been set aside for someone else.

The professor was subsequently denied tenure, and after his internal grievance was denied, he sued the university in a state court. He claimed the university tolerated and condoned an ethnically hostile work environment and that the director retaliated against him for opposing discriminatory practices. The director further said he was denied tenure based on his national origin. A jury sided with the professor with respect to his retaliation claim and awarded him $400,000 in back pay, $175,000 in compensatory damages and $100,000 in punitive damages. The university appealed. The state supreme court upheld the verdict with respect to the retaliation claim. **While a rational jury could have reached a contrary verdict, there was enough evidence to support the conclusion that tenure was denied because the professor opposed the university's hiring practices.** The jury was entitled to credit his testimony over that of the university's witnesses. Moreover, the proximity between his refusal to participate in the interview and the denial of tenure supported his retaliation claim. *Shoucair v. Brown Univ.*, 917 A.2d 418 (R.I. 2007).

◆ *A Missouri professor's due process claim against a private college failed because she did not show the college engaged in state action.*

The professor claimed male professors with similar responsibilities in her department were paid about $13,000 more annually than females. The college initially renewed her appointment for the 2006-07 term, but the college president then informed her that she would be placed on leave with pay and that she would not be reappointed for 2007-08. The college denied her grievance without a hearing. She then filed bias charges with state and federal agencies before suing the college's board of trustees for due process violations, retaliation, sex and age discrimination, breach of contract, tortious interference with her contract of employment and violation of the Equal Pay Act.

The court rejected the due process claim because the professor failed to show the private college had engaged in any state action. Next, the court granted the motion to dismiss the retaliation claim. The professor had admitted the college took no action relating to her employment after she filed the grievance. The claim of tortious interference with a contractual relationship was also dismissed, as such claims can be filed only against a third party. However, the court retained the discrimination claims. Both Title VII and the state's human rights act allowed punitive damage awards in cases of discrimination with malice or reckless indifference to federally protected rights. *Reed v. Board of Trustees of Columbia College*, No. 07-04155-CV-W-NKL, 2007 WL 4365749 (W.D. Mo. 2007).

◆   *An adjunct Virginia State University (VSU) professor failed to identify any constitutional violation that would allow him to proceed with a federal case.*

The adjunct professor applied for several full-time openings, but he was not chosen for any of them. When his teaching contract expired, VSU did not renew it. The adjunct claimed it chose not to renew his contract based on his African-American race. He also said VSU illegally failed to consider his military service when it made its hiring decisions. The adjunct sued VSU and several officials in a federal district court for discrimination based on race and age. He also alleged violation of his constitutional rights under the First Amendment and the Fourteenth Amendment. After the court dismissed the constitutional claims against VSU and the officials in their official capacities, the officials sought dismissal of the claims filed against them as individuals.

The court noted that the adjunct made only a passing reference to the First Amendment and the Fourteenth Amendment in his complaint. Under a generous reading of the complaint, the only constitutional violation he could have possibly identified was an unlawful deprivation of a property interest in continued employment. However, the adjunct failed to offer any facts to show he had a legitimate property interest in the positions he sought. **His unilateral expectation of continued employment was not enough to show a constitutional violation.** The motion to dismiss the constitutional claims against the officials in their individual capacities was granted. *Bland v. Virginia State Univ.*, No. 3:06CV513-HEH, 2007 WL 1991041 (E.D. Va. 7/5/07).

◆   *An Ohio university did not breach its employment contract when it fired a medical department professor who was a native of India.*

The professor worked in the department of psychiatry under a one-year, non-tenured contract. The university renewed his contract for a second year, when it also hired a new department chair. The professor alleged the chair disliked him because he was Indian. At the end of the year, the chair notified him his contract would not be renewed. A university grievance committee found the non-renewal decision was not motivated by discrimination or personal animosity. The professor sued the university in a state court for breach of contract and intentional infliction of emotional distress. He added claims against the department chair for intentional infliction of emotional distress. The court awarded judgment to the university and chair, and the professor appealed.

The Court of Appeals of Ohio held that all employment in the state is "at-will" so that either party may sever the employment relationship at any time and for any reason. The renewal of an untenured professor is discretionary. Since the professor had not published or applied for funding for the past two years, he failed to fulfill his contract performance requirements. The university had a legitimate reason not to renew his contract. The court affirmed the judgment, rejecting the professor's claims for intentional infliction of emotional distress against the university and chair as they did not engage in outrageous conduct. *Adityanjee v. Case Western Reserve Univ.*, 806 N.E.2d 583 (Ohio Ct. App. 2004).

◆ *A professor from the University of Redlands lost her discrimination case because she failed to prove she was denied tenure because she is Jewish.*

A professor in the university's art department applied for tenure in 1995. The Faculty Review Committee subsequently denied her tenure. An appeals committee recommended tenure, but the university president ultimately decided not to grant tenure, advising her to apply the next year. Once again, she was denied tenure. The appeals committee concluded her review was not fair because the dean may have been prejudiced against her. It recommended she be allowed to reapply in three years. The president upheld the denial and rejected the committee's recommendation to allow the professor to reapply, finding no prejudice by the dean. The professor sued the university for breach of implied contract, breach of implied covenant of good faith and fair dealing, fraud, and religious discrimination. A state superior court ruled for the university, and the professor appealed. The California Court of Appeal concluded that the denial of tenure was not related to the fact that she was Jewish, but was instead due to academic politics at the university.

The court conceded the professor may have been treated unfairly, but it did not find any of the university's decisions about denying her tenure were related to religion. A reasonable juror would conclude that any perceived prejudice was based on the incident with her colleague and not the fact that she was Jewish. Even if various faculty members made comments about her not teaching classes on certain Jewish holidays, this did not demonstrate discrimination since she suffered no adverse consequences for not teaching on those days. The court affirmed the trial court's decision. *Slatkin v. Univ. of Redlands*, 88 Cal.App.4th 1147, 106 Cal.Rptr.2d 480 (Cal. Ct. App. 2001).

C. Collegiality and Animosity

◆ *Lack of collegiality was a valid basis upon which to discharge a tenured North Carolina State engineering professor.*

After gaining tenure at North Carolina State University, the professor was given unsatisfactory performance reviews for three straight years. A faculty hearing committee found he was not incompetent, but university trustees discharged him for incompetence of service. Among the university's findings was a lack of collegiality with colleagues that had become so disruptive that the professor's department was unable to operate efficiently. A state court upheld the discharge, and he appealed to the Court of Appeals of North Carolina.

On appeal, the professor claimed that tenured professors cannot be discharged on grounds other than incompetence, misconduct or neglect of duty under the state university code. The court rejected this argument, as the discharge was for incompetence – one of the permissible reasons for discharge under the code. A **university regulation authorized discharge for incompetence when a tenured professor had unsatisfactory reviews for two straight years. Moreover, disruptive behavior may also constitute incompetence.** The professor's due process claim failed because the university followed the relevant code provisions. Since there was "ample evidence" that he disrupted his department to the point that its functions and operations were impaired, the discharge was affirmed. *Bernold v. Board of Governors of the Univ. of North Carolina*, 683 S.E.2d 428 (N.C. Ct. App. 2009).

◆ *A federal district court refused to reverse an Iowa university's decision that a professor with several years of experience should not be granted tenure.*

The professor occupied a tenure-track position, with tenure becoming available in the sixth year of employment. A university promotion and tenure document noted that decisions relating to promotion involved subjective considerations. The university denied the professor's request for an early promotion in his fifth year, and the next year, only 12 of 29 faculty members voted for promotion. After his internal appeals were turned down, he sued the university regents in the state court system, claiming the decision to deny tenure was arbitrary, capricious and an abuse of discretion. The court ruled against him, noting that university officials had expressed concerns about the lack of impact of his scholarship and his low number of publications. On appeal, the Court of Appeals of Iowa noted that **the subjective process of deciding whether to award tenure should be left to the professional judgment of educators**, unless it was shown that they acted in a way that was arbitrary or capricious. As no such showing was made in this case, the court affirmed the judgment for the university regents. *Meltzer v. Board of Regents*, No. 08-0345, 2008 WL 5412225 (Iowa Ct. App. 12/31/08).

◆ *A tenured Arkansas professor did not show any causal connection between his dismissal and his filing of a lawsuit four years earlier.*

The professor claimed he was removed as department chair in violation of his constitutional rights. To settle his lawsuit, the university paid him a nominal sum and agreed to use its best efforts to promote a spirit of harmony within the department. After the settlement, friction developed between the professor and the new chair. Following a series of insubordinate acts by the professor, the chair told him he could not teach during a summer session. When the professor went to a class he would have taught and started filming it, he was removed by university security and warned that further disruptions would result in his dismissal. A short time later, he filmed students as they registered for classes and was again removed by security. The professor did not appear at a meeting called by the university chancellor, and he was soon dismissed. In a federal district court action against university officials, the professor accused the chair and university of retaliating against him for filing a lawsuit. He also claimed race discrimination and due process violations. The court ruled for the university.

On appeal to the U.S. Court of Appeals, Eighth Circuit, the university asserted Eleventh Amendment immunity. The professor provided no authority to support his argument that the university could not claim immunity because it did not timely raise this defense. The fact that he could go back to court to enforce the settlement agreement did not deprive the university from asserting an immunity defense. The retaliation claim failed because he did not show a causal connection between a protected activity and his dismissal. In any event, the university had legitimate reasons for its decision. **There was evidence that the professor was insubordinate, refused to attend meetings and acted unprofessionally.** No due process violation occurred, since he did not show university officials acted arbitrarily and he did not comply with university procedures. As a result, the judgment was affirmed. *Satcher v. Univ. of Arkansas at Pine Bluff Board of Trustees*, 558 F.3d 731 (8th Cir. 2009).

◆ *A federal district court dismissed an Illinois professor's constitutional rights violation claims.*

The professor was disciplined after having confrontations with other faculty members. After a no-confidence vote by the faculty, he lost his position as a member and chair of a college personnel committee. He was also removed from the University Council Personnel Committee position. The professor sued university officials in a federal district court for denial of due process and equal protection rights. The court dismissed the claims against the board and officials on Eleventh Amendment grounds, finding they were not subject to constitutional claims for damages. The claims of deprivation of property and liberty without due process lacked merit. Although the professor had a property interest in his employment as a tenured faculty member, he did not have any interest in membership on committees. As he did not show damage to his good name, reputation, honor or integrity, the court dismissed his claim based on deprivation of a liberty interest. Since the university did not take adverse employment action against the professor, such as termination, demotion, or a loss of pay and benefits, he failed to allege any significant legally cognizable injury, and the case was dismissed. *Ganesan v. NIU Board of Trustees*, No. 02 C 50498, 2003 WL 22872139 (N.D. Ill. 2003).

◆ *Even though collegiality was not listed as a specific factor for tenure or promotion review, a university could consider it when evaluating a teacher.*

A teacher at a Maryland university sought an early review for tenure and a promotion. When both were denied, she sued the university for breach of contract, asserting that it had improperly considered **"collegiality" (defined by the court as "the capacity to relate well and constructively to the comparatively small bank of scholars on whom the ultimate fate of the university rests" and as "the relationship of colleagues")** in its decision-making process. She claimed that the university could only evaluate teaching, research and service. The university claimed that although nothing in the contract mentioned collegiality, it was inherently a part of the contract and therefore a proper consideration in both tenure and promotion decisions.

The Court of Special Appeals of Maryland ruled in favor of the university, finding that **collegiality was a proper factor for review**. It noted that the American Association of University Professors had even contemplated as much in its Statement on Professional Ethics. **Collegiality plays an important role in both teaching and service.** Finding insufficient evidence that the university breached either the contract or its implied covenant of good faith and fair dealing, the court ruled that the teacher's claim could not succeed. *Univ. of Baltimore v. Iz*, 716 A.2d 1107 (Md. Ct. Spec. App. 1998).

D. Handbooks and Procedures

◆   *A private Minnesota university did not breach a professor's contract when it decided not to grant her application for tenure.*

A university faculty handbook called for evaluation of tenure cases by an academic council, which then made tenure recommendations to the university president. The president had final authority regarding all tenure decisions. The academic council recommended denying the professor's application for tenure, and the university president accepted the recommendation. After a hearing, the council reversed itself and recommended tenure. But the president again denied the application, and the professor sued the university and its president in a state court for breach of contract and breach of the covenant of good faith in employment. All the claims were dismissed, and the professor appealed.

Before the Court of Appeals of Minnesota, the professor claimed the faculty handbook created a contract and required it to grant her tenure. She argued that the president was obligated to grant tenure to candidates who met applicable criteria for tenure and were recommended for tenure by the academic council. **The court affirmed the judgment, finding that the handbook set out procedures for candidates seeking tenure but explicitly reserved final tenure decisions for the president.** *Nash-Marshall v. Univ. of Saint Thomas*, No. A07-2028, 2008 WL 3290383 (Minn. Ct. App. 8/12/08).

◆   *A trial court was ordered to re-examine claims that changes to an employment handbook wrongfully deprived professors of vested tenure rights.*

Until 2002, the Metropolitan State College of Denver was a part of the Colorado State Colleges System. At that time, the state removed the college from the system and created a board of trustees to govern it. In 2003, the board issued a new handbook describing the rights of professional personnel at the college. The new handbook superseded one that had been in place since 1994, and it included some changes that did not sit well with tenured professors. For example, it did not afford tenured faculty priority over nontenured faculty in the event of a layoff. In addition, it removed the requirement that the college try to relocate dismissed faculty and eliminated a hearing committee procedure that was used when tenured faculty members sought to challenge their dismissal.

Five tenured professors filed a state court action against the board of trustees, claiming the new handbook breached their employment contracts and violated their procedural due process rights. The court held the new handbook did not breach their employment contract. It also rejected the due process claim, because none of the professors had been subjected to dismissal or layoff under the terms of the new handbook. **On appeal, the Court of Appeals of Colorado held the board lacked authority to unilaterally modify handbook provisions that afforded the professors substantive and vested rights.** Provisions in the new handbook relating to priority and relocation in the event of layoffs affected the professors' substantive rights. It was up to the trial court to determine whether those rights were vested. The new handbook violated the professors' due process rights because it allowed the college president to institute and resolve dismissal proceedings. Based on these and other errors, the case was returned to the lower court. *Saxe v. Board of Trustees of Metropolitan State College of Denver*, 179 P.3d 67 (Colo. Ct. App. 2007).

In 2008, the Supreme Court of Colorado rejected further appeal of the action. *Saxe v. Board of Trustees of Metropolitan State College of Denver* 2008 WL 698945 (Colo. 2008).

◆ *When Harvard University followed its handbook in denying tenure, a professor's breach of contract action against it was dismissed.*

After an associate professor of government at Harvard was denied tenure, he grieved the matter, claiming that Harvard's provost was biased against him and influenced the ad hoc committee that had recommended against tenure. The reviewing committee ruled that the grievance was without merit, and the professor sued for breach of contract. A state court refused to dismiss the lawsuit, but the Appeals Court of Massachusetts reversed, holding that the lawsuit should have been dismissed. Nothing in the university's handbook prevented the provost from submitting an opinion regarding the professor's abilities. Also, there was no requirement that the ad hoc committee be composed of specialists in the professor's field. Since **Harvard did not violate the tenure evaluation procedures outlined in its handbook**, the breach of contract lawsuit should have been dismissed. *Berkowitz v. President & Fellows of Harvard College*, 789 N.E.2d 575 (Mass. App. Ct. 2003).

The Supreme Court of Massachusetts denied a petition for further review in 2003. *Berkowitz v. President & Fellows of Harvard College*, 440 Mass. 1101 (Mass. 2003).

◆ *A professor lost her challenge to tenure denial by failing to follow procedural court rules.*

An assistant professor of health, physical education, recreation and coaching was evaluated for tenure after five years. She was rated above average in teaching and service, but below average in scholarly activity, and was denied tenure. She sued the university under Title VII and the Fourteenth Amendment, asserting equal protection violations. After pretrial judgment was granted to the university, the professor appealed to the Seventh Circuit, which affirmed. Here, the professor committed procedural errors by failing to comply with local court rules. Also, she was unable to show an equal protection violation. She was not treated differently than other similarly situated tenure candidates, and **she had no liberty interest claim because the university did not make any stigmatizing remarks in connection with the denial of tenure**. *Hedrich v. Board of Regents of Univ. of Wisconsin System*, 274 F.3d 1174 (7th Cir. 2001).

IV. INVESTIGATIONS, HEARINGS AND PROCEDURES

A. Investigations

When public institutions and administrative agencies investigate discrimination charges, they are bound to respect the due process rights of public employees during such investigations.

◆ *A Minnesota community college did not violate a part-time English instructor's right to due process by declining to renew his contract after an investigation established he had sexually harassed a student.*

The instructor's contracts ran from semester to semester. Near the end of his sixth consecutive semester, the college legal affairs director advised him that a student had filed a sexual harassment complaint against him. According to the student, the instructor had spent weeks coming to the bookstore to stare at her while she worked, trying to talk to her and asking her out despite her repeated refusals. The legal affairs director told the instructor to stay away from the bookstore. She did not, however, give him written notice or a copy of applicable college policies and procedures, or tell him he could submit a written response to the allegations. At a later interview, the director failed to give the instructor notices required by state law. After interviewing the instructor, the student and three witnesses, she wrote up a report concluding he had violated the college's sexual harassment policy. After she completed her report, she threw away her notes. The college notified the instructor it would not renew his contract, and he sued the college and various officials in a state court for violating his due process rights and illegally disposing of evidence.

The court held for the college, and the instructor appealed. The Court of Appeals of Minnesota found the instructor had to establish he was deprived of a constitutionally protected property or liberty interest in continued employment. **He could not show any property interest in continued employment because the terms of his contract called only for part-time, temporary employment that ended each semester.** The court was not persuaded by his argument that ordering textbooks for the classes he expected to teach showed he had a property interest in continued employment. A liberty interest in continued employment can arise when government action is so damaging to an employee's reputation that it impairs his or her chance of getting another job. In this case, the college did not publicize either the letter informing the instructor he would not be rehired or the investigator's sexual harassment report. The court affirmed the judgment for the college. *Phillips v. State*, 725 N.W.2d 778 (Minn. Ct. App. 2007).

◆ *A Colorado university improperly released an audit report to the media without providing a name-clearing hearing.*

The University of Colorado at Denver (UCD) investigated a managing director for fiscal misconduct. An auditors' report found evidence that he had granted employees paid time off without required approval. The director also gave a subordinate paid time off to prepare for a foreign teaching assignment and approved a termination date that was seven days beyond the date on which a subordinate actually stopped working. The director's supervisor told him he would be assigned other duties for 30 days and then discharged. However, the director did not receive a copy of the audit report until two weeks later. Meanwhile, the UCD newspaper ran an article detailing the report. Another article appeared in a local paper. After the director was discharged, he said the release of the report created a stigma on his reputation and prevented him from applying for jobs he otherwise would have sought. In his federal lawsuit against UCD, the director claimed his due process rights were violated when the audit report was disseminated before any hearing. A federal district court ruled against him, and he appealed to the U.S. Court of Appeals, Tenth Circuit.

The court found enough evidence to create a factual issue as to whether the damaging statements in the audit report were false. The director said he believed he had the authority to grant administrative leave without the approval of his supervisor, and insisted he had made no misrepresentation in allowing an employee to take time off to teach. As to the third incident, the director said the employee worked a full day on each day of her last week of employment. The court found this evidence was important, because **UCD could not prove fiscal misconduct unless it showed the director acted intentionally**. As factual issues existed as to whether the charges of fiscal misconduct were adequately supported, the case was returned to the district court for further proceedings. *Evers v. Regents of the Univ. of Colorado*, 509 F.3d 1304 (10th Cir. 2007).

◆ *A private college had to disclose certain records to the EEOC in the following case.*

A professor, who had been employed at a Pennsylvania private college for three years, was denied tenure after he was reviewed by the school's Professional Standards Committee. The committee, composed of the dean and five faculty members, recommended that tenure not be granted to the professor. The committee's recommendation was also reaffirmed by the college's grievance committee. The professor then filed a complaint with the EEOC alleging discrimination based on his French national origin. The EEOC issued a subpoena for the committee's records. Although the EEOC offered to accept the records with names deleted, the school refused to disclose them.

The EEOC then filed suit in federal district court to compel the college to comply with the subpoena. The district court ordered disclosure of the records and the college appealed. The court of appeals affirmed, holding that **although the disclosure might burden the tenure process or invade the privacy of other professors, the records had to be disclosed because they were "relevant" to the EEOC's case**. The college appealed to the U.S. Supreme Court, but its petition for review was denied. *Franklin & Marshall College v. EEOC*, 476 U.S. 1163, 106 S.Ct. 2288, 90 L.Ed.2d 729 (1986).

◆ *The U.S. Supreme Court required a university to comply with an EEOC subpoena seeking peer review information.*

After the University of Pennsylvania, a private institution, denied tenure to an associate professor, she filed a charge with the EEOC alleging discrimination based on race, sex and national origin in violation of Title VII. During its investigation, the EEOC issued a subpoena seeking disclosure of the professor's tenure-review file and the tenure files of five male faculty members identified as having received more favorable treatment. The university refused to produce a number of the tenure-file documents and asked the EEOC to modify the subpoena to exclude "confidential peer review information." The EEOC refused and successfully sought enforcement of its subpoena through a federal district court. The U.S. Court of Appeals, Third Circuit, affirmed and rejected the university's claim that policy considerations and First Amendment principles of academic freedom required recognition of a qualified privilege or the adoption of a balancing approach that would require the EEOC to demonstrate a showing of need to obtain peer review materials.

The U.S. Supreme Court then held that **a university does not enjoy a special privilege requiring a judicial finding of necessity prior to access of peer review materials**. The Court was reluctant to add such a privilege to protect "academic autonomy" when Congress had failed to do so in Title VII. The Court also stated that "academic freedom" could not be used as the basis for such a privilege. The Court affirmed the lower court decisions. *Univ. of Pennsylvania v. EEOC*, 493 U.S. 182, 110 S.Ct. 577, 107 L.Ed.2d 571 (1990).

B. Hearings and Procedures

◆ *When a property right to employment exists, due process requires that the employee receive notice and an opportunity to be heard before discipline.*

In two consolidated cases, the U.S. Supreme Court considered what pretermination process must be afforded a public employee who can be discharged only for cause. In the first case, a security guard hired by a school board stated on his job application that he had never been convicted of a felony. Upon discovering that he had in fact been convicted of grand larceny, the school board summarily dismissed him for dishonesty in filling out the job application. He was not afforded an opportunity to respond to the dishonesty charge or to challenge the dismissal until nine months later. In the second case, a school bus mechanic was fired because he had failed an eye examination.

The mechanic appealed his dismissal after the fact because he had not been afforded a pretermination hearing. The Supreme Court held that **because the employees possessed a property right in their employment, they were entitled to a pretermination opportunity to at least respond to the charges against them**. The pretermination hearing need not fully resolve the propriety of the discharge, but should be a check against mistaken decisions. The Court held that in this case, the employees were entitled to a pretermination opportunity to respond, coupled with a full-blown administrative hearing at a later time. *Cleveland Board of Educ. v. Loudermill*, 470 U.S. 532, 105 S.Ct. 1487, 84 L.Ed.2d 494 (1985).

◆ *When the disciplinary action is something less than termination, the protections afforded by due process are not the same as required in* Loudermill.

A police officer employed by a Pennsylvania state university was arrested in a drug raid and charged with several felony counts related to marijuana possession and distribution. State police notified the university of the arrest and charges, and the university's human resources director immediately suspended the officer without pay pursuant to a state executive order requiring such action where a state employee is formally charged with a felony. Although the criminal charges were dismissed, university officials demoted the officer because of the felony charges. The university did not inform the officer that it had obtained his confession from police records and he was thus unable to fully respond to damaging statements in the police reports. He filed a federal district court action against university officials for failing to provide him with notice and an opportunity to be heard before his suspension without pay.

The court granted pretrial judgment to the officials, but the U.S. Court of Appeals, Third Circuit, reversed and remanded the case. The U.S. Supreme Court stated that the court of appeals had improperly held that a suspended public employee must always receive a paid suspension under *Cleveland Board of Educ. v. Loudermill*, above. The Court held that **the university did not violate due process by refusing to pay a suspended employee charged with a felony pending a hearing**. It accepted the officials' argument that the Pennsylvania executive order made any pre-suspension hearing useless, since the filing of charges established an independent basis for believing that the officer had committed a felony. The Court noted that the officer here faced only a temporary suspension without pay, and not employment termination as in *Loudermill*. The Court reversed and remanded the case for consideration of the officer's arguments concerning a post-suspension hearing. *Gilbert v. Homar*, 520 U.S. 924, 117 S.Ct. 1807, 138 L.Ed.2d 120 (1997).

◆ *University of North Carolina (UNC) employees must follow UNC employment-dispute-resolution procedures before filing a lawsuit.*

An associate professor completed a probationary year and earned a two-year employment contract. The agreement specified it was "subject to and governed by" UNC's code. A month before his contract was up, the university notified the professor that he would not be rehired. Instead of pursuing an appeal, he sued UNC for wrongful termination. A court dismissed the case, finding it lacked jurisdiction (authority) to hear it. The professor had not exhausted his administrative remedies by completing university appeals before suing. On appeal, the Court of Appeals of North Carolina affirmed the judgment. **North Carolina law required UNC employees to complete university procedures intended to resolve employment disputes before going to court.** As a result, the judgment for UNC was affirmed. *Johnson v. Univ. of North Carolina*, 688 S.E.2d 546 (N.C. Ct. App. 2010).

◆ *A Kentucky community and technical college professor was afforded due process before being demoted for poor job performance.*

The professor received three consecutive negative performance evaluations. After the third, she appealed, but the college president agreed with the evaluations and the college notified her she would be demoted to a temporary, part-time adjunct position. A letter informing the professor of the decision cited her violations of administrative policies and procedures, and her poor job performance. The letter notified her she was on leave without pay and told her she had a right to a pre-demotion hearing. The professor received an administrative hearing where she was represented by counsel and was given the opportunity to show why she should not be demoted. The college allowed her to submit additional information after the hearing, but the college president informed her in writing that she would be demoted. The college then sent the professor a letter advising her of her appeal rights, but later informed her that the demotion was final. This letter outlined reasons for the decision, including job carelessness, poor behavior toward students and staff, and failure to follow security procedures. The letter advised the professor that she had not been discharged and indicated she remained eligible for substitute duties.

The professor sued the college in a state court, claiming it violated her due process rights. The court dismissed her complaint, and she appealed to the Court of Appeals of Kentucky. **The court affirmed the decision, noting that procedural due process is a flexible concept.** Its key components are notice and an opportunity to be heard. In this case, the professor acknowledged that she was given adequate written notice of the charges against her. She also acknowledged that she received a chance to be heard and to present her evidence. As the professor received all the process she was due, the trial court's decision was affirmed. *Bassett v. Board of Regents*, No. 2006-CA-002131-MR, 2007 WL 2687399 (Ky. Ct. App. 9/14/07). In 2008, the Supreme Court of Kentucky denied further consideration of the case.

◆ *An employee on probationary status could not show a California university violated his due process rights.*

The University of California hired the employee under a union contract providing for an initial six-month probationary period. During this time, the university had discretion to fire probationary employees without following collective bargaining grievance procedures. While the employee was still on probation, he was fired for sexual harassment of a co-worker. He sued the university in a federal district court for due process violations. He also argued the university violated his Fourteenth Amendment liberty rights by publicly disclosing the sexual harassment allegation that had been made against him.

The court held for the university, and the employee appealed. The U.S. Court of Appeals, Ninth Circuit, **explained that to be entitled to due process in the form of notice and a hearing, an employee must demonstrate a property interest in employment**. There was no due process violation in this case, as the employee knew he was still in his probationary term and had no property interest in continuing employment. While public employers can violate employee liberty interests by publicly disclosing sexual harassment allegations, the university committed no violation here. The employee could not prove that any co-workers had learned about the sexual harassment charges from the university. Moreover, he would have to tell prospective employers about the charges himself. As the university had been properly granted pretrial judgment, the court affirmed the judgment. *Whitworth v. Regents of Univ. of California*, 274 Fed.Appx. 559 (9th Cir. 2008).

◆ *An Ohio university football coach was allowed to discover and present information to a trial court before it resolved his breach of contract claim.*

The coach became aware that some of his players were conducting voluntary throwing sessions. He knew players could get hurt unless there was some organization to these workouts. An NFL scout arrived at the university looking for game films and information about a senior quarterback. During the visit, the coach allegedly directed the quarterback while the scout watched. The coach's supervisor reprimanded the coach in writing, stating that such contact with players outside NCAA-approved dates was unacceptable. The university investigated allegations that the coach violated the NCAA rules during a pre-season camp. After the investigation, the university suspended him.

The university held a hearing before a five-person faculty committee, then voted to dismiss the coach. He appealed through a grievance process, but the grievance committee rejected the appeal as untimely. The coach sued the university in a state court for breach of contract. The court awarded pretrial judgment to the university, and the coach appealed to the Court of Appeals of Ohio. There, he alleged the trial court had erred by granting judgment without providing him an opportunity to conduct the pretrial fact-finding process called "discovery." The court agreed, finding **the evidence was not developed in a way necessary to properly determine a motion for summary judgment**. It vacated the judgment and returned the case to the trial court to allow discovery. *Kaczkowski v. Ohio Northern Univ.*, No. 6-05-08, 2006 WL 1312401 (Ohio Ct. App. 5/15/06).

◆ *A federal district court held an Illinois university did not violate an employee's constitutional due process rights.*

The employee worked as the university's director of printing. He earned average or above-average job evaluations for 13 years. The university then conducted a financial analysis which showed the office of printing services had a deficit of over $1.1 million. The director's supervisor told him the deficit must be eliminated in one year, even though university policy usually allowed three years to do so. The director alleged most of the deficit was caused by a lease agreement for several hundred copiers. The supervisor and a financial affairs director then began to manage the university's photocopy business themselves. A year later, the university fired the director. He sued the university in a federal district court, alleging it violated his due process rights.

The director argued that the university had disregarded an investigatory recommendation. The court explained that the director had confused state-created procedural requirements with constitutionally protected interests. **A state statute or regulation must guarantee more than a right to certain procedures to rise to the level of a constitutionally protected right.** A right to notice, a hearing, an appeal or an investigation does not create a Fourteenth Amendment Due Process Clause right. The court dismissed the case. *Bant v. Board of Trustees of Univ. of Illinois*, No. 05-2132, 2006 WL 91327 (C.D. Ill. 1/12/06).

◆ *The Supreme Court of Nevada was liable to a tenured professor for breach of contract because it discharged him based on outdated evaluations.*

The university gave the professor consecutive unsatisfactory evaluations, which was cause for termination. It filed a complaint against the professor with its administrative code officer and scheduled a hearing. The parties reached a settlement under which the professor agreed to resign at the end of the academic year. The university agreed to cancel the hearing and offer him a non-tenured teaching contract. The professor refused to sign an employment contract without guaranteed language and sued the university for breach of contract in a Nevada trial court. The court prohibited the university from using the unsatisfactory evaluations as a basis for firing the professor. It ordered the university to continue the professor's employment unless it revoked his tenure.

The university filed another administrative complaint against the professor based on the unsatisfactory evaluations, which were now six years old. It decided its own six-month deadline for hearings did not apply to the time of the settlement and its present administrative complaint. After a hearing, the university fired the professor. He sued the university a second time, alleging the prior court order prohibited the university from using the old evaluations as a basis for termination. **The court held for the professor, and the university appealed. The Supreme Court of Nevada held the university breached the settlement by holding the hearing based on an outdated complaint that included the prior evaluations.** The court found the hearing violated the terms of the settlement agreement and held the university breached the agreement when it unilaterally determined it could proceed with a new hearing. *State of Nevada, Univ. and Community System v. Sutton*, 103 P.3d 8 (Nev. 2004).

◆   *The Court of Appeals of North Carolina held state law precluded administrative review of layoff actions involving state university employees.*

Permanent state funding reductions forced the University of North Carolina at Chapel Hill to eliminate staff positions in various departments. Three employees who were included in the reduction of force pursued grievances that were upheld under university procedures. All three employees filed petitions with the state office of administrative hearings (OAH), alleging they were improperly laid off. A state trial court denied the university's dismissal motions and held the OAH had jurisdiction to determine if just cause supported the layoffs. **The state court of appeals held the OAH only had jurisdiction to hear state employee cases involving demotion, retaliation for opposition to discrimination and disputes relating to veterans preferences.** The state legislature enacted a law that intentionally excluded reductions in force based on procedural violations from OAH jurisdiction. The court directed the trial court to grant the university's dismissal motions. *Univ. of North Carolina v. Feinstein*, 590 S.E.2d 401 (N.C. Ct. App. 2003).

◆   *A university was not liable for firing a professor for harassment prior to a hearing.*

A professor at a New York university was rumored to have sexually harassed a female student. Although no grievance or complaint was filed under the university's grievance procedures, the university took the student's information, gathered other information, and decided to fire the professor. When the student failed to appear at the arbitration hearings mandated by the collective bargaining agreement, the termination was rescinded and the charges against the professor were dismissed. He nevertheless sued the university for failing to follow its own rules when disciplining him. A jury awarded him $25,000 in damages, but the Second Circuit Court of Appeals reversed. Here, the professor failed to show that the university was required to follow the grievance procedures exclusively when making a finding that an employee had engaged in illegal discrimination. Because the university's grievance procedures gave it the flexibility to discipline the professor without formal hearings, there was no breach of duty by the university. *Garcia v. State Univ. of New York at Albany*, 320 F.3d 148 (2d Cir. 2003).

◆ *College officials were not entitled to immunity in a lawsuit brought by a teacher accused of misconduct and barred from campus.*

A music instructor at a Nebraska public college taught for 29 years before retiring. He directed a performance group called "Chorale" in addition to teaching, and continued to work in a part-time capacity after he retired until the college eliminated his position. At that time, the college informed him it was banning him from campus, pending an investigation into alleged embezzlement. The college's letter also accused him of permitting Chorale to have inappropriate sexual overtones in their performances. He sued the college and its officials under 42 U.S.C. § 1983, alleging violations of his substantive and procedural due process rights as well as his free speech and freedom of association rights under the First Amendment. The college and officials asserted qualified immunity and sought a dismissal. A federal court dismissed the substantive due process claims, but refused to dismiss the others.

The Eighth Circuit Court of Appeals affirmed. **The instructor was entitled to a name-clearing hearing because the accusations of dishonesty and immorality were stigmatizing and were known by faculty members at several campuses.** He had a liberty interest in his name and reputation, and the college officials were not entitled to qualified immunity after refusing to provide the hearing. Finally, since the college was a public forum, its officials should have determined whether banning the instructor from campus was the least restrictive way to serve a compelling interest. They were not entitled to qualified immunity on the First Amendment claims either. *Putnam v. Keller*, 332 F.3d 541 (8th Cir. 2003).

◆ *An at-large professor might have been qualified for another position so as to avoid a reduction in force.*

A university hired a dean for its college of business and management, but because of a faculty restructuring, gave him an "at-large" executive appointment. Later, the college merged with the college of professional studies and he was retained as a tenured professor. Finally, a financial crisis caused a reduction in force (RIF), in which he lost his job. He sued the university, claiming that he should have been exempt from the RIF because of his status as an at-large professor. The court ruled for the university, and the D.C. Court of Appeals affirmed in part. Here, **the university had the authority to conduct a RIF and release faculty members.** However, the university never made an initial finding as to whether the professor might have qualified for placement in another department because of his at large status. Thus, that issue had to be remanded to the university. *Hahn v. Univ. of Dist. of Columbia*, 789 A.2d 1252 (D.C. 2002).

◆ *A police officer whose contract was not renewed could not sue for due process violations.*

A Kentucky university hired a police officer under an annual contract. It later suspended him with pay for his involvement in the dubious arrest of several students. He did not challenge the suspension. When the university refused to renew his contract the following year, he sued it under 42 U.S.C. § 1983, asserting due process and equal protection violations. A federal court ruled in favor of the university, and the Sixth Circuit affirmed. It noted that he could not succeed because **he could not show that he had a legitimate expectation of continued employment with the university**. The university's personnel manual did not create a property interest in employment, nor did it require the university to reappoint him. *Baker v. Kentucky State Univ.*, 45 Fed. Appx. 328 (6th Cir. 2002).

◆ *Even if a university violated an employee's procedural due process rights, he did not suffer any harm so as to be entitled to judicial relief.*

A paraprofessional library assistant at a South Carolina university was accused of sexual harassment. Although no formal charges were filed, he was issued several reprimands, which were withdrawn from his file after he challenged them. Several years later, his new assistant accused him of gender discrimination and of making sexual advances toward males in a specific library. The director of the Equal Opportunity Programs (EOPs) office notified him of the allegations but failed to provide him with witness names or details. After yet another complaint, the university temporarily reassigned the employee, then issued him a reprimand and permanently reassigned him, still without providing him with witness names or details of its investigation.

The employee sued the university for violating his due process rights, and a federal court ruled against him. The Fourth Circuit affirmed, noting that even though the EOP office may have violated the employee's procedural due process rights, he could not show that he was deprived of a property interest in employment. **He only had a right to continued employment with the university, not to continued employment in a particular position. Also, he did not suffer a reduction in pay** upon his reassignment. *Parkman v. Univ. of South Carolina*, 44 Fed.Appx. 606 (4th Cir. 2002).

◆ *A North Dakota professor was properly fired where he was able to confront witnesses and challenge evidence in two hearings before his termination.*

A university professor served as chairman of the physics department until his relationships with other faculty members deteriorated and he was removed as chairman. He criticized the department in a number of letters that he sent to university officials and local newspapers. Subsequently, the university received numerous complaints from students about his poor teaching performance. More than 90% of his introductory students transferred out of his class in one semester. The university then sent him a letter of termination that listed six grounds for his firing, including his libelous conduct, his disciplinary record, and his lack of cooperation with faculty members. He obtained a hearing before a special review committee, which ruled in his favor, but the president of the university rejected the committee's findings.

The committee on faculty rights then upheld the dismissal. The professor sued the university in a federal district court under 42 U.S.C. § 1983 for violating his First and Fourteenth Amendment rights. The court ruled for the university, and the professor appealed to the Eighth Circuit. It noted that while two of the professor's letters addressed matters of public concern, most of them did not. The professor could not claim First Amendment protection for all the letters, and the allegedly libelous material in the unprotected letters could be used as a reason for termination. Also, **the professor received due process in that he was given notice of the charges against him and an opportunity to respond**. Thus, his Fourteenth Amendment claim could not succeed. *de Llano v. Berglund*, 282 F.3d 1031 (8th Cir. 2002).

◆ *A Wisconsin professor had six months to seek review of his tenure denial.*

The health, physical education, recreation and coaching department at a Wisconsin university evaluated an assistant professor it was considering recommending for tenure. Her teaching and service were above average, but her research was below average because none of the four articles she had submitted for publication had been published. The department decided not to recommend tenure. A grievance panel determined that the department should have considered her manuscripts. However, when the executive committee met, she had to submit revised drafts because she failed to keep copies of the originals. The committee refused to consider the revised drafts and voted to deny tenure. When she later sought judicial review, the university sought to dismiss her petition because it was not filed within the statutory 30-day deadline for contested tenure cases. A trial court dismissed the petition, but the Wisconsin Court of Appeals reversed. **Cases involving denial of tenure were not contested cases, but rather uncontested.** As such, she had six months to petition for review, and her petition was timely filed. The court remanded the case for further proceedings. *Hedrich v. Board of Regents of Univ. of Wisconsin System*, 635 N.W.2d 650 (Wis. Ct. App. 2001).

V. WRONGFUL DISCHARGE

"Employment at-will" exists in the absence of an oral or written contract of employment. When an employee works "at will," the law presumes the employment relationship may be terminated by either party at any time for any reason. However, an employer may not discharge an employee for an unlawful reason, such as reporting illegal or fraudulent conduct or agreeing to give testimony in an action that may be adverse to the employer's interests.

◆ *A New Jersey university's refusal to hire a wrestling coach for a full-time paid position may have been a retaliatory response to his previous complaints.*

After volunteering as an assistant wrestling coach for some time, the coach received a series of one-year appointments as a part-time, salaried coach. Midway through the last of the appointments, the head wrestling coach told the coach he would be resigning and that he would recommend him for the job. The coach was hired as a part-time head coach. During the next season, he complained to the school's athletic director about equipment and facilities. When university officials decided to eliminate the wrestling program, the coach solicited donations, helped save the program and won honors for his coaching. Near this time, members of the team were illicitly videotaped while showering.

The university's athletic director planned to fire an assistant for failing to promptly report the discovery of the videotape, and the coach complained that female coaches who engaged in misconduct were treated more leniently. The university created a new full-time job for a head wrestling coach/coordinator of student staffing. The athletic director offered the job to another candidate, and the coach sued the university in a federal district court, claiming he was denied the job due to his previous complaints. The court denied the university's motion for pretrial judgment. **Although the university claimed it hired another candidate for legitimate reasons, factual issues existed as to its true motivation for passing over such a successful coach.** *Sabol v. Montclair State Univ.*, No. 06-3214 (DMC), 2008 WL 2354553 (D.N.J. 6/3/08).

◆ *A University of Washington (UW) employee's state-law claim of retaliation was rejected by a federal district court.*

The employee worked in UW's Computing and Communications (C&C) Department. He used his UW e-mail account to send a vulgar e-mail to the United Way. UW issued the employee a letter of counsel, but a month later he received a favorable performance review and a raise. The employee filed a complaint with the UW department of human resources, claiming a co-worker had distributed a harsh critique of his work and that his supervisor failed to address it. He also claimed he was perceived differently by others who learned about the United Way e-mail, and that he was denied an interview for a job based on the critique and e-mail. The employee then resigned to accept another job at UW. He was placed on home assignment for the duration of his two-week notice period. The employee complained that the C&C Department had discriminated and retaliated against him, but the UW complaint resolution office found the complaint unfounded. He then sent harassing e-mails to several UW officials, leading to the termination of his employment.

The employee sued UW in a federal district court for retaliation. However, the claim was filed under a state law that makes it unlawful to discharge an employee who has opposed unlawful employment practices. **The court granted UW's motion for pretrial judgment, because the employee did not show he opposed any practice forbidden by the state law against discrimination.** He did not show how a critique of his work, or his supervisor's alleged failure to intervene regarding criticism, constituted behavior prohibited by the statute. Even if the employee could show he engaged in protected conduct, his claim would fail because he was fired for sending harassing e-mails. The court awarded pretrial judgment to UW. *Cooper v. Univ. of Washington*, No. C06-1365RSL, 2007 WL 3356809 (W.D. Wash. 11/8/07).

◆ *The Court of Appeals of Michigan interpreted the term "public body" broadly to allow an employee to pursue a whistleblower action.*

The U.S. Department of Education (DOE) investigated student financial assistance programs at a Michigan college. An administrator who cooperated with the DOE was later discharged. She sued the college in state court, relying on a state whistleblower statute to support her claim that she was fired for participating in the DOE investigation. The court held the college, finding the DOE was not a "public body" under the whistleblower law. The administrator appealed to the Court of Appeals of Michigan, which noted the power to arrest was not the only factor to consider when determining whether an agency was a "law enforcement agency" under the whistleblower law. Instead, it was appropriate to consider the extent of the DOE's overall power to detect and punish legal violations.

The DOE has broad investigatory powers, including the power to gain access to people and documents and to issue subpoenas. DOE officials are authorized to execute warrants and make arrests. **In light of the broad powers granted to the DOE, the appeals court concluded the DOE was a "law enforcement agency" within the meaning of the state whistleblower law.** It reversed and remanded the case for further proceedings. *Ernsting v. Ave Maria College*, 274 Mich. App. 506, 736 N.W.2d 574 (Mich. Ct. App. 2007).

◆ *A federal district court held Connecticut College did not cause a director of development emotional distress during termination proceedings.*

After the director of development had worked for the college about two years, a newly hired vice president stated at a meeting that he perceived her position to be a "senior major gift officer" and not director of development. A month later, the acting vice president of development and alumni relations gave the director a negative performance evaluation. The college soon demoted her to a position designated "senior development officer of major gifts." The director's next performance evaluation was critical of her performance and a month later, the college discharged her. The director sued the college in a federal district court for negligently inflicting emotional distress, among other claims. The college moved for dismissal of the emotional distress claim.

The court stated that the time period identified by the director as the basis for her emotional distress claim involved routine employment matters such as job performance evaluations, work assignments, job transfers and title transfers. While these actions may have played a part in the employment action, they did not occur during a "termination process." **A claim for negligent infliction of emotional distress must be based on conduct during the termination itself, not during the time leading up to it.** Since the employee offered insufficient evidence of negligent conduct by the university at a relevant time, the court dismissed the case. *Stitt v. Connecticut College*, No. Civ. A. 3:04 CV577 (CFD), 2005 WL 646218 (D. Conn. 2005).

◆ *The Supreme Court of Iowa held that opposition to a co-worker's discharge was not "protected activity."*

Drake University investigated a security officer for an arrest he made during the annual Drake Relays. The officer was placed on desk duty for three months, then discharged. A university shift sergeant defended the officer's actions and offered to testify on his behalf. The university asked the sergeant to stop discussing the incident with the press, but he continued to talk openly about it. The university then demoted him one rank, resulting in a pay cut. The sergeant resigned and sued the university in an Iowa court, asserting he was constructively discharged for engaging in protected activity. The court awarded the university summary judgment. The state appeals court affirmed.

The state supreme court held that to succeed in a wrongful discharge claim, the sergeant had to establish that his advocacy established a clearly defined public policy that would be undermined by his termination. He would also have to show his termination resulted from his participation in a protected activity and for no other reason. **The court found that opposing a co-worker's wrongful termination was not a "protected activity" under state law.** While public policy protected employees offering truthful testimony at legal proceedings, there was no indication the discharged officer had intended to sue the university. The court affirmed the judgment for the university. *Shoop v. Drake Univ.*, 672 N.W.2d 335 (Iowa 2003).

◆ *A Florida District Court of Appeal held a whistleblower complaint was properly dismissed by the state human relations commission.*

After being discharged, a community college provost filed a complaint with the Florida Commission on Human Relations, accusing college trustees of violating the state whistleblower act. The commission dismissed her complaint because the college was not a "state agency" under state law. The provost appealed to a state district court of appeal. The court found the list of statutory terms for the definition of "state agency" included any official, officer, commission, board or department of the executive branch of state government. For the provost to establish the commission's jurisdiction to investigate her claim, she would have to show the board of trustees was part of the executive branch. However, state law described community colleges as state political subdivisions and emphasized the difference between political subdivisions and state agencies. **As the board of trustees was not a board of the executive branch of state government, the commission lacked jurisdiction to investigate the complaint.** *Caldwell v. Board of Trustees Broward Community College*, 858 So.2d 1199 (Fla. Dist. Ct. App. 2003).

◆ *An Illinois court denied a professor's claims against a university for defamation, breach of contract and invasion of privacy.*

A divinity school was considering an associate professor for tenure when the administration received complaints about the way he ran his classes. A tenure committee conducted an investigation and learned that students considered him rude and abrasive. They reported he deviated from class topics and was unprofessional. School administrators spoke with the professor several times about these concerns and warned him that failure to change his conduct would result in termination. The professor denied the charges and the school suspended him. He claimed the charges harmed his professional reputation and that communications to students and faculty about termination constituted defamation. He sued the school for defamation and breach of contract. The court dismissed the defamation claim and characterized the termination of his contract as a "buy-out," since it paid the professor in full.

The professor appealed. The Appellate Court of Illinois rejected contract claims relating to the university handbook, which allowed the interviewing of students about classroom decorum. **The university did not breach his contract by failing to renew it after extending the tenure review process.** Under the faculty constitution, notice of termination was to be given by March 1 of the year, except in cases of moral turpitude. Since the professor did not receive notice by this deadline, he argued colleagues and students would infer he was fired on grounds of moral turpitude. The court rejected his claim and affirmed the judgment. The invasion of privacy claim failed because the professor did not show the university put him in a false light. *Green v. Trinity Int'l Univ.*, 801 N.E.2d 1208 (Ill. App. Ct. 2003).

◆ *Project documents did not prevent a university from eliminating an employee's position.*

A university assigned an employee to work on a project updating the university's financial software system for Y2K compatibility. Several months later, the employee's position was eliminated as part of a reorganization and, after he unsuccessfully applied for a number of other jobs, he was fired. He sued the university for breach of contract, asserting that the project work plans amounted to a contract. The university asserted that the work plans did not constitute an employment contract and that, even if they did, it had not breached the contract. A court found in favor of the university, and the California Court of Appeal affirmed. **The work plans did not prohibit the university from conducting the reorganization or from firing the employee when it had no work for him.** *Jenkins v. California Institute of Technology*, No. B153627, 2002 WL 31529092 (Cal. Ct. App. 2002).

◆ *A university employee could not show that he was fired because of complaints he made about co-workers stealing.*

A receiving clerk in the maintenance department at a Florida university complained to university security officers that his supervisor and co-workers were stealing university property. He was then allegedly subjected to certain retaliatory actions, including a glued office lock, a smoke-filled office, and interference with his radio transmissions. He later asked to take a leave, but his request was rejected when the university determined that he had already exhausted his leave time. He took the time off anyway and was fired. **He sued the university for retaliation under the state whistleblower act,** and a state court ruled against him. The Florida District Court of Appeal affirmed. Here, even if the employee's complaint about stealing was protected speech, he failed to show a causal connection between his complaint and his firing. For being absent without leave, he would have been fired regardless of the complaint. Also, as for the retaliatory actions, he was unable to prove that management was either implicated in the attacks or that it condoned them. *Amador v. Florida Board of Regents*, 830 So.2d 120 (Fla. Dist. Ct. App. 2002).

CHAPTER SIX

Employment Practices and Labor Relations

I. PRIVACY RIGHTS

In City of Ontario, California v. Quon, *this chapter, the U.S. Supreme Court cautioned courts against departing from established law when interpreting privacy rights in electronic forums such as texting. It said "the judiciary risks error by elaborating too fully on the Fourth Amendment implications of emerging technology before its role in society has become clear." Despite changing technology, courts continue to focus on what rights of privacy a public employee may reasonably expect. This inquiry includes evaluation of any applicable employment policies, such as acceptable use policies.*

The Fourth Amendment standard of reasonableness applies to searches of public employees as well as their workspaces, offices and computers. Courts reviewing public employee privacy cases typically balance the employee's reasonable expectations of privacy against the government employer's interest in supervision, control and workplace efficiency. In O'Connor v. Ortega, 480 U.S. 709 (1987), the U.S. Supreme Court held public employees have a reasonable expectation of privacy in their personal workspaces, desks and file cabinets. Acceptable use policies and other workplace rules place limits on reasonable privacy expectations.

A. Electronic Data and Communications

◆   *A California city did not violate a police officer's rights by reviewing text messages on his department-owned pager to find the cause of excess charges.*

A city police department policy reserved management rights to monitor and log all employee e-mail and Internet use without notice. **Employees were informed in a city computer use policy that they had "no expectation of privacy or confidentiality when using these resources."** The department later obtained pagers that could send and receive text messages. If a pager sent and/or received more than an allowed number of characters per month, an additional fee was charged. Employees were notified at a meeting that the city computer policy applied to use of the pagers. The officer's monthly pager usage soon exceeded his text character allotment, and a supervisor reminded him that text messages were like e-mail messages under the policy and were eligible for auditing. The officer's pager use continued to exceed the wireless provider's monthly limit and he agreed to pay for the overages. After several months of collecting overage fees from various officers, the supervisor decided to find out if the character limit was too low or if officers were using pagers for personal messages. Transcripts of text messages obtained from the wireless service revealed that many messages on the officer's pager were not work-related, and that some were sexually explicit. After an investigation, the officer and several others sued the department in a federal district court for Fourth Amendment violations. The court found the officer had a reasonable expectation of privacy. A jury found the supervisor had acted to ensure that officers were not paying for work-related costs. After the U.S. Court of Appeals, Ninth Circuit, reversed the decision, the U.S. Supreme Court held the review of the transcript was a search for Fourth Amendment purposes. Government employees do not lose their Fourth Amendment rights by virtue of their public employment. Public employees have a reasonable expectation of privacy, and government investigations are judged by a "reasonableness" standard. The department made clear that the computer policy applied to text messages, and that users had no expectation of privacy when using city communications systems.

The Court held it was reasonable for the officer to expect privacy in text messages sent on his department pager. Principles of law applying to government searches of employee offices applied in the electronic sphere, particularly the Court's decision in *O'Connor v. Ortega*, this chapter. A government employer's search was reasonable if it was justified at its inception and not excessively intrusive in light of the reasons for the search. The search in this case was justified at its inception, since reasonable grounds existed for investigating pager usage. As the jury found, the search was intended to determine if the character limit on pagers was meeting department needs. This was a legitimate, work-related rationale and the Supreme Court found no

Fourth Amendment violation. A reasonable employee would be aware that sound management principles might require the audit of text messages to determine if the pagers were being used appropriately. As the Court found the search was permissible in scope and motivated by legitimate work-related purposes, it held the department did not violate the officer's rights or the rights of those with whom he communicated. *City of Ontario, California v. Quon*, 130 S.Ct. 2619 (U.S. 2010).

◆ *Officials properly seized an Oklahoma university department head's personal laptop computer as part of a child pornography investigation.*

The case involved a department head at Oklahoma State University (OSU). Another OSU employee reported finding child pornography in a box belonging to the department head. A university dean and associate dean seized the box and turned it over to university police. After legal counsel was consulted, a decision was made to seize the desktop computer in the department head's office. Two members of the university's computer information services security office went to the office and saw a laptop computer on a table near his desk. Although the department head was not present, the laptop was running. The screen showed a university-supported e-mail program. The laptop also showed spreadsheets that appeared to include university records. The security specialists took the hard drive from the desktop computer and also seized the laptop. The contents were retained by the university's police department.

The department head sued university officials, including one of the security specialists, in a federal district court. He claimed the seizure violated the Fourth Amendment. The court relied heavily on the U.S. Supreme Court's ruling in *O'Connor v. Ortega*, above. **It found the search was reasonable, as the purpose was to investigate suspected misconduct involving the possibility that child pornography was being stored on computers located in an on-campus office.** The personal laptop computer was open and running when the security specialists entered the department head's office. The laptop was showing an e-mail program that was supported by the university as well as spreadsheets that looked like they contained university records. Under these circumstances, the search was justified at its inception, and its scope was reasonable. Therefore, the search did not violate the Fourth Amendment. The remaining state-law claim was dismissed. *Soderstrand v. State of Oklahoma*, 463 F.Supp.2d 1308 (W.D. Okla. 2006).

◆ *The Tennessee Court of Appeals applied Florida decisions in finding public school Internet records and e-mails were not open to public inspection.*

A Tennessee citizen made a written request to a county education board to view and inspect digital records of Internet activity, including e-mails sent and received, Web sites visited, and the identity of Internet service providers used during school hours or stored on school-owned computers. A trial court judge reviewed the requested records privately and found they were not accessible under the state Public Records Act (PRA).

The citizen appealed to the Court of Appeals of Tennessee, asserting the digital records or documents were open to public inspection because they had been made during business hours or were stored on the school's computers.

The court found the PRA's clear purpose favored the disclosure of public records. The PRA defined "public record" to include documents, papers, electronic data processing files and other material "made or received pursuant to law or ordinance or in connection with the transaction of official business by any governmental agency." The PRA did not limit access to records based on the time a record was created or the place the record was produced or stored. The trial court judge had properly inspected documents in private to decide if they were "made or received pursuant to law or ordinance or in connection with the transaction of official business." **The Supreme Court of Florida has rejected arguments that placement of a document in a public employee's file made the document a "public record."** The Tennessee PRA definition of "public records" nearly matches the definition used in the Florida Law. The Tennessee court stated that while it was not bound by Florida decisions on public records, it found them well-reasoned and applicable. The trial court did not commit error in privately reviewing the records, and the judgment was affirmed. *Brennan v. Giles County Board of Educ.*, No. M2004-00998-COA-R3-CV, 2005 WL 1996625 (Tenn. Ct. App. 2005).

◆   *A Florida high school teacher accused of exchanging sexually explicit e-mails with students did not have to turn over all his home computers for inspection by his school board for use in an employment termination hearing.*

The board suspended the teacher for misconduct for exchanging e-mails and instant messages with students that were sexually explicit and made derogatory comments about staff members and school operations. An administrative law judge issued an order allowing a board expert to inspect the hard drives of the teacher's home computers to discover if they had relevant data for use against him in a formal termination hearing.

The teacher appealed, arguing production of the home computer records would violate his Fifth Amendment right against self-incrimination and his privacy rights. **The court noted that computers store bytes of information in an "electronic filing cabinet."** It agreed with the teacher that the request for wholesale access to his personal computers would expose confidential communications and extraneous personal information such as banking records. There might also be privileged communications with his wife and his attorney. The only Florida decision discussing the production of electronic records in pretrial discovery held **a request to examine a computer hard drive was permitted "in only limited or strictly controlled circumstances," such as where a party was suspected of trying to purge data**. There was no evidence that the teacher was attempting to thwart the production of evidence in this case. The court held the broad discovery request violated the teacher's Fifth Amendment rights and his personal privacy. It reversed the administrative order allowing the board to have unlimited access to his home computers. *Menke v. Broward County School Board*, 916 So.2d 8 (Fla. Dist. Ct. App. 2005).

◆   *A Florida District Court of Appeal held personal e-mail fell outside the current definition of public records.*

The case involved a newspaper's request for e-mails sent from or received by municipal employees on government-owned computers. The court of appeal held personal e-mail was not "made or received pursuant to law or ordinance." **Although digital in nature, "there was little to distinguish a personal e-mail from personal letters delivered to public employees through a government post office box and stored in a government-owned desk."** The court noted the state supreme court has held "only materials prepared 'with the intent of perpetuating and formalizing knowledge' fit the definition of a public record." The court denied a publisher's request to compel a municipality to release all e-mail sent from or received by two employees on their government-owned computers. *Times Publishing Co. v. City of Clearwater*, 830 So.2d 844 (Fla. Dist. Ct. App. 2002).

◆ *The Second Circuit upheld discipline against a New York state employee for downloading personal tax programs on the state-owned computer he used.*

The state had a policy prohibiting use of state equipment for personal business. The employee came under suspicion of neglecting his duties, and the state authorized an investigation of his computer usage. A list of file names revealed non-standard software was loaded on the computer, and additional searches determined the employee loaded a personal tax preparation program on it. The employee challenged the search of his computer in a federal district court. The court awarded pretrial judgment to the state.

On appeal, the U.S. Court of Appeals, Second Circuit, found no Fourth Amendment violation. The court held that **although the employee had a reasonable expectation of privacy in his office computer, the investigatory searches by the state were upheld as reasonable. The searches of his computer were reasonably related to the objectives of the search and not excessively intrusive** in light of the nature of his suspected misconduct. *Leventhal v. Knapek*, 266 F.3d 64 (2d Cir. 2001).

B. Employee Search and Seizure

Searches and seizures conducted by government employers implicate the Fourth Amendment. Because these searches are not carried out to enforce criminal laws, the courts consider them "administrative searches," which may be justified by the need to protect campus safety and ensure order.

◆ *After being criminally prosecuted for stalking a colleague, a professor filed an unsuccessful civil action against the University of New Hampshire.*

The professor was arrested for disorderly conduct and stalking of another University of New Hampshire professor who accused him of kicking over a garbage can in a lobby and screaming repeatedly. He was also accused of threatening another professor three times and was suspended and banned from campus pending an investigation. After the criminal charges were dismissed, the university reinstated the professor, but he filed a federal lawsuit for violating his First, Fourth, Fifth, Ninth and Fourteenth Amendment rights.

The professor asserted that his arrest for disorderly conduct violated his Fourth Amendment rights and constituted an unreasonable seizure. The court rejected this claim, as people can be arrested based on offenses that are defined as mere "violations" under the state's criminal code. Moreover, the arrest was based on a valid warrant. While the professor argued that an arrest for stalking violated his rights because it was based on a "singular frustrated outburst," the court rejected this theory. A warrant is valid if it is supported by probable cause, which was satisfied in this case by a law enforcement officer's belief that the professor threatened a colleague three times. **According to the court, the standard of probable cause is not difficult to meet, requiring only a reasonable belief that a crime has been committed.** Since the arrest warrant for stalking was supported by probable cause, there was no violation of the Fourth Amendment and the university was entitled to judgment on the claims of false arrest and stalking. *Collins v. Univ. of New Hampshire*, No. 09-cv-78-JM, 2010 WL 1052220 (D.N.H. 3/15/10).

◆ *A court upheld a jury's decision to award $1.65 million to a professor whose laboratory contents were cleared out while he was at a conference.*

Upon accepting adjunct work at the University of the District of Columbia (UDC), the professor brought course materials, research data and lab equipment from another institution, where he had created materials and notes for 20 different courses. UDC had renewed his contract annually for several years when he accused it of reneging on a promise to grant him tenure. The professor filed a lawsuit against UDC. During settlement negotiations, UDC's provost told him to vacate his lab because the space was needed for other programs. After several delays, UDC hired a contractor to clear out the lab while the professor was at a conference. No inventory was made and the movers may have "thrown stuff out." The professor found that 90% of his belongings were gone and that some of his property had been thrown into trash dumpsters.

In a lawsuit against UDC, the professor sought compensation for course materials, research data, scientific instruments and other items. Since most of the property was unique or had no fair market value, he offered testimony from a collaborating biomedical engineering researcher and engineering professor to establish its value. He claimed that class materials he developed for 21 different courses had been taken, and that he lost at least 10 ongoing research projects. A jury found UDC liable for trespass, conversion and negligence and set the damages at $1.65 million. UDC sought a new trial, but the District of Columbia Court of Appeals held the valuation testimony was admissible, rejecting UDC's argument that the experts lacked subject-matter knowledge. **The experts had extensive research experience, were familiar with the professor's work, and articulated their methodologies for estimating damages.** As the jury had reasonably found UDC destroyed much of the professor's life work and ruined his career, the damage award was affirmed. *Trustees of the Univ. of the District of Columbia v. Vossoughi*, 963 A.2d 1162 (D.C. Ct. App. 2009).

◆ *Random searches of public employees must be justified by "major safety concerns" to meet the reasonableness standard of the Fourth Amendment.*

A West Virginia school board implemented a random, suspicionless drug testing policy on employees in 47 "safety sensitive positions." Included were teachers, coaches, cabinetmakers, handymen, plumbers and the district superintendent. Teachers and their employees' association petitioned a state court to prevent implementation of the policy, and the case was removed to a federal district court. It noted drug testing is a "seizure" under the Fourth Amendment. A 19-year veteran teacher testified that he never witnessed a school employee coming to work in an impaired state. And the district superintendent admitted there had been no instances of any student injuries due to a drug- or alcohol-impaired teacher. When a state agency conducts a search, there must ordinarily be individualized suspicion of wrongdoing. **Safety concerns must be of sufficient magnitude to outweigh employee privacy interests in order to uphold an employee testing program.**

The Supreme Court has found special safety needs outweigh employee privacy interests where there are major safety concerns such as a risk of great harm to people and property. In order to justify a search with no reasonable suspicion of a substance violation, the safety interest identified by the state must be concrete. The court found teachers and other school employees did not have a reduced privacy interest by virtue of their public employment. They were not in "safety sensitive" positions according to a line of Supreme Court cases upholding testing programs justified by threats to safety from railroad accidents, failed interdiction of illegal drugs smuggled across national borders and impaired workers at nuclear reactors. The risk of harm stated by the board was speculative, and it did not outweigh the employees' privacy interests. The court issued a preliminary order to prevent the implementation of the policy. *American Federation of Teachers – West Virginia, AFL-CIO v. Kanawha County Board of Educ.*, 592 F.Supp.2d 883 (S.D. W.Va. 2009).

◆ *Three Ohio university police officers who arrested a school janitor for criminal menacing could not be sued for false arrest.*

The janitor reportedly lost his temper after the co-worker ignored a sign he had posted on a restroom door asking people to use a different bathroom. When the janitor told him to leave, the co-worker refused. Furious, the janitor went to their manager. The co-worker followed the janitor to the manager. The janitor threatened the co-worker, who called university police. The co-worker told the officers he was worried because he believed the janitor was capable of violence.

The officers arrested the janitor and charged him with criminal menacing. The janitor sued the university and nine employees in a federal district court. The court held the officers did not have qualified immunity, and they appealed. The U.S. Court of Appeals, Sixth Circuit, held public officials are protected by immunity unless they violate clearly established federal law. **It is clearly established that arrests based upon probable cause do not violate the Fourth Amendment. Sixth Circuit precedent allows police to base probable cause on credible eyewitness reports.** The co-worker stated the janitor had threatened him, and the manager verified his account. As the officers had probable cause for the arrest, the court reversed the judgment. *Franklin v. Miami Univ.*, 214 Fed.Appx. 509 (6th Cir. 2007).

◆ *The special needs of public employers justify allowing them to avoid the warrant and probable cause requirements of the Fourth Amendment.*

The U.S. Supreme Court held that the search of a public employee's office was reasonable when the measures adopted were reasonably related to the objectives of the search and not excessively intrusive in light of its purpose. The

Court held that workplace searches by government employers "should be judged by the standard of reasonableness under all the circumstances."

The Court announced a case-by-case standard for evaluating employee privacy expectations, stating that a public employee's expectation of privacy in the workplace may be reduced by actual office practices, work procedures or rules. Acceptable-use policies governing employee usage of computers and e-mail are examples of such workplace procedures or rules. *O'Connor v. Ortega*, 480 U.S. 709 (1987).

C. Video Surveillance

◆ *California officials were immune to invasion of privacy claims based on the videotaping of an employee's wedding and part of her honeymoon.*

A California teacher submitted a workers' compensation claim for a back injury. She underwent disc replacement surgery and was married while still on disability leave. The School Insurance Program for Employees (SIPE) and the teacher's school district hired an investigator to surreptitiously attend her wedding and obtain videotape of her. The investigator went to the wedding and represented himself as a guest. He videotaped the ceremony and the reception. The day after the wedding, the investigator videotaped the teacher and her husband while they sunbathed on the balcony of a rented room. The teacher sued the district, SIPE and others in a state superior court for invasion of privacy and negligence. The court dismissed the case, and the teacher appealed.

The Court of Appeal of California held that SIPE and the school district were only liable for injuries as provided by state Government Code Section 815. The code immunized public employees for injuries caused by instituting or prosecuting any judicial or administrative proceeding within the scope of their employment. This was true even if an employee acted maliciously and absent probable cause. If the employee had immunity, so did the employing public entity. The court rejected the teacher's claim that SIPE and her district "intended to harass her," not to conduct an investigation or disciplinary action. **The investigation was an essential step to a judicial or administrative proceeding and was "cloaked in immunity."** The investigation was within the scope of the investigator's employment. For this reason, the district and SIPE were entitled to government code immunity and there was no liability for either agency under the government code. The government Tort Claims Act did not authorize invasion of privacy suits against a public employee. *Richardson-Tunnell v. School Insurance Program for Employees (SIPE)*, 157 Cal.App.4th 1065, 69 Cal.Rptr.3d 176 (Cal. Ct. App. 2007).

◆ *A Massachusetts state college did not violate an employee's privacy rights by videotaping her without her knowledge.*

The employee worked in the college's small business development center. Many employees and volunteers had keys to the office and were allowed to enter and leave after business hours. Visitors did not have to check in at the front desk before entering. The college learned a former client who was being investigated for criminal activity had entered the building without permission after hours. Without informing the employee the college installed a hidden security camera on the rear wall of the office. For three weeks, she went to a rear work area, unbuttoned her blouse and applied ointment to a severe sunburn. The area was under video surveillance, but tape recordings did not show any images of her. The employee learned about the videotaping and sued the college in a state court for violating her Fourth Amendment privacy rights.

The court held the college was protected from liability by qualified immunity, and the employee appealed. **The Supreme Judicial Court of Massachusetts stated a person's constitutional right to privacy is violated only if an alleged invasion of privacy occurs where a person has a reasonable expectation of privacy.** Generally, a person's reasonable expectation of privacy on business premises is less than the expectation of privacy in a home. While the law recognizes some privacy interests in business premises, people cannot have a reasonable expectation of privacy in open places. The office was open to the public all day and visitors did not have to check in. Volunteers and employees could get into the office at any time with keys supplied by the college. There was no absolute guarantee of privacy, even when the employee locked the front door before she applied ointment. Despite her efforts to discreetly conduct personal and private acts in the office, she had no objectively reasonable expectation of privacy there. Accordingly, the court affirmed the judgment for the college. *Nelson v. Salem State College*, 446 Mass. 525, 845 N.E.2d 338 (Mass. 2006).

D. Personnel Records

State data privacy acts protect the confidentiality of public employee personnel files. Common law rules of defamation may also provide a basis for legal action against a school district or its officers for wrongful disclosure of private facts or erroneous factual statements.

1. Media Access

◆ *A Pennsylvania newspaper and reporter had a right to see current and past salary information for certain employees of a state university.*

The reporter asked the State Employees' Retirement System (SERS) for salary information on state university employees. The state right-to-know act provides that "public records" kept by a government agency are accessible for inspection. A "public record" is "any account, voucher or contract dealing with the receipt or disbursement of funds by an agency." However, any record or document which would prejudice or impair a person's reputation or personal security is not considered a public record. Before SERS responded to the request, it notified the university.

The university and employees claimed the salary information was private and protected from release by the Constitution. The State Employees' Retirement Board granted the request, finding the information was a public record. The case reached the Supreme Court of Pennsylvania, which held it was proper to disclose the requested information under the state's right-to-know act. The SERS' fiduciary duties extended to investment matters but were not applicable to requests for salary information. The court rejected the argument that disclosure was barred by the federal Gramm-Leach-Bliley Act, which protects the privacy of consumer information held by financial services industry institutions. Finally, the court rejected the employees' argument that disclosure would violate their right to privacy. **Although a privacy exception in the right-to-know law excused disclosure that would "prejudice or [impair] a person's reputation or personal security," the exception did not apply because the employees' privacy rights did not outweigh the public interest** in information about the disbursement of state funds. *Pennsylvania State Univ. v. State Employees' Retirement Board*, 594 Pa. 244, 935 A.2d 530 (Pa. 2007).

◆   *The private consideration of applicants for a university president violated the Minnesota Open Meetings Law and Government Data Practices Act.*

The University of Minnesota Board of Regents searched for a new president for the university. Some applicants requested anonymity, and the board voted to screen them privately. The board denied information requests by media organizations about unsuccessful candidates. The organizations sued the board in the state court system for an order forcing disclosure of the information and enjoining the university from holding closed meetings. The court entered summary judgment for the media, and the board appealed.

The state court of appeals noted that **the government data privacy act made public all personnel data on current and former applicants for employment by a statewide agency**. The names of applicants were considered "private data," except for finalists. Since the university was a statewide agency, and because the candidates were deemed "finalists," the court held the data practices act applied to procedures for selecting a university president. The only exception to the open meetings law applied to disciplinary proceedings, and did not apply in this case. Accordingly, the court affirmed the decision to grant the media organizations' motion. *Star Tribune Co. v. Univ. of Minnesota*, 667 N.W.2d 447 (Minn. Ct. App. 2003).

2. Disclosure to Third Parties

◆   *California State University (CSU) trustees did not violate the state open meetings act by discussing a former chancellor's status in a closed session.*

A former CSU chancellor wanted to return to CSU as a trustee professor. Anticipating his return would result in publicity, he scheduled a closed session of the board of trustees. At the meeting, the board approved his return as a trustee professor. The president of the union representing faculty members sued the board under the state open meetings act, claiming the subject matter required a public session, and seeking an order to disclose what happened in the session. A state superior court rejected the action, and the union appealed.

The Court of Appeal of California held **an open meetings act exception applied to meetings held to consider the appointment, employment, evaluation of performance, or dismissal of a public employee**. The court held that disclosure in this case would run counter to the policy of shielding employees from unwarranted embarrassment and publicity. The board simply wanted to discuss the former chancellor's vested right to return as a professor, and to address any questions. As the superior court did not commit error, the judgment was affirmed. *Travis v. Board of Trustees of California State Univ.*, 161 Cal.App.4th 335, 73 Cal.Rptr.3d 854 (Cal. Ct. App. 2008).

◆   *The Family Educational Rights and Privacy Act (FERPA) did not prevent an Ohio community college from disclosing prior complaints against an instructor accused of sexually harassing a student.*

In a federal district court action against the college, it was claimed that an instructor's supervisor knew of past misconduct and that the college and supervisor failed to take adequate steps to eliminate the risk he posed. During pretrial activity, the student sought rosters from classes taught by the instructor for the four years prior to the harassment she claimed. She also sought "every document relevant to any student complaint/concern" about the instructor." The college denied the requested information, arguing it could not be disclosed under FERPA. The court disagreed, finding some prior student complaints could be relevant. Complaints that were similar to the student's would support charges that the college and supervisor were aware of prior misconduct. The court concluded that the request should be limited to prior complaints of alleged sexual harassment. **There was insufficient evidence to show that class rosters were relevant to the student's claims**, and FERPA did not bar the request for prior student complaints relating to alleged sexual harassment. *Briggs v. Board of Trustees Columbus State Community College*, No. 2:08-CV-644, 2009 WL 2047899 (S.D. Ohio 7/8/09).

◆   *Michigan law permitted a public university to decline disclosing a record containing personal information, if disclosure would be a privacy invasion.*

The Michigan Federation of Teachers submitted a Freedom of Information Act (FOIA) request to the University of Michigan (UM) for employee names, home addresses, home phone numbers, job titles, pay rates, and work contact information. UM provided most of the information, including home addresses and phone numbers for about 21,000 employees who had given permission to publish this information in a staff and faculty directory. As to the remaining 16,406 employees, UM denied the request on privacy grounds. The Michigan Federation of Teachers and School Related Personnel sued UM in a state court, seeking the remaining addresses and phone numbers. The court held employee home addresses and phone numbers were personal information and not likely to contribute to the public's understanding of how the government works.

The case reached the Supreme Court of Michigan, which explained that **public entities may refuse to disclose a public record, if the record includes information of a personal nature and disclosure "would constitute a clearly unwarranted invasion of an individual's privacy."** The court expanded the definition of "information of a personal nature" to include private or confidential information. Employee home addresses and phone numbers were clearly of a private and confidential nature. Disclosure of this information could subject employees to potential abuses, such as having it used for marketing purposes. Disclosure could also place employees in physical danger if their information fell into the wrong hands. The court held disclosure was unwarranted because it would reveal little or nothing about the conduct of the university and would do nothing to advance the public policy behind the FOIA. *Michigan Federation of Teachers and School Related Personnel v. Univ. of Michigan*, 481 Mich. 657, 753 N.W.2d 28 (Mich. 2008).

◆ *A Missouri college did not violate an untenured professor's right to privacy by confirming to another institution that he was employed there.*

The professor signed a contract to be a full-time, tenure-track professor of business administration during his second year at the college. A representative from DeVry University called the college's human resources (HR) department. She gave the department the professor's Social Security number and asked if he was working full time at the college. The HR department confirmed that he was. The representative then asked the HR department if it knew the professor was on disability leave from DeVry. The HR department said it did not. The DeVry representative said the professor committed insurance fraud by claiming he was disabled when he was not. DeVry discharged the professor. The college soon reduced its staff and told the professor his contract would not be renewed.

The college's long-term disability carrier denied the professor's application for benefits. The professor was told to file another claim seeking benefits for a period during which he was not working and receiving a full salary. The professor continued to teach at the college, but sued the college and several officials in a state court for privacy rights violations. **The court found the only evidence the professor presented was the phone call between DeVry and the HR department. He did not indicate any confidential information was shared when the HR department confirmed he worked at the college.** The court granted the university's motion to dismiss the case. *Fish v. William Jewel College*, No. 05-00025-CV-W-DW, 2006 WL 2228975 (W.D. Mo. 8/3/06).

II. LABOR RELATIONS

The National Labor Relations Act (NLRA), as amended by the Labor Management Relations Act (LMRA), 29 U.S.C. § 141, et seq., governs unionization and collective bargaining matters in the private sector, including private education. States are also subject to the dictates of the act. The NLRA was passed to protect the rights of employees to organize, or to choose not to organize, and to ensure that commerce is not interrupted by labor disputes. Managerial employees are unprotected by the NLRA.

A. Appropriate Bargaining Units

◆ *The Supreme Court held a public university could require faculty to emphasize undergraduate instruction without bargaining over the new rule.*

The Ohio legislature passed a statute requiring state universities to adopt faculty workload policies and made them an inappropriate subject for collective bargaining. The law was enacted to address the decline in the amount of time faculty spent teaching, as opposed to time spent on research. Any university policy prevailed over the contrary provisions of collective bargaining agreements. One university adopted a workload policy pursuant to the law and notified the collective bargaining agent that it would not bargain over the policy. As a result, the professors' union filed a state court action, seeking an order that the statute violated public employee equal protection rights.

The Supreme Court of Ohio struck down the statute, finding the collective bargaining exemption was not rationally related to the state's interest of encouraging public university professors to spend less time researching at the expense of undergraduate teaching.The U.S. Supreme Court accepted the university's appeal, and held that the state supreme court had not applied the correct standard of review under the Equal Protection Clause. In equal protection clause cases that do not involve fundamental rights or suspect classifications, there need only be a rational relationship between disparity of treatment and some legitimate government purpose. In this case, the disputed statute met the rational relationship standard. Ohio could reasonably conclude that the policy would be undercut if it were subjected to collective bargaining. **The state legislature could properly determine that collective bargaining would interfere with the legitimate goal of achieving uniformity in faculty workloads.** The Ohio Supreme Court decision was reversed and remanded. *Cent. State Univ. v. American Ass'n of Univ. Professors, Cent. State Univ. Chapter,* 526 U.S. 124, 119 S.Ct. 1162, 143 L.Ed.2d 227 (1999).

◆ *An exclusive bargaining representative should have the sole voice in discussing employment-related matters with the employer.*

Minnesota community college faculty members brought suit against the State Board for Community Colleges. **The faculty alleged that a state statute requiring public employers to engage in official exchanges of views only with their professional employees' exclusive representatives on certain policy questions violated their First Amendment rights.** Under the statute, public employers were required to bargain only with the employees' exclusive bargaining representative. The statute gave professional employees, such as college faculty members, the right to "meet and confer" with the employer on matters outside the scope of the collective bargaining agreement.

The faculty members objected to the "meet and confer" provision, saying that rights of professional employees within the bargaining unit who were not members of the exclusive representative were violated. The U.S. Supreme Court held that the "meet and confer" provision did not violate the faculty members' constitutional rights. **There was no constitutional right to force public employers to listen to the members' views.** The fact that an academic setting was involved did not give them any special constitutional right to a voice in the employer's policymaking decisions. Further, the state had a legitimate interest in ensuring that its public employer heard one voice presenting the majority view of its professional employees on employment-related policy questions. *Minnesota Community College Ass'n v. Knight,* 465 U.S. 271, 104 S.Ct. 1058, 79 L.Ed.2d 299 (1984).

◆ *In certain circumstances, faculty members at private educational institutions can be considered managerial employees.*

Yeshiva University's faculty association had petitioned the National Labor Relations Board (NLRB) for certification as bargaining agent for all faculty members. The NLRB granted certification but the university refused to bargain. After the U.S. Court of Appeals declined to enforce the NLRB's order that the university bargain with the union, the NLRB appealed to the U.S. Supreme Court, which upheld the appeals court. The Supreme Court's ruling was based on its conclusion that Yeshiva's faculty were managerial employees. It stated:

> The controlling consideration in this case is that the faculty of Yeshiva University exercise authority which in any other context unquestionably would be managerial. **Their authority in academic matters is absolute.** They decide what courses will be offered, when they will be scheduled, and to whom they will be taught. They debate and determine teaching methods, grading policies, and matriculation standards. They effectively decide which students will be admitted, retained, and graduated. On occasion their views have determined the size of the student body, the tuition to be charged, and the location of a school. When one considers the function of a university, it is difficult to imagine decisions more managerial than these. To the extent the industrial analogy applies, the faculty determines within each school the product to be produced, the terms upon which it will be offered, and the customers who will be served.

The Court noted that its decision applied only to schools that were "like Yeshiva" and not to schools where the faculty exercised less control. **Schools where faculty do not exercise binding managerial discretion do not fall within the scope of the managerial employee exclusion.** *NLRB v. Yeshiva Univ.*, 444 U.S. 672, 100 S.Ct. 856, 63 L.Ed.2d 115 (1980).

◆ *A District of Columbia court remanded an NLRB decision recognizing a bargaining unit for college faculty members.*

Approximately 60 full-time faculty members at LeMoyne-Owen College attempted to form a collective bargaining unit. The college denied the request because it considered them managerial employees who were exempt from NLRA coverage. The faculty petitioned the NLRB for recognition as a bargaining unit. The college opposed the petition, citing the Supreme Court's decision in *NLRB v. Yeshiva Univ.*, above, as controlling precedent. The NLRB regional director found the college's faculty were not managerial employees and certified the bargaining unit. The college sought review, arguing the regional director deviated from *Yeshiva* and other precedents.

The NLRB found the college guilty of an unfair labor practice when it refused to bargain with the new bargaining unit. The college petitioned for review of the NLRB's order. The District of Columbia Circuit Court remanded the case. While deference is generally afforded to the NLRB's authority to certify bargaining units, the decision in this case departed from precedent without explanation. The NLRB had an obligation to explain itself. The college made a reasoned argument based on the *Yeshiva* case. The regional director did not explain why the college's argument should be rejected. The court remanded the case to the NLRB for further proceedings. *LeMoyne-Owen College v. NLRB*, 357 F.3d 55 (D.C. Cir. 2004).

◆ *A Michigan court upheld a determination by the State Employment Relations Commission to deny a petition to merge two bargaining units.*

Kendall College of Art and Design is a sub-unit of Ferris State University that retains its academic governance and operates autonomously. The Ferris Faculty Association, which represented full-time faculty members at the university, petitioned to add the Kendall bargaining unit to its bargaining unit. The Kendall unit was composed of full-time and part-time faculty members.

The Michigan Employment Relations Commission denied the petition, and the association appealed. The Court of Appeals of Michigan explained a commission's determination of appropriate bargaining units was factual, and could not be disturbed unless there was a lack of competent, material, and substantial evidence. In reaching its decision, the commission focused on Kendall's academic autonomy from the university and the differences between the two educational institutions. The court rejected the association's argument that the commission erred in considering the bargaining history of the Kendall union. **Bargaining history is a relevant factor in considering whether a bargaining unit is appropriate.** The commission acknowledged the need "to avoid fractionalization or multiplicity of bargaining units." As the Kendall bargaining unit served its members well, it was an appropriate bargaining unit. The commission's decision was affirmed. *Ferris Faculty Ass'n v. Ferris State Univ.*, No. 243885, 2004 WL 144671 (Mich. Ct. App. 2004).

◆ *The Second Circuit refused to enforce a National Labor Relations Board (NLRB) order requiring a New York college to bargain with a union because supervisors belonged to the union.*

The Security Department Membership (SDM) is the organization certified by the NLRB to represent Quinnipiac College's security personnel in collective bargaining. Quinnipiac refused to bargain with SDM, maintaining the organization was improperly certified because it included supervisors, who are excluded from collective bargaining under the NLRA. SDM was certified to include six dispatchers, four traffic-control officers, two shift supervisors and 18 assistant supervisors, four of whom act as shift supervisors at certain times. Quinnipiac objected to the inclusion of the two shift supervisors and the assistant supervisors who acted as shift supervisors. The NLRB conducted a hearing in response to the college's objection, but concluded the shift supervisors were not "supervisors" under the act. The board ordered Quinnipiac to bargain with SDM, but the college refused. The NLRB petitioned the U.S. Court of Appeals, Second Circuit to enforce the order.

The NLRA defines "supervisor" as an employee who has the authority to hire, transfer, suspend, lay off, recall, promote, discharge, assign, reward, discipline or responsibly direct other employees, or address grievances. According to the Second Circuit, Quinnipiac's shift supervisors made assignment decisions based on their own expertise and experience, despite the existence of college procedures. Shift supervisors also disciplined employees. Although security directors had to review any disciplinary procedures taken by the shift supervisors, they still amounted to a supervisor's duty. Lastly, the shift supervisors responsibly directed other security employees. In declining to enforce the NLRB's order, the Second Circuit remanded the matter, with the suggestion that the board review the membership of SDM and consider eliminating the shift supervisors from the bargaining unit. *NLRB v. Quinnipiac College*, 256 F.3d 68 (2d Cir. 2001).

◆   *A state labor relations board used incorrect tests to determine whether two employees were "confidential employees" who were ineligible for the union.*

A union sought to represent all classified and specialist employees at an Illinois college. In the representation election, the union won by a single vote. The college challenged the result, asserting that two of the employees should not have been allowed to vote because they were "confidential employees" under the state labor relations act. One was a secretary; the other was a research associate – both reported to an assistant vice president for administrative affairs. An administrative law judge determined that the employees were confidential employees, and the state labor relations board upheld that decision.

The Appellate Court of Illinois reversed and remanded the case, finding that the board used the wrong tests to determine whether the employees were "confidential." Here, **although the college asserted that the employees were going to be performing duties related to the collective bargaining process, they had not yet done so.** Thus, the board should have determined whether there was a reasonable expectation that future job duties would satisfy the definition of a confidential position. *One Equal Voice v. Illinois Educ. Labor Relations Board*, 777 N.E.2d 648 (Ill. App. Ct. 2002).

B. Agency Fees

"Agency-shop agreements" entitle unions to charge "agency fees" to employees who are not union members, but who enjoy the representation of unions. The U.S. Supreme Court has held public sector agency-shop arrangements raise First Amendment concerns that individuals may have to contribute to unions as a condition of public employment. **In Abood v. Detroit Board of Educ.,** *below, the Court held unions cannot use agency fees for ideological purposes that are unrelated to collective bargaining.*

◆   *The U.S. Supreme Court upheld a Washington law requiring public employee unions to obtain affirmative authorization from nonmember employees before using agency fees for election-related purposes.*

Washington law permits public employee unions to charge nonmembers who are in the collective bargaining unit an "agency fee" that is equivalent to full union membership dues. In 1992, state voters approved an initiative that prohibited unions from spending the agency fees collected from union nonmembers unless the expenditure was "affirmatively authorized by the individual" nonmember. The initiative became Section 760 of the Fair Campaign Practices Act. The Washington Education Association (WEA) faced separate state court actions claiming it used nonmember agency fees for election-related purposes without the affirmative authorization of union nonmembers. The Supreme Court of Washington held the affirmative authorization requirement violated the First Amendment. The State of Washington and other parties appealed to the U.S. Supreme Court.

The court held *Abood* **and later decisions did not require public sector union to obtain affirmative consent before spending nonmember agency fees for purposes unrelated to collective bargaining**. The Court said Section 760 was a "modest limitation" on the extraordinary power of a private union over public employees to prohibit the use of agency fees for election-related purposes. This did not violate the First Amendment. In fact, the Court stated "it would be constitutional for Washington to eliminate agency fees entirely." The Court vacated the state court decision, finding Section 760 was a constitutional condition that presented no realistic threat of official suppression of ideas. *Davenport v. Washington Educ. Ass'n*, 551 U.S. 177 127 S.Ct. 2372, 168 L.Ed.2d 71 (2007).

◆ *Compelled agency fees cannot be used to support political viewpoints.*

In 1977, the U.S. Supreme Court held that the First Amendment prohibited states from compelling teachers to pay union dues or agency fees where their labor unions used the fees for purposes that were unrelated to collective bargaining. Compelled support of collective bargaining representatives implicated free speech, freedom of association, and freedom of religion concerns. However, some constitutional infringement on those rights was justified in the interest of peaceful labor relations. Thus, as long as the union acted to promote the cause of its membership, individual members were not free to withdraw their financial support. However, **compelled agency fees could not be used to support political views and ideological causes that were unrelated to collective bargaining issues**. *Abood v. Detroit Board of Educ.*, 431 U.S. 209, 97 S.Ct. 1782, 52 L.Ed.2d 261 (1977).

◆ *In order to justify agency fees, the activities for which the fees are collected must be germane to collective bargaining activity, be justified by the government's interest in labor peace (and the avoidance of free riders), and present only an insignificant burden on employee speech.*

The exclusive bargaining representative of the faculty at a state college in Michigan entered into an agency-shop arrangement with the college requiring nonunion bargaining unit employees to pay a service or agency fee equivalent to a union member's dues. Employees who objected to particular uses by the unions of their service fee brought suit under 42 U.S.C. § 1983, claiming that using the fees for purposes other than negotiating and administering the collective bargaining agreement violated their First and Fourteenth Amendment rights. A federal district court held that certain collective bargaining expenses were chargeable to the dissenting employees. The U.S. Court of Appeals affirmed, and the U.S. Supreme Court granted certiorari. The Court first noted that chargeable activities must be "germane" to collective bargaining activity and be justified by the policy interest of avoiding "free riders" who benefit from union efforts without paying for union services. It then stated that **the local union could charge the objecting employees for their *pro rata* share of costs associated with chargeable activities of its state and national affiliates, even if those activities did not directly benefit the local bargaining unit**. The local could even charge the dissenters for expenses incident to preparation for a strike, which would be illegal under Michigan law. However, lobbying activities and public relations efforts were not chargeable to the objecting employees. The Court affirmed in part and reversed in part the lower courts' decisions and remanded the case. *Lehnert v. Ferris Faculty Ass'n*, 500 U.S. 507, 111 S.Ct. 1950, 114 L.Ed.2d 572 (1991).

◆ *A union's objection procedures for challenging nonmembers' dues were constitutional.*

Two University of Alaska professors challenged their union's procedures for calculating nonmember dues. Under the collective bargaining agreement, if they declined union membership, they had a choice of either objecting to the use of their dues for unrelated union activities (and paying a reduced agency fee) or requesting arbitration to determine if the nonmember fee was accurate. Under the second option, the arbitrator had the option of raising the amount. A federal court ruled that the union's procedure was constitutional, and the Ninth Circuit Court of Appeals affirmed. Here, the procedures complied with the requirements set forth by the U.S. Supreme Court in *Chicago Teachers Union v. Hudson*, 475 U.S. 292 (1986). **The professors received an adequate explanation of the basis for calculating the agency fee, and they were provided with a reasonably prompt opportunity to challenge the amount of the fee before an impartial decisionmaker.** *Carlson v. United Academics-AAUP/AFT/APEA AFL-CIO*, 265 F.3d 778 (9th Cir. 2001).

◆ *An Illinois local failed to provide adequate procedural protections to non-bargaining unit members who objected to its nonrepresentational activities.*

In federal court, a group of non-bargaining unit members, employed by a university as clerical employees, filed a class action suit against the union. The nonmembers asserted that the union's fair share fee collection procedure failed to provide sufficient safeguards, thereby violating the First and Fourteenth Amendments. The union moved to dismiss the complaint. The court interpreted the union's response as a pretrial judgment motion and ruled in favor of the union. The employees appealed.

The Seventh Circuit reversed. Pursuant to the Illinois Educational Labor Relations Act (IELRA), the amount of fair share fees "can neither exceed union dues nor include any costs related to supporting candidates for political office." In *Chicago Teachers Union v. Hudson*, 475 U.S. 292 (1986), the U.S. Supreme Court required a union to satisfy the following three prongs in collecting these fees: (1) provide "an adequate explanation of the basis for the fee"; (2) provide the nonmember with a reasonable opportunity to protest the fee amount; and (3) establish "an escrow account for the amounts in dispute." Here, the union had the university collect 100% of union dues from both members and nonmembers, even though the fair share fee calculated for two of the disputed years amounted to about 85% of full dues. When an objection was filed, the nonmember fees were then held in an escrow account, which could not be accessed by the union. **The collection of fees, based on an advance reduction approach, was not as problematic as the dispute resolution procedure.** Under the IELRA, objectors were deprived of 15% of their funds for a year, a portion of which was not even being disputed. In addition, the fee objections had to be renewed annually. These burdens violated the *Hudson* test. *Tavernor v. Illinois Federation of Teachers*, 226 F.3d 842 (7th Cir. 2000).

◆ *Massachusetts' highest court held expenses related to a two-day strike by university faculty were not germane to collective bargaining.*

Public school teachers and state university instructors sued the Massachusetts Teachers Association (MTA) for charging them agency fees for activities the teachers claimed were not part of doing business as a bargaining representative. The Massachusetts Labor Relations Commission examined the MTA's expenditures for 1990–1991 to determine which expenses were chargeable to nonunion members and which were not. The commission concluded that the MTA had demanded $26.77 in excess service fees from each of the nonunion members. The Supreme Judicial Court of Massachusetts modified the commission's decision. It found the MTA's accounting expenses were chargeable, except for the 14 hours the accounting staff devoted to non-chargeable activities. **The union president and vice president's salaries were overhead and therefore chargeable in proportion to the union's overall chargeable activities.** Discussions the union had about a statewide strike to publicize the condition of public education funding were not chargeable.

Expenses related to days when faculty at the University of Massachusetts at Amherst withheld services to protest the lack of funding for their collective bargaining agreement were also not chargeable, even though the university administration approved of and participated in the protest. Because the faculty had withheld services, the two-day action was a strike, and the expenses incidental to it were not chargeable. Nor were the costs of flyers distributed during commencement exercises at the University of Massachusetts at Boston chargeable to nonunion members. However, expenses related to an article that appeared in a union magazine providing pointers on how to communicate during a strike or some other unusual event were chargeable. *Belhumeur v. Labor Relations Comm'n*, 432 Mass. 458, 735 N.E.2d 860 (Mass. 2000).

C. Collective Bargaining

In NLRB v. Catholic Bishop of Chicago, *this chapter, the U.S. Supreme Court held the First Amendment prevents inquiry by the National Labor Relations Board (NLRB) into a school's religious mission.*

◆ *As the NLRB had no jurisdiction over a church-affiliated Wisconsin college, it could not order the college to bargain with a faculty union.*

The NLRB ordered Carroll College to recognize and bargain with the collective bargaining agent of its faculty. The college appealed to the federal court system, asserting its religious environment and affiliation with the United Presbyterian Church placed it beyond NLRB jurisdiction under *NLRB v. Catholic Bishop of Chicago* and *Univ. of Great Falls v. NLRB*, this chapter. It also said faculty members were managerial employees who were not covered by the National Labor Relations Act. The case reached the U.S. Court of Appeals, District of Columbia Circuit, which stated that the First Amendment religion clauses preclude NLRB review of church-affiliated schools.

The court applied the three-part *Great Falls* analysis to determine whether the college had a "substantial religious character" that exempted it from NLRB review. It found **the college held itself out to students, faculty and the community as providing a religious educational environment**. Second, the college was a nonprofit, and third, it was affiliated with the Presbyterian Church. The court found the college easily satisfied the *Great Falls* test. In assessing religious affiliation, it was unnecessary to show the college was sponsored or controlled by a church. Since the NLRB had no jurisdiction over the college, the NLRB could not order it to recognize and bargain with the union. *Carroll College v. NLRB*, 558 F.3d 568 (D.C. Cir. 2009).

◆ *A Kansas professor's refusal to hold office hours at a particular community college campus justified her discharge for insubordination.*

The college denied the professor's request for mileage reimbursement for her trips between a satellite campus in Leavenworth and its main campus in Kansas City. The disagreement escalated, and she filed a grievance over the college's decision to assign her to the main campus. College trustees denied the grievance but failed to issue a timely decision. The professor believed she was entitled to the relief requested in her grievance and insisted on having her office in Leavenworth, even though she was not assigned to teach any courses there.

A college provost ordered the professor to hold office hours on the Kansas City campus. Although her caseload included online instruction, the provost noted that a relevant master contract required her to hold five office hours per week on campus. When the professor resisted, she was suspended without pay. College trustees discharged the professor for insubordination. A hearing officer found the provost had the sole authority to set class schedules and assign office locations, and further agreed that the professor had been insubordinate. She appealed to the state court system, where the Court of Appeals of Kansas rejected her argument that the hearing officer's decision was unsupported by evidence. **The college provost had the authority to assign faculty to specific work locations.** The professor failed to show that work locations could be changed only with her consent. The master contract required faculty members who taught online courses to hold at least five office hours per week on campus. There was substantial evidence that the professor refused to comply with the provost's order and was insubordinate. As the record showed she acted in an antagonistic and unprofessional manner, the judgment was affirmed. *Heflin v. Kansas City Kansas Community College*, 224 P.3d 1201 (Kan. Ct. App. 2010).

◆ *A union's waiver of employee rights to negotiate an intellectual property policy survived the expiration of a collective bargaining agreement. For that reason, refusal to negotiate the policy was not an improper labor practice.*

The City University of New York (CUNY) adopted a policy in 1972 addressing intellectual property developed by its employees. The policy was not the subject of collective bargaining between CUNY and the Professional Staff Congress (PSC), which represented CUNY employees. The parties' 1996-2000 collective bargaining agreement expired, and PSC demanded that the intellectual property policy be negotiated. CUNY asserted Article 2 of the expired agreement constituted a waiver by the union to negotiate particular items, including the policy. Article 2 authorized CUNY's board of trustees to alter existing bylaws or policies "respecting a term or condition of employment" after giving PSC notice and an opportunity to consult. PSC filed an improper practice charge with the state public employment relations board (PERB). The parties reached a new agreement covering 2000-2002, and the PSC withdrew its proposal on the intellectual property policy. The new agreement carried forward Article 2, unchanged from the prior agreement. Just before expiration of the 2000-2002 agreement, PSC again sought to negotiate the intellectual property policy. An administrative law judge held CUNY committed an improper practice by refusing to negotiate the policy.

The PERB held PSC waived its right to negotiate the intellectual property policy in Article 2. The case reached the Court of Appeals of New York, which held the resolution of improper practice charges was generally within PERB's discretion. Article 2 granted CUNY the right to unilaterally alter bylaws and policies respecting terms or conditions of employment that did not conflict with the agreement. Article 2 explicitly referred to "terms and conditions of employment," and it was not confined to "management prerogatives." **The court held the intellectual property policy was squarely within the coverage of Article 2, since it was never a part of a collective bargaining agreement and did not conflict with any terms of the current agreement.** Civil Service Law Section 209-a(1)(e) required employers to continue all terms of an expired agreement while a new one was being negotiated. This enhanced the negotiating process by preserving the status quo pending a new agreement. As the PERB had correctly determined the status quo and found the Article 2 waiver remained in effect, the court reinstated its decision. *Professional Staff Congress-City Univ. of New York v. New York State Public Employment Relations Board*, 7 N.Y.3d 458, 857 N.E.2d 1108 (N.Y. 2006).

◆ *A private Ohio university professor could not proceed with his state-law breach of contract claim because it was preempted by federal labor law.*

Wilberforce University and its faculty members have a collective bargaining agreement governing the criteria and procedures for the promotion of professors. An associate professor received a negative recommendation for a full professorship, and he withdrew his application. He waited too long to submit materials when another opportunity for promotion arose, and he later submitted an incomplete application. After being denied a promotion for a third time, he filed a grievance. However, he did not follow procedures outlined in the collective bargaining agreement. The professor sued the university and its officials in a federal district court for breach of contract. The university sought dismissal of the case, arguing it was preempted by Section 301 of the federal Labor Management Relations Act (LMRA), which calls for the resolution of collective bargaining disputes by reference to federal law. The court agreed that the state law claim of failure to promote was preempted by the LMRA. **Proof of the state law claim and other rights claimed by the professor required interpretation of the collective bargaining agreement.** As Section 301 preempted the contract claim, the case was dismissed. *Grisby v. Wilberforce Univ.*, No. 3:05-cv-014, 2007 WL 1989593 (S.D. Ohio 7/6/07).

◆ *A California court rejected a nurse's claim that her dismissal from a student clinic violated her due process and collective bargaining rights.*

A nurse practitioner who worked at a university clinic examined a student and determined she was 24 weeks pregnant. The student wanted to abort the pregnancy, but the nurse recommended against it, saying the pregnancy was too advanced. The nurse later urged the student to put the baby up for adoption and told her that a colleague at the clinic was interested in adopting it. A supervisor learned of the plan and admonished the nurse for unethical conduct. The student later had the baby, and the colleague took it home from the hospital.

The university discharged the nurse, and her grievance was denied. She requested a hearing that was later cancelled by a union representative based on insufficient notice of witnesses and the university's refusal to allow her to issue subpoenas. A hearing was held in the nurse's absence, and the hearing officer upheld the dismissal. The nurse appealed to a state trial court, which dismissed the case. The Court of Appeal of California found the nurse had no right to invoke arbitration. It also rejected her claims that the hearing officer was biased and the proceedings were inherently unfair. The university's failure to provide her with a witness list seven days before the hearing did not prejudice her case. By then, the nurse had already gone through the grievance procedure and knew the identity of the witnesses. Her inability to subpoena witnesses did not render the process unfair. **Since the nurse voluntarily failed to appear for her hearing, she could not now complain it was unfair to hold it in her absence.** The judgment was affirmed. *Nelson v. Regents of the Univ. of California*, No. D040623, 2004 WL 339340 (Cal. Ct. App. 2004).

◆ *A union could use a university's e-mail system to contact members where the collective bargaining agreement did not prohibit it.*

The union representing Oregon University System employees negotiated a collective bargaining agreement that allowed union officers and stewards to "have access to electronic bulletin boards under specified conditions." The union then began using e-mail to transmit information to its members' work computers. The university objected to this practice, claiming that the bargaining agreement did not allow the union to use e-mail in that way. After two arbitrators determined that the university could prohibit union officials from using the e-mail system, the Oregon Court of Appeals determined that the union's use of e-mail neither violated the terms of the bargaining agreement nor breached its duty of good faith and fair dealing. **The bargaining agreement was silent with respect to the union's use of e-mail.** Thus, there was no breach of contract and no bad faith. *Oregon Univ. System v. Oregon Public Employees Union, Local 503*, 60 P.3d 567 (Or. Ct. App. 2002).

◆ *Adjunct faculty members were allowed to join a union in New Hampshire.*

A labor association seeking to represent 147 adjunct faculty members at a New Hampshire state college petitioned for certification by the Public Employees Labor Relations Board (PELRB). The university system opposed the petition, arguing that adjunct faculty are temporary employees who are excluded from bargaining because of their temporary status. A hearing officer granted the petition, allowing instructors who were currently teaching, and those who had taught two of the last three semesters, to join the union. The PELRB upheld that decision, and the adjunct faculty voted for the union.

The case reached the Supreme Court of New Hampshire, which found that there is some expectation that adjunct faculty members will return annually – they are compensated for longevity. The court affirmed the PELRB's decision that **adjunct faculty members are not temporary employees**. Even though the contracts they signed did not include an expectation of continued employment, that fact did not necessarily diminish the adjunct faculty members' **reasonable expectation of continued employment**. The fact that adjunct instructors taught one-third of the college's courses indicated that they were not just "last-minute" hires. The court remanded the case to consider who was eligible for union membership. The PELRB did not provide an explanation for why only adjuncts who were currently teaching or who had taught two of the last three semesters were eligible. *In re Univ. System of New Hampshire*, 795 A.2d 840 (N.H. 2002).

◆ *Hawaii could not enact a law eliminating state university employee rights to collectively bargain.*

A Hawaii law prohibited the state university system from negotiating over "cost items" during the 1999-2001 biennium. Because wages, hours, pensions, and other terms and conditions of employment were "cost items," public employee unions sued, seeking a declaration that the law was unconstitutional. The Hawaii Supreme Court struck down the law. Even though the state constitution gave the legislature the ultimate authority over collective bargaining "as provided by law," that authority was granted within the framework of existing **federal law that granted employees the right to bargain collectively**. Since the law would deny public employees the right to bargain collectively, it could not stand. *United Public Workers, AFSCME, Local 646, AFL-CIO v. Yogi*, 62 P.3d 189 (Haw. 2002).

◆ *The D.C. Circuit adopted a test for determining whether a religious institution can exempt itself from NLRB jurisdiction for collective bargaining.*

The University of Great Falls, which is operated by the Sisters of Providence (a Roman Catholic religious order) refused to recognize or bargain with the Montana Federation of Teachers. The university maintained that the NLRB lacked jurisdiction because the school was a religiously run institution, and also asserted that the Religious Freedom Restoration Act barred the NLRB from ordering it to engage in collective bargaining. The union petitioned the NLRB for relief, and the regional director examined the university's mission, courses and operation before ruling that the NLRB had jurisdiction.

The NLRB upheld that determination, and the university appealed to the U.S. Court of Appeals, D.C. Circuit. The appellate court vacated the NLRB's decision and order. It stated that the NLRB had improperly engaged in an examination of the university's religious character. The court adopted **a three-part test for determining whether an institution can avail itself of the exemption in *NLRB v. Catholic Bishop of Chicago***, see Chapter Four, Section I.B, where the Supreme Court held the NLRB did not have jurisdiction over religious institutions. Under this test, an institution must: 1) provide a religious educational environment and hold itself out as such, 2) be organized by a nonprofit, and 3) be "affiliated with, or owned, operated or controlled directly or indirectly, by either a recognized religious organization or with an entity, membership of which is determined, at least in part, with reference to religion." Here, the university easily passed that test. As a result, the NLRB did not have jurisdiction, and the university did not have to bargain with the union. *Univ. of Great Falls v. NLRB*, 278 F.3d 1335 (D.C. Cir. 2002).

◆ *A law allowing Hawaii to postpone employees' pay by a few days was unconstitutional.*

To remedy a budget crisis, Hawaii passed a law authorizing the state to postpone by a few days, at six different times, the dates on which state employees were to be paid. It also declared that the postponements were "not subject to negotiation" by the state employees' unions. University of Hawaii faculty members and their union sued in federal district court to stop the state from implementing the law, and the district court granted the injunction. The case then reached the Ninth Circuit Court of Appeals, which affirmed. It held that **the law violated the U.S. Constitution's Contract Clause by substantially impairing the state's obligation to honor its collective bargaining agreements with the unions**. The law not only changed the employees' pay dates, but also removed "the whole subject from the bargaining table." It could not be justified as reasonable and necessary because there were less drastic ways to reduce the state's financial obligations. *Univ. of Hawaii Professional Assembly v. Cayetano*, 183 F.3d 1096 (9th Cir. 1999).

◆ *Where a no-smoking policy was not included in a collective bargaining agreement, a university did not have to bargain over the policy.*

The University of Alaska's Board of Regents adopted a policy that excluded smoking from university facilities that were open to the public. It later amended the policy to prohibit smoking in motor vehicles. Prior to the adoption of the policy, the union representing certain university employees formally requested bargaining. One union member learned of the revised smoking policy but continued to smoke in the vehicle assigned to him. He was censured for smoking in the vehicle and circulated a petition signed by 30 union members asking the union to negotiate the non-smoking policy.

The union presented the proposal to the university, which refused to bargain, asserting that the policy was a permissive subject for which it had no obligation to bargain. The parties reached a collective bargaining agreement that was ratified by the union membership containing no express reference to the non-smoking policy. The agreement contained a reservation of rights clause stating that bargaining unit members agreed to follow all university policies not specified in the agreement and reserving the right to change university policies. The union filed an unfair labor practice against the university, asserting that the non-smoking policy was a mandatory subject of bargaining. The state labor relations agency determined that the policy was a mandatory subject of bargaining, but that the union had contractually waived it by executing the collective bargaining agreement. On appeal, the Supreme Court of Alaska observed that **because the collective bargaining agreement contained no**

specific reference to the non-smoking policy, the union had contractually waived its right to bargain on that issue. The union could also be deemed to have waived its right to bargain under the reservation of rights section of the agreement. The court affirmed the agency ruling that the union had waived bargaining on the policy by entering into the agreement. *Univ. of Alaska v. Univ. of Alaska Classified Employees Ass'n*, 952 P.2d 1182 (Alaska 1998).

D. Arbitration

◆ *Because a settlement voided an earlier pact to arbitrate any employment dispute, a coach could sue Duke University for defamation.*

In 2006, three Duke men's lacrosse team members were accused of rape. The head lacrosse coach resigned, and the parties executed a release to resolve any matters regarding his separation. The release declared an intent to cancel all earlier agreements between the parties but said nothing about arbitrating any future claims that might arise. Two years later, the coach sued Duke and a senior vice president in the state court system for defamation. Duke sought to force him to arbitrate the claims, asserting they were subject to an arbitration agreement in the university's employment policy. The court denied the request, and Duke appealed. The Court of Appeals of North Carolina found the release clearly rescinded all earlier agreements to arbitrate. **There was no doubt that the release stated the intent of both parties to cancel all earlier agreements, and it discharged their duties under previously existing contracts.** The coach was not bound to arbitrate his libel and slander claims and could proceed with his action. *Pressler v. Duke Univ.*, 685 S.E.2d 6 (N.C. Ct. App. 2009).

◆ *An arbitrator wrongfully placed the burden on a Pennsylvania university to show it had good reason to deny tenure to a probationary faculty member.*

The university denied the professor tenure because she failed to demonstrate the requisite scholarly growth. Her professional union filed a grievance on her behalf under the relevant collective bargaining agreement (CBA). After the grievance was denied at all levels, the matter proceeded to arbitration, where an arbitrator held in the professor's favor. He ordered her reinstated as a probationary faculty member who was eligible for reconsideration for tenure. The university appealed to the state court system.

The case reached the Commonwealth Court of Pennsylvania, which noted courts generally defer to the decisions of arbitrators when parties have agreed via a CBA to use arbitration to resolve disputes. **However, an arbitrator's decision is not entitled to deference unless it "draws its essence" from the CBA.** In this case, the CBA did not expressly state which party bore the burden of proof in a grievance proceeding regarding tenure. **The agreement between the university and union specified that tenure candidates had the burden of showing requirements for tenure had been met.** The arbitrator should have consulted this agreement and placed the burden of proof on the professor. The arbitrator's award was vacated, and the case was remanded for additional proceedings. *Slippery Rock Univ. of Pennsylvania v. Ass'n of Pennsylvania State College and Univ. Faculties*, 916 A.2d 736 (Pa. Commw. Ct. 2007).

◆   *The Vermont State Colleges Federation did not unlawfully retaliate against a faculty member by declining to accommodate her scheduling request.*

The faculty member worked part time at a state college. The applicable collective bargaining agreement required the college to give priority to full-time faculty and administrators in scheduling matters. The faculty member filed a grievance when she was not assigned a schedule that accommodated her child care and commuting needs. She later complained about a new schedule. The department decided not to change the new schedule and she filed another grievance, this time for retaliation for her earlier grievance.

A grievance board found the college could have made some adjustments and was unlawfully motivated by the prior grievance. On appeal, the Supreme Court of Vermont found the faculty member did not present any direct evidence of a discriminatory motive. The court disagreed with the board's findings that the timing of the new schedule was suspicious, and that the college treated the faculty member less favorably than others. **The court noted an adverse employment decision following a successful grievance is not necessarily suspicious. The court said the faculty member presented no other evidence to infer the college retaliated because of her earlier grievance.** There was no basis to infer the timing was suspicious or that the college was unlawfully motivated. The court reversed the board's decision. *Grievance of Rosenberg v. Vermont State Colleges*, 852 A.2d 599 (Vt. 2004).

III. OVERTIME AND WAGE DISPUTES

While wages are typically covered by contract, they may also be subject to the requirements of the Fair Labor Standards Act (FLSA) and state wage laws. Instructors are typically exempt from FLSA overtime coverage, as they are considered professional employees. The FLSA requires employers to pay covered workers the prevailing minimum wage and any earned overtime.

◆   *A University of Washington (UW) faculty salary policy that guaranteed raises for "meritorious" faculty did not apply to extension lecturers.*

In 2002, the Washington legislature did not appropriate funds for UW employee pay raises. Faculty members filed a class action against UW in a state court for breach of contract. The class consisted of professors, associate professors, artists, full-time lecturers, senior lecturers and principal lecturers. After the case was settled, a second class action was filed by part-time lecturers who claimed they had been wrongfully excluded from the prior case. UW settled the second action, only to face a third class action by extension lecturers.

After the trial court certified a class of extension lecturers, it agreed with UW that they were not university faculty and were thus not entitled to salary increases referenced in the faculty salary policy. On appeal, the Court of Appeals of Washington held **a breach of contract claim required proof of "a promise of specific treatment in a specific situation," justifiable reliance on the promise, and a breach of the promise**. But the lecturers could not even show the handbook applied to them. Their appointments were part of a UW educational outreach program that was separate from UW academic faculty appointments. The education outreach program had a separate manual that did not incorporate UW's faculty handbook. As the extension lecturers were not "faculty," the faculty salary policy in the handbook did not apply to them. No promise of a raise was made to them under the faculty salary policy. The judgment for UW was affirmed. *Carosella v. Univ. of Washington*, 154 Wash.App. 1038 (Wash. Ct. App. 2010).

◆ *A New York university was forced to face a collective FLSA action based on a student's preliminary showing that she was not paid for overtime work.*

A Hofstra University undergraduate assistant was paid a $700 stipend to be a football team manager. Since she held other on-campus jobs, she claimed she was entitled to overtime compensation for all hours worked beyond 40 hours a week. Hofstra's student employment handbook forbade students from working more than 25 hours per week when school was in session and 35 when classes were in recess. No student was to work on campus more than 40 hours a week, and extra care was to be taken to make sure the 40-hour limit was not exceeded when a student worked in more than one department. **The student said Hofstra routinely disregarded these policies and that she worked at least 40 hours per week as the football team manager.** In her federal lawsuit, she accused Hofstra of violating the Fair Labor Standards Act (FLSA), since she regularly worked more than 40 hours a week but was not paid overtime.

The student moved the court to certify a collective FLSA action. She also sought an order requiring Hofstra to provide her with names, addresses, e-mail addresses, Social Security numbers and dates of employment of all students who had worked as undergraduate or graduate assistants in the previous six years. The court held the student was similarly situated to the other undergraduate and graduate assistants, and it conditionally certified a collective action of students who were not paid minimum wage or did not receive overtime pay. The class was limited to students who had worked for Hofstra in the previous three years. Hofstra was required to provide the names and addresses of those students, but no additional information. *Summa v. Hofstra Univ.*, No. CV 07-3307(DRH)(ARL), 2008 WL 3852160 (E.D.N.Y. 8/14/08).

◆ *A Georgia university did not breach a professor's employment contract when it recalculated his salary following a demotion.*

When the professor acquired tenure, the university paid him an annual salary of $49,537. It then appointed him to an associate vice president position at a salary of $70,000. Over the next three years, the professor entered into a series of one-year contracts, each providing for a pay increase. The university then decided to eliminate the associate vice president position. It notified the professor in writing of its decision and gave him the option of returning to the classroom at an annual salary of $54,341. The professor argued his salary computation was wrong, but his appeal failed. He sued the university in a state court for breach of contract. The court awarded summary judgment to the university, and the professor appealed to the Court of Appeals of Georgia.

The court found the university had compared the professor's salary to those of others in his department. The head of the department earned $59,472 for the same academic year and the salaries of three associate professors who worked for the university for similar or longer time periods than the professor were less than his. The court found the terms of the professor's contract were unambiguous. **As the contract was clear, the trial court had the discretion to determine its terms.** The court affirmed the judgment. *Homer v. Board of Regents of the Univ. System of Georgia,* 613 S.E.2d 205 (Ga. Ct. App. 2005).

◆ *A California trade school qualified as an institution of higher learning, and its instructors were professionals who did not qualify for overtime pay.*

The school received state accreditation and became a degree-granting institution in 2002. Its instructors held certificates of authorization for service under the Education Code. The state division of labor standards enforcement notified the school its instructors were not exempt from overtime pay under an administrative wage order. The school sought a declaration that its instructors were exempt from overtime pay as professional employees. A state trial court agreed, and held the instructors were exempt from the overtime wage order.

The state court of appeal held the school qualified as a "college." It complied with statutory requirements to obtain accreditation. **The "teaching exception" was not limited to institutions granting bachelor's or higher degrees.** The division relied on outdated records and evidence in arguing trade schools did not meet the definition of "higher learning." Instead, the boundaries of California's education system had expanded to include a much broader category of institutions. **Since the professional exemption was not limited to instructors at institutions granting baccalaureate degrees or higher, the school's instructors were entitled to the professional exception**, and the court affirmed the judgment. *California School of Culinary Arts v. Lujan,* 112 Cal.App.4th 16, 4 Cal.Rptr.3d 785 (Cal. Ct. App. 2003).

◆ *A New York court held that a fee required by medical schools from physicians as a condition of employment violated state Education Law.*

Ophthalmologists who worked as full-time assistant professors at Columbia University wanted to continue practicing ophthalmology and remain on the faculty. In exchange for allowing them to change their appointments to part time, Columbia requested that they pay a 10% "Dean's Tax" on all their practice income. When they refused, their appointments were terminated. The doctors sued Columbia in a state trial court, which held in their favor. A state appellate division court held that the **payment of the "Dean's Tax" as a condition of employment constituted illegal fee-splitting**. Because the doctors were no longer employees, and because Columbia was no longer providing them with benefits, facilities or malpractice insurance, the request was a violation of law. The court directed Columbia to review the applications for part-time appointments and affirmed the judgment. *Odrich v. Trustees of Columbia Univ.,* 764 N.Y.S.2d 448 (N.Y. App. Div. 2003).

◆ *A teacher who also worked for the university as a nurse was entitled to an accounting over discrepancies in her pay.*

As part of her contract, a Mississippi nursing school teacher was required to work at a school-operated clinic. Although she would earn more income by doing so, she also had to contribute half of any earnings over $10,000 to the clinic. In practice, the clinic held her earnings until the end of the year, then paid her share. The agreement between the parties specified that all disputes were to be arbitrated. When the teacher noticed that she received only $767 one year, while the clinic kept $6,000, she requested an explanation and an accounting. The dean refused the request and then fired the teacher when she refused to continue working at the clinic. She filed a petition for an accounting with the Mississippi Chancery Court, and the university sought to compel arbitration. The court held that **the teacher was entitled to an accounting** and that the university waived its right to demand arbitration. On appeal, the Mississippi Supreme Court ruled that the university did not waive its right to demand arbitration by delaying its demand. However, the teacher was entitled to an accounting, which was not subject to arbitration. *Univ. Nursing Associates PLLC v. Phillips*, 842 So.2d 1270 (Miss. 2003).

◆ *Two part-time Washington community college instructors were not entitled to overtime wages.*

Part-time instructors from five community colleges in Washington brought a lawsuit alleging that the colleges violated the state's Minimum Wage Act by failing to compensate them for overtime work. Their wages were determined by multiplying their classroom hours by a negotiated hourly rate that included payment for time spent on course preparation, grading and office hours. However, they asserted that they were not exempt professional employees paid on a salary basis because the colleges docked their pay for time missed after all their accrued sick and annual leave was exhausted. The case reached the Washington Supreme Court, which ruled against them. It noted that as long as **their predetermined wages were not subject to reduction because of variations in the quality or quantity of work performed**, they still could be considered salary-basis employees. Under U.S. Department of Labor regulations adopted by the court, deductions for missed time after accrued sick and annual leave expire do not alter an employee's professional status. *Clawson v. Grays Harbor College Dist. No. 2*, 61 P.3d 1130 (Wash. 2003).

◆ *A coach obtained over $135,000 for fraud and Fair Labor Standards Act (FLSA) violations after the athletic director who hired him refused to pay him.*

The athletic director at an Illinois community college hired a basketball coach in March 1999 and promised him a teaching position in physical education for the following fall. The coach began his duties right away, but was not paid. In August, he filled out paperwork for the teaching position. He also made informal complaints to the athletic director, then filed a formal complaint regarding the payment of wages. After the athletic director told him he would not be paid for the work he had done the previous seven months, he sued under the FLSA. A jury awarded him $10,562 on that claim, as well as $52,526 in compensatory damages for the athletic director's fraud and $75,000 in punitive damages. The Seventh Circuit Court of Appeals found sufficient evidence to support the jury's determination that **the coach had justifiably relied on the athletic director's misrepresentations to his detriment**. The award in favor of the coach was reinstated. *Hefferman v. Board of Trustees of Illinois Community College Dist. 508*, 310 F.3d 522 (7th Cir. 2002).

◆ *Probationary campus police officers were not entitled to overtime for attending EMT classes.*

A Massachusetts university hired four campus police officers as probationary employees. As a condition of employment, the officers were required to obtain and retain certification as emergency medical technicians within one year of their hire date. The four officers took the EMT course at the university and completed the course. Although they were not paid for attending EMT classes after work, they were compensated when EMT classes occurred during their regular working hours. They sued the university under the FLSA, seeking overtime pay for time spent working toward their EMT certification. The case reached the U.S. Court of Appeals, First Circuit, which held **the Portal-to-Portal Act permits an employer to avoid paying an employee for activities that are "preliminary or postliminary" to the principal activities the employee is engaged to perform**. Here, that condition was satisfied because the officers were attending the EMT classes during their probationary period, and they did not perform any EMT-related work until after obtaining certification. Thus, they could be characterized as students during their probationary period for purposes of avoiding overtime compensation. *Bienkowski v. Northeastern Univ.*, 285 F.3d 138 (1st Cir. 2002).

IV. LEAVES OF ABSENCE

The Family and Medical Leave Act of 1993 (FMLA), 29 U.S.C. §§ 2601–2654, makes available to eligible employees up to 12 weeks of unpaid leave per year: 1) because of the birth of a son or daughter of the employee and in order to care for such son or daughter; 2) because of the placement of a son or daughter with the employee for adoption or foster care; 3) in order to care for the spouse, or a son, daughter, or parent, of the employee, if such spouse, son, daughter or parent has a serious health condition; or 4) because of a serious health condition that makes the employee unable to perform the functions of the position of such employee. 29 U.S.C. § 2612.

To be eligible for leave, an employee must have been employed by the covered employer for at least 12 months, and must have worked at least 1,250 hours during the 12-month period preceding the start of the leave. 29 U.S.C. § 2611. If the employer provides paid leave for which the employee is eligible, the employee may elect, or the employer may require the employee, to substitute the paid leave for any part of the 12 weeks of leave to which the employee is entitled under the act. When the need for leave is foreseeable, the employee must provide reasonable prior notice. An employer may require medical certification to support a claim for leave, and may require, at its own expense, a second opinion. An employer is under no obligation to allow the employee to accrue seniority or other employment benefits during a leave.

◆ *A Texas career services director could not pursue FMLA claims, as she did not prove she requested leave and was discharged for unprofessional conduct.*

The director injured herself at work and took a few days off to have back surgery. When she returned to work, she used a cane to walk. The director maintained that she advised her supervisor that her doctor suggested she take a medical leave, but the supervisor later denied any such conversation. A short time later, a staff member notified the supervisor that the director had engaged in unprofessional conduct with students and staff. This included counseling students to file complaints against the supervisor and seek tuition refunds because of his alleged management deficiencies. After the misconduct was corroborated by other employees, the supervisor discharged the director.

In a federal district court lawsuit against the supervisor and others, the director claimed interference with her FMLA rights, retaliation and various state law violations. The case reached the U.S. Court of Appeals, Fifth Circuit, which found her FMLA claims failed. **In order to succeed with a case for interference with FMLA rights, it must be shown that an employee took a leave that was protected by the FMLA.** There was no proof in this case that the supervisor even knew that the director had requested leave. The director's retaliation claim failed because she could not counter evidence of her unprofessional conduct. A lower court judgment against her was affirmed. *Burris v. Brazell*, 351 Fed.Appx. 961 (5th Cir. 2009).

◆ *A maintenance worker at a Seattle community college failed to show an FMLA violation or discrimination against him based on disability.*

After the worker compiled a record of chronic tardiness and absenteeism, he asked to change schedules. The college did not want to let him work the shift he sought because doing so would leave him unsupervised for three hours. However, the worker was permitted to work his desired shift on a trial basis. Even with the later start time, he continued to be late or absent and missed safety meetings. After the college reclassified the worker to a lower-paying position, he filed a federal district court action under the FMLA and the Americans with Disabilities Act (ADA). The court held he did not show he had a disability under the ADA. Even if he was disabled, he did not show the college failed to accommodate him, since he was offered a position with a later start time. The court rejected the worker's claim that the college violated the FMLA by ending a period of FMLA leave without justification. **He never commenced an FMLA leave.** Although the worker said the college retaliated against him for filing a complaint under the state industrial safety and health act, he did not show the college was aware that he had filed the complaint or that it took action against him because of it. *Elkins v. North Seattle Community College*, No. C08-1466RSL, 2009 WL 3698516 (W.D. Wash. 11/3/09).

◆ *A college did not violate the FMLA or Americans with Disabilities Act (ADA) by denying a professor's request to work on campus three days a week.*

The professor typically worked only three days per week on campus. When his department changed its policy to require full-time staff members to be on campus for at least four hours a day for at least four days a week, the professor did not comply. He then took leave under the FMLA due to stress-related problems. He told the college that his department chair was "the source of his physical problems." When the professor returned to work, the college granted him a temporary transfer away from the department chair. He was also offered a transfer to a non-teaching position under a different supervisor. After the professor failed to report for this job, the college considered him to have resigned. He sued the college in a federal district court for violations of the ADA and FMLA. The court held for the college, and the professor appealed.

On appeal, the U.S. Court of Appeals, Third Circuit, held the professor did not show he had a disability under the ADA. Despite being treated for panic attacks and agoraphobia, he did not show he had a substantial limitation of a major life activity. The court also rejected the professor's claim that the college wrongly discharged him instead of granting him additional leave. **He was not eligible for FMLA leave because he did not have a "serious health condition"** as defined by the act. Even if he was FMLA-eligible, he took more leave than he was entitled to receive. As a result, the judgment was affirmed. *Lloyd v. Washington & Jefferson College*, 288 Fed.Appx. 786 (3d Cir. 2008).

◆ *A Vanderbilt University (VU) research assistant failed to prove a connection between her requests for leave and her discharge.*

The research assistant received several warnings about performance issues. After she told a supervisor she was pregnant, she was placed on performance improvement counseling (PIC). Her job performance continued to slip, and she took a leave of absence under the FMLA. While she was on leave, she and her husband were discovered using a lab computer after work hours. The research assistant filed an internal discrimination complaint while she was on leave, saying Vanderbilt issued the PIC because she was pregnant.

The research assistant's supervisors issued a final PIC for failing to follow instructions. The next day, she took another leave of absence under the FMLA. Her job performance did not improve upon her return to work, and her employment was terminated. The research assistant sued VU for retaliation based on taking her FMLA leave. She added claims for pregnancy and national origin discrimination. **The court held that to prevail in an FMLA claim for retaliation, the research assistant had to show a causal link between the leave and her discharge.** However, VU began counseling her about her work performance before she took FMLA leave, even before it learned she was pregnant. The evidence showed the discharge was due to poor work performance. As the research assistant could not show a link between the leave and the discharge, the case was dismissed. *Zhu v. Vanderbilt Univ.*, No. 3:06-0460, 2007 WL 2963980 (M.D. Tenn. 10/5/07).

◆ *A federal appeals court held FMLA posting requirements are met when the employer posts notices on its intranet site.*

A Massachusetts employee was involved in an accident and took a leave of absence from his supervisory job. The employer sent him a letter that provided information about the FMLA and told him the leave was being counted as FMLA leave. The employer also asked the employee to provide a medical certification regarding his condition. He provided a disability claim form signed by a physician and was given 15 weeks of leave. The employer later discharged the employee after he failed to return to work. He filed a federal district court action claiming the employer failed to post FMLA notices.

The court held for the employer, and the employee appealed. The U.S. Court of Appeals, First Circuit, noted the employer posted an adequate FMLA notice on its intranet Web site. This defeated the claim that employees did not receive notice of their FMLA rights. The site was accessible to all employees while they were at work, and the employee admitted he had used it at work. The court rejected the claim that the employer violated the FMLA because the site could not be accessed from home. **FMLA regulations only required that notice be posted at the workplace.** The district court's decision was affirmed. *Dube v. J.P. Morgan Investor Services*, 201 Fed.Appx. 786 (1st Cir. 2006).

◆ *An Iowa university did not violate the Equal Protection Clause by allowing mothers, but not fathers, the benefit of paid leave after childbirth.*

The university's parental leave policy allowed biological mothers to take sick leave for any pregnancy-related temporary disability. A male employee filed administrative complaints against the university, then sued the university in a federal district court. He alleged the policy violated the Equal Protection Clause of the Constitution. The case became a class action lawsuit when the employee was certified to represent similarly situated biological fathers who worked for the university. A federal district court held for the university, and the employee appealed to the U.S. Court of Appeals, Eighth Circuit.

The court found the policy did not allow mothers to use accrued sick leave after their disability ended. The time off was disability leave even though mothers often cared for a newborn during that time. The employee contended the university did not require proof of a disability for a leave, of six weeks or less. He submitted an affidavit from his wife that she fully recovered from childbirth in four weeks. The court held the university reasonably established a period of presumptive disability. It did not need to review medical records for each employee. **The court held the distinction between biological mothers and fathers was rationally related to legitimate concerns.** As the policy did not violate the Equal Protection Clause, the judgment was affirmed. *Johnson v. Univ. of Iowa*, 431 F.3d 325 (8th Cir. 2005).

◆ *A federal district court decided to further consider the case of a Tennessee university employee whose son had attention deficit disorder (ADD).*

The university allowed the employee to start work an hour late so she could get her son on his school bus. Even with this accommodation, she had problems getting to work on time, and she eventually violated the university's absenteeism and tardiness policy. The employee was referred for written performance improvement counseling, but she continued to perform poorly. After the university warned her she would be fired if she did not improve, it followed through by terminating her employment. The employee sued the university in a federal district court for violated her rights under the FMLA.

The FMLA allows employees to take leave to care for a child's physical or psychological needs. The university said while ADD is a "serious health condition" as defined by the FMLA, it considered the request for leave to be only a request for a change in schedule. The court found information from the child's doctor could be read as a request for a schedule change, which was not provided by the FMLA. **The court found it unclear whether the employee had to be home to care for her son's physical or psychological needs – which were covered under the FMLA – or merely to get him on the bus,**

which was not. As there was insufficient evidence for the court to rule at this point, a trial would have to be held to resolve these issues. *Wiseman v. Vanderbilt Univ.*, No. 3:04-0946, 2005 WL 3055661 (M.D. Tenn. 11/14/05).

◆   *An Illinois college did not retaliate against an employee by terminating her because she asked to take time off.*

The college instituted a dress code that prohibited employees from wearing shorts. The employee arrived at work wearing maternity shorts. The college denied her request for an exemption from the dress code and suspended her. The employee returned to work dressed in compliance with the dress code, but the college president told her that her conduct was "the grossest form of insubordination that he had seen in his 34 years at the College." The college board voted to approve the president's recommendation to fire the employee.

The employee sued the college in a federal district court, alleging it violated the FMLA by firing her before she became entitled to exercise her FMLA rights. To prevail on her FMLA claim, the court held she had to show the college fired her to prevent her from taking leave she was entitled to take. **Under the FMLA, an employee must provide sufficient notice to qualify for the leave.** For leave that is foreseeable, such as for the birth of a child, the employee must give at least 30 days advance notice. The employee said she told the college months in advance that she was pregnant and intended to take leave. **Employees are not required under the FMLA to mention the FMLA by name. They only need to give a college enough information to put it on notice that FMLA leave would be necessary.** The court concluded the employee gave sufficient notice. However, it did not find proof that she would not have been terminated had she not requested leave. As there was evidence of other reasons for the firing, the court held the college did not retaliate against the employee and dismissed the case. *Sample v. Rend Lake College*, No. 04-CV-4161-JPG, 2005 WL 2465905 (S.D. Ill. 10/5/05).

◆   *A New York employee could proceed with his claim that a university violated his rights under the FMLA.*

The university hired the employee as a security guard and later promoted him to Director of Security Services. He began suffering from depression and anxiety due to personal and professional problems relating to a co-worker who had accused him of participating in administrative charges. The employee asked the university for a one-month vacation followed by a medical leave for mental health problems. After the employee left for his vacation, his supervisor sent him a letter discharging him immediately for poor performance and neglect of duties. The employee sued the university in a federal district court for FMLA violations by denying medical leave and firing him.

The court referred the case to a federal magistrate judge, who stated the FMLA defines "serious health condition" as an illness, injury, impairment, or physical or mental condition that involves inpatient care in a hospital or continued treatment by a health care provider. **Stress and depression can constitute a serious health condition for FMLA purposes.** The magistrate judge explained that because the evidence about the seriousness of the employee's health condition differed, summary judgment was improper. He recommended denial of the request for summary judgment. *Tambash v. St. Bonaventure Univ.*, No. 99CV967, 2004 WL 2191566 (W.D.N.Y. 2004).

◆ *A federal court held a New York university did not violate an employee's FMLA rights by terminating her position while she was on FMLA leave.*

A research nurse was placed on medical leave for being intoxicated at work. The university did not inform her it considered her leave to be under the FMLA. It sent the nurse a letter, stating the conditions of her leave and its concern with her performance. The university agreed to take no adverse action if she confirmed her admittance into a treatment program. The letter stated the university would consider the time she spent receiving treatment to be medical leave, and it continued to pay her for 12 weeks. The nurse applied for a professional assistance program, but the treatment center later reported she had relapsed. Doctors did not recommend she return to work, and the university discharged the nurse for failing to submit the reports required by the letter.

The nurse sued the university in a federal district court, alleging it interfered with her FMLA rights by firing her while she was on medical leave. She said the university violated the FMLA by not informing her she was being placed on FMLA leave, requiring the progress reports, and discharging her. The court held the nurse did not prove she was denied any FMLA benefits. The university granted her 12 weeks of paid leave, and **was not obligated to offer her a position after she took leave. The nurse was incapable of performing the job's essential functions.** The university could discharge her while she was on leave, as long as it did not do so because she took FMLA leave. The court dismissed the case. *Geromano v. Columbia Univ.*, 322 F.Supp.2d 420 (S.D.N.Y. 2004).

◆ *A New York university did not violate an employee's FMLA rights by denying his leave request.*

The employee had attendance problems, but no disciplinary action was taken against him. He stopped reporting to work and applied for workers' compensation benefits. When the employee's benefits were cut off, he applied for leave under the FMLA. He submitted an incomplete FMLA form request. The university rejected medical information supplied by his chiropractor and scheduled another physical examination. After the examination, the employee did not return to work. The university terminated his employment, and he sued the university in a federal district court for FMLA violations. The court granted the university's motion for summary judgment and the employee appealed.

The U.S. Court of Appeals, Second Circuit, noted the FMLA does not specifically define "willfully," but the U.S. Supreme Court has addressed the issue. Under the Supreme Court's rationale, if the university acted reasonably, but not recklessly, in determining its legal obligation to the employee, then its actions were not willful. The statute of limitations for bringing an FMLA claim differs depending on whether the employer's conduct is considered "willful." The employee filed his complaint against the university more than two years after the alleged incident occurred. If the university's behavior was considered willful, the employee had three years to file his claim. **Because the court**

found the university did not act willfully, the statute of limitations was only two years, and the judgment was affirmed. *Porter v. New York Univ. School of Law*, 392 F.3d 530 (2d Cir. 2004).

◆ *An employee failed to show that she was discriminated against for requesting maternity leave.*

A university employee held a position classified as half-faculty/half-staff. When she requested maternity leave, she claimed that the university began to retaliate against her by requiring her to teach summer school and by reducing her accrued maternity leave. When she sued for discrimination under state law, the case reached the Minnesota Court of Appeals.

The court held that even though the employee had presented a *prima facie* case, **the university had set forth a legitimate, nondiscriminatory reason for its adverse actions**. First, the employee had wrongly accrued maternity leave at the full-staff rate. Second, she was given the summer school assignment based on her past summer teaching experience. Because she could not show that the university's reasons for its actions were actually a pretext for discrimination, she could not succeed on her claim against it. *Cierzan v. Hamline Univ.*, No. C4-02-706, 2002 WL 31553931 (Minn. Ct. App. 2001).

V. EMPLOYEE BENEFITS

Like their counterparts in the public sector, many private schools offer a broad range of employment benefits to employees. These benefit programs are subject to federal civil rights laws such as Title VII and the Equal Pay Act as well as income tax laws. Employer-employee disputes concerning benefits will generally be resolved according to contract law rules (see Section I).

A. Retirement Benefits

◆ *An Ohio university did not have to establish an early retirement incentive plan under state law based on the size of an employee's "state employing unit."*

A student affairs department employee who had worked for 26 years at the University of Toledo was one of 85 employees who lost their jobs due to layoff. She claimed the university had to establish an early retirement incentive plan under Ohio law. The case reached the Court of Appeals of Ohio, which held **the layoff was not large enough to trigger the legal obligation to establish an early retirement incentive plan** under Ohio R.C. Section 145.298 and state regulations. The law required a state entity to establish a plan based on the number of layoffs in an "employing unit." The number was the lesser of 350 or 40% of the employees in the employing unit. While the employee claimed this requirement was triggered by counting all 85 employees who lost their jobs, the court disagreed. It found the university correctly argued that the student affairs department was the relevant "employing unit" in this case. Only four employees in the department lost their jobs. As a result, the university did not have to establish an early retirement incentive plan. *State ex rel. Edgeworth v. Univ. of Toledo*, 185 Ohio App.3d 48, 923 N.E.2d 175 (Ohio Ct. App. 2009).

♦ *A professor could not enroll in an early retirement program because he waited too long to submit his application.*

An Ohio state university instituted an early retirement incentive program, which Ohio law authorized as long as enrollment did not exceed 5% of eligible employees. A professor/associate dean applied for the program but then withdrew his application. He later attempted to resubmit his application, but the university denied his request. After resigning, the professor sued, seeking an order that he be enrolled in the early retirement program. A state court ruled in his favor, but the Court of Appeals of Ohio reversed. Here, the university had improperly expanded the program to allow more than 5% of eligible employees to participate. As a result, even though the professor's initial application would have placed him in the eligible 5%, his resubmitted application came after the 5% threshold had already been met. He was ineligible for the program. *Bee v. Univ. of Akron*, No. 21081, 2002 WL 31387127 (Ohio Ct. App. 2002).

♦ *A New York professor could pursue a lawsuit for unpaid pension benefits.*

After 10 years teaching, a tenured assistant professor was notified that he would be reassigned to an administrative position. While trying to agree on a position, the professor performed no services for the university, which then stopped paying his salary and began dismissal proceedings against him. The university did not complete the proceedings because it determined that he had abandoned his job. When he sued for reinstatement and back pay, a New York court dismissed the case on the grounds that he should have filed an Article 78 proceeding against the university. An appellate division court reversed the judgment, but the lawsuit was dismissed when he failed to appear. He later sued for unpaid salary and pension contributions, asserting that the university had never formally fired him. A federal district court dismissed the case, but the U.S. Court of Appeals, Second Circuit, reversed the judgment in part, finding that **if his employment status claim was valid, he might be able to succeed on his pension claim**. However, his claim for unpaid salary had been properly dismissed. *Yoon v. Fordham Univ. Faculty and Administrative Retirement Plan*, 263 F.3d 196 (2d Cir. 2001).

♦ *Where a university reasonably modified a retirement plan, it was not liable for violating the Employee Retirement Income Security Act (ERISA).*

A professor employed by a New York private university retired in 1977 and began receiving benefits under the school's contributory retirement plan. The board of trustees amended the plan periodically to provide cost of living adjustments (COLAs) to plan members or their beneficiaries. Subsequently, the retirement committee amended the COLA, and the board of trustees amended the plan again to provide that "the retirement committee shall have exclusive authority and discretion to construe any disputed term." After the retirement committee denied the professor's claim for additional benefits, he filed suit against the retirement plan and the university under ERISA in a state trial court.

The case was ultimately transferred to a U.S. magistrate judge. The magistrate judge granted the university's motion for pretrial judgment, and the professor appealed to the U.S. Court of Appeals, Second Circuit. The retirement committee claimed it had properly modified the earlier increases by calculating what each retiree's monthly benefit would have been under the amended COLA, subtracting the value of increases actually given, and adding the difference to each retiree's monthly benefits. The professor contended that the base figure to which the above formula would be applied should include all prior COLAs. The court ruled that **the retirement committee had discretion to construe any uncertain or disputed term**. Consequently, the court applied the arbitrary and capricious standard of review. Because the retirement committee's interpretation of the statute was reasonable, the court affirmed the magistrate judge's ruling in favor of the university. *Jordan v. Retirement Committee of Rensselaer Polytechnic Institute,* 46 F.3d 1264 (2d Cir. 1995).

B. Other Benefits

◆   *A police instructor was not entitled to disability benefits because his injuries predated his membership in the state retirement system.*

The instructor was involved in two automobile accidents during his employment by a state university. He had been involved in an accident prior to his employment by the university that caused severe injuries to his spine, for which he underwent spinal fusion surgery and received psychiatric treatment for post-traumatic stress disorder. After going to work for the university, the instructor was involved in another motor vehicle crash and was diagnosed as having a sprain. His third accident occurred when he was going to work. After this accident, the instructor underwent a second cervical fusion operation. He applied for disability benefits based on his cervical injury and mental illness. A medical board denied his request, and a hearing officer upheld the denial.

The state retirement system adopted the hearing officer's findings, and the instructor appealed to the Court of Appeals of Kentucky. The court found medical testimony supported the hearing officer's finding that the instructor's physical and mental disabilities resulted from the first automobile accident and predated his university employment. The court rejected his argument that his injuries from the third accident occurred during the course of his employment because he changed his route to obtain water for use in his police training class. The record showed the instructor traveled just a mile out of his way and was not on campus when the accident occurred. **The university did not file an accident report or a workers' compensation claim, which would have indicated the accident was in the course of his employment.** The court affirmed the denial of benefits. *Morris v. Kentucky Retirement Systems,* No. 2002-CA-001570-MR, 2003 WL 21834980 (Ky. Ct. App. 2003).

◆   *Community college teachers who did not work during the summer were not entitled to state-paid health care benefits.*

Two teachers at community colleges in Washington worked under contract for each quarter they taught at more than 50% of a full-time schedule. They did not teach during the summer. When the teachers sued to get state-paid health benefits for the summer months, a state trial court held they were not employees during the summer.

The Washington Court of Appeals found that while **the teachers worked a nine-month period, they did so under quarterly contracts and did not**

qualify as career seasonal/instructional employees. Also, despite the fact that they did not qualify for unemployment in the summer (because they received reasonable assurances of employment for the following quarter), they were not technically employed during that time. *Mader v. Health Care Authority*, 37 P.3d 1244 (Wash. Ct. App. 2002).

◆   *A New Hampshire college could provide less insurance benefits for mental illnesses than for physical illnesses.*

A college professor was treated for depression through medication and outpatient medical care. The college funded its own health care plan, which contained an annual limit of $3,000 for outpatient mental health benefits and a lifetime cap of $10,000. After the professor reached the lifetime cap, he filed a grievance, arguing that the cap violated a state statute and the collective bargaining agreement by providing less benefits for mental illnesses than physical illnesses. An arbitrator ruled that neither the state statute nor the bargaining agreement had been violated, and the Supreme Court of New Hampshire upheld that decision. **Because the college was not an insurer, it was not subject to the statute requiring equal health insurance coverage for mental and physical illnesses.** *Marshall v. Keene State College*, 785 A.2d 418 (N.H. 2001).

C. Discrimination

◆   *A Michigan nonprofit corporation lacked standing to challenge a policy of providing benefits to same-sex domestic partners of state university employees.*

The corporation sued state entities to challenge the benefits policy, claiming it violated a state constitutional provision which requires a marriage to be between a man and a woman. The corporation claimed the policy resulted in an illegal expenditure of state funds and violated state laws relating to marriage and divorce. A state court held the corporation did not have standing to file the suit. On appeal, the Court of Appeals of Michigan held that **to establish a right to bring a lawsuit, a party must have an injury that can be redressed by a favorable court decision**. The corporation did not show it suffered an injury that was different from any "injury" to the public at large. The only injury claimed was that the policy was "at odds with that which [it] seeks to promote." This vague assertion was not enough to show the type of concrete injury needed for a party to proceed in court. As the corporation lacked standing to challenge the policy, the decision for state officials was affirmed. *American Family Ass'n of Michigan v. Michigan State Univ. Board of Trustees*, 276 Mich.App. 42, 739 N.W.2d 908 (Mich. Ct. App. 2007).

◆   *An Ohio university employee lacked standing to challenge a university policy granting health insurance benefits to same-sex partners of employees.*

Miami University (MU) made health insurance benefits available to same-sex domestic partners of university employees. To receive benefits for a domestic partner, employees were required to submit an affidavit attesting to the existence of a same-sex domestic partnership. For the 2004-05 academic year, the university paid about $100,000 in premiums for domestic partner insurance coverage, which was about .5% of its total budget for faculty and staff compensation. Five months after the university adopted the policy, Ohio voters approved a state constitutional amendment recognizing only marriages between men and women. It also barred the state from creating or recognizing a legal status for unmarried couples that "approximate[d] the design, qualities, significance or effect of marriage." An MU employee sued the university and its board of trustees to challenge the same-sex benefits policy. He sought a declaration that the policy violated the constitutional amendment and an order forcing the university to discontinue application of the policy.

A state court entered judgment for MU. On appeal, **the Court of Appeals of Ohio held the insurance premiums were funded by private party donations and not tax money**. Therefore, the employee could not claim a right to challenge the policy based on his status as a taxpayer. The court rejected his argument for a public-right standing to pursue his claim. The judgment for the university was affirmed. *Brinkman v. Miami Univ.*, No. CA2006-12-313, 2007 WL 2410390 (Ohio Ct. App. 7/27/07).

◆ *A California institute could not discontinue disability benefits to an employee who turned 65 because he was not receiving pension benefits.*

A research scientist at a California research and education institute was diagnosed with Parkinson's disease and took a medical leave of absence. He eventually became eligible to receive long-term disability benefits through the institute's insurance plan, but he retained his employee status and his right to return to work if his health improved. While still receiving his disability benefits, he turned 65 years old and became eligible for retirement. Had the scientist chosen to retire, his pension benefits would have been slightly more than his disability benefits. **Although he did not retire (and thus did not receive pension benefits), the institute offset his disability benefits with the amount of pension benefits he would have received by retiring, thereby reducing his income to zero.** The scientist filed suit against the institute in state court, alleging violations of the Age Discrimination in Employment Act (ADEA) and a state statute. The institute cross-claimed for the amount of disability benefits it had inadvertently paid him after he turned 65, removed the case to federal court and filed a motion to dismiss. The motion was granted and the employee appealed to the U.S. Court of Appeals, Ninth Circuit.

The court noted that this was not a case of double dipping, which the ADEA was designed to prevent. In order to preclude employees from receiving both long-term disability benefits and pension benefits for which the employee is eligible, the ADEA allows employers to offset the amount of disability benefits with the amount of pension benefits. The institute argued that since the employee was eligible to retire, he was eligible to receive the pension benefits, and therefore it could offset them. The court disagreed. **Because the employee had not retired, he was not receiving any pension benefits.** The court also noted that the ADEA expressly prohibits any employee benefit plan from requiring or permitting involuntary retirement. The primary effect of the institute's policy was to leave an employee without an income unless he or she retired, and the court held that a reasonable person in the employee's position would feel that he had no choice but to retire. Finding that **the offsetting of long-term disability benefits is only allowed when pension benefits are being paid concurrently,** the court found that the institute's disability plan violated the ADEA. The district court's decision was reversed. *Kalvinskas v. California Institute of Technology*, 96 F.3d 1305 (9th Cir. 1996).

VI. UNEMPLOYMENT AND WORKERS' COMPENSATION

A. Unemployment Benefits

The Federal Unemployment Tax Act (FUTA), 26 U.S.C. § 3301, et seq., establishes a federal program to compensate people temporarily unemployed. Although the federal Department of Labor oversees the program, states meeting specific criteria administer it. A major exemption from coverage, in Section 3309(b)(1) of the act, states: "This section shall not apply to service performed ... in the employ of (A) a church or convention or association of churches, or (B) an organization which is operated primarily for religious purposes and which is operated, supervised, controlled, or principally supported by a church or convention or association of churches."

◆   *An Illinois college instructor was not entitled to unemployment benefits while working reduced hours during summer session classes.*

The instructor worked as an adjunct and part-time adult education teacher during fall, spring and summer terms. He was scheduled to teach during the next summer session at a reduction in work hours. He filed for unemployment benefits, which the college opposed on grounds of his part-time employment status. A claims adjudicator agreed with the college that the instructor was ineligible for benefits because he had a reasonable assurance of returning to work in the fall, as he had done the previous four years. The instructor appealed, arguing his claim was not filed "between successive terms" since higher education institutions do not consider summer session a "term."

A hearing referee affirmed the adjudicator's decision, as did the state board of review. Appeal reached the Appellate Court of Illinois, which noted he was scheduled to teach during the summer months, in contrast to educators who are employed only during the spring and fall. The court held the instructor had applied for unemployment benefits between academic terms as opposed to during academic terms. An "academic year" included two semesters – fall and spring – and was differentiated from "summer session." For this reason, the court did not agree with the instructor that the summer session was intended to be included as an "academic term" under state law. **A key inquiry into eligibility for unemployment benefits is whether the instructor has a contract or reasonable assurances of future work.** Since the instructor's reduced summer work schedule did not change the fact that he always had a reasonable expectation of returning for work in the fall, unemployment benefits were properly denied. *Kilpatrick v. Illinois Dep't of Employment Security*, 928 N.E.2d 545 (Ill. App. Ct. 2010).

◆ *An Ohio community college athletic director was not entitled to a name-clearing hearing after his unemployment compensation proceedings.*

The athletic director (AD) was accused of accepting $800 to rent space and failing to turn it over to the college. His employment was terminated, and a local television station reported he had been fired for embezzlement. When the AD applied for unemployment compensation benefits, the college opposed his application, maintaining that he was discharged due to theft, dishonesty and possible embezzlement. A hearing officer held the employee had been properly terminated, but noted he denied doing anything wrong and was not criminally charged. Instead of appealing to a state court, he sued the college in a federal district court, asserting a right to a name-clearing hearing.

The court held that to show entitlement to a name-clearing hearing, the AD had to show the college made public comments about his discharge. Moreover, the comments had to be false and stigmatizing, not just statements about job performance, incompetence, neglect of duty or malfeasance. While the AD established these elements, the court found he had received an adequate name-clearing hearing in his unemployment compensation case, where he had enjoyed full procedural protections. *Welling v. Owens State Community College*, 535 F.Supp.2d 886 (N.D. Ohio 2008).

◆ *A New York university adjunct professor could keep his benefits despite improperly stating he had no reasonable assurance of continued employment.*

The professor filed for and received unemployment insurance benefits after the end of the spring semester of 2004. On his application for benefits, he denied that he was filing the claim between academic terms or years. The university rehired the professor for two courses in the fall 2004 semester. An administrative hearing law judge (ALJ) then found the professor received a reasonable assurance of continued employment and willfully misrepresented this on his application for benefits. The ALJ held he was ineligible to receive benefits, charged him with a recoverable overpayment and assessed a penalty.

The case reached the New York Supreme Court, Appellate Division. **The court held New York Labor Law Section 590(10) precludes an employee from receiving unemployment insurance benefits during the time period between two successive academic years, or terms, where he or she had received a reasonable assurance that he would perform services in the same capacity for those academic years or terms.** Because the professor taught three courses during the spring 2004 term and only two courses during the fall 2004 semester, the appellate court agreed with the board. The professor could not meet the economic standard of earning in the fall 2004 semester of at least 90% of what he earned during the spring 2004 semester. He therefore could keep the benefits he had already received. *In re Kendall*, 30 A.D.3d 863, 817 N.Y.S.2d 715 (N.Y. App. Div. 2006).

◆ *The Court of Appeals of Minnesota held a university was justified in firing an employee for repeatedly seeking loans from students.*

The employee worked at the university as a receptionist and administrative assistant. Her supervisor learned she was borrowing money from students. She told the employee this was inappropriate and instructed her not to do it again. The employee agreed and promised not to do it anymore. After the employee borrowed money from a student for a third time, the university fired her. The state department of employment and economic development denied her request for unemployment compensation benefits. The employee asked the Court of Appeals of Minnesota to review the commissioner's decision.

Under Minnesota Statutes Section 268.095, an employee discharged for misconduct does not qualify for unemployment compensation benefits. The statute says employment misconduct includes acts that evince a serious violation of the standards of behavior the employer has a right to reasonably expect of an employee. The court explained the university's policy about behavior did not have to be express. When the supervisor pointed out to the employee that her conduct was inappropriate, she made the employee aware of the behavior the school reasonably expected. The employee had agreed that borrowing money from students was inappropriate. When she continued to ask students for loans, she committed employment misconduct. The court affirmed the denial of unemployment compensation benefits. *Brown v. National American Univ.*, 686 N.W.2d 329 (Minn. Ct. App. 2004).

◆ *The Supreme Court of Hawaii held that a student, who was also a university employee, was not entitled to receive unemployment benefits.*

The student attended the University of Hawaii for five consecutive academic years. He was hired as a university peer counselor full time during a summer when he did not attend school. The student resumed his studies at the university that fall. The next year, he filed an unemployment insurance claim. The state Department of Labor and Industrial Relations determined the wages from his summer job could be considered for the purpose of unemployment benefits, since he was not enrolled or regularly attending classes during the summer session. An appeals officer found the student's services could be considered for benefits. A state trial court noted Hawaii law made students ineligible for unemployment benefits if they were enrolled or regularly attended classes while working for a university. The court applied a "primary relationship test," which focused on the student's primary relationship to the university. It held the student's services were excluded from the unemployment statute's definition of "services." The Supreme Court of Hawaii held that **because the student attended classes full time for five consecutive academic years, his primary relationship was that of a student.** He would have been ineligible for summer work with the school without his status as a student. Since the summer job was excluded from the code's term "employment," the court affirmed the judgment. *Univ. of Hawaii v. Befitel*, 100 P.3d 55 (Haw. 2004).

B. Workers' Compensation

An award of workers' compensation benefits is typically an employee's exclusive remedy for an injury in the course and scope of employment. This precludes personal injury suits by employees in most cases. A large group of cases in this area involves determining whether a student at a university may be deemed an "employee" based on performing on-campus jobs.

◆ *A Pennsylvania State University employee who made insufficient efforts to regain employment lost his workers' compensation benefits.*

The employee received workers' compensation benefits for almost two years after injuring his shoulder. He then applied for a disability pension. The university petitioned for modification of the employee's compensation benefits, asserting work was available for him. A workers' compensation judge agreed with the university and substantially reduced the employee's benefits. Two years later, the university petitioned to suspend his benefits entirely based on voluntarily retirement and withdrawal from the work force. It presented the testimony of a vocational rehabilitation specialist, who identified several jobs the employee could perform. In response, the employee said he had registered with a career services organization and had checked Web sites and newspapers for job openings. Although there was no documentation to confirm these claims, the judge denied the university's suspension petition, finding he sought employment and did not voluntarily remove himself from the work force.

A workers' compensation board affirmed the ruling, and the university appealed to the Commonwealth Court of Pennsylvania. The court held that when a claimant accepts a pension, he or she is presumed to have left the work force and a former employer is generally entitled to have benefits suspended. In this situation, the employee could avoid suspension by showing he was seeking employment or that his work-related injury forced his retirement. According to the court, the employee failed to show he made a good-faith effort to find employment. **Searching the Internet and newspaper ads was not enough. Instead, the employee had to show he actually applied for work or did something more to try to land a job.** Since he failed to show he sought employment in good faith, he was not entitled to further workers' compensation benefits. *Pennsylvania State Univ. v. Workers' Compensation Appeal Board*, 948 A.2d 907 (Pa. Commw. Ct. 2008).

◆ *A Michigan court reversed a grant of workers' compensation benefits to a university employee that was based on alleged harassment by her supervisor.*

The employee claimed psychological injury based on her supervisor's repeated harassment at work. A workers' compensation magistrate granted her application for benefits, finding she suffered a work-related psychiatric condition "that was significantly contributed to by actual events of her employment." The magistrate also found the employee showed she was disabled. The Court of Appeals of Michigan reviewed the case. It explained that to prove an entitlement to benefits based on a mental disability, the employee had to show a mental disability caused by an event that occurred in connection with her employment. Moreover, she had to show her perception of the event was "grounded in fact or reality," when viewed objectively. A key question was whether the employee reasonably perceived her supervisor's actions as racist, vindictive or discriminatory. In awarding benefits, the magistrate had failed to address this crucial question. An award of benefits could not be justified on the basis of the current record. Therefore, the court returned the case to a magistrate for further proceedings.

Any disability in this case ended when the employee's psychologist released her to return to work. Although the university refused to allow her to return to work because its own doctor had not cleared her, she nonetheless had the capacity to return to a job of a comparable salary as of the date of her release by her own psychologist. In the event that a magistrate found the employee was entitled to benefits, the award could not extend beyond the date on which her psychologist released her to return to work. *Swinton v. Michigan State Univ.*, No. 280135, 2008 WL 4604096 (Mich. Ct. App. 10/7/08).

◆ *A resident assistant at a North Carolina university was limited to workers' compensation benefits for contracting asthma in a dormitory.*

A North Carolina State University student enlisted as a naval reserve and entered the Navy's Nuclear Propulsion Officer Candidate Program. A Navy physical did not reveal any significant abnormalities, and he was declared "fit for full service." The university hired the student as a resident advisor for a residence hall. Near the start of his second year of work, he resigned due to mold and mildew in living spaces of the hall. A month after resigning, the student was diagnosed with a permanent asthmatic and respiratory condition. The Navy granted him a medical waiver, and he went to work at a naval air station in Florida after graduating. Another physical resulted in the revocation of his medical waiver, and the Navy later ruled that his asthma disqualified him from serving. The student sought to recover $150,000 from the university under the state Tort Claims Act for exposing him to a substandard and unhealthy environment when he was a resident advisor.

An administrative commission agreed with the university that the exclusive remedy was a claim for workers' compensation benefits. On review, the Court of Appeals of North Carolina held **the state workers' compensation act is the exclusive remedy for any employee who is injured in the course and scope of employment.** Since the student was an employee of the university while he attended classes there, his injuries arose out of the course of his employment. For this reason, the commission had correctly found the workers' compensation act was his exclusive remedy. *Christopher v. North Carolina State Univ.*, 661 S.E.2d 36 (N.C. Ct. App. 2008).

◆ *Columbia University could not avoid a worker's negligence claim on the basis that workers' compensation was his exclusive remedy.*

A temporary employment agency assigned the employee to kitchen work at Columbia. While working there, he was injured when he slipped and fell on a wet, greasy floor. The worker sued Columbia for negligence. Under state law, he would be unable to sue Columbia for negligence if it was his employer because negligence claims against employers are generally barred by the exclusive remedy provisions of the state's workers' compensation law.

The temporary agency was the worker's employer. It paid his salary and benefits, and it set his assignments. **A special employment relationship does not exist unless an entity has completely transferred control over the employee to another entity.** Columbia argued that it met this test, and it asked the trial court for judgment on this basis. The court denied the motion, and

Columbia appealed. A state appellate division court held the evidence did not conclusively establish the existence of a special employment relation between the worker and Columbia. Uncontradicted evidence showed that no one at Columbia told him how to do his job or supervised him. There was a factual question as to whether the agency transferred control to Columbia to an extent that would justify the conclusion that Columbia became a special employer. Columbia was properly denied judgment on this issue. *Bellamy v. Columbia Univ.*, 50 A.D.3d 160, 851 N.Y.S.2d 406 (N.Y. App. Div. 2008).

◆ *A Minnesota appeals court upheld a decision for a college and chemistry professor who were blamed for a student accident in a chemistry lab.*

The student was hurt while participating in a summer research program. He was paid a stipend and permitted to live in a campus dormitory at no charge. The student was seriously hurt when a chemistry flask exploded and chemical debris ignited his clothes. He sued the college, chemistry professor and several college officials for personal injury in a state court. The court noted that Minnesota law generally makes workers' compensation the exclusive remedy for employees injured on the job. It denied a motion for pretrial judgment.

The state appeals court said the facts related to the student's activities were not developed enough to support a determination regarding whether he was acting as an employee when hurt. The state workers' compensation act treated medical residents as employees but said nothing about how to treat other student workers. **The determination of whether an individual should be treated as an employee or a student depends on the context.** Deciding whether a student is an "employee" for purposes of the workers' compensation act required an analysis of purposes and character of the work performed. Because neither side offered detailed information about the nature of the work the student performed, the court upheld the trial court's decision. *Lindsay v. St. Olaf College*, No. A06-2137, 2008 WL 223119 (Minn. Ct. App. 1/29/08).

◆ *A Florida District Court of Appeal held a student who was injured while interning was not an "employee" under state workers' compensation law.*

A student at the University of Central Florida was injured when she was pushed into a wall. After the university advised her it was not responsible for her injuries, she sought workers' compensation benefits. A workers' compensation judge determined the student was entitled to benefits. Even though the student did not receive pay from the school board, the judge reasoned she was an employee because the internship was required for her to earn a degree. The board appealed to a state district court of appeal, which noted the workers' compensation statute defined "employee" as a person who received remuneration from an employer for performing work or a service.

Although the student received a benefit as a result of the internship, she was merely a participant in an internship course. This participation did not make her an "employee" under the state's workers' compensation law. Nor did a separate state law provision, which gave students in teacher preparation programs the "same protection of law" as certified educators, entitle the student to benefits. That provision did not supersede state workers' compensation law, which defined "employee" in a way that excluded the student from its coverage. Finally, the student was not covered under a workers' compensation law provision applicable to volunteers. This provision was not applicable, as she was at the school to complete a required course. The decision of the workers' compensation judge was reversed, and the case was remanded. *Orange County School Board v. Powers*, 959 So.2d 370 (Fla. Dist. Ct. App. 2007).

◆ *Missouri's labor and industrial relations commission erred in finding a sexual harassment incident could not trigger workers' compensation eligibility.*

The employee worked as a licensed practical nurse for about 21 years. Most of that time, she worked in the outpatient dialysis department. The employee was sexually harassed while administering dialysis treatment to a male patient. She notified the nurse in charge about the incident. After the employee left work that day, she broke down emotionally. She then took vacation time and began psychiatric treatment. The employee was diagnosed with depression and post-traumatic stress disorder. She took medication and received counseling. She resigned from her job because of the incident.

A vocational expert determined the employee was permanently and totally disabled due to emotional problems. The employee filed a claim for workers' compensation benefits. An administrative law judge (ALJ) found she failed to prove the stress was extraordinary and unusual. According to the ALJ, the employee had no physical injury and should be denied compensation. **The case reached the Missouri Court of Appeals, which explained that the employee's mental injury claim was based on a physical assault. Accordingly, it resulted from a traumatic incident, not work-related stress.** The employee was not required to prove the stress was extraordinary or unusual. The Missouri Workers' Compensation Act requires compensation of employees for personal injury arising out of and in the course of employment. The court reversed the decision and returned the case to administrative levels to determine if the employee deserved compensation. *Jones v. Washington Univ.*, 199 S.W.3d 793 (Mo. Ct. App. 2006).

◆ *The Court of Appeals of South Carolina held an administrative assistant who was hurt on the job could collect lifetime workers' compensation benefits.*

In 2000, the administrative assistant hurt herself when she fell at work. She had a previous history of injury, including a 1973 spinal injury from a car accident. As a result of the 2000 work accident, the assistant began using a walker and lost her ability to control her bowels. Because of these problems, the assistant became able to carry out only menial tasks and was unable to pursue additional vocational training. She sought lifetime medical care and weekly compensation benefits for life. The workers' compensation commission determined the assistant was entitled to lifetime benefits. The decision was largely based on the testimony of a treating physician. The university asked a state court to review the order, but the court affirmed it. The university appealed to the Court of Appeals of South Carolina.

The court of appeals held S.C. Code Section 42-9-10 provides that any person who is found totally and permanently disabled and is paraplegic from an injury is to receive workers' compensation benefits for life. The university argued the circuit court was wrong in determining the assistant was paraplegic because the statute did not differentiate between complete and incomplete paraplegia. The court of appeals found the circuit court had reasonably relied on the physician's testimony. The university offered no evidence to refute the court's interpretation that the term "paraplegic" included incomplete paraplegia. *Reed-Richards v. Clemson Univ.*, 631 S.C. 304, 638 S.E.2d 77 (S.C. Ct. App. 2006).

◆   *The Kentucky Workers' Compensation Board reasonably determined the disability benefits of a library assistant who was injured on the job.*

The library assistant felt pain and numbness in her right hand, arm, shoulder and neck while she was working on an exhibit. She reported the injury to her supervisor and missed a day of work before returning with restrictions. The employee continued to work until the university disallowed her from doing so because of her doctor's restrictions. She applied for workers' compensation benefits. A hearing was conducted by an administrative law judge (ALJ), who issued an opinion favoring the university. The employee appealed to the state Workers' Compensation Board, arguing the ALJ had erred by assigning only an 8% functional impairment rating instead of a "3 multiplier" to her benefits. She claimed the ALJ improperly determined the date of her maximum medical improvement (MMI). The board affirmed the MMI date and the 8% impairment findings. It reversed the finding on the multiplier and returned the case to the ALJ to reconsider the number applied.

The employee petitioned the Court of Appeals of Kentucky for review. She asserted that because the ALJ incorrectly assigned the MMI, she lost temporary total disability payments, which stop on the date of an employee's MMI. The court found the ALJ had based the MMI date on notes by the employee's orthopedic surgeon. The surgeon had stated the employee was able to return to work on a specific date, with restrictions. **The court affirmed the ALJ's decision on the MMI date, finding the ALJ had every right to believe the evidence of one doctor over another.** The court refused to review the issue of whether the correct multiplier was applied. The board had returned that issue to the ALJ, and the court was not authorized to direct the ALJ to make specific findings. *Crawford v. Univ. of Louisville*, No. 2005-CA-000137-WC, 2005 WL 2045940 (Ky. Ct. App. 8/26/05).

CHAPTER SEVEN

Employment Discrimination

I. RACE AND NATIONAL ORIGIN DISCRIMINATION

Title VII of the Civil Rights Act of 1964, later amended in 1991, 42 U.S.C. § 2000e, et seq., prohibits discrimination in employment based upon race, color, sex, religion or national origin. It applies to any institution, affecting commerce, which has 15 or more employees. Title VII exempts employment decisions based on religion, sex or national origin where these characteristics are "bona fide occupational qualifications reasonably necessary to the operations of that particular business or enterprise." The First Amendment also may preclude consideration of such claims against religious schools. However, no such exemptions exist for race-based discrimination. Other federal statutes cover discrimination based upon age and disability.

The prohibition against race and national origin discrimination in employment extends to all "terms or conditions of employment," including hiring and firing decisions, promotions, salary, seniority, benefits, and work assignments. Title VII applies to both public and private institutions.

A. Race Discrimination

◆   *A federal appeals court held Emory University did not discharge an employee based on his race in violation of 42 U.S.C. § 1981 and Title VII.*

In addition to his Section 1981 and Title VII claims, the employee alleged retaliation, wage bias, hostile environment and negligent retention. He claimed harassment and said that nothing was done after he consistently complained to human resources personnel. The employee asserted retaliatory action such as a demotion, denial of requests for office staff and space, and failure to award larger raises. To support his claims of wrongful termination and retaliation, the employee pointed to a Caucasian woman's rapid rise in job rank. He claimed the university did not truly discharge him for performance reasons and that the university did not place him into another position, as it had done for others.

A federal district court held for the university and the employee appealed to the U.S. Court of Appeals, Eleventh Circuit. The court found the program he was hired to develop required less of his time than in the past. Evidence showed the employee's remaining job duties were shared by lower-paid employees after he was discharged. This evidence defeated the employee's claim that the stated reasons for discharge were a pretext for discrimination. The wage bias claim failed because he was not similarly situated to the employees to whom he compared himself. They had different job responsibilities. There was not enough evidence to support his hostile environment claim. **The employment actions he relied on to support this claim were not severe or pervasive enough to alter the terms or conditions of his employment.** The court held a negligent retention claim could not survive, and the judgment for Emory was affirmed. *Hill v. Emory Univ.*, 346 Fed.Appx. 390 (11th Cir. 2009).

◆   *A single incident of racial discrimination was not enough to support a Title VII claim of hostile work environment.*

Appalachian State University (ASU) hired an African-American clerical worker. A Caldwell Community College (CCC) employee who was at ASU to pick up mail used a racial epithet in a conversation with an ASU secretary. The clerical worker said the secretary expressed agreement with the comment, and he claimed that ASU failed to take action to address the incident despite his complaints. The clerical worker later sued ASU and CCC in a federal district court for race discrimination under Title VII. He alleged no other incidents of discrimination. The court stated that to prove a hostile work environment exists, an employee must show harassment that is so severe or pervasive that it alters his or her working conditions and creates an abusive environment.

Hostile work environments generally result from repeated instances of harassment rather than single, isolated occurrences. Factors to consider in determining whether a hostile environment exists include the frequency of the conduct, whether the conduct is physically threatening or humiliating, and whether it unreasonably interferes with an employee's work performance. As the clerical worker was unable to show the hostility in his work environment was so severe that it altered his employment conditions or created an abusive atmosphere, the claims against both institutions failed. *Blue v. Appalachian State Univ.*, No. 5:07cv108, 2009 WL 703851 (W.D.N.C. 3/16/09).

◆ *An Hispanic candidate for an associate professor job failed to show his application was rejected based on his race, color or national origin.*

The candidate sought an associate professor position in the anthropology department at Montclair State University (MSU). Job announcements generated about 52 applications for the job, which were reviewed by a six-member hiring committee. A hiring committee narrowed the field to three. A Caucasian applicant was eventually chosen, and the Hispanic candidate filed a federal district court lawsuit against MSU for race, color and national origin discrimination under Title VII. The court held for MSU, and the candidate appealed to the U.S. Court of Appeals, Third Circuit.

Although the court found the candidate satisfied the preliminary elements of his case by showing he was qualified for the job and it was awarded to a non-Hispanic candidate, he failed to prove the reasons given by MSU for not hiring him were a pretext for discrimination. MSU said it chose another candidate because he did not have the qualifications it sought for the job. Specifically, the candidate's research focused on great apes, whereas the department was looking for someone who was an expert in the study of the social and cultural aspects of disease or health patterns. In addition, the candidate did not provide much evidence of past successful teaching performance. **Since MSU had legitimate and nondiscriminatory reasons for its decision, and there was not enough evidence to show a pretext, he did not prove MSU's decision was discriminatory** and the judgment was affirmed. *Sarmiento v. Montclair State Univ.*, 285 Fed.Appx. 905 (3d Cir. 2008).

◆ *An Arkansas professor could not base a federal discrimination lawsuit on a generalized charge that he was treated unfairly.*

The professor claimed he was mistreated, disrespected and harassed by two colleagues. He added that one of them referred to him as a "weed," which he understood as a racial remark. The professor said he was pressured to resign after he complained of the harassment. His federal district court action asserted race discrimination under Title VII and age bias under the Age Discrimination in Employment Act. When the case came before the court, the professor said he did not want to pursue an age discrimination claim. He also said he did not "really want to pursue a racist claim" either. Instead, he said his "main concern" was that he had been treated unfairly at work. A federal magistrate judge recommended that the case be dismissed, noting that **mere unfair treatment does not create a cause of action under federal employment discrimination law**. Since the allegations of unfair treatment were not enough to support any of the claims, the district court accepted the magistrate judge's recommendation and dismissed the case. *Annan v. Southern Arkansas Univ.*, No. 08-CV-1050, 2008 WL 4899527 (W.D. Ark. 11/12/08).

♦ *A federal court held that an African-American professor failed to show he was denied a promotion to a post as a full professor based on his race.*

The professor became the first tenured African-American professor in the University of Louisville (UL) history department in 1992. However, he began complaining to department officials about institutional segregation at UL. This included criticism of the department chair. In 2003, the professor filed an administrative complaint of race discrimination against UL. Near this time, he sought promotion to full professor. A UL personnel committee recommended against the promotion for lack of superior achievement in teaching, research and creative activity or service. Based on the committee's recommendation, the department faculty voted against the professor's application. He sued UL, the history department and several UL employees in a federal district court for race discrimination under Title VII and state law. He also said he was subjected to a hostile work environment and retaliation. After the court ruled for UL and each of the officials, the professor sought reconsideration.

The court declined to alter its earlier ruling. **The professor did not show he was replaced by a person of a different race or that similarly situated employees were treated more favorably.** In fact, he was not even competing with another professor for promotion. Nor did the professor show evidence indicating all full professors in the history department were white. As a result, the court denied the motion for reconsideration. *Tyler v. Univ. of Louisville*, No. 3:06-CV-151-R, 2008 WL 4683018 (W.D. Ky. 10/22/08).

♦ *A Texas professor was denied a merit salary increase based on poor job performance, not his race.*

The professor began working at Texas A&M University in 1972. He became a full professor in 1999, and he was the only black, tenured professor there at the time of his lawsuit. The professor claimed A&M paid him less than three white colleagues on the basis of his race. The claim referred to a "constant" component granted to all faculty members. The other was a merit component that included an evaluation of each faculty member's annual evaluation scores. For the 2005-06 school year, A&M granted the professor a pay increase representing the constant component, but denied a merit increase. The professor claimed race bias, noting three white colleagues were given merit raises for the same time period. The court rejected the claim that the merit increases to the white colleagues proved race discrimination. It was undisputed that the colleagues earned higher evaluation scores, and that **the professor had the lowest annual evaluation score of all professors in his department**. As the white colleagues had higher annual evaluation scores, the court awarded judgment to A&M. *Green v. Texas A&M Univ. System*, No. H-07-1115, 2008 WL 416237 (S.D. Tex. 2/14/08).

♦ *A white assistant coach was allowed to go forward with a Title VII claim that he was discharged based on his marriage to an African-American woman.*

The coach claimed college athletic directors made numerous racially biased remarks, including disparaging comments about his African-American wife. The team's performance declined, and it experienced off-court problems. The team was investigated for possible rules infractions. An athletic director's report criticized the coaching staff, but proposed retaining the coaches under improvement plans. Following some discussion, the college president and two other officials decided to fire the white assistant coach and an assistant of African-American heritage. The assistant coach claimed an athletic director referred to an African-American employee as a "jungle bunny" and to his wife as an "Aunt Jemima." The assistant coach sued the college and its officials in a federal district court. However, the court awarded judgment to the college.

On appeal, **the U.S. Court of Appeals, Second Circuit, held Title VII's prohibition of race discrimination applied to discrimination claims based on a relationship with another person**. The court reasoned that an employee is subjected to bias based on race when an adverse job action is taken because an employer disapproves of interracial association. Three other federal appeals courts – the Fifth, Sixth and Eleventh Circuits – have reached the same conclusion. As the assistant coach was a member of a protected class, he could proceed with his Title VII claim. It did not hurt his claim that the college retained the white head coach, who was also in an interracial relationship, because the head coach had a long-term contract and was considered too expensive to fire. Even though the college stated the assistant coach was fired based on the team's declining performance, he produced enough evidence for a jury to conclude he was fired at least partially because of his wife's race. The judgment was vacated, and the case was returned to the district court for further proceedings. *Holcomb v. Iona College*, 521 F.3d 130 (2d Cir. 2008).

◆ *A Louisiana university football coach identified factual issues about the motive for his discharge that prevented pretrial dismissal of his lawsuit.*

The University of Louisiana at Lafayette (ULL) fired the coach after three losing seasons. He claimed ULL violated state law by removing him as coach because he is an African-American. ULL claimed he was fired for his losing record, a significant drop in attendance during his tenure, and a budget crisis.

The court held for ULL, and the coach appealed to the Court of Appeal of Louisiana. The court held the coach proved he was a qualified African-American who was removed from his post and replaced by a white male. He also offered evidence to rebut ULL's reasons for releasing him. As to the team's win/loss record during his tenure, the coach said ULL knew the team was weak and that it would take time to turn the program around. He also produced evidence showing attendance actually increased during his first year. Budget difficulties began long before the coach arrived. A previous coach was provided counseling when the administration disagreed with his decisions. Under the circumstances, **the coach raised a question regarding whether the reasons given for his removal were really a pretext for race discrimination**. As the trial court had improperly awarded judgment to ULL, the case was returned to the lower court for further proceedings. *Baldwin v. Board of Supervisors for the Univ. of Louisiana System*, 961 So.2d 418 (La. Ct. App. 2007).

◆ *A federal district court in Tennessee rejected a professor's claims that she was denied a promotion because of her race and sex.*

An Austin Peay State University professor applied for a promotion to associate professor. In denying the application, a promotion committee said she failed to use her time effectively. The committee again failed to recommend the professor for promotion three times. She sued the university in a federal district court for race and sex discrimination. The professor added claims that she was subjected to a hostile work environment and retaliation. The court found claims relating to the first promotion denials were time-barred. The only direct evidence offered by the professor was an incident in which a noose was hung from a tree. However, nothing connected this to the promotion process.

With respect to one promotion denial, the professor claimed two white men who received tenure were similarly situated to her. **But the tenure process is different from the promotion process, and neither one of the two men sought a promotion. Therefore, they were not similarly situated to the professor.** As she did not show a promotion was denied due to race or sex, the evidence did not support her discrimination claims. The court rejected the retaliation claims, as the professor did not show the university took adverse action against her because she engaged in protected activity. *Prather v. Austin Peay State Univ.*, No. 3:05-cv-1068, 2007 WL 2688546 (M.D. Tenn. 9/11/07).

◆ *Auburn University did not discriminate against an African-American employee by declining to reclassify her job.*

According to the employee, Auburn classified her position lower than for the same jobs performed by white employees. She also claimed the university failed to promote her and retaliated against her for complaining about disparities between African-American and white employee salaries and classifications. The employee sued Auburn in an Alabama federal district court, alleging it violated Title VII. In an attempt to support her claims, she compared herself to several other employees. **The court found comparison with one of the other employees inappropriate because that employee held a different position and worked in a different department.**

The employee did not identify other employees appropriate for comparison as they had different job duties. The court also found no evidence to show any different treatment was based on race. The employee did not show a causal connection between her complaints about disparities and the failure to reclassify her position. As the university offered legitimate nondiscriminatory reasons for its failure to reclassify the employee, the court awarded pretrial judgment to Auburn. The employee appealed to the U.S. Court of Appeals, Eleventh Circuit, contending the district court erred by concluding the employees she compared to herself were not similarly situated. She said the other employees' job duties were essentially the same and that the university's reasons were a cover-up for race discrimination. The court determined the decision by the district court was proper and affirmed the judgment for Auburn. *Johnson v. Auburn Univ.*, 193 Fed.Appx. 955 (11th Cir. 2006).

◆ *The University of Minnesota did not deny promotions to an African-American employee based on his race or create a hostile work environment.*

The employee worked as a university delivery person. He was later rejected for promotion three times. The employee contended these rejections were based on his race. After his supervisor called him "tan" and he overheard a parking attendant saying the word "niggers," he filed discrimination charges with state and federal agencies. The complaints were dismissed, but the employee sued the university in a federal district court for race discrimination in violation of Title VII. The court awarded judgment to the university, and the employee appealed to the U.S. Court of Appeals, Eighth Circuit.

Courts rely on the test established in *McDonnell Douglas Corp. v. Green*, 411 U.S. 792 (1973), to analyze Title VII race discrimination claims. **If the employer articulates a legitimate, nondiscriminatory reason for adverse employment action against an employee who is in a "protected class," the employee must show the reason is a pretext for discrimination.** The university stated it did not promote the employee because other applicants were more qualified. The court agreed, as the selected applicants were more qualified for the positions than the employee on specific test results and interviews. **Infrequent racial comments were not enough to create a hostile work environment.** As the employee did not prove the university was trying to cover up race discrimination, the court affirmed the judgment. *Sallis v. Univ. of Minnesota*, 408 F.3d 470 (8th Cir. 2005).

B. National Origin Discrimination

◆   *A Maryland community college responded to threats against a professor, defeating his national origin discrimination and retaliation lawsuit.*

After the professor received anonymous threats based on national origin, the community college investigated and reported the incidents to police. E-mails were sent out soliciting evidence of hate crimes, and certain students were removed from his classes. The college provided the professor with on-campus escorts, and asked the police to check in with him at home. No perpetrator was ever identified and the professor filed a charge against the college with the Equal Employment Opportunity Commission (EEOC). Meanwhile, a student accused him of sexual harassment and others told college investigators that he made inappropriate remarks to them. The community college learned he had viewed pornography and dating sites on a college computer in violation of its Internet policy. Based on a pattern of disruptive behavior such as accusing staff of forging documents and criticizing teaching evaluators, the college fired him.

The professor filed a federal district court action against the community college for hostile work environment and retaliation. The court held for the college and the U.S. Court of Appeals, Fourth Circuit, affirmed the judgment. It held **the college was not liable for a hostile work environment based on the threats because it took reasonable action to address and correct the situation**. Since the college had valid reasons for firing the professor that were unrelated to his EEOC charge, his retaliation claim also failed. He was unable to counter evidence that the reason for discharge was his own misconduct. *Latif v. Community College of Baltimore*, 354 Fed.Appx. 828 (4th Cir. 2009).

◆   *A University of Texas (UT) accountant could not proceed with a state court discrimination case because she did not file a timely administrative charge.*

In 1999, the accountant was fired for unsatisfactory work performance and failure to follow instructions. In 2000, she filed a discrimination lawsuit against UT in a state court. The case was dismissed for failure to file an administrative charge. Nine years later, the accountant filed an administrative charge with the Texas Human Rights Commission for retaliation and discrimination based on her national origin. The case returned to the trial court, which held she failed to file an administrative charge within 180 days of the discriminatory conduct.

On appeal, the accountant argued that her 2009 administrative charge was timely because UT had committed a "continuing violation" of her rights. The Court of Appeals of Texas explained that the continuing violation doctrine applies when a party commits a series of related acts, and one or more of them occurs within the applicable limitations period. Of the 21 incidents of claimed discrimination in this case, only one occurred within 180 days from the date of filing of the administrative complaint. That incident involved a reprimand for a cluttered desk. However, **being reprimanded for having a cluttered desk was not an "adverse job action" that would support a discrimination claim**. Since the complaint did not allege any actionable discrimination within the filing period, the case had been properly dismissed. *Olivarez v. Univ. of Texas at Austin*, No. 03-05-00781-CV, 2009 WL 1423929 (Tex. Ct. App. 5/21/09).

◆   *A university that provided a research associate with an office, phone and business cards was not her employer under Title VII of the Civil Rights Act.*

The University of Utah granted the research associate a one-year appointment in its civil and environmental engineering department. She shared an office, phone and mailbox with other workers. However, the university did not pay her a salary or contribute Social Security or other taxes on her behalf. The associate used her own computer. The university did not monitor her day-to-day activities, but retained an ownership interest in the work she produced. After the university declined to renew the associate's contract, she claimed discrimination based on national origin and gender, and she sued the university in a federal district court. The court dismissed the case, finding the associate could not sue under Title VII because she was not a university employee.

On appeal, the U.S. Court of Appeals, Tenth Circuit, found that **the key inquiry was whether the university controlled "the means and manner by which the work [was] accomplished."** In affirming the conclusion that the associate was not an employee, the court relied heavily on the fact that the university exercised very little control over her daily activities. The associate was free to pursue any research activities she chose, and her research was not supervised. The university did not pay her a salary, and it provided only minimal supplies to her. The associate was different from faculty members because she had no teaching or administrative obligations. As the university exercised little control over her activities, she was not an employee and her Title VII claim failed. *Xie v. Univ. of Utah*, 243 Fed.Appx. 367 (10th Cir. 2007).

◆   *A Virginia university was not motivated by discrimination when it chose not to renew a temporary professor's contract.*

The professor was a Nigerian national who was hired under a nine-month contract for a non-tenure track position in the agriculture department. He was relocating from Australia, and he said the department chair e-mailed him about the possibility of reimbursement for moving expenses. But the written contract did not mention reimbursement. During his first semester of work, a colleague and students made repeated complaints about him. Despite the complaints, the department chair gave the professor a favorable evaluation. The next semester, another colleague began complaining about the professor. Students continued to complain about him, but the university again renewed his contract. However, it did not offer him a tenure-track position. Similar problems recurred the next year, and other faculty members complained about his condescending attitude.

After learning that his contract would not be renewed, the professor sued the university and officials in a federal district court, claiming his contract was not renewed based on his national origin and age. He also said the university breached a contract by disregarding a promise to pay his moving expenses. The court held for the university, and the professor appealed to the U.S. Court of Appeals, Fourth Circuit. It found **a reasonable jury could not find that the decision not to renew his contract was based on national origin or age discrimination**. Instead, the decision was based on the many problems the professor had at work. He did not dispute that colleagues who co-taught classes with him complained about him and said they would not work with him again. There was simply no evidence of national origin discrimination. The court also rejected the breach of contract claim, finding a statement in the e-mail from the department chair regarding possible moving reimbursement did not create an enforceable contract. The court affirmed the judgment. *Ilozor v. Hampton Univ.*, 286 Fed.Appx. 834 (4th Cir. 2008).

◆   *The removal of an instructor from a math course by a Kansas university was based on his inability to teach the course, not on his national origin.*

As part of his training, the instructor was assigned to teach a five-week math course under the mentorship of another instructor. When he began teaching, students began to complain about him almost immediately. The instructor improperly disclosed a student's personal academic information. As a result, he was removed from the course and told to retake an earlier portion of the training. The instructor sued the university in federal district court, alleging discrimination based on his Pakistani heritage. The court rejected his claim because he could not show he was able to teach the course in a satisfactory manner. **The university did not take an adverse action against the instructor when it instructed him that he needed to be retrained.** The retraining requirement did not significantly affect his employment status. Throughout the retraining, the instructor continued to receive pay. The court granted the university's motion for summary judgment. *Shinwari v. Univ. of Phoenix*, No. 05-1167-JTM, 2006 WL 3021116 (D. Kan. 10/23/06).

◆   *A Jamaican-born employee was entitled to keep a $15,000 verdict in a federal discrimination lawsuit against an Illinois community college because she showed she was treated differently than an American-born employee.*

The employee worked for as coordinator of six child development centers run by the community college. One of her duties was to secure funding for the centers, including $500,000 from the Illinois Department of Human Services (IDHS). The college suspended the employee for 30 days without pay for taking a two-week vacation without completing the application for IDHS funding for the current school year. It then discharged her. The employee sued the college in a federal district court for national origin discrimination. The court denied the university's motion for pretrial judgment on the suspension claim. However, the college was entitled to judgment on her wrongful termination charge because there was evidence of insubordination. The suspension claim went before a jury. The employee presented evidence that an African-American supervisor said she thought the employee displayed a "plantation mentality." She also provided evidence that the university did not discipline a non-Jamaican employee who sent in a late application for an IDHS contract. The jury awarded the employee $15,000 on the suspension claim.

The university appealed to the Seventh Circuit, which found the evidence tended to show a difference of opinion as to whether the non-Jamaican employee was treated differently from the employee. It held the district court did not err in denying the college's motion for summary judgment on the suspension claim. **The district court ruling on the termination claim was upheld, as the employee did not counter evidence that she was unresponsive and insubordinate to instructions.** *Waite v. Board of Trustees of Illinois Community College Dist. No. 508*, 408 F.3d 339 (7th Cir. 2005).

Section 1981 of the Civil Rights Act (42 U.S.C. § 1981) makes it unlawful for any person or entity to discriminate on the basis of race in the making and enforcement of contracts, therefore providing an alternative basis to Title VII for race discrimination claims in employment cases. Section 1981 applies not only at the initiation of contracts, but also at any time during the life of the contract. It is also used by private contractors attempting to hold an entity liable for race discrimination in contract cases.

◆ *An Arizona community college faced a 42 U.S.C. § 1981 claim based on a decision not to promote an African-American advisor to a managerial job.*

The community college hired the advisor into its disability resources and services office. After 10 years, the office sought a manager, and the advisor applied for the job. He was not even interviewed, based on his alleged lack of qualifications. The advisor sued the college and several officials in a federal district court for race discrimination under Title VII, 42 U.S.C. § 1981 and 42 U.S.C. § 1983. **The court dismissed the Title VII claims against the officials, since "employees" cannot be held personally liable under Title VII.** Section 1981 and Section 1983 claims against two of the officials failed because the officials were not involved in the selection process. A community college manager who was a member of the hiring committee declared the advisor was the best candidate for the job and said a meeting was held just to exclude him because of his race. The court said her statement and the advisor's testimony were sufficient reasons to let a jury decide whether the college was being truthful about its decision. *McIntosh v. Maricopa Community College Dist.*, No. CV-07-0760-PHX-DGC, 2009 WL 364021 (D. Ariz. 2/12/09).

When the manager later gave more evidence at a deposition, she admitted she had only second-hand information about the meeting to decide whether to grant the employee an interview. She said she only had a "gut feeling" that the meeting was secretive in nature. The deposition testimony also revealed that the manager was removed from the hiring committee and never attended a meeting regarding the position. As the deposition did not yield direct evidence of a discriminatory motive, and the circumstantial evidence provided by the deposition was not specific or substantial, the court awarded pretrial judgment to the college. *McIntosh v. Maricopa Community College Dist.*, No. CV-07-0760-PHX-DGC, 2009 WL 1286197 (D. Ariz. 5/8/09).

◆ *A Chinese-born professor failed to show he was denied tenure because of his race or national origin when a university did not select him for an award.*

The year before the assistant professor's tenure review, he won a teacher-of-the-year award. The next year, when the assistant professor was facing his tenure review, a tenured full professor said in a faculty meeting that he would no longer accept Chinese graduate students. The assistant professor claimed the department head retaliated against him by influencing faculty members to vote against him. The department head told the assistant professor he would not be granted tenure. The assistant professor sued the members of the board of trustees, alleging the university discriminated against him on the basis of race or national origin and violated his First Amendment speech rights.

A federal district court held for the board members, and the assistant professor appealed. The U.S. Court of Appeals, Seventh Circuit, held he could not prove the department head or the professor who made the anti-Chinese remark had a final say in the tenure decision. The assistant professor had insufficient evidence to warrant a trial based on indirect discrimination. The university showed that a Caucasian assistant professor had superior credentials in terms of funding and invited presentations. By contrast, **the assistant professor had several identifiable weaknesses related to funding, scholarship, and supervising grad students**. Judgment had been properly granted on the First Amendment claim that his selection of an award recipient was protected speech and that the head retaliated against him. *Sun v. Board of Trustees of the Univ. of Illinois*, 473 F.3d 799 (7th Cir. 2007).

◆ *A Muslim job applicant failed to show an Ohio college based its decision not to hire him upon his race.*

The applicant was denied a full-time tenure-track position as an assistant professor of mathematics despite over 10 years of teaching experience and an extensive record of publishing. A hiring committee eliminated him from consideration because he had recently been denied tenure by another university and submitted outdated reference letters. One of the letters indicated concern about the applicant's performance. The college selected a white person for the position who had formerly studied under the department chair as a student. The applicant sued the college in a federal district court, alleging it violated Title VII of the Civil Rights Act and Section 1981. The court dismissed the case.

The applicant appealed to the Sixth Circuit, which held that **to prevail in a Section 1981 race discrimination case, there must be proof of intentional discrimination**. The applicant argued the district court did not properly consider preferential treatment for the white applicant as proof of intent to discriminate. The court disagreed, finding the department chair's preference for the white applicant, whom he knew personally, did not prove discrimination. The court accepted the college's position – that the applicant was not one of the most qualified candidates and that the former student was the most likely to succeed – as legitimate, nondiscriminatory reasons for its actions. The judgment was affirmed. *Amini v. Oberlin College*, 440 F.3d 350 (6th Cir. 2006).

◆   *A North Carolina college did not discriminate against a white professor when it dismissed him for violating the college policy on grades.*

The professor asked the college registrar to change one of his student's grades, without giving a reason. Both times the dean rejected his requests. The professor stated a reason on the third request. His immediate supervisor approved the third request and passed it along to the dean. Because the reason given was unacceptable, the dean again rejected it. The dean met with the professor to discuss the grade change. The college then offered the professor a one-year terminal contract for disregarding the college policy. The professor sued the college in a state court, alleging breach of contract and race discrimination under 42 U.S.C. § 1981. A jury found the college discriminated against the professor and the court awarded him $68,495.

The college appealed to the Court of Appeals of North Carolina, which noted the professor had based his race discrimination claim solely on alleged different treatment from a similarly situated African-American employee. The court explained that the African-American employee was a department chair and the professor was not. They also did not have the same supervisor. **Because the employees were not similarly situated, the professor could not prove discrimination. The college offered a legitimate nondiscriminatory reason for offering the professor a terminal contract and there was no evidence of pretext.** The court vacated and remanded the judgment. *Miller v. Barber-Scotia College*, 605 S.E.2d 474 (N.C. Ct. App. 2004).

◆   *The U.S. Supreme Court held that persons of Arab descent are protected from racial discrimination under 42 U.S.C. § 1981.*

The case involved an Arab-American Muslim professor who sued St. Francis College in a U.S. district court after St. Francis denied his tenure request. The Pennsylvania district court ruled that Section 1981, which forbids racial discrimination in the making and enforcement of any contract, does not reach claims of discrimination based on Arab ancestry. It held that Arabs were Caucasians, and that since Section 1981 was not enacted to protect whites, the Arab professor could not rely upon that statute. The professor appealed. The U.S. Court of Appeals, Third Circuit, reversed in favor of the professor, and St. Francis appealed to the U.S. Supreme Court.

Section 1981 states that "[a]ll persons shall have the same right to make and enforce contracts ... as is enjoyed by white citizens...." In affirming the court of appeals' decision, the Supreme Court noted that although Section 1981 does not use the word "race," the Court has construed the statute to forbid all racial discrimination in the making of private as well as public contracts. It observed that all who might be thought of as Caucasian today were not thought to be of the same race at the time Section 1981 became law. The Court cited several sources to support its decision that **for the purposes of Section 1981, Arabs, Englishmen, Germans and certain other ethnic groups are not to be considered a single race**. If the professor could prove that he was subjected to intentional discrimination because he was an Arab, rather than solely because of his place of origin or his religion, he would be entitled to relief under Section 1981. The court of appeals' decision in favor of the professor was affirmed, and the case was remanded for trial. *St. Francis College v. Al-Khazraji*, 481 U.S. 604, 107 S.Ct. 2022, 97 L.Ed.2d 749 (1987).

◆ *An Ohio professor's federal lawsuit against a university failed because he was not a member of a protected class under Section 1981 and similar laws.*

A professor at the University of Toledo was disciplined after the National Science Foundation accused him of plagiarism. The professor sued the university and various officials under 42 U.S.C. §§ 1981, 1983 and 1985(3). He also sued under state law. An Ohio federal court granted pretrial judgment to the university, and the Sixth Circuit affirmed. **The professor could not succeed on his Section 1981 and Section 1985(3) claims because he was not a member of a protected class.** Nor could he define himself as a class of one – this is allowed only under egregious circumstances, which were not present here. The court held a Section 1983 claim against the school could not succeed because universities are not "persons" under that statute, and the Eleventh Amendment bars suits against state entities in federal court. The Section 1983 claim against the various officials also failed because the professor did not specify that he was suing them in their individual capacities. The court refused to extend jurisdiction over the state-law claims and dismissed the lawsuit. *Underfer v. Univ. of Toledo*, 36 Fed.Appx. 831 (6th Cir. 2002).

II. SEX DISCRIMINATION

Sex discrimination is prohibited by Title VII, the Equal Pay Act, and state statutes. These laws apply to public and private institutions of higher education. Colleges and universities may not engage in sexually discriminatory employment practices unless the employee's gender is a bona fide occupational qualification. The First Amendment may preclude sex discrimination claims against religious schools where the position involved is a religious one.

A. Different Treatment

◆ *Michigan State University (MSU) defeated a gender bias claim by a male faculty candidate despite evidence that female candidates were preferred.*

After twice being denied tenured positions, the candidate filed an internal complaint for gender discrimination. A few months later, he claimed his work laboratory was substantially reduced in size. The candidate sued MSU in a state court for gender bias and retaliation. MSU conceded that a dean involved in the hiring process had shown a preference for female candidates, but argued this was irrelevant because the candidate was not qualified for either job. He did not hold a relevant doctoral degree, and was not an otherwise competitive applicant. MSU asserted that the candidate was also subject to discipline for assaulting a student. After the trial court held for MSU, the case came before the Court of Appeals of Michigan. **Despite the dean's bias toward females,**

the candidate was considered equally with other applicants in the early screening process. As the lower court found, MSU would have rejected him even if gender bias did not play a role in the hiring process. There was no evidence that the candidate's laboratory space was reduced in retaliation for his internal complaint of gender discrimination. *Dybas v. Michigan State Univ.*, No. 281547, 2009 WL 2195110 (Mich. Ct. App. 7/23/09).

◆ *An Ohio community college did not commit age or gender discrimination by refusing to hire an overqualified candidate as an academic advisor.*

Sinclair Community College created and advertised two entry-level academic advisor positions. Nearly 200 women and more than 80 men applied for the jobs. Of nine finalists, the search committee chose to interview only one man, who was 59 years old at the time and had over 20 years of experience as a university director of academic advising. The new positions at Sinclair were entry level and paid much less than the director's current job. After Sinclair chose two women for the vacancies who were younger and less experienced than the director, he sued the community college in an Ohio court for sex and age discrimination. While the director stated a case of age discrimination, he could not pursue the claim because the college gave valid, nonbiased reasons for not hiring him. The court found the gender disparity was not caused by favoritism, but by the fact that women dominate the field of academic advising.

The case reached the Court of Appeals of Ohio, which agreed with the director that he had a more impressive resume than the women who were hired. But his resume was not so impressive that an employer would have been compelled to hire him. **The college considered him overqualified for an entry-level job.** It had a good reason to hire the women, who had experience with Ohio community colleges. The court held the trial court had properly granted judgment to the college. *Silberstein v. Montgomery County Community College Dist.*, No. 23439, 2009 WL 3977080 (Ohio Ct. App. 11/20/09).

◆ *A New York university employee did not show she was assigned a negative performance evaluation because she complained about sex discrimination.*

The employee received a poor job performance evaluation after she complained to supervisors about sex discrimination. As a result of the poor evaluation, her employment contract was not renewed, and she sued the university in a federal district court for retaliation under Title VII. The court awarded pretrial judgment to the university, and the employee appealed to the U.S. Court of Appeals, Second Circuit. It agreed with the lower court that **the university provided multiple, documented and nondiscriminatory reasons for the negative job evaluation**. Records showed the employee mismanaged programs and failed to meet revenue expectations. Since she did not show these reasons were a pretext for retaliation, the judgment was affirmed. *Malacarne v. City Univ. of New York*, 289 Fed.Appx. 446 (2d Cir. 2008).

◆ *The discharge of a North Carolina campus police officer for various insubordinate acts did not violate Title VII.*

The officer refused to comply with an instruction to wear a tie, which led to a written warning for unacceptable personal conduct. She filed a grievance but was told that she was not eligible to do so because she was not a permanent employee. The officer later struck a guard rail while driving her patrol car on campus. A report indicated she did not contact her superior until she realized he had learned about the accident. A week later, the officer met with a fellow officer at the university's cafeteria for breakfast during her shift, even though officers were prohibited from eating with other officers while on duty.

A university police captain ordered the officer not to charge a student for a misconduct incident as this would violate university policy. Because the officer refused his order, she was placed on administrative leave. After an investigation, the officer was discharged for unacceptable personal conduct and insubordination. She sued the university in a federal district court for sex discrimination. **The court held the officer did not show she was performing her job in a satisfactory manner at the time of discharge.** She failed to follow instructions, violated a rule against eating with other officers while on duty, and issued two criminal citations to a university student even though she knew it was against university policy. On appeal, the U.S. Court of Appeals, Fourth Circuit, affirmed the decision for the reasons stated by the district court. *Hooper v. State of North Carolina*, 222 Fed.Appx. 271 (4th Cir. 2007).

◆ *A professor who was turned down for a tenure-track position did not show the denial was based on her gender or ethnicity.*

The professor applied for a tenure-track professorship at the University of Texas-El Paso (UTEP). UTEP instead offered her a visiting professor position, which she accepted. The professor soon reapplied for the tenure-track position, but was not offered the job. She appealed unsuccessfully within the university, then sued UTEP in a federal district court. The professor claimed UTEP denied her a promotion on the basis of her Hispanic origin and gender.

The district court noted UTEP had stated nondiscriminatory reasons for its decision that were not shown to be false. Specifically, UTEP said it rejected the professor for the job due to her lack of experience in strategic management, level of potential for publishing, and level of collegiality with UTEP faculty during her employment as a visiting professor. As she did not convince the court that any of these reasons were false, the court held for UTEP. On appeal, the U.S. Court of Appeals, Fifth Circuit, noted that **UTEP set forth legitimate, nondiscriminatory reasons for declining to hire the professor for a tenure-track position. She could prevail only by showing these reasons were pretextual.** As the professor's own testimony was not enough to show UTEP's stated reasons were false, the court affirmed the judgment. *Alvarez-Diemer v. Univ. of Texas-El Paso*, 258 Fed.Appx. 689 (5th Cir. 2007).

◆ *A 13-year veteran Indiana university tennis coach was allowed to pursue a claim that she was fired from her job based on her gender.*

In the coach's final year as head coach of the women's tennis team at Indiana University-Purdue (Indianapolis), the team had its best season ever and qualified for the National Collegiate Athletic Association tournament for the first time. It also had the highest grade point average of all athletic teams at the school. Despite her performance, the university discharged the 53-year-old coach for violating rules requiring coaches "to treat others with dignity and respect" and to "exhibit a higher standard of behavior." About a month later, the university hired the 23-year-old sister of the men's tennis coach to replace her.

The coach sued the university in a federal district court for gender and age discrimination. The court held for the university, and she appealed to the U.S. Court of Appeals, Seventh Circuit. **The court found evidence that the university treated similarly situated male employees more favorably than the coach.** Specifically, there was evidence that the men's soccer coach and the men's tennis coach committed the same rules violations as the coach. The male coaches were provided with progressive discipline, while the female was not. The university never warned her she was in danger of losing her job and simply told her they were looking to move in a "new, different direction." Under these circumstances, it was improper to dismiss the gender bias claim. However, the dismissal of her age bias claim was affirmed. *Peirick v. Indiana Univ.-Purdue Univ. Indianapolis Athletic's Dep't*, 510 F.3d 681 (7th Cir. 2007).

◆   *A Maryland university did not fire an assistant professor based on gender.*

The head of the department considered the assistant professor to be a top-notch researcher. The university sometimes paid overload compensation, which must be recommended and approved by the dean's office and approved by the provost. It is paid when teaching or research exceeds the normal workload. The assistant professor asked the chair for overload compensation for overtime hours she claimed to have logged and for additional child care expenses. The chair strongly endorsed her request and noted her extraordinary efforts in attracting research grants and contracts. The university rejected the request for overload compensation. After that, the assistant professor's relationships with university staff and faculty members began to deteriorate. She accused the department head and other faculty members of sex discrimination. She filed a formal complaint with the Equal Employment Opportunity Commission.

The university received allegations that the assistant professor had engaged in scientific misconduct in connection with the grant for which she sought overload compensation. After an investigation, the university discharged her for professional misconduct and willful neglect of duty. The assistant professor sued the university and others in a federal district court for sex discrimination. The court found no evidence of discrimination. **The university had a legitimate, nondiscriminatory reason for every action it took.** The U.S. Court of Appeals, Fourth Circuit, affirmed the judgment in a brief opinion. *Britton v. Univ. of Maryland at Baltimore*, 206 Fed.Appx. 282 (4th Cir. 2006).

◆   *A Florida graduate student was considered an "employee" under Title VII but could not prove employment discrimination by a university.*

The student conducted cancer research in a university professor's lab. The university gave her the highest possible performance rating in her first three reviews, but a professor voiced concerns about her attendance, lab notebooks and poor communication. He said the student failed to obey instructions, was argumentative, disrespected colleagues and lacked focus. She left a message for a school staff member that she needed time off because of a severe hand injury. The student never notified her professor, and the university replaced her with a male. The student sued the university for sex discrimination in violation of Title

VII. The university argued Title VII did not apply because she was a student, not an employee. The court found she was an employee, but held the male was not a similarly situated or comparable employee and held for the university.

The U.S. Court of Appeals, Eleventh Circuit, applied an economic realities test to determine if the student was an employee for purposes of Title VII. She worked in the lab to satisfy lab work, publication and dissertation requirements of her program. These factors led the court to view her as an employee. **The decision not to renew the student's appointment was based on employment reasons, such as attendance, rather than academic reasons.** She was paid for her work and received benefits, sick pay and annual leave. The court held the university offered a nondiscriminatory reason for discharging her. The professor expressed concerns about her performance months before she took a leave of absence. As she could not establish the university's nondiscriminatory reason for its action was a pretext, the court affirmed the judgment. *Cuddeback v. Florida Board of Educ.*, 381 F.3d 1230 (11th Cir. 2004).

◆ *A Pennsylvania chaplain's sex discrimination claims against a Catholic university were dismissed under the Title VII "ministerial exception."*

The chaplain worked as director of the university's Center for Social Concerns. She then became the university chaplain. Allegations surfaced that the university's president had an affair with a subordinate, and he took a leave of absence. Another female employee accused him of sexual harassment. The chaplain claimed the university attempted to cover up the president's misconduct. The university demoted the chaplain by restructuring her position as head of the division and reduced much of her responsibilities and her decision-making authority. The chaplain sued the university in a federal district court, alleging it retaliated against her based on her conduct and her sex. The court stated the ministerial exception precludes courts from questioning the reason for a religious university's employment decision. The chaplain was a ministerial employee in light of how important her role was in supporting the school's spiritual and pastoral mission. The court held she performed a "ministerial" function at the university, and declared it could not hear her Title VII claims. The U.S. Court of Appeals, Third Circuit, agreed to hear the case.

The court joined seven other federal circuit courts that have recognized the ministerial exception. **Title VII exempts religious educational institutions from its anti-discrimination requirements to the extent that their decisions are based on religious preferences.** The chaplain's Title VII discrimination and retaliation claims were barred. As resolution of her fraudulent misrepresentation and breach of contract claims did not limit the university's free exercise rights, these claims were not precluded. However, the chaplain failed to plead fraud with sufficient particularity, and the claim was properly dismissed. The breach of contract claim required further consideration by the district court. *Petruska v. Gannon Univ.*, 462 F.3d 294 (3d Cir. 2006).

◆ *A Wisconsin civil rights act provided no protection to a female teacher, because her position was a religious one, and the statute did not apply.*

A part-time female teacher employed by a Wisconsin Roman Catholic theological seminary was selected to organize, develop, and lead the newly implemented department of field education. The purpose of the department was to increase seminary students' pastoral development outside the classroom. The Catholic Church promulgated an administrative policy requiring that directors of field education be experienced priests. Based on these policy guidelines, the seminary declined to renew the director's contract. The director challenged the seminary's action with the Labor Industry Review Commission, alleging sex discrimination in violation of the Wisconsin Fair Employment Act.

At a hearing, an administrative law judge determined that the seminary was sectarian and found the Equal Rights Division lacked jurisdiction over it. On appeal, the Court of Appeals of Wisconsin held the Equal Rights Division could investigate employment discrimination complaints but **could not enforce employment discrimination laws against religious associations when the employment position served a "ministerial" or "ecclesiastical" function**. As a general rule, if the employee's primary duties consist of teaching, spreading the faith, church governance, supervision of a religious order, or supervision or participation in religious ritual and worship, he or she should be considered ministerial or ecclesiastical. Because the director performed several of these duties, the Equal Rights Division was constitutionally precluded from enforcing the employment act against the seminary. *Jocz v. Labor and Industry Review Comm'n*, 538 N.W.2d 588 (Wis. Ct. App. 1995).

◆   *An Equal Employment Opportunity Commission (EEOC) investigation and lawsuit was impermissibly entangled with religion, as they interfered with the selection and training of clergy.*

A Catholic university hired a nun as an associate professor. Her tenure application was denied, and she appealed to a school committee, alleging differential treatment. The university responded that her scholarship, measured primarily by her publications, was not up to its standards. She filed a complaint with the EEOC, which filed suit on her behalf against the university, alleging sex discrimination and retaliatory conduct. The trial judge dismissed the case, finding that the application of Title VII to the case would violate the Free Exercise and Establishment Clauses. The professor appealed.

The professor argued that the district court improperly used **the ministerial exception, which exempts the selection of clergy from Title VII,** and similar statutes. The court of appeals found that the exception did apply since the professor's duties included spreading the faith and participation in religious worship. The court held that the EEOC's investigation and lawsuit violated the First Amendment since they resulted in an impermissible entanglement with religious decision-making and interfered with a procedure of critical importance to the Catholic Church: its ability to select and train its clergy. The university's interest in employing faculty of its choice outweighed the government's interest in eliminating discrimination and, therefore, the professor's claims were barred by the Free Exercise and Establishment Clauses. The district court's decision was affirmed. *EEOC v. Catholic Univ. of America*, 83 F.3d 455 (D.C. Cir. 1996).

◆ *A Pennsylvania labor foreman was provided further opportunities to show she was wrongfully denied a promotion because of her gender.*

Slippery Rock University posted a vacancy for a locksmith position. The posting stated that two years of experience was required. The foreman applied for the position along with three males. The university did not choose her for the vacancy, instead selecting a younger male carpenter. When the carpenter was later promoted, the university again posted the locksmith position. This time, it said three years of locksmithing experience was needed. However, it did not conduct interviews or fill the position on a permanent basis.

The foreman sued the university, claiming it denied her the job based on her gender and age. A federal district court rejected the claims, saying the foreman lacked the requisite experience for the job and was unqualified. She appealed, claiming the carpenter also lacked required experience. The U.S. Court of Appeals, Third Circuit, reversed the district court's decision. **The fact that a male without the "required experience" was hired for the job showed that something less than this was sufficient to meet the actual requirements.** As the district court mistakenly relied on the foreman's lack of experience to conclude she was not qualified for the job, the judgment was reversed and the case was remanded for further proceedings. *Scheidemantle v. Slippery Rock Univ. State System of Higher Educ.*, 470 F.3d 535 (3d Cir. 2006).

◆ *The Supreme Court of Iowa reversed a trial court judgment ordering a university to pay $3 million to a student employee who was sexually harassed.*

The student attended a doctoral program and worked as a research assistant to a male professor. She accompanied him to Russia to help him run a month-long cultural and educational exchange program for high school students. When they arrived at their hotel, the student learned the professor had arranged for them to share a two-room suite with both beds in one room. The student told the professor she was uncomfortable with the sleeping arrangements and insisted one of the beds be moved to the other room. The professor was very angry, but relented. He later told the student she could "kiss her Ph.D. good-bye." At other times on the trip, the professor touched her and told her details of his sex life. When the student returned home, she filed a sexual harassment complaint against the professor. After he admitted his misconduct, the college reassigned the student to another professor. Although the college directed the professor to have no contact with the student, he continued to pester her, and she filed a formal complaint. The university found the professor violated its sexual harassment policy and suspended him. It tried to fire him, but it dropped the proceeding after he was diagnosed with terminal colon cancer.

The student sued the university in a state court for sexual harassment and retaliation in employment and education for failing to protect her from sexual harassment. A jury awarded her more than $3 million, and the university appealed. **The Supreme Court of Iowa held Title VII administrative procedures must be followed. Employees may sue a university for violating Title VII only after they exhaust available administrative procedures.** The court held that because the student did not allege retaliation in her complaints to the federal and state agencies, she failed to exhaust her administrative remedies. It reversed the jury verdict for the student and ordered a new trial on her sex discrimination claim. *McElroy v. State,* 703 N.W.2d 385 (Iowa 2005).

◆ *The U.S. Supreme Court held that a Title VII "charge" did not have to be verified by oath or affirmation at the time it was filed with the Equal Employment Opportunity Commission (EEOC).*

Five months after a Virginia college denied tenure to a professor, he faxed a letter to an EEOC field office claiming he had been subjected to gender, national origin and religious discrimination. He then filed charges with the state and, 313 days after the denial of tenure, he filed a verified "Form 5 Charge of Discrimination." When he sued the college under Title VII, the college sought to dismiss the case on the grounds that he had failed to comply with the 300-day statute of limitations. A federal court found that the faxed letter was not a "charge" of discrimination within the meaning of Title VII, and that the verification could not relate back to the letter. The Fourth Circuit agreed, but the U.S. Supreme Court reversed, noting that **the faxed letter to the EEOC could qualify as a "charge" under Title VII**, and that the verification could relate back to the letter. Nothing in Title VII required the charge to be verified at the time it was made. The Court remanded the case for further proceedings. *Edelman v. Lynchburg College*, 535 U.S. 106 (2002).

◆ *The Supreme Court held the statute of limitations for a Title VII case began to run on the date a teacher was denied tenure, not his final employment date.*

A black Liberian teacher taught at a state-supported Delaware college. A faculty committee on tenure recommended that he not be given tenure, and the college faculty senate and board of trustees agreed. The college offered him a one-year "terminal contract" in accordance with state policy. After the teacher had signed the terminal contract without objection, the grievance committee denied his grievance. The teacher then attempted to file a complaint with the EEOC. However, he was notified that he would first have to exhaust state administrative remedies if he wanted to file a claim under Title VII. After a state agency waived its jurisdiction, the EEOC issued a right-to-sue letter.

The teacher then sued the college for discriminating against him on the basis of his national origin in violation of Title VII and 42 U.S.C. § 1981. The district court dismissed the teacher's claims as untimely because the Title VII complaint had not been filed with the EEOC within 180 days and the Section 1981 claim had not been filed in federal court within three years. The U.S. Court of Appeals, Third Circuit, reversed, holding that the limitations periods for Title VII and Section 1981 did not begin to run until the teacher's terminal contract expired. The U.S. Supreme Court reversed the judgment, finding that **both the Title VII and Section 1981 claims were untimely**. The teacher's complaint did not state that the college discriminated against him on the basis of national origin; it simply concentrated on the college's denial of tenure. The teacher had failed to make out a *prima facie* case of employment discrimination under Title VII, because he had stated no continuing violation of his civil rights. In fact, the teacher had received essentially the same treatment accorded to other teachers who were denied tenure. The statute of limitations began to run when the teacher was denied tenure, specifically, on the date when the college had offered him a terminal contract. *Delaware State College v. Ricks*, 449 U.S. 250, 101 S.Ct. 498, 66 L.Ed.2d 431 (1980).

◆ *The Supreme Court ruled that a state administrative proceeding on a Title VII discrimination claim filed in state court could be appealed to the federal court system when the state proceeding remained unreviewed by state courts.*

The University of Tennessee Agricultural Extension Service discharged a black employee, allegedly for inadequate work and misconduct on the job. The employee requested a hearing under the state Uniform Administrative Procedures Act to contest his termination. Before his administrative hearing took place the employee also filed a claim in a federal district court under federal civil rights laws, alleging that his dismissal had been racially motivated.

The court entered a temporary restraining order halting a hearing, but it later allowed the hearing to go forward. The hearing officer determined that the dismissal had not been racially motivated. The university moved to dismiss the employee's federal court lawsuit because it already had been resolved in the administrative hearing. The district court agreed and dismissed the case. The Sixth Circuit reversed, allowing the case to remain in federal court. The university appealed the decision to the U.S. Supreme Court, which held that the case should be heard by the district court. It ruled that **a state administrative proceeding on a Title VII claim not reviewed by a higher state board could be heard in federal court**. Since the decision made at the employee's administrative hearing was not reviewed by the state courts, it had no preclusive effect. The employee had the right to introduce his claim anew. *Univ. of Tennessee v. Elliot*, 478 U.S. 788, 106 S.Ct. 3220, 92 L.Ed.2d 635 (1986).

◆ *In an employment discrimination lawsuit filed under Title VII, the aggrieved party bears the burden of proving employer pretext.*

In an employment discrimination case against a state college, a federal district court ruled that the college had discriminated against a professor on the basis of sex. The U.S. Court of Appeals, First Circuit, affirmed the decision, ruling that Title VII of the 1964 Civil Rights Act, 42 U.S.C. § 2000e, *et seq.*, required the college to prove absence of discriminatory motive. The U.S. Supreme Court held that this burden was too great. It ruled that **in an employment discrimination case, the employer need only "articulate some legitimate, nondiscriminatory reason for the employee's rejection."** In other words, the employee has the burden of proving that the reason for the employee's rejection was a mere pretext. The Court vacated the court of appeals' decision and remanded the case for reconsideration under the lesser standard. *Trustees of Keene State College v. Sweeney*, 439 U.S. 24, 99 S.Ct. 295, 58 L.Ed.2d 216 (1978).

B. Harassment

Sexual harassment is a form of sex discrimination which violates Title VII of the Civil Rights Act of 1964, Title IX of the Education Amendments of 1972 and state antidiscrimination laws. To pursue a harassment claim under

Title VII, there must be "adverse employment action," which alters the terms and conditions of employment. In order to prove a harassment case under federal law, there must be severe or pervasive harassment based on gender, such as unwelcome sexual advances or requests for sexual favors.

Sexual comments may constitute harassment if they affect a person's employment, or create an intimidating, hostile or offensive work environment.

◆ *Virginia's highest court upheld the firing of a university business manager after his second violation of a sexual harassment and discrimination policy.*

The business manager volunteered at a local youth boxing club that was seeking to raise funds by selling calendars with attractive young women posing in boxing settings. A supervisor who worked for the business manager at the university asked female students if they would be interested in posing. The two interviewed a student and asked her if she would be interested in posing in a bathing suit or short shorts. During the meeting, the manger told the student she should not eat a piece of candy she was reaching for because "you will look like a little refrigerator with your head on top." The comment upset the student, and she reported it. A formal investigation of the manager was begun for violating the university's sexual harassment and discrimination policy. He filed a grievance, but a hearing officer upheld the discharge on grounds that this was the manager's second harassment policy violation in three years.

A state court reversed the decision, and the court of appeals affirmed the judgment. On appeal, the Supreme Court of Virginia noted that the business manager did not assert how the hearing officer's decision contradicted the law. Both courts had improperly focused on federal court cases interpreting sexual harassment under Title VII. While the lower courts had found federal decisions persuasive, the hearing officer had rejected sexual harassment as a basis for the decision. **The hearing officer noted this was the business manager's second relevant offense in three years.** He had previously violated the policy when he used a university computer to access pornography. Since the business manager did not identify any applicable law that the hearing officer's decision contradicted, the lower courts lacked any basis for reviewing the decision. The court reversed the lower court decisions and entered a final judgment reinstating the hearing officer's decision. *Virginia Polytechnic Institute and State Univ. v. Quesenberry*, 277 Va. 420, 674 S.E.2d 854 (Va. 2009).

◆ *A federal district court held a sexual harassment claim cannot be based on conduct that is merely "bizarre."*

A New York college administrator was appointed to a regular, tenure-track position in 2003. A married, heterosexual female faculty member told others in her department that they "meant a lot to her" and were "very important to her." The administrator made several vague complaints to superiors about the faculty member, saying the two "did not always see eye to eye" and were involved in an "unhealthy relationship." She then told the faculty member of her intent to resign and seek a position elsewhere within the college. The faculty member stated she was unhappy as she was concerned about covering her teaching load.

The administrator moved to another department, but continued to collaborate with the faculty member on a grant. She later resigned as co-administrator of the grant, asserting her relationship with the faculty member affected her psychologically. The administrator sued the college in a federal district court, alleging a hostile work environment based on sex. The court found the incidents of allegedly harassing conduct were all facially neutral. The faculty member never made any sexual remarks to the administrator and did not touch her. **The administrator admitted that the faculty member's conduct toward her was not romantic in nature.** Instead, she characterized it as "bizarre." As there was not enough evidence to establish sexual harassment, the court dismissed the case. On appeal, the U.S. Court of Appeals, Second Circuit, found that while the faculty member's conduct was unwelcome or inappropriate, no reasonable jury could find that it took place because of gender. There was no evidence that her conduct was based on sex, and thus no hostile work environment under Title VII. No "adverse employment action" supported a retaliation claim, and the judgment was affirmed. *Guarino v. St. John Fisher College*, 321 Fed.Appx. 55 (2d Cir. 2008).

◆   *An Illinois university did not subject an employee to a sexually hostile environment or treat her differently from her male counterparts.*

The employee worked for the university as a building services worker. She claimed male supervisors called her degrading and obscene names, although not to her face. The employee also asserted that a male employee asked her to join him on his boat for "a weekend of drinking and other things." School officials suspended her for insubordination and failure to follow departmental guidelines and practices. The employee sued the university in a federal district court, alleging it violated Title VII for allowing a sexually hostile environment.

The court found the employee did not present any evidence that the university treated her less favorably than the males. While there had been offensive conduct, there was no showing this was frequent, severe, threatening or humiliating. On appeal, the U.S. Court of Appeals, Seventh Circuit, held that **to establish a claim for Title VII sex discrimination, there had to be "adverse employment action."** Adverse employment action typically involves an economic injury, like suspension without pay. Because the employee voluntarily left her job, she was not subjected to economic injury. **An employment action is "adverse" only if it alters the terms and conditions of employment.** As the university did not change the terms or conditions of the employee's job, she could not prevail in a Title VII case and the judgment was affirmed. *Whittaker v. Northern Illinois Univ.*, 424 F.3d 640 (7th Cir. 2005).

◆   *A court rejected a police officer's claim that a Pennsylvania university discriminated against her based on her need to produce breast milk at work.*

The university granted the officer's request for permission to express milk during breaks after she returned from maternity leave. However, supervisors refused to provide her a courtesy transport from her foot patrol to headquarters, where she expressed the milk. The officer claimed she was treated differently from colleagues in other ways and was assigned to menial tasks. She quit and sued the university in federal district court for race and pregnancy discrimination. The court held for the university, and the officer appealed.

The U.S. Court of Appeals, Third Circuit, explained that **to prove she was** subjected to a hostile work environment, the officer had to show harassment that was so "severe or pervasive" that it changed the terms and conditions of her employment and created an abusive environment. In addition, she needed to show she was subjected to conduct that was offensive both subjectively and objectively. It was clear that the conduct in this case was subjectively offensive. However, the officer did not show she was subjected to conduct that a reasonable person in her position would have found to be hostile or abusive. Other officers who were placed on light duty were also assigned menial tasks. The university provided breaks to express breast milk and switched the officer to a patrol route that was closer to headquarters. As no reasonable jury could conclude the university created a hostile work environment in violation of Title VII, the court upheld the judgment. *Page v. Trustees of the Univ. of Pennsylvania*, 222 Fed.Appx. 144 (3d Cir. 2007).

◆ *A Mississippi federal district court held an employee failed to establish a university did not promote her because of her sex.*

The university did not select the employee for the position of office manager. **She insisted that she was not chosen because she refused sexual advances by her supervisor.** The employee sued the university in a federal district court for discrimination based on her sex, claiming a violation of Title VII. The university argued the employee failed to establish sex discrimination because it selected another female applicant for the position. The supervisor testified that 20 applicants applied for the position and that he interviewed 16 females. The court rejected the employee's arguments. It said her alleged failure to accept the supervisor's advances were insufficient to support her claim that he sexually harassed her. *Turner v. Jackson State Univ.*, No. 3:04CV623LS, 2006 WL 1139931 (S.D. Miss. 4/25/06).

◆ *A federal district court declined to dismiss a Wisconsin university employee's sexual harassment claim.*

The employee claimed her manager harassed her repeatedly during the three years that she worked for a university bookstore. She sued the university in a federal district court, alleging his conduct violated Title VII. The university admitted there had been a touching incident but denied anything further. It argued the manager's conduct was not sexual harassment under Title VII. The court held each case must be analyzed on its own facts to determine whether the conduct is actionable. **Factors to consider include the frequency and severity of the discriminatory conduct, whether the conduct was physically threatening or humiliating or merely offensive, and whether the harassment interfered with the employee's job performance.** The court held the employee presented enough evidence to proceed to trial. While each incident may not have seemed physically or verbally abusive, the conduct continued for a considerable time. The court denied the dismissal motion and set the case for trial. *Gray v. Board of Regents of the Univ. of Wisconsin System*, No. 04-C-562, 2006 WL 314416 (E.D. Wis. 2/9/06).

◆ *An Alabama university did not violate Title VII when it declined to renew the contract of a former dean of students.*

The dean claimed her supervisor made indirect sexual advances and comments toward her. The supervisor told the dean he wanted to come visit her at home sometime, and that women sleep with their bosses to keep their jobs and get promotions. The supervisor denied he made sexual advances or comments toward the dean. After a poor performance evaluation, the supervisor told the dean the university was not renewing her contract.

The dean sued the college in a federal district court for violating Title VII. The court held sexual harassment is a form of sex discrimination which violates Title VII. **Unwelcome sexual advances, requests for sexual favors, and comments of a sexual nature may constitute sexual harassment if they affect an individual's employment, or create an intimidating, hostile or offensive work environment.** The court found the dean did not present evidence that the supervisor threatened to fire her if she refused to comply. She never let the supervisor know she was uncomfortable about his sexual remarks. No evidence supported the dean's contention that the decision not to renew her contract was connected to sexual advances. Even after the dean turned down her supervisor's advances, he appointed her dean of students. The court granted the university's motion for summary judgment. On appeal, the U.S. Court of Appeals, Eleventh Circuit, found the lower court had correctly held the dean did not satisfy the burden of proof framework established by *McDonnell Douglas Corp. v. Green.* It affirmed the judgment for the college. *Hammons v. George C. Wallace State Community College*, 174 Fed.Appx. 459 (11th Cir. 2005).

◆ *A professor did not suffer any adverse action under Title VII because she retained her position and benefits.*

A Georgia university assistant professor received excellent performance evaluations and was chosen for a candidate selection committee to fill a vacant position. She was upset by the majority's recommendation to hire a male for the position and allegedly shook her fist at other committee members. The faculty voted not to renew the professor's contract on the grounds that she was insulting and hostile to colleagues. School deans rejected the faculty's recommendation based on her previous positive performance evaluations.

The faculty voted not to renew her contract and the deans did not interfere with the decision. Although the faculty senate eventually voted to retain the professor, she sued the university and officials in a federal district court for First Amendment and Title VII violations. The court held for the university, and the professor appealed. The Eleventh Circuit Court of Appeals found she suffered no serious or tangible effects from the university's actions. Moreover, any emotional distress was too insubstantial to be considered adverse employment action. **Since the professor did not suffer any adverse action under Title VII, there was no basis for a First Amendment retaliation claim. The court explained that "an important condition of employment" must be involved in a First Amendment retaliation claim.** She did not suffer a reprimand, demotion, or discharge, so the court affirmed the judgment. *Stavropoulos v. Firestone*, 361 F.3d 610 (11th Cir. 2004).

♦ *A Louisiana women's basketball coach won a Title VII sexual harassment claim against a university based on the athletic director's misconduct.*

The athletic director was the coach's supervisor. She claimed he asked her out about once a month despite her repeated refusals, and made sexually oriented remarks about her appearance and clothing. The coach said the athletic director told her if she "was nice," she would not have to worry about losing her job and he would buy her nice things. According to the coach, after she continued to refuse the athletic director's advances, he began to interfere with her coaching. She sued the university in a state court for violating Title VII. A jury found the athletic director sexually harassed the coach, and the court held the university liable for his conduct. The university appealed.

The Court of Appeal of Louisiana explained that sexual harassment did not always come in the form of sexual advances. Any harassment or unequal treatment that occurred only because of sex violated Title VII if it was sufficiently pervasive. **Sexual harassment included unwelcome sexual advances, requests for sexual favors – and other conduct of a sexual nature – where the conduct unreasonably interfered with work performance or created an intimidating, hostile or offensive work environment.** The court agreed with the jury that the athletic director had subjected the coach to unwelcome sexual harassment, and affirmed the judgment. *Brooks v. Southern Univ.*, 877 So.2d 1194 (La. Ct. App. 2004).

♦ *"A tangible employment action" occurs when a supervisor threatens an employee with discharge unless the employee acquiesces to sexual demands.*

A secretary for a California university began a sexual relationship with her supervisor. She later stated her belief that he would discharge her if she did not comply with his advances. After their relationship ended, she requested a transfer. The university denied the request and established a committee to investigate her sexual harassment allegations. The committee found insufficient evidence of sexual harassment, but it offered the secretary a position working for a female professor in a different department. She rejected the offer and sued the university and supervisor for sexual harassment.

A federal district court awarded summary judgment to the university, finding the secretary did not suffer a "tangible employment action." **The secretary appealed to the Ninth Circuit, which held an employee can establish a "tangible employment action" by showing she complied with a supervisor's sexual demands to avoid termination.** If there is a tangible employment action under Title VII, the employer can be held vicariously liable for the supervisor's unlawful conduct. The court found the secretary did not show her continued employment was conditioned upon consenting to sexual relations with the supervisor. Although he created an uncomfortable environment, there was no evidence establishing a connection between continuing employment and his request for sex. The court noted the university investigated the allegations as soon as it learned of them. Even though it did not think there was sufficient evidence of sexual harassment, it offered to transfer the secretary and asked the supervisor to resign. As the university took reasonable corrective measures, the court affirmed the judgment. *Holly D. v. California Institute of Technology*, 339 F.3d 1158 (9th Cir. 2003).

◆ *A university was liable for its agent's harassing behavior, but its good faith efforts to end the harassment prevented an award of punitive damages.*

A Louisiana woman worked as an office manager for a doctor at Tulane University and later began a consensual sexual relationship with him. After the relationship ended, she claimed that he began to harass her – breaking into her desk, searching her belongings and stripping some of her job duties. Her mental health suffered, and she eventually left Tulane. When she sued the doctor and the university under Title VII, a federal court dismissed the claims against the doctor, but allowed the claims against the university to go to a jury.

The jury awarded her $300,000 in compensatory damages plus over $128,000 in wages. The court dismissed her claim for punitive damages. On appeal, the Fifth Circuit found sufficient evidence that the doctor harassed the manager because of her gender and not just because of the failed relationship. Since he was acting as an agent of the university by doing so, the jury verdict against the university was proper. Also, punitive damages had appropriately been denied because despite the doctor's behavior, **the university acted in good faith to end the harassment by putting her on paid administrative leave and seeking another position for her within the university system.** *Green v. Administrators of Tulane Educ. Fund*, 284 F.3d 642 (5th Cir. 2002).

Title IX of the Education Amendments of 1972 prohibits sex discrimination by all recipients of federal funding. In Davis v. Monroe County Board of Educ., *526 U.S. 629 (1999), the U.S. Supreme Court first held federal funding recipients could be liable under Title IX for student-on-student harassment.*

The Court established a three-part test for institutional liability in Davis *for peer sexual harassment: (1) sexual harassment by peers; (2) deliberate indifference by officials who have actual knowledge of the harassment; and (3) harassment so severe, pervasive and objectively offensive it deprives the student of access to educational opportunities. A teacher's knowledge of peer harassment is sufficient to create "actual knowledge" that may trigger liability.*

In Fitzgerald v. Barnstable School Committee, *129 S.Ct. 788 (U.S. 2009), the Court held Title IX does not bar students from advancing parallel gender discrimination claims against federally funded institutions under 42 U.S.C. Section 1983. Section 1983 is a federal statute that creates no rights itself, but enforces rights created by federal laws and the Constitution.*

While Title IX claims may be brought against any recipient of federal funds, there is no individual liability for school officials or employees under Title IX. The Supreme Court thus held in Fitzgerald *that "parallel and concurrent Section 1983 claims will neither circumvent required procedures, nor allow access to new remedies." Title IX reaches only federal funding recipients. By contrast, Section 1983 Equal Protection claims can be brought against individuals, municipalities and other government entities. Where activities and defendants are subject to liability under both Title IX and the Equal Protection Clause, the standards of liability are not the same.*

◆ *An Arizona community college could lawfully prohibit a transgendered instructor from using a women's restroom.*

After the college received complaints about the instructor's use of the women's restroom, it banned her from doing so until she could prove that she had completed sex reassignment surgery. After the complaints were received, the college declined to renew her employment contract. The instructor sued the college in a federal court for gender bias under Title VII. She also alleged a violation of Title IX, and raised constitutional claims under 42 U.S.C. § 1983.

After the district court ruled for the college, appeal reached the U.S. Court of Appeals, Ninth Circuit. According to the court, **gender stereotyping is direct evidence of sex discrimination**. Transgender individuals can sue for sex discrimination based on the theory that they were subjected to discrimination because they did not conform to "socially constructed gender norms." As a result, **employers cannot discriminate against a transgender employee solely because the employee does not behave in a way that the employer believes is gender-appropriate**. By alleging that the college's actions against her were motivated by impermissible gender stereotypes, the instructor stated a preliminary case of gender bias. But the college produced evidence that it barred her from using the women's restroom for safety-related concerns. Since the instructor could not show this was pretextual and that its real reason for the ban was illegal gender bias, her Title VII claim failed. The court also affirmed the judgment on related Title IX and equal protection claims. *Kastl v. Maricopa County Community College Dist.*, 325 Fed.Appx. 492 (9th Cir. 2009).

◆ *A North Carolina university police officer alleged sufficient facts to support Title VII claims that she was sexually harassed by a supervisor.*

The officer claimed the supervisor made lewd remarks, touched her inappropriately and accosted her in a parking lot. She complained to other supervisors, who offered her no assistance. The officer claimed the harassment caused her mental distress and depression. She received psychiatric treatment and eventually lost her job at the university. The officer sued the university in a federal district court under Title VII for hostile work environment, adding a Title IX claim for sexual harassment and a claim for constitutional rights violations by the university and its officials. The university sought dismissal.

The court relied on *Shaw v. First Union Nat'l Bank*, 202 F.3d 234 (4th Cir. 2000), to test the Title VII hostile work environment claim. It held **the officer demonstrated harassment that was sufficiently pervasive or severe to create an abusive work environment. The supervisors who did not assist her had actual knowledge of harassing behavior which created an unreasonable risk of harm.** While the supervisors were potentially liable for failing to act, punitive damages were unavailable against university officials. The university's motion to dismiss the case was denied. *Alston v. North Carolina A&T State Univ.*, 304 F.Supp.2d 774 (M.D.N.C. 2004).

◆ *A women's basketball coach lost a Title VII suit against Delaware State University. She should have filed a Title IX claim instead.*

The university fired the coach for poor job performance, but she claimed it was due to her frequent complaints that the women's athletic program did not receive the same benefits as the men's program. A U.S. District Court held that the coach "confused discrimination based on her sex with discrimination based on her association with women's athletics." **She did not demonstrate that she**

was discriminated against for being a woman, as opposed to being fired for her complaints about the women's athletic program. Her retaliation claim also failed because it addressed an activity protected under Title IX of the Education Amendments of 1972, rather than Title VII. Despite the coach's claim that she suffered retaliation for complaining about a potential Title IX violation, she did not show she suffered retaliation for complaining about discrimination based on her sex, as required by Title VII. The court granted pretrial judgment to the university. The U.S. Court of Appeals, Third Circuit, affirmed the judgment. It held the coach admitted her allegations were based on her opposition to university funding disparities, and not sex. *Lamb-Bowman v. Delaware State Univ.,* 39 Fed.Appx. 748 (3d Cir. 2002).

C. Equal Pay Issues

The Equal Pay Act (EPA) requires that employers pay males and females the same wages for equal work. Employees are protected by the EPA as long as the employer is engaged in an enterprise affecting interstate commerce. The EPA has been interpreted by the courts to require only that the jobs under comparison be "substantially" equal. Strict equality of the jobs under comparison is not required.

The EPA requires equal pay for jobs involving "equal skill, effort, and responsibility, and which are performed under similar working conditions, except where such payment is made pursuant to (i) a seniority system; (ii) a merit system; (iii) a system which measures earnings by quantity or quality of production; or (iv) a differential based on any other factor other than sex." Many cases alleging disparate pay rates based on sex include claims under Title VII and analogous state laws. If employers can prove that the difference in pay is for a reason other than the difference in sex, they do not have to provide the same pay and benefits. It is for the employer to show that such a factor exists and that it is the real reason for the difference.

◆ *An Indiana university did not discriminate against a female professor who was denied a salary award given to some of her male peers.*

A university task force evaluated gender inequities at the university, with a particular focus on salary differences. After conducting a review, the task force reported that male professors tended to have higher mean salaries than female professors at all rank levels. It recommended a professional excellence program to reward tenured full professors who demonstrated excellence in scholarship, teaching and service. The professor was the only woman eligible in the college of liberal arts and sciences the first two years the awards were offered. The university made the awards only to male professors for both years.

The professor filed a grievance with the faculty appeals committee, then sued the university for sex discrimination. A federal district court held for the university. The professor appealed to the Seventh Circuit, which agreed with her argument that the denial of an award was an adverse employment action by the university. Adverse employment actions include denial of a raise, failure to promote, and termination. The court found the award was not a raise, but more closely resembled a bonus. The university contended it had a legitimate nondiscriminatory reason for not paying the award to the professor. For both years, it determined other professors exceeded her overall performance in the areas of teaching, scholarship and service. The professor alleged these reasons were a cover-up for sex discrimination. She said the existence of an "old boys' club" proved discrimination. **The court found the existence of an old boys' club did not in itself establish a cover-up. It accepted the university's reasons as legitimate and nondiscriminatory, and affirmed the judgment.** *Farrell v. Butler Univ.*, 421 F.3d 609 (7th Cir. 2005).

◆   *The U.S. Court of Appeals, Ninth Circuit, held a female professor failed to show a California university violated the Equal Pay Act.*

The professor claimed the university paid her male colleagues substantially more money than it paid her for the same kind of work. She sued the university in a federal district court for violating the EPA. The professor specifically pointed to a discrepancy between herself and the male employees in annual raises. The court dismissed the case, finding she did not show her total compensation was less than the average total compensation earned by her male colleagues for substantially equal work. **The court said the comparison of annual raises alone does not violate the EPA, which compares "wages." The act defines wages to include all payments made to an employee and all forms of compensation.** The professor appealed to the Ninth Circuit, which agreed with the reasoning of the district court and affirmed the judgment. *Ghirardo v. Univ. of Southern California*, 156 Fed. Appx. 914 (9th Cir. 2005).

◆   *A Wisconsin university lecturer earned a trial to determine if a university violated the Equal Pay Act by paying males more than she received.*

The lecturer was an untenured senior lecturer in the university's business school who was not on a tenure track. She taught business statistics, a required course for all business school students. Three of her male colleagues earned more money per course than she did. Two taught management courses and one taught a marketing course. The lecturer asked the department chair to perform a gender equity review of her salary. The dean concluded her pay was appropriate. The lecturer sued the university in a federal district court, alleging it violated the EPA by paying more money to the male lecturers.

The court explained that to determine whether the university violated the EPA, it must compare job requirements, not individuals. Under the EPA, the university could lawfully pay the male lecturers more than the female lecturer based on seniority, a merit system, a system which measured earnings by production, or another reason besides sex. The university argued that the difference between the lecturer's salary and the salaries of the other three lecturers was valid because she did not teach in the core area of the business school. According to the lecturer, the university failed to prove her skill, effort and responsibility were different from those of the male lecturers. The court found a genuine issue of fact concerning whether the lecturer and the male lecturers had the same skill and responsibility and put forth the same effort. For that reason, it denied the university's motion for dismissal, and ordered that the case proceed to trial. *Mullins v. Board of Regents of the Univ. of Wisconsin System*, No. 05-C-581-S, 2006 WL 641079 (W.D. Wis. 3/10/06).

◆ *An Ohio university did not discriminate or retaliate against a female professor who was paid less than a male counterpart.*

The university hired the professor at $2,000 less per year than a newly hired male professor in the same department. When she learned of the salary difference two years later, the university honored her request to begin to adjust her salary so it would eventually equal his pay. Three years later, the professor was promoted to full professor. She took sabbatical leave, and over the next three and a half years, she taught at the university only one semester. The professor then sued the university in a federal district court, stating her salary was lower than eight other full-time professors in her department and $13,314 less than the male professor who was hired at the time of her hire.

The court held for the university, and the professor appealed to the U.S. Court of Appeals, Sixth Circuit. It held that **to prevail under a Title VII sex discrimination claim, the professor had to prove she was treated differently from similarly situated members of a non-protected class**. The court found the university offered legitimate, nondiscriminatory reasons for paying her less than the male professor. The disparity was based on merit differences awarded during her absences and budgetary constraints. Because the professor had no evidence to counter the university's nondiscriminatory reasons, the court affirmed the judgment. *Harrison-Pepper v. Miami Univ.*, 103 Fed.Appx. 596 (6th Cir. 2004).

◆ *A Minnesota assistant women's hockey coach lost his EPA and Title VII action because he did not prove he suffered any adverse employment action.*

The assistant coach learned the university paid him $13,000 per year less than a female assistant coach. He complained to the director of women's athletics, and then asserted the head coach retaliated against him and gave him a poor performance evaluation. The male assistant coach resigned and sued the university in a federal district court for EPA and Title VII violations. **The court noted the female assistant coach performed many job duties that the male assistant coach did not perform, such as recruiting and public relations. Their positions were not "substantially equal" under the EPA.**

The male assistant coach appealed to the Eighth Circuit, which upheld the EPA ruling. **It also rejected his Title VII retaliation claim because the performance evaluation was not an "adverse employment action."** The assistant's discomfort with the situation was not enough to create an adverse employment action under Title VII. As his working conditions were not so intolerable as to force his resignation, the court affirmed the judgment for the university. *Horn v. Univ. of Minnesota*, 362 F.3d 1042 (8th Cir. 2004).

◆ *A Louisiana professor failed to show an EPA violation because she did not show her job was "substantially equal" to a male professor's.*

The professor worked as an adjunct for nine years before becoming a tenured associate. The university turned her down twice for a full professorship before doing so after 11 years. She claimed the university violated the EPA by paying her less than a male professor doing the same work she did and that she was more experienced than anyone else in her department. The professor sued the university in a state court for EPA violations. The case went before a jury, which rejected the university's evidence that the pay disparity reflected the different starting dates and annual performance reports of the two professors. The university appealed to the Court of Appeal of Louisiana, which held the **professor did not show her job was substantially equal to that of the male professor or involved the same skills**. Because of this, she failed to show an EPA violation, and the court reversed the judgment. *Ramelow v. Board of Trustees of Univ. of Louisiana*, 870 So.2d 415 (La. Ct. App. 2004).

◆ *The Second Circuit affirmed a jury verdict of $117,929.98 to a female professor who sued Marist College under the EPA and Title VII.*

After the jury rendered its verdict for the professor, both sides appealed different aspects of the decision. The college argued that the verdict should be overturned because the professor did not make specific comparisons with her male counterparts, but rather the group as a whole. Thus, the university argued that the professor failed to state a *prima facie* case.

The professor claimed that a special jury verdict form erroneously instructed the jury to ignore her claim under Title VII if it found that any violation of the EPA by the college was not willful. The appeals panel rejected the college's argument, finding that the five variables the professor's expert used to isolate comparable positions were effective. The variables were rank, years of service, division, tenure status and degrees earned. Turning to the professor's argument on appeal, the circuit court pointed out that while the EPA and Title VII must be construed in harmony, particularly where claims made under the two statutes arise out of the same discriminatory pay policies, another consideration comes into play. One of the major differences between the EPA and Title VII is the requirement regarding intent. **Under Title VII, a plaintiff alleging disparate treatment must demonstrate discriminatory intent, while an EPA plaintiff does not have to make this showing.** Accordingly, the jury verdict form was appropriate. The district court decision was upheld. *Lavin-McEleney v. Marist College*, 239 F.3d 476 (2d Cir. 2001).

D. Pregnancy Discrimination

Pregnancy discrimination is prohibited by Title VII, the Pregnancy Discrimination Act (42 U.S.C. § 2000e(k)), and analogous state laws.

◆ *A federal district court refused to grant summary judgment to a university accused of retaliating against an adjunct professor for filing an earlier lawsuit.*

In a federal district court action filed in 1998, the adjunct professor claimed the university did not reappoint her because of her pregnancy. Her Title VII suit was settled in 2000, with the university agreeing to appoint the adjunct to teaching jobs for spring and fall in 2001. But as a result of a clerical error, she was not offered the fall assignment, and she threatened to sue to enforce the settlement agreement. Three years later, the adjunct did so, this time claiming the university declined to reappoint her in retaliation for the first action. The court found there was a possible causal connection between the first lawsuit and the decision not to reappoint her some time later. In addition, there was evidence that the professor who decided not to reappoint the adjunct played a role in evaluating her and had objected to the terms of the settlement.

There was enough evidence for a jury to infer retaliation in this case. Also, although the college claimed the decision not to reappoint the adjunct was based on student complaints, it did not produce any written records of complaints. **There was evidence that professors with equal or lower student evaluation scores were reappointed.** Thus, pretrial judgment was improper. *Rumain v. Baruch College of City Univ. of New York*, No. 06 Civ. 8256 (PKC) (MHD), 2008 WL 4866019 (S.D.N.Y. 11/6/08).

◆ *Columbia University did not subject an employee to "adverse employment action" by changing her supervisor.*

The employee worked as an associate director for the university until the associate dean decided to restructure her department. The employee continued to report directly to the associate dean. Upon learning she was pregnant, she informed the executive director. The associate dean soon decided the employee was to report to the executive director as part of the restructuring. The employee suspected the decision was based on her pregnancy. She told the associate director she was having a high risk pregnancy, and she took disability leave. Meanwhile, the associate dean criticized her performance. The employee sued the university in a federal district court for pregnancy discrimination under Title VII, the Pregnancy Discrimination Act, and state law.

The court found the employee did not prove the university subjected her to adverse employment action. It said **the assignment to report to a different supervisor was not a demotion or an "adverse employment action."** The executive director was senior to the employee in title and grade, and the change did not affect her title, grade, salary or benefits. The court explained that criticizing an employee was not an adverse employment action. **"Adverse employment actions" include demotion, termination, or a change that results in significantly diminished material responsibilities.** As the employee did not establish any of these, the court awarded summary judgment in favor of Columbia. *Palomo v. Trustees of Columbia Univ. in City of New York*, No. 03 Civ. 7853 (DLC), 2005 WL 1683586 (S.D.N.Y. 7/20/05).

◆ *A federal district court let a pregnancy discrimination claim by an Oklahoma childcare employee proceed to trial.*

The employee worked as a childcare attendant at a university childcare center. She said her manager rolled her eyes and "congratulated' her in a hateful manner when she told her she was pregnant. The employee claimed after she became pregnant, the manager refused to consult with her and allowed other employees to harass her about her pregnancy. The employee gave her supervisors statements from a physician advising her to stop working because of pregnancy complications. She took FMLA leave and returned to work after the childbirth. The employee then gave her supervisors doctors' notes stating she could not lift over 20 pounds, which meant she could pick up infants but not toddlers. The center told her she could not work with restrictions.

The employee sued the university for pregnancy discrimination. The university moved for summary judgment, arguing she could not perform the job because lifting was required. The court disagreed, holding **the university did not conduct an independent evaluation to determine if the weight restrictions actually prevented the employee from performing her job**

duties. It denied the university's motion for summary judgment and scheduled the case for trial. *Borchert v. The State of Oklahoma*, No. 04CV0839 CVE/SAJ, 2006 WL 228913 (N.D. Okla. 1/30/06).

III. RELIGIOUS DISCRIMINATION

Title VII generally prohibits religious discrimination. However, religious hiring preferences are permitted if the institution is substantially "owned, supported, controlled, or managed" by a religious organization or if the curriculum "is directed toward the propagation of a particular religion."

◆ *An Illinois university defeated a religious discrimination claim by a Muslim professor, but a federal district court let his retaliation claim proceed.*

A probationary, tenure-track professor at Illinois State University (ISU) learned that another Muslim employee was not selected for a position, and became involved in an internal investigation. The professor believed his low student ratings were based on prejudice against him because of his color and national origin. When the professor learned he would not be offered another contract, he sued ISU in a federal district court. The court held for ISU on the professor's race, national origin and religious discrimination claims because he "failed to demonstrate a convincing mosaic of circumstantial evidence" indicating bias. He had a history of poor scores and his ratings were below the school average. But the court found enough evidence of bias to proceed with the professor's retaliation claim. **He complained of illegal discrimination and adverse employment action that was linked to his complaint.** As a result, the retaliation claim survived pretrial dismissal. *Abuelyaman v. Illinois State Univ.*, No. 07-1151, 2009 WL 3837012 (C.D. Ill. 11/13/09).

◆ *A Texas court reinstated a former university librarian's claim that she was discharged based on her Christian faith.*

The librarian claimed she was subjected to a hostile work environment based on her religion. She stated she was asked to view a computer image of "Jesus in a satan costume," and was subjected to anti-Christian comments such as "Christianity is a 'cop out'" and "Catholics are paying for forgiveness." According to the librarian, her supervisor instructed her to turn off her Christian radio programs when others were present in the library. She complained to a school dean about the supervisor's conduct, but about five months later, the university discharged her. In a state court lawsuit against the university, the librarian claimed she was fired based on her religion and in retaliation for complaining about a hostile work environment. She also asserted a claim for hostile work environment. The court held for the university.

On appeal, the Court of Appeals of Texas reversed the judgment on the religious discrimination claim. Although the lower court had found it was untimely filed, the court of appeals found this was error. On the other hand, the hostile work environment claim failed because the administrative complaint did not identify any acts of harassment occurring within 180 days from the date of the complaint. **The court affirmed the judgment on the retaliation claim,**

based on the delay of over five months between the time the librarian filed a complaint with the dean and the date of her discharge. Without more evidence that her complaint caused her discharge, the retaliation claim failed. *Bartosh v. Sam Houston State Univ.*, 259 S.W.3d 317 (Tex. Ct. App. 2008).

◆ *A Jewish professor failed to show she was denied tenure by an Illinois University on the basis of her religion.*

A university committee recommended the professor for tenure, but a dean noted a personality conflict and warned her not to politicize the tenure process. During a meeting, the dean told a university vice president that the professor had missed work and university events on Jewish holidays. The dean recommended against tenure, citing her lack of service on committees and negative comments by students. The dean also pointed to declining enrollment in her department. The university committee recommended against her tenure, and the university vice president and president agreed. The professor filed an unsuccessful grievance with the university, then commenced a federal district court action for discrimination. The court held for the university.

On appeal, the U.S. Court of Appeals, Seventh Circuit, noted that the professor had accused the dean of religious bias. However, no higher-ranking persons were accused of this. The dean explained that tenure was denied for nondiscriminatory reasons such as the professor's lack of committee service, negative student comments and declining enrollment in her program. The dean's allegedly biased comments did not show these reasons were false. **The dean was a subordinate participant in the tenure process, making it unlikely that there was a causal connection between a discriminatory motive and the denial of tenure.** There was not enough evidence to show the reasons given for the denial were a cover for discrimination. Finally, the court affirmed the rejection of a claim of tortious interference with prospective employment. No evidence showed the dean had acted recklessly or with an intent to injure the professor. The decision of the district court was affirmed. *Adelman-Reyes v. Saint Xavier Univ.*, 500 F.3d 662 (7th Cir. 2007).

◆ *A physical altercation, not improper discrimination, motivated the discharge of a New York university employee.*

A supervisor accused the employee of punching the time card of a co-worker who was not at work. Their argument culminated in physical contact. The employee's union filed a grievance on her behalf but later declined to arbitrate it. The university determined the employee started the fight, but she denied this and sued the university in a federal district court for discrimination based on her race, age, religion and color. The court held the employee did not state a claim of age discrimination. Because the university concluded she had struck the supervisor and that the supervisor had not struck her back, the two were not subject to the same disciplinary standards. There was no evidence to support the employee's claim that the person who investigated the incident was biased against her for any reason. The employee admitted that she struck the supervisor, and that act justified her termination.

The employee asserted she was discriminated against based on her Christian faith, and she supported this allegation by contending that a supervisor once said she disliked people who "pretend they're Christian." The employee further claimed that religious materials she left on a break room table were moved to the floor. **The court found these incidents did not prove religious bias by the university. It rejected the employee's remaining claims and dismissed the case.** On appeal, the U.S. Court of Appeals, Second Circuit, held the employee raised an inference of discrimination because she claimed the supervisor had struck her first. However, even if this was true, she did not show the reasons given for her discharge were false. There was also no evidence of age discrimination, or any showing that an investigation of the incident had been biased. As the employee did not show the explanation for her discharge was a pretext for discrimination, the judgment for the university was affirmed. *Mincey v. Univ. of Rochester*, 262 Fed.Appx. 319 (2d Cir. 2008).

◆ *A Missouri university did not discriminate against a doctor by refusing to rehire him because of license suspensions and criminal conduct.*

The doctor sued the university in a federal district court, alleging it violated Title VII when it did not hire him because the Catholic Church did not approve of his divorce. The university stated it did not rehire him because of medical license suspensions in Missouri and Illinois, criminal conduct, failure to provide a complete residency application, and past unprofessional conduct. **The court found the university had legitimate nondiscriminatory reasons for not rehiring the doctor.** He presented no evidence to show the decision was motivated by discrimination instead of the reasons it offered. The court granted the university's motion for summary judgment and dismissed the case. *Kaminsky v. Saint Louis Univ. School of Medicine*, No. 4:05CV1112 CDP, 2006 WL 2376232 (E.D. Mo. 8/16/06).

In a brief memorandum opinion, the U.S. Court of Appeals, Eighth Circuit, held that even if the doctor had shown discrimination, the university produced sufficient nondiscriminatory evidence to deserve pretrial judgment. The district court judgment was affirmed. *Kaminsky v. St. Louis Univ. School of Medicine*, 226 Fed.Appx. 646 (8th Cir. 2007).

◆ *A Georgia state university did not violate a Christian cheerleading coordinator's constitutional right to the free exercise of her religion.*

Two Jewish cheerleaders complained to the athletic department that the coordinator discriminated against them because of their religion. They said the coordinator treated them unfavorably and used her position to encourage students to pray, study the Bible and engage in other religious practices. The university placed the coordinator on probation, and it informed her she would be discharged if she continued to violate the university's policy on religious discrimination. She read a statement to the cheerleading squad, stating a Jewish cheerleader had accused her of religious discrimination and that the claim was without merit. The university fired the coordinator, who filed a federal lawsuit.

A federal district court held the university was entitled to Eleventh Amendment immunity. The terms of the coordinator's probation letter simply mandated that she keep her religious activities separate from the cheerleading program. **As the university did not compromise her religious beliefs or prevent her from doing anything essential to exercising**

her religion, the court dismissed the case. *Braswell v. Board of Regents of the Univ. System of Georgia*, 369 F. Supp. 2d 1371 (N.D. Ga. 2005).

◆ *A Minnesota business college discharged an instructor for his poor performance, not his Muslim religion.*

The college hired the instructor to teach computer programming. There were soon complaints about his teaching. A student complained that the instructor did not respect students and refused to answer their questions. Several students claimed his presentation and lecture styles were ineffective. The college held an annual review and rated the instructor as "meeting expectations" in all categories. His next annual review was unfavorable. The university placed the instructor on probation and told him if he did not improve his performance, he would be discharged. After he failed to follow the conditions of his performance improvement plan, the college discharged him. The instructor sued the college in a federal district court, alleging it discriminated against him based on religion. The college argued the instructor failed to adequately perform his job. **The court agreed, finding evidence that he did not meet the legitimate employment expectations of the college. The college was entitled to summary judgment.** *Eldeeb v. Career Educ. Corp.*, No. Civ. 04-2932PAMRLE, 2005 WL 2105500 (D. Minn. 8/30/05).

◆ *A federal district court dismissed Title VII religious discrimination charges by a former employee of the University of Rochester.*

The employee was Iranian and a Muslim. His supervisor was Jewish and had lived in Israel. The supervisor noticed the employee's performance problems during the first few months of his employment, and documented them in a warning letter stating he might face termination if his work did not improve. The employee stated the supervisor began treating him differently after he found out he was Muslim and born in Iran. He sued the university in a federal district court for discrimination based on religion and national origin. **The court found examples of the employee's poor performance adequately demonstrated a nondiscriminatory reason for firing him. The employee offered no evidence to refute the university's explanation or to show its actions were actually a pretext for hostility toward Iran or Muslims.** The firing of a Muslim employee two months after the September 11 terrorist attacks did not establish a connection between the decision to fire him and his religion or national origin. The court noted the employee's performance problems arose before September 11. This was not a case where a sudden change in a performance evaluation followed a precipitating event. The court granted the university's motion for summary judgment. *Sasannejad v. Univ. of Rochester*, 329 F.Supp.2d 385 (W.D.N.Y. 2004).

◆ *A Texas professor was unable to establish that a university improperly fired him based on his religious beliefs.*

The professor asserted that as the only Jewish professor in a predominantly Arab or Muslim department, he was subjected to a hostile work environment. He contended the university required him to teach a course on his Sabbath, while accommodating Muslim colleagues during Ramadan. A colleague observed the professor's class and found that he was not teaching or applying the required subjects. His supervisor rated his performance "unsatisfactory" and "unacceptable," and the university discharged him. The professor sued the university in a state court for age and religious discrimination. The court awarded the university summary judgment, and the professor appealed.

The Court of Appeals of Texas held that to prevail in his religious discrimination claim, the professor had to show the university knew of his good-faith religious beliefs, that they conflicted with a job requirement, and that he suffered an adverse employment action for failing to comply with the requirement. In view of the substantial evidence indicating the professor's performance was poor, the court concluded the university had legitimate, nondiscriminatory reasons for discharging him. *Brauer v. Texas A&M Univ.*, No. 13-01-868-CV, 2003 WL 22415369 (Tex. Ct. App. 2003).

◆   *An Orthodox Jewish professor's claims of religious discrimination, hostile work environment and retaliation were allowed to go to trial.*

At the start of an Orthodox Jewish professor's first year as an associate professor in the School of Education at William Paterson College of New Jersey, her department chair allowed her to arrange her schedule around religious holidays. Also, she did not count as sick days the days she missed for religious holidays. During her third year of employment, she was charged sick days for religious holidays. She also was charged a sick day for a Jewish holiday that fell on a day she was not scheduled to teach. The professor was continually asked why she could not attend meetings on Friday nights and Saturdays, even though she had explained her wish to observe the Sabbath. After her termination, she sued under Title VII and the New Jersey Law Against Discrimination for religious discrimination, hostile work environment and retaliation. A U.S. district court granted pretrial judgment to the university.

On appeal, the U.S. Court of Appeals, Third Circuit, held the district court applied the wrong standard to the hostile environment claim. The court should have asked **whether a reasonable fact finder could view the evidence as showing that the professor's treatment was attributable to her religion**. Although the college provided legitimate nondiscriminatory reasons for its decision not to retain the professor, she was able to cast doubt on the legitimacy of those reasons such that the lawsuit could proceed. *Abramson v. William Paterson College of New Jersey*, 260 F.3d 265 (3d Cir. 2001).

IV. AGE DISCRIMINATION

The Age Discrimination in Employment Act (ADEA), 29 U.S.C. § 621, et seq., prohibits age discrimination against individuals at least 40 years of age. As part of the Fair Labor Standards Act, it applies to institutions with 20 or more employees and which affect interstate commerce.

A. ADEA

◆   *A university administrative assistant failed to prove that the non-renewal of her contract was motivated by race or national origin discrimination.*

The administrative assistant began working for the university in 1995 when she was already over 40. She received good performance evaluations until a new dean arrived at her department in 2000. The new dean assigned the assistant to work with the university outreach coordinator, who soon took maternity leave and left the assistant with many of her job duties. An Asian-American assistant dean agreed to help her and at the same time became her supervisor. But the assistant dean found her job performance deficient. Two others involved in the review process disagreed and submitted positive appraisals at about the same time. The dean later recommended that the university not rehire the assistant. She was replaced by a person of Hispanic origin. The administrative assistant sued the university in a federal district court for race, national origin and age discrimination. She also claimed officials retaliated against her and engaged in a conspiracy to discriminate against her.

The court held for the university, and the assistant appealed to the U.S. Court of Appeals, Third Circuit. The court held the allegations did not prove race discrimination. An assertion that the university wanted to diversify its staff was purely speculative, and the fact that the assistant dean and president were not Caucasian failed to prove racial bias. **There was no evidence that the university's affirmative action guidelines had been improperly applied or that the timing of the opening for the administrative assistant's old job was suspicious.** The age discrimination claim failed because the university produced evidence of unsatisfactory job performance. Despite the positive job evaluations from some supervisors, the court found the administrative assistant did not prove the negative ones from the other supervisor were a pretext for bias. The court affirmed the judgment for the university. *Hunter v. Rowan Univ.*, 299 Fed.Appx. 190 (3d Cir. 2008).

◆ *The U.S. Supreme Court held employees may bring "disparate impact" actions under the ADEA. Disparate impact actions do not require proof of intentional age discrimination. Instead, they require an employee to show an employment policy has the effect of discriminating on the basis of age.*

The city of Jackson, Mississippi increased the salaries of all employees in 1999. Those with under five years of experience received comparatively higher raises than more experienced employees. The city justified the action as a way to remain competitive and "ensure equitable compensation to all employees."

A group of veteran police officers, most over 40 years old, claimed the city's action constituted discrimination on the basis of age. The officers sued the city in a federal district court for ADEA violations, alleging both disparate treatment and disparate impact. The court held for the city, and the U.S. Court of Appeals, Fifth Circuit, affirmed the judgment. The Supreme Court agreed to review the disparate impact claim. It compared the ADEA with Title VII of the Civil Rights Act of 1964. **Except for substitution of the word "age" for "race, color, religion, sex, or national origin," the language of the ADEA and Title VII was identical.** Title VII disparate impact claims have long been recognized by the Court. The Court stated the ADEA authorizes potential recovery for disparate impact cases, in a manner comparable to Title VII disparate impact claims for race, religion or sex discrimination. **Employees alleging an employer practice has a disparate impact on a class of employees need not show the practice is intentional.** While the Court held the officers were entitled to bring a disparate impact claim under the ADEA, they could not show the city violated the ADEA in this case. The Court noted the ADEA's coverage for disparate impact is narrower than that of Title VII. Under the ADEA, an employer can treat workers differently if the employer is motivated by reasonable factors other than age. The Court found Congress had narrowed the ADEA's scope because there is often a connection between age and ability to perform a job. The city's decision to make itself competitive in the job market was based on a reasonable factor other than age. As the employees could not prove the increase had a disparate impact on them, the Court affirmed the judgment. *Smith v. City of Jackson*, 544 U.S. 228 (2005).

◆ *The U.S. Court of Appeals, Eighth Circuit, held that replacement by a substantially younger person is necessary to prove age discrimination.*

A Minnesota university promoted an employee to serve as a dean at the age of 62. He had a heart attack three years later, and learned of rumors indicating he wanted to retire and that a plan had been developed to replace him. The dean denied the rumors in a formal letter to the university president. He stated he was profoundly disturbed by the rumors and accused the president of trying to force his resignation. The next year, the university reorganized, and a newly hired provost/vice president soon recommended replacing the dean. The reasons stated were the dean's creation of a divisive environment, ineffective handling of conflicts, and favoritism and bias in personnel evaluations. The dean's permanent replacement was 64 years old at the time of his appointment. The dean sued the university in a federal district court for ADEA violations. The court held for the university, and the dean appealed.

The Eighth Circuit explained that the ADEA bars employers from taking age-based adverse employment actions against employees who are 40 or older. **The U.S. Supreme Court held in a 1996 case that the replacement of a 68-year-old by a 65-year-old was "very thin evidence" of discrimination.** The Eighth Circuit held the dean did not prove age discrimination based on his replacement by an employee who was only two-and-a-half years younger than he was. **The university had legitimate nondiscriminatory reasons for demoting him, and the court did not "sit as a super-personnel department and second guess" its decisions.** The dean's other discrimination and retaliation claims failed for the same reasons. The court affirmed the judgment for the university. *Lewis v. St. Cloud State Univ.*, 467 F.3d 1133 (8th Cir. 2006).

◆ *A federal district court held a 56-year-old professor was fired because he was not qualified and did not follow university procedures.*

The professor had taught night classes as an adjunct professor in the university's college of business (COB) since 1985. His academic background was in the field of education. In 2002, the university hired a new dean for its COB and prepared for an accreditation visit. The university took steps to ensure that adjunct faculty were teaching courses in which they had academic and professional credentials. As a result, the university stopped using the professor to teach courses at its COB. He was given the chance to teach marketing courses at the university, but he failed to comply with a policy that required students to purchase their books from the student bookstore.

The university then discharged the professor, and he filed a federal court action for violation of the ADEA. **The court held age was not a factor in the university's decision. Instead, the discharge was based on the professor's lack of qualifications to teach the classes he formerly taught.** He also failed to order course books through the university's book store, as required by university policy. There was no violation of the ADEA. *Anhalt v. Cardinal Stritch Univ.*, No. 04-C-1052, 2006 WL 3692631 (E.D. Wis. 12/12/06).

◆ *The U.S. Court of Appeals for the Second Circuit held a New York university did not assign fewer courses to a professor because of his age.*

The university assigned the tenured professor a courseload of four courses for an academic year. He believed his tenure entitled him to teach at least five courses, and he sued the university in a federal district court under the ADEA. The court ruled for the university, and the professor appealed. The Second Circuit held the professor did not establish adverse employment action. **The assignment of four courses was not a "materially adverse change" in the terms and conditions of his employment. Material changes include termination, a demotion evidenced by a decrease in wages, or a less distinguished title.** The average courseload for a tenured professor was fewer than four, and the professor claimed no wage loss. The court held that even if the professor had managed to show an adverse employment action, he submitted no evidence to support an inference that the assignment of classes was based on his age. The judgment for the university was affirmed. *Boise v. Boufford*, 121 Fed.Appx. 890 (2d Cir. 2005).

◆ *The Supreme Court held state employees could not sue their employers under the ADEA.*

Two associate professors at the University of Montevallo sued the university in an Alabama federal court under the ADEA. They alleged that the university had discriminated against them on the basis of their age, that it had retaliated against them for filing charges with the Equal Employment Opportunity Commission, and that its College of Business, where they were employed, used an evaluation system that had a disparate impact on older faculty members. The university sought to dismiss the action on the grounds of Eleventh Amendment immunity, and the district court agreed, finding that the ADEA did not eliminate the state's immunity. A group of current and former faculty and librarians of Florida State University and Florida International University filed suit against the Florida Board of Regents under the ADEA, alleging that the board refused to require the two state universities to allocate funds to provide previously agreed-upon market adjustments to the salaries of eligible university employees. They maintained that this failure had a disparate impact on the base pay of older employees with a longer record of service.

The court refused to dismiss the action. On appeal, the Eleventh Circuit consolidated the cases and held the ADEA did not abrogate (do away with) state Eleventh Amendment immunity. The U.S. Supreme Court noted that **although the ADEA contains a clear statement of Congress' intent to eliminate the states' immunity under the Eleventh Amendment, such action exceeded Congress' authority under Section 5 of the Fourteenth**

Amendment (which grants Congress the power to enact laws under the Equal Protection Clause). Although state employees cannot sue their employers for discrimination under the ADEA, they are not without remedies. Every state has age discrimination statutes, and almost all of them allow the recovery of money damages from state employers. *Kimel v. Florida Board of Regents*, 528 U.S. 62, 120 S.Ct. 631, 145 L.Ed.2d 522 (2000).

1. Applicability to Religious Schools

◆ *The ADEA did not to apply to pervasively religious Missouri seminary.*

A Missouri seminary allegedly dismissed an employee because of his age. He sued the seminary in a federal district court under the ADEA. The seminary brought a motion for pretrial judgment, stating that the ADEA was inapplicable because the institution was pervasively religious. The court agreed. It considered the U.S. Supreme Court's decision in *NLRB v. Catholic Bishop of Chicago*, 440 U.S. 490, 99 S.Ct. 1313, 59 L.Ed.2d 533 (1979), in which the Court held the National Labor Relations Act (NLRA) inapplicable to church-operated schools. The court ruled that although the ADEA was a remedial statute rather than a regulatory statute such as the NLRA, the ruling in *Catholic Bishop* applied here. Because application of the ADEA could implicate enforcement by the EEOC, government regulatory powers were involved. Thus, **since the potential existed for impinging the seminary's religious freedoms, the court ruled that the ADEA was inapplicable**. It granted the seminary's motion for pretrial judgment. *Cochran v. St. Louis Preparatory Seminary*, 717 F.Supp. 1413 (E.D. Mo. 1989).

◆ *An Ohio federal court held that the ADEA could be applied to a religious institution.*

An employee at Xavier University, an institution operated by the Order of Jesuits, sued the university under the ADEA in an Ohio federal court. The university asserted that the court had no authority to rule on the case because the university, as a religious institution, was exempt from the ADEA's provisions. The court observed that because the ADEA gave no indication that religious institutions were exempt from its provisions, the issue became whether application of the ADEA to the university would violate the Free Exercise and Establishment Clauses of the First Amendment.

The court held for the employee, noting that the Fourth Circuit held in *Ritter v. Mount St. Mary's College*, 814 F.2d 986 (4th Cir. 1987), that **application of the ADEA to a religious institution did not present a significant risk of infringement on the institution's First Amendment rights**. Here, the facts gave no indication that enforcement of the ADEA would violate the religion clauses of the First Amendment. Accordingly, the university was not entitled to have the case dismissed. *Soriano v. Xavier Univ.*, 687 F.Supp. 1188 (S.D. Ohio 1988).

2. Defenses

The Eleventh Amendment protects state entities from private lawsuits but not from suits filed by the federal government. Thus, the U.S. Equal

Employment Opportunity Commission (EEOC) may sue state entities for violating the Age Discrimination in Employment Act. See EEOC v. Board of Supervisors for the Univ. of Louisiana System, *559 F.3d 270 (5th Cir. 2009).*

◆   *A federal appeals court dismissed age bias claims against the University of Missouri because a lower court did not rule on a qualified immunity issue.*

A University of Missouri professor filed a lawsuit in federal court against the university, his department chair and department administrator, claiming age discrimination and hostile work environment. He added claims for federal due process and equal protection violations and state law tortious interference with his employment contract. The defendants filed a motion to dismiss the case, arguing the professor did not state valid claims for due process or equal protection violations. They also argued they had qualified immunity from the due process and equal protection claims. Without addressing the issue of qualified immunity, the district court granted the defense motion to dismiss the equal protection claim. The chair and administrator appealed to the U.S. Court of Appeals, Eighth Circuit, arguing that the district court improperly rejected their qualified immunity defense. The court explained that it could not grant the requested review because the lower court did not rule on qualified immunity. The district court did not even mention qualified immunity in its decision. **Since the district court did not make a finding with respect to the qualified immunity issue, there was nothing to review** and the appeal was dismissed. *Mitra v. Curators of the Univ. of Missouri,* 322 Fed.Appx. 467 (8th Cir. 2009).

◆   *A former women's basketball coach failed to show the decision to buy out the last year of her contract was motivated by age or gender bias.*

After the University of Miami exercised its contractual right to buy out the last year of the coach's contract, she filed a state court action for discrimination based on age and gender. A trial court held for the university, finding at least three legitimate business reasons for its decision. In addition, the court ordered the coach to pay the university's attorneys' fees. A Florida District Court of Appeal explained that once the university offered legitimate, nondiscriminatory reasons for its action, the burden shifted to the coach to show the claimed reasons for its actions were a pretext for bias. She tried to meet this burden with evidence about the university's treatment of other coaches, but the court found this evidence was insufficient. **Since the university provided a legitimate reason for its decision that was not pretextual, the trial court had properly ruled for the university on the discrimination claims.** However, the court held the trial court should not have awarded attorneys' fees to the university, since the coach's claims were not "frivolous, unreasonable, or without foundation." *Labati v. Univ. of Miami,* 16 So.3d 886 (Fla. Dist. Ct. App. 2009).

◆   *Texas Tech University's decision to eliminate a college director's position was based on budgetary reasons, not age discrimination.*

The director had worked for Texas Tech University since 1990, and she earned outstanding job evaluations for several years. But some time later, several of her former and then-current subordinates filed written complaints stating she was an inflexible authoritarian who created an unpleasant work environment. After these complaints, the director was placed on paid leave and later offered a separation agreement. When the director took a medical leave, her supervisor reassigned some of her job duties to others. The director claimed the changes constituted a demotion, and she filed an age, sex and disability discrimination claim with the Equal Employment Opportunity Commission (EEOC). After being reassigned to a different job that she also considered a demotion, the university informed her the job was being eliminated as a cost-saving measure.

The director filed another EEOC charge, then sued the university in the state court system for age and sex discrimination as well as retaliation. The court awarded the university pretrial judgment, and the Court of Appeals of Texas agreed to review the case. On appeal, the court agreed with the lower court that the university had a legitimate reason for eliminating the director's position. She did not show this was a pretext for discrimination. **The university provided detailed information showing the decision to eliminate the position was made as part of an effort to reduce operating expenses.** The retaliation claim failed because the person who eliminated the position was unaware of the EEOC complaint. As a result, the judgment was affirmed. *Ptomey v. Texas Tech Univ.*, 277 S.W.3d 487 (Tex. Ct. App. 2009).

◆ *A federal court rejected a 57-year-old Illinois applicant's claim that she was not hired as a university enrollment counselor based on her age.*

The university sought applicants who had a general knowledge of the higher education market to contact and enroll prospective students. The applicant was invited to participate in a group assessment with about 10 other applicants, even though the university had already chosen two younger candidates, contingent on background checks. The university then filled other jobs by hiring people aged 31 or younger. The applicant sued the university in a federal district court for violating the Age Discrimination in Employment Act (ADEA). The university sought pretrial judgment, arguing she failed to show she applied for the four positions that opened after she initially submitted her resume. **The court found no age discrimination, because the university showed the individuals chosen for employment were better qualified than the applicant.** Each of the selected applicants held a bachelor's degree, which the candidate lacked. She also had no background in higher education. Because she did not present enough evidence to support her age discrimination claim, the court granted the university's motion for pretrial judgment. *Czubernat v. Univ. of Phoenix*, No. 07 C 2821, 2008 WL 2339570 (N.D. Ill. 6/4/08).

◆ *New York University (NYU) did not discriminate against a 70-year-old teacher by firing him for making inappropriate comments.*

NYU refused to reappoint the teacher after learning he made inappropriate comments during a class and was rude to the staff. The university presented evidence that he had commented during class that his phone number was "just for girls." This violated NYU's internal sexual harassment policy. The teacher claimed the reasons alleged for the employment decision were false. He insisted the remarks were merely jokes and did not offend the other female students. NYU replaced him with a teacher who was substantially younger. The teacher sued the university in a federal district court for age discrimination.

The court said whether female students found the comments offensive

was irrelevant, since the teacher's remarks violated the harassment policy. The teacher said the allegation he had been rude to members of the staff was a cover-up for unlawful age discrimination. He said he had always been polite and cooperative with staff. The court found the evidence supported the university's contention that the teacher was rude. It accepted NYU's legitimate, nondiscriminatory reasons for not reappointing him. As the teacher failed to prove the university's reasons were a cover-up for age discrimination, the court granted NYU's motion for summary judgment. *Chapkines v. New York Univ.*, No. 02CIV6355(RJH)(KNF), 2005 WL 167603 (S.D.N.Y. 1/25/05).

◆ *The U.S. Court of Appeals, Eleventh Circuit, held a Florida university did not reject an applicant because of his age.*

A 70-year-old white male applied for three positions at a university in Florida. The university rejected the applications. The applicant sued the university in a federal district court, alleging it refused to hire him because of his age, in violation of the ADEA. The court dismissed the case and the applicant appealed. The Eleventh Circuit found the university had legitimate, nondiscriminatory reasons for not hiring him. The university wanted to reduce turnover by filling the positions with faculty who had ties to the area. The applicant had no ties to central Florida, and one interviewer thought he was boring and unenthusiastic. **No evidence was presented to show the university lied about its reasons for not hiring him.** As the applicant failed to prove the reasons given by the university for not hiring him were untrue, the court affirmed the judgment. *Hillemann v. Univ. of Cent. Florida*, 167 Fed.Appx. 747 (11th Cir. 2006).

◆ *A Maryland employee did not prove a violation of the ADEA when she was laid off by a state university after 33 years of employment.*

The university laid off the employee, allegedly due to budget constraints. She later learned the university had not laid off younger employees and that the school had replaced her with a younger employee. The employee sued the university in a federal district court, alleging it discriminated against her because of her age. The employee alleged 10 of the 11 employees the university laid off for budget reasons were over 40. The university argued it was an arm of the state and was therefore protected from liability by the Eleventh Amendment. The court agreed, finding **Maryland courts have consistently held the state's public universities are arms of the state that are entitled to immunity.** The university's choice of autonomy from the University of Maryland did not deprive it of immunity. The court granted the university's request to dismiss the case. *Laney v. Morgan State Univ.*, No. Civ. CCB-04-1719, 2005 WL 1563437 (D. Md. 6/30/05).

3. Evidence of Discrimination

◆ *An employee who lasted only three days at a Pennsylvania university failed to show discrimination based on her race or age.*

The employee claimed she was assigned to a small office with child-sized furniture and no phone or computer. The people she was supposed to supervise shared a larger office that had adult-sized furniture, a phone and a computer. The employee became sick and dizzy in her office because it was too hot. She told a supervisor about the problem, but when she reported for her third day of work, she was told she was being fired because she had complained about her office. The university later filled the post with a black female over age 40.

In a federal district court action against the university and supervisor, the employee alleged race-based claims of wrongful termination, disparate treatment and hostile work environment under Title VII. She also claimed age discrimination under the ADEA. The court explained that the employee did not show other employees were treated more favorably than she was. She did not identify circumstances indicating race played a role in the decision to discharge her. The court also rejected the age discrimination claim, as **the employee did not show she was replaced by someone who was younger than her by a margin that allowed for an inference of bias**. She was either 43 or 44 at the time of her discharge, and she was replaced by someone over 40. This was not enough of an age difference to permit a finding of age discrimination. None of the evidence showed the employee was subjected to severe, extreme or pervasive discrimination. The court awarded pretrial judgment to the university on all the claims. *Beaubrun v. Thomas Jefferson Univ.*, 578 F.Supp.2d 777 (E.D. Pa. 2008).

◆ *A candidate for a college instructor job failed to prove age discrimination.*

The college hired the candidate, who was in his 50s, as a sociology instructor under a temporary teaching appointment that was renewed on a semester-by-semester basis. A full-time, tenure-track appointment to teach sociology became available the next academic year. The position attracted 29 applicants, including the candidate. Applicants ranged in age from 27 to 55. The candidate performed poorly on a teaching demonstration and was not selected as a finalist. The position was awarded to a candidate in his early 30s who had teaching experience, a doctorate degree, and had presented an interactive technology-based teaching demonstration that impressed the college hiring committee. The candidate sued the college in a federal district court for violating the Age Discrimination in Employment Act. The court held the college offered a legitimate, nondiscriminatory reason for its decision.

Specifically, the college said it decided not to hire the candidate because he performed poorly during his teaching demonstration. The hiring committee believed he did not demonstrate qualities they believed to be important, including the ability to engage students and interact effectively with them. The candidate did not show these reasons were false. There was no other evidence showing the college decided not to hire him based on his age. Therefore, the college's motion for summary judgment was granted. *Salerno v. Ridgewater College*, No. 06-1717, 2008 WL 509001 (D. Minn. 2/8/08).

◆ *A Tennessee university did not violate the ADEA by changing a 69-year-old professor's position and decreasing his lab space.*

The professor had worked for the university for nearly 30 years when a newly hired pathology department chairman asked whether he would consider early retirement. The professor told him he had no intention of retiring any time soon, and claimed the chairman then began a series of retaliatory actions, including orders to vacate his lab and office space. The chairman offered him several employment options, but they all meant a lower salary and several included early retirement. The professor sued the university in a federal district court for age discrimination. The court dismissed the case, and he appealed to the Sixth Circuit. **The court found no adverse employment action under the ADEA. The reduction in lab space did not affect salary or job status. Any proposal to reduce the professor's salary was never carried out, and threats alone are not an adverse action.** The professor presented no evidence the job changes significantly decreased his responsibilities. As he could not prevail on his claim of age discrimination without evidence of an adverse employment action, the court affirmed the judgment for the university. *Mitchell v. Vanderbilt Univ.*, 389 F.3d 177 (6th Cir. 2004).

B. Retirement

◆   *The Alabama Legislature had the authority to set a mandatory retirement age of 70 for Alabama State University board members.*

An Alabama State University board member reached the age of 70 before his second 12-year term expired. The terms of an amended state law barred him from serving on the board for his full term. In an attempt to block removal, the board member sued state and university officials in the federal court system for Equal Protection violations. He claimed the law discriminated on the basis of age without a rational basis and treated trustees at Alabama State University differently than trustees at other Alabama public universities. A district court held for the university, and the board member appealed. On appeal, the U.S. Court of Appeals, Eleventh Circuit, applied a deferential rational basis review. It found the law did not involve a fundamental right or suspect classification.

The court referenced *Gregory v. Ashcroft*, 501 U.S. 452 (1991), in which the U.S. Supreme Court upheld what the Eleventh Circuit said was "a remarkably similar retirement provision." **The court said that the age limit for trustees in this case satisfied rational basis review.** As for the claim that the law set an age limit for the trustees of some state universities but not others, the court dismissed this as frivolous. It held the legislature possessed the leeway to take such an approach. The appeals court also upheld the lower court's determination that no existing statutory exception saved the board member from application of the mandatory retirement age rule. The lower court's ruling was affirmed. *Clark v. Riley*, 595 F.3d 1258 (11th Cir. 2010).

◆   *A federal district court held Cornell University did not discriminate against a professor because of her age.*

When the professor was 50 years old, the university told her she would not be offered a fourth five-year reappointment when her contract expired. Instead, it offered her a one-year assignment that would require travel between Ithaca and New York City. The university said the change was being made due to budget problems. Midway through the contract, the professor accepted the university's offer of early retirement. She continued to perform work for the university for several months. She then sent the university a $25,000 bill for her services. The university refused to pay the amount claimed by the professor, and she sued the university in a federal district court for ADEA violations. She claimed the university replaced her with a younger employee and that it fired six other females over 40 for budgetary reasons. The court said the professor failed to show the university subjected her to an adverse employment action.

Action must be "more disruptive than a mere inconvenience or an alteration of job responsibilities" to be "adverse." While termination is clearly an adverse employment action, the professor did not suffer adverse employment action because the university did not discharge her. Rather, it chose not to renew her appointment. The university extended the professor's employment for an additional year after the term of her reappointment expired, and kept her salary and benefits the same. She terminated her employment when she volunteered to resign and accept early retirement. The court dismissed the case and the employee appealed. The U.S. Court of Appeals, Second Circuit, applied the wrong standard in assessing the dismissal motion. **The employee alleged an unofficial policy to guarantee her lifetime employment that was now being precluded on the basis of her gender and age.** She also asserted a valid Equal Pay Act claim, based on the claim that male employees were paid more for similar work. While the employee had taken an early retirement package, she did so to preserve benefits she would have enjoyed if her job was secure. Two state law claims had been properly dismissed, but the discrimination claims were returned to the district court for further proceedings. *Leibowitz v. Cornell Univ.*, 445 F.3d 586 (2d Cir. 2006).

C. State Statutes

◆ *New Jersey's highest court held a community college dean could pursue a claim that her contract was not renewed because of age discrimination.*

In 2001, when the dean was 69 years old, she was informed by the college's acting president by letter that her contract might not be renewed for job performance. She had over 26 years of experience working for the community college at that time. The dean obtained a reprieve, but three years later she was informed that her contract would not be renewed when it expired for performance reasons. At the time, the dean was over 70 years old. She filed a state-law claim of age discrimination. The trial court ruled against her, and she filed an appeal. On appeal, the New Jersey Superior Court, Appellate Division, held the state Law Against Discrimination (LAD) does not allow employers to discriminate against employees who are age 70 or older.

Appeal then reached the Supreme Court of New Jersey, which held the LAD permits employers to refuse to accept for employment any person who is over the age of 70. **The court held the protection extended by the LAD applied to the nonrenewal of an existing employee's contract.** It found that the refusal to renew the contract of an employee over 70, on the basis of age, was a prohibited discriminatory act under the LAD. For this reason, the appellate division's decision for the dean was affirmed. Although the parties advised the court that the case had been settled, the case was found not moot because it involved an important matter of public interest. *Nini v. Mercer County Community College*, 202 N.J. 98, 995 A.2d 1094 (N.J. 2010).

◆   *A New Jersey university computer specialist's age bias case failed because he did not show that friction at work was due to age discrimination.*

At the time of the dispute, the specialist was 43 years old. His supervisor found he had poor interactions with co-workers and customers, and he had a string of unsatisfactory performance evaluations. The specialist was disciplined and twice suspended. He claimed his supervisor told him three times he was "too old." Following an investigation, the New Jersey Division of Civil Rights found the specialist did not prove age discrimination. He sought review by a state court, which upheld the civil rights division's ruling. It found that by choosing to file his complaint with the division instead of suing, the specialist chose his forum. The division did not act unfairly or unreasonably, and the evidence did not corroborate the claim of age discrimination. Instead, **the record showed the specialist was disciplined for legitimate reasons relating to his poor job performance.** *Bostanci v. New Jersey City Univ.*, No. EJ06WB-53199, 2009 WL 972673 (N.J. Super. Ct. App. Div. 4/13/09).

The specialist sued the university in a federal district court for wrongful discharge, retaliation and harassment under Title VII, the Age Discrimination in Employment Act (ADEA) and the New Jersey Law Against Discrimination. The court considered the argument that a claim under the ADEA was barred by the Eleventh Amendment. While the court found sovereign immunity generally protects states from ADEA claims, sovereign immunity does not always protect state political subdivisions. To be entitled to Eleventh Amendment immunity, the university had to be an "arm of the state." The university did not present a detailed argument relating to why it should be considered an arm of the state. As a result, the court held it did not meet its burden to show it was immune to the ADEA claim. However, the court granted a motion to dismiss the Title VII claim. Title VII bars discrimination based on race, color, religion, sex or national origin. As the specialist's claims were based on age discrimination, his Title VII was dismissed. The court also denied a motion to dismiss the New Jersey Law Against Discrimination claims. *Bostanci v. New Jersey City Univ.*, No. 08-4339 (SRC), 2009 WL 2488183 (D. N.J. 8/11/09).

◆   *The Court of Appeals of Missouri upheld an award of more than $1.2 million to a baseball coach for age discrimination.*

The coach was over the age of 40 at the time of his hiring. His team had a winning record every year, and 80% of his players graduated. After he pursued an administrative charge of age bias in 1998, the university reduced his job to a half-time position, cut his pay in half and eliminated his benefits. It also moved his office to a basement near a swimming pool. During the same time his position was cut to part time, the university classified a younger compliance officer who worked 5.5 hours per day as a full-time employee. An assistant basketball coach who was under 40 and had far less experience than the baseball coach received a higher salary. The baseball coach sued the university in the state court system for violating the Missouri Human Rights Act. A jury awarded him $225,000 in actual damages and $1,050,000 in punitive damages.

On appeal, the court upheld the punitive damage award, finding that state law specifically authorized it. The court found the evidence was sufficient to support the punitive damages award. **Evidence showed younger employees**

were treated better with respect to pay, hours and benefits. The baseball field did not comply with National Collegiate Athletic Association requirements, and coaches who were hired after the baseball coach were given nicer offices in an athletic complex. The amount of scholarship money allotted for baseball was low compared with the amount allotted for other sports. **The university discontinued the coach's medical insurance with knowledge that he was a cancer survivor.** The court rejected the university's argument that the amount awarded exceeded reasonable compensation for any injury he suffered. The verdict against the university was upheld. *Brady v. Curators of the Univ. of Missouri*, 213 S.W.3d 101 (Mo. Ct. App. 2006).

◆   *A Pennsylvania law school did not violate a state anti-discrimination act when it discharged an employee who was over 40 years old.*

   The law school asked the employee to resign shortly before it merged with a Pennsylvania university. The law school and employee entered into a separation agreement and general release placing him on administrative leave at full salary with full benefits. In return for signing the agreement and giving up his right to unemployment benefits, the employee agreed not to make any claims under the Pennsylvania Human Relations Act (PHRA). However, he filed age discrimination charges against the university with state and federal civil rights agencies. Later, the employee sued the university and law school in a state court, alleging they violated the PHRA. He argued the agreement was invalid because it did not meet the requirements of the Older Workers Benefit Protection Act. The court held for the university and law school. The employee appealed to the Superior Court of Pennsylvania. **The court held the agreement was binding unless the employee proved fraud, duress or other circumstances to invalidate it.** Contracts are interpreted according to their plain language, and the court found this contract was clear. It affirmed the judgment for the university and law school. *Griest v. Pennsylvania State Univ. & Dickinson School of Law*, 897 A.2d 1186 (Pa. Super. 2006).

◆   *A graduate student could not sue for discrimination under Kentucky's employment laws because she was not an employee of the university.*

   A 44-year-old graduate student studying psychology received a Regent's Fellowship that provided her with full tuition and a yearly stipend. She lost her fellowship after her third year of study due to her failure to have her thesis proposal approved by a department committee. She remained in the graduate program for another year, but was subsequently dismissed. The student filed an unsuccessful grievance, then sued for sex and age discrimination in violation of Kentucky law and the university handbook. A state court held the student had no cause of action under the state discrimination statutes because she was not an employee of the university. The Kentucky Court of Appeals affirmed. **It rejected the student's assertion that her duties as a psychologist during her studies resembled employee duties, not academic work.** Although the student may have developed a therapist-patient relationship with one clinic patient, it was clear that nearly all of her duties and activities were in connection with her academic work rather than providing a service to the university, and therefore, an employer-employee relationship did not exist. *Stewart v. Univ. of Louisville*, 65 S.W.3d 536 (Ky. Ct. App. 2001).

V. DISABILITY DISCRIMINATION

Section 504 of the Rehabilitation Act of 1973, 29 U.S.C. § 794, prohibits discrimination against qualified individuals with disabilities in programs or activities receiving federal financial assistance. The Americans with Disabilities Act of 1990 (ADA), 42 U.S.C. § 12101, et seq., extends this protection to both private and public employees, and prohibits discrimination against employees who are associated with disabled individuals.

In 2008, Congress broadened certain ADA provisions to correct Supreme Court decisions that interpreted the Act differently than Section 504. Congress expected the ADA's definition of "disability" would be interpreted consistently with how courts were interpreting the definition of "handicapped individual" under Rehabilitation Act Section 504. Congress singled out Sutton v. United Air Lines, Inc., *527 U.S. 471 (1999) and* Toyota Motor Mfg., Kentucky, Inc. v. Williams, *534 U.S. 184 (2002) as cases in which the Supreme Court interpreted "substantially limits" more restrictively than Congress intended.*

The 2008 Amendments addressed the term "disability" – defined as "a physical or mental impairment that substantially limits one or more major life activities" of an individual. "Disability" under the ADA is to be construed in favor of broad coverage "to the maximum extent permitted by the terms of this Act." The term "substantially limits" is to be interpreted consistently with Congressional findings and purposes. U.S. Public Laws 110-325 (S. 3406), 110th Congress, Second Session. "ADA Amendments Act of 2008." 29 U.S.C. § 705, 42 U.S.C. §§ 12101-03, 12106-14, 12201, 12205a.

A. Liability

◆ *A Louisiana professor did not show an ADA violation when his request to limit faculty meetings to 20 minutes to accommodate his back pain was denied.*

The professor received poor evaluations for several years. Twenty years after being hired, he was subjected to a formal faculty performance review. A review panel found formal remediation was necessary. The professor asked the university to limit faculty meetings to 20 minutes to accommodate his chronic back pain. Instead, the university notified him it was initiating his termination for not cooperating with a remediation committee. After the professor was fired, he sued the university for violation of the Contracts Clause and his tenure rights. The court awarded pretrial judgment to the university and he appealed.

On appeal, the U.S. Court of Appeals, Fifth Circuit, held the professor did not mention his constitutional and tenure claims in his brief and thus lost the right to appeal them. His ADA claims failed because his requests for a more accessible office were made so long before he filed suit that they were outside the statute of limitations. **An employee who challenges the denial of an accommodation must show why a requested accommodation is reasonable.** But the professor did not show his request to limit faculty meetings to 20 minutes was reasonable. As his ADA and other claims failed, dismissal was proper. *Windhauser v. Board of Supervisors for Louisiana State Univ. & Agricultural and Mechanical College,* 360 Fed.Appx. 562 (5th Cir. 2010).

◆ *A Kentucky court found Eastern Kentucky University (EKU) did not discriminate against a professor by refusing her an extension to earn her Ph.D.*

The professor told EKU she expected to get her Ph.D. almost immediately. She had to earn the degree by the end of the 1998-99 school year or face termination. But the professor was diagnosed with breast cancer at the start of her probationary period. She went through a mastectomy and chemotherapy. A few years later, with her deadline approaching, the professor asked EKU for more time to earn her Ph.D. She was granted one extension, but her request for another was denied. When the professor failed to complete her Ph.D. on time, EKU refused to give her another contract, and she sued EKU in a state court.

The court awarded EKU judgment on the professor's disability and gender discrimination claims. She appealed to the Court of Appeals of Kentucky, which found she could not make a case for disability or gender discrimination. **Both claims required the professor to be qualified for a position. She did not show this, as her job required the Ph.D she had yet to earn.** The question of whether EKU had reasonably accommodated her disability (or whether a jury should decide that question) was moot. As a result, the court found the lower court had properly held for EKU. *Murray v. Eastern Kentucky Univ.*, No. 2008-CA-000561-MR, 2009 WL 4722760 (Ky. Ct. App. 12/11/09).

◆ *An American University driver may proceed with a disability discrimination lawsuit based on denial of permission to use a restroom.*

The driver claimed he was fired after being wrongfully denied the accommodation of using a restroom during a car trip between Washington, D.C., and Philadelphia. He sued the university and its president, claiming violations of the ADA and the District of Columbia Human Rights Act based on failing to accommodate his disability. A federal district court explained that the employee had to show he had a disability of which the university had notice, that he could perform the essential functions of his job with a reasonable accommodation, and that the university refused to provide the accommodation.

The court held a reasonable jury could conclude he had an impairment. **Evidence showed the employee had a physiological disorder or condition that affected his digestive system.** A jury could also find his condition substantially limited the major life activity of waste elimination, based on evidence that he needed to use a restroom up to 15 times a day. There was also evidence that the university had notice of this condition. The employee told university officials about his condition and the limitations it placed on his ability to travel. As factual issues existed regarding whether he could perform the essential functions of his job, the court held it was up to a jury to decide if he was qualified for the job, and whether the university refused to accommodate his condition and terminated his employment based on his condition. *Green v. American Univ.*, 647 F.Supp.2d 21 (D.D.C. 2009).

◆ *A counselor at an Arizona community college could proceed with an ADA claim, even though she threatened her department chair.*

The counselor suffered a brain injury in a car accident. The injury impaired her ability to regulate her emotional responses. When the college tried to discharge her, she filed a federal disability discrimination claim.

A settlement was reached renewing the counselor's contract and providing her with a job coach for nine months. The agreement required her to comply with college policies and procedures. However, the counselor was accused of shouting at and speaking disrespectfully to a student in a class. Months later, a new department chair met with her to review her job responsibilities. She reminded the counselor that she was to work 35 hours each week, and that she had failed to do so in the previous week. After the meeting, the counselor became upset and threatened the chair. She then called an associate dean of student services to say she had experienced a breakdown. The college placed the counselor on leave and asked her to submit to fitness-for-duty examinations. One of the examining psychologists concluded she was unable to function as a counselor. As all open positions at the college involved interaction with students, the counselor's employment was terminated.

The counselor sued the college in a federal district court for ADA violations. Although the college argued no accommodations would permit her to serve as a counselor, the court held a jury could find that a job coach would enable her to do this work. While the college argued the counselor had violated its violence policy by threatening the department chair, the court said conduct resulting from a disability is "part of the disability" and not a separate basis for discharge. Pretrial judgment was not allowed on the termination claim. **As an examination to determine whether a threat will be carried out is consistent with business necessity, the college could require one.** *Menchaca v. Maricopa Community College Dist.*, 595 F.Supp.2d 1063 (D. Ariz. 2009).

◆ *A Connecticut community college did not discriminate against an assistant professor when it declined to renew her teaching contract.*

A year after being hired to teach computer courses, the professor had major surgery and her mother died. She told a supervisor she was under psychiatric care, but she did not provide a diagnosis or other details. The college denied the professor's requests for only lower-level class assignments and that she not be required to teach both day and evening classes. Students began to complain that she had "stopped teaching" and was relying on a student to facilitate class discussions. A supervisor assigned the professor a poor performance evaluation, saying she was unprepared for class. After the college did not renew the professor's contract, she filed a federal district court action accusing it of disability discrimination under the ADA and sex discrimination under Title VII. **The court noted she only vaguely alleged having a mental impairment, and she failed to show she had a disability as defined by the ADA.** There was enough evidence to show her contract was not renewed due to her poor job performance. As no reasonable jury could conclude the decision was motivated by sex discrimination, the court held for the community college.

On appeal, the U.S. Court of Appeals, Second Circuit, found no evidence that the professor had an impairment that met the ADA definition of disability. She also did not show she had any record of a qualifying disability. Since the professor did not demonstrate that her contract was not renewed because of a disability, the judgment for the community college was affirmed. *Mastrolillo v. State of Connecticut*, 352 Fed.Appx. 472 (2d Cir. 2009).

◆ *The University of Pennsylvania did not violate the ADA when it denied a former employee's application for reemployment.*

The employee applied for any open administrative or clerical position. He submitted his resume and described his prior work experience, but he did not mention he had been diagnosed with bipolar disorder. When the employee did not receive an interview, he sued the university in a federal district court for disability discrimination. The court ordered him to be examined by a psychiatrist. The employee withdrew a claim based on an "actual disability" and preserved his ADA claim based on a "perceived disability." The court then ordered the applicant to undergo a psychiatric evaluation. After the applicant refused to undergo the evaluation, the court dismissed the case.

The employee appealed to the U.S. Court of Appeals, Third Circuit, asserting there was no need for a psychiatric evaluation. He said since the claim he was pursing focused on his "being regarded as disabled" – not on his actual abilities – the court had to focus on the reactions and perceptions of persons interacting with him. The court rejected this argument. It explained that **because the employee allegedly had a major psychiatric illness, the district court needed to evaluate whether he was "regarded as disabled."** Because he had been previously diagnosed as having bipolar disorder, his mental state was in controversy, and the judgment was affirmed. *Parker v. Univ. of Pennsylvania*, 128 Fed.Appx. 944 (3d Cir. 2005).

◆ *A Harvard University staff assistant with bipolar disorder was permissibly discharged due to his egregious misconduct.*

The employee was diagnosed with bipolar disorder and sometimes had periods of mania on the job. His disorder started to adversely affect his work after 15 years at Harvard. He established a Web site where he criticized the pay scale. The employee updated his Web site at work on his personal laptop. Shortly after the employee created the Web site, he became severely manic. He was loud and animated as he told co-workers about Harvard's wage policies and invited them to view the Web site. In the university's main Museum lobby, he sang, clapped and danced to protest songs that were posted on his Web site. He was hospitalized for an episode of paranoia. Soon after that, staff members and police officers approached the employee and asked him to leave. When he refused, the officers arrested him, and the university later discharged him.

The employee sued Harvard in a state court for violating the ADA. Harvard contended the employee could not establish he was a "qualified handicapped person" under the ADA. Harvard relied on *Garrity v. United Airlines*, 421 Mass. 55 (1995). In *Garrity*, the Massachusetts Supreme Judicial Court held if an employee's "egregious misconduct" is adverse to the interests of the employer and violates employer rules, the employee may not claim ADA protection. The court found the employee's misconduct was egregious and that Harvard fired him promptly after the misconduct. It granted Harvard's motion for summary judgment. On appeal, the supreme judicial court noted that its *Garrity* decision was consistent with the view adopted by the majority of courts facing the issue of egregious employer misconduct under federal law. This was so even though Congress had only granted express permission to employers to hold alcoholics to the same standard of conduct as other employees, even though their disability caused the misconduct. **The court held disabled employees were not entitled to disability law protection if they engaged in egregious misconduct that would be sufficient to result in the discharge of a non-disabled employee.** Noting that *Garrity* was meant to apply to all disability-related misconduct, and not just alcoholism-related misconduct, the court affirmed the judgment. *Mammone v. President and Fellows of Harvard College*, 446 Mass. 657, 847 N.E.2d 276 (Mass. 2006).

◆ *The U.S. Supreme Court concluded that Congress exceeded its authority by allowing monetary damage awards against states in ADA cases.*

According to a 2001 U.S. Supreme Court decision, Congress did not identify a history and pattern of irrational employment discrimination against individuals with disabilities by the states when it enacted the ADA. For this reason, the states were entitled to Eleventh Amendment immunity from such claims. As a result, **two state employees were unsuccessful in their attempt to recover money damages under the ADA from their state employer for disability discrimination.** *Board of Trustees of Univ. of Alabama v. Garrett*, 531 U.S. 356, 121 S.Ct. 955, 148 L.Ed.2d 866 (2001).

B. Defenses

To be covered by the ADA, an employee must have a disabling condition that substantially limits the ability to engage in a major life activity such as work. So a primary ADA defense is that the employee has no disability under the Act. Another common ADA defense is that employers need not offer job accommodations that result in the elimination of essential job functions.

◆ *A New York community college security guard with a foot injury was entitled to use a cane at work.*

For 29 years, the guard worked a 3:00 p.m. to 11:00 p.m. shift at the college. As the result of a work injury, he began to limp. The college sought medical documentation of the guard's disability. When he provided documents showing he had been diagnosed with reflex sympathetic dystrophy and a crush injury, the college denied that he was a person with a disability and said he did not need accommodation under the ADA. The guard sued the college in a federal district court for ADA, Title VII, equal protection and due process violations.

The court refused to award the college pretrial judgment on the ADA claim. There was evidence that the guard's foot injury was a disability under the ADA. **To prove the existence of a disability under the ADA, he had to show the injury substantially limited his ability to perform the major life activity of walking.** The court found evidence of substantial pain from the injury and that it was likely to be permanent. It also found enough evidence for a jury to find that using a cane would help the guard perform the essential functions of his job. His request to use a cane was "a plausible accommodation" with a negligible cost to the community college. For this reason, the college was denied pretrial judgment. *Schroeder v. Suffolk County Community College*, No. 07-CV-2060, 2009 WL 1748869 (E.D.N.Y. 6/22/09).

◆ *A Florida professor's claim that he was discharged because his employer thought he was an alcoholic will not be dismissed prior to a trial.*

The professor began teaching as an adjunct professor and soon became a full-time associate professor. A few years later, he began missing meetings and showing signs of alcohol abuse. His divorce became final near this time. An associate dean arrived unannounced at the professor's residence and concluded he was under the influence of alcohol. The professor was placed on medical leave. The university told him he would be deemed to have resigned if he did not submit a leave of absence form and physician's certification by a specified date. It then discharged him after he did not submit the forms on time.

The professor sued the university under the Rehabilitation Act, claiming it discharged him because it "regarded" him as an alcoholic. Alcoholism can be a disability under the Rehabilitation Act when the individual claiming protection is not currently abusing alcohol. The court rejected the university's claim that pretrial judgment should be granted based on the professor's failure to actively participate on a dissertation review committee. A factual dispute existed as to whether active participation on the committee was an essential job function and as to whether he adequately performed it. **The court also rejected the university's argument that it accommodated the professor by placing him on leave and making its employee assistance program available to him.** These steps did not conclusively establish it met its duty to reasonably accommodate him. *Gardiner v. Nova Southeastern Univ.*, No. 06-60590 CIV, 2006 WL 3804704 (S.D. Fla. 12/22/06).

◆ *The U.S. Court of Appeals, Eleventh Circuit, held a Florida university could not claim Eleventh Amendment immunity under Title II of the ADA.*

Students at a Florida university requested sign-language interpreters, auxiliary aids, and note-takers. When the requests were denied, a disability rights association sued the university in a federal district court, alleging it violated Title II of the ADA. The court found the university was immune from liability under the Eleventh Amendment. The association appealed to the Eleventh Circuit. The court stayed the appeal until the U.S. Supreme Court decided *Tennessee v. Lane*, 541 U.S. 509 (2004), which concerned the ability of disabled citizens to sue for access to the courts under Title II. In *Lane*, the Supreme Court decided Title II constituted a valid exercise of Congressional power under the Fourteenth Amendment in cases implicating the fundamental right of access to the courts. The Eleventh Circuit **held Title II of the ADA constituted a valid exercise of Congress's enforcement power under the Fourteenth Amendment in cases involving access to public education**. Since Congress had acted within its power, Eleventh Amendment immunity was abrogated. The court reversed the judgment and remanded the case to the district court for further proceedings. *Ass'n for Disabled Americans v. Florida Int'l Univ.*, 405 F.3d 954 (11th Cir. 2005).

◆ *A narcoleptic hospital resident could be fired where he couldn't perform his duties due to his impairment.*

An anesthesiology resident at a New York university hospital failed to respond to his emergency beeper on three occasions and was fired. He was later diagnosed with narcolepsy. He then sued the hospital and various physicians for disability discrimination, and the defendants sought to have the case dismissed. After a trial court dismissed the doctors from the suit, the New York Supreme Court, Appellate Division, dismissed the hospital. Although the resident suffered from a disability, which caused the behavior that got him fired, **the hospital had asserted a legitimate reason for firing him** – his narcolepsy prevented him from performing the essential functions of the job. *Timashpolsky v. SUNY Health Science Center at Brooklyn*, 761 N.Y.S.2d 94 (N.Y. App. Div. 2003).

◆ *Generally, a seniority system takes precedence over ADA accommodation.*
In a case involving an airline employee with a bad back, who was seeking a mailroom position, **the U.S. Supreme Court held that as a general rule, an accommodation under the ADA is not reasonable if it conflicts with an employer's seniority rules.** However, employees may present evidence of special circumstances that make a "seniority rule exception" reasonable in a particular case. *US Airways, Inc. v. Barnett*, 535 U.S. 391, 122 S.Ct. 1516, 152 L.Ed.2d 589 (2002).

C. Contagious Diseases

In 1998, the U.S. Supreme Court held that a person with HIV was protected by the Americans with Disabilities Act (ADA), despite the fact that she was not yet exhibiting symptoms of the disease. Since HIV substantially impaired her ability to reproduce, she could not be excluded unless her condition presented a direct threat to the health and safety of others. Bragdon v. Abbott, 524 U.S. 624, 118 S.Ct. 2196, 141 L.Ed.2d 540.

◆ *The Supreme Court held that a person with a contagious disease was entitled to the protections of the Rehabilitation Act.*
A Florida elementary school teacher was discharged because of her continued recurrence of tuberculosis. She sued the school board under Section 504 of the Rehabilitation Act. A federal district court dismissed her suit, but the Eleventh Circuit held persons with contagious diseases fall within Section 504's coverage. The case then reached the U.S. Supreme Court, which held that **tuberculosis was a disability under Section 504**. The disease attacked the teacher's respiratory system and affected her ability to work. It would be unfair to allow an employer to distinguish between a disease's potential effect on others and its effect on the afflicted employee in order to justify discriminatory treatment. Accordingly, she was entitled to reinstatement or front pay if she could show that despite her disability, she was otherwise qualified for her job with or without a reasonable accommodation. *School Board of Nassau County v. Arline*, 480 U.S. 273, 107 S.Ct. 1123, 94 L.Ed.2d 307 (1987).

◆ *The transfer of an HIV-positive employee was not discriminatory where the employee had committed infractions that resulted in risks to others.*
A New York medical college employed a phlebotomist who was HIV positive. The college had a policy in place requiring employees to wear gloves

on both hands when drawing blood. After the employee violated that policy on at least three occasions, the college reassigned her to the billing department. The employee brought suit against the college in a state trial court, alleging that it had discriminated against her based on her HIV-positive disability. The case was transferred to the New York Supreme Court, Appellate Division, which held that **the college did not discriminate against the employee by reassigning her**. The court noted that the employer was unaware of any similar infractions by any other employees. Thus, it had provided a legitimate, nondiscriminatory reason for the transfer that was supported by substantial evidence. *Friedel v. New York State Division of Human Rights*, 632 N.Y.S.2d 520 (N.Y. App. Div. 1995).

VI. RETALIATION

A. Generally

Title VII prohibits an employer from retaliating against an employee for opposing an unlawful employment practice, or for making a charge, testifying, assisting, or participating in any manner in a discrimination investigation, proceeding or hearing. In Robinson v. Shell Oil Co., *519 U.S. 337 (1997), the Supreme Court held a former employee of a corporation could bring a retaliatory discrimination lawsuit against his former employer after he was given a negative employment reference following his filing of an Equal Employment Opportunity Commission complaint.*

◆ *A federal court refused to dismiss retaliation claims brought by a former dean at Gallaudet University, a higher education institution for deaf persons.*

According to the dean, many Gallaudet students and staff espoused "Deaf Culture," which includes a belief that deaf persons should use only American Sign Language (ASL) to communicate. While the dean used ASL, she used other methods such as hearing amplification and lip-reading. When Deaf students staged protests over the appointment of a new university president, the board of trustees revoked the appointment. According to the dean, the only basis for this was the perception that the new president wasn't "Deaf enough." She suggested the movement was biased and later said Gallaudet faculty, staff and alumni supported the protesters while she stood behind the president. The dean claimed her responsibilities were reduced and that she was excluded from administrative decisionmaking. She claimed university staff retaliated against her and spread lies about her. After the dean sued the university in a federal court for retaliation under state and federal law, Gallaudet sought dismissal.

The court allowed a retaliation claim under Section 601 of Title VII. **Section 601 does not explicitly prohibit retaliation – but the court held Section 601 retaliation claims are implicitly allowed.** The court held the dean made a valid Title VII case by showing Gallaudet took adverse actions against her because of her advocacy for minority students. The court also found she stated a claim under the District of Columbia Human Rights Act, which prohibits retaliation for exercising civil rights or for aiding or encouraging others to do so. The dean had supported a president whose appointment was revoked for what she alleged were discriminatory reasons. She also said that she suffered the same discrimination – being seen as not "Deaf enough." Finding the dean had stated valid retaliation claims, the court refused to dismiss the case. *Kimmel v. Gallaudet Univ.*, 639 F.Supp.2d 34 (D.D.C. 2009).

◆ *A university manager may pursue a claim that she was retaliated against for her complaints that a staff member was being treated unfairly due to race.*

The manager complained several times that she believed a refusal to implement a performance improvement plan for an African-American employee constituted race discrimination. The manager was told that the employee "had a history" with the university and that any action against her could result in a discrimination lawsuit. She felt the process followed for the employee was not equitable because it subjected her to such intense scrutiny. The manager filed a state court complaint alleging opposition to discriminatory employment practices. The case reached the Court of Appeals of Minnesota, which held she was not required to show that the employer's practices were actually discriminatory. **Instead, she needed to show only that she had a good-faith, reasonable belief that the employment practices she opposed were discriminatory.** The complaint set forth reasonable grounds for the belief that the university was treating the employee differently on the basis of her race. *Bahr v. Capella Univ.*, 765 N.W.2d 428 (Minn. Ct. App. 2009).

◆ *A Massachusetts general accounting director who complained about college financial practices could not claim retaliation under Title VII.*

The accounting director complained that a male co-worker's financial information was erroneous and in violation of state regulations. According to the director, illegal changes were made to the college's general ledger system. She said her supervisor retaliated against her for making these complaints and that instead of disciplining the co-worker, the supervisor discriminated against her and created a hostile work environment. The director took a leave of absence, claiming her supervisor had caused her to suffer a nervous breakdown. While she was on leave, an audit determined that her job performance was unsatisfactory. The college discharged the director, and she filed an administrative complaint for gender discrimination. She then filed a federal district court action against the college and some co-workers for gender discrimination and retaliation under Title VII. The court dismissed the case.

Appeal reached the U.S. Court of Appeals, First Circuit, which found the administrative complaint put the college on notice of possible gender bias. For this reason, the director's gender bias claim was reinstated. There is no individual liability under Title VII, so the lower court had properly disposed of the claims against the individual co-workers. **To prove her claim of unlawful retaliation under Title VII, the director had to show she opposed an unlawful employment practice under Title VII or participated in an investigation, proceeding or hearing under Title VII.** Since the financial improprieties she reported had nothing to do with Title VII, the court held this claim failed. *Fantini v. Salem State College*, 557 F.3d 22 (1st Cir. 2009).

◆ *A federal appeals court refused to disturb a verdict for a Grambling State University police chief who was fired after trying to hire a white job applicant.*

Grambling State University (GSU) is a historically black Louisiana institution of higher learning. After receiving approval to create an assistant police chief position, the chief followed the hiring procedures that had been explained to him. After reviewing the qualifications of four candidates, he recommended a white applicant for the job. A supervisor blocked the application, and the chief believed she was doing so based on race. Less than a week after the chief made a written inquiry about the status of the application, GSU fired him. He sued GSU in a federal district court for violations of Title VII and state law. GSU countered that the chief was discharged for not following proper hiring procedures, his rudeness at an interdepartmental meeting, and a harassment complaint by a co-worker.

A jury returned a unanimous verdict for the chief and awarded him $140,000 in compensatory damages. Appeal reached the U.S. Court of Appeals, Fifth Circuit, which upheld the compensatory damages award. **It found the chief's opposition to GSU's refusal to hire an applicant based on his race could be protected activity under Title VII.** There was also enough evidence for a jury to conclude GSU treated the applicant differently than others based on race. The compensatory damages award was justified, and the court held the lower court should have awarded the chief attorneys' fees. The case was returned to the district court for this purpose. *Tureaud v. Grambling State Univ.*, 294 Fed.Appx. 909 (5th Cir. 2008).

◆ *No violation of Title VII occurred when a university employee was laid off after he complained that his supervisor was showing favoritism toward a lover.*

An Oklahoma State University (OSU) employee complained that his supervisor showed favoritism to a person he was having an affair with and then retaliated against him. After being laid off, he sued OSU in a federal district court for retaliation and age discrimination. OSU responded that the layoff was part of a restructuring. To prove retaliation, the court held the employee had to show he engaged in protected activity and suffered an adverse employment action as a result. However, he did not participate in a Title VII investigation, proceeding or hearing, and he could not show he opposed an unlawful employment practice. Since opposition to an affair is not protected conduct under Title VII, the employee could not proceed with his retaliation claim.

On appeal to the U.S. Court of Appeals, Tenth Circuit, the employee claimed he was subjected to a hostile work environment based on his reporting of the affair. The court held this was simply a re-hash of his invalid retaliation claim. **There was no evidence of a hostile work environment or unlawful discrimination.** As the supervisor's affair and favoritism were not enough to pursue a Title VII case, the court rejected the appeal. *Anderson v. Oklahoma State Univ. Board of Regents*, 342 Fed.Appx. 365 (10th Cir. 2009).

◆ *Two University of Denver professors did not show they were subjected to a hostile work environment or that they were retaliated against under Title VII.*

In their lawsuit against the university and several officials, the professors claimed retaliation after they engaged in more than 20 acts of protected conduct over a two-year period. They said they were subjected to public humiliation at a department meeting after they complained that they were treated unfavorably during a search for an assistant professor. The professors also said the Spanish section of their department was abolished after they complained about hostile work environment and discrimination. A federal district court dismissed the case, and the professors appealed to the U.S. Court of Appeals, Tenth Circuit.

The court held that to prove retaliation, the professors had to show they engaged in protected opposition to bias, and that adverse employment action was taken against them. Moreover, there had to be a causal connection between the protected activity and the adverse employment action. The court held *Burlington Northern & Santa Fe Railway Co. v. White*, this chapter, required the professors to show that a reasonable person would have found the action taken against them was materially adverse in a way that dissuaded them from filing discrimination charges. The professors did not show this. The conduct they found humiliating consisted of colleagues rolling their eyes, laughing, snickering and making comments to one another while they talked. As this was insufficient to show they were subjected to an adverse action, the case was properly dismissed. **Title VII does not establish a workplace civility code.** *Somoza v. Univ. of Denver*, 513 F.3d 1206 (10th Cir. 2008).

◆ *Actions taken against a Nebraska professor did not form the basis of a retaliation claim.*

The professor had worked at Creighton University for 10 years when a colleague filed a sexual harassment claim against her. A four-person committee investigated the charge and recommended discharging the professor. Instead, the university's president placed her on probation under close monitoring. She was forbidden from contact with her accuser and required to undergo a year of psychological counseling and training. The professor filed discrimination charges against Creighton, claiming she was placed on probation based on her national origin. She then sued the university in a federal district court, alleging 21 counts of retaliation. The court ruled for the university, and the professor appealed to the U.S. Court of Appeals, Eighth Circuit. **The court found none of the actions noted by the professor were harmful enough to constitute a "materially adverse" job action.** For example, the decision to alter her teaching schedule did not cause any significant harm. Nor was the professor's allegation that she received "the silent treatment" and was ostracized by other faculty members sufficient to show retaliation. As no link between the charge and alleged retaliation was demonstrated, the judgment was affirmed. *Recio v. Creighton Univ.*, 521 F.3d 934 (8th Cir. 2008).

◆ *An employee's unreasonable complaint of sexual harassment was not protected activity that could form the basis for a retaliatory discharge claim.*

A supervisor called a meeting to address tension among staff members of the employee's department. During the meeting, a male co-worker became "angry and out of control," yelling sexual comments at the employee. The co-worker was fired the next day, but the employee claimed she had been sexually harassed at the meeting by both the co-worker and supervisor. After interviewing other witnesses, the director concluded there was no basis for this charge. She also concluded the employee engaged in similar misconduct and also deserved to be fired. The employee sued the college in a federal district court for sexual harassment and retaliatory discharge. **The court held the retaliatory discharge claim failed because the employee could not reasonably have believed she was subjected to sexual harassment at the meeting.** Instead, the evidence indicated she made the allegation to avoid being disciplined for her own misconduct. In addition, the co-worker's comments were made in anger and not as a sexual request. *Middleton v. Metropolitan College of New York*, 545 F.Supp.2d 369 (S.D.N.Y. 2008).

◆   *The U.S. Supreme Court held the reassignment of a female to more arduous and dirtier work was evidence of retaliation by her employer.*

The employee worked in the maintenance way department of a railway company. Her primary responsibility was to operate a forklift. The employee was the only woman in her department. She complained that her immediate supervisor told her women should not be working there. The company disciplined the supervisor but also transferred the employee from forklift duty to standard track laborer tasks. The employee who transferred her said the reassignment reflected co-workers' complaints that a "more senior man" should have the "less arduous and cleaner job of forklift operator." The employee filed two complaints with the Equal Employment Opportunity Commission (EEOC), claiming that the company discriminated against her in violation of Title VII. She was suspended without pay for insubordination but was later reinstated with back wages. The employee sued the company in a federal district court for unlawful retaliation under Title VII.

Following a jury trial, the jury held in favor of the employee. The U.S. Court of Appeals, Sixth Circuit, affirmed the judgment and the U.S. Supreme Court agreed to review the case. The Court held the anti-retaliation provision of Title VII provides that an employer may not discriminate against an employee or job applicant because he or she has opposed a practice prohibited by Title VII. The Sixth Circuit had held that to prevail on a Title VII retaliation claim, employees must show they suffered an "adverse employment action." An "adverse employment action" is defined as a "materially adverse change in the terms and conditions" of employment. The Court held the scope of the anti-retaliation provision extended beyond workplace or employment-related retaliatory acts and harm. **The anti-retaliation provision must prohibit employers from action that is serious enough to deter victims of discrimination from complaining to the EEOC.** Petty slights, minor annoyances, and simple lack of good manners will not create such a deterrence. The jury had correctly found the employer's actions were "materially adverse." An indefinite suspension without pay could act as a deterrent to complaints, even though in this case the employee was later reinstated. *Burlington Northern & Santa Fe Railway Co. v. White*, 548 U.S. 53 (2006).

◆   *A Utah instructor failed to prove a university failed to renew her three-year teaching contract based on her gender, national origin or retaliation.*

The instructor claimed the university declined to renew her contract because she assigned some students poor grades. She said the failure to renew her contract was based on her gender and/or national origin, and she added a claim for hostile work environment. The instructor sued the university in a federal district court. It stated that to prove discrimination, she needed to show that she was doing satisfactory work. The instructor failed to satisfy this requirement. The facts showed she could not establish and maintain authority in her classroom. The instructor failed to respond to messages from the chair of her department. There were no facts showing the employment environment at the university was objectively hostile. **To prove retaliation, the instructor had to show she had engaged in a protected activity.** The instructor claimed she was retaliated against for academically penalizing students. The court held this was not protected behavior that can support a retaliation claim. *Mejia v. Univ. of Utah*, No. 1:05-CV-53 TS, 2007 WL 391586 (D. Utah 2/1/07).

◆ *The U.S. Supreme Court held the broad prohibition of discrimination on the basis of sex in Title IX extends to retaliation claims.*

The Supreme Court held **Title IX covers retaliation against a person for complaining about sex discrimination. Retaliation is an intentional act that is a form of discrimination, since the person who complains is treated differently than others.** A program that retaliates against a person based on a sex discrimination complaint intentionally discriminates in violation of Title IX. The Court held a private right of action for retaliation was within the statute's prohibition of intentional sex discrimination. **Title IX did not require the victim of retaliation to also be the victim of discrimination.** Retaliation against individuals who complained of sex discrimination was intentional conduct violating the clear terms of Title IX. *Jackson v. Birmingham Board of Educ.*, 544 U.S. 167, 125 S.Ct. 1497, 161 L.Ed.2d 361 (2005).

◆ *A Massachusetts university did not fire a professor in retaliation for supporting his wife's sexual harassment claim against a department head.*

The professor and his wife worked in the university's biochemistry and molecular biology department. A department head criticized the professor for certain fees charged by the research lab founded by the professor and his wife. He said imposing such fees indicated the professor lacked a cooperative spirit and collegiality. The professor and wife filed a grievance, asking the university to remove the information from their personnel files. The grievance was resolved when the department head agreed his letter was a private communication that did not belong in university files. The university later reduced the professor's teaching assignments after he received negative comments on student evaluations. His evaluations remained poor for several years, and the university eventually held hearings and decided to fire him.

The professor sued the university and two department heads in a Massachusetts trial court for retaliation in violation of Title VII and a Massachusetts anti-discrimination law. The court awarded judgment to the university and department heads, and the professor appealed to the Supreme Judicial Court of Massachusetts. He argued a court could infer the causal connection between support of his wife's complaint and the actions taken against him from the timing and sequence of events. **The court held the professor did not prove a causal link merely by showing that one event**

followed another. His performance and department funding problems begin before his wife filed her complaint. As the time span between endorsing the sexual harassment complaint and adverse employment action was too long, the court affirmed the judgment. *Mole v. Univ. of Massachusetts*, 442 Mass. 582, 814 N.E.2d 329 (Mass. 2004).

B. Defenses

◆   *A sign-language instructor could not show he was denied a promotion by a Connecticut community college in retaliation for filing discrimination claims.*

After 13 years of working for the community college, the instructor filed two civil rights charges against it that were eventually settled. He then applied for promotion to an assistant professor position. But the college began to receive complaints from students about his class performance. The instructor filed a new charge of retaliation with the state civil rights agency, claiming the real reason he was denied promotion was his earlier charges of discrimination. He then sued the college board in a state court, which held for the board. On appeal, a state appellate court found it is illegal to retaliate against an employee for filing a discrimination charge. While the instructor had filed a charge, and the college knew about it, he could not show the college refused to promote him because of the charge. Instead, **the lower court properly found the college denied the instructor a promotion because of the numerous student complaints against him.** It was reasonable to conclude there was no causal connection between his charge and the college's decision not to promote him. The court affirmed judgment for the board. *Ayantola v. Board of Trustees of Technical Colleges*, 116 Conn.App. 531, 976 A.2d 784 (Conn. App. Ct. 2009).

◆   *A tenured Louisiana State University (LSU) professor could pursue a retaliation claim based on a demand that she forfeit her sabbatical pay.*

For most of her time at LSU, the professor believed she was discriminated against based on her gender. She went on sabbatical leave and took leave under the Family and Medical Leave Act to care for her son. LSU considered her to have abandoned her job and asked her to return some of her sabbatical pay. The professor filed an administrative complaint, then sued LSU in a federal district court under state and federal law. She included a retaliation claim under Title VII. The court dismissed all her claims as time barred. She appealed to the U.S. Court of Appeals, Fifth Circuit, which found the lower court had properly dismissed most of her claims. **Most of the discriminatory conduct occurred more than 300 days before the professor filed her administrative complaint.** But the letter asking her to repay part of her sabbatical pay occurred within 300 days of her charge. Accordingly, a retaliation claim based on the sabbatical pay issue was returned to the lower court. *Ikossi-Anastasiou v. Board of Supervisors of Louisiana State Univ.*, 579 F.3d 546 (5th Cir. 2009).

◆   *An appeal of a verdict on a New York college vice president's retaliation claim led to a $400,000 reduction in a punitive damage award.*

The college fired the vice president days after she filed a sex discrimination complaint. She sued the college in a federal district court for sex discrimination and retaliation. A jury found the discharge was in retaliation for her sex discrimination complaint, and it awarded her $75,000 in compensatory damages and $425,000 in punitive damages. The college sought to overturn the judgment or obtain a new trial, arguing that its president had discharged the vice president before he learned she had filed her complaint. Therefore, the college claimed the action could not have been in retaliation for the complaint.

The court found enough evidence for the jury to find the president fired the vice president after he learned of the discrimination complaint. He did not ask her for her keys or other college property before she left. Nor did the college prove the firing was based solely on dissatisfaction with the vice president's job performance. Although the court upheld the verdict, it found the punitive damage award was excessive. **The reasonableness of a punitive damage award depends largely on the reprehensibility of a defendant's conduct.** In this case, there was no violence, threats or evidence of repeated misconduct. Under the circumstances, the most a jury could reasonably award in punitive damages was $25,000. *Norris v. New York City College of Technology*, No. 07-CV-853, 2009 WL 82556 (E.D.N.Y. 1/14/09).

◆ *A teaching assistant's retaliation claim failed because he did not engage in "protected activity" within the meaning of the law.*

An Iranian national began working as a graduate teaching assistant at a Missouri university while in a chemistry Ph.D. program. The student appealed a grade he received in an advanced inorganic chemistry course, accusing the professor of mismanaging the course and assigning grades capriciously. After a hearing, the grade was not changed. The teaching assistant later complained to a university international affairs office about compliance with Department of Homeland Security regulations regarding foreign nationals. He also complained to the university affirmative action office about an investigation into the transmission of anonymous e-mails to a female student.

The chemistry department dismissed the teaching assistant without stating a reason, and he withdrew as a student. He sued the university and its officials in a federal district court for retaliation. The court held for the university, and the assistant appealed to the U.S. Court of Appeals, Eighth Circuit. **The court held that to prove retaliation, he needed to show he had engaged in a protected activity, and that the university took adverse action against him on that basis.** The court held the assistant did not engage in any "protected activity." His complaints regarding grades, Department of Homeland Security regulations and the student affairs office related to his status as a student, whereas his retaliation claim related to his status as an employee. Because none of the activities related to his status as an employee, the assistant could not prove his retaliation claim. The decision for university officials was affirmed. *Bakhtiari v. Lutz*, 507 F.3d 1132 (8th Cir. 2007).

◆ *Four Illinois university police officers failed to prove claims that they were assigned to work at a particular university campus based on their race.*

The officers patrolled two university campuses, one of which was located in a predominantly black residential area in East St. Louis. Due to its smaller size, duties at the East St. Louis campus were deemed less strenuous than those at the Edwardsville campus. After the officers were denied promotions to sergeant positions, they were discharged for insubordination and other reasons. The officers sued the university in a federal district court, claiming the university violated Title VII by disproportionally assigning them to the East St. Louis campus based on race. The court held for the university, and the officers appealed. The U.S. Court of Appeals, Seventh Circuit, held **the assignments did not constitute a materially adverse employment action**. Three of the four officers had asked to work at the East St. Louis campus at some point, and their complaints regarding assignment location involved nothing more than subjective preference. There was no evidence that assignments were made with regard to race or in retaliation for complaining about discrimination. *Nichols v. Southern Illinois Univ.-Edwardsville*, 510 F.3d 772 (7th Cir. 2007).

◆ *The U.S. Court of Appeals, Eleventh Circuit, reinstated an academic advisor's Title VII retaliation claim.*

The advisor claimed his direct supervisor began making unwanted sexual advances soon after he was hired. He said that she told him to meet her at her home for a "mandatory meeting," but that when he arrived, she made an overt sexual advance. According to the advisor, he rejected the advance and the supervisor then overloaded him with work and verbally abused him. He claimed that when he applied for a promotion, the supervisor verbally attacked him in his office, spit in his face, and knocked papers out of his hands.

The advisor filed a formal written sexual harassment complaint against the supervisor, and he claimed she then threatened him. He called campus police and filed a protection order against her. The advisor later gave the dean a copy of the police report and protection order, then claimed she withdrew her recommendation for the promotion and discharged him for unprofessionalism. A federal district court held the university did not violate Title VII, and the advisor appealed. The U.S. Court of Appeals, Eleventh Circuit, vacated the district court's decision and remanded the case. It held **a call to police might qualify as protected activity under Title VII**. If this was the case, then the police report could not serve as a legitimate basis for job termination. Under the university's rationale, an employee could be fired for reporting a rape by a supervisor. At this stage of the case, the court was required to view the facts in the light most favorable to the advisor. As a result, the case was returned to the lower court for more proceedings. *Scarbrough v. Board of Trustees Florida A&M Univ.*, 504 F.3d 1220 (11th Cir. 2007).

◆ *An Alabama university did not retaliate against an employee for reporting sexual harassment by her supervisor.*

The employee claimed her supervisor subjected her to unwelcome sexual attention. She said he implied he would allow her to obtain further training opportunities only if she gave in to his sexual demands and that he threatened to fire her. The employee sought a higher-paying position, but she did not mention any problems with her supervisor. Later, the supervisor refused to sign the employee's time sheet. She complained about him to the university's human resource department. For the first time, the employee told the university her supervisor had made sexual advances toward her. The university placed her on paid leave and instructed her to file a written statement about harassment. The university investigated the complaint and interviewed the supervisor. He stated he had engaged in consensual sex with the employee.

The university reassigned the employee to a different supervisor. She sued the university in a federal district court for retaliation. **The court held an employer can only be held liable for a Title VII sexual harassment claim if there is a tangible employment action, such as discharge or demotion, or the harassment was sufficiently severe to change the employee's working conditions.** The court agreed with the university that there was no adverse employment action in this case. Although the supervisor apparently threatened to fire the employee, no evidence was presented to show he actually tried to do this. The court granted the university's motion for summary judgment. *Arnold v. Tuskegee Univ.*, No. 3:03CV-515-F, 2006 WL 47507 (M.D. Ala. 1/9/06).

◆ *The U.S. Court of Appeals, Tenth Circuit, held the University of Kansas had legitimate, nondiscriminatory reasons for denying tenure to an adjunct professor and did not retaliate against her on the basis of disability.*

A University of Kansas assistant professor was denied tenure, then discharged. She sued the university in a federal district court for discrimination under Title VII. She was then appointed to an adjunct lecturer position, but was denied principal investigator (PI) status, which would have allowed her to act as a director of grant applications. Meanwhile, a jury ruled for the university in her discrimination lawsuit. The next month, the professor applied for an administrative position with the university, but was not interviewed for it. Claiming the university denied her the administrative position and PI status in retaliation for filing her Title VII lawsuit, she brought a second action against the university in a federal district court for retaliation. The court granted summary judgment to the university, and the professor appealed.

The U.S. Court of Appeals, Tenth Circuit, held that to establish adverse employment action under Title VII, the professor had to show the university acted in a way that meant a significant change in her employment status. The court found the decisions to confer the adjunct lecturer title on the professor and deny her PI status were not significant changes in employment. The university's decision not to hire the professor as an administrator was not retaliation. **The university presented legitimate, nondiscriminatory reasons for declining to hire her for that position.** Because the professor offered no evidence to show the school's non-discriminatory reasons were a pretext for discrimination or retaliation, the court affirmed the judgment. *Annett v. Univ. of Kansas*, 371 F.3d 1233 (10th Cir. 2004).

◆ *A three-year lapse between reported sexual harassment and the discharge of a Wisconsin professor doomed her retaliation claim.*

A research scientist with the U.S. Department of Veteran Affairs (VA) worked part time as an associate professor of neurology at a Wisconsin medical college. When she charged another professor with sexual harassment, her supervisor at the college warned her filing a sexual harassment charge could be a "career limiting move." However, the supervisor investigated her complaint. Three years later, the professor lost her VA research position. The college then discharged her because her VA research responsibilities were the basis of her faculty appointment. The professor sued the college in a federal district court for retaliation in violation of Title VII. The court granted the college's motion for summary judgment and the professor appealed.

The U.S. Court of Appeals, Seventh Circuit stated that **a Title VII claim based on retaliation required evidence of statutorily protected activity that results in adverse employment action. The professor's retaliation claim failed because of the time lapse between her sexual harassment complaint and her discharge three years later.** The delay was too great to imply a causal connection between protected activity and adverse employment action. The supervisor's comment that a complaint could be a "career limiting move" was not direct evidence of retaliation. As the professor did not show she was treated less favorably than similarly situated employees, the court affirmed the decision. *Myklebust v. Medical College of Wisconsin*, 97 Fed.Appx. 652 (7th Cir. 2004).

C. Causal Connection

◆   *An Illinois college instructor did not prove a causal connection between her complaint of sexual harassment and her discharge.*

A college vice president learned that the instructor used inappropriate language and gossiped with co-workers. Based on reports and observations, the supervisor issued a written warning and prepared a corrective action notice requiring her to immediately stop gossiping. However, the instructor refused to sign it. The next day, the supervisor learned she was spreading rumors that he was having a gay affair. Following an investigation, the regional vice president fired the instructor. A few days later, the instructor claimed that the supervisor had sexually harassed her. After filing an administrative complaint, the instructor sued the college in a federal district court for sexual harassment. She also claimed the college retaliated against her for reporting sexual harassment.

The court found the instructor did not assert any conduct so severe or pervasive that a reasonable person would find a hostile work environment. In addition, she did not show her supervisor's behavior toward her negatively affected her work. This defeated her sexual harassment claim. **To prove retaliation, the instructor had to show there was a causal connection between her post-discharge letter and the decision to fire her.** But there was no evidence that the vice president who made the termination decision was aware of any sexual harassment allegations at the time the decision to fire her was made. The court awarded pretrial judgment to the college. *Bozek v. Corinthian Colleges*, No. 07 C 4303, 2009 WL 377552 (N.D. Ill. 2/13/09).

◆   *A white Virginia professor failed to produce enough evidence to prove his claim that he was forced out of a historically black university based on his race.*

The professor worked at Virginia State University (VSU) for 40 years. He claimed he was forced into retirement when VSU officials took a series of actions designed to force his early departure. The professor said VSU cancelled a three-year grant, overloaded him with increased teaching duties, sided with a student in a grading dispute and shut off his e-mail. In his federal district court lawsuit against the university and several individual defendants, he claimed race discrimination and retaliation.

To support his discrimination claims, the professor said VSU's president called him "a fat fool" and a "fat stupid son of a bitch," and told him to "get out of my face." On one occasion, the president abruptly changed direction and walked away when he saw the professor walking toward him on campus. The president had also barred the professor from attending a luncheon. The court found this evidence did not indicate hostility based on race or color. Therefore, the president did not establish illegal discrimination. **The court also rejected the retaliation claim, because the professor did not show a causal connection between his participation in prior lawsuits involving VSU and adverse job actions taken against him.** Finally, the court rejected a breach of contract claim and granted pretrial judgment to VSU. *Stronach v. Virginia State Univ.*, 631 F.Supp.2d 742 (E.D. Va. 2008).

◆ *An Alabama university showed it did not fire an employee based on retaliation for turning her down for another job.*

The university discharged the employee, saying it wanted to achieve standardization and save money by outsourcing her tasks. It also denied her a job as an associate director of student housing, as she lacked relevant experience. The employee sued the university in a federal district court for discrimination based on gender and for retaliation. The court held for the university, and she appealed to the U.S. Court of Appeals, Eleventh Circuit. **The court held the gender discrimination claim failed because the university stated a legitimate and nondiscriminatory reason for the termination – saving costs and standardization.** Similarly, the retaliation claim failed because the individual who was chosen to fill the post had more relevant experience. The district court's ruling was affirmed. *Cashman v. Univ. of Alabama Board of Trustees*, 260 Fed.Appx. 216 (11th Cir. 2007).

◆ *A Tennessee community college discharged an African-American professor in retaliation for accusing the college of unlawful discrimination.*

The professor complained of racial discrimination during his 25-year career and filed several complaints with the college's affirmative action office. He also filed racial discrimination charges with the U.S. Equal Employment Opportunity Commission. The college received criticism from the professor's students and colleagues about how he managed a psychology course. The department removed the professor from that class and eventually relieved him of his teaching duties for unsatisfactory performance. He attempted to meet the requirements of a performance plan but was not given the entire fall term, as promised, to complete it. The college discharged the professor, and he sued the college and others in a federal district court, alleging it violated Title VII by opposing an unlawful employment practice enumerated under Title VII.

The district court dismissed the action, but the U.S. Court of Appeals, Sixth Circuit, returned the case to the district court for further consideration. A jury awarded the professor $320,000 in compensatory damages, and the college appealed. The Sixth Circuit found sufficient evidence for a reasonable jury to have found the college unlawfully retaliated against him in violation of Title VII. To succeed on a Title VII retaliation claim, an employee must demonstrate he or she was fired in retaliation for opposing a discriminatory practice. **The professor presented ample evidence to support a causal connection between his termination and retaliation for his discrimination complaints.** Front pay was an appropriate way to compensate him for future loss. *Cox v. Shelby State Community College*, 194 Fed.Appx. 267 (6th Cir. 2006).

CHAPTER EIGHT

Intellectual Property

I. COPYRIGHT LAW

State and federal copyright laws protect original works of authorship by creating exclusive rights for the owner to make copies of the work, prepare derivative works, distribute copies of the work, and perform or display the work publicly. See 17 U.S.C. § 106. Copyright protection for an original work exists even if no copyright is registered. See 17 U.S.C. § 408(a). Registration is required in order to initiate a copyright infringement action. Employers are presumed to own the copyright to works prepared by their employees within the scope of their employment, unless a specific written agreement says otherwise.

A. Fair Use

Educators and others are entitled to make "fair use" of copyrighted works for the purposes described in 17 U.S.C. § 107. The statute lists four factors to assure such use is not for commercial purposes. In Stewart v. Abend, *495 U.S. 207 (1990), the U.S. Supreme Court held the primary factor in fair use cases is the effect that use will have on the work's potential market or value.*

17 U.S.C. § 107 states:

The fair use of a copyrighted work, including such use by reproduction in copies … for purposes such as criticism, comment, news reporting, teaching (including multiple copies for classroom use), scholarship, or research, is not an infringement of copyright. In determining whether the use made of a work in any particular case is a fair use the factors to be considered shall include –

(1) the purpose and character of the use, including whether such use is of

347

a commercial nature or is for nonprofit educational purposes;

(2) the nature of the copyrighted work;

(3) the amount and substantiality of the portion used in relation to the copyrighted work as a whole; and

(4) the effect of the use upon the potential market for or value of the copyrighted work.

◆ *A Massachusetts federal court refused to find file-sharing falls under the fair use exception to the Copyright Act. Instead, it held a student infringed four recording company copyrights and must pay $675,000 in damages.*

The "fair use exception" is a limit on the virtual monopoly a copyright holder has over a work. The exception allows a limited, free use of the work for a worthy public purpose, such as education that does not harm the copyright holder's market interest. A student shared music files he downloaded even after court decisions clarified that file-sharing is a copyright violation. Applying the four fair use factors and weighing the equities, the court declined to find the student had made fair use of the files. His purpose and the character of his use of the music was personal enjoyment. **The court found music should enjoy "robust copyright protections."** The court held the effect of the student's use of music would be destructive to the market. No one would purchase iTunes songs if they could get them for free. The court implored Congress to amend the statute to reflect the reality of file-sharing in the face of this case and thousands of suits like it. The record companies were entitled to a judgment, and the student had to pay $675,000 in damages. *Sony BMG Music Entertainment v. Tenenbaum*, 672 F.Supp.2d 217 (D. Mass. 2009).

◆ *Forcing a university to disclose the identities of students accused of illegally downloading copyrighted music did not violate student privacy rights.*

Several recording companies filed a federal copyright infringement lawsuit against 14 University of Kansas students for illegally downloading copyrighted music files. The companies discovered the Internet protocol addresses used to access the files but were unable to discover the names of the students. A university log enabled identification of the students. A federal district court allowed the companies to subpoena the university for student names, addresses, telephone numbers, e-mail addresses and media access control addresses.

The court noted the university was free to try to quash the subpoena and avoid disclosing the information. Two students moved to quash the subpoenas, claiming disclosure would violate their privacy rights and FERPA. The court rejected the claim that student privacy interests outweighed the companies' interest in discovering their identities. **A person who uses the Internet to download copyrighted music without consent is engaging in the exercise of speech only to a limited extent.** Disclosing student identities would not violate privacy rights because the companies made a preliminary showing of copyright infringement, and the request for identifying information was specific enough to lead to disclosure of appropriate information. There was no other way to gain access to the requested information, and identifying the students was essential to a successful copyright infringement claim. In any event, the students could not reasonably expect a great degree of privacy, as they opened their computers to others for file-sharing. While FERPA generally bars federally funded educational institutions from disclosing specified student records, otherwise protected information may be disclosed pursuant to a valid court order. In this case, the limited scope of the subpoenas made it unlikely that information relating to student identities would become public. Therefore, the court held disclosing the information would not violate their privacy. *Interscope Records v. Does 1-14*, 558 F.Supp.2d 1176 (D. Kan. 2008).

◆   *A court denied a recording company's request to force Virginia Tech to reveal the names of students accused of illegally sharing files on the Internet.*

When the company filed a federal copyright infringement action, the students could be identified only by Internet Protocol (IP) addresses. The court authorized the company to seek to identify the students by serving a subpoena on Virginia Tech. In response, Virginia Tech provided the company identifying information for six students. It withheld the name of one student based on a prior court order and offered nothing about the remaining four. The company moved the court for an order requiring Virginia Tech to identify them. Virginia Tech claimed it was entitled to Eleventh Amendment immunity in the case.

Finding the doctrine of sovereign immunity was inapplicable to a subpoena request, the court denied Virginia Tech's motion. **Virginia Tech was not treated as a party simply because it was served with a subpoena, and was not entitled to immunity since it was not a party to the case.** However, it was appropriate to deny the company's motion because Virginia Tech had already complied with the subpoena. The company did not dispute the assertion that Virginia Teach was unable to provide names because many students lived in the dorm rooms at relevant times. Virginia Tech produced an affidavit from its chief information officer indicating that student names are not associated with the assignment of IP addresses. By producing the network session file logs, Virginia Tech complied with the subpoena. While the company's motions were denied, the court authorized it to serve more subpoenas to seek the names of all students who lived in the dorm rooms involved. *Arista Records LLC v. Does 1-14*, No. 7:08cv00205, 2008 WL 5350246 (W.D. Va. 12/22/08).

◆   *A Missouri teacher was unable to convince a federal appeals court that his materials deserved the protection of U.S. copyright and patent laws.*

The teacher designed an "Out of Area Program" for use by teachers to respond to student disruptions. He claimed he developed and implemented the program during his employment with the school district. The teacher asserted the school district continued using materials he developed after it discharged him. He sued the district in a federal district court for patent and copyright infringement. The court dismissed the case, finding the teacher's program was a "business idea" that was excluded from federal copyright protection.

The teacher appealed to the U.S. Court of Appeals, Federal Circuit, which noted that **general concepts and ideas are beyond the protection of copyright law. Copyright law protects the expression of an idea, but not ideas themselves.** The court found a hall pass used at the school during the relevant time period had the same language as the teacher's program. The school's hall pass was not otherwise like the teacher's materials. The court found the limited use of similar functional language did not constitute copyright infringement, even if the district had deliberately copied it. Fragmentary words and phrases were not protected by copyright law. **Forms of expression directed solely at functional considerations did not exhibit the minimal level of creativity to warrant federal copyright protection.** The teacher failed to provide any evidence that he had been issued a U.S. patent, and he could not maintain a patent infringement action without one. As the district court had properly dismissed the case, its judgment was affirmed. *Clark v. Crues*, 260 Fed.Appx. 292 (Fed. Cir. 2008).

◆   *The U.S. Supreme Court has held that publishing companies must obtain permission from freelance writers before reusing their works.*

In 2001, the U.S. Supreme Court determined that permission was required for inclusion of freelancers' works in electronic databases. Copyright law allows publishers to reuse freelancers' contributions when a collective work, such as a magazine issue or an encyclopedia, is revised, but the Court said that **massive databases such as NEXIS do not fit within that provision of the law because they are not revisions of previously published collective works**. The decision was the result of a lawsuit that was filed against New York Times Co., Newsday Inc., Time Incorporated Magazine Co., LEXIS/NEXIS and University Microfilms International, alleging violation of freelance writers' copyrights in articles they wrote that were included in complete issues of the publishers' products. *New York Times Co., Inc. v. Tasini*, 533 U.S. 483, 121 S.Ct. 2381, 150 L.Ed.2d 500 (2001).

◆   *An Illinois professor could pursue her copyright claims against a publisher, but could not pursue claims against a college that formerly employed her based on how her books were used after being sold.*

The professor taught the course "Smart Foreclosure Buying" at City Colleges of Chicago. She authored a book of the same name, which she copyrighted and used as a text. When the professor stopped teaching the class, the college offered it with a new instructor, but still used the professor's initials in a catalogue. The professor advised the text's publisher by phone, letter and fax to stop printing the book, but it continued printing and selling the text and stopped paying her royalties. The professor sued the college in a federal district court to force it to stop offering courses using her book or its title as a course name. She added federal copyright and trademark claims against the publisher and an instructor, claiming the college engaged in false advertising, fraud and deceptive business practices. The court held the professor did not state a valid claim, and she appealed to the U.S. Court of Appeals, Seventh Circuit.

The court reversed the decision to dismiss the copyright claims against the publisher, noting the professor said she had mailed the publisher a letter of termination. Although the publisher claimed it never got the letter, **oral licenses and terminations are generally allowed**. A jury could reasonably determine the publisher had some notice of the professor's intent to withdraw her consent to publish the text, especially since it stopped paying her royalties. Although it reversed the decision on the copyright claims against the publisher, the court affirmed the ruling with respect to the copyright claims against the new instructor and the college. The professor could not pursue claims based on how the books were used after they were sold. **Once a copy of a work has been sold, the buyer may use it as he pleases so long as he does not create a new copy or derivative work.** The court also found a valid claim for trademark violation against the college. Finally, the professor stated a valid claim against the college for false advertising, fraud and deceptive business practices based on the continued use of her initials in the course catalog. *Vincent v. City Colleges of Chicago*, 485 F.3d 919 (7th Cir. 2007).

◆ *A federal district court held FERPA did not bar a university from disclosing the names of students accused of illegally downloading music files.*

Music publishers sued six unnamed persons for copyright infringement. An investigation revealed that the persons used an online media distribution system to download and/or distribute copyrighted music without authorization. The publishers identified the persons by an Internet protocol address assigned when the files were improperly accessed. They were also able to determine that Georgetown University was the Internet service provider used to access the files. The publishers asked a federal court for an order requiring the university to disclose the identities of the persons so they could pursue their claims.

The court stated that it had wide discretion over pretrial discovery matters. As an educational institution, Georgetown was subject to FERPA. Although FERPA protects personal information relating to students from disclosure, such information can sometimes be released pursuant to a court order. **Disclosure may be permitted in a judicial proceeding if it is shown that the requested information is sufficiently relevant to the litigation.** The court held the music publishers made a sufficient showing of good cause to gain access to the information they sought, as it was critical to the pursuit of their claims. In fact, the copyright infringement action would stall completely if the requested information was not provided. For that reason, the court granted the record companies' motion for expedited discovery. However, a subpoena to gain the requested information was to be limited to names, physical addresses, e-mail addresses, and media access control addresses. In addition, the publishers were to use personal information relating to the students only for the purpose of protecting their copyrighted materials. FERPA required the university to notify affected students before turning over the identifying information. *Warner Brothers Records v. Does 1-6*, 527 F.Supp.2d 1 (D.D.C. 2007).

◆ *A New York university defeated a media foundation's claims for copyright infringement and breach of contract.*

The parties contracted to produce public service announcements. The foundation alleged the university breached the contract by refusing to pay additional compensation as a condition of producing the announcements. It also contended the university violated federal copyright law by displaying copyrighted material at a fundraiser for a commercial purpose. The foundation sued the university in a federal district court for breach of contract and violation of the "fair use" provision of copyright law. The court allowed the case to go before a jury, and after a trial, it found for the university. The foundation appealed to the U.S. Court of Appeals, Second Circuit.

The court held the foundation breached the contract with the university by demanding extra compensation. To determine if the university satisfied the fair use requirements of 17 U.S.C. § 107, the court considered: 1) the purpose and character of the use, including whether such use is of a commercial nature or is for nonprofit educational purposes; the 2) nature of the copyrighted work; 3) the amount and substantiality of the portion used in relation to the copyrighted work as a whole; and 4) the effect of the use upon the potential market for or value of the copyrighted work. The court determined the fair use issue was properly presented to the jury. **Copyright law permits the reproduction or distribution of a copyrighted work as long as it is not done for commercial reasons.** The judgment was affirmed. *New York Univ. v. Planet Earth Foundation*, 163 Fed.Appx. 13 (2d Cir. 2005).

◆   *The U.S. Court of Appeals for the First Circuit rejected a Tufts University visiting lecturer's claims based on the terms of a publishing contract.*

The lecturer had co-authored the second and third editions of an undergraduate textbook with a professor and director of the graduate nutrition program at another college. The third edition agreement assigned all present and future copyrights of the third and future editions to the book's publisher. The lecturer and professor contracted with the same publisher for a fourth edition that increased the lecturer's share of royalties from 25 to 40%. The professor failed to meet deadlines set by the agreement, and the publisher suggested she assign more work to the lecturer. The professor refused, and the lecturer notified the publisher she was withdrawing from the project. She also stated her revisions could not be used without her permission. The publisher sent the lecturer an acknowledgement that she would receive 12.5% of the fourth edition royalties – half her compensation under the third edition agreement. She signed the acknowledgement, but later discovered her revisions were included in the fourth edition and that the professor was listed as its sole author.

The lecturer copyrighted her revisions and brought a multi-count federal district court complaint against the publisher and professor for copyright infringement and breach of contract. The court held the lecturer had assigned her copyright interest to the publisher under the fourth edition revisions. The publisher was not obligated to terminate its contract with the professor when she failed to meet her deadlines. The First Circuit affirmed the decision, holding the lecturer could not claim a copyright interest in her fourth edition revisions. She had "assigned … all present and future copyrights" of the third and future editions to the publisher. **The publisher was the sole copyright owner of the third edition, and consequently the fourth "revised edition." There was no breach of contract by the publisher, because it had the option to extend the deadlines and did so for legitimate financial reasons.** *Zyla v. Wadsworth*, 360 F.3d 243 (1st Cir. 2004).

◆   *By refusing to pay permission fees to copyright holders, a copy shop violated the Copyright Act.*

A commercial copy shop reproduced substantial segments of copyrighted works and bound them into "coursepacks," which were sold to students so that they could fulfill reading assignments given by professors at the University of

Michigan. The copy shop acted without the permission of the copyright holders, claiming that the fair use doctrine eliminated the need for it to obtain permission. The fair use doctrine states that the fair use of a copyrighted work for teaching, scholarship or research, among other uses, is not an infringement of copyright. In this case, a number of copyright holders sued the copy shop claiming that its reproduction of material was not fair use. A federal court agreed and awarded damages against the copy shop for willful infringement.

On appeal, the U.S. Court of Appeals, Sixth Circuit, noted that by reproducing copies for students without paying the copyright holders the permission fees that other copy shops paid, **the copy shop was reducing the potential market for or the value of the copyrighted works.** Since one of the potential uses of a copyright is to grant a license to reproduce part of the work for use in a classroom, and since the copyright holders were willing to grant those licenses, by refusing to pay the permission fees, the copy shop violated the Copyright Act. The court also noted that the purpose and character of the use was of a commercial nature, that the material being reproduced was creative in nature, and that the amount and substantiality of the reproduced segments in relation to the works as a whole were quite large (between 5 and 30%). The court affirmed the finding that the copy shop had infringed the copyright holders' rights. However, it refused to find that the infringement had been willful, and remanded the case for reconsideration of damages. *Princeton Univ. Press v. Michigan Document Services*, 99 F.3d 1381 (6th Cir. 1996).

B. Work-For-Hire

Employers are presumed to own the copyright to works prepared by their employees within the scope of their employment, unless they have agreed otherwise in writing. See 17 U.S.C. § 201(a), also referred to as Section 201(b) of the Copyright Act of 1976. The work of independent contractors is considered "work for hire" under a written agreement for specially ordered or commissioned work used as a contribution to a collective work, part of a motion picture or other audiovisual work, a translation, supplementary work, compilation, instructional text, test or test answer, or an atlas.

Agency principles help determine whether a professor's work is covered by the work-for-hire doctrine. Section 228 of the Restatement (Second) of Agency deems a work to be "for hire" only if the work is of the type the faculty member was hired to create, was created substantially within the space and time limits of the job, and was motivated at least partly by a purpose to serve the university. Professors are expected to produce intellectual property in the scope of their employment, and those who conduct research, write and publish scholarly articles and create other forms of intellectual property receive better performance evaluations, more promotional opportunities and higher pay.

◆ *The Supreme Court of Kansas held the work-for-hire doctrine did not prevent a state university and the employee association representing its faculty from entering into a memorandum of agreement on intellectual property rights.*

The university and Kansas Board of Regents proposed a policy to retain ownership and control over any intellectual property created by the faculty. The faculty association rejected the policy. The board responded it was not required to negotiate over the policy because intellectual property rights were not a "condition of employment." According to the board, the question of intellectual property rights was a management prerogative and was preempted by state and federal law. The board then adopted a policy giving some intellectual property rights to faculty, but without meeting and conferring with the association.

The state public employee relations board (PERB) held the university had no duty to meet and confer with the faculty association, because the subject was preempted by state and federal law. The case reached the Supreme Court of Kansas, which found neither state nor federal law preempted the subject of intellectual property from being included in a memorandum of agreement. **The work-for-hire doctrine was only a presumption regarding the ownership of copyrights, and it allowed parties to contract for particular ownership rights. The doctrine operated as a default provision, unless the parties agreed otherwise.** The court found Congress contemplated that parties could negotiate the ownership of a copyright. The federal Patent Act also allowed parties to assign patent ownership rights. Federal law did not preempt any kind of intellectual property rights from being covered by a memorandum of understanding or other written agreement. The court reversed the decision with directions to return the case to the PERB for further proceedings. *Pittsburg State Univ./Kansas National Educ. Ass'n v. Kansas Board of Regents/Pittsburg State Univ.*, 280 Kan. 408, 122 P.3d 336 (Kan. 2005).

◆ *Brown University retained its copyrights to photographs taken by a member of its staff under the "works-for-hire" doctrine.*

Brown University hired a full-time professional photographer to capture images of academic life and natural campus settings for its publications. He was also allowed to shoot pictures on his own initiative. The university purchased photographic equipment for him, arranged for student assistants, and provided him access to the university's darkroom. Brown's copyright policy contained a provision regarding the ownership of copyrightable materials.

After 24 years, Brown severed its relationship with the photographer as part of a reduction in force. He sued Brown in a federal district court, claiming ownership of 97 photographs in his possession. The court focused on the **"Works Made for Hire" Section** of the Copyright Act of 1976. **The court explained that ownership rights of works by an employee typically vest with the employer.** It determined the photographs were "works for hire" owned by Brown. **The court distinguished between the photographs and the "faculty exception" from the works-for-hire rule.** Equitable considerations often mandate that a scholar retain the copyright to works, notwithstanding the works-for-hire doctrine. The faculty exception did not apply in this case because Brown officials often directed what images should be photographed. There was no document indicating a conveyance of ownership rights to the photographer. The language of the policy was too imprecise to support the photographer's claim of such a transfer. He did not think about copyright ownership in the photos until after his relationship with Brown was severed. As a result, the court held for Brown. *Foraste v. Brown Univ.*, 290 F.Supp.2d 234 (D.R.I. 2003).

C. Standardized Tests

◆ *New York's Standardized Testing Act requires testing agencies to file reports on standardized tests with the Commissioner of Education and also requires the filing of copyrightable test questions.*

The American Association of Medical Colleges (AAMC), a nonprofit educational association, sponsors a medical school testing program, the central feature of which is the MCAT exam. The AAMC holds copyrights in the MCAT test forms, test questions, answer sheets, and reports. When the state of New York enacted the Standardized Testing Act, requiring disclosure of this copyrighted information, the AAMC sued to enjoin the application of the act. It claimed that the Act was preempted by the federal Copyright Act and moved for pretrial judgment, which the court granted. The court found that the purpose and character of the use was noncommercial and educational, and that disclosure of the test questions would prevent their reuse.

The Second Circuit Court of Appeals reversed, finding that there were issues of fact that precluded a grant of pretrial judgment. If the disclosure of material were considered "fair use," then there would be no Copyright Act violation. However, if the state act facilitated infringement, then the Copyright Act would preempt it. **Here, the state's goal of encouraging valid and objective tests was laudable, and there was a question of fact as to whether the test questions could be used again after being disclosed.** As a result, the fourth and most important fair use factor – the effect of the use upon the potential market for or value of the copyrighted work – did not necessarily weigh in favor of the AAMC. The court remanded the case for further proceedings. *Ass'n of American Medical Colleges v. Cuomo*, 928 F.2d 519 (2d Cir. 1991).

◆ *A federal court agreed with four educational testing agencies, including the College Entrance Examination Board, that the required disclosure of test questions under a New York law violated federal copyright law.*

New York education law requires college testing services to file copies of their test questions and statistical reports with the state education commissioner. A number of testing agencies claimed that the statute violated federal copyright law, and filed a lawsuit against the governor and other state officials. In view of the result in a similar case filed by the Association of American Medical Colleges, the parties entered into a stipulation under which the testing agencies disclosed questions for only some of the tests administered in the state and were allowed to administer a fixed number of undisclosed tests. The court then considered a motion by the agencies for temporary relief. The agencies argued that the compelled disclosure of the test questions violated federal copyright law and did not meet the fair use exception to federal copyright law. The state argued that **the public had an interest in ensuring the fairness and objectivity of standardized admission tests** and had a strong need to evaluate the scoring process. It also claimed that disclosure did not violate copyright laws because of the lack of any commercial purpose.

The court agreed with the testing agencies that the disclosure of test

questions violated federal copyright law and issued a preliminary injunction. The court also found that the agencies were entitled to the presumption of irreparable injury that normally accompanies the showing of copyright infringement. However, because of the many factual issues existing in the case, the court issued an order preserving the status quo, under which only some tests administered in the state would be subject to the disclosure law pending further proceedings. *College Entrance Examination Board v. Pataki*, 889 F.Supp. 554 (N.D.N.Y. 1995).

Three of the testing agencies sought an order completely barring enforcement of the state law or alternative relief. A fourth agency submitted a statement indicating that it would comply with the order by disclosing three testing forms administered in New York during the test year and an additional form traditionally administered in the state in low-volume administrations.

The testing agencies asserted that the wording of the preliminary order would prevent the Graduate Record Examination (GRE) program from offering at least one administration in the state, and that the status quo provision of the order did not account for changing circumstances in testing from year to year. They further asserted that the preliminary order contravened **the principle in copyright infringement cases that the status quo sought to be preserved is the state of non-infringement**. The court held that the preliminary order struck the correct balance between competing interests, including that of the students who would take the examinations. There was no need to strictly comply with the rule that the status quo to be preserved is a state of non-infringement, since the parties had agreed by stipulation to provide for limited disclosure of test forms. The court modified the preliminary order to accommodate the GRE program's phase-out of paper and pencil administrations. *College Entrance Examination Board v. Pataki*, 893 F.Supp. 152 (N.D.N.Y. 1995).

D. Due Process Issues

◆   *A tenured University of Michigan professor had an insufficient property interest in an idea to gain any protection of it as his intellectual property.*

In 1995, the professor wrote drafts for a design center in the university's Department of Aerospace Engineering. The drafts were revised by another professor and turned into an abstract. The first draft proposal listed two co-authors, and the second listed three others. The proposal identified a design center with resident visitors of different specialties, with a focus on Russian designers. The university obtained funding for the center and built it in 1999. The professor sued the university in the state court system asserting violation of his due process and intellectual property rights. The court held for the university, and he appealed. On appeal, the Court of Appeals of Michigan held the university had no fiduciary duty to the professor. A fiduciary relationship exists only "when there is confidence reposed on one side and a resulting superiority and influence on the other." The court disagreed with the professor's claim to a property interest in the design center. He prepared drafts for the center in 1995 with various others. The proposal indicated there were already programs for visiting designers. The university had previously hired retired designers to teach courses. The court held the protection of an idea under a property theory "requires that the idea possess property-like traits."

Moreover, "ideas themselves are not subject to individual ownership or control. They do not rise to the level of property and are not in themselves protected by law." The professor could not "own the idea" of a design center or a visiting designer program that already existed in other forms. The professor asserted the university's rules and policies made him "automatically the principal investigator" of the proposal. The court disagreed, finding no such rule or policy "promising or even hinting at how those benefits accrued to him." **In order to have a constitutionally protected interest, a person must have more than an abstract need or desire for it. There must be a legitimate claim of entitlement.** A party's unilateral expectation is insufficient to create a property interest protected by procedural due process. The court held that as the professor did not show any legitimate property interest in his idea, he could not allege a due process claim. *Kauffman v. Univ. of Michigan Regents*, No. 257711, 2006 WL 1084330 (Mich. Ct. App. 4/25/06). The Supreme Court of Michigan denied further review. *Kauffman v. Univ. of Michigan Regents*, 477 Mich. 911, 722 N.W.2d 823 (Mich. 2006).

II. PATENTS

A patent is a legally protected property interest that gives the owner the right to exclude others from making, using, selling, offering for sale, or importing the invention covered by the patent. Patents generally run for a period of 20 years from the effective filing date of the patent application. To be patentable, an invention must be useful, new or novel, and non-obvious.

Unlike copyright law, there is no federal patent law provision on work-for-hire. Patent ownership is instead resolved by common law. The federal Patent Act also allows parties to assign patent ownership rights. In determining who owns the patent rights to an invention, courts look at the nature of the relationship between the inventor and the employer. Where the inventor is hired to invent something, the employer retains all patent rights; and where the inventor is hired under a general contract of employment, the inventor will retain ownership rights. However, most cases fall somewhere in between these two: for example, where a university hires a professor or a graduate student to teach and do research. The ambiguity this creates has led colleges and universities to enter into pre-employment assignments of intellectual property rights that specifically lay out the rights of both parties. Sometimes this is done by written agreement – other times, by use of a faculty handbook.

With respect to patent rights, professors usually are required to assign creations and patent rights to the colleges and universities that employ them in exchange for a percentage of the royalties. The issue becomes trickier when dealing with graduate students. Some universities require graduate students to assign patent rights, while others do not.

A number of states have enacted statutes to limit the extent to which employers can claim an interest in employee inventions. However, those statutes generally provide that if the employer provides resources, or if the invention relates to the employer's business, the employer can require assignment of intellectual property rights. It is only where the employer has no involvement at all that the employee can claim full rights to an invention.

Literal infringement refers to the misappropriation of all essential elements in a patent. Infringement under the doctrine of equivalents results when a device performs the same function as the patented device in substantially the same way to achieve the same result.

A. Ownership and Inventorship

◆ *Vanderbilt University was unable to show that two of its scientists contributed to the invention of an erectile dysfunction treatment and method.*

Vanderbilt sued ICOS Corporation in a Delaware federal district court, asserting that two of its scientists should be added as joint inventors of patented compounds and methods for treating erectile dysfunction. These included tadalafil, a PDE5 inhibitor which is the active ingredient in Cialis. According to Vanderbilt, its scientists were among the first to discover PDE5 in the late 1970s, and they continued to work on related research. Vanderbilt retained ownership of the intellectual property under an underwriting and license agreement with Glaxo, Inc. Glaxo later assigned all its rights, title and interest in the patented compounds to ICOS. Vanderbilt then sought to correct inventorship of the patents in a federal district court. The court found no evidence that Vanderbilt scientists conceived of tadalafil's specific chemical structure. Vanderbilt appealed to the U.S. Court of Appeals, Federal Circuit.

According to the court, federal patent law permits joint inventorship by one or more inventors who are not physically working together. However, each inventor needs to perform part of the task and make some contribution to the inventive thought and the final result. **For persons to be joint inventors, there must be some element of joint behavior, such as collaboration or working under common direction.** Vanderbilt could not counter ICOS' evidence that an ICOS researcher independently discovered the compounds to be tested for PDE5 inhibition. While Vanderbilt claimed ICOS' research was done more than 10 years after Glaxo did the same work, the court found no evidence of joint collaboration on the invention. Vanderbilt failed to present clear and convincing evidence that the ICOS researcher could not have independently identified the compound. Since the parties' stories were equally plausible and there was no clear and convincing evidence of joint invention, the judgment for ICOS was affirmed. *Vanderbilt Univ. v. ICOS Corp.*, 601 F.3d 1297 (Fed. Cir. 2010).

◆ *A federal district court was instructed to reconsider a case that originally appeared before it in 1997 to determine whether certain products infringed on patents under the doctrine of equivalents.*

The University of California (UC) and Abbott Labs claimed patents for inventions to improve methods for identifying and classifying chromosomes to detect abnormalities associated with genetic disorders, degenerative diseases and cancer. They sought to employ a staining technique to allow rapid and highly sensitive detection of chromosomal abnormalities in both metaphase and interphase cells using standard clinical and laboratory equipment. The patent claims were directed at blocking, selectively removing or screening repetitive sequences. UC and Abbott Labs, as the owner and exclusive licensee of the patents, sued a manufacturer in a federal district court for a preliminary order to prohibit it from manufacturing and selling certain products. The court held UC and Abbott could not prevail on a patent infringement claim based on limitations for "morphologically identifiable chromosome or cell nucleus," and "heterogeneous mixture of labeled unique sequence nucleic acid fragments." They also did not show their product met a blocking nucleic acid limitation under the doctrine of equivalents. The court later issued pretrial judgment to the manufacturer as to two of its products.

On appeal, the U.S. Court of Appeals, Federal Circuit, considered UC and Abbott's claim that the district court misconstrued the phrase "heterogeneous mixture of labeled unique sequence nucleic acid fragments." The manufacturer's products contained repetitive sequences found in prior art, while the patents referred to unique sequence fragments. The court found it was erroneous to characterize the patent as prior art. However, the lower court correctly found the products did not infringe upon a second patent, which employed a mixture including repetitive sequences. The original patent claim did not include the phrase "unique sequence." This was a response to three separate enablement rejections by a claims examiner. **The prosecution history demonstrated how the inventor intended to limit the invention.** The non-infringement judgment was affirmed as to the first patent. However, as to the second patent, the lower court improperly applied prosecution history to the "blocking nucleic acid" limitation. The court returned this claim to the lower court for reconsideration of whether the manufacturer had infringed the patent under the doctrine of equivalents. *Regents of Univ. of California v. Dakocytomation Cal., Inc.*, 517 F.3d 1364 (Fed. Cir. 2008).

◆ *A patent licensee could pursue claims against a competitor under the California unfair competition law and the Lanham Act, but not the Florida Deceptive and Unfair Trade Practices Act.*

Optivus Technology claimed to be the exclusive licensee of two proton beam therapy system patents. The University of Florida signed a non-binding letter of intent with Optivus regarding the proton beam therapy systems. After the letter expired, Florida considered other vendors and awarded a contract to Ion Beam Applications (IBA), which competed with Optivus in the same market. Optivus sued IBA in a federal district court for infringement of the patents. Loma Linda University Medical Center, as assignee of Optivus, became a party. Optivus added claims against IBA for unfair competition under California and Florida law, as well as violation of the Lanham Act. IBA counterclaimed against Optivus, seeking an order declaring the proton beam patents invalid in view of a neutron therapy facility in use at the University of Washington. The California unfair competition claim was based on the theory that IBA marketed a medical device that was not approved by the U.S. Food and Drug Administration (FDA). The district court refused to consider the California unfair competition law claim. The court held for IBA on the Florida

Unfair Trade Act and Lanham Act claims, as well as a claim for intentional interference. The court found both patents invalid and ruled there was no patent infringement. Optivus appealed to the U.S. Court of Appeals, Federal Circuit.

The court agreed with Optivus that the district court should have ruled on the significance of an FDA letter. The district court had thus improperly dismissed the California state law unfair competition claim. The court considered the claim under the Florida Unfair Trade Act and noted the University of Florida had selected IBA as its vendor after the expiration of the letter of intent with Optivus. **At the time IBA was selected, only a "consumer" could bring a claim under the Florida Deceptive and Unfair Trade Practices Act.** For this reason, the district court properly awarded summary judgment to IBA on Optivus' Florida law claim. **The district court had found Optivus did not show a business relationship existed after the letter of intent expired.** The court of appeals found no error in this conclusion. Any business relationship between Optivus and Florida ended with the expiration of the letter. The court stated that to prevail on its Lanham Act claim, Optivus would have to show IBA made a false and material statement of fact that caused the University of Florida to award the contract to IBA. The court disagreed with the district court's findings in favor of IBA regarding false statements about financing. It reversed the judgment on the Lanham Act claim for further consideration of IBA's alleged statements. Loma Linda asserted the lower court improperly found the patents invalid. It claimed modification of the University of Washington's neutron therapy facility would result in a "death ray." The court disagreed, finding the combination of prior art references by the district court had been proper. **The patent was invalid as obvious, in view of Washington's neutron therapy facility.** The patent for a safety system for a multi-room proton beam therapy facility was written with expansive, highly inclusive language. **As Loma Linda did not rebut this evidence, the judgment of patent invalidity was correct.** *Optivus Technology, Inc. v. Ion Beam Applications, S.A.*, 469 F.3d 978 (Fed. Cir. 2006).

◆ *A federal district court held a Yale University chemistry professor defrauded Yale of a patent for an invention.*

The professor claimed he invented a chemical mass spectrometry device and that its patent was issued to him in July 1992. However, Yale's internal patent policy gave it the right of first refusal to patent any faculty inventions. The professor sued Yale in a federal district court, alleging it violated the Connecticut Unfair Trade Practices Act. Yale counterclaimed for an accounting and assignment of the patent. It also said the professor breached his contract and committed fraud and theft. After a trial, the court held the professor breached Yale's internal patent policy, to which he was contractually bound. Yale was entitled to patent the invention and receive all related royalties. The court found the professor misrepresented the importance and commercial viability of the invention. He discouraged Yale from preparing and filing a patent application while secretly preparing an application in his own name. The professor refused to assign the patent to Yale, in breach of the internal patent policy. The court found he purposefully engaged in fraud and committed larceny and civil theft, and ordered him to assign his patent rights to Yale.

On appeal to the U.S. Court of Appeals, Second Circuit, the professor argued that Yale's longstanding patent policy was preempted when the National Institutes of Health (NIH) accepted his ownership of the patent. The court found the only evidence of NIH acceptance was a letter acknowledging receipt of a patent license form signed by the professor. **This did not indicate the NIH had found he was the owner of the patent.** Even if NIH had so found, it would have violated controlling law. The court affirmed the judgment for Yale. *Fenn v. Yale Univ.*, 184 Fed.Appx. 21 (2d Cir. 2006).

◆ *A medical school student at a private New York university did not prove he contributed to a professor's patented treatment for glaucoma.*

The university owned a patent involving the use of prostaglandins in treating glaucoma. A long-time professor at the university was the named inventor of the patent. In 1980, the professor agreed to a proposal by the student to perform a one-semester ophthalmology research elective. He directed the student to begin his project by reviewing a faculty member's papers on prostaglandins and intraocular pressure (IOP). At the time, the professor had published several papers on the effects of prostaglandins on the IOP in animals such as rabbits and owl monkeys. The student conducted experiments in the lab that showed topical application of single doses of prostaglandin reduced IOP in rhesus monkeys and cats. After the student left the university, the professor conceived the patent while studying the effects of repeated prostaglandin application on the IOP in rhesus monkeys. He applied for the patent in 1982, and it was issued in 1986. When the student found out about the patent, he sued the university and professor in a federal district court, asking to be added as a co-inventor. The trial court granted summary judgment for the university and the professor. It found the student failed to present evidence of inventorship.

On appeal, **the U.S. Court of Appeals, Federal Circuit, held the student had to show he contributed to the conception of the invention in order to be considered one of the inventors of the patent.** The court found the student did not have an understanding of the claimed invention. He also did not discover that prostaglandins have an effect on IOP, or conceive of the idea of the use of prostaglandins to reduce IOP in primates. Furthermore, the student did not collaborate with the professor in developing a glaucoma treatment. **He simply carried out an experiment done previously by the professor on different animals.** The court held the student's contribution was insufficient to support his claim of co-inventorship and affirmed the judgment. *Stern v. Trustees of Columbia Univ. in the City of New York*, 434 F.3d 1375 (Fed. Cir. 2006).

◆ *A pharmaceutical company had to pay $54 million in damages for fraudulently obtaining a patent based on work by university researchers.*

Two University of Colorado researchers worked under an agreement with a pharmaceutical company. They discovered certain multivitamins were not supplying proper amounts of iron to pregnant women and published an article suggesting a reformulation to increase iron absorption. The researchers sent an advance copy to the doctor they had been working with at the company. The company then obtained a patent on the reformulation of the multivitamin without notifying the university. It copied and plagiarized portions of the article in the patent application. The university foundation sued the company in a federal district court for wrongfully obtaining the patent. The court found the company liable for fraudulent nondisclosure. It noted the company would have had to pay the university for the rights to the reformulation, and calculated the royalty rates at approximately $22 million. The court held the university could recover equitable damages for unjust enrichment of $23 million. It also ordered exemplary damages in the amount of $500,000 for each inventor, based on the company's "clandestine and deceptive conduct," and "fraud, malice, and willful and wanton misconduct." *Univ. of Colorado Foundation v. American Cyanamid Co.*, 216 F.Supp.2d 1188 (D. Colo. 2002).

The U.S. Court of Appeals, Federal Circuit, rejected the company's argument that the damage award for unjust enrichment created a state-based patent law that was inconsistent with the federal statutory scheme. The court held this was not the issue in this case. The unjust enrichment claim was based on the wrongful use of research and did not interfere with the federal patent scheme. The researchers satisfied state law requirements for unjust enrichment, as it would be unjust to allow the company to retain profits acquired through misconduct. **The district court had properly awarded damages based on incremental profits that were directly attributable to the misconduct. The court upheld the district court's findings establishing inventorship.** Clear and convincing evidence indicated the researchers were the sole inventors of the patent. Substantial evidence supported the damage award, including the award of exemplary damages, and the court affirmed the judgment for the researchers and university. *Univ. of Colorado Foundation v. American Cyanamid Co.*, 342 F.3d 1298 (Fed. Cir. 2003).

◆   *The corporate sponsor of genetic research at a state university was the rightful owner of a patentable invention.*

A molecular biologist assigned all intellectual property rights arising out of his research at Washington State University (WSU) to WSU by agreeing to the terms of WSU's faculty manual. WSU had in turn assigned its intellectual property rights to a corporate sponsor under a research collaboration agreement. The biologist began research on a plant fat metabolism project, for which he also used a laboratory at Ohio State University (OSU). He discovered the FAD2 gene, one of several genes that encoded the fatty acid desaturase enzyme. The sponsor and biologist entered into an agreement recognizing him and another scientist as the inventors of the FAD2 gene and assigning his entire right, title and interest in the gene to the sponsor. The biologist further agreed to cooperate with the sponsor's patent application. He later refused to cooperate until he received a reasonable royalty. The sponsor sued the biologist in a federal district court for a declaratory judgment that it exclusively owned the FAD2 gene, and to enforce his contract duties. The biologist counterclaimed for a declaration that he was the sole owner and inventor of the FAD2 gene and requesting rescission of his assignment. The court held for the sponsor.

On appeal, the Sixth Circuit held that while the Federal Circuit has exclusive jurisdiction over federal patent law, this was a contract dispute. It held inventorship is an issue of patent law, but ownership of a patent is not a federal patent law question. **The WSU faculty manual established a legally**

binding contract between the biologist and WSU. Faculty members assigned their ownership of intellectual property to WSU, which in turn assigned ownership to the sponsor under the research collaboration agreement. The consequence of these two agreements was that all rights to the FAD2 patent were transferred to WSU, and then to the sponsor. OSU had waived any rights to the FAD2 patent. Even if it did not, **the faculty manual obligated the transfer of the biologist's intellectual property rights to WSU.** Summary judgment for the sponsor was affirmed. *E.I. Du Pont de Nemours & Co. v. Okuley*, 344 F.3d 578 (6th Cir. 2003).

◆ *A West Virginia university could not compel a student to assign second-generation patents to it under the university's patent policy.*

The student created a "half-wave bifilar contrawound toroidal helical antenna." He asked the university to submit patent applications for the antenna, and it did so. The student changed his mind and received a patent for the same invention. He then filed another application to provoke an interference with the university's application for second-generation patents. The university sued the student in a federal district court for breaching his duty to assign the patent as required by a university policy, and the student counterclaimed for breach of an implied contract. The district court issued an order for the university.

On appeal, the Federal Circuit held the student in breach of his obligation to assign the applications. He refused to sign the university's assignment forms and drafted new ones that only conveyed the rights to patent applications listed in the district court order. The court granted the university's motion to enforce the order and denied the student's motion for relief. The case reached the Federal Circuit again. The university argued the student's assignments failed to include three second-generation patents. **The court held the original assignment covered only the exact invention, its "immediate lineal descendants" and similar categories. The second-generation patents were excluded from these categories**, and the professor was not obligated to assign them to the university. **The university could not use its patent policy to compel assignment of the second-generation patents.** As the ownership of these patents had not been decided yet, the case was reversed and remanded. *Univ. of West Virginia v. VanVoorhies*, 342 F.3d 1290 (Fed. Cir. 2003).

◆ *A university's patent policy validly required two researchers to assign all rights to their inventions to the university.*

The University of New Mexico's patent policy stated that all inventions developed during the course of research funded by the university or employment at the university belonged to the university. The policy also required the inventors to cooperate with the university in the patent process. Two researchers of chemical compounds completed work that led the university to submit 11 different patent applications regarding two compounds. The researchers assigned their rights in the patents to the university.

Two years later, the university submitted five continuation-in-part patent applications, and the researchers did not assign their rights under these applications to the university. When the university entered into a licensing agreement with a company regarding the two compounds, a dispute arose over the ownership of the patents. A New Mexico federal court assigned a special master, who concluded that the researchers had to assign their rights to one of the compounds to the university. With respect to the second compound, the court conducted a trial and determined that the university owned those patents as well. On appeal, the Federal Circuit largely affirmed. The researchers were to be listed as inventors, but **the university's patent policy, which was incorporated into the researchers' employment contracts, clearly made the university the owner of the patents**. *Regents of the Univ. of New Mexico v. Scallen*, 321 F.3d 1111 (Fed. Cir. 2003).

B. Validity of Patents

When competing applicants for a patent on the same invention cannot settle their differences privately, either party may seek to have the matter resolved by the U.S. Patent and Trademark Office via a procedure known as a patent interference proceeding. The purpose of these proceedings is to determine priority of invention between competing applicants. Sometimes, an applicant can ask that an interference proceeding be conducted even after the patent it seeks has been granted to another applicant.

◆   *A patent claimed by a New York university was invalid because it did not comply with the written description requirement of federal patent law.*
Researchers at the University of Rochester developed a method for identifying a prostaglandin synthesis inhibitor. The university received two U.S. patents, one of which was based on a method that inhibited PGHS-2 prostaglandins. After four pharmaceutical manufacturers began using the method, the university filed a federal district court action against them for patent infringement. The court held the patent did not meet statutory written description requirements and merely described a theory, not an invention. The patent did not satisfy statutory enablement grounds, as it did not allow those skilled in the art to make and use the invention without undue experimentation.

The university appealed to the Federal Circuit. It held **the patent failed the written description requirement, as its description was "vague." It did not disclose the structure or physical properties of any compounds.** While it was not necessary for the university to describe the exact chemical compound of an inhibitor, its description of a non-steroidal compound that inhibits the activity of the PGHS-2 gene product was insufficient for statutory purposes. **It would not provide a researcher, skilled in this area, with sufficient information to understand what it claimed to accomplish and how to perform the method.** The court affirmed the judgment for the manufacturers. *Univ. of Rochester v. G.D. Searle & Co.*, 358 F.3d 916 (Fed. Cir. 2004).

◆   *Inventions by a pharmaceutical concern and a university were separately patentable as their molecules had different chemical structures.*
Eli Lilly and Co. filed a reissue application surrendering a patent covering deoxyribonucleic acid (cDNA), a sequence code for human protein C. At the same time, Lilly filed a patent interference claim against the University of Washington concerning a university-held patent that also related to the

sequence of human protein C. The university denied any interference, asserting the cDNA molecules had different chemical sequences. The Board of Patent Appeals and Interferences agreed, finding Lilly's invention was not the same as the university's. Lilly was dissatisfied with the board's ruling and moved to define the interfering subject matter by proposing two alternative constructions of the cDNA: a narrow construction and a broad construction. The board applied a two-part test and rejected Lilly's contentions. Regardless of whether the claim was construed as a genus or a species, Lilly's reissue application and the university's claim did not define the "same patentable invention." There was no interference-in-fact, and the matter was dismissed. Lilly appealed to the Federal Circuit, which explained that under 37 C.F.R. § 1.601(n), the "'same patentable invention' means that the one invention of one party anticipates or renders obvious the other party's invention." Since the claimed interference involved genus/species inventions, it was unclear whether the genus claim or the species claim was invented first.

The court found it possible that both a genus claim and a species claim could be separate, patentable inventions. The director resolved the issue by presuming that both Lilly's invention and the university's invention were "prior art." This meant that the university's invention was assumed to be prior art of Lilly's invention and vice versa. Although the court acknowledged Lilly's assertion that a one-way test should be applied, it was within the director's discretion not to accept it. The court upheld the use of the two-way test and affirmed the board's decision. *Eli Lilly & Co. v. Board of Regents of Univ. of Washington*, 334 F.3d 1264 (Fed. Cir. 2003).

◆   *A university and its licensee could not patent a discovery about the best time to harvest and eat certain vegetables.*

Johns Hopkins University owned three patents based in part on the discovery of the beneficial effects of harvesting and eating broccoli and cauliflower at the two-leaf stage, when they contain the highest levels of glucosinates and Phase 2 enzymes, which reduce the risk of developing cancer. The patents also contained a method for preparing the sprouts in order to increase their protective properties. The university licensed the patents to a company, then joined the company in a lawsuit against competitors for violating the patents. The defendants asserted that the portions of the patents that referred to the eating and growing of sprouts should be invalidated by prior art. A Maryland federal court ruled in favor of the defendants. On appeal, the Federal Circuit Court of Appeals noted that under 35 U.S.C. § 101, a patent can be obtained for inventing or discovering any new composition of matter or any new improvement thereof.

The university and its licensee did not create a new kind of sprout or develop a new growing method. They merely discovered that the vegetables contained glucosinates and Phase 2 enzymes (anti-cancer agents). Those elements were inherent in the sprouts. Since prior art unquestionably included growing, harvesting and eating the sprouts, the patents were invalidated to the extent they tried to protect that activity. The judgment was affirmed. *Brassica Protection Products, LLC v. Sunrise Farms*, 301 F.3d 1343 (Fed. Cir. 2002).

C. Defenses

The Eleventh Amendment to the U.S. Constitution generally bars claims against state defendants, including state colleges and universities. States can waive immunity from suit.

◆ *The Eleventh Amendment bars federal court lawsuits by private parties against states under the Patent Remedy Act and the Lanham Act.*

In 1999, the Supreme Court decided two cases involving the same parties and the same dispute. In *Florida Prepaid Postsecondary Educ. Expense Bd. v. College Savings Bank*, 527 U.S. 627, 119 S.Ct. 2199, 144 L.Ed.2d 575, **the Court held that Congress' abrogation, under the Patent Remedy Act, of states' sovereign immunity from patent infringement suits was not constitutional**. Building on its earlier decision in *Seminole Tribe of Florida v. Florida*, 517 U.S. 44, 116 S.Ct. 1114, 134 L.Ed.2d 252 (1996), where it held that Congress does not have the power to abrogate a state's sovereign immunity under Article I of the Constitution, the Court found that Congress had overstepped its bounds. Although patents can be considered property within the meaning of the Due Process Clause, there was no indication here that the Patent Remedy Act had been enacted under the authority of the Fourteenth Amendment. Rather, the legislation was authorized by Article I and thus improperly removed states' sovereign immunity.

The case arose after College Savings Bank, which owned and marketed a patented investment methodology designed to finance the costs of college education, discovered that the state of Florida was selling a similar product. The bank brought separate actions against the state for patent infringement and false advertising under the Lanham Act. In the patent infringement action, the Court determined that Florida could not be sued without its consent where it had merely engaged in interstate commerce. In the false advertising action, the Court held that **the Trademark Remedy Clarification Act also did not validly abrogate states' Eleventh Amendment immunity from a suit brought under the Lanham Act**. Although Congress may remove a state's sovereign immunity under Section 5 of the Fourteenth Amendment, there must be a property interest involved for it to do so. However, there was no property interest at stake in a false advertising suit under the Lanham Act. Further, the state of Florida had not constructively waived its immunity by engaging in interstate commerce. *College Savings Bank v. Florida Prepaid Postsecondary Educ. Expense Board*, 527 U.S. 666, 119 S.Ct. 2219, 144 L.Ed.2d 605 (1999).

◆ *A state university that voluntarily submits itself to the jurisdiction of the federal court system waives its Eleventh Amendment immunity with respect to the claims involved.*

The University of Missouri filed an application for a patent of an unspecified invention. While the application was pending, a company filed an application to patent the same invention. The company's application proceeded more quickly, and it was granted while the university's remained pending. The university responded by instituting an interference proceeding. After a six-year interference proceeding, the U.S. Patent and Trademark Office held the company was not entitled to the patent. The university was awarded priority and the office held it was entitled to the patent. The company appealed to a federal district court. The university moved for dismissal, arguing it was immune from suit in the federal courts under the Eleventh Amendment.

The district court agreed with the university, and the company appealed. The U.S. Court of Appeals, Federal Circuit, explained that a state does not waive its Eleventh Amendment immunity merely by participating in the federal patent system. In this case, however, the university asked the U.S. Patent and Trademark Office to conduct litigation-type activity, and it participated in that activity without claiming immunity. **When a state voluntarily submits itself to the jurisdiction of the federal court system, it waives its state immunity with respect to the claims raised.** In this case, an appeal to federal court was built into the U.S. Patent and Trademark Office proceeding by statute. Therefore, by instituting and participating in the proceeding, the university subjected itself to federal court jurisdiction. The appeals court reversed the decision and remanded the case for further proceedings. *Vas-Cath, Inc. v. Curators of the Univ. of Missouri*, 473 F.3d 1376 (Fed. Cir. 2007).

III. TRADEMARKS

A trademark, defined at 15 U.S.C. § 1127, is any word, name, symbol or device, or any combination thereof used to identify and distinguish goods, including a unique product, from those manufactured or sold by others, and to indicate the source of the goods, even if the source is unknown.

Service marks are identical to trademarks in all respects except that they are intended to indicate the origin of services, rather than goods. Trade dress is defined as the total image of a product, and includes features such as size, shape, color, color combinations, texture, graphics or sales techniques.

◆ *Section 43(a) of the Lanham Act, 15 U.S.C. § 1125(a), creates a federal cause of action for unfair competition in interstate commercial activities. It forbids unfair trade practices involving infringement of trade dress, service marks or trademarks, even in the absence of federal trademark registration. See, for instance,* Two Pesos, Inc. v. Taco Cabana, Inc., *505 U.S. 763 (1992).*

Under Section 43(a), civil liability exists in cases where a person "on or in connection with any goods or services, ... uses in commerce any word, term, name, symbol, or device, or any combination thereof, or any false designation of origin, false or misleading description of fact, or false or misleading representation of fact, which—

(A) is likely to cause confusion, or to cause mistake, or to deceive as to the affiliation, connection, or association of such person with another person, or as to the origin, sponsorship, or approval of his or her goods, services, or commercial activities by another person, or

(B) in commercial advertising or promotion, misrepresents the nature, characteristics, qualities, or geographic origin of his or her or another person's goods, services, or commercial activities ..."

According to one court, the "touchstone test" for a violation of Section

43(a) is the likelihood of confusion resulting from the defendant's adoption of a trade dress similar to the plaintiff's. See Original Appalachian Artworks, Inc. v. Toy Loft, Inc., *684 F.2d 821 (11th Cir. 1982).*

◆ *A federal court rejected the University of South Carolina's bid to gain trademark rights in a mark resembling one that was already trademarked and was in use by the University of Southern California.*

The University of South Carolina filed an application to trademark its logo, which includes the letters "SC." South Carolina wanted to use the mark on hats, baseball uniforms, T-shirts and shorts. The University of Southern California opposed the registration of the mark, as it had previously registered a trademark that protects the letters "SC." It argued that allowing the proposed mark would create a likelihood of confusion. South Carolina filed a counterclaim seeking cancellation of Southern California's mark. South Carolina claimed the mark falsely suggested an association with the State of South Carolina. The Trademark Trial and Appeals Board refused to register South Carolina's proposed mark, finding it would create a likelihood of confusion among consumers. The board pointed out that the marks were identical and would appear on the same classes of goods and in the same channels of trade. South Carolina's counterclaim for cancellation of Southern California's mark was also rejected, as South Carolina did not show the initials "SC" are "uniquely and unmistakably associated" with South Carolina. On appeal, the U.S. Court of Appeals, Federal Circuit, held the evidence supported the board's conclusion.

Allowing registration of the mark would create a likelihood of confusion, since the marks were the same and would appear on the same kinds of goods and in the same channels of trade. The court upheld the decision to reject South Carolina's counterclaim for cancellation of Southern California's mark. To win on this claim, South Carolina had to show Southern California's mark was "unmistakably associated" with another person or institution. South Carolina did not make this showing, as "SC" refers to many entities other than the state of South Carolina. The initials "SC" do not uniquely point to the state of South Carolina. The Trademark Trial and Appeals Board's decision was affirmed. *Univ. of South Carolina v. Univ. of Southern California,* 367 Fed.Appx. 129 (Fed. Cir. 2010).

◆ *A federal district court retained an action by a former star basketball player who claimed the NCAA is unfairly profiting from the use of his image.*

Ed O'Bannon led the UCLA men's basketball team to the 1995 NCAA championship. According to O'Bannon, the NCAA required all student-athletes to sign a form authorizing the NCAA's use of their names and likenesses for promotional purposes. He claimed the forms were signed under duress and required student-athletes to give up all rights to the commercial use of their images, even after graduation. O'Bannon sued the NCAA for violation of federal antitrust law. He said the NCAA engaged in price-fixing by setting a price of zero for the use of his image. He added claims for unjust enrichment and an accounting. The Collegiate Licensing Company (CLC), described as the NCAA's licensing arm, was added as a party. The NCAA and CLC sought to dismiss the claims. The court explained that to prove a federal antitrust violation, O'Bannon had to show a contract, a combination or conspiracy that unreasonably restrained trade, and a restraint that affected interstate commerce.

The court found sufficient facts to avoid dismissal with respect to each of these elements. **O'Bannon alleged the existence of agreements among the NCAA, its members, CLC and distributors of products containing his images. He sufficiently alleged that a relevant collegiate licensing market existed, and that NCAA and CLC actions had significant anticompetitive effects.** There was an effect on interstate commerce. The court also preserved a claim of unjust enrichment. *O'Bannon v. National Collegiate Athletic Ass'n*, No. C 09-1967 CW, 2010 WL 445190 (N.D. Cal. 2/8/10).

♦ *A state court rejected a Michigan State University football team manager's attempt to challenge a decision to have the Nike logo appear on team apparel.*

The manager claimed the appearance of the logos on the uniforms created confusion as to whether Michigan State student-athletes were personally endorsing Nike products. A state court held for the university, and the manager appealed on his state consumer protection act claim. The state court of appeals explained that he lacked standing to act as a private attorney general, as he did not suggest any injury from a deprivation of constitutional rights to himself or student-athletes at Michigan State. **The manager did not identify any student-athlete who objected to wearing the Nike logo.** The court also rejected his challenge under the state consumer protection act. As the manager did not identify any loss, the judgment was affirmed. *Sternberg v. Michigan State Univ.*, No. 281521, 2009 WL 131737 (Mich. Ct. App. 1/20/09).

♦ *A federal appeals court affirmed a decision for four major universities that sued an apparel manufacturer for federal trademark infringement.*

Louisiana State University, Ohio State University, the University of Oklahoma, and the University of Southern California held registered trademarks for their names and abbreviations. However, the institutions had no trademarks specifically relating to their color schemes. A clothing manufacturer sold t-shirts in color schemes and logos that were associated with the universities. Retailers displayed them alongside officially licensed merchandise, and the universities sued the manufacturer for trademark infringement. A federal district court found that even though the universities did not hold trademarks for their color schemes, the colors were associated with them closely enough to be entitled to trademark protection.

The manufacturer admitted it used the colors with the intent of identifying the universities. Since there was a likelihood of confusion regarding the source of the shirts, the court held the manufacturer violated the universities' trademark rights. A jury awarded the universities about $10,500 in actual damages and nearly $36,000 in lost profits. On appeal, the U.S. Court of Appeals, Fifth Circuit, found the universities established ownership of legally protectable marks. While they did not hold trademarks in their color schemes, each had acquired a "secondary meaning." **Secondary meaning occurs when the main reason for a mark is to identify the source of a product.** The universities had used their respective color schemes since the late 1800s, and they demonstrated a likelihood of confusion for consumers. The court rejected the manufacturer's argument that it made fair use of the color schemes and was not liable for trademark infringement. **The fair use doctrine does not apply when the use creates a likelihood of confusion.** *Board of Supervisors for Louisiana State Univ. Agricultural and Mechanical College v. Smack Apparel Co.*, 550 F.3d 465 (5th Cir. 2008).

◆ *The University of Texas at Austin (UT) will be allowed to proceed with several trademark violation claims against an electric company that used several logos resembling UT's familiar longhorn steer logo.*

UT first requested that the company stop using the logo in 2002, claiming it had a longtime registered trademark depicting the silhouette of a longhorn steer. The owner refused, noting he had used the silhouette with certain embellishments since 1998. UT sued the company in a federal district court in 2006 for state and federal trademark claims. The company asserted the case was time-barred because UT knew it used the logo by 1999 and unreasonably delayed filing a lawsuit. The court referred the case to a federal magistrate, who denied the company's motion to award it pretrial judgment based on unreasonable delay. There was evidence that UT had objected with a cease and desist letter to the company soon after learning of the company's logo. The company did not deserve pretrial judgment on the basis of acquiescence, even though there was evidence it had done work for UT in the past and that its trucks with logos were often parked on UT's campus.

The court found UT correctly argued that its trademark and unfair competition claims should not be dismissed prior to further court activity. Trademark infringement occurs when a person, without consent, uses in commerce any reproduction, counterfeit, copy or imitation of a registered mark in connection with the sale, distribution or advertising of goods or services, when the use is likely to cause confusion or deception. **The court found that for both trademark infringement and unfair competition purposes, a "likelihood of confusion" means that confusion is probable, not just possible.** The court refused to dismiss the case at this early stage, finding UT showed a likelihood that the company logo suggested a UT affiliation or endorsement. However, the longhorn logo was not sufficiently famous to establish a basis for monetary relief based on federal dilution under the Lanham Act. The mark was not a household name, despite evidence of retail sales of UT products near $400 million in 2005-06. Only the claim based on federal dilution was dismissed. *Board of Regents of University of Texas System v. KST Electric, Ltd.*, 550 F.Supp.2d 657 (W.D. Tex. 2008).

◆ *A federal district court approved a settlement involving a university that included too much personal information on credit card receipts.*

University of Pittsburgh students who had purchased sporting event tickets over the Internet filed a federal district court action asserting they had been given receipts displaying more than the last five digits of their credit cards and/or card expiration dates. At the time, the practice violated the Fair and Accurate Credit Transaction Act (FACTA). The parties executed a settlement agreement that called for each class member to receive a ticket to one of two University of Pittsburgh football games. The court granted preliminary approval of the agreement. **Congress then amended the FACTA to eliminate a private cause of action based on a seller's inclusion of an expiration date on a receipt.** The amendment said a party could not be deemed to have been in willful noncompliance with the statute simply by virtue of printing an expiration date on a receipt. The amendment applied to transactions that occurred between specified dates. The court rejected the university's petition to vacate the settlement agreement, since it was a binding contract. The amendment did not apply to any action that became final after Congress acted. *Colella v. Univ. of Pittsburgh*, 569 F.Supp.2d 525 (W.D. Pa. 2008).

◆   *Texas Tech University won a $3.1 million judgment against a retailer who continued to sell unlicensed university merchandise after the termination of a longstanding contract between the parties.*

The retailer was one of 450 university licensees that sold a total of $8 million in licensed products annually. He failed to account for the university's share of royalties, and the license was terminated in 2003. However, the retailer continued selling unlicensed merchandise through 2005, when Texas Tech sued him in a federal district court for trademark infringement, unfair competition, breach of contract, trademark dilution and injury to business reputation.

The court held Texas Tech's marks were protectable under trademark law because they were distinctive and not functional. The color scheme of Texas Tech apparel and merchandise identified and distinguished it. The scheme was associated with the university since the 1920s. The products were easily recognized, and they signalled to the public that they were licensed by Texas Tech. The commercial impression created by the unlicensed products was identical to the impression created by the university's products. The strength of the marks was undeniable, and they deserved broad protection. In addition, the retailer sold licensed products right alongside unlicensed ones. Consumers were likely to be confused by the sales of similar goods at the same stores. Each of the factors regarding the potential confusion for consumers presented by the retailer's use of the trademarks weighed in favor of the university. Texas Tech was also entitled to judgment on the unfair competition claims, for the same reasons that supported the trademark infringement claims. **Unfair competition occurs when an individual passes off the products of another by virtue of their substantial similarity.** The retailer had sold unlicensed products with identical marks since the license was revoked in 2003. The retailer clearly breached his contract with Texas Tech by continuing to sell licensed products after the contract was terminated. He further breached the contract by trying to register the phrases "Wreck 'em Tech" and "Raiderland" with the U.S. Patent and Trademark Office. **The Lanham Act permits the owner of a violated trademark to recover all the infringer's profits plus any damages and costs.** Texas Tech showed the retailer's profits during 2004-05 totalled more than $2.8 million. The university was entitled to these profits as well as the royalties due under the contract. The court awarded the university a total of more than $3.1 million on all its claims. *Texas Tech Univ. v. Spiegelberg*, 461 F.Supp.2d 510 (N.D. Tex. 2006).

◆   *The Nebraska Supreme Court denied an apparel store owner's claim for damages and injunctive relief against the University of Nebraska for wrongful use of a registered trade name.*

In late 1995, the Nebraska Athletic Department created an Authentic Shop, which would sell to the public apparel and equipment identical to that used by its teams and staff. The university began this process by test-marketing the idea to gather purchasing statistics for a new store. That same year, the university's board of regents filed an application with the Nebraska secretary of state to register the trade name "Husker Authentics" for the purpose of selling licensed goods. However, because the university did not file the requisite proof of publication of the name with the secretary and the county clerk as required by law, the registration was canceled without notice to the university. Taking all this in was Brent White, who owned and operated two businesses, Nebraska Spirit and Team Spirit Industries. White was well aware of the university's plans to open a store in 1997, which would, he believed, be a direct competitor with his stores. The day White learned that the university's registration of the trade name had been canceled because of improper publication, he filed his own application for registration of the trade name Husker Authentics. The Collegiate Licensing Company (CLC), the university's exclusive licensing agent, then got involved in the dispute. White had the CLC's approval to produce and manufacture the university's indicia from 1995 to 1998. The CLC sent White a letter claiming he was in violation of his license agreement and that failure to transfer his registration to the university within 15 days would result in immediate termination of his licensing agreement. White then canceled his agreement with CLC. Ignoring White's preemptive strike, the university opened a store called Husker Authentic on Aug. 27, 1997. Seven days later, White filed a petition requesting that the school be enjoined from using the disputed trade name. Later that month, White added a damages claim.

The university argued, among other things, that there had been a violation of common-law and statutory trade name and trademark rights. A state district court considered the arguments and found for the university, concluding that White's registration had been improperly granted because he had not actually used the trade name prior to registration. White appealed. The Nebraska Supreme Court found the district court's decision to be correct, but on different grounds, citing the work the university had done in test-marketing the concept. It further concluded that this afforded the school the common-law right to the trademark and any subsequent registration was therefore invalid. **Because the university owned the common-law right to "Husker Authentics," White could not properly register the disputed trademark.** The lower court's cancellation of White's registration was upheld. *White v. Board of Regents of the Univ. of Nebraska*, 260 Neb. 26, 614 N.W.2d 330 (Neb. 2000).

CHAPTER NINE

School Liability

I. NEGLIGENCE

Negligence results from the failure to use reasonable or ordinary care. To impose liability on a person or an institution there must be a legal duty. This is determined by the foreseeability of the risk of harm that caused injury. If an injury is a foreseeable result of negligent or intentional conduct, a legal duty exists, and liability may follow. Once a duty on the part of the institution is shown, liability exists if there was a breach of that duty, an injury or loss caused by the breach, and some damages. A pattern of negligence by schools and colleges that shows conscious disregard for safety may be "willful misconduct," a form of intentional conduct discussed in Section II of this chapter.

A. Duty of Care

◆ *The University of the District of Columbia was not liable for injuries sustained by a student who was attacked in an on-campus parking garage.*

Two assailants demanded money from the student, and one of them stabbed her in the face. She was able to escape, but the criminals were never apprehended. The student and her husband sued the university for negligence, claiming it should have taken safety precautions to prevent the attack. After a jury awarded $300,000 to the student and $100,000 to her husband, the case went before the District of Columbia Court of Appeals. It explained that a party may be held liable for negligence when there is a duty, a breach of that duty causing injury, and proof that the injury was proximately caused by the breach. **When injury results from an intervening criminal act, the injured party cannot recover for negligence unless the criminal act is so foreseeable that it creates a duty on the part of the defendant to guard against it.** This required some evidence that the university had "an increased awareness" that there was a risk of a violent, armed attack in its parking garage.

It was not enough to show there was a general possibility that a crime could occur in the garage. Although there was some evidence of crime on campus, none of the incidents involved a weapon, and none were committed in a parking garage or caused serious injury. Finding the university could not have foreseen the attack, the court held for the university. *Board of Trustees of Univ. of Dist, of Columbia v. DiSalvo*, 974 A.2d 868 (D.C. Ct. App. 2009).

◆   *A Massachusetts college was not liable for the death of a 20-year-old man who drank at a college party and then drove his car.*

The administrator of the man's estate sued the college for negligence in a state court, alleging that it failed to monitor its alcohol policy and prevent underage drinking. Before the Court of Appeals of Massachusetts, the administrator said the death was foreseeable because college students are known to behave irresponsibly. As an alternate argument, the administrator said social values and customs within the college community enabled the college to foresee and prevent the death. Noting that the man did not even attend the college, the court rejected any claim that the college owed him a duty to prevent his death. **While the college had policies relating to alcohol, they did not create a duty to someone outside the college community.** In addition, there was no special relationship between the man and the college that created a duty of care. The fact that the college owned the building where the party took place did not, by itself, create a special relationship and a resulting duty by the college. The man was in the best position to prevent the harm he suffered, as he could have decided not to drink and drive. The college was not responsible for his death. *Brody v. Wheaton College*, 74 Mass.App.Ct. 1105, 904 N.E.2d 493 (Table) (Mass. App. Ct. 2009).

◆   *A New York university could not be held liable for a slip and fall in a campus stairwell after a winter storm.*

A pedestrian slipped and fell on a stairwell, where she said there was a mix of water and icy snow on the stairs. In a state court personal injury action, the university argued that it was entitled to judgment because it did not know about or create the condition on the stairs. The court refused to award pretrial judgment, and the university appealed to a state appellate division court. An appellate panel found no evidence that the university knew students were tracking in snow and ice. **"A general awareness" that stairs become wet when ice and snow are tracked into a building was not enough to establish that the university knew of the particular condition that caused the fall.** As the university established it neither created nor knew of the condition that caused injury, the judgment was reversed. *Wartski v. C.W. Post Campus of Long Island Univ.*, 63 A.D.3d 916, 882 N.Y.S.2d 192 (N.Y. App. Div. 2009).

◆ *Parents of a University of Kansas (UK) freshman who fell to his death from a ledge outside his seventh-floor dorm room were unable to hold UK liable.*

The student fell to his death after removing window screens and going onto a ledge to smoke a cigarette. His blood alcohol level at the time was .16. The parents filed a wrongful death suit in a state court against UK, saying the ledge presented a dangerous condition that the university should have corrected.

After the court awarded pretrial judgment to UK, the parents appealed. The Court of Appeals of Kansas explained that a "discretionary function exception" insulates government entities from liability when harm results from an entity's performance of, or failure to perform, a discretionary duty or function. While the parents argued that the exception did not apply because UK was obligated to use reasonable care to protect their son, the court disagreed. Any duty of UK did not require it to warn of known and obvious dangers such as stepping out onto the ledge. UK was not required to take any extraordinary steps to minimize the obvious risk of danger from going out onto the ledge. **Universities are not required to protect their students from their own reckless and negligent acts and are not insurers of student safety.** The court affirmed the judgment for UK. *Wellhausen v. Univ. of Kansas*, 40 Kan.App.2d 102, 189 P.3d 1181 (Kan. Ct. App. 2008).

◆ *Under New York law, students could not be liable for injuries to another student at a party unless it was foreseeable that she would get drunk.*

A 19-year-old Ithaca College sophomore drank alcohol at a party. She then fell from a balcony and was seriously hurt. Her parents sued Ithaca in a state court, claiming the college was liable because the balcony and railings were unsafe and negligently designed. Ithaca sought contribution from five students who shared the apartment and from the architect who designed the balcony and railings. The college claimed the injuries were caused, at least in part, by the fact that the students who hosted the party supplied the student with alcohol. The trial court denied pretrial judgment to a student who had provided alcohol. But another who did not know the student was at the party until after the accident avoided liability. On appeal, a New York Appellate Division Court affirmed the judgment. Under state law, the students could not be liable unless it was foreseeable that someone at the party would get drunk, engage in a fight, and cause an injury. That showing was not made. **There was no common law claim based on negligent provision of alcohol to underage drinkers.** *O'Neill v. Ithaca College*, 56 A.D.3d 869, 866 N.Y.S.2d 809 (N.Y. App. Div. 2008).

◆ *A Mississippi university was required to defend a negligence claim alleging it was liable for the rape of a 14-year-old girl on its campus in 1993.*

The student claimed she was raped by two 15-year-old boys on the campus of Jackson State University (JSU) during a National Youth Sports Program. As part of the program, JSU leased a bus and transported participating children from their homes to the JSU campus. Both boys had prior histories of trouble in the program. One had been expelled from the program for fighting, and the other had been threatened with expulsion for fighting on a bus and on campus. The girl was dropped off at the wrong location on campus, where both boys raped her in a restroom. The boys later pled guilty to raping her. Her parents sued JSU and its officials in the state court system for negligence. The court awarded judgment to JSU, but the Supreme Court of Mississippi returned the case to the trial court in 2000. It again granted judgment to JSU.

The case returned to state's highest court in 2007. **The court focused on the question of whether the rape was foreseeable to JSU officials. If it was, then the university could be held liable for negligence.** The court held that a reasonable juror might conclude JSU could have foreseen that, by leaving the girl and two boys unattended and unsupervised, JSU placed her in danger of "some violent act or impermissible sexual act." A jury could find that JSU knew there were 63 crimes reported on campus in the 10 months preceding the rape, including other rapes. It could also find JSU was on notice that the girl had been in the boys' restroom prior to the date of the rape, and that the boys who committed the rape had violent tendencies. The court remanded the case for trial. *Glover v. Jackson State Univ.*, 968 So.2d 1267 (Miss. 2007).

◆ *The Supreme Court of Louisiana held a student's suicide note could not be admitted as evidence to support a negligence claim against a university.*

The student committed suicide at her parents' home by hanging herself. According to the parents, the university failed to properly supervise fraternal organizations on campus, and fraternity members sexually assaulted and raped her. The parents sued a fraternity, the university, and others in a state court, alleging their negligence caused the student to kill herself. She had written a suicide note that said "[a]ll I wanted was to forget about what happened & all it brought me was debt." The university and the fraternity challenged the parents' right to have the suicide note admitted into evidence. The court allowed most of the letter into evidence. The rest of the note was inadmissible because it was not a "dying declaration," which is an exception to the evidence rule on hearsay. The case reached the Supreme Court of Louisiana.

The court explained that hearsay statements are unreliable when admitted through someone other than the person who actually said them. Dying declarations are exempt from the hearsay rule because the likelihood that people will lie at the time of death is highly improbable. To be admitted into evidence, a dying declaration must address impending death, when a person realizes he or she is going to die immediately. The control of the student over her fate distinguished the suicide note from a true dying declaration. A suicide note is planned and in anticipation of death. **The court held the parents failed to show a connection between the rape and the suicide. The student killed herself months after the rape.** The supreme court held the lower court erred in allowing the note to be admitted as a dying declaration into evidence. It reversed the judgment and sent the case back to the district court to determine if the fraternity or the university should be held negligent. *Garza v. Delta Tau Delta Fraternity National*, 948 So.2d 84 (La. 2006).

◆ *An Ohio university was not liable for the rape of a student that took place in a university dormitory because the rape was not foreseeable.*

The student lived in a co-ed dorm with separate communal bathrooms for male and female students. She was raped while she was taking a shower in a dorm bathroom. Her attacker was never caught. The student sued the university in a state court for negligence, asserting it breached a duty of care by failing to install locks on the bathroom or shower doors. The court held for the university, but the Court of Appeals of Ohio reversed the judgment. It found the trial court had improperly admitted testimony by an expert witness. When the case was retried, the trial court held the university liable for negligence and awarded the student $100,000 for her injuries, pain and suffering. The university brought another appeal to the Court of Appeals of Ohio. According to the university, it did not owe the student a duty to protect her from rape by an unknown intruder. It claimed it was not liable because the attack was unforeseeable.

The court noted that while the university had a duty to warn or protect its students from known criminal conduct of third persons, it was not an insurer of student safety. If the attack was not foreseeable, the university was not liable for negligence. To determine whether an incident was foreseeable, Ohio courts apply the "totality of circumstances test." This test considers prior similar incidents, the propensity for criminal activity to occur on or near the location, and the character of the business. In this case, the trial court had found evidence that the university knew criminal activities occurred on campus, in classrooms, and in dorms, presenting a risk of harm to female students in a co-ed dorm. The court of appeals rejected these findings, as **the evidence was not specific enough to show the university could have foreseen this attack. The university did not breach its duty of care to the student**, and the court reversed the judgment. *Shivers v. Univ. of Cincinnati*, No. 06AP-209, 2006 WL 3008478 (Ohio Ct. App. 10/24/06).

◆ *The Supreme Court of Montana held a state university was liable for injuries to a child who fell on library stairs.*

The child slipped between the stairway balusters of a second-story open stairwell and fell approximately 20 feet to the concrete floor. He suffered three skull fractures from the fall. The mother sued the state in a Montana trial court, alleging negligence. The court found the state had a duty of care to the child and breached that duty, so it was liable for the fall. The state appealed to the Supreme Court of Montana. **The court held the state had a duty to maintain the balcony and staircase at the university library so they were safe for ordinary public use.** The court found the risk of falling was foreseeable because the state knew the distance between the staircase balusters was 11 to 12 inches. As the state failed to cure, remove or warn the public about the stairway defect, the court affirmed the judgment. *Henricksen v. State of Montana*, 84 P.3d 38 (Mont. 2004).

◆ *The Supreme Court of Utah held a university was not liable for injuries to a student who fell on an icy sidewalk during a class field trip.*

As part of an earth sciences curriculum, the student attended a field trip to examine fault lines in Salt Lake County. An instructor told students to walk on icy and snowy sidewalks through a condominium complex. The student fell and was injured when a classmate slipped and grabbed him for support. The student sued the university in a state court for negligence. The case reached the Supreme Court of Utah, which reviewed whether the university had a special relationship with the student that created a legal duty of care.

The court held that a special relationship can be created between an instructor and a student in higher education settings, because a college student will at times defer to an instructor's superior knowledge, skill, and experience. In this case, the instructor's directive that students cross the condominium sidewalk was not a command the student should have felt he had to obey. The court found it was unreasonable to believe the student would think his academic success could be affected if he refused to take a dangerous route so he could view fault lines. **The instructor did not exert the type of control in an academic setting required to create a special relationship.** As no special relationship existed, the court held the university had no legal duty to protect the student, and could not be held liable for his injuries. *Webb v. Univ. of Utah*, 125 P.3d 906 (Utah 2005).

◆ *A Minnesota university was not liable for injuries to a cheerleader who injured her spine while participating in a pyramid stunt during a practice.*

The cheerleader fell and suffered a cervical spine fracture when the squad tried to perform a pyramid stunt. She later admitted she knew the stunt was risky, but felt pressured to attempt it. The cheerleader sued the university for negligence in a state court. The court found the university had no duty to protect her and held for the university. The cheerleader appealed to the Court of Appeals of Minnesota. **The court held that to prevail on her negligence claim, the cheerleader had to establish first that the university owed her a duty of care. A university is not required to guarantee student safety.**

The court found that courts in Utah, Indiana and Louisiana have found no special relationship exists between a university and a student-athlete. While the university handled some administrative tasks for cheerleading programs, it exerted minimal control over cheerleaders. The university did not provide a coach to direct practices or otherwise impose rules on participants. The court noted the university did not profit from cheerleading programs. The university was not in a position to protect the student and could not have been expected to do so. Nothing suggested the cheerleader was vulnerable. Because there was no special relationship in this case, the university did not owe her a duty of care, and the court affirmed the judgment. *Vistad v. Board of Regents of Univ. of Minnesota*, No. A04-2161, 2005 WL 1514633 (Minn. Ct. App. 6/28/05).

◆ *A Delaware university was not negligent when its security officers responded to a student's 911 call within two minutes.*

The student heard someone outside the door of her dormitory room about 5:00 a.m. She called campus security, but by the time the security office picked up the call, she had hung up. The student was afraid the person would get in, so she jumped out her window, injuring herself. She crawled back into the building and hid in a men's room on the first floor. A university security officer arrived at the dorm room less than two minutes after the call was received.

When security arrived at the room, no one answered and there were no signs of an attempted break-in. Officers searched the grounds nearby. About an hour later, the student emerged from the men's room and the university quickly transported her to a hospital. The student sued the university in a Delaware trial court, alleging the school security personnel were negligent by failing to promptly respond to her 911 call. **The court held that to prevail on her claim of negligence, the student had to show the university owed her a duty of care and that it breached the duty.** While the university owed a duty to the student to protect her in her dorm, she failed to present any evidence of a breach of that duty. Evidence indicated university personnel acted professionally and effectively in responding to the incident. The court granted the university pre-trial judgment. *Pochvatilla v. Univ. of Delaware*, No. Civ.A. 03C-11-015 SCD, 2005 WL 434495 (Del. Super. Ct. 2/3/05).

◆   *The Court of Appeals of Tennessee held a state university was not liable to a non-student actress who fell during a rehearsal.*

The play took place in a theater in the round with several concentric descending steps encircling the theater. Glow tape was placed on set pieces to help actors and stagehands place sets and props on the stage during blackouts. During a rehearsal, a cast member complained she could not see well enough to make out the entrances and that more glow tape was needed near her entrance. A non-student actress then broke her ankle after attempting to stand on the darkened stage. The actress sued the state, claiming the university negligently failed to place glow tape on the edge of the stage.

The Tennessee Claims Commission found the actress 100% at fault for her injuries. She appealed to the Court of Appeals of Tennessee, which agreed with her argument that theaters owed a duty to actors and actresses to exercise reasonable care. However, that did not make them liable for risks that could not be reasonably foreseen. **The court found the actress did not prove the university knew or should have known she would fall because no glow tape was on the edge of the stage.** The other cast member's complaint that glow tape should be placed on set pieces did not put the university on notice there was a dangerous condition in another part of the stage. When the theater was blacked out, the actors were not supposed to be on stage. The court held the actress failed to establish the state was negligent. *Fox v. State of Tennessee*, No. E2003-02024-COA-R3-CV, 2004 WL 2399822 (Tenn. Ct. App. 10/27/04).

◆   *A California college was not liable for a student's off-campus injuries.*

A student at a California community college was thrown from a pickup truck while on a homework assignment for a course designed to train guides for horse-packing trips. She became a paraplegic and sued the college and instructor, alleging negligence in planning and supervising the assignment. The California Court of Appeal held the college had no duty to protect the student during an off-campus assignment. **As a general rule, colleges and their employees are not liable for off-campus student injuries. Here, neither the instructor nor any other employee supervised the assignment.** *Stockinger v. Feather River Community College*, 4 Cal. Rptr. 3d 385 (Cal. Ct. App. 2003).

◆   *A university did not have a greater duty to protect a 15-year-old student than it had to its other students.*

A 15-year-old matriculated at the University of Alabama and performed well her first semester. However, she then began drinking, doing drugs, and was rumored to be engaged in sexual activity with football and basketball players. On two occasions, university officials confronted her about the rumored sexual activity, which she denied. Later, she stopped attending classes and failed out of school. She then sued the university under Title IX, alleging that the university had a duty to prevent her from engaging in sexual activity that interfered with her classroom performance, which it breached. She asserted that the college stood *in loco parentis* (in the place of her parents) because of her age. An Alabama federal court disagreed. **Even though high schools stand *in loco parentis*, and even though she was of high school age, the university did not have increased obligations toward her.** Further, she had denied engaging in any sexual activity when confronted by university officials. Thus, the court dismissed the case. *Benefield v. Board of Trustees of Univ. of Alabama at Birmingham*, 214 F.Supp.2d 1212 (N.D. Ala. 2002).

◆ *A Florida university owed a student a duty to use reasonable care in assigning her to a practicum location.*

A graduate student in psychology at a private Florida university was assigned to an internship (practicum) at a family services agency that was about 15 minutes away from the university's campus. One evening, while leaving the agency, the student was abducted at gunpoint, robbed and sexually assaulted. She sued the university, alleging that it had been aware of a number of criminal incidents that had occurred at or near the agency's parking lot and that it had breached its duty of care to her by assigning her to an unreasonably dangerous internship site. The university sought to dismiss the case, arguing that it did not owe the student a duty of care because it did not own, operate or control the parking lot where the abduction had taken place. A trial court agreed.

The case reached the Florida Supreme Court. It noted that **because the university required the student to take the internship, and because it assigned her to a specific location, it also assumed the duty of acting reasonably in making that assignment.** Since the university had knowledge that the internship location was unreasonably dangerous, a jury would now have to decide whether the university acted reasonably in placing the student there. The jury also would have to consider the student's knowledge that the internship site was unreasonably dangerous, and assess fault accordingly. *Nova Southeastern Univ. v. Gross*, 758 So.2d 86 (Fla. 2000).

B. Premises Liability

◆ *A woman who fell on a college campus could not recover damages because the college did not have notice of a dangerous condition where she fell.*

The woman was catering an event at the college when she slipped and fell in a restroom. She claimed she did not remember falling, but she said she heard others say the floor was slippery and that there was "something" on it. College employees examined the floor and found the texture of the tile in front of the sink smoother than the rest of the floor. When the woman sued the college in a state court, her expert witness offered the opinion that the college had maintained a hazardous condition due to the presence of glassware polish on the tile floor. The court entered an order that barred the woman's expert from testifying about the alleged existence of a foreign substance on the floor, since this was based on speculation. The court then awarded judgment to the college. On appeal, the court explained that **an expert cannot offer a mere conclusion. Instead, the expert must provide the "why and wherefore" of his opinion.** In this case, the conclusion that a foreign substance contributed to the fall was speculation. The lower court permissibly barred the expert from testifying that a foreign substance contributed to a slippery condition, and the college was entitled to judgment. *Byrd v. Salem Community College*, L-172-06, 2009 WL 2015128 (N.J. Super. Ct. App. Div. 7/14/09).

◆   *Morehead State University was not liable for injuries sustained by a blind student who slipped and fell on candy on the floor of an on-campus restroom.*

Four witnesses testified that pieces of candy the size of marbles were "strewn everywhere" on the restroom floor after the student fell. There was no evidence indicating how the candy got on the floor. A cleaning staff of 63 employees was responsible for maintaining 44 campus buildings. The building where the fall took place was cleaned twice a day. A maintenance worker testified that the bathroom where the fall took place was inspected and cleaned before the accident. A hearing officer dismissed the case, and appeal reached the Court of Appeals of Kentucky. It found substantial evidence supporting the decision for the university. **Evidence showed the restroom was cleaned before and after the fall. There was enough evidence to support a conclusion that the university reasonably maintained the property**, justifying a decision for the university. *Glass v. Morehead State Univ.*, No. 2008-CA-001018-MR, 2009 WL 2192739 (Ky. Ct. App. 7/24/09).

◆   *A fraternity could not be held liable for the death of a drunken student who trespassed on its property at Cornell University.*

While looking for a party, the student and his friend parked their car in a fire lane within the private driveway of a fraternity house. There was no party at the house, and a fraternity member questioned the pair. They did not respond and began walking to the rear of the house, where a five-foot-high fence and foliage protected pedestrians from a deep gorge. The student made it beyond the fence and through the foliage and then fell 80 feet to his death. His parents sued the fraternity in a state court, claiming it negligently maintained its premises.

The court rejected the fraternity's claim that the gorge was an open and obvious hazard and that the fence was a reasonable protective measure. The court denied pretrial judgment to the fraternity, and appeal reached a state appellate division court. It held that judgment should have been awarded to the fraternity because it was not foreseeable that a drunken student would trespass onto its property, go over the fence, and fall into the gorge. A property owner's duty to maintain property in a reasonably safe condition is determined by the foreseeability of harm. **When an injured party's presence on property is not reasonably foreseeable, the property owner cannot be held liable for injury.** In this case, there was nothing to indicate that visitors, guests or others were reasonably foreseeable users of the area where the death occurred. *Elwood v. Alpha Sigma Phi, Iota Chapter of Alpha Sigma Phi Fraternity*, 62 A.D.3d 1074, 878 N.Y.S.2d 499 (N.Y. App. Div. 2009).

◆   *A Delaware college was not liable for injuries to a student who fell while stepping off a sidewalk, since it did not cause a defective condition.*

The student tripped on uneven pavement near the college campus and hurt himself. At the time, a construction company was working on the road and the abutting sidewalks and curbing. The student sued the college and construction company in a state court for negligence. He claimed the college knew or should have known that the pavement was unsafe. The court granted the college's motion for pretrial judgment. **Under state law, abutting landowners are liable for injuries caused by a defective sidewalk only if they cause the defect or have a statutory duty to repair it.** In this case, there was no evidence that any state law or local ordinance made the college responsible for maintaining the sidewalk. Instead, evidence showed the city was responsible to maintain the sidewalk. There was no evidence that the college caused the defect that led to injury. *Lawson v. Wilmington College of Delaware*, No. 07C-07-027 JTV, 2009 WL 27301 (Del. Super. Ct. 1/5/09).

◆   *A Tennessee university could be liable for injuries contractors sustained while performing repairs on the school's premises.*

A maintenance supervisor discovered a malfunctioning switchgear in an electrical equipment cabinet and called in outside help when he discovered unusually high voltage was present. He told the contractor's service manager that high voltage was present but did not relay this information to the two contractors who arrived to fix the problem. The two men began to work on the equipment and were injured when a high-voltage arc of electricity generated a flash of light and ball of fire. Both men sued the university in the state court system for negligence, claiming it misstated the voltage. They also faulted the university for failing to provide warning signs and failing to maintain its electrical equipment. The case reached the Supreme Court of Tennessee.

The court explained that a premises owner who hires an independent contractor and offers information regarding the repair has a duty to make sure the information is accurate. If the university employees told the contractors that the equipment carried only 480 volts, the university had a duty to make sure that information was correct. The university was also potentially liable to the contractors on a theory of negligent misrepresentation. Under that theory, a person or entity that supplies false information to others with respect to business transactions can be liable for losses suffered as a result of reliance on the information. In this case, a disputed issue remained as to whether university employees supplied false information to the contractors about the voltage in the equipment. It would be improper to award pretrial judgment to the university. The case was remanded for additional proceedings. *Bennett v. Trevecca Nazarene Univ.*, 216 S.W.3d 293 (Tenn. 2007).

◆   *A Texas student could not rely on a university safety manual to prove the university knew about the dangerous condition that caused his fall.*

While walking to a class on campus, the student tripped on a water hose and broke his knee. In his state court negligence lawsuit, the university claimed immunity under the state tort claims act. Under the act, the university was not liable for injuries caused by a premises defect unless it knew about a dangerous condition on its premises and failed to warn others about it. The court rejected the student's claim that a university safety manual, which required walking areas to be kept unobstructed, created a fact issue about whether the university had knowledge of the condition that caused his fall. A trial court agreed and denied the university's motion for summary disposition. The state appeals court affirmed the judgment, but **the Supreme Court of Texas held the manual was not evidence that the university knew about the hazard that caused the fall**. While the manual warned of the danger created when flexible cords were placed across paths of travel, it did so while discussing indoor safety. Nothing in the manual suggested that the hose created an unreasonable risk of harm. As a result, the lower court decisions were reversed, and the case was dismissed. *Univ. of Texas-Pan American v. Aquilar*, 251 S.W.3d 511 (Tex. 2008).

◆ *A Utah student failed to produce expert testimony showing her fall was caused by defective stairs, defeating her negligence action.*

The student and her husband sued the university for negligence and loss of consortium, saying the student's fall was caused by a failure to maintain the stairs. They did not present any expert testimony and relied primarily on the student's account. A state trial court held an affidavit and report from a university emergency response team were admissible under state rules of evidence. It also held expert testimony was needed to prove causation. The Court of Appeals of Utah said the state rules of evidence took precedence in this case. The reviewing court also affirmed the finding that expert testimony was needed to show a causal link between the allegedly defective stairs and the injury. Only in "the most obvious cases" are plaintiffs excused from proving causation via expert testimony. **Without the benefit of expert testimony, a fact-finder would need to resort to speculation regarding what really caused the injury.** The trial court's decision for the university was affirmed. *Fox v. Brigham Young Univ.*, 176 P.3d 446 (Utah Ct. App. 2007).

◆ *A Texas man who fell while trying to enter a building at Southern Methodist University (SMU) could not pursue claims for his injuries.*

The man played cello for the Dallas Chamber Orchestra, which occasionally rehearsed at the building where he was injured. When he arrived on campus, he chose to try to carry his cello up some steps into the building instead of using an available ramp. He tripped and fell as he climbed the stairs, injuring his fingers. The man sued the university to recover for his injuries, claiming the stairs were too steep. The case reached the Court of Appeals of Texas, which affirmed the judgment for SMU. The duty owed by SMU to the man depended on whether he was an invitee or a licensee. **An "invitee" is invited onto premises and is owed a higher duty of care than a "licensee," who enters the premises by permission, not invitation.** The man was not an invitee because he did not enter the premises at the university's invitation. Instead, he was a licensee on the day he was hurt, meaning SMU owed him only a slight duty of care. SMU did not breach this duty, as the man was aware of the condition of the stairs. Therefore, he could not recover for his injuries. *Osadchy v. Southern Methodist Univ.*, 232 S.W.3d 844 (Tex. Ct. App. 2007).

◆ *An Indiana college did not owe the parent of a student any duty to exercise reasonable care because he was not an "invitee" under state law.*

The parent slipped on some loose gravel on a campus walkway while walking toward a restroom. He severely injured his left arm and sued the college for negligence. A state court held for the college. On appeal, the Court of Appeals of Indiana explained that a landowner's duty in negligence cases depends on the legal status of the visitor. The duty owed varies depending on whether the visitor is an invitee, a licensee or a trespasser. The highest duty of care is owed to invitees, who are owed a duty of reasonable care. Licensees are those who enter premises for their "own convenience, curiosity or entertainment." The duty owed to licensees is the duty not to "willfully or wantonly" injure them or to "increase [their] peril." The law offers the least protection to trespassers. The court held that under the circumstances, "no reasonable person could conclude Ivy Tech extended an invitation" to the parent to use its public restrooms. **As a licensee, the parent needed to prove the college willfully or wantonly injured him or increased his peril.** However, he did not even allege that the college did so. Because the parent was aware of the loose gravel and it was not a latent danger, the judgment was affirmed. *Gilpin v. Ivy Tech State College*, 864 N.E.2d 399 (Ind. Ct. App. 2007).

◆ *The U.S. Court of Appeals, Second Circuit, held a college was not liable for a student's attack in her dorm.*

A student attended a college in New York. She was assaulted at knifepoint in her dorm room by an attacker who was wearing a mask. The student had left the door to her room slightly ajar. At the time of the attack, the college had a security policy that required all outer doors to its residential halls be locked 24 hours a day. The policy also required visitors to register in the lobby. Despite the policies, students held and propped open doors so people could enter without registering. The student sued the college in a federal district court for negligence. The court dismissed the complaint, and the student appealed.

The U.S. Court of Appeals, Second Circuit, disagreed with the district court's conclusion that the attack was unforeseeable because of the low history of on-campus crime. In each of the previous five years, there had been significant events and a security reporting firm reported there were other assaults on campus that were not documented. The district court's analysis of foreseeability was flawed because it assumed that only actual prior crimes could put the college on notice of the risk of future crimes. A jury could reasonably find suggestions by a security company hired by the college were enough to alert the school to the possibility that intruders might commit a crime. **While the court found the attack was foreseeable, the student failed to establish a causal connection between negligence by the college and her attack.** Because the attacker was never caught or identified, the student did not show the university caused her attacker to gain access to the building. While New York law did not require her to identify her assailant, she had to provide some evidence that her attacker was an intruder, and she failed to do so. The judgment was affirmed. *Williams v. Utica College of Syracuse Univ.*, 453 F.3d 112 (2d Cir. 2006).

◆   *The Court of Appeals of Mississippi held a university was not liable for a visitor's shooting of a student on campus.*

A Mississippi state university had welcome centers located at the main and rear entrances to the campus. During the hours the centers were open, a member of the campus police department was stationed at each center and was to log in each non-student visitor who entered the campus. The police officers were allowed to suspend the log-in process during public events. One evening, three non-students entered the campus in a car. They were not asked to log in. The non-students rode around the campus, threw beer bottles at students and became involved in a number of fights. One of the non-students drew a gun and shot into a crowd that had gathered to watch the fighting. A bullet hit a student and he underwent surgery to remove it.

The student sued the university in a Mississippi trial court for negligence. The court held the student could not prove a connection between the reckless disregard by the police officers and the student getting shot. He appealed to the Court of Appeals of Mississippi, contending that had the police conducted log-in procedures, they would have become suspicious and would not have admitted the non-students. The court disagreed. It emphasized that because the log-in procedure did not require a search for weapons, the outcome would have been the same. **The court agreed with the trial court that the student failed to prove a causal connection between the police officers' conduct and his injuries.** It affirmed the judgment. *Johnson v. Alcorn State Univ.*, 929 So.2d 398 (Miss. Ct. App. 2006).

◆   *A Maryland university was not negligent when it assigned a student to live with a roommate who had a prior record of fighting.*

The student was in the process of moving out of the room when the roommate accused him of breaking a fish tank. The roommate hit the student in the jaw, requiring him to undergo surgery and have his mouth wired shut. The student sued the university for negligence in a state trial court. The case went before a jury. The student presented evidence of the roommate's disciplinary history at the university. He had been involved in fights with other students. The university had suspended the roommate and allowed him to return only after he completed a conflict resolution counseling program.

The Court of Special Appeals of Maryland held the university and student had a landlord-tenant relationship. As a landlord, the university had to take reasonable security measures to eliminate foreseeable harm. **The university could not have foreseen the incident based on the roommate's prior fights with other students. No previous fights had taken place in a dormitory, nor were there weapons incidents or criminal charges.** The university did not breach its duty to protect the student from injury. On further appeal, the Court of Appeals of Maryland held the university could not have reasonably foreseen what happened. The roommate had no history of violence under similar circumstances. Even the student did not believe the roommate was dangerous. He knew about the roommate's prior incidents and did not ask for a new room or roommate. The judgment for the university was affirmed. *Rhaney v. Univ. of Maryland Eastern Shore*, 388 Md. 585, 880 A.2d 357 (Md. 2005).

◆   *The Court of Appeals of Georgia held a college could not be held liable for*
the abduction of a student from a campus parking lot.

The student had parked her car in a campus parking lot. When she returned
to her car the next afternoon, an assailant reached into the window and punched
her several times in the face. He then forced his way in, drove to another area
and raped the student. She escaped when the car stopped at a red light. The
student later sued the college in a state court for negligence. The court denied
her motion for pretrial judgment, and she appealed to the court of appeals.

A college is generally not liable for the criminal acts of a third party
unless it could have reasonably foreseen such an act. The assault would be
considered foreseeable if it was substantially similar to previous criminal
activities that occurred on or near the premises, and a reasonable person would
have taken ordinary precautions to protect persons from the risk. Courts review
the location, nature and extent of prior criminal activities and their likeness,
proximity or other relationship to the crime in question. The previous activity
must have attracted the college's attention to a dangerous condition. The court
found no evidence of similar occurrences in the campus parking lot. The
college could not have foreseen the attack. The lot was a common area used by
many students, and a confrontation with an attacker could be very brief. The
court affirmed the judgment for the college. *Agnes Scott College v. Clark*, 273
Ga.App. 619, 616 S.E.2d 468 (Ga. Ct. App. 2005).

C. Defenses

1. Immunity

State laws preclude liability in many tort cases against public institutions.
Such laws confer immunity on public entities unless they cause injury through
conduct that is willful, wanton or grossly negligent.

◆   *A spectator who slipped and fell in front of a stadium at the University of*
Texas could not recover damages for her injuries.

The spectator was hurt when she slipped and fell on a removable drainage
trench cover. The metal cover was slippery at the time of the fall because of
rain. The spectator sued the university in a state court, claiming the trench cover
was a premises defect. Under the tort claims act, state entities are immune from
claims based on discretionary decisions. Despite an engineer's statement that
the metal cover was used as the result of a discretionary design decision, the
court refused to dismiss the case. The Court of Appeals of Texas held that the
university had immunity if incorporating the cover into the sidewalk was a
discretionary act. **A "discretionary act" requires the exercise of judgment**
and occurs when "the law does not mandate performing the act with such
precision that nothing is left to discretion or judgment." The engineer's
statement established that the decision to place the cover in the sidewalk was
discretionary. As a result, the university had state tort act immunity from the
lawsuit. *Univ. of Texas v. Amezquita*, No. 03-06-00606-CV, 2009 WL 1563533
(Tex. Ct. App. 6/4/09).

◆   *A personal injury action by the grandparent of a University of Michigan (UM) student was barred by state law immunity.*

The grandparent fell from a chair tethered to a riser in a UM auditorium after she watched a student performance. She sued the university in a state court, claiming the riser should have had guard rails to help prevent patrons from falling. The court noted **the state governmental immunity law provides a broad grant of immunity from tort liability to government agencies when they perform governmental functions**. The court found a public building exception barred UM's claim to immunity. On appeal, the Court of Appeals of Michigan explained that the public building exception does not allow claims based on design defects. In this case, the grandparent claimed her injuries were caused by design defects. Therefore, the public building exception did not apply, and immunity barred her claims. *Hetherington v. Univ. of Michigan Regents*, No. 07-000036-MZ, 2009 WL 692444 (Mich. Ct. App. 3/17/09).

◆   *A woman who was injured when she fell down a flight of stairs at Texas Southern University (TSU) could proceed with her lawsuit.*

The woman fell down stairs in an area where a work order had recently been issued to repair a loose handrail. A supervisor had signed off on the work order. The woman sued TSU in a state court for negligence. TSU responded by claiming state law immunity, but the court denied pretrial dismissal. TSU appealed to the Court of Appeals of Texas. It explained that state agencies such as TSU were immune from suit unless immunity was waived. An exception to immunity exists when a condition of personal or real property causes personal injury or an injury is caused by a premises defect. **To prove liability on a premises defect theory, the woman had to show TSU would be liable under the circumstances if it were a private person.** According to the court, she met this requirement by producing evidence that work orders were created for the handrail and that repairs were made to it. Since there was enough evidence to go forward with the claims, the judgment was affirmed. *Texas Southern Univ. v. Gilford*, 277 S.W.3d 65 (Tex. Ct. App. 2009).

◆   *Texas A&M officials could be sued for a 1999 bonfire collapse that killed 12 students and injured 27 others. The claims were not barred by immunity.*

In one of several lawsuits resulting from the tragic bonfire incident, a state court denied the officials' motion for pretrial dismissal. On appeal, the Court of Appeals of Texas explained that an action against a government employee in his or her official capacity is a suit against the government. On the other hand, an action against a government employee in his or her individual capacity seeks to impose personal liability. **Sovereign immunity applies only to claims against officials who are sued in their official capacities.** A&M officials claimed they were being sued in their official capacities because the acts that formed the basis for their claims were taken while they were acting within the course and scope of their employment. The court agreed with the plaintiffs, noting they had filed their claims against the officials in their individual capacities. The judgment for the officials was thus reversed. *Bowen v. Comstock*, No. 10-05-00295-CV, 2008 WL 2209722 (Tex. Ct. App. 5/28/08).

◆ *Immunity barred a claim by a Michigan community college student who tripped and fell over an electrical floor socket in a campus lab.*

In a state court lawsuit against the community college, the student asserted negligent maintenance of a dangerous and defective condition, failure to keep the floor free of improperly raised, protruding floor-mounted electrical boxes, and creation of a dangerous condition by failing to properly repair and/or maintain the premises. Under Michigan law, community colleges and other government entities are immune to such claims unless an exception applies. A state court held the public building exception applied since there was a claim based on a failure to properly repair or maintain public buildings. After the court denied the college's motion for summary disposition, appeal reached the Court of Appeals of Michigan. It reversed the judgment, finding that in reality, **the student was asserting a design defect claim**. Public building exception language relating to "dangerous or defective conditions" did not remove the requirement for claims to allege failure to repair and maintain premises. As a design defect was alleged, the court reversed the judgment. *Collins v. Oakland County Community*, No. 282351, 2009 WL 794686 (Mich. Ct. App. 3/26/09).

◆ *Eleventh Amendment immunity defeated a former student's claim that a community college violated the Constitution by dismissing her from campus.*

Students complained to a lab facilitator about a "chemical smell" surrounding the student caused by a hair product. She later argued with the lab instructor about closing a door, and he asked her to leave. When she refused, the instructor called campus security to escort her out. After a third incident of disruption, the college barred the student from campus. She sued the college in a federal district court, claiming the removal from campus violated her First and Fourteenth Amendment rights. The court held **the college was entitled to Eleventh Amendment immunity, as it was an entity that was an "arm of the state."** *Davis v. Cent. Piedmont Community College*, No. 3:07-cv-424-RJC, 2008 WL 5120616 (W.D.N.C. 12/4/08).

◆ *A Texas recreational use statute barred claims by a bicyclist who was injured while riding on a university campus.*

Water from an oscillating sprinkler knocked the bicyclist to the ground, injuring her. She sued the university in state court for gross negligence. The university claimed immunity under the state tort claims act, which applied to claims arising out of discretionary decisions. It also asserted the claim was barred by the state recreational use statute. The court denied the university's motion to dismiss the case, and the university appealed. The Supreme Court of Texas held the state tort claims act did not bar the claim, as it was based on the university's implementation of a policy decision to irrigate its campus. However, **the claim was barred by the state's recreational use statute**. That law limited the liability of landowners who open their property to recreational use by immunizing them from claims unless there was gross negligence or intent to cause injury. As the bicyclist could not show the university intended to injure her or was grossly negligent, the lower court's ruling was reversed. *Stephen F. Austin State Univ. v. Flynn*, 228 S.W.3d 653 (Tex. 2007).

◆   *A Michigan university had immunity from liability for injuries to a high school student who fell and was injured at a university football stadium.*

The student participated in a band camp sponsored by her high school that was held on the campus of Central Michigan University (CMU). While watching a band performance at CMU's football stadium, she left her seat to use a restroom. She tripped and fell while walking up some steps, injuring her hand and wrist. The student sued CMU for negligence in a state court. The court held for CMU, finding it had government immunity under state law. On appeal, the state appeals court agreed that the university was immune and that no statutory exception applied. An exception requiring government agencies to repair and maintain public buildings did not apply. The band camp was not open to the public, so the stadium was not a "building" under the law. A proprietary function exception to immunity was also inapplicable, as there was no government activity designed to produce a profit in this case. CMU merely allowed the high school to use its facilities, and fees it charged the high school covered costs only. **Since neither exception applied, the university was immune to the student's suit, and the judgment was affirmed.** *Williams v. Cent. Michigan Univ.*, No. 276445, 2008 WL 942268 (Mich. Ct. App. 4/8/08).

◆   *An immunity provision barred a personal injury action by a student who slipped and fell on a wet floor during a lifeguard training class.*

A University of Kansas (KU) student hurt her elbow and side when she fell on a wet floor in a health and education center. She sued KU and its Board of Regents for negligence in state court, seeking damages for medical expenses and pain and suffering. The board claimed immunity under a state recreational use exception to liability. The student argued that the exception did not apply because the health and education center was used primarily for the education of university students and only incidentally for public recreation.

The court held for the board. On review, the Court of Appeals of Kansas explained that the recreational use exception applied as long as the facility was intended or permitted to be used for recreational purposes. **The test for application of the exception was "whether the property has been used for recreational purposes in the past or whether recreation has been encouraged."** The exception could apply even if the injury did not result from purely recreational use of the facility. The court noted that the center was owned and operated by the university and located on its campus. Although students and faculty used the facility, it could also be rented out by general public groups. Under these circumstances, it was clear that the board intended and actually permitted the facility to be used for recreational purposes. As a result, the exception applied and the board was not held liable. *Marks v. Kansas Board of Regents*, 157 P.3d 1129 (Kan. Ct. App. 2007).

◆   *A Kentucky university was immune to a claim of negligence in the case of a student who was assaulted, raped and set on fire in her dormitory room.*

Three days after being brutally attacked in her dorm room at Western Kentucky University, the student died from her injuries. Two men who were not residents of the dorm were later charged in the case. The administrators of the student's estate filed negligence claims in a suit against the university in state court. The court dismissed the case, and the state appeals court affirmed the judgment. The case reached the Supreme Court of Kentucky.

The court explained that governmental immunity extends to state agencies that perform governmental functions. At the same time, immunity does not extend to state agencies that are not created to perform a governmental function. Officials of state agencies can also be entitled to immunity if the agency itself is immune to suit. When sued in their official capacities, these officials enjoy the same immunity as the state agency. The university operated the dorm as part of its statutory duty to provide college instruction, and therefore it was not performing a proprietary function. **As the dormitory operation was a discretionary function, the university was entitled to immunity.** Because the claims against the university were barred by immunity, the claims against the officials in their official capacities were also barred. *Autry v. Western Kentucky Univ.*, 219 S.W.3d 713 (Ky. 2007).

◆ *A Kansas state university was immune from liability in a case filed by a student who slipped and fell on an icy crosswalk.*

The student stated it was snowing lightly at the time of her fall. She testified that snow that had fallen earlier had been pushed off the crosswalk. She thought the snow had probably refrozen to form ice. The university had 13 landscaping employees responsible for snow removal. Most of them started work at 6:30 a.m. and were instructed to begin their shifts by walking the campus in search of any hazardous conditions needing immediate attention. Employees were to sprinkle ice melting compound on hazardous spots, remove the ice, or report the problem to a manager.

The student stated the employees negligently failed to inspect and treat the crosswalk on the morning she fell, and sued the university in a state court. The court granted summary judgment to the university, finding it was immune from liability under the Kansas Torts Claims Act. The student appealed to the Court of Appeals of Kansas. **The court agreed with the university that the only exception to state immunity is injury caused by an employee's affirmative act. By contrast, an employee's failure to act has no bearing on liability.** As the student did not allege any affirmative act by a university employee, the court held the university was immune from liability under the act and affirmed the judgment. *Owoyemi v. Univ. of Kansas*, 91 P.3d 552 (Kan. Ct. App. 2004).

◆ *A state university could not be held liable for a resident advisor's murder at the hands of a student.*

A graduate student at Purdue University worked as a resident advisor (RA) and reported to campus police that a student had marijuana in his dorm room. He later discovered that the student's roommate had cocaine on him and reported that to the police as well, despite a death threat from the roommate. Later, the roommate shot the RA, then killed himself. The RA's estate sued the university, the campus police and various officials for wrongful death, asserting violations of 42 U.S.C. § 1983. A trial court dismissed the action, but the Indiana Court of Appeals reversed in part. Although **the university and the campus police were "arms of the state" under Section 1983 and thus immune from liability under the Eleventh Amendment**, the university officials and individual police officers were "persons" under Section 1983 and could be sued. The court also noted that the state never assumed a duty to protect the RA, and it did not have a "special relationship" with him such that a duty to protect could be inferred. The court remanded the case for further proceedings against the individual defendants. *Severson v. Board of Trustees of Purdue Univ.*, 777 N.E.2d 1181 (Ind. Ct. App. 2002).

◆ *A New Jersey state university was entitled to charitable immunity.*

A student at Montclair State University fell down an amphitheater staircase on campus, fracturing his ribs and elbow. He spent several days in the hospital and sued the university for damages. The university asserted that it was immune under the New Jersey Charitable Immunity Act, and a trial court agreed. Because the student was a "beneficiary" under the act, the university was entitled to charitable immunity. The appellate division court reversed that decision, but the New Jersey Supreme Court reinstated the trial court's ruling. Here, the university was formed for a nonprofit purpose; it was organized for educational purposes; and it was promoting those goals at the time the student (beneficiary) was injured. **Nothing in the act required that an entity be a private nonprofit institution in order to qualify for charitable immunity.** As a result, the public university was entitled to have the lawsuit against it dismissed. *O'Connell v. State of New Jersey*, 795 A.2d 857 (N.J. 2002).

◆ *Two students who were injured while traveling to another college to play a soccer game could not sue their college because of state law immunity.*

Two members of a community college soccer team were injured when the van they were riding in was involved in a highway accident. While traveling to another college for a soccer match in a van owned by the community college and driven by an assistant coach, the van blew a tire. The coach lost control of the vehicle, causing it to travel across two lanes of oncoming traffic and to flip several times. The players sued the college and the coach to recover for their injuries. The college claimed it could not be sued, citing a California statute that granted immunity to colleges for field trips or excursions in connection with school-related social, educational, cultural, athletic or college band activities to and from places. The statute provided that **persons taking such field trips or excursions are deemed to have waived all claims against the college or the state for any injuries that might result**. The California Court of Appeal affirmed the trial court's grant of pretrial judgment in favor of the college. Since extracurricular sports programs are "school-related athletic activities," the trip to the other college was covered by the immunity statute, and the students' lawsuit could not succeed. *Barnhart v. Cabrillo Community College*, 90 Cal.Rptr.2d 709 (Cal. Ct. App. 1999).

2. Assumption of Risk

Assumption of risk is an affirmative defense to negligence. If the defense is proven, the claimant cannot recover on a negligence claim. To prove the defense, a university or college must show the claimant had knowledge of the risk, appreciated the risk, and voluntarily confronted it. Because the risk of injury is inherent and obvious in many sports, assumption of risk often bars recovery in negligence actions brought by student-athletes. Institutions may further limit their liability in this area by requiring students to sign waivers and releases prior to engaging in hazardous activities.

◆ *A New York appeals court allowed a student to proceed with a claim that his college was liable for his hand injury at the college fitness center.*

The student was hurt when 140 pounds on a jammed weight machine suddenly dislodged and fell onto his hand. He sued the college in the state court system. The college argued it could not be held liable because it did not have notice of any dangerous condition. But a college custodian admitted that jamming had been a recurring problem with the machine, which had been repaired several times. The court denied the college's request for pretrial judgment. On appeal, a state appellate division court found evidence that the college was on notice that the machine created a danger. There were relevant factual issues regarding whether an accessory weight was being used at the time of injury. There was a possibility that use of the accessory weight caused the jam that led to injury. **There would have to be further consideration of the college's claim that the student ignored a warning label on the machine by placing his hand underneath the weights.** This created the possibility that comparative fault principles applied. Since further consideration of the facts was warranted, the trial court's decision was affirmed. *Beglin v. Hartwick College*, 67 A.D.3d 1172, 888 N.Y.S.2d 320 (N.Y. App. Div. 2009).

◆ *An ice skater's claim that the University of Delaware failed to properly supervise skaters at its rink was not barred by the assumption of risk doctrine.*

After she began skating, the skater noticed others were frequently going in the wrong direction and "running into people." About an hour later, she saw a child skating toward her at a high rate of speed. While trying to avoid him, the skater fell and was seriously injured. She later sued the university in a state court for negligently failing to supervise skaters, allowing an unsafe condition, and failing to adequately warn or protect her against a dangerous condition.

The university sought pretrial judgment, arguing that the claims were barred because the skater assumed the risk of skating. The skater argued that the assumption-of-risk doctrine did not bar her claims because the risk of a dangerous, erratic skater is not a risk that is normally associated with a public skating session. The court explained that in Delaware, primary assumption of risk applies when an individual expressly consents to relieve the defendant of an obligation and to take the chance of being injured as a result of a known risk. Secondary assumption of risk applies when a person voluntarily encounters a known and unreasonable risk. **The court held that the primary assumption-of-risk doctrine did not apply because the skater never relieved the university of its duty to reasonably supervise the premises.** The university did not show she assumed the risk of reckless conduct by other skaters. Further consideration was required to determine whether the university could have prevented the fall. *Farrell v. Univ. of Delaware*, No. 07C-09-175 PLA, 2009 WL 3309288 (Del. Super. Ct. 10/8/09).

◆   *A Georgia student who ran across a street to join a fight voluntarily assumed a risk of injury.*

A Morris Brown College student was killed after being struck on the head with a glass bottle during a fight. His parents sued the college in the state court system for wrongful death. The trial court denied judgment to the college. On appeal, the Court of Appeals of Georgia explained that **adults of ordinary intelligence are deemed to be aware that they risk injury to themselves when they voluntarily join a fight**. Even when a person enters an altercation with the intention of breaking it up, he is responsible for any injury he suffers. In this case, the student ran across a street to voluntarily join a fight that had already begun. Under a state law doctrine known as "the rescue doctrine," individuals may recover for their injuries even though they assumed a risk of harm – but only if the injured party was acting to rescue someone from harm and the rescue was made necessary by another party's negligence. The court held that the rescue doctrine did not apply in this case, because the student chose to interject himself into the fight. As he assumed the risk of injury, the judgment against the college was reversed. *Cornelius v. Morris Brown College*, 299 Ga.App. 83, 681 S.E.2d 730 (Ga. Ct. App. 2009).

◆   *A federal district court rejected a college's bid to dismiss a claim filed against it by a student who was severely injured by a saw.*

While using a compound meter saw at the college, the student's shirt sleeve was pulled into the machine and his arm was partially amputated. Instructions from the manufacturer advised users not to operate the saw while wearing long sleeves, but the student did not read them. He sued the college in a federal district court, claiming it negligently failed to train and supervise his use of the saw. After the college joined the manufacturer and a retailer of the saw as parties, all sides filed motions for pretrial judgment. The court held that the student did not show the saw's warning label proximately caused his injury. **Failure to provide adequate warnings cannot be said to cause an injury if the injured party admits he knew of the risks that caused injury.** Since the student admitted he knew of the risks associated with placing his hand in the path of a moving saw blade, he could not show the absence of any particular warning caused his injury. However, the court denied the college judgment regarding its claim that it lacked a duty to play the role of parent to its students. Even accepting that argument, the court held the college had potential liability under ordinary negligence principles. Because factual issues existed on the question of negligence, the college's motion was denied. Factual issues were present as to whether the student was negligent in operating the saw. The court found that the assumption of risk doctrine did not apply because it was not beyond question that he had "voluntarily and knowingly proceeded in the face of an open and obvious danger." *Hawkins v. Waynesburg College*, No. 07-5, 2008 WL 2952888 (W.D. Pa. 7/30/08).

◆   *The parent of a Maryland student was unable to pursue a negligence case because she assumed the risk of injury by trying to cross an icy parking lot.*

The parent drove to the university to deliver gas money and other supplies to her daughter after about 22 inches of snow had fallen in the vicinity. As soon as she drove into the parking lot near her daughter's dormitory, she noticed it had not been cleared of ice and snow. Although the parent made it to her daughter's room safely, she fell and broke her leg in the icy lot while returning to her car. She sued the university in state court for negligent failure to clear the lot of snow and ice. She also claimed negligent hiring, training and supervision based on the failure of university employees to clear the lot in a timely manner. A Maryland trial court held the parent voluntarily assumed the risk of injury by walking on the snow and ice. The state court of special appeals reversed the decision, finding that a jury should decide whether to bar her negligence claim.

On appeal, the Court of Appeals of Maryland held the parent had voluntarily assumed the risk of injury when she chose to cross the icy lot. She could have found another way to get the money to her daughter. There was no evidence that the parent was forced to confront the danger of walking on ice and snow against her will. She understood she was taking a chance when she chose to cross the lot. **It was clear that a person of normal intelligence would have understood the risk presented. In assumption of risk cases, the claimant relieves the defendant of its duty of care by voluntarily choosing to encounter a known risk.** For that reason, the university's failure to clear the lot was irrelevant. The decision against the university was reversed. *Morgan State Univ. v. Walker*, 397 Md. 509, 919 A.2d 21 (Md. 2007).

◆ *A New York community college student who broke her leg during a backpacking class may have assumed the risk of an activity that injured her.*

The student's instructor required students to go over a rope tied to two folding chairs without touching it. The student was unable to do so and told her teammates to continue the activity without her. The instructor encouraged her to try doing it again with assistance, but she fell when doing so. The student sued the county for personal injury in the state court system. The county claimed she could not recover because she assumed the risk of attempting the move suggested by the course instructor. The court denied the motion, and the county appealed to a state appellate division court. **Under the legal doctrine of assumption of risk, a "voluntary participant is deemed to have consented to apparent or reasonably foreseeable consequences of engaging in the sport."** A question of fact existed as to whether the student had voluntarily assumed the risk of engaging in the maneuver that caused her fall. The trial court correctly denied the county pretrial judgment. *Calouri v. County of Suffolk*, 43 A.D.3d 456, 841 N.Y.S.2d 598 (N.Y. App. Div. 2007).

◆ *A California college was not liable to a student injured during a peace officer training class where he practiced arrest and control techniques.*

The student attended a class called "Arrest Communications and Firearms," which satisfied requirements prescribed by the state Commission on Peace Officer Standards and Training. Students performed techniques and maneuvers for controlling suspects by role-playing in teams of two. One student played the role of an officer and the other played a suspect. Three police officers taught the class. One of the officers demonstrated four maneuvers the students were to carry out. An officer saw the student perform each maneuver at least once. The student was injured when his partner pulled him down. He hit his neck on the partner's knee, causing a herniated cervical disc. The student sued the college in a state court for negligence. The court held for the college and the student appealed to the Court of Appeal of California.

The court discussed the doctrine of primary assumption of risk, which applies to activities or sports where "conditions or conduct that otherwise might be viewed as dangerous often are an integral part of the sport itself." Skiing is an example of such a sport. Careless conduct by others could also be an inherent risk in a specific sport or activity. The court explained that **during dangerous activities, the integral conditions of the sport or the inherent risks of careless conduct by others render the possibility of injury obvious and negate the duty of care usually owed for those particular risks**. The takeover maneuvers in the student's class bore a similar risk of injury inherent in many sports. The court found careless conduct by others was an inherent risk. Imposing a duty to eliminate the risk of injury from the activity in this situation would chill vigorous participation in learning the maneuvers. Because of the nature of the classroom activity and the lack of evidence that the college acted recklessly, the court held the action was barred by the doctrine of primary assumption of the risk. The judgment for the college was affirmed. *Saville v. Sierra College*, 133 Cal.App.4th 857, 36 Cal.Rptr.3d 515 (Cal. Ct. App. 2005).

◆   *A Rhode Island university was not liable for injuries to a student who fell while walking at night on campus.*

The student lived in a university dormitory. He fell while on an unlighted pathway on an unpaved embankment on the side of a road on campus. The student sued the university in a state trial court for negligence. The case was heard by a jury. It ruled in favor of the university. The student filed a motion for a new trial. After the court denied the motion, he appealed to the Supreme Court of Rhode Island. The student argued the trial court overlooked evidence about defects in the asphalt where he fell. He also claimed the area was commonly used by students. The court held the trial court judge had properly reviewed the evidence and assessed the credibility of the witnesses. The judge had found the student was not credible. The court agreed with the trial court's finding that the student tripped on crumbled asphalt, not a defect in a campus walkway. **The trial court made a well-supported finding that the area of the fall was not an existing pathway and the student could have used an existing route instead of the one he chose.** The judgment for the university was affirmed. *Candido v. Univ. of Rhode Island*, 880 A.2d 853 (R.I. 2005).

◆   *A student's personal injury action was barred because she signed the university's release.*

A student registered for a seven-week basic rock-climbing course at Cornell University. As part of the registration process, she watched a safety video and signed a release, which precluded her from holding the university liable for any injuries caused by use of the climbing wall and for injuries that resulted from her own negligence. She also signed a contract promising not to climb above a yellow "bouldering" line without required safety equipment. On the day of her fall, she was climbing above the yellow "bouldering" line without safety equipment. She lost her footing and fell, then sued the university for her injuries. The university moved to dismiss the matter based on the release. The trial court granted the university's motion, and the New York Supreme Court, Appellate Division, affirmed. **The release language was unambiguous. It pointed out the dangers of rock climbing, and it clearly stated that the university could not be held responsible.** *Lemoine v. Cornell Univ.*, 769 N.Y.S.2d 313 (N.Y. App. Div. 2003).

D. Damages

Damage awards generally reflect the nature of the injury and the conduct of the parties. Compensatory damages compensate an injured party for his or her injuries such as medical expenses or pain and suffering. Punitive damages, on the other hand, are not designed to compensate for loss. Instead, they punish the offending party because of the party's willful and wanton conduct.

◆   *A New York court preserved a $4 million verdict for a student who was injured when she fell into an open manhole on a college campus.*

The student stepped into an open manhole at 1:00 a.m. one morning and hurt her right leg. About three weeks after the fall, she experienced swelling and pain. She eventually was diagnosed with blood clots in both legs. In a state court action for negligence, a jury found negligence by the college had caused the student's injuries. The court substantially reduced a multi-million dollar verdict to reflect future pain and suffering in the amount of $1.5 million and future medical expenses of $3.36 million. The college appealed to a New York Appellate Court, seeking to set aside the verdict for insufficiency of evidence.

The court found enough evidence for a jury to conclude that the fall caused a recurrence of the student's underlying medical condition. The award of $3.36 million for future medical expenses was supported by testimony indicating she would need to take blood-thinning medicine for the rest of her life, at a cost of about $5,000 per month. Since the college did not show these estimates were inaccurate, the award for future medical expenses was upheld. The court also upheld the decision to award $300,000 for past pain and suffering. This figure did not materially deviate from awards in comparable cases. However, the $1.5 million awarded for future pain and suffering was not justified. After the student was released from a hospital, she was able to walk, exercise and go to the gym. **While she endured some long-term limitations and effects from the fall, her injuries were not debilitating, permanent or life-changing, and did not justify an award of $1.5 million.** A new trial on damages for future pain and suffering was required, unless the student agreed to accept only $450,000 for her future pain and suffering. *Nolan v. Union College Trust of Schenectady*, 51 A.D.3d 1253, 858 N.Y.S. 2d 427 (N.Y. App. Div. 2008).

◆   *A Louisiana university was liable for failing to protect patrons from getting hit by foul balls when they entered a baseball park.*

A visitor went to a baseball game held on a university baseball field. She was struck in her right eye by a foul ball near the ticket booth along the third-base side of the field. The visitor suffered a fracture and permanent ocular blindness resulting in permanent 10/200 vision in her right eye. She sued the university in a state trial court for negligence. The court awarded the visitor $485,000, and the university appealed to the Court of Appeal of Louisiana. The court explained that ballpark owners cannot be held responsible for every foul ball in common areas. There are certain areas of a ballpark where protection is required. One such area is the main entrance, where people have to enter to buy a ticket. **The university could have reasonably anticipated there would be foul balls in the main entrance area.** There was sufficient evidence to support the jury's finding that the baseball park presented an unreasonably dangerous condition to those who entered and that the university had notice of the defect. The court affirmed the judgment. *Reider v. Louisiana Board of Trustees for State Colleges and Universities*, 897 So.2d 893 (La. Ct. App. 2005).

◆   *The Court of Appeals of Ohio held a university was liable for injuries to an operations manager of a mobile production unit.*

The manager got hurt when he was on the university's campus setting up for television coverage of a basketball game. He spoke to a university representative, who told him to run cables beside two large air conditioning units. The units were housed inside a dimly lit brick enclosure. Based on what the university representative told him, the manager thought the power was on the other side of the enclosure. He tossed the cable over a wall and over one of the air conditioner units, but it fell short. The manager entered into the darkness, took two steps and fell into a large pit. He injured his head, wrist and elbow. After two surgeries, the manager got a staph infection. He sued the university for negligence in a state trial court. The court found the university had breached its duty of care to the manager and caused his injuries.

The university appealed to the Court of Appeals of Ohio, arguing expert medical testimony was required to establish a connection between the manager's original injuries and the staph infection. The court of appeals disagreed. Expert testimony is needed only where the internal complexities of the body are at issue. The court found the staph infection was not internal or elusive, so the trial court needed to focus only on the location and nature of the infection to determine a connection. A court could sufficiently understand the infection and its connection to the surgery without expert medical testimony. **The court also rejected the university's contention that the operations manager played a part in getting hurt by stepping into the brick enclosure.** It was unclear whether a university representative lulled him into a false sense of safety by directing him to the area without warning him of the danger of the pit. The court affirmed the judgment. *Dixon v. Miami Univ.*, No. 04 AP-1132, 2005 WL 3316963 (Ohio Ct. App. 12/8/05).

◆   *A Vermont university was liable for over $2 million in damages for hazing.*

A five-year veteran of the Navy enrolled in the Military College of Vermont of Norwich University under a Navy Reserve Officer Training Corps scholarship. He lasted for only 16 days, during which he was subjected to, and observed, repeated instances of hazing by upperclassmen. After withdrawing from school, he sued the university for assault and battery, infliction of emotional distress and negligence, asserting that it was vicariously liable for the actions of the upperclassmen. A jury returned a verdict in the student's favor, awarding him almost $500,000 in compensatory damages and $1.75 million in punitive damages. The Supreme Court of Vermont affirmed the compensatory damage award against the university, but reversed the award of punitive damages, finding no evidence of malice on the university's part. Here, **the university had charged the upperclassmen with "indoctrinating and orienting" the student.** As a result, this was not a simple case of student-on-student hazing for which the university could not be held liable. Because the upperclassmen were acting as agents of the university, it breached its duty of care toward the student. The court also found that the nearly $500,000 in compensatory damages awarded by the jury was not clearly erroneous. *Brueckner v. Norwich Univ.*, 730 A.2d 1086 (Vt. 1999).

II. INTENTIONAL CONDUCT

Institutions may be found liable for the intentional acts or omissions of their personnel. Courts have found colleges and universities liable for intentional acts of third parties on or near campuses. In those cases, courts may hold the institution should have foreseen the potential for misconduct.

A. Instructor Misconduct

◆ *A Tennessee court rejected a battery claim filed by a student against her instructor, who forcibly removed her from a nursing class.*

The student learned she would be removed from the program because of a D grade. She said a vice president of student affairs eventually phoned her to say her grade appeal had been granted. Based on this assurance, the student went to class on the first day of the semester. She said that when she got to class, the instructor asked her why she was there and then physically removed her from the room. In a state court lawsuit against the instructor and other university officials, the student asserted claims of battery, conspiracy to commit battery, and intentional infliction of emotional distress. The court dismissed the case, and the student appealed. The Court of Appeals of Tennessee rejected the student's battery claim. **Not every touching without consent amounts to a battery. Certain classes of employees, including police officers and teachers, "are expected to touch people at times in order to direct their movements."** In this case, the alleged touching of the student by the class instructor was not offensive enough to constitute a battery.

The instructor apparently believed the student was not supposed to be in his class. The student did not say she was injured as a result of the contact. Since her conspiracy claim was premised on the meritless battery claim, it failed as well. There was no evidence supporting the student's claim that the instructor had conspired with university administrators to keep her out of the classroom "by any means necessary." An emotional distress claim failed, as it was based on conduct that was not extreme or outrageous. The judgment for the university and officials was affirmed. *Runions v. Tennessee State Univ.*, No. M2008-01574-COA-R3-CV, 2009 WL 1939816 (Tenn. Ct. App. 7/6/09).

◆ *Common lawsuits against university instructors include those claiming intentional infliction of emotional distress, defamation, or sexual misconduct.*

An Arkansas student claimed an anatomy professor performed a breast examination on her in his classroom. At the time, the rest of the class had left the room, and the door was closed. The student said she was "stunned, shocked and scared" when the professor performed the examination. After the student complained to a university official, the professor resigned. She sued him in a federal district court for violating her substantive due process rights. She added a state law claim based on outrage. Applying a "shocks the conscience" standard, the court found the complaint supported a substantive due process claim. The court also refused to dismiss the outrage claim. **To prove this claim, the student needed to show the professor caused her severe emotional distress through extreme and outrageous conduct.** The facts as alleged in her complaint were sufficient to avoid dismissal. Under the circumstances, a factual issue existed as to whether the professor acted with the intent necessary to prove a due process violation or the tort of outrage. The question of his intent was a matter of credibility that was best left for a jury. *Thompson v. Guntharp*, No. 3:07-CV-00010 GTE, 2007 WL 2769597 (E.D. Ark. 9/24/07).

◆ *Yale University defeated a student's claim that her drama instructor's vulgar behavior intentionally inflicted emotional distress upon her.*

The student was on stage when her instructor announced he changed the title of a play to "Metamorphosis Revisited Or Rock Out with Your Cock Out." He instructed male actors to simulate masturbation as they stood next to the student. After they carried out the simulation, the instructor called out "that was great!" The student complained to the department chair and questioned the artistic value and justification for the activities. She claimed that the rest of the year, faculty and students subjected her to macho and "frat house" behavior.

The student sued the university in a federal district court for intentional infliction of emotional distress. **The court explained that liability for intentional infliction of emotional distress requires proof of conduct that exceeds "all bounds usually tolerated by decent society." Conduct that is merely insulting or displays bad manners or results in hurt feelings is insufficient to prove intentional infliction of emotional distress.** The court held a reasonable jury could not find the conduct here constituted extreme and outrageous behavior. Connecticut courts have generally held that mere insults or verbal taunts do not rise to the level of extreme and outrageous conduct. While the adaptation of the play may have been tasteless it did not subject the student to conduct that exceeded all bounds tolerated by decent society. The court granted the university's motion for dismissal. *Greenhouse v. Yale Univ.*, No. 3:05 CV1429 (AHN), 2006 WL 473724 (D. Conn. 2/28/06).

B. Employee Misconduct

◆ *The sexual assault of a minor non-student by an Indiana university bus driver was not caused by negligence on the university's part.*

The university did not conduct a criminal history check when it hired the driver. He had been convicted of battery and furnishing alcohol to a minor, but he failed to reveal this information on his job application. On a day when he was not working for the university, the driver asked a minor to accompany him on a trip to a retail store. Using his own truck, the driver took the minor to a campus garage where the buses were parked, then molested him inside a bus.

The minor sued the university board of trustees in a state court for negligence. The court held for the university, and the student appealed. The Court of Appeals of Indiana held that to prevail on his claim of negligent hiring/retention, the minor needed to show the university breached a duty it owed to him. However, as he was not a university student, the university did not owe him a duty to exercise reasonable care in hiring the driver. The minor also failed to show the university owed all members of the public a duty to refrain from hiring individuals with criminal backgrounds. The driver was not acting within the scope of his employment at the time of the attack. **An employer can be liable for the criminal acts of an employee only if there is a sufficient association between the criminal acts and acts the employee is authorized by the employer to take.** The trial court's ruling was affirmed. *J.B. v. Board of Trustees of Vincennes Univ.*, 883 N.E.2d 229 (Ind. Ct. App. 2008).

◆ *A discharged female employee could not proceed with a claim of intentional infliction of emotional distress against university officials.*

The employee discovered a male university employee was earning nearly $10,000 more annually than she was for doing essentially the same job. She filed administrative claims of discrimination against the university, then sued the university, supervisors and a human resources representative in a federal district court. The employee claimed violations of the Equal Pay Act, the Fair Labor Standards Act, Title VII, and the state fair employment practices act. She added a state law claim for intentional infliction of emotional distress, saying supervisors continuously harassed her for filing the administrative complaint.

The employee claimed supervisors denied her access to files she needed to do her job and took away significant job responsibilities. She said they had a "shadow" follow her around at work and subjected her to discipline without cause. According to the employee, these actions caused her to suffer from sleeplessness and anxiety. **The court held that to prevail on an emotional distress claim, the employee had to show conduct that was extreme and outrageous, and that it caused her to suffer severe emotional distress.** The court rejected the claim, because she did not show the conduct was extreme or outrageous. The employee's allegations did not indicate conduct that "transcended the bounds of civilized society," and she did not allege she was subjected to any public ridicule or humiliation. In short, she did not allege facts sufficient to support her claim of intentional infliction of emotional distress. The motion to dismiss the claim was granted. *Jamilik v. Yale Univ.*, No. 3:06 CV 0566 (PCD), 2007 WL 214607 (D. Conn. 1/25/07).

◆ *A university instructor's physical assault of a student did not result in school liability because the assault was not in furtherance of the school's business and therefore fell outside the scope of employment.*

A student at a New York university enrolled in a noncredit karate course offered during the summer session. The class was held in the school's physical education building. According to the student, he was told by the instructor to do a reverse push-up. After he refused, believing that it was unsafe, the instructor struck him several times. He was taken to the hospital and later sued the school in the Court of Claims for his injuries. The school asserted that it should not be held vicariously liable for the student's injuries because the instructor was not an employee but an independent contractor.

The court noted that although there was an issue as to whether students could reasonably believe that the instructors of the noncredit courses were employees of the school, it did not need to resolve this issue since the karate instructor's conduct was outside the scope of his employment. **The school did not authorize the use of violence and such actions were not within any discretionary authority given to the instructor.** The assault was not in furtherance of the school's business and therefore fell outside the scope of employment. The school could not be held vicariously liable for such actions. *Forester v. State*, 645 N.Y.S.2d 971 (N.Y. Ct. Cl. 1996).

C. Third-Party Misconduct

Liability for third-party misconduct can arise when someone connected with a university is injured by a third party off campus, or when an individual not affiliated with the institution enters campus and injures someone connected with the institution. Typically, third-party misconduct involves some type of criminal behavior, such as physical or sexual assault.

◆   *The Court of Appeals of Georgia reinstated negligence claims filed by a student who was beaten by a classmate with a baseball bat.*

The classmate attacked and beat the student in a dormitory shower, allegedly because he believed the student was a homosexual and "glanced at him in an inappropriate way." He was later convicted of assault and battery and sentenced to prison. The student sued the college in a state court for negligence and related claims. The court dismissed the case, finding insufficient evidence of foreseeability. The court of appeals disagreed, finding that at this stage of the case, the student was not required to come forward with evidence that the harm he suffered was foreseeable. He was only required to allege facts which, if proven, created a factual issue on the question of whether the harm he suffered was foreseeable. In Georgia, **a college or university has a duty "to exercise ordinary and reasonable care for a student's safety and to take reasonable steps to protect against foreseeable acts of violence on its campus."** The student claimed the college should have been aware of a danger to him and that it had failed to address harassment of students believed to be homosexual. *Love v. Morehouse College*, 287 Ga.App. 743, 652 S.E.2d 624 (Ga. Ct. App. 2007).

◆   *A Tennessee court affirmed a $300,000 judgment for a student who was attacked while walking to her dorm.*

To get to her dorm, the student had to go down a stairwell in a parking garage. When she got to the bottom of the steps, she was attacked by a man who hit her on the head with a brick. The student suffered severe injuries, including permanent brain damage. Her family filed a state claims commission action against the university for negligently creating or maintaining a dangerous condition. The claims commissioner found the university created a dangerous condition by failing to provide and maintain adequate lighting on the steps. He awarded the student $300,000 – the maximum amount available. The case reached the Court of Appeals of Tennessee, which upheld the award. There was enough evidence to support a finding that the lighting on the stairwell was inadequate, creating a dangerous condition. In addition, **the history of crime near the garage justified a finding that the attack was foreseeable**. A university expert testified that there were 55 thefts at the garage in 2001-02. The university had breached a duty of care to the student, and the court affirmed the commission's decision. *Smith v. State*, No. E2007-00809-COA-R3-CV, 2008 WL 699062 (Tenn. Ct. App. 3/17/08).

◆   *A Texas student's claims against a university arising from sexual assault were dismissed on grounds of state immunity and untimeliness.*

The student was sexually assaulted by an acquaintance who was also a student at the university. The student obtained an emergency protective order, which she presented to an associate dean. She was unaware that the associate dean knew the attacker. According to the student, the associate dean tried to convince her not to pursue charges against the attacker and to forgive him. Eventually, the associate dean admitted that she knew the attacker. She added that if the student did not drop her claim against the attacker, she would find continuing at the medical school to be difficult. The attacker was disciplined under the Student Code of Conduct. Two years later, the victim sued the university, the associate dean and the attacker, alleging assault, intentional infliction of emotional distress, retaliation and constitutional rights violations.

A federal district court noted the Eleventh Amendment shields states from claims for money damages unless Congress has abrogated that immunity. This did not happen here. **Since the university was a state entity, it was entitled to Eleventh Amendment immunity.** The associate dean was also entitled to immunity because she was sued in her official capacity as an employee of the university. The court then turned to the issue of timeliness and determined the student had waited too long to file her lawsuit. All of the events described in the complaint occurred more than two years before the student sued. Even though administrative proceedings had taken place at the university within that two-year period, the statute of limitations was not tolled, because those proceedings did not prevent the student from exercising her legal right to sue. The court dismissed the claims against the university defendants. *Maltbia v. Coffie*, No. H-06-834, 2007 WL 43793 (S.D. Tex. 1/5/07).

◆   *A Massachusetts university was not liable for the murder of a student in his off-campus apartment because the risk of injury to him was not foreseeable.*

The student leased the apartment where he was murdered from a private landlord. On the day of the murder, another tenant let the perpetrators into the building. The student's estate sued the university for wrongful death and negligence. The court granted the university's motion for pretrial judgment on grounds that **the university had no duty to provide security for the student** or to prevent his murder. **Although there had been four burglaries at the building in the six months before the murder, there was no evidence that they involved violence or that any other violence occurred in the building**. The building was privately owned and managed, and the university was not in the best position to take the steps needed to ensure the student's safety. *Doyle v. Gould*, 22 Mass.L.Rptr. 373 (Mass. Super. Ct. 2007).

◆ *A New York university was not liable for injuries to a student who was injured when another student struck him with a chain.*

The student was injured when another student hit him on the head with a tow-truck chain during a fight on campus. Another fight involving different students had occurred on campus earlier that day. The university campus security officers went to the location of the second fight immediately after it started and apprehended the student with the chain. They called police and emergency medical services to the scene, and they appeared within minutes of the call. The student sued the university in a state court for negligence. The court denied the university's motion for pretrial judgment, and it appealed.

A New York appellate division court explained that **as a property owner, the university had a duty to exercise reasonable care to protect the student from reasonably foreseeable criminal or dangerous acts committed by third persons on campus**. The university did not breach its duty because it could not have foreseen the attack on the student. The other fight involving different students could not have put the university on notice of the fight between the student and his attacker. Even if the university had known of the later fight, the student failed to show what could have been done to stop it. The trial court should have granted the university's motion, and the judgment was reversed. *Ayeni v. County of Nassau*, 794 N.Y.S.2d 412 (N.Y. App. Div. 2005).

◆ *The Supreme Court of Texas held a state university was not liable for the stabbing of a student actor during a school play.*

The university had no theater curriculum, but it offered a voluntary student drama club whose members received no grades or class credit for participating. The club director and his wife told actors to use a real knife in a play, in violation of a university policy prohibiting deadly weapons on campus. During the second performance of the play, an actor missed a stab pad worn by the student and drove the knife into the student's chest, puncturing his lung. The student sued the university in a Texas court, alleging the university was liable for his injuries. The court held for the student, and the university appealed. The state court of appeals reversed the decision, finding the director, his wife, and faculty advisors were not "employees" under the Texas Tort Claims Act. For that reason, the university was protected by governmental immunity. The Supreme Court of Texas found the advisors were university employees under the act. But the director and his wife had no employment contract with the university. **The university had only a minimal degree of control over them that did not indicate employee status. The court held the university was protected from liability by governmental immunity.** It reversed the judgment. *Texas A&M Univ. v. Bishop*, 156 S.W.3d 580 (Tex. 2005).

◆ *An Ohio appellate court held a university was entitled to question a student who started a fire in a dormitory.*

The fire killed another student who was asleep in his dorm room. Investigators determined the fire was caused by a student who lit paper towels in a stairwell of the dorm. The father of the student who died sued the university, alleging its negligence contributed to his son's death. The university sued the student who started the fire for contribution. A settlement was reached between the student who set the fire and the father. The student asserted that because he entered into an agreement with the father in good faith, the court should dismiss the university's action against him. The university contended the court should permit it to question the student to evaluate whether the agreement was entered into in good faith. The court denied the university's request to question him about the incident. It found the student entered into a settlement agreement with the father in good faith, and it dismissed the action against him. The university appealed to the Court of Appeals of Ohio.

According to the university, the trial court erred by declining its request to question the student to determine if the agreement was completed in good faith. **The court held the university should be allowed to assess whether the settlement agreement was in good faith.** If it was not, the university could seek contribution. The court reversed the judgment and remanded the case to the trial court for further proceedings. *Cohen v. Univ. of Dayton*, 164 Ohio App.3d 29, 840 N.E.2d 1144 (Ohio Ct. App. 2005).

◆ *An Alabama district court found a state university was not liable for the murder of a freshman residing in a dormitory.*

The student was a freshman at the university and lived in a dormitory room. A stranger entered the dormitory without authorization and murdered her in her room. Her parents sued the university in a federal district court for civil rights violations. They argued the student's relationship with the university was involuntary, such that it had a "special relationship" to her. This meant the university would have a duty to protect her from violence by a third party. The parents argued this relationship arose from a university requirement that all freshmen live on campus. The court disagreed. The student voluntarily attended the university and was not in its custody. She was able to retain her liberty and therefore had no special relationship to the university. The court also rejected the parents' due process claim based on deliberate indifference to a risk of serious injury to the student. **The university did not know about or disregard a risk to the student's health and safety.** The court found the university was entitled to qualified immunity and dismissed the case. *Griffin v. Troy State Univ.*, 333 F. Supp.2d 1275 (D. Ala. 2004).

◆ *Lawsuits filed against Texas A&M after a tragic bonfire accident were allowed to continue by a federal appeals court.*

In 1999, a bonfire stack collapsed on the campus of Texas A&M University, killing 12 students and injuring 27 others. A university special commission report exonerated university officials, finding that their actions did not rise to the level of deliberate indifference. However, numerous lawsuits arose, alleging violations of 42 U.S.C. § 1983 under a state-created danger theory. A federal district court dismissed the lawsuits, but the Fifth Circuit reversed and remanded the case. The court held the record supported a finding of deliberate indifference. The plaintiffs presented evidence that university officials allowed the bonfire stack to increase over the years to a pile of burning trash weighing more than 3 million pounds. A university official had described the stack as the "most serious risk management activity at the university." Nevertheless, university officials did not use their authority to control the stack's building or destruction. The plaintiffs even asserted that the university encouraged students to add to the stack as a "marketing tool to lure prospective students" and to gain alumni donations. Based on all this evidence, the Fifth Circuit found that the plaintiffs established their Section 1983 claim. The district court's decision was reversed, and the case was remanded. *Scanlon v. Texas A&M Univ.*, 343 F.3d 533 (5th Cir. 2003).

◆ *The University of Maine may have been negligent in failing to prevent a sexual assault that occurred in one of its dorms.*

A student participated in a pre-season summer soccer program at the University of Maine. The university allowed participating students to live on campus during the program. The student stayed in a dorm and attended a fraternity party, after which a young man offered to escort her back to her dorm. When she reached her room, the man followed her in and sexually assaulted her. The student and her parents sued the university for negligence and breach of an implied contract. The court granted pretrial judgment to the university. She appealed. The Supreme Judicial Court of Maine reversed the dismissal of the negligence claim. It found that the university owed a duty of care to the student. Under Maine law, **a business (such as the university) has a duty to protect its "invitees" from reasonably foreseeable danger. A sexual assault in a college dormitory is foreseeable** and is one of the reasons the university went through the trouble of establishing safety measures in the dorms.

In this case, the student had never seen or met with the resident assistant on her floor; there were no group meetings offering instruction on rules and regulations regarding safety within the dorms; and there were no signs posted in the dorms informing residents who should or should not be allowed in. The negligence claim was allowed to proceed, but the court affirmed the dismissal of the contract claim. *Stanton v. Univ. of Maine System*, 773 A.2d 1045 (Me. 2001).

◆ *A New York college could declare an alumnus "persona non grata" and bar him from campus.*

Over the course of his nine years at a college, a student exhibited disruptive behavior on campus and began receiving psychiatric treatment. His mother allegedly warned a nurse that he might act violently at his graduation ceremony, and security guards questioned him shortly before the ceremony began. However, the ceremony took place without any trouble. A month later, the student was declared "persona non grata" by the college and was barred from the campus. He eventually sued the college and the nurse. A state court ruled for the defendants, and the New York Supreme Court, Appellate Division, affirmed. Here, **since he had graduated, he was no longer a student and was not entitled to due process as a result of the college barring him from campus.** Further, his claims against the nurse could not succeed because he could not show that she breached a duty to keep information confidential. *Godinez v. Siena College*, 733 N.Y.S.2d 262 (N.Y. App. Div. 2001).

III. BREACH OF CONTRACT

Colleges and universities can be liable for breach of contract even where they have immunity from lawsuits for negligence or other torts. In order for a contract to exist, there must be some enforceable promise, not just general representations of the kind typically found in student handbooks.

◆ *Since they failed to present evidence of a specific promise, two Minnesota students failed to prove breach of contract by their university.*

The students were accepted into the Master of Arts in Instruction program at St. Mary's University of Minnesota. The program is designed for students who want to teach but have not obtained an undergraduate education degree. The students had to complete a number of prerequisites before they could be recommended for licensure as teachers. They said that the program director promised them that all the courses they needed would be offered. However, the university did not offer the courses they needed at their campus. Instead of pursuing alternative options, one student applied for a teaching license, which was denied. The other student also failed to secure a license, and they sued the university in a state court for breach of an educational contract.

Appeal reached the Court of Appeals of Minnesota. It stated a general rule for breach of contract claims by students against educational institutions. **Breach of contract claims are available only if the institution failed to perform on specific promises to a student, and only if the claims would not involve "an inquiry into the nuances of educational processes and theories."** The court rejected a claim based on failure to provide the students all math classes they needed for licensure. Course requirements vary from student to student and are subject to change. The evidence showed that the program director said only that she would request that the courses be offered. Nor did the college breach a contract by declining to accept life experience as an alternate for course requirements. Review of the decision to reject life experiences as an acceptable substitute would involve an impermissible inquiry into the nuances of educational process and theory by the court. There was no evidence that the university promised the pair it would recommend them for licensure even if they failed to satisfy all applicable program requirements. *Clem v. St. Mary's Univ. of Minnesota*, No. A09-1231, 2010 WL 773596 (Minn. Ct. App. 3/9/10).

◆ *Representations to incoming students in a university's medical department brochure were not sufficiently definite to form an enforceable contract.*

A Massachusetts Institute of Technology student overdosed on Tylenol with codeine during her freshman year. She was hospitalized and admitted to a psychiatric hospital for one week. While receiving treatment there, the student revealed she suffered from mental health problems and had cut herself when she was in high school. A psychiatrist at the university's mental health services department diagnosed the student with adjustment disorder. He recommended further therapy when she returned for her sophomore year. When the student returned after summer break, she told a dean she was thinking about suicide.

The dean sent her to the mental health department for an immediate assessment. The psychiatrist stated the student had passive suicidal ideation but he did not believe she was at risk of hurting herself. Her mental health problems resurfaced about five months later. The psychiatrist decided the student should be admitted for observation at the university infirmary. After she was examined, she was allowed to return to the dorm. Shortly thereafter, the student died from self-inflicted thermal burns. Her parents sued the university in a state court, asserting representations in the university's medical department brochure and in its medical department bylaws created an enforceable contract. **The court held the representations in the brochure and bylaws were only generalized representations of the purpose and medical services available to the school community. Such statements are not definite and are too vague to form an enforceable contract.** There was no evidence of specific promises made by the university. The court held there was no contract and awarded the university pretrial judgment. *Shin v. Massachusetts Institute of Technology*, 19 Mass. L. Rptr. 570 (Mass. Super. 2005).

◆ *The receipt of funds from a state is just one factor to consider in determining whether a state university is entitled to immunity.*

The Rosa Parks Legacy contracted with Troy University to use the name and image of Rosa Parks in connection with the operation of the Rosa Parks Library and Museum. A dispute developed between the parties, and the Parks Legacy sued the university in a state court for breach of contract. It sought to block the university from using Rosa Parks' name or image and particularly from making a movie that was to feature her image. The Parks Legacy named the university's president as a party, and it sought compensatory and punitive damages. The university and president filed motions to dismiss the action based on the immunity provisions of the Alabama Constitution. The court denied their motions, and they sought review by the Supreme Court of Alabama.

The court noted that the state's constitution broadly immunizes state defendants from liability. The state "shall never be made a defendant in any court of law or equity." This provision barred claims not only against the state but against state agencies, employees and officials, including state institutions of higher learning. The Parks Legacy argued the university was not immune from suit because it was not wholly funded by the state. The court rejected this argument, noting **the receipt of funds from the state is just one factor to consider in determining whether an entity is a state entity**. The university president also enjoyed immunity. The nature of the claims against her showed she was being sued in her official capacity, and a suit against a state agent in his or her official capacity is essentially a suit against the state. *Ex parte Troy Univ.*, No. 1051318, 2006 WL 3759341 (Ala. 12/22/06).

♦ *A North Carolina university could be sued for breach of contract, but not for an intentional tort.*

The dealer for a piano manufacturer entered into a contract with a North Carolina university to loan the university a number of pianos in exchange for the right to service the university's other pianos. When the contract ended, the dealer and the manufacturer sued the university for breach of contract, conversion and property damage, claiming that the university returned the pianos in damaged condition and that the university improperly retained 14 pianos. The university sought to dismiss the lawsuit on grounds of sovereign immunity. The North Carolina Court of Appeals noted that the state's tort claims act allows state entities to be sued for negligence. However, conversion is an intentional tort (wrongfully depriving another of it property) and that action had to be dismissed. The breach of contract action, on the other hand, could continue because **when the university entered into the contract, it impliedly agreed to be sued for damages if it breached the contract**. Also, the property damage claim was a breach of contract claim that could proceed. The court remanded the case. *Kawai America Corp. v. Univ. of North Carolina at Chapel Hill*, 567 S.E.2d 215 (N.C. Ct. App. 2002).

♦ *A public college was shielded from liability by the state tort immunity act.*

An employee at an Illinois public college worked under a series of one-year contracts. He complained to college officials that his supervisor subjected him to physical and verbal abuse that caused him physical and psychological problems. When the supervisor gave him a negative evaluation, his contract was not renewed. He then sued the college for breach of contract, battery and intentional infliction of emotional distress. He also sued the supervisor. A jury returned a verdict in his favor, but the Appellate Court of Illinois reversed in part. The court found that **the Illinois Tort Immunity Act shielded the college from liability for the battery and emotional distress claims**. Also, the college was not liable for breach of contract. Here, the college had to provide three months' notice of non-renewal to avoid a breach. The court held that it did so by postmarking the notice on March 31 – the last day it could provide notice. Even though the employee did not receive the notice until early April, it was deemed timely because it was postmarked in March. Finally, however, the court held that the supervisor could be held liable for battery and emotional distress. *Valentino v. Hilquist*, 785 N.E.2d 891 (Ill. App. Ct. 2003).

♦ *A university was determined to have breached its agreement with a philanthropist; it could not claim that the money was a gift.*

A private California university asked a philanthropist to endow a professional chair at one of its research centers. After a number of conversations and the exchange of several letters, the philanthropist agreed to endow the chair. However, the university later selected an existing faculty member for the chair in violation of the endowment terms and also failed to fund the chair. The philanthropist sued for breach of contract, promissory fraud and misappropriation. A state trial court dismissed the action, finding that no contract existed and that the philanthropist made a gift to the university. The California Court of Appeal reversed, finding that **the contract (partially verbal and partially written) existed**. The letters confirmed the verbal agreement; they did not make up the agreement exclusively. The philanthropist could sue the university. *Glenn v. Univ. of Southern California*, No. BC 236256, 2002 WL 31022068 (Cal. Ct. App. 2002).

IV. INSURANCE

Insurance policies may provide coverage for both first- and third-party claims. Third-party claims generally involve liability policies and lawsuits for negligence by employees. Unless an exclusion in the policy specifically exempts a claim from coverage, an insurer may be required to defend and indemnify the policyholder in any lawsuit arising from an injury to a third party.

◆   *Insurers were obligated to defend and indemnify a New York college that was sued by a man who was injured at a volleyball tournament.*

The man was hurt when a referee's platform collapsed. He sued the college and the tournament sponsor for his injuries. The college asserted cross-claims against the sponsor, which was obligated to indemnify the college by contract. Although the college was listed as an additional insured party on the sponsor's liability policies, the insurers denied a request by the college for defense and indemnification. The college sued the insurers in a state court, which held for the college, ruling that the sponsor had contracted to defend and indemnify it. The insurers were also required to defend and indemnify the college because it was named as an additional insured and because the contractual liability provision of the insurance policy obligated them to do so.

On appeal, a state appellate division court noted that the injured party had settled his case for $75,000. Despite the settlement, the case was not moot because the settlement reserved the right to pursue an appeal regarding the college's responsibilities. **The court found the parties had expressly agreed that the sponsor would indemnify the college against all claims for damages based on injuries during the tournament.** The fact that the college was named as an additional insured on the policy created a duty on the part of the insurers to provide a defense. The trial court's ruling was affirmed. *Balyszak v. Siena College*, 63 A.D.3d 1409, 882 N.Y.S.2d 335 (N.Y. App. Div. 2009).

◆   *The U.S. Court of Appeals, Third Circuit, held a private college's breach of contract claim against its insurance carrier could proceed to trial.*

The college purchased a policy that covered repairs necessary to return property to pre-fire condition. It bought a separate "Ordinance and Law Endorsement" that covered loss to the undamaged portion of a building if it had to be fixed to comply with any ordinance or law. The insurance carrier denied coverage for fire damage caused to the upper floors of a dormitory. The college sued the carrier in a federal district court for breach of contract, contending the endorsement provided coverage for repair and renovation costs required by the Americans with Disabilities Act (ADA). It asserted that the endorsement covered numerous accessibility upgrades made to the building because they had to be done to comply with the ADA. The court held the protections of the ADA did not apply to dormitory space on the second, third and fourth floors of the building. It found they were akin to apartments. The court held for the carrier, and the college appealed to the U.S. Court of Appeals, Third Circuit.

The court held the repairs to the dormitory were alterations within the meaning of the ADA because they included remodeling, renovation or reconstruction. **The court agreed with the college's contention that because dorms are part of boarding colleges, they are places of education.** The ADA prohibited denying disabled students reasonable accommodations that would allow them to live in its dorms. The court held the ADA applied to all four floors of the dormitory. It reversed the judgment. *Regents of Mercersburg College v. Republic Franklin Insurance Co.*, 458 F.3d 159 (3d Cir. 2006).

◆   *A liability insurer did not have to defend a university accused of fraud.*

A Florida university failed to disclose in its catalog that its physical therapy program's accreditation status was probationary. When the applicable accrediting organization withdrew the program's certification, the students who had enrolled in the program became ineligible to take the physical therapy licensing examination. They sued the university for breach of contract, fraud in the inducement, and violation of the Florida Deceptive and Unfair Trade Practices Act. The university sought to have its liability insurer defend and indemnify it in the action, but the Florida District Court of Appeal ruled in favor of the insurer. Here, the insurance policy covered any bodily injury caused by an occurrence, and defined "occurrence" as an accident. However, **the students were alleging intentionally fraudulent conduct by the university. Fraud in the inducement could not be accidental.** Thus, the university would have to defend itself in the action. *Barry Univ. v. Fireman's Fund Insurance Co. of Wisconsin*, 845 So.2d 276 (Fla. Dist. Ct. App. 2003).

◆   *An excess insurer had to contribute to a Colorado university's defense costs.*

A Colorado professor sued a university in state court for denial of tenure, wrongful termination, defamation and breach of contract, among other claims. Eighteen months later, she filed a second lawsuit against the university in federal court, but chose not to include the defamation claim. The lawsuits were consolidated in federal court, and a question of insurance coverage then arose – namely, which insurer (primary or excess) had to pay the costs of defending the university. The primary insurer was held to have the responsibility for defending the first lawsuit because of the defamation claim – the only claim it was potentially liable for paying. **The excess insurer had to contribute $50,000 to the second lawsuit** (where no defamation claim was presented and the primary insurer could not be liable) even though the two cases were consolidated. Here, even though the cases were consolidated and the primary insurer had the primary obligation to defend the lawsuit, the second lawsuit retained its separate identity for purposes of allocating defense costs. *Farmington Casualty Co. v. United Educators Insurance Risk Retention Group, Inc.*, 36 Fed.Appx. 408 (10th Cir. 2002).

◆   *A Missouri medical school could not obtain reimbursement from its insurer for a settlement.*

The medical school agreed to buy land from an energy company that it intended to convert into a parking lot. Before the sale closed, the school's contractor began working on the site, struck and ruptured an underground storage tank, and caused the release of coal tar wastes. The company sued the school and contractor for negligence and trespass, and the school's insurer initially defended it. It withdrew from the defense after a federal court concluded it had no duty to defend. That decision was later reversed. After a court found that the contractor had not trespassed because it had implied permission to work on the site, a settlement was reached. The school then sued its insurer for indemnification. A federal court ruled in favor of the insurer, and the Eighth Circuit affirmed. Here, the policy excluded environmental contamination claims, and the contractor was found not to have trespassed (the only claims the insurer could have been liable for). Thus, **even though the insurer breached its duty to defend the school, it did not have to indemnify the school for the settlement**. *Royal Insurance Co. of America v. Kirksville College of Osteopathic Medicine*, 304 F.3d 804 (8th Cir. 2002).

◆   *A North Dakota university was entitled to insurance coverage for damage from a flood.*

After a record rainfall, the Red River flooded, and the city of Grand Forks shut down two sanitary sewer lift stations that serviced the University of North Dakota campus. As a result, water entered 22 campus buildings through the sewer system and damaged boiler and machinery equipment. The university's insurer denied coverage on the grounds that the sewer backup actually was caused by flooding, which was excluded by the policy. The university asserted that the damage was caused instead by the sewer backup, and that the policy therefore provided coverage. In the lawsuit that followed, a jury ruled in favor of the university, finding that the flood was not the efficient proximate cause of the damage. (Efficient proximate cause is the predominating cause of the loss, though not necessarily the last act in the chain of events, nor the triggering cause of the loss.) **The jury determined that the sewer backup, not the flood, was the efficient proximate cause of the damage.** The North Dakota Supreme Court affirmed, noting that the jury had properly considered the evidence before finding that the sewer backup caused the loss. Accordingly, the court upheld the jury's award of $3.35 million to the university. *Western National Insurance Co. v. Univ. of North Dakota*, 643 N.W.2d 4 (N.D. 2002).

◆   *City University of New York (CUNY) did not have to compensate Carnegie Hall Corporation for damages resulting from a student fall at graduation.*

CUNY's licensing agreement with Carnegie Hall allowed CUNY to use the hall for the 1994 graduation ceremony of the university's technical college. The agreement required CUNY to obtain comprehensive general liability insurance to cover any claims arising out of the event, but CUNY never obtained the required coverage. During the ceremony, a graduating student fell on a staircase and sued Carnegie Hall for failing to keep the staircase in a reasonably safe condition. The hall's insurance company ultimately paid $41,987 in settlement fees and defense costs. Carnegie Hall and the insurance company sued CUNY for reimbursement because the university failed to get insurance coverage, as mandated by the license agreement. A New York claims court determined that CUNY owed the hall's insurer compensation and granted pretrial judgment in the plaintiffs' favor, but a state appellate division court disagreed.

The court held neither Carnegie Hall nor the insurer had any basis for recovery against CUNY. Carnegie Hall had no ground to seek damages from CUNY because it did not incur any financial loss – its insurer paid the expenses related to the student's lawsuit. In addition, **the insurer was not entitled to recover settlement and defense costs. It was not a party to the license agreement, and it did not claim to be a third party to the agreement.** Therefore, any basis for recovery was based on its status as the subrogee of Carnegie Hall. New York's high court previously has ruled that recovery for the breach of a contract requiring the purchase of insurance is limited to the cost of obtaining substitute coverage, and not defense costs. Accordingly, the case was dismissed. *Carnegie Hall Corp. v. City Univ. of New York*, 729 N.Y.S.2d 93 (N.Y. App. Div. 2001).

◆ *By giving its insurer late notice of an occurrence that could lead to a lawsuit, a university lost coverage.*

Vanderbilt University conducted a study in the 1940s to track the absorption of iron in pregnant women. The women unknowingly ingested a solution containing radioactive iron isotopes. In the 1960s, a follow-up study revealed a higher incidence of cancer among the participants. In 1985, the Department of Energy requested information relating to the study for a congressional hearing. In 1994, the women and their children filed a class action lawsuit against Vanderbilt, which was settled for $10 million in 1998. When Vanderbilt sought insurance to cover the loss, its excess insurer denied coverage because of the late notice. A federal court ruled in favor of the insurer, and the Sixth Circuit Court of Appeals affirmed. **Under the policy, Vanderbilt had to notify the insurer of an "occurrence" as soon as possible.** Here, the occurrence was deemed to have happened in the 1960s when the follow-up study was conducted (or at the very latest, in 1985). By failing to give notice until the lawsuit was filed in 1994, Vanderbilt prejudiced the insurer's ability to defend and thus was not entitled to be reimbursed for the settlement. *U.S. Fire Insurance Co. v. Vanderbilt Univ.*, 267 F.3d 465 (6th Cir. 2001).

◆ *An insurer could seek reimbursement for a student's medical expenses by joining the student's individual action.*

A University of Tennessee student was permanently injured while participating in a track meet. The student and his parents filed a claim against the university with the Tennessee Claims Commission. The matter was settled between the parties, except for the student's subrogation claim seeking $1,026,666 in reimbursement to his insurer for medical expenses. The Claims Commission denied the subrogation claim because the student did not assert the claim in his pleadings and because his insurer was not joined as a party to the action. Initially, the Tennessee Court of Appeals affirmed the commission's determination and found that the insurer should file its own claim to obtain compensation. The student then notified the Claims Commission that he was joining the insurer to the action, but the commission denied the joinder request as too late. The appellate court reversed the commission's decision. It held that the commission was in error when it struck the student's pleadings regarding joinder of the insurer, even though the pleadings were untimely. The panel noted that **the university was previously advised of the subrogation claim and would not be prejudiced if the claim was included, since the commission had not yet decided whether the insurer was entitled to reimbursement**. The case was remanded for a trial on the insurer's claim. *Hartman v. Univ. of Tennessee*, 38 S.W.3d 570 (Tenn. Ct. App. 2000).

V. PRIVATE INSTITUTIONS

Like their public counterparts, private colleges and universities are not liable for negligence unless they breach a legal duty. In most situations, institutions have a duty to exercise only "reasonable care" in their activities.

A claimant in a tort case must show a legal duty, breach of the duty that proximately caused an injury, and damages. There is no liability for injuries caused by sudden, unexpected, or unforeseeable acts. Institutions organized exclusively for religious, charitable, or educational purposes may be entitled to claim charitable immunity.

◆   *Private institutions must exercise reasonable care to protect students from foreseeable criminal or dangerous acts by third persons.*

A New York private college student was punched in the face by a classmate during a classroom altercation. He sued the college in the state court system for negligently failing to prevent the attack. The court held for the college, and the student appealed. The New York Supreme Court, Appellate Division, held that **to prove negligence, there must be a breach of a legal duty that proximately caused damages. The court noted that colleges generally have no duty to shield students from dangers presented by other students.** However, **they must exercise reasonable care to protect students from reasonably foreseeable criminal or dangerous acts committed by others**, including other students. In this case, the college did not breach any duty, because the injury was the result of a "sudden, unexpected, and unforeseeable act." Because the attack was not foreseeable, the college's failure to prevent it was not negligent. The judgment was affirmed. *Luina v. Katharine Gibbs School New York*, 830 N.Y.S.2d 263 (N.Y. App. Div. 2007).

◆   *A private Connecticut university was not liable for harassment of a student based on his religion.*

The student attended a doctoral program in management systems. He claimed one of his professors suggested he adopt some Chinese heritage and culture, and that another remarked that he had a "mind like a computer." The student told the professor his mental abilities came from God. The professor responded, "It doesn't come from God, it comes from David, from the Jewish religion." A third professor allegedly made a remark about the student being Catholic. The student claimed several other faculty members also harassed him, delayed his presentation of his doctoral thesis, and prevented him from taking classes. He sued the university, claiming it violated state and federal laws when it harassed him based on his religion. The student alleged the university violated his federal civil rights, as protected by 42 U.S.C. § 1983. **The university argued it was a private entity that could not be sued for federal civil rights violations.** The student contended that as the university received some federal funding, the court should further determine if its acts or decisions would be considered functions of the state. The court agreed with the university and granted its motion for summary judgment. *Martin v. Univ. of New Haven*, 359 F.Supp.2d 185 (D. Conn. 2005).

◆ *A student who was shot could proceed with his lawsuit against a college and a fraternity for negligence.*

A Missouri student enrolled in a private college for the summer semester and moved into a fraternity house. After a confrontational phone call, the student attempted to lock the front door, but the latch malfunctioned and popped open. Ten minutes later, two men entered the house and shot him. He sued the college and the fraternity for negligence, asserting that they breached a duty to maintain the premises in good repair. The college and fraternity maintained that they had no duty to prevent a third person from performing an intentional criminal act, and that even if they had a duty to maintain and repair the house, the student could not show that a breach of that duty caused his injuries under the law. A state court granted pretrial judgment to the defendants, but the Missouri Supreme Court reversed. It found issues of fact as to **whether the student was in a landlord-tenant relationship with either of the defendants so as to impose a duty of care**. There also was a jury question as to whether the breach of that duty was the proximate cause of the student's injuries. *Letsinger v. Drury College*, 68 S.W.3d 408 (Mo. 2002).

◆ *Where an insured board member at a private college made misrepresentations to the board of trustees to obtain a personal advantage for his company, and where the college lost $2 million as a result, the college's errors and omissions policy did not provide coverage for the loss.*

A Texas Christian College purchased a "school leaders errors and omissions" policy that insured it against wrongful acts committed by directors and officers of the school. Subsequently, a member of the board of trustees convinced the board to invest $2 million of its endowment funds in a company that accepted accounts receivable as security for short-term loans. However, he did not disclose that the company had a negative net worth, that he was a 49% owner of the company, or that he also was a salaried employee of the company. **When the investment failed, the college obtained the board member's resignation, then sued him and his company for misrepresentation of certain facts and for making false statements.**

The college obtained a judgment against the board member for $1.8 million and against the company for $2 million. Unable to collect on the judgments, it sought to collect under its errors and omissions policy. The insurer denied coverage under the "fraud or dishonesty" exclusion and the "personal profit or advantage" exclusion. A Texas federal court held that the two exclusions applied to bar coverage, and the college appealed to the U.S. Court of Appeals, Fifth Circuit. The appellate court affirmed. It noted that **the exclusion for "any claim arising out of the gaining in fact of any personal profit or advantage to which the Insured is not legally entitled" applied to bar coverage**. Here, the board member clearly gained a personal advantage by his company's receipt of the $2 million in endowment funds from the college. Despite the fact that the board member did not ultimately make a profit, he did gain a personal advantage by his wrongful acts. As a result, the insurer had no obligation to pay out under the policy. *Jarvis Christian College v. National Union Fire Insurance Co.*, 197 F.3d 742 (5th Cir. 1999).

◆ *A Virginia college and professor were not entitled to charitable immunity where the professor was not acting on behalf of a charitable institution at the time he injured a beneficiary.*

A professor at a Virginia college established a program with the Boys and Girls Club of Hampton Roads, under which students in the professor's recreation programming class were required to spend six hours observing the children and volunteering at the club. The students were required to return to the classroom, design programs for the children, then implement the programs at the club. The professor went to the club to observe his students and help them out when needed. While he was there observing one day, a student asked him to watch a door leading to the weight room. She was giving a talk on wellness and body conditioning to 13- to 18-year-olds and wanted to keep younger students not involved in the program out of the room. The professor closed the door, amputating the right thumb of a minor who had his hand on the doorframe. The minor sued the professor and the college, who sought to dismiss the action on the basis of charitable immunity.

The Supreme Court of Virginia noted that the club was a charity and that the minor was a beneficiary of the club. However, **it refused to award the defendants charitable immunity because, at the time of the injury, the professor was not engaged in the work of the charity. Rather, he was carrying out his duties as a professor**, observing a student and acting as a "doorkeeper." The court remanded the case for further proceedings. *Mooring v. Virginia Wesleyan College*, 514 S.E.2d 619 (Va. 1999).

◆ *The New Jersey charitable immunity statute provided protection to a religious university in a negligence lawsuit arising from the university's operation of a pub on campus.*

A Catholic university in New Jersey operated a pub on campus solely for students and their guests. The pub was not operated for profit, it was subsidized by the student government association, and its employees were students. A 21-year-old senior at the university went with several friends to the pub and slipped in a puddle that was apparently left when a serving cart was moved. He sued the university in a state trial court seeking to recover for his injuries. The court denied the university's motion for a directed verdict, and a jury returned a verdict in favor of the student. The university appealed to the Superior Court of New Jersey, Appellate Division.

On appeal, the court noted that the university had deemed the pub to be part of a student's socialization process and a factor in the development of a well-rounded person. The question was whether the state's charitable immunity statute applied to the university while it was running the pub for students and their guests. **Under the statute, nonprofit corporations, societies or associations organized exclusively for religious, charitable, or educational purposes could not be held liable for negligence where the person injured as a result of the negligence was a beneficiary, to whatever degree, of the works of the nonprofit corporation, society or association.** Because the student was a beneficiary of the university to some degree while patronizing the pub, the university was entitled to charitable immunity under the statute. The court noted that the fact that the pub had since been replaced by a campus coffee house was not critical to the immunity analysis. Since the university had reasonably concluded that a campus experience ought to include opportunities to mature in an environment enriched not only by study and classes, but by diverse forms of social interchange within the university setting, the student was a beneficiary at the time of his injury, and the university was entitled to immunity. *Bloom v. Seton Hall Univ.*, 704 A.2d 1334 (N.J. Super. Ct. App. Div. 1998).

CHAPTER TEN

University Operations

I. GOVERNMENT REGULATION

A. Public Records and Freedom of Information

◆ *The Florida public records law did not shield the NCAA from disclosing to the media documents from investigation reports it kept on a secure website.*

Florida State University (FSU) learned that staff members gave improper assistance to student-athletes. It conducted an investigation, then turned over its findings to the NCAA. Months later, the NCAA issued FSU a formal notice of allegations to initiate disciplinary proceedings for the reported misconduct. An NCAA committee issued an infractions report and imposed penalties for academic misconduct, including the forfeiture of some games. To prepare an appeal, FSU lawyers viewed documents posted on a secure NCAA Web site.

The Associated Press (AP) sought disclosure of the NCAA documents in a state court action. They sued the NCAA, FSU and its officials and attorneys under Florida Chapter 119. A state court held for the AP, finding the documents were "public records" as they were received by a state agency and not exempt under federal laws (they contained no information directly related to a student). After the court ordered disclosure of the documents, the NCAA appealed. A Florida District Court of Appeal found that Chapter 119 had a public policy of keeping public records open for personal inspection and copying. The state policy of open government made it appropriate to resolve any doubt in favor of disclosure. The court held that **the Public Records Law applied to documents**

maintained on a computer in the same way that it would apply to those kept in a file cabinet. A document may qualify as a public record if it was prepared by a private party, if it was received by the government and used in the transaction of public business. The term "received" referred to examination of a document on a remote computer, as had taken place in this case. The requested documents did not reveal the identity of any student, so federal law did not prohibit disclosure. Since the documents in this case were "received" by FSU lawyers in connection with public business, the Public Records Law applied, and the documents had to be disclosed. Rejecting other NCAA arguments based on constitutional grounds, the court affirmed the judgment. *NCAA v. Associated Press*, 18 So.3d 1201 (Fla. Dist. Ct. App. 2009).

◆ *A Michigan university police report had to be reviewed by a trial court judge in chambers to consider if parts of it were exempt from public disclosure.*

Three men were arrested in connection with an assault on the campus of Michigan State University (MSU). A news organization asked MSU for a copy of its police incident report related to the incident. The request was filed under the state Freedom of Information Act (FOIA). The organization had already published a story with the names of three men who were arrested for the assault, but it wanted additional information from the report, such as personally identifiable information relating to victims, witnesses, and police officers. The report also included photographs and statements from the responding officers and others. MSU officials denied the request, saying disclosure would violate individual privacy rights and interfere with the law enforcement investigation.

The case reached the Michigan Court of Appeals, which held MSU did not show FOIA privacy and law enforcement exemptions applied. It held the trial court had wrongfully failed to review the report to decide if parts of it could be separated and disclosed without violating privacy rights or interfering with the investigation. Appeal reached the Supreme Court of Michigan, which held that unless a FOIA exemption provided otherwise, the relevant time to consider was when the public body asserted the exemption. **The passage of time and the course of events after asserting a FOIA exception did not affect whether a public record was initially exempt from disclosure.** This part of the appeals court decision was reversed, and the case was returned to the trial court. Upon return to that court, the judge was to inspect the police incident report in chambers to determine what information was exempt from disclosure, to make particularized findings regarding disclosure or nondisclosure, and to separate any exempt material from nonexempt material. *State News v. Michigan State Univ.*, 481 Mich. 692, 753 N.W.2d 20 (Mich. 2008).

◆ *Two Wisconsin veterans could not proceed with a court challenge to a proposal to change the name of a university football stadium.*

In 1945, the city of La Crosse chose the name Veterans Memorial Stadium for the football facility at the University of Wisconsin-La Crosse (UWL). Between 2000 and 2005, the name of the facility was changed three times. The veterans said the 2000 and 2001 name changes violated Wisconsin's open meetings and public records laws and UWL policies. They claimed the changes resulted from "malfeasance" by UWL's board of regents. A state circuit court dismissed the case, finding that the veterans failed to show they had suffered any injury and thus lacked standing to pursue their claims.

The Court of Appeals of Wisconsin agreed with the trial court that the veterans lacked standing to challenge the name change. **To have standing, or the legal right to bring an action, a party must show he has suffered an injury or has been threatened with an injury as a result of the other party's conduct.** In addition, the injury must be to a legally protectable interest. The veterans did not allege any direct personal injury as a result of the name changes. Their concern that the name changes did not sufficiently honor veterans was not a "direct personal injury" that gave them the right to bring an action against UWL. The court affirmed the judgment for UWL. *Nedvidek v. Kuipers*, No. 2006AP3077, 747 N.W.2d 527 (Table), 2008 WI App 51, 2008 WL 516781 (Wis. Ct. App. 2/28/08).

After granting a petition by the veterans to review the case, the Supreme Court of Wisconsin found the case did not present any novel questions or lead to the development of the law. For this reason, it found the review petition had been improvidently granted, and dismissed the appeal. *Nedvidek v. Kuipers*, 766 N.W.2d 205 (Wis. 2009).

◆ *Massachusetts' highest court held incident reports and other documents held by a private university police department were not "public records."*

A student newspaper asked two municipal police departments and Harvard University's police department for all records related to certain incidents listed on the university department's weekly log of complaints, including incident reports and correspondence. The municipal police departments supplied the documents to the newspaper, but the university asserted it did not have to comply with the public records law because it was not a public entity.

The newspaper asked a state court for an order requiring the university to release the documents. The court dismissed the case, ruling that private university officers were not governmental employees. Accordingly, documents they made or received were not "public records." The newspaper appealed to the Supreme Judicial Court of Massachusetts, arguing the appointment of some university officers as special state police officers or deputy sheriffs vested them with broad police powers. Under this theory, they were subject to public records law requirements. **The court held the university records were not covered by the state public records law, and did not have to be disclosed.** The judgment for Harvard was affirmed. *Harvard Crimson v. President and Fellows of Harvard College*, 445 Mass. 745, 840 N.E.2d 518 (Mass. 2006).

◆ *The Supreme Court of Iowa held a state university could not shield its financial records from public view by outsourcing certain university functions.*

University financial records were managed by a private nonprofit foundation that had been incorporated by the university in 1958. In 2002, the university and foundation renewed an elaborate service agreement. In the agreement, the university expressed its desire to engage the expertise of the foundation as an independent contractor to provide advice, coordination, and assistance in fundraising, development, and in the operation, accounting and fund investment management of those areas. A group of citizens sought a state court order to view university tax and financial records under the Iowa Freedom of Information Act, I.C.A. § 22.1, *et seq.* The act creates a public right to view governmental records. The court held the foundation was not a government body under the act, so its documents were not "public records."

On appeal, the Supreme Court of Iowa stated "public records" included documents or other information belonging to the state, school corporation, or nonprofit corporation whose facilities are supported with property tax revenue, and relate to the investment of public funds. **The court held the foundation was performing a government function through the contract with the university, so its records were subject to public disclosure.** It said a government body may not outsource its functions to a private corporation and then keep the information from the public. In executing the service agreement, the university, a government body, contracted away its ability to raise money and manage its finances to what was assumed to be a nongovernment body. The university had attempted to do indirectly what it could not do directly – avoid disclosure of what would otherwise be public records. The court held the Freedom of Information Act prevented this result, and it reversed the judgment. *Gannon v. Board of Regents of State of Iowa*, 692 N.W.2d 31 (Iowa 2005).

◆   *A federal district court held the U.S. Department of Agriculture (USDA) failed to properly document a refusal to disclose information to a university under the federal Freedom of Information Act (FOIA).*

An Illinois university requested documents under the FOIA from the USDA. When the USDA failed to respond more than a year later, the university sued it in a federal district court. The USDA admitted it did not respond to the request and provided the documents the university had asked for. The USDA then argued the case was moot because it had complied with the FOIA. The court noted the U.S. Court of Appeals, District of Columbia Circuit, held in *Vaughn v. Rosen*, 484 F.2d 820 (D.C. Cir. 1973), **that a federal agency must submit an index to explain the reasons why information was withheld or redacted**. This index is known as a "Vaughn index." Because the USDA failed to submit a Vaughn index, the court could not assess whether its reasons for redacting information or refusing to disclose materials were legitimate. The court denied the university's motion for summary judgment and ordered the USDA to submit a Vaughn index. *Northwestern Univ. v. U.S. Dep't of Agriculture*, 403 F.Supp.2d 83 (D.D.C. 2005).

◆   *A university had to disclose faculty booklists to a competitor of the campus bookstore under the New York Freedom of Information Law .*

A bookstore seeking to compete with the on-campus bookstore run by Barnes & Noble attempted to obtain faculty booklists. When informal attempts failed, it got an advisory opinion stating that the lists constituted records under New York's Freedom of Information Law (FOIL), then submitted formal requests to university faculty members and the university's records access officer. A few faculty members responded, but the records officer did not. The following semester, the same result was achieved. The bookstore then sued the university to compel it to comply with the FOIL, and a trial court dismissed the action. The supreme court, appellate division, reversed. **Course syllabi and**

written booklists constitute "records" under the FOIL because they are held by an agency. It did not matter that the lists were kept by individual faculty members. Regardless of whether the university required the lists to be turned in to the records office, if they existed and someone requested them, they had to be made available. Here, the records existed, and the records officer was required to make them available. *Mohawk Book Co. Ltd. v. SUNY*, 732 N.Y.S.2d 272 (N.Y. App. Div. 2001).

B. Aliens and Immigration

◆   *A Muslim scholar was entitled to further consideration of a claim that he was improperly denied a visa without an opportunity to show he did not knowingly support an organization that gave support to terrorist groups.*

The federal Immigration and Nationality Act (INA) makes an alien who has afforded material support to terrorist organizations ineligible for a visa. The American Academy of Religion and the American Association of University Professors sued the Department of Homeland Security in a federal court, challenging the exclusion of Tariq Ramadan from the U.S. Ramadan is a well-known Muslim scholar who shuns violence and has spoken out against terrorism and radical Islam. However, the U.S. revoked his visa because he admitted making donations to an organization that supported terrorist groups. This was a direct violation of the INA. Finding the government excluded him for legitimate reasons, the court held for the U.S.

The organizations appealed to the U.S. Court of Appeals, Second Circuit, arguing that the visa was improperly rejected in violation of a First Amendment right to hear Ramadan's views. The court upheld a statutory provision making contributors to terrorist organizations ineligible for visas. **A knowledge requirement provision of the INA required a consular officer to find that Ramadan knew his contributions provided material support to a terrorist organization, and to confront him and afford him an opportunity to deny this.** Since the record did not establish that the consular officer who denied the visa confronted Ramadan with the claim that he knowingly gave support to Hamas, the court returned the case to the district court for further consideration. Ramadan would be entitled to an opportunity to demonstrate by clear and convincing evidence that he did not know he was supporting a terrorist organization. *American Academy of Religion v. Napolitano*, 573 F.3d 115 (2d Cir. 2009).

◆   *A federal court ordered the University of Pittsburgh to retain a research assistant while she pursued administrative charges of unlawful discrimination.*

The research assistant worked at the university until her supervisor told her that her contract would end due to insufficient funding. If the contract ended on the stated date, the research assistant's visa would expire and she would be forced to return to Russia. She claimed that the decision to end her employment was motivated by national origin discrimination. To support this claim, she noted that her supervisor had hired and/or retained similarly situated Korean employees while non-renewing her contract. A federal district court granted the research assistant's request for an injunction and ordered the university to retain her while she filed administrative charges of discrimination. She showed a reasonable probability of succeeding on the merits of her discrimination claim since she was let go while similarly situated Korean employees were retained. **In addition, if relief was denied, she would either have to return to Russia voluntarily or be subject to immediate deportation.** *Karakozova v. Univ. of Pittsburgh*, No. 09cv0458, 2009 WL 1652469 (W.D. Pa. 6/11/09).

◆ *A California court found federal immigration law preempted a state law permitting undocumented aliens to qualify for resident tuition.*

The California Legislature enacted Assembly Bill 540, which became Section 68130.5 of the state Education Code. The law exempted some students without lawful immigration status from nonresident tuition rates at public institutions of higher learning. Section 68130.5 placed those seeking to legalize their immigration status on the same footing as students who had graduated from California high schools, students who had attended a California high school for at least three years, and current students registered at state institutions of higher education. A group of university students who could not claim resident status under Section 68130.5 sued the state university system in a California superior court. The court explained that California and nine other states have similar laws allowing certain undocumented students to apply for in-state tuition rates at public universities and colleges. However, since the federal government had yet to offer any opinion on the validity of these state laws, the court held federal immigration law did not preempt Section 68130.5.

On appeal, the Court of Appeal of California reversed the judgment. It held Section 68130.5 was preempted by federal law. **Title 8, Section 1623 of the U.S. Code prohibited any alien who was not lawfully present in the U.S. from eligibility for any postsecondary education benefit on the basis of residency within a state, unless a citizen or national of the U.S. was eligible for such a benefit on equal terms.** According to the court, in-state tuition was a "benefit" since it was some $17,000 cheaper than out-of-state tuition at the University of California. A three-year residency requirement in Section 68130.5 was deemed "a surrogate residence requirement." A vast majority of California high school students who attended school in the state for three years were state residents. As the superior court improperly decided the federal law question, the judgment was reversed for further proceedings. *Martinez v. Regents of Univ. of California*, 83 Cal.Rptr.3d 518 (Cal. Ct. App. 2008).

The Supreme Court of California granted review of the case. *Martinez v. Regents of Univ. of California*, 87 Cal.Rptr.3d 198 (Cal. 2008).

◆ *A federal district court rejected a Wisconsin Ph.D. candidate's second lawsuit claiming that he was wrongfully terminated from a graduate program.*

Marquette University dismissed the candidate for not maintaining adequate grades, and he sued the graduate committee chair for discrimination. Marquette tried to intervene in the case, but the court denied the request and awarded pretrial judgment to the chair. The candidate filed a second lawsuit, this time alleging Marquette had breached a contract with him. The court granted Marquette pretrial judgment, explaining that it did not have jurisdiction to hear the case. The complaint involved a private contract dispute and did not present a federal question. Nor could the candidate establish federal jurisdiction by showing diversity of citizenship between the parties. Although he stated he was a resident of China, the court noted **an alien admitted to the U.S. is deemed to be a citizen of the state where he is domiciled**. Therefore, the candidate did not show a diversity of citizenship that would justify federal court jurisdiction. Even if the court had jurisdiction to hear the candidate's claim, his prior lawsuit arose out of the same set of events and was thus barred. *Zhou v. Marquette Univ.*, No. 07-CV-958, 2008 WL 2714659 (E.D. Wis. 7/7/08).

◆ *Yale University could no longer employ an alien student because students who are not enrolled are ineligible for on-campus employment.*

Yale had hired the student, a Turkish citizen, to work as a full-time research assistant. According to the student, Yale breached the terms of contracts when it refused to pay him money it allegedly owed him. The student had dropped the only course he had been enrolled in, which meant he lost his status as a student. The Appellate Court of Connecticut upheld a state trial court decision in favor of Yale. **It could no longer employ or pay the student because immigration law provides that once a student is no longer enrolled, he is ineligible for an on-campus employment benefit.** *Keles v. Yale Univ.*, 98 Conn. App. 901, 908 A.2d 28 (Conn. App. Ct. 2006).

The Supreme Court of Connecticut refused to consider a further appeal. *Keles v. Yale Univ.*, 281 Conn. 916, 917 A.2d 998 (Conn. 2007).

◆ *The right to rebut a presumption of nonresidence extends even to aliens with visas living in state.*

The University of Maryland granted "in-state" tuition status only to students domiciled in Maryland, or, if a student was financially dependent on the student's parents, to students whose parents were domiciled in Maryland. The university also could deny in-state status to individuals who did not pay the full spectrum of Maryland state taxes. The university refused to grant in-state status to a number of students, each of whom was dependent on a parent who held a "G-4 visa" (a nonimmigrant visa granted to officers and employees of international treaty organizations and members of their immediate family). The university stated that the holder of a G-4 visa could not acquire Maryland domicile because the holder was incapable of showing an essential element of domicile – the intent to live permanently or indefinitely in Maryland.

After unsuccessful appeals at the administrative level, the students brought a class action lawsuit in federal court seeking declaratory and injunctive relief. The students alleged that university policy violated the Equal Protection Clause. A federal district court granted relief, stating that the G-4 visa could not create an irrebuttable presumption of nondomicile. On appeal, the U.S. Supreme Court stated that the case was controlled by the principles announced in *Vlandis v. Kline*, this chapter, that **when a state purports to be concerned with domicile, it must provide an individual with the opportunity to present evidence bearing on that issue**. Federal law allows aliens holding a G-4 visa to acquire domicile in the United States. However, the question of whether such domicile could be acquired in Maryland was a question of state law. Since no controlling precedent had been decided by the state's highest court, the Supreme Court declined to rule and certified the question to the Maryland Court of Appeals for resolution. *Elkins v. Moreno*, 435 U.S. 647, 98 S.Ct. 1338, 55 L.Ed.2d 614 (1978).

◆ *The Supreme Court struck down a university policy that restricted an alien's right to acquire domicile in a state and thus qualify for in-state tuition.*

The University of Maryland's student fee schedule policy denied students whose parents held nonimmigrant alien visas in-state status, even if they were domiciled in the state, thus denying them preferential fee and tuition schedules. The U.S. Supreme Court found the policy to be in violation of the Supremacy Clause of the U.S. Constitution. The Court stated that the university's policy conflicted directly with the will of Congress as expressed in the Immigration and Nationality Act of 1952. In passing the Immigration and Nationality Act, Congress explicitly decided not to bar nonimmigrant aliens such as these the right to acquire domicile in the United States. **The university's policy denying these aliens "in-state" status, solely on the basis of their immigration status, amounted to a burden not contemplated by Congress** in admitting them to the United States. Thus, the University of Maryland's student fee schedule, as applied to these aliens, was held to be unconstitutional. *Toll v. Moreno*, 458 U.S. 1, 102 S.Ct. 2977, 73 L.Ed.2d 563 (1982).

C. Residency

◆ *The University of Illinois violated its own regulation by refusing to classify a student as a state resident.*

The student's family resided in Iowa, but his mother was a faculty member at a community college in Illinois. A university regulation governing residency defined "resident" to include any dependent of a faculty member who worked at an Illinois state-supported institution of higher education on at least a quarter-time basis. The university refused to classify the student as an Illinois resident on grounds that community colleges were not state-supported public institutions of higher learning. The student's father presented information from the state community college board which indicated the college received 35.4% of its annual budget from state funds. He also sent the officials a definition of "public institutions of higher education" from the Illinois Code that included both four-year and community colleges. University officials maintained that only dependents of employees at four-year universities qualified for in-state tuition reduction. The parents appealed the university's decision.

An Illinois circuit court upheld the decision, and the parents appealed. The Appellate Court of Illinois found the university's regulation defined "resident" to include the dependent of someone employed at least one-quarter time as a faculty member of a "state-supported institution of higher education in Illinois." State support for four-year public universities had fallen so much in recent years that it was questionable whether they received more funding from the state than community colleges. The university received about 31% of its total revenue from the state, while the community college received 34% of its revenue from the state. The college's receipt of local funding did not negate its status as a "state-supported institution." Community colleges were both state supported and locally supported, and they were not excluded from being considered state-supported public institutions under the regulation. **The court held the university's board was bound to comply with its own regulation.** It rejected the university's additional reasons for denying the student resident status and reversed the judgment. *Dusthimer v. Board of Trustees of Univ. of Illinois*, 368 Ill.App.3d 159, 857 N.E.2d 343 (Ill. App. Ct. 2006).

The Supreme Court of Illinois denied further review in *Dusthimer v. Board of Trustees of Univ. of Illinois*, 222 Ill. 606, 862 N.E.2d 233 (Ill. 2007).

◆ *A Maryland state university's presumption against in-state residency for all students who depended upon out-of-state sources did not violate equal protection principles. However, university administrators may not have applied the presumption in a constitutional manner.*

Four students who were enrolled in professional and post-graduate degree programs at a state university sued the university board of regents in a state court, claiming the board violated their constitutional rights by refusing to classify them as in-state residents. This decision denied them a substantial tuition reduction offered to Maryland residents, which the students claimed was a violation of equal protection principles. The university system presumed that students who were not financially independent were residing in the state primarily for the purpose of attending a college or university, if they remained financially dependent upon a nonresident. A state court held for the board and the students appealed to the Court of Special Appeals of Maryland.

The court stated no single definition could mechanically determine a person's domicile. The most important factors for determining domicile were where a person actually lived and where he or she voted, although a number of other factors also had weight. **The court held the university system's presumption was valid. The source of a student's financial support was related to the issue of residence.** However, there was evidence that some administrators did not allow students to challenge the presumption by treating the financial dependency presumption as irrebuttable. **The absence of uniformity in standards or criteria under the tuition policy violated equal protection principles.** The students were in the state during the time they attended the university, and each satisfied many other traditional domicile factors. The court vacated the lower court order for the board and remanded the case for further activity. *Bergmann v. Board of Regents of the Univ. System of Maryland*, 167 Md. App. 237, 892 A.2d 604 (Md. Ct. Spec. App. 2006).

◆ *State residency requirements for favorable tuition rates are subject to the due process right of students to present evidence about their residency.*

Connecticut required nonresidents enrolled in the state's university system to pay tuition and other fees at a higher rate than state residents. It also created an irreversible and irrebuttable statutory presumption that if the legal address of a student, if married, was outside the state at the time of application for admission or, if single, was outside the state at some point during the preceding year, the student remained a nonresident as long as the student remained enrolled in Connecticut schools. Two students, one married, one single, who were both residents of Connecticut, challenged the presumption, claiming that it violated the Fourteenth Amendment's guarantee of due process and equal protection. A three-judge district court panel upheld the students' claim.

The U.S. Supreme Court held that **the Due Process Clause does not permit states to deny a student the opportunity to present evidence that the student is a bona fide resident of the state, and thus entitled to in-state tuition rates,** on the basis of an irrebuttable presumption of nonresidence. Such a presumption is not necessarily true, and the state had reasonable alternatives in making residency determinations. *Vlandis v. Kline*, 412 U.S. 441, 93 S.Ct. 2230, 37 L.Ed.2d 63 (1973).

◆   *The Court of Appeals of Kansas held that a student who moved to Kansas to attend law school could not claim resident tuition status.*

The student, who was born in England, came to Kansas in May 1999 and moved to Colorado in July 1999. He lived there until March 2002. He signed a contract to build a house in Kansas, contingent on his acceptance to the law school there. He was accepted and he and his wife finalized the purchase of a house in Kansas in June 2002. The university denied the student's application to be reclassified as a Kansas resident for the 2003 fall semester. The residence committee found he did not satisfy the residency requirements and denied his appeal. A state district court agreed, and the student appealed.

The court of appeals noted several state law factors determined if a student was a Kansas resident. **These included a continuous presence in Kansas, employment in the state, payment of resident income taxes, reliance on in-state sources of financial support, commitment to an education program indicating an intent to remain permanently, and owning a home in Kansas.** The committee found the purchase of the house was contingent on the student's acceptance to the law school. This did not demonstrate an intent to remain in Kansas permanently. All of the other factors could be considered routinely performed by temporary residents of Kansas. The court found the committee's decision was supported by substantial competent evidence and it affirmed the district court judgment. *Lockett v. The Univ. of Kansas, Residence Appeals Committee*, 33 Kan. App.2d 931, 111 P.3d 170 (Kan. Ct. App. 2005).

◆   *The Board of Regents of the University of Wisconsin System had immunity against a student's equal protection challenge.*

The student attended a Wisconsin state university for five semesters after graduating from a high school in Colorado. The university charged him the nonresident tuition rate of $9,000 per semester. At the same time, the tuition for residents was about $2,500 per semester. Tuition for students who were residents of Minnesota was only slightly higher because of a reciprocity agreement between Wisconsin and Minnesota. The student sued the board of regents in a federal district court, claiming the tuition policy violated the Equal Protection Clause of the Constitution.

The court held the board of regents was immune from liability under the Eleventh Amendment and dismissed case. The student appealed to the U.S. Court of Appeals, Seventh Circuit. The court held that the board was an arm of that state that qualified for immunity under the Eleventh Amendment. As

Congress did not surrender state immunity in Section 1983 actions, the student's action against the board was barred, and the judgment was affirmed. *Joseph v. Board of Regents of the Univ. of Wisconsin System*, 432 F.3d 746 (7th Cir. 2005).

D. Zoning and Land Use

◆   *The Supreme Court of Vermont upheld the state environmental court's approval of a college building project over the objections of several neighbors.*

The college proposed to renovate an existing building in Burlington and build a new 18,000 square-foot building on the same lot to create 49 new student rooms that could house 94 students. A development review board conditionally approved the project and neighbors appealed to the Vermont Environmental Court. After a hearing and a site visit, the court approved the application with conditions, finding the project satisfied city density and setback requirements. On appeal, the Supreme Court of Vermont considered a claim by the neighbors that the lower court order had permitted a project exceeding the city's maximum allowable density and setback requirements.

The court deferred to the city's approach of treating each group of four dormitory rooms as a "single dwelling unit." Using this approach, the court upheld the environmental court's conclusion that the project complied with city density requirements. While neighbors complained that the lot was not a "corner lot" and thus violated setback requirements, the court disagreed. It found that **the neighbors sought to have the court "rewrite the zoning ordinances to declare that large lots cannot be corner lots under the City's definition of that term."** Since the lot was a "corner lot" as defined by the city, the environmental court did not commit error in allowing the project with conditions. *In re Champlain College Maple Street Dormitory*, 186 Vt. 313, 980 A.2d 273 (Vt. 2009).

◆   *A New Jersey court rejected claims that a zoning board improperly approved a university's plan to build a dormitory in a residential area.*

A group of neighbors objected to the construction of a three-story dormitory at Monmouth University. The local board of adjustment granted several variances for the project, which was planned in an area zoned for low-density residential uses. The neighbors sued Monmouth in the state court system, claiming several board members should have been disqualified from the application based on their financial or personal involvement with the university. The court upheld the decision, and the neighbors appealed.

A New Jersey appellate division court acknowledged that **the state Municipal Land Use Law has a conflict of interest provision that bars board of adjustment members from acting on any matter on which they have any personal or financial interest**. But none of the board members in this case came within the scope of this law. Some members were alumni of the university, but they were inactive and did not contribute substantially to Monmouth. No board members or any of their family members were currently students at the university. As none of the connections noted by the neighbors could reasonably be expected to impair the independence or objectivity of a board member, the judgment was affirmed. *Hughes v. Monmouth Univ.*, 394 N.J. Super. 193, 925 A.2d 741 (N.J. Super. Ct. App. Div. 2007).

◆ *The Court of Appeals of North Carolina upheld a decision to grant a university's request for an order to close a road running along its property.*

The university asked the Town of Chapel Hill to close part of Laurel Hill Road to promote safety, unify the grounds of the North Carolina Botanical Garden, and provide better teaching and visitor experiences. The town council adopted an order to permanently close a section of the road. A nearby property owner filed a state court petition to vacate the order. The court dismissed the petition and affirmed the order of the town council. The owner appealed to the Court of Appeals of North Carolina. He contended the trial court erred in failing to conduct an evidentiary hearing and in refusing to allow him to present evidence at the hearing on his petition.

The court noted the owner did not contest the procedures at the town hearing and did not contend the trial court violated other applicable local requirements. **The town held three public hearings on the proposed road closing in two months. Those hearings were the proper place for the owner to present evidence, not the trial court.** The court affirmed the judgment upholding the town's decision. *Houston v. Town of Chapel Hill*, 177 N.C.App. 739, 630 S.E.2d 249 (N.C. App. 2006). The state's highest court denied review in *Houston v. Town of Chapel Hill*, 639 S.E.2d 449 (N.C. 2006).

◆ *A New York court held a city commission had no rational basis to deny an application by Cornell University to build a parking lot in a historic district.*

Cornell intended to replace some existing residence halls with new housing and create a parking lot nearby. The city planning board approved the building proposal, but it denied the request for a parking lot. Two years later, the commission designated a new historic district that included the parking lot site. The historic district consisted of about 10 acres of land and three buildings in an area zoned exclusively for educational use. Near the buildings were a shared lawn and other landscaping. Cornell proposed to place the parking lot in a wooded area. The Ithaca city landmarks preservation commission denied the application, but a state trial court annulled the commission's decision.

The commission appealed to the New York Supreme Court, Appellate Division. Under the Ithaca city code, proposed improvements within a historic district may be approved if they will not have a substantial adverse effect on the aesthetic, historical or architectural significance and value of the landmark. The court found the parking lot, which was to be located within the wooded area, would have a minimal effect on the original landscape. It would not be visible to the public, and 85% of the existing lawn would be retained. **The court rejected the commission's argument that the parking lot was not a valid educational use. Colleges and universities are generally allowed to locate facilities for accessory uses on their properties that are reasonably related to their educational purposes.** The parking lot was a qualified accessory use to the student residences and instructional facilities. The commission did not consider what conditions could reasonably be imposed to mitigate any adverse effect on the landscape. Instead, it simply assumed the public would be offended by a change to the landscape. The court held the commision's decision was arbitrary and capricious, and it affirmed the judgment for Cornell. *Cornell Univ. v. Beer*, 16 A.D.3d 890 (N.Y. App. Div. 2005).

◆ *A federal district court upheld a District of Columbia zoning board order concerning a campus plan.*

The District zoning board approved the university's campus plan for 2000-2010, but its order imposed several conditions, including a cap on student enrollment. The university had already admitted a substantial number of its students for the next semester. The order also directed that if the university failed to meet a requirement to house 70% of buildings on campus, it would be barred from erecting nonresidential buildings on campus while it was noncompliant. A federal district court granted the university's request to prevent enforcement of the order. The board then issued a corrected final order that also imposed a cap on housing with certain housing requirements for undergraduates. The university amended its federal district court complaint to include a due process claim. The court found the board's order was not rationally related to its legitimate purpose and violated due process. The U.S. Court of Appeals, D.C. Circuit, reversed in part, noting that **the zoning board did not violate the university's substantive due process rights by imposing the housing restrictions**. Since students are not a suspect class deserving of heightened protections, the board's zoning regulations would be constitutional if they were rationally related to a legitimate governmental interest. Preservation of the residential character of an adjoining neighborhood was a legitimate governmental interest, and the zoning restrictions were upheld. *George Washington Univ. v. Dist. of Columbia*, 318 F.3d 203 (D.C. Cir. 2003). The case was remanded to the district court, where the university argued the board's final order was an unconstitutional taking of its property.

To determine if government action amounts to a taking of property, a court considers the economic impact, any interference with reasonable investment-backed expectations, and the character of government action. The court found the final order did not deprive the university of all economic benefits from the property. The university did not show the order diminished the property value. The court held the order did not interfere with the university's reasonable investment-backed expectations because it knew the property was subject to governmental regulation. To assess the character of the government's action, courts consider whether the action advances a "common good" or "public purpose." Because of the potential impact on the surrounding neighborhood, the court held the board's order advanced a common good or public purpose. **The conditions imposed by the order did not constitute a taking of property,** and the court dismissed the university's complaint. *George Washington Univ. v. Dist. of Columbia*, 391 F.Supp.2d 109 (D.D.C. 2005).

◆ *A Massachusetts zoning board's density regulation was invalid as applied to a college campus under state law.*

Boston College (BC) applied to the Newton Board of Aldermen for special permits to construct three buildings. It also sought an exemption from the parking requirements of a local zoning ordinance. The purpose of the construction project was to provide additional space for academic functions, faculty offices and dining facilities. The board denied the application and BC sued the board in a state court, alleging violation of the Dover Amendment, a state law barring zoning ordinances that prohibit or restrict the use of land for educational purposes. The court held the board unreasonably applied its dimensional and density regulations to the building project, but was reasonably justified in denying a parking waiver. The parties appealed.

The Court of Appeals of Massachusetts noted that **a municipality could reasonably regulate parking, open spaces, and buildings used for educational purposes**. The floor area ratio density requirement of the local zoning ordinance was invalid as applied to the BC middle campus. The entire middle campus was "nonconforming" under the ordinance, with the practical result that enforcement would require BC to always secure a special permit to construct any building there. Strict compliance with the density requirement would thwart an "educational use" and was invalid. The trial court correctly found the denial of a waiver for more parking spaces was unreasonable. The court affirmed the decision. *Trustees of Boston College v. Board of Aldermen of Newton*, 793 N.E.2d 387 (Mass. App. Ct. 2003).

◆ *A city could require certain landlords of college students to comply with a lodging house ordinance.*

Six owners of condominium units in the city of Worcester leased the units to students at the College of Holy Cross. Four unrelated students lived in each unit. When the condo owners refused to obtain permits as operators of lodging houses, the city filed complaints against them in housing court. The court found the lodging ordinance unconstitutionally vague, but the Appeals Court of Massachusetts vacated that opinion and found the ordinance valid. Here, **the ordinance clearly defined a lodging house as a "dwelling unit that is rented to four or more persons not constituting a family."** Moreover, the ordinance was rationally related to a legitimate governmental interest: creating quiet neighborhoods and limiting the number of unrelated people living together. The condo owners were subject to the ordinance. *City of Worcester v. Bonaventura*, 775 N.E.2d 795 (Mass. App. Ct. 2002).

◆ *If a city improperly targeted a private university for designation as a historic district, it could be liable for an equal protection violation.*

The city of Evanston, Illinois, asked Northwestern University to voluntarily contribute to the cost of city services. Northwestern refused to do so. A group of citizens then formed an association that sought to designate parts of the city and parts of the university as a National Historic District. The Department of the Interior approved the designation over Northwestern's objections. Northwestern then sued the city under 42 U.S.C. § 1983 for violating its constitutional rights, and the city moved for dismissal. The district court granted the motion in part. However, it found that Northwestern could proceed on two causes of action. First, under the "vindictive action equal protection" part of the lawsuit, **Northwestern alleged that the city had an improper motive (hostility to the university) and that it was treated unequally as a result.** This claim had to proceed to trial. Also, Northwestern claimed that the city imposed an unconstitutional condition on its right to be exempt from property taxation under the charter granted to it by the state in 1851. It asserted that an alderman suggested university property could be excluded from the historic district if the university agreed to surrender its tax-exempt status. This claim also deserved a trial. *Northwestern Univ. v. City of Evanston*, No. OOC7309, 2002 WL 31027981 (N.D. Ill. 2002).

◆   *The U.S. Supreme Court found the Religious Freedom Restoration Act (RFRA) unconstitutional as applied to state actions.*

The case involved a building permit for the enlargement of a church. It was denied on the ground that the church building was part of a historical district. The Supreme Court held that the church could not use the RFRA to obtain the permit because the RFRA proscribed state conduct that the Fourteenth Amendment did not even prohibit. However, the Supreme Court did not address the question of whether the RFRA was unconstitutional in all respects. It limited its analysis to state actions. Accordingly, the RFRA still may provide protections against federal actions. *City of Boerne, Texas v. Flores*, 521 U.S. 507, 117 S.Ct. 2157, 138 L.Ed.2d 624 (1997).

E. State and Local Regulation

◆   *Wisconsin taverns that banned drink specials in response to pressure from municipal officials could claim immunity in an antitrust suit.*

Concerned about binge drinking by its students, officials at the University of Wisconsin, Madison pressured city officials to prohibit taverns from using weekend drink specials to lure customers. When officials threatened to pass an ordinance that would ban the practice by all taverns, a group of tavern owners announced at a news conference that they were giving in to the demands and would no longer offer drink specials. Some students at the University of Wisconsin accused the taverns of unlawful price-fixing and brought a state court antitrust action against them. The court held that the antitrust claim was barred based on the city's public health and safety concerns.

Appeal reached the Supreme Court of Wisconsin, which held the taverns were immune to the antitrust claim. **When legislators enacted the antitrust law, they intended to permit municipalities to take anti-competitive actions.** It was reasonable to find the regulation was intended to supersede competition in alcohol sales. Cities can regulate alcohol, as long as doing so serves an important public interest. Municipal immunity extended to the taverns because it was essentially the city that was responsible for the taverns' decision to "voluntarily" end the weekend drink specials. Since the lower courts correctly held for the taverns, the court affirmed the judgment. *Eichenseer v. Madison-Dane County Tavern League*, 748 N.W.2d 154 (Wis. 2008).

◆   *A Texas law violated the First Amendment by requiring private postsecondary schools to obtain a certificate of authority or accreditation before granting degrees or using the name "seminary."*

In an effort to stop "diploma mills," Texas passed a law that barred schools from using the words "college," "university," "seminary" and other specified terms in their names unless they first obtained a certificate of authority from the state. The law also restricted the designations schools could use regarding educational attainment. HEB Ministries, Inc., which operated a school it called the Tyndale Theological Seminary and Bible Institute, was assessed an administrative penalty of $173,000 for violating the state law. In response, it sued the state for a declaratory judgment that the law violated the Establishment Clause and the Free Exercise Clause of the First Amendment. An intermediate court ruled for the state, and HEB Ministries appealed.

The Supreme Court of Texas held that **the state law violated the Establishment Clause by requiring private postsecondary institutions to obtain a certificate of authority or accreditation before granting degrees or using the word "seminary" in their names**. In addition, the law violated the Free Exercise Clause because it forced a party to either comply with state standards and compromise its religious mission or forgo the use of restricted terms. The decision of the intermediate court was reversed. *HEB Ministries, Inc. v. Texas Higher Educ. Coordinating Board*, 235 S.W.3d 627 (Tex. 2007).

◆ *The Supreme Court of Alabama held a lower court should have dismissed an action to determine the term of office for an Auburn University trustee.*

The dispute centered on whether the appointment of a replacement trustee was intended to complete the unexpired term of a previous trustee or was instead for a full seven-year term. After receiving an opinion from the state attorney general, the university determined the trustee was serving out the remainder of his predecessor's term, not a full seven-year term. The trustee agreed to give up his seat. When the governor sought to fill the vacancy, another trustee of the university filed a state court action, seeking a declaration that the trustee was entitled to serve a full seven-year term. The trial court restrained the governor's appointing committee from meeting or acting to appoint a new trustee. **The supreme court reversed the judgment, finding the individual who filed the action had no standing to bring it.** He could not show any actual injury to his rights as a public official, and he was not prevented from performing his duties. *Ex parte Richardson*, 957 So.2d 1119 (Ala. 2006).

◆ *The Court of Appeal of California held a community college was required to perform an environmental study before moving a campus shooting range.*

The college proposed a new site for a shooting range used for firearms courses offered in its criminal justice programs. It obtained approval by county and city governments, but a report indicated high levels of lead contamination at the new site. A public interest group alleged violation of state Environmental Quality Act requirements for an environmental study. A state superior court disagreed, finding the site change was not a "project" under the act.

The Court of Appeal of California stated that under the act, **a "project" is defined as "an activity which may cause either a direct physical change in the environment, or reasonably foreseeable indirect physical change in the environment" by a person or agency receiving public funds**. Even though dismantling and removing the range would be accomplished incrementally, these actions were all part of a single project. The college argued the lead abatement aspect of the move was exempt from the act, as the cleanup would cost less than $1 million. The court held that while lead abatement was exempt, this did not relieve the college of its responsibility to conduct an initial study of the project. **The decision was reversed and remanded with instructions for an environmental study.** *Ass'n for a Cleaner Environment v. Yosemite Community College Dist.*, 10 Cal.Rptr.3d 560 (Cal. Ct. App. 2004).

◆ *New York City was not allowed to ban a private educational institution's distribution of free magazines via news racks because the proposed ban arbitrarily singled out certain kinds of publications.*

A private institution that offered short, nonaccredited courses in New York City sought to distribute its magazine free of charge by way of news racks placed on city sidewalks. The city contended that the news racks were unsightly, unsanitary and unsafe. It also asserted that the magazine was "commercial speech," which is entitled to a lesser degree of First Amendment protection, and that the ban on all commercial speech through sidewalk news racks was constitutional. The New York Court of Appeals observed that the city's arguments missed the central point in the case: **"a government official or employee may not exercise complete and unregulated discretion, in the absence of duly enacted guidelines, ... to decide which publications may be distributed via [news racks]."** Here, the city's action against the institution was taken without the benefit of any regulatory guidelines. The city's action therefore violated the First Amendment, which requires that government action regulating "speech" be undertaken pursuant to clear guidelines that leave little room for arbitrary decisions. The decision to ban the sidewalk magazine news racks was illegal. *City of New York v. American School Publications*, 509 N.E.2d 311 (N.Y. 1987).

◆ *In 1982, the Supreme Court ruled that a Pennsylvania taxpayer group lacked standing to challenge a governmental conveyance of surplus property to a private religious college. The Court ruled that the group could show no injury to itself or any of its members as a result of the conveyance.*

Congress enacted the Federal Property and Administrative Services Act, 40 U.S.C. § 471, *et seq.*, to dispose of surplus property and authorize its transfer to public or private entities. This statute authorized the education secretary to dispose of surplus real property for schools. The secretary was permitted to take into account any benefit accruing to the U.S. from any new use of the transferred property. In 1973, the Secretary of Defense and General Services Administration declared a Pennsylvania army hospital site surplus property. In 1976, the secretary conveyed part of the property to a Christian college. Although the appraised value of the property was $577,500, the secretary computed a 100% public benefit allowance, permitting the college to acquire the property for no cost. **A taxpayer group advocating the separation of church from state learned of the conveyance and sued the college and U.S. government**, claiming that the conveyance violated the Establishment Clause. The court dismissed the complaint, ruling that the taxpayers lacked standing under prior decisions of the U.S. Supreme Court. The U.S. Court of Appeals, Third Circuit, reversed the decision, and the Supreme Court agreed to hear an appeal by the college and the U.S. government.

The Court stated that Article II of the Constitution limited the judicial power of courts to cases and controversies. Litigants were entitled to bring a lawsuit only by showing some actual or threatened injury. Without such a showing, lawsuits were to be dismissed for lack of standing. In this case, the taxpayers had alleged injury from deprivation of fair and constitutional use of their tax dollars. This allegation was insufficient to confer standing in federal courts. Taxpayers were proper parties only to allege the unconstitutionality of congressional actions under the Taxing and Spending Clause and were required to show that the action went beyond the powers delegated to Congress. **Courts were not available to taxpayers to vent generalized grievances of government conduct or spending.** The complained-of statute arose under the Property Clause, and therefore the taxpayers had no standing to complain about the property transfer. The Court reversed the court of appeals' decision. *Valley Forge Christian College v. Americans United for Separation of Church and State*, 454 U.S. 464, 102 S.Ct. 752, 70 L.Ed.2d 700 (1982).

F. Licensing

◆   *Wyoming's amended Private School Licensing Act did not violate the rights of a private educational institution.*

A Wyoming corporation offered post-secondary degrees to students in 17 international learning centers. It operated under a license granted in 2003. In 2006, amendments to the Private School Licensing Act significantly changed state licensing requirements. Prior to the change, institutions could obtain licensure by paying fees and posting a bond. Under amended law, all private post-secondary institutions had to become accredited within five years unless they obtained a good cause extension. The amended law imposed minimal standards for institutions and provided for state investigation and evaluations to implement state rules. An emergency rule required all private post-secondary degree-granting institutions to submit applications to the state and provide proof of an application for accreditation from an association approved by the U.S. Department of Education. The corporation attempted to renew its license under the old law but the department rejected its application.

The corporation sued the state education department in the Wyoming court system, which held for the department. On appeal, the Supreme Court of Wyoming denied each of the corporation's constitutional claims. There was no differentiation among new state regulations, as the corporation argued, defeating an equal protection claim. As the lower court found, the new law did not create classes of institutions that were accredited or not. Instead, the law required all trade, correspondence, distance education, technical, vocational, business or other private schools to be accredited. There was no improper delegation of legislative authority based on the requirement of accreditation by an approved association. The amended law was not so vague as to be constitutionally void. The court held that **the state had authority to regulate private institutions under its police powers**. As none of the corporation's arguments had merit, the court affirmed the judgment. *Newport Int'l Univ. v. State of Wyoming, Dep't of Educ.*, 186 P.3d 382 (Wyo. 2008).

◆ *The Michigan Department of Education could deny a license to operate to the owner of a trade school teaching casino gambling.*

A Michigan resident applied to the proprietary school unit of the department of education for a license to operate a private trade school teaching casino gambling. The board denied his application because gaming was considered criminal behavior in Michigan. The applicant appealed to a Michigan trial court. The trial court reversed, and the board of education appealed to the Court of Appeals of Michigan.

The court of appeals noted that public policy did not completely prohibit casino gambling as evidenced by the legislature's decision to legalize millionaire parties and to allow casino gambling on Indian reservations. On further appeal, the Supreme Court of Michigan reversed. It adopted the dissenting opinion from the lower court, which stated that **licensing the proposed school would violate public policy**. If the school were allowed to teach casino gambling, it would be teaching behavior that was currently defined as illegal under Michigan law. *Michigan Gaming Institute v. State Board of Educ.*, 547 N.W.2d 882 (Mich. 1996).

◆ *A corporation that provided review courses for nursing school graduates had to pay an annual renewal licensing fee for each location.*

The corporation offered courses that prepared nursing school graduates for state certification exams. It operated at five different locations in the state. The review courses were held in hotel meeting rooms, college auditoriums or hospital conference rooms. The California legislature modified the Private Postsecondary and Vocational Education Reform Act to increase the annual renewal fee for nondegree granting institutions from $225 to a range of $600 to $1,200, depending on size. The corporation made a single $1,200 payment but refused to make a separate payment for each of its course sites.

A lawsuit arose, and a California trial court found that a separate fee could be charged for each location. The California Court of Appeal, First District, noted that because the corporation's educational sites were 50 miles from corporate headquarters and were held in places such as hotel conference rooms, they were neither branches nor satellites subject to separate annual fees under the act. However, since the legislature provided that each site be inspected by the governing council, the court inferred a legislative intent to require separate annual fees for each site. **As long as the governing council used some "reasonable method" of estimating the administrative costs of the entire program, its annual fee interpretation was reasonable.** Thus, the court of appeal required the corporation to pay an annual fee for each site. *RN Review for Nurses, Inc. v. State*, 28 Cal.Rptr.2d 354 (Cal. Ct. App. 1994).

◆ *A board for community colleges should have provided an occupational school with a hearing prior to terminating the school's license.*

A private Colorado occupational school was licensed to do business by the State Board for Community Colleges and Occupational Educations. A new statute revised licensing requirements, and the school was required to renew its license. The board's vice president rejected the school's application because it had not employed an independent accountant or utilized accepted accounting procedures as required by the new statute. The school filed a 42 U.S.C. § 1983 action in a Colorado district court against the vice president and the board. It alleged that both had failed to provide a hearing prior to terminating the school's license and had failed to provide an impartial tribunal.

A trial court determined that neither the board nor its vice president could be sued under 42 U.S.C. § 1983 and dismissed the case. The Colorado Court of Appeals found that the board was a state regulatory body that was entitled to immunity from suits for damages. Next, the court determined that **the vice president's failure to grant the school a pre-deprivation hearing was not a clear violation of its constitutional rights**. The vice president therefore had immunity on the claim for damages under Section 1983. However, the board's refusal to grant the school a pre-deprivation hearing potentially violated its statutory rights. On remand, the school could sue for injunctive relief. *National Camera, Inc. v. Sanchez*, 832 P.2d 960 (Colo. Ct. App. 1991).

G. Desegregation

◆ *A longstanding court battle to end racial segregation in Alabama colleges and universities could not be used to force changes in state K-12 funding.*

The suit was filed in 1981, when a group of black citizens claimed the state perpetuated a segregated university system. They said admissions standards at historically white institutions disqualified disproportionate numbers of black applicants. The citizens claimed historically black institutions were plagued by unfair funding and facility policies. In 1991, a federal district court ordered the state to encourage greater racial integration at its colleges and universities. Four years later, it entered a decree that ordered numerous additional changes to the state's higher education policies. Among other things, it required more flexible admissions policies and increased integration of faculty and administration at all state colleges and universities. The court also required the state to increase its funding of historically black institutions. Over the next eight years, the state and the plaintiffs "worked tirelessly" to make the changes required by the court. From 1990-2004, the state increased its annual funding of higher education by $340 million. During this time, undergraduate and graduate degrees awarded to black students increased by over 96%. In 2009, the plaintiffs filed a motion to require the state to provide better funding for K-12 schools. They sought an order invalidating property tax limitations imposed by the state constitution.

The plaintiffs said a funding crisis in the state's K-12 schools resulted in segregation at its colleges and universities. The district court denied the motion, and the plaintiffs appealed. On appeal, the U.S. Court of Appeals, Eleventh Circuit, explained that the case had always been about segregation in the state's higher education system. The plaintiffs' motion was about reforming the state's K-12 school funding system. Because the motion raised a claim relating to school finance rather than desegregation, it could not be pursued. The plaintiffs tried to link the inadequacy of K-12 funding with segregation at higher levels by proposing a chain of causation. Property tax limitations resulted in underfunded public schools, leading to the diversion of higher education funds to lower education. This diversion resulted in higher tuition rates and decreased black student enrollment at state colleges and universities. **Under** *U.S. v.*

Fordice, below, race-neutral state policies governing higher education can be challenged under the Constitution if they are traceable to a system of segregation. The court found the asserted relationship between the underfunding of the state's K-12 schools and segregation in Alabama colleges and universities was too attenuated and based on too many unpredictable premises. The judgment for the state was affirmed. *Knight v. Alabama*, 476 F.3d 1219 (11th Cir. 2007).

◆   *Where a state perpetuates policies and practices that can be traced to a segregative system and that have segregative effects, the policies will be considered unconstitutional unless there is sound educational justification for them and it is not practical to eliminate them.*

Mississippi maintained a dual system of public education at the university level – one set of universities for whites, and another set for blacks. In 1981, the State Board of Trustees issued "Mission Statements" to remedy this, classifying the three flagship historically white institutions (HWI) as "comprehensive" universities, redesignating one of the historically black institutions (HBI) as an "urban" university and characterizing the rest as "regional" institutions. However, the universities remained racially identifiable. A federal court found that state policies need merely be racially neutral, developed in good faith, and not contribute to the racial identifiability of each institution. It held that Mississippi was currently fulfilling its duty to desegregate. The U.S. Court of Appeals, Fifth Circuit, affirmed. The U.S. Supreme Court granted review.

The Supreme Court held that the district court had applied the wrong legal standard in ruling that Mississippi had brought itself into compliance with the Equal Protection Clause. **If a state perpetuates policies and practices traceable to its prior dual system that continue to have segregative effects, and such policies are without sound educational justification and can be practicably eliminated, the policies violate the Equal Protection Clause.** This is true even if the state has abolished the legal requirement that the races be separated and has established neutral policies. The proper inquiry is whether existing racial identifiability is attributable to the state. Applying the proper standard, several surviving aspects of Mississippi's prior dual system were constitutionally suspect. First, the use of higher minimum ACT composite scores at the HWIs, along with the state's refusal to consider high school grade performance was suspect. Second, the unnecessary duplication of programs at HBIs and HWIs was suspect. Third, the mission statements' reflection of previous policies to perpetuate racial separation was suspect. Finally, the state's policy of operating eight universities had to be examined to determine if it was educationally justifiable. *U.S. v. Fordice*, 505 U.S. 717, 112 S.Ct. 2727, 120 L.Ed.2d 575 (1992).

On remand, a federal court **entered a remedial decree prohibiting the state from maintaining remnants of the prior segregated system** and mandating specific relief in areas of admissions and funding. However, the court refused to order the relief requested by the complaining parties, which would significantly increase the number of African-Americans accepted for regular admission at state universities. The complaining parties claimed that the district court order's reliance on a summer remedial program to boost African-American admissions was inappropriate, and the parties appealed to the Fifth Circuit. The court agreed with the complaining parties that the district court's order affirming the elimination of many remedial courses had to be reconsidered, along with its finding that use of college entrance scores as a criterion for scholarships was not traceable to the illegal system of segregation. The court remanded for clarification the status of a proposal to merge two universities to eliminate unnecessary program duplication, as well as questions of increasing the other-race presence at two HBIs and issues of accreditation and funding. The court affirmed many aspects of the district court decision as consistent with the *Fordice* decision, significantly affirming its decision to maintain admissions standards that ensured educational soundness. *Ayers v. Fordice*, 111 F.3d 1183 (5th Cir. 1997).

H. Delegation of Police Power

◆   *A Michigan court properly entered a personal protection order (PPO) against a student who was accused of stalking one of her professors.*

A professor at Wayne State University filed a petition for a PPO against a student who sent her inappropriate e-mails of a sexual nature. She said the student left a magazine at her office that included an article about love with her picture pasted on it with disturbing comments. The professor said the student then continued to contact her after she was told not to. The court granted the petition, taking into account three prior PPOs issued against the student in other cases, including one that involved another instructor. The Court of Appeals of Michigan held the evidence relating to the other PPOs was admissible because it was relevant to show a scheme or plan of harassing college instructors. Even without the evidence relating to the prior PPOs, there was enough evidence to support the entry of a PPO. **On at least two occasions, the student engaged in acts of what the state harassment law called "unconsented contact" that caused emotional distress to the professor.** Under applicable provisions of state law, this was enough to show the student stalked the professor. As a result, the lower court had properly entered the PPO, and its judgment was affirmed. *Hilgendorf v. Lee*, No. 270335, 2007 WL 1713114 (Mich. Ct. App. 6/14/07).

◆   *The Appeals Court of Massachusetts held in favor of a university that faced charges it had illegally arrested a university alumnus.*

A student at the university had an abuse prevention order against a university alumnus, which required him to stay at least 30 yards away from her. However, as she was leaving a university building one day, she spotted the alumnus parked in a car across the street. The student went back inside the building and called university police to report a violation of the protection order. She gave a description of the car. The alumnus had left the campus area by then. University police officers confirmed there was an order and saw where the student said the alumnus had been parked. The area was within 30 feet of where the student had been at the time. Based on information he had been given, a university police officer stopped and arrested the alumnus on a public street near the university. The university sent him a letter notifying him he was barred from entering campus. The alumnus sued the university in a trial court, alleging the university police lacked the authority to arrest him, among other claims. He asserted a brochure titled "Benefits for Alumni of Boston University" created a contract between himself and the university.

The court awarded summary judgment to the university. The alumnus appealed to the Appeals Court of Massachusetts. He contended university police were not authorized to arrest him on a public street near the university. **The court found the university officer who arrested the alumnus was appointed as a special state police officer, with the same power to make arrests as regular police officers for any criminal offense committed in or about university property.** The officer had probable cause to arrest the alumnus, and the letter barring him from campus did not breach any contract, as he alleged. The court found the officer's authority extended to the area surrounding the campus, and it affirmed the judgment for the university. *Young v. Boston Univ.*, 64 Mass. App. Ct. 586 (Mass. App. Ct. 2005). The Supreme Judicial Court of Massachusetts denied further review in *Young v. Boston Univ.*, 445 Mass. 1107, 838 N.E.2d 577 (Mass. 2005).

II. ACCREDITATION

Regional and other accrediting institutions have been sued by private schools upon withdrawal of accreditation. The cases suggest: 1) actions of accrediting institutions do not constitute "state action" triggering due process requirements, 2) a school may maintain a breach of contract lawsuit against an accrediting institution if the institution fails to follow its own rules and procedures, and 3) if an accrediting institution's procedures are fair, its decision to revoke accreditation will likely be upheld.

A. Grants of Accreditation

◆   *Where an accreditation foundation's denial of accreditation to a college of art and design was supported by substantial evidence, it did not qualify as arbitrary or unreasonable.*

In 1995, Savannah College of Art & Design sought accreditation for its interior design program from the Foundation for Interior Design Education Research. Although a team of evaluators' report generally praised the program, it recommended the denial of accreditation. The foundation's board of trustees accepted the recommendation. Savannah College appealed, and a second on-site evaluation also recommended denial of accreditation for poor student achievement. Believing it had been treated unfairly, Savannah turned to the foundation's appeals panel, which determined that the denial of accreditation was supported by substantial evidence and consistent with other schools' accreditation reports. After the college threatened legal intervention, the foundation sued for a declaration that its decision to reject accreditation was lawful. In response, the college filed counterclaims against it. A federal court granted pretrial judgment to the foundation and dismissed all of the counterclaims. The school appealed to the Sixth Circuit.

The court held the foundation's denial of accreditation was neither

arbitrary nor discriminatory. Savannah College argued that the foundation's method of evaluation deviated from the usual evaluative process and was therefore discriminatory. The court agreed that the process in this case differed, but to the college's favor. The foundation would not normally send a second evaluation team, but it did so in this case to ensure fairness. Savannah's final argument claimed the foundation acted arbitrarily because the college's interior design program closely resembled other accredited programs. The court disagreed and affirmed the judgment, finding the foundation's decision was based on substantial evidence. *Foundation for Interior Design Educ. Research v. Savannah College of Art & Design*, 244 F.3d 521 (6th Cir. 2001).

◆ *A federal court refused to force the American Bar Association (ABA) to provisionally accredit a law school.*

After a religious university acquired a non-accredited law school, it applied for provisional accreditation from the ABA. The ABA rejected the application. The following year, the university applied again, and again was rejected. A group of graduates, students and instructors then sued the ABA seeking a preliminary injunction to force provisional accreditation. The university also filed a third application for provisional accreditation. A Florida federal district court refused to grant the injunction, finding no evidence that irreparable harm would befall the plaintiffs if the injunction was not granted. While the third application was pending, **graduates still could be admitted to practice in other states, and they could seek a waiver of the 12-month rule on sitting for the Florida Bar Exam** from the state supreme court. *Staver v. American Bar Ass'n*, 169 F.Supp.2d 1372 (M.D. Fla. 2001).

◆ *An Oregon law allowing certain schools to be exempted from requirements that out-of-state schools were not exempted from, was struck down.*

A private Washington university with a branch campus in Oregon was accredited by the Northwest Association of Schools and Colleges (NASC). Following NASC accreditation, the Oregon Office of Educational Policy and Planning (OEPP) continued to review non-Oregon schools every three years. The statute provided that "no school ... shall confer ... any degree ... without first having submitted the requirements for such degree to the [OEPP] and having obtained the approval of the director." However, an amendment exempted Oregon schools in good standing with the NASC from OEPP review. The university filed suit in an Oregon circuit court, seeking a declaration that the statute violated the Commerce Clause. The circuit court held for the university and severed a portion of the amendment. The court of appeals affirmed but invalidated the exemption in its entirety. The Oregon Supreme Court allowed the university's petition for review solely on the issue of remedy.

The university contended that the entire amendment had been improperly invalidated. The supreme court disagreed, ruling that the statute as severed was not capable of being executed in accordance with legislative intent. The legislature had intended both to continue the exemption from OEPP authority for Oregon schools that were members of the NASC and to remove the exemption from OEPP authority for out-of-state schools, even if those schools were NASC members. However, the dominant intent of the amendment was to ensure that Oregon branch campuses of the out-of-state schools had the same level of faculty and facilities as their main campuses. **As partial severance would subject these out-of-state schools to lesser scrutiny, the court ordered the amendment severed in its entirety.** The court of appeals' ruling was affirmed. *City Univ. v. Office of Educ. Policy*, 885 P.2d 701 (Or. 1994).

B. Claims of Fraud

◆ *A Georgia court refused to certify a class action by students who alleged fraud by a university, because their claims required a case-by-case review.*

According to the students, the education they received was "not worth the cost." They claimed the university engaged in fraudulent recruiting practices. Although the university was continuously accredited during the time in question, the students asserted that the accreditation was obtained through false representations including inflated employment rates for university graduates. They filed a state court action against the university and its parent corporation, seeking damages because they had paid tuition and incurred loans but were unable to find employment in their respective fields of study. The court found no reason to certify the case as a class action, and on appeal, the Court of Appeals of Georgia agreed. **The students had introduced a great deal of individualized evidence that required a case-by-case review.** For this reason, the court found their claims not suitable for class certification. As determining whether each student was adversely affected by some aspect of the university's operation would "require a separate mini-trial," the court affirmed the judgment denying class certification. *Diallo v. American Intercontinental Univ.*, 301 Ga.App. 299, 687 S.E.2d 278 (Ga. Ct. App. 2009).

◆ *A law school graduate who could not take a bar exam after attending an unaccredited Massachusetts law school could not proceed with fraud claims.*

At the time of the student's admission, the school was not accredited by the American Bar Association (ABA). This meant graduates could not sit for a state bar examination. Upon learning that the ABA was recommending a provisional accreditation, the school sent prospective students a letter expressing confidence that accreditation was forthcoming. But a disclaimer was included in the law school catalogue, which stated that it did not represent it would be approved prior to the graduation of any matriculating student. The ABA denied the school accreditation near the time the student enrolled.

Further attempts to gain accreditation failed, and the student was unable to transfer to another school. He graduated but was unable to sit for a state bar examination due to the school's lack of accreditation. The student sued the school for fraudulent misrepresentation in a federal district court. The case reached the U.S. Court of Appeals, First Circuit, which held that to prevail, **the student had to show he relied on a false representation and acted on it to his detriment. He also had to show his reliance on the false statement was reasonable.** But the student did neither. His claim that he relied on statements regarding accreditation was contradicted by his transfer attempt after the school indicated its difficulties gaining accreditation. The student's transfer application strongly suggested he did not believe the assurances regarding accreditation. Even if the student did rely on the statements of assurance regarding the school's chances at accreditation, reliance was not reasonable. As a result, the court affirmed a lower court judgment for the law school. *Rodi v. Southern New England School of Law*, 532 F.3d 11 (1st Cir. 2008).

◆   *A university's failure to gain accreditation for its Master of Social Work program did not violate students' due process rights.*

Governor's State University instituted a Master of Social Work Program in 1997. Three years later, university officials informed graduate students enrolled in the program that the National Council of Social Work Education had denied the university's application for accreditation. As a result, graduates were not permitted to sit for a licensing examination in Illinois. Graduating students discussed the accreditation problem with university officials at a board meeting. Additional students remained outside, protesting. A month later, graduate students were invited to an alumni fundraising dinner. The university limited the number of entrances and exits and permitted the students to picket only in the vestibule area. Instead of attending the dinner, the students peacefully protested the university's actions. Security guards removed the students from the premises and refused to allow them to re-enter the grounds.

A group of students sued the university, its president and trustees in a federal district court for due process and speech rights violations. The court held for the university, and the students appealed. The U.S. Court of Appeals, Seventh Circuit, held the students did not show any arbitrary government action in violation of the Due Process Clause. **While the university was responsible for ensuring its programs were accredited, the students had adequate remedies at law to resolve their complaints.** The trustees were not involved in the dinner event, and did not prevent the protesters from attending. The university president did not retaliate against the students for their protests. The actions of security guards were merely a response to overcrowding. The court held summary judgment was properly entered for the university and its officials. *Galdikas v. Fagan*, 342 F.3d 684 (7th Cir. 2003).

◆   *A class of students was allowed to sue an accrediting agency for fraud after the agency improperly extended the accreditation of a school.*

A District of Columbia vocational school applied to an accrediting agency for accreditation in 1985. The agency granted the school an accreditation that was to expire in two years. Despite areas of concern, including curriculum, instructional materials, clarity of the school's mission statement and the school's financial status, the agency granted the school a series of automatic extensions until November of 1988. A number of students who had enrolled during this period began to notice that the school did not carry through on all of its promises. The students filed suit against the accrediting agency in the U.S. District Court for the District of Columbia, alleging that the agency was liable for fraud because it extended the accreditation of the school without knowledge of whether the school met its standards for accreditation.

On cross-motions for pretrial judgment, the court determined that **the class of students had established a *prima facie* case of fraud** under District of

Columbia law. The elements of a cause of action for fraud are 1) a false representation, 2) in reference to a material fact, 3) made with the knowledge of its falsity, 4) with the intent to deceive, and 5) on which action is taken in reliance upon the representation. Here, there were issues of fact that precluded the granting of pretrial judgment for either party. The motions for pretrial judgment were denied. *Armstrong v. Accrediting Council for Continuing Educ. & Training, Inc.*, 961 F.Supp. 305 (D.D.C. 1997).

◆ *A fraud claim brought by nursing students against a school that had allegedly misrepresented its accreditation status failed where the students could not show that they relied on the school's misrepresentation.*

A Missouri nursing school graduated its first class of students in 1984. The school was accredited by the Missouri State Board of Nursing. It also was a "candidate for accreditation" with the North Central Association for Colleges and Schools (NCA). The NCA recommended that the school's brochure state that it was a "candidate for accreditation by the NCA." However, the brochure actually stated that the school "has ... been granted [NCA] candidacy for review status" and that "accreditation for [the school] is expected in 1983." In 1981, a letter from the student services coordinator restated the above-quoted information to the class of 1984. However, the students were not apprised of the NCA accreditation status prior to their graduation, and the school was not formally accredited until 1987. This accreditation status did not apply retroactively to the class of 1984. Members of the class of 1984 filed suit in a Missouri trial court, alleging that the school intentionally misrepresented its accreditation status, which limited their job prospects, advanced education and future earning power. The trial court granted the school's motion for pretrial judgment, and the students appealed.

The Missouri Court of Appeals held that **although misrepresentation of a material fact by silence may amount to actionable fraud, the students failed to show they relied on the school's allegedly fraudulent statements in enrolling or remaining enrolled in the program**. Because the students failed to establish the reliance element of fraud, the court refused to address the issue of whether the school had a duty to disclose all material facts related to the anticipated accreditation. The holding of the trial court was affirmed. *Nigro v. Research College of Nursing*, 876 S.W.2d 681 (Mo. Ct. App. 1994).

C. Withdrawal of Accreditation

◆ *A small college in Tennessee failed in its attempt to reverse an accrediting agency's decision to remove its accreditation.*

Hiwassee College lost its accreditation by the Southern Association of Colleges and Schools (SACS) based on its troubled financial condition. The college sued the SACS in a federal district court, claiming that SACS failed to meet its own requirements relating to removal of accreditation. It asserted that SACS denied it due process of law under the Higher Education Act (HEA) and the Due Process Clause of the Fifth Amendment. The court held the SACS was entitled to judgment as a matter of law, and the college appealed. The U.S. Court of Appeals, Eleventh Circuit, held the college did not have an express or implied right of action to bring a claim against SACS under the HEA statute. **Nothing indicated Congress intended to create a private right of action in the HEA. The court held the SACS was not a government actor and therefore was not required to comply with Fifth Amendment due process requirements.** Nor did SACS fail to meet any common law duty to provide the college with due process in connection with the accreditation decision. The college never asserted that it was in compliance with the agency's accreditation criteria. The judgment was affirmed. *Hiwassee College, Inc. v. Southern Ass'n of Colleges and Schools*, No. 07-13033, 2008 WL 1701694 (11th Cir. 4/14/08).

◆   *Where a decision to withdraw accreditation was not arbitrary, a federal court should not have ordered the agency to continue the accreditation.*

The Commission on Occupational Education Institutions (COEI) is part of the Southern Association of Colleges and Schools (SACS). It was set up to accredit postsecondary, nondegree granting institutions. In March 1988, COEI conducted an on-site inspection of a cosmetology school's campuses to determine whether to reaffirm accreditation. After finding various problems (violations of dual accreditation and of refund and disclosure policies, and failure to submit an annual report for 1986), COEI dropped the school's accreditation. Since this was a prerequisite for the students' receipt of federal financial assistance, the school sued COEI and SACS to stop the disaccreditation. A federal court issued an injunction preventing SACS from withdrawing the school's accreditation for at least one year, and it further ordered SACS to pay the school's attorneys' fees and costs.

During the SACS appeal to the U.S. Court of Appeals, Fifth Circuit, five of the school's six campuses closed. The school voluntarily relinquished SACS accreditation for the other campus. This rendered the validity of the injunction moot. However, the court of appeals found that it had to reach the merits of the case because of the question of attorneys' fees and costs. The court then noted that **there had been clear evidence that the school had been in violation of the dual accreditation policy set by COEI**. The district court had incorrectly found that COEI's policy language was vague. It should have accorded COEI's accreditation decisions greater deference. Thus, the court reversed the district court's award to the school and held that it was not entitled to attorneys' fees and costs. *Wilfred Academy v. Southern Ass'n of Colleges and Schools*, 957 F.2d 210 (5th Cir. 1992).

III. CONSTRUCTION AND OUTSIDE CONTRACTS

◆   *A New Jersey court revived a claim against a company that provided snow and ice removal services to Rider University (RU).*

A student slipped and fell on a patch of black ice after leaving a piano lesson on campus. She was about 16 feet from the building she had exited. A private contractor was responsible for clearing building entrances and the perimeter of campus buildings to a distance of eight feet. Typically, arrangements to remove snow and ice beyond the eight-foot perimeter were made informally by the contractor and RU. An RU facilities director said he told the contractor that de-icing was needed in various areas of the campus beyond the eight-foot perimeter on the morning of the student's fall. He said this included the area where she later fell and that the contractor had previously agreed to provide de-icing for the entire campus when conditions were icy.

The student sued the contractor in a state court for negligence based on its failure to remove the black ice. In response, the contractor filed a third-party complaint against RU for contribution and indemnification. RU sought dismissal under a state law immunity provision, but the court instead granted the contractor pretrial judgment. A New Jersey Appellate Division Court reversed the decision, finding that the lower court had to resolve a number of fact issues. **The case was returned to the lower court so it could determine if the area where the student fell was within the scope of the oral agreement.** It would also have to consider if the ice was reasonably observable and whether the time period between notice of the need for additional services and the fall was sufficient to allow de-icing. *Besner v. UNICCO Service Co.*, No. A-4804-07T2, 2009 WL 483225 (N.J. Super. App. Div. 1/29/09).

◆ *A federal district court refused to find an American university breached a contract to enter into an affiliation agreement with an Israeli college.*

In 1994, the college began partnering with American institutions to offer courses at a campus in Israel. It began a search to replace New England College. The search led it to Southern New Hampshire University (SNHU), which initially decided not to go forward with the affiliation. Two years later, negotiations proceeded to a point where the parties signed affiliation and academic supervision agreements. The agreements outlined the responsibilities of each party with respect to curriculum, faculty, admission criteria and other details. They also outlined contractual obligations. The president of SNHU signed the documents, and the Israeli college president then signed them. Five months later, SNHU's president decided not to move ahead with the affiliation. The college then sued SNHU for breach of contract in a federal district court.

SNHU claimed that the parties had a memo of understanding but not a contract. The court denied the college pretrial judgment. **There were disputed facts about what happened at meetings leading up to the signing of the two documents, and it was unclear whether an agreement to enter into a binding contract was conditioned on SNHU's completion of due diligence.** *Israel College-Educational Horizons, Ltd. v. Southern New Hampshire Univ.*, No. 05-cv-392-JD, 2008 WL 187606 (D.N.H. 1/17/08).

◆ *A university that did a thorough environmental impact evaluation of a construction project did not have to file an environmental impact statement.*

A New York state university planned five separate campus housing projects, including a 116-unit building for which it filed a full environmental assessment form that was supported by an environmental site assessment report. A lawsuit nevertheless ensued, seeking to compel the university to file an environmental impact statement and seeking a temporary injunction to prevent construction until such statement was filed. The New York Supreme Court, Appellate Division, ruled that the university did not have to file an environmental impact statement because its thorough study of the environmental effects of construction concluded that there would not be an adverse impact on wetlands, cultural resources, groundwater, air quality, solid waste, removal of vegetation, wildlife or open space such that the project should be stopped. **In light of the university's thorough evaluation, the project could proceed.** *Forman v. Trustees of State Univ. of New York*, 757 N.Y.S.2d 180 (N.Y. App. Div. 2003).

◆ *A university was entitled to money from a contractor who underbid a project and then sought to recoup its losses as additional work.*

The University of Alaska solicited bids for fixing a drainage problem involving an access road and gravel pad surfaces at a research facility. **It accepted the lowest bid but then experienced problems with the contractor.** The contractor first obtained a one-week extension, then sought approval for extra materials, extra work and the payment of additional money. The university rejected the claims. When the contractor failed to finish the project on time, the ground froze, and it was unable to complete the project. Both the university and the contractor sought financial reimbursement, and a hearing officer determined that the contractor underbid the project, then sought to recover its losses as additional work. However, the university also owed some additional monies to the contractor. The case reached the Supreme Court of Alaska, which largely upheld the hearing officer's determinations. It refused, however, to grant the university liquidated damages because the university had entered into an agreement with the contractor's bonding company regarding the hiring of another contractor to finish the project. *Lakloey, Inc. v. Univ. of Alaska*, No. 5-9690, 2002 WL 1732561 (Alaska 2002).

◆ *Fact issues prevented a court from granting pretrial judgment to a university on a breach of contract claim involving an electrical contractor.*

A New York university hired an electrical contractor to perform work on a biomolecular medicine and residential tower. Shortly after the contract was signed, the project fell behind schedule. The electrical contractor blamed the construction manager and inadequate security, which led to vandalism and theft, forcing the electrical contractor to redo some work. Eventually, a lawsuit was filed, with the electrical contractor asserting that the university breached the contract by failing to pay for work performed, and the university asserting that it had to correct and complete work the electrical contractor was supposed to finish. A New York court granted pretrial judgment to the university, but the Supreme Court, Appellate Division, reversed. **Evidence existed indicating that the electrical contractor performed its obligations under the contract.** The court remanded the case for further proceedings. *F. Garofalo Electric Co. v. New York Univ.*, 754 N.Y.S.2d 227 (N.Y. App. Div. 2002).

◆ *A coffee shop breached its lease agreement with a university by refusing to pay rent after a competitor opened a shop on campus.*

An Ohio university entered into a 10-year lease with a coffee shop for one of the sections of its food court. The university agreed that competition between like products among shops would be strongly discouraged. Later, another coffee seller opened a location in the student center, and the coffee shop stopped paying rent. The university sued it for breach of contract, and the coffee shop defended by asserting that the university breached the non-compete agreement of the lease by allowing the competitor onto the university campus. The Ohio Court of Claims ruled for the university, finding it only had a duty not to allow competitors into the food court. **Since the competitor was not located in the court with the coffee shop, the university did not breach the non-compete agreement.** The court ordered the coffee shop to pay the university over $37,000 in damages for past-due rent and common area charges. *Kent State Univ. v. Univ. Coffee House, Inc.*, 776 N.E.2d 583 (Ohio Ct. Cl. 2002).

◆   *West Virginia's highest court set forth five factors to be used in determining whether a construction project is a public project.*

West Virginia University and the West Virginia University Foundation (a private, nonprofit corporation) began planning and developing a layout for the construction of a building to be known as the University Services Center. After a bidding process, a developer agreed to build the center at its own cost and risk. The foundation would then purchase the site and lease the building to the university. When an affiliation of construction trades sued for a declaration that the proposed construction was a public project governed by state wage and competitive bidding laws, the university and the nonprofit foundation moved for pretrial judgment. A state court granted the motion, finding that the foundation was not a state agency, and its connection to the university did not convert the construction into a public project. The West Virginia Supreme Court of Appeals listed five factors to be used in determining whether a construction project is a public project. It held **the lower court record was not sufficiently developed to determine whether public funds had been used on the project**. Further, the building was now completed, and there was no indication of wage violations. *Affiliated Construction Trades Foundation v. Univ. of West Virginia Board of Trustees*, 557 S.E.2d 863 (W. Va. 2001).

◆   *A university could not recover from a contractor for an explosion and fire several years after the construction of a power plant.*

The University of Colorado contracted with a construction company to build a co-generation power facility on its Boulder campus. The contract contained a provision stating that **acceptance of the work would constitute a release of all claims against the company**, and also contained a 12-month warranty period. However, the university purchased an extended five-year warranty from the subcontractor that furnished the gas turbine engines for the facility. After the facility had been in operation for three and a half years, a combination of events caused a backup in one engine, resulting in an explosion and fire. The university sued the contractor and subcontractor for breach of contract, breach of warranty, negligence and strict liability. A state court ruled for the defendants, and the Colorado Court of Appeals affirmed. Here, the contractor's warranty and the release clearly protected it from liability. Also, with respect to the subcontractor, the jury's ruling was not unsupported by the evidence. *Regents of the Univ. of Colorado v. Harbert Construction Co.*, 51 P.3d 1037 (Colo. Ct. App. 2001).

◆ *The U.S. Supreme Court held a choice of law clause in a construction contract superseded arbitration rights found in the Federal Arbitration Act.*

An electrical contractor contracted with a California university to install conduits. The contract contained a clause in which the parties agreed to arbitrate disputes relating to the contract. The contract also contained a choice-of-law clause that stated that it would be governed by the law of the place of the project's location. A dispute arose concerning overtime compensation, and the contractor made a formal request for arbitration. The university sued the contractor in a California trial court for fraud and breach of contract. **The contractor claimed that it was entitled to arbitration under the contract and the Federal Arbitration Act (FAA).** The court granted the university's motion to stay arbitration under a California statute that permits a stay when arbitration is the subject of pending court action. The contractor appealed to the California Court of Appeal, which affirmed the trial court's decision. The court of appeal acknowledged that although the contract affected interstate commerce, the California statute applied because of the contractual choice-of-law clause. The California Supreme Court denied the contractor's petition for discretionary review, but the U.S. Supreme Court agreed to hear its appeal.

On appeal, the contractor reiterated its argument that the court of appeal's ruling on the choice-of-law clause deprived it of its federally guaranteed right to arbitration under the FAA. The Supreme Court ruled that **the FAA did not confer a general right to compel arbitration. Rather, it guaranteed the right to arbitrate according to the manner provided for in the parties' contract.** The court of appeal had correctly found that the contract incorporated California law. The FAA was not undermined by the state law that permitted a stay of arbitration. The Court affirmed the court of appeal's decision for the university. *Volt Information Sciences v. Board of Trustees of Leland Stanford Junior Univ.*, 489 U.S. 468, 109 S.Ct. 1248, 103 L.Ed.2d 488 (1989).

CHAPTER ELEVEN

School Finance

I. PUBLIC ASSISTANCE TO SCHOOLS

A. Federal Funding

1. Compliance

◆ *A conservative advocacy group lacked standing to enforce the Solomon Amendment on behalf of its student-members in a federal court.*

Under the Solomon Amendment, a college or university can lose federal funds if the U.S. Secretary of Defense determines the institution does not allow military recruiting on campus on terms at least equal to those allowed other employers. The Young America's Foundation (YAF) informed the Secretary of Defense that some students and faculty prevented or disrupted military recruiting at the University of California at Santa Cruz (UCSC) and prevented YAF members from meeting with military recruiters at campus job fairs. When the Secretary took no action under the Solomon Amendment, the YAF asked a federal court to order him to withhold funds from UCSC. The court dismissed the case, and the YAF appealed to the U.S. Court of Appeals, D.C. Circuit. The court held the YAF lacked standing to bring the action. Organizations may sue to enforce the rights of members if at least one member has the right to bring the lawsuit on her own behalf. But since none of these member-students did, the YAF lacked standing. **The YAF could not demonstrate that ordering the Secretary of Defense to withhold funds from UCSC would provide student-members greater access to military recruiters** at job fairs. *Young America's Foundation v. Gates*, 573 F.3d 797 (D.C. Cir. 2009).

♦   *The U.S. Supreme Court held that the government may show a violation of*
Title IV of the Higher Education Act without proving specific intent to injure or
defraud by a defendant.

A private, nonprofit technical school in Indiana participated in the
Guaranteed Student Loan (GSL) program authorized by Title IV of the Higher
Education Act. The program required the school to make refunds to the lender
if a student withdrew from school during a term. If the school failed to refund
loans to the lender, the student – and if the student defaulted, the government –
would be liable for the full amount of the loan. The treasurer of the school
conferred with the school's owners and initiated a practice of not making GSL
refunds. As a result, the school owed $139,649 in refunds.

After the school lost its accreditation, a federal grand jury indicted the
treasurer for "knowingly and willfully misapplying" federally insured student
loan funds in violation of 20 U.S.C. § 1097(a). A federal district court
dismissed the indictment because it lacked an allegation that the treasurer
intended to injure or defraud the U.S. The Seventh Circuit reinstated the
prosecution, and the U.S. Supreme Court affirmed the decision. The Court held
Section 1097(a) did not require the specific intent to injure or defraud. **If the**
government can prove the defendant misapplied Title IV funds knowingly
and willfully, that is sufficient to show a violation of Section 1097(a).
Bates v. U.S., 522 U.S. 23, 118 S.Ct. 285, 139 L.Ed.2d 215 (1997).

♦   *Federal assistance may be conditioned on compliance with federal law.*

Section 12(f) of the Military Selective Service Act denied federal financial
assistance under Title IV of the Higher Education Act to male students between
the ages of 18 and 26 who did not register for the draft. Applicants for
assistance were required to file a statement with their institutions attesting to
their compliance with the Selective Service Act. A group of students who had
not registered for the draft sued the selective service system to enjoin
enforcement of Section 12(f). A federal district court held that the act was a bill
of attainder (a law that imposes a penalty on a group of people without a trial)
because it singled out an identifiable group that would be ineligible for Title IV
aid based on their failure to register. The court also held that the compliance
requirement violated the Fifth Amendment. On appeal, the Supreme Court
rejected the claims that the law was a bill of attainder and upheld the law.
The law clearly gave non-registrants 30 days after receiving notice of
ineligibility for federal financial aid to register for the draft and thereby
qualify for aid. Furthermore, the bill of attainder prohibition in the
Constitution applies only to statutes that inflict punishments on specified
groups or individuals such as "all Communists." The Court also held that the
denial of aid based on these requirements was not "punishment." The Court
stated that **if students wish to further their education at the expense of their**
country, they cannot expect the benefits without accepting their fair share
of governmental responsibility. Finally, the law did not violate the Fifth
Amendment because there was nothing forcing students to apply for federal
aid. *Selective Service System v. Minnesota Public Interest Research Group*, 468
U.S. 841, 104 S.Ct. 3348, 82 L.Ed.2d 632 (1984).

◆ *Private schools whose students receive federal funds are deemed to be recipients of federal assistance. Therefore, even a college with an unbending policy of rejecting all forms of government assistance was required to comply with federal laws because its students received federal grants and loans.*

A private college, which had an "unbending policy" of refusing all forms of government assistance in order to remain independent of governmental restrictions, was asked by the Department of Education (DOE) to supply "assurance of compliance" with Title IX, which the college refused to do on the ground that it was receiving no federal funding. The DOE disagreed, saying that because the school enrolled large numbers of students receiving federal Basic Educational Opportunity Grants (BEOGs), it was receiving financial assistance for purposes of Title IX. The DOE then cut off student financial assistance based on the college's failure to execute assurances of compliance.

Students and the college brought suit challenging the termination of financial assistance. **The Supreme Court held that the college was a recipient of federal financial assistance and was thus subject to Title IX. This was so despite the fact that only some of the college's students received BEOGs and even though the college did not receive any direct federal financial assistance.** The college was obliged to submit assurance of compliance, but only with regard to the administration of its financial aid program, in order for students to continue to receive federal aid. *Grove City College v. Bell*, 465 U.S. 555, 104 S.Ct. 1211, 79 L.Ed.2d 516 (1984).

◆ *A federal law that cuts off financial aid to students convicted of drug-related offenses did not violate the Fifth Amendment.*

A federal statute located at 20 U.S.C. § 1091(r) cuts off federal grant, loan or work assistance to any student who is convicted of an offense involving the sale or possession of a controlled substance. A student advocacy group sued the U.S. Department of Education Secretary, claiming the law was unconstitutional because it punished them criminally a second time for the same offense in violation of the Double Jeopardy Clause of the Fifth Amendment.

A federal district court rejected the group's arguments. On appeal, the U.S. Court of Appeals, Eighth Circuit, analyzed whether punishment imposed by the statute was civil or criminal in nature. **The fact that the law suspended eligibility and did not impose penalties, and the fact that an administrative agency determined eligibility indicated that Congress intended a civil sanction, not a criminal one.** The court also found the statute's scheme was not so punitive that it could be deemed to levy a criminal penalty. Application of the relevant factors weighed in favor of a finding that the statute did not impose criminal punishment. Therefore, there was no violation of the Double Jeopardy Clause, and the judgment was affirmed. *Students for Sensible Drug Policy Foundation v. Spellings*, 523 F.3d 896 (8th Cir. 2008).

◆ *A federal court lacked jurisdiction to determine whether the U.S. Department of Education (DOE) improperly listed a college as closed.*

A Puerto Rico college participated in the Pell Grant program under a Program Participation Agreement (PPA). In February 1995, the Puerto Rico Treasury Department shut down the school due to a tax debt. The department placed locks on the college's doors, and students were forced to vacate the premises. The college reopened about two weeks later. As a result, the DOE placed the college on a list of "closed schools" and stopped treating it as a participating school in the Pell Grant program. The college claimed the DOE breached its PPA contract and sued the DOE. The U.S. Court of Federal Claims dismissed the complaint, but the U.S. Court of Appeals for the Federal Circuit vacated the decision and remanded the case to the lower court. On remand, the court again dismissed the case. The DOE did not breach any contract with the college by failing to provide it with a hearing. Under federal regulations governing PPAs, the agreement automatically expired when the college failed to hold classes for two weeks. **As the agreement automatically expired, no hearing was needed. The court also held it lacked jurisdiction to determine whether the DOE improperly placed the college on its list of closed schools.** *San Juan City College v. U.S.*, 74 Fed.Cl. 448 (Ct. Claims 2006).

In 2007, the district court granted the college's request for a time extension. The U.S. Court of Appeals, Federal Circuit, affirmed this decision without an opinion. *San Juan City College v. U.S.*, 258 Fed.Appx. 316 (Fed. Cir. 2007).

2. Government Authority

◆ *A private college was not covered by the Privacy Act because participation in a student financial assistance program did not make it a federal agent.*

An Illinois student's father died, and her mother was unable to comply with her college's requests for verification of income. As a result, she did not receive federal financial aid for one school year. The college allowed the student to register for classes and treated her tuition as an "unpaid debt." Although she qualified for federal aid, the college's financial aid office refused to issue her funds because she was not in good standing. The student's mother then took out private loans to cover her tuition. The student completed the requirements for her bachelor's degree that year – but the college refused to grant her a degree because her tuition for the previous year remained unpaid. The student and her mother sued the college and the U.S. Department of Education (DOE) in a federal district court for violating the federal Privacy Act. **The court found the Privacy Act is intended to protect citizens from the improper disclosure of personal information by government agencies.** The court awarded pretrial judgment to the college because it is not a government agency. The DOE was also entitled to judgment because it had not maintained the financial information in this case. Instead, the college kept it. The court rejected the argument that the college was a DOE agent that could be held liable for record-keeping. *Lengerich v. Columbia College*, 672 F.Supp.2d 599 (N.D. Ill. 2009).

◆ *A Florida law restricting state universities from spending funds on travel to "terrorist states" was an impermissible embargo on the exchange of ideas, culture and academia that also intruded on federal authority.*

An Act Relating to Travel to Terrorist States restricted state universities from spending both "state" and "nonstate" funds on activities related to travel to "terrorist states" as designated by the U.S. Department of State. A sponsoring Florida legislator declared the act was intended to prevent public funds from assisting Cuba's communist regime. A group of university faculty members claimed the act violated the Constitution and filed a federal district court action against state officials to bar its enforcement. Some of the faculty members argued that the act would hamper their research in nations such as Cuba and Iran. The court noted that the act restricted the use of both "state" and "nonstate" funds. It found the design and intent of the law took in more than spending, as it made a political condemnation of the designated countries.

A spending limitation on "state funds" could be justified as within the legislature's discretion. State officials claimed the funding restrictions for travel to designated countries did not prevent individuals from traveling "on their own dime." The court disagreed, finding the act not only prevented use of private and federal funds for travel, it effectively foreclosed travel to, and research in, the designated countries by preventing universities from disbursing funds and conducting other travel and research activities. The act made it impossible for individuals to travel to Cuba. **Characterizing the act as "essentially an impermissible 'embargo' on the exchange of ideas, culture and academia," the court found it was outside the realm of permissible state activity.** Restrictions on the use of "nonstate" funds for activities related to travel to the designated countries was also an obstacle to federal authority in international relations. The faculty members were entitled to pretrial judgment regarding the restrictions on the use of "nonstate" funds. *Faculty Senate of Florida International Univ. v. Roberts*, 574 F.Supp.2d 1331 (S.D. Fla. 2008).

◆ *A government agency could seek a refund of grant money to equalize the amounts spent by it and by the university foundation awarded the grant.*

A nonprofit foundation for a California university submitted a project proposal designed to retrain defense engineers for positions in small businesses or manufacturing. The estimated cost of the program was $1,179,544, and the foundation sought $593,166 from a federal grant program administered by the National Science Foundation (NSF). The NSF awarded the foundation $550,000 under a three-year grant that required the foundation to essentially match the grant funds, and to maintain detailed accounting records of all costs as well as of the matching funds. When the NSF later suspected that the foundation was not meeting its financial obligations, an audit was conducted, and a recommendation was made that the NSF should seek a refund of approximately $140,000. The foundation sued to prevent the NSF from obtaining a refund, but a Virginia federal court ruled in favor of the NSF.

The U.S. Court of Appeals, Fourth Circuit, affirmed the judgment, finding that **the foundation had breached the terms of the grant regarding its obligation to fund or obtain funding for approximately half the costs of the program**. The foundation also had improperly stated certain amounts paid to the engineers as matching funds. As a result, the lower court had properly required the foundation to refund part of the grant money to the NSF. *California State Univ. Fullerton Foundation v. National Science Foundation*, 26 Fed.Appx. 263 (4th Cir. 2002).

◆   *A private university did not meet the eligibility requirements for student financial assistance programs under Title IV of the Higher Education Act.*

In 1991 and 1992, the DOE found the university system, Sistema Universitario Ana G. Mendez, was not eligible for Title IV programs dealing with Pell grant programs. As a result of the DOE's finding, **the university system was responsible for refunding to the federal government $1,712,540 in student grant funds** that were disbursed from 1989 to 1991. The secretary of education's determination was based on the fact that the university system failed to license its additional campuses. When filling out its Title IV application forms, the university system did not report these campuses under the "additional locations" section. It also failed to obtain prior approval from the Puerto Rico Commission on Higher Education for most of the satellite locations. The university system filed an administrative challenge, but a DOE administrative law judge affirmed its $1.7 million liability. The university system appealed to a federal district court, which reversed the administrative decision, finding the satellite campuses were licensed. However, it also found that the certifications did not necessarily constitute legal authorization under the Higher Education Act. On remand, the DOE determined that the certifications did not constitute legal authorization. The district court affirmed.

The university system then asked the U.S. Court of Appeals for the First Circuit to determine whether the Higher Education Act gives the secretary of education the final word on whether a university program is legally authorized by a state under the act and is therefore eligible for Title IV funding. The First Circuit held that **the Higher Education Act does not explicitly give either the secretary of education or the states the exclusive right to determine "legal authorization."** However, the court reasoned that it is not impermissible or unreasonable to allow the secretary to make that determination. The DOE's finding of liability was affirmed. *Sistema Universitario Ana G. Mendez v. Riley*, 234 F.3d 772 (1st Cir. 2000).

◆   *The U.S. Court of Appeals, Second Circuit, upheld federal regulations published under Title IV of the Higher Education Act as representing a reasonable interpretation of the statute.*

Title IV of the Higher Education Act, 20 U.S.C. § 1091b(a), requires college and post-secondary vocational training schools that receive federal funds for student financial aid programs to establish a fair and equitable policy for refunding unearned tuition and other costs when a student receiving such aid fails to enter or prematurely leaves the intended program. Subsection (b) declares that an institution's refund policy shall be considered fair and equitable if the refund is at least the largest of the amounts provided under state law, the institution's nationally recognized accrediting agency formula, or the statutorily described formula for pro rata refunds.

A regulation issued by the Secretary of Education (found at 34 C.F.R. § 668.22(b)(4)) provided that schools had to deduct "any unpaid charges owed by the student for the period of enrollment for which the student has been charged." Former regulations had put the risk of student nonpayment on the government. A coalition of vocational training schools in New York sought a federal district court injunction against the operation of the regulation. The court granted the injunction, but the U.S. Court of Appeals, Second Circuit, vacated the injunction and stated that **Section 668.22(b)(4) represented a reasonable interpretation of the statute**. The statute set a minimum refund amount but did not bar the secretary from asking for a larger amount. *Coalition of New York State Career Schools Inc. v. Riley*, 129 F.3d 276 (2d Cir. 1997).

B. State Funding

◆ *A Wisconsin federal judge refused to order the University of Wisconsin (UW) to fund a conservative student group from student fees.*

UW student fees funded registered student organizations. "Collegians for a Constructive Tomorrow-Madison" (CFACT) missed an application deadline for funding set by the student services finance committee (SSFC), and the application was rejected. CFACT appealed, arguing its conservative viewpoint was the real reason SSFC denied it eligibility. After a student government panel upheld the decision, CFACT filed a federal district court action against UW, alleging denial of equal access to UW's student activity fee forum based on its viewpoint. The court denied the organization's request for a preliminary order requiring UW to fund it. It found a limited pool of money for student groups meant both sides faced equal harm. **Denying the injunction would hinder the group's ability to convey its expressive message on campus, but granting it would cause the same harm to other student groups.** UW successfully refuted the claim that SSFC granted eligibility to other groups that missed the deadline. The court denied the injunction. *Collegians for a Constructive Tomorrow-Madison v. Regents of Univ. of Wisconsin System*, No. 09-C-0514, 2010 WL 898794 (W.D. Wis. 3/9/10).

◆ *The New York Supreme Court, Appellate Division, held that the state could review a nonpublic educational institution's certification of a student's eligibility for a state grant.*

A New York private college accepted and certified a group of students who had previously attended a local community college as eligible for state Supplemental Tuition Assistance Program (STAP) grants. The STAP grants provided tuition assistance to New York students whose educational deficits were so great that they would not be considered admissible to a college-level program. The state denied the college's request for STAP award and a New York trial court affirmed the denial. On appeal by the college, the appellate division court held that **the state had both the authority and the obligation to review a nonpublic educational institution's certification of a student's eligibility for a STAP grant**. The regulatory scheme did not contemplate awards to students with successful college experience who had previously received funds pursuant to the Tuition Assistance Program. The appellate court affirmed the trial court's denial of STAP funds. *Touro College v. Nolan*, 620 N.Y.S.2d 558 (N.Y. App. Div. 1994).

♦   *A university could not maintain a race-based scholarship program where past discrimination did not justify it.*

The University of Maryland maintained a merit scholarship program open only to African-American students. It alleged that the program redressed prior constitutional violations against African-American students by the university, which had formerly been segregated by law. A student of Hispanic descent attempted to obtain a scholarship under the program, but was denied on the basis of his race. He filed a lawsuit against the university and a number of its officials in the U.S. District Court for the District of Maryland. The court granted summary judgment to the university, and the student won reversal from the U.S. Court of Appeals, Fourth Circuit. On remand, the parties again filed cross motions for summary judgment, and the district court again awarded summary judgment to the university.

The case was again appealed to the court of appeals. It determined that the district court had improperly found a basis in the evidence for its conclusion that a remedial plan of action was necessary. It also had erroneously determined that the scholarship program was narrowly tailored to meet the goal of remedying past discrimination. The court had misconstrued statistical evidence presented by the parties and had erroneously found a connection between past discrimination and present conditions at the university. **The reasons stated by the university for maintaining the race-based scholarship – underrepresentation of African-American students, low retention and graduation rates and a negative perception among African-American students – were legally insufficient.** The court reversed the summary judgment order for the university and awarded summary judgment to the student. *Podberesky v. Kirwan*, 38 F.3d 147 (4th Cir. 1994).

C. Student Default

Section 523(a)(8) of the U.S. Bankruptcy Code does not allow the discharge of student loans in bankruptcy. However, a bankruptcy court may permit the discharge of student loan debt if the student can show it would impose an undue hardship to repay the loans. In addition to the test for "undue hardship," a bankruptcy court may consider exceptional circumstances that strongly suggest a continuing inability to repay, such as a disability, and a student's failure to take advantage of forebearances or deferments.

The bankruptcy code does not define "undue hardship" and the courts have struggled with its meaning. In the case of In re Frushour, 433 F.3d 393 (4th Cir. 2005), The U.S. Court of Appeals, Fourth Circuit, held that having a low-paying job does not in itself cause undue hardship, especially when the debtor has not tried to get a job that pays more. Government-backed student-loan debt is ordinarily not discharged in Chapter 7 proceedings.

♦   *A Wisconsin university violated federal law by denying a transcript to a teacher whose tuition debt had been discharged in a bankruptcy proceeding.*

An art teacher stopped making payments midway through the first year of her master's degree program. By the time she completed the program, she owed the university over $6,000 in tuition. A federal bankruptcy court discharged this debt. During and after the bankruptcy proceeding, the university denied the teacher's requests for a copy of her transcript. **Under the U.S. Bankruptcy Code, creditors cannot take actions to collect a debt until a bankruptcy proceeding ends.** The code also bars creditors from taking action to collect debts that have been discharged. The teacher said the university violated both provisions when it denied her requests for her transcript. A bankruptcy judge ordered the university to provide the teacher a copy of her transcript and to pay her damages and attorneys' fees. On appeal, **the U.S. Court of Appeals, Seventh Circuit, said students have a right to receive copies of their transcripts.** It found a right to receive a transcript "is essential to a meaningful property right in grades." Finding the university violated the Bankruptcy Code by refusing to provide the teacher with a copy of her transcript, the court affirmed the judgment. *In re Kuehn*, 563 F.3d 289 (7th Cir. 2009).

◆ *A disabled student borrower's request to have her student loan debt discharged was rejected by a federal appeals court.*

A former Illinois college student took out federal loans totalling $13,250. She later defaulted on them and filed a series of applications with the U.S. Department of Education (DOE) to discharge her debt on the basis of her disability. Although the former student produced letters from her physician declaring her inability to work, the DOE denied the application for discharge.

When the student sought judicial review of the denial, her doctors provided 10 years of medical records. Based on the new evidence, the court sent the case back to the DOE. But the DOE found her physician failed to explain why she was completely unable to work, and the DOE again denied discharge. A federal district court upheld the decision, and appeal went before the U.S. Court of Appeals, Seventh Circuit. It found that **to discharge a student loan debt on the basis of disability, the student had to show she was "permanently and totally disabled."** To do so, she had to establish she was unable to work because of an injury or illness that was expected to continue indefinitely or result in death. The student did not meet this standard. Her physician provided few details about her condition, and the DOE was not required to accept his conclusory assertions. *Boutte v. Duncan*, 348 Fed.Appx. 151 (7th Cir. 2009).

◆ *A Utah college graduate was not entitled to have about $88,000 in student loan debt discharged during bankruptcy proceedings.*

The graduate had a degree in Middle East studies and formerly worked as an interpreter. As a single parent, she did not apply for a job for over 10 years, and received $1,100 per month in government benefits. When the graduate filed for bankruptcy, she asked the court to discharge her student loan debt. A bankruptcy court instead held the debt was not dischargeable in bankruptcy because requiring her to repay it would not impose an undue hardship on her.

A federal district court affirmed the decision. The graduate appealed to the U.S. Court of Appeals, Tenth Circuit, arguing she had medical conditions precluding full employment. But the only evidence she offered regarding her condition was her own testimony, and she admitted that no doctor had ever told her she was unable to work. **Instead, the court focused on her failure to apply for a job in more than 10 years and her failure to repay any portion**

of the debt when she received lump sums of cash. Her decision to use $1,000 of that money for dance lessons and $4,000 of it for orthodontic work indicated she did not act in good faith. In addition, she had turned down an opportunity to consolidate her student loan debt. Because the graduate failed to meet the applicable test, the court affirmed the denial of her request for discharge of her student loan debt. *In re Roe*, 295 Fed.Appx. 927 (10th Cir. 2008).

◆   *A New York court rejected a graduate's claim that a college wrongfully intercepted his state tax refunds to recoup money he owed for tuition.*

A college intercepted the graduate's state tax refunds after obtaining a civil court judgment against him for failing to pay his tuition. He filed a state court action to force the return of the intercepted refunds. The graduate claimed he had already paid back his student loans and did not owe more tuition. He claimed the college failed to apply the intercepted refunds to his loans. After a trial, the court dismissed the case, and the graduate appealed. A New York Appellate Division Court agreed with the lower court's decision that the case was meritless. The judgment authorizing interception of the graduate's state tax refunds was obtained in a suit to recover sums previously awarded to him as federal Pell grants and state awards. **Those sums were used to pay his tuition, and the college was obligated to repay them to state and federal agencies.** As a result of this obligation, the college was entitled to recoup tuition amounts the graduate did not pay. The graduate failed to show the civil court judgment that served as the basis for intercepting the funds was not properly entered. As a result, the court affirmed the judgment for the college. *Onitiri v. CUNY*, 55 A.D.3d 808, N.Y.S.2d 294 (N.Y. App. Div. 2008).

◆   *An Ohio court reversed a decision that excused a suspended student from repaying student loan funds he had received.*

The student compiled a history of using profanity and raising his voice when calling the university's financial aid office. He received repeated warnings about his behavior. The university approved a financial aid package on the assumption that the student would be taking a certain number of courses. When officials learned he would not be taking all the classes, his financial aid was decreased. The student called the financial aid office and used profanity. He told a financial aid office employee that "if he could reach through the phone, he would slap her." Shortly after his outburst, the student received a student loan check of $2,600. The university suspended him for misconduct.

The student's appeal was denied, and the university adjusted his account and sued him in a state court to recover $1,700 of the financial aid it gave him. He said he was not required to pay back the money because the suspension was unjust. The court agreed, saying the university had "demanded full payment for classes never given." The university appealed to the Court of Appeals of Ohio, which reversed the judgment. It found **the student had undisputedly received a loan check and spent the money**. Some of the funds were used to purchase a computer. Under the circumstances, the trial court abused its discretion and the case was returned to it for more proceedings. *Franklin Univ. v. Ickes*, 181 Ohio App.3d 10, 907 N.E.2d 793 (Ohio Ct. App. 2009).

◆ *A federal court denied a Pennsylvania law school graduate's request to have her student debt discharged in bankruptcy.*

At the time of her bankruptcy filing, the graduate had accumulated over $150,000 in student loan debt and repaid only $622. She was 36 years old, in good health and earning more than $51,000 a year. The graduate sought discharge of her student loan debt on grounds of undue hardship. **The court found the graduate failed to show she would be unable to maintain a minimal standard of living if she had to repay the debt.** Her net income at the time of the proceedings exceeded her monthly expenses by almost $500. In addition, she had the option of reducing her expenses. The court noted that the graduate had indulged in luxuries beyond her basic needs. She was young and healthy, and she had marketable skills. Therefore, she did not show she would be unable to repay her student loans in the future. As the graduate's efforts to repay her student loan debt had been "negligible," her request to discharge the debt was denied. *Johnson v. Access Group*, 400 B.R. 167 (M.D. Pa. 2009).

◆ *A husband and wife who failed to make a good-faith effort to repay their student loans could not discharge their student loan debt.*

The couple received student loans in connection with their studies at several North Carolina universities. The husband had a degree in information systems and obtained work as a programmer. He was later laid off, then went to work at a home improvement store. The store fired the husband because of "excessive daytime sleepiness." The wife worked as a music teacher at a middle school. In 2002, 2003 and 2004, the couple earned about $75,500, $78,300 and $64,100, respectively. In December 2004, they asked a court to discharge their student loan debt in connection with their ongoing bankruptcy proceedings. At the time, they had a combined total debt of about $120,500. The bankruptcy court considered whether they showed they would not be able to maintain a minimum standard of living if they had to repay the loans; whether their current state of financial affairs was likely to continue for a significant part of the loan repayment period; and whether they made a good-faith effort to repay the loans.

The court found that the pair satisfied each part of the test, and it discharged their student loan debts. The case reached the U.S. Court of Appeals, Fourth Circuit, which determined the couple did not make a good-faith effort to obtain employment and maximize their income. The wife did not work during the summer, and the husband did not show that his medical condition completely prevented him from working. The monthly budget they submitted to the court showed $75 for Internet service, $80 for cell phones, $60 for satellite television and $68 for a YMCA membership. In the three months prior to their bankruptcy filing, the couple spent a combined total of $4,600 on consumer expenditures. These expenditures were not necessary to maintain a minimal standard of living and were evidence that the couple did not make a good-faith effort to minimize expenses. **The record also showed the pair failed to make loan payments for a period of time when they were financially able to do so, and they did not adequately pursue loan consolidation options.** The decision to discharge the student loan debt was reversed. *In re Mosko*, 515 F.3 319 (4th Cir. 2008).

◆   *A debtor was not required to present expert medical evidence to support his*
claim for discharge of his student loans due to his medical condition.

The student accumulated nearly $95,000 in student loan debt while earning
master's degrees from Saint Louis University. His student loans became due
while he underwent chemotherapy for Hodgkin's disease. The treatments made
him too weak to work, and he was approved for economic hardship deferments
in 2000 and 2001. The student filed for bankruptcy and was then diagnosed
with vascular necrosis. The condition caused him to suffer severe pain in his
hips, shoulders and knees. He underwent two shoulder surgeries and began
taking multiple pain medications. He also expected to undergo surgery on both
hips and his other shoulder. The student was the only witness at his bankruptcy
proceeding, where he said he performed computer jobs that required him to do
nothing more than move a computer mouse with his left hand. In addition, he
claimed his condition was getting worse. The bankruptcy court considered
records indicating the student had a monthly income of $868 and monthly
expenses of $3,575. Based on the evidence presented, the bankruptcy court
found it would be an undue hardship for him to repay his student loans.

The creditor sought review by the U.S. Court of Appeals, Sixth Circuit. It
argued the student was required to provide expert medical evidence showing
his condition was likely to last throughout the repayment period of the loans. It
also claimed he had failed to show he made a good-faith effort to repay his
loans. **The court rejected the argument that expert medical evidence was**
needed to show entitlement to discharge. Under the circumstances, requiring
corroborating medical evidence would only serve to place an additional,
unnecessary burden on the student. His account of his medical status and
history was not disputed. The court also rejected the argument that the student
did not make a good-faith effort to repay the loans based on his failure to apply
for a particular repayment option. *In re Barrett,* 487 F.3d 353 (6th Cir. 2007).

◆   *The U.S. Department of Education could intercept a 67-year-old disabled*
Washington man's Social Security benefits to offset a delinquent student loan.

The man failed to repay federally reinsured student loans he incurred
between 1984 and 1989 under the Guaranteed Student Loan Program. The
loans were reassigned to the Department of Education, which certified the debt
to the U.S. Department of Treasury through the Treasury Offset Program. The
U.S. began withholding a portion of the man's Social Security benefits to offset
his debt, part of which was over 10 years delinquent. He sued the U.S. in a
federal district court, alleging the offset was barred by the 10-year statute of
limitations contained in the Debt Collection Act of 1982. The federal district
court dismissed the case, and the U.S. Court of Appeals, Ninth Circuit,
affirmed. The U.S. Supreme Court agreed to review the case.

The court noted the Debt Collection Act permits U.S. agency heads to
collect an outstanding debt by "administrative offset." However, Section 407(a)
of the Social Security Act limits the availability of benefits to offset a debt. The
Court explained that the Higher Education Technical Amendments of 1991
"sweepingly eliminated time limitations as to certain loans." This included the
student loans in this case. The Debt Collection Improvement Act of 1996
clarified that, notwithstanding any other law, including Section 407, all

payments due under the Social Security Act were subject to offset. **The Court held the Debt Collection Improvement Act clearly made Social Security benefits subject to offset. Moreover, the Higher Education Technical Amendments removed the 10-year limit that would otherwise bar an offset of Social Security benefits.** The Court rejected the man's argument that Congress could not have intended in 1991 to repeal a statute of limitations as they concerned Social Security benefits that were not made available for offset until 1996. Congress did not have to foresee all the consequences of a statutory enactment. It was also unnecessary for Congress to explicitly mention Section 407 in the Higher Education Technical Amendments. The Court concluded that the Debt Collection Improvement Act gave the U.S. the authority to use Social Security benefits to offset debts. The retention of the 10-year limit on debt collection in the Higher Education Technical Amendments did not apply in all contexts, including this administrative offset. It affirmed the judgment for the U.S. *Lockhart v. U.S.*, 546 U.S. 142 (2005).

◆ *An Ohio university failed to recoup a tuition subsidy it provided to a medical student who broke her promise to practice medicine in the state.*

Tuition subsidies are available to out-of-state residents who attend Ohio University and agree to practice medicine in Ohio for at least five years after they complete an in-state medical program. A California resident completed the program but returned to California without fulfilling the five-year obligation. The university sued her for breach of contract, seeking to recover about $94,000 – the subsidized cost of educating her. It obtained a default judgment on its claim. Before the university could collect on the judgment, the student filed for bankruptcy, seeking to discharge the debt to the university.

Under Chapter 7 bankruptcy law, a debtor generally remains obligated to repay an educational loan or an "educational benefit." The bankruptcy court held for the student, finding that her obligation was not a loan or the repayment of an educational benefit. The university then appealed to the Bankruptcy Appellate Panel (BAP) of the Ninth Circuit. The BAP held that **to qualify as a "loan," the agreement must indicate definite repayment terms. In addition, the repayment obligation must be a reflection of the benefit received.** As the contract did not require the student to repay the value of the educational services she received, the subsidy did not qualify as an "educational benefit" within the meaning of the bankruptcy law. The Ninth Circuit adopted the opinion of the BAP. *In re Hawkins*, 469 F.3d 1316 (9th Cir. 2006).

◆ *A California vocational school did not have a right to invoke an arbitration clause in a loan note that a student executed with a lender.*

The student borrowed money from Sallie Mae to finance his enrollment at a vocational institution. He executed a loan note with an arbitration clause by which he agreed to arbitrate any claim arising from "the relationships which result from this note." The student later joined a class action suit that accused the institution of making misrepresentations that induced students to enroll in its classes and violating disclosure provisions of the state education code. The institution filed a motion to compel arbitration, claiming it was a third-party beneficiary of the arbitration provision. It also argued that the scope of the note's arbitration provision should be initially decided by an arbitrator. A California superior court denied the motion, and the Court of Appeal of California affirmed the judgment. It held the institution was not a party to the note that included the arbitration clause. **The reference to relationships resulting from the note's execution did not include the one between the student and institution.** Nothing in the note told students that the institution was an intended third-party beneficiary of the arbitration clause, and there was no equitable reason to give the institution the benefit of it. *Smith v. Microskills San Diego L.P.*, 153 Cal.App.4th 892, 63 Cal.Rptr.3d 608 (Cal. Ct. App. 2007).

◆ *The Georgia state medical education board could recoup a scholarship awarded to a student who breached a contract.*

The student received more than $40,000 in return for an agreement with the board to practice medicine in a Georgia community with a population of 15,000 or less. She claimed she could relocate to a qualifying community only if the board paid her "funds necessary to rent a building, purchase equipment and hire competent staff." **The Court of Appeals of Georgia found no merit to the student's claim that the board was obligated to help her find work in a qualifying community.** There was no evidence that the board breached the contract by not paying her all the funds due under the contract or rescinded the contract. In an earlier order, the court of appeals held that state law authorized the award of treble damages under the contract. It reversed a lower court order limiting the board to the amount of her scholarship. *Calabro v. State Medical Educ. Board*, 283 Ga.App. 113, 640 S.E.2d 581 (Ga. Ct. App. 2006).

II. ESTABLISHMENT CLAUSE ISSUES

The Establishment Clause of the First Amendment prohibits Congress from making any law respecting an establishment of religion. It was construed by the U.S. Supreme Court through the 1980s as prohibiting financial assistance by government agencies to religious schools and colleges.

In 1997, the Court decided Agostini v. Felton, *521 U.S. 203, 117 S.Ct. 1997, 138 L.Ed.2d 391, an important private school finance case in which the Court abandoned the presumption that the presence of public employees on parochial school grounds creates a symbolic union between church and state that violates the Establishment Clause. Under* Agostini, *government assistance to private schools must not result in government indoctrination or endorsement of religion. The recipients of government assistance must not be defined by reference to their religion, and the assistance must not create excessive entanglement between church and state.*

◆ *An Arkansas city bond issue to finance a Christian university building project was upheld as a neutral benefit available to any entity seeking funding.*

An Arkansas city issued bonds to fund building projects at a private Christian university. Before issuing the bonds, a local housing board required the university to agree that the facilities being financed would not be used for sectarian instruction or religious worship. The university agreed to repay the bonds and all expenses, operate and maintain the financed facilities as a four-year, degree-granting institution, and maintain its nonprofit status. After the city approved the bonds, several residents sued the university in a federal district court for constitutional violations. They claimed the bond issue violated the Establishment Clause and provisions of the Arkansas Constitution.

The court held the city did not act to advance or inhibit religion. The bond issue had a secular purpose and did not have the effect of advancing or inhibiting religion. There was no risk that issuing the bonds would result in any religious indoctrination, and no evidence supported the residents' claim that the bonds had the primary effect of promoting or fostering religion. Moreover, no evidence showed government funds were being used for religious purposes. The tax benefits of the bonds were neutrally available. Issuance of the bonds did not create an excessive entanglement with religion. The bonds were issued to finance buildings that were to be used for the nonsectarian purpose of buildings for higher education. **The court cited U.S. Supreme Court decisions indicating that the government may provide aid to religiously affiliated institutions of higher learning.** The court also concluded that the issuance of the bonds did not violate the state constitution. *Gillam v. Harding Univ.*, No. 4:08-CV-00363BSM, 2009 WL 1795303 (E.D. Ark. 6/24/09).

◆   *Colorado violated the Establishment Clause by denying scholarship funding to state colleges it deemed to be "pervasively sectarian."*

Colorado provided scholarships to in-state students who attended private colleges except for those that were "pervasively sectarian." Some confusion existed among state officials regarding eligibility criteria. When the state law provision excluding pervasively sectarian schools was enacted in 1977, U.S. Supreme Court precedents indicated the states could not provide financial aid to pervasively sectarian schools. But the Supreme Court modified its Establishment Clause jurisprudence in cases such as *Agostini v. Felton*, above.

Colorado never repealed the statutory provision that barred funding to pervasively sectarian schools, and state officials determined Colorado Christian University (CCU) was "pervasively sectarian." CCU filed a federal district court challenge to the denial of its application for public funding, claiming religious Free Exercise, Establishment Clause and Equal Protection violations. The court held for state officials, and CCU appealed to the U.S. Court of Appeals, Tenth Circuit. **The court explained that the Establishment Clause permits "evenhanded funding" of education through student scholarships.** Federal law did not require the state to discriminate against CCU with respect to funding, and it also prevented the state from permissibly doing so. Instead, religions must be treated neutrally and without discrimination or preference by the state. **Making scholarships available to students who attended "sectarian" but not "pervasively sectarian" schools discriminated among religious institutions.** Proof of discriminatory intent was not required to invalidate the challenged provision as unconstitutional. The state law required intrusive judgments by officials relating to questions of religious belief or practice. This type of entanglement between government and religion violated the Establishment Clause, requiring reversal of the judgment for state officials. *Colorado Christian Univ. v. Weaver*, 534 F.3d 1245 (10th Cir. 2008).

◆   *The U.S. Supreme Court approved of the state of Washington's choice to exclude devotional theology candidates from a state scholarship program.*

Washington law created the Promise Scholarship Program, which made state funds available to qualified students for their educational costs. To be eligible, students had to meet certain performance standards and income limits, and enroll at least half-time in an eligible postsecondary institution in the state. The program excluded scholarships for theology majors, but students who attended religiously affiliated schools could still obtain scholarships so long as they did not major in theology and the institution was accredited. A student who received a Promise Scholarship enrolled as a double major in pastoral ministries and business at a private Christian college. A college financial aid administrator advised him he could not use the scholarship to pursue a devotional theology degree and could only receive program funds by certifying he would not pursue a theology degree. The student sued state officials in a federal district court for violating the Free Exercise, Establishment, Speech and Equal Protection Clauses. The court awarded summary judgment to the state, but the Ninth Circuit reversed the decision.

The U.S. Supreme Court held **the program was not a state expression of disfavor against religion**, as the student argued. The program did not impose civil or criminal sanctions on any type of religious service or rite. **There was no Free Exercise Clause violation, as the program did not require students to choose between their religious beliefs and a government benefit.** The state had only chosen not to fund a distinct category of instruction. The training of ministers was essentially a religious endeavor that could be treated differently than training for other callings. There was no evidence of state hostility toward religion. **The program permitted funding recipients to attend pervasively religious schools, and nothing in its text or the state constitution suggested anti-religious bias.** The state interest in denying funds to theology majors was substantial, and the program placed only a minor burden on recipients. The Court reversed the judgment. *Locke v. Davey*, 540 U.S. 712, 124 S.Ct. 1307, 158 L.Ed.2d 1 (2004).

◆   *A federal appeals court held taxpayers could not sue to force a Catholic university to repay federal funds it received for a teacher quality initiative.*

The federal Department of Education (DOE) awarded the University of Notre Dame a one-time, $500,000 grant for a program called Alliance for Catholic Education. The program trained and placed teachers in underserved Catholic schools. Two private taxpayers sued the secretary of the DOE to block payment of the grant money, claiming it would violate the Establishment Clause. But they did not file a motion for a preliminary injunction, and by the time the district court heard the case the money had already been paid. As a result, the district court dismissed the case as moot. On appeal to the U.S. Court of Appeals, Seventh Circuit, the taxpayers agreed any request for injunctive relief was moot. But they argued they could still seek to force Notre Dame to repay the money by having the court order the DOE to seek recoupment.

The court rejected the taxpayers' argument on the basis that it was up to the DOE to decide whether to file an enforcement action to recoup the money. The DOE's decision was not judicially reviewable. However, the district court could order Notre Dame to repay the money if the disbursement violated the Establishment Clause. In the meantime, the U.S. Supreme Court made it clear in *Hein v. Freedom from Religion Foundation*, 127 S.Ct. 2553 (U.S. 2007), that **taxpayers who claim a congressional appropriation violates the Establishment Clause can sue for injunctive relief only**. When the Notre Dame case later reached the Supreme Court for review, the Court vacated the decision and returned it to the Seventh Circuit for reconsideration. On remand, the appeals court held the district court had properly dismissed the case as moot. *Laskowski v. Spellings*, 546 F.3d 822 (7th Cir. 2008).

◆ *Missouri's highest court held the city of St. Louis could constitutionally fund the construction of an arena at a Jesuit university.*

St. Louis University's philosophy is "to teach young men and women ... to follow their Judeo-Christian conscience." The president is a Jesuit, as are nine of its 42 trustees. However, the university is not owned or controlled by any church. When the university decided to construct a new 13,000-seat arena, it sought financial assistance from the city under a state law that authorizes the provision of assistance to encourage urban renewal. Since the proposed site for the arena was in a blighted area, the city authorized funding for the project. The Masonic Temple Association of St. Louis filed a federal court action against the city, claiming it violated the establishment clauses of the state and federal constitutions by providing public aid to a religious institution.

After Masonic's suit was dismissed, the university filed a state court action, seeking a declaration that the funding was valid. The court granted summary judgment for the university. On appeal, the Supreme Court of Missouri rejected the argument that university bylaws proved it was a religious institution. **Mere affiliation with a religion does not prove a college or university is controlled by a religious creed.** Although they clearly indicated a religious affiliation, neither the bylaws nor the university's mission statement showed the school was controlled by a religious creed. The university convinced the court that its primary mission was education and not indoctrination. Moreover, the purpose of the arena was not to advance religion. Instead, its purpose was to provide a venue for secular student and community events in a blighted area of the city. Because Masonic did not show the university was controlled by a religious creed, the city did not violate the state constitution. *Saint Louis Univ. v. Masonic Temple Ass'n of St. Louis*, 220 S.W.3d 721 (Mo. 2007).

◆ *The U.S. Supreme Court held the First Amendment did not prevent the state of Washington from providing financial assistance directly to an individual with a disability attending a Christian college. However, the Supreme Court of Washington held on remand that the assistance violated the state constitution.*

A visually impaired Washington student sought vocational rehabilitative services from the Washington Commission for the Blind pursuant to state law. The law provided that individuals with visual disabilities were eligible for educational assistance to enable them to "overcome vocational handicaps and to obtain the maximum degree of self-support and self-care." However, because the plaintiff was a student at a Christian college intending to pursue a career of service in the church, the Commission for the Blind denied him assistance. The

Washington Supreme Court upheld this decision on the ground that the First Amendment to the U.S. Constitution prohibited state funding of a student's education at a religious college. The U.S. Supreme Court took a less restrictive view of the First Amendment and reversed the Washington court. The operation of Washington's program was such that the Commission for the Blind paid money directly to students, who could then attend the schools of their choice. The fact that the student in this case chose to attend a religious college did not constitute state support of religion because "the decision to support religious education is made by the individual, not the state." The First Amendment was therefore not offended. *Witters v. Washington Dep't of Services for the Blind*, 474 U.S. 481, 106 S.Ct. 748, 88 L.Ed.2d 846 (1986).

On remand, the Washington Supreme Court reconsidered the matter under the Washington State Constitution, which is far stricter in its prohibition on the expenditure of public funds for religious instruction than is the U.S. Constitution. **Vocational assistance funds for the student's religious education violated the state constitution because public money would be used for religious instruction.** The court rejected the student's argument that the restriction on public expenditures would violate his right to free exercise of religion. The court determined that the commission's action was constitutional under the Free Exercise Clause because there was no infringement of the student's constitutional rights. Finally, denial of the funds to the student did not violate the Fourteenth Amendment's Equal Protection Clause because the commission had a policy of denying any student's religious vocational funding. The classification was directly related to the state's interest in ensuring the separation between church and state as required by both state and federal constitutions. The court reaffirmed its denial of the student's tuition. *Witters v. State Comm'n for the Blind*, 771 P.2d 1119 (Wash. 1989).

◆ *For more than a generation, courts have analyzed Establishment Clause cases under the framework established by the following decision.*

In *Lemon v. Kurtzman*, the Court invalidated Rhode Island and Pennsylvania statutes that provided state money to finance the operation of parochial schools. The Rhode Island statute provided a 15% salary supplement to parochial school teachers who taught nonreligious subjects using public school teaching materials. The Pennsylvania statute authorized payment of state funds to parochial schools to help defray the cost of teachers' salaries, textbooks and other instructional materials. Reimbursement was limited, however, to the costs of secular subjects, which also were taught in the public schools. The Supreme Court evaluated the Rhode Island and Pennsylvania programs using its **three-part test: First, the statute must have a secular legislative purpose; second, its principal or primary effect must be one that neither advances nor inhibits religion; finally, the statute must not foster "an excessive government entanglement with religion."**

Applying this test to the two state programs in question, the Court held that the legislative purpose of the programs was a legitimate, secular concern with maintaining high educational standards in both public and private schools. The Court did not reach the second inquiry because it held that the state programs failed under the third inquiry. The Rhode Island salary supplement program excessively entangled the state with religion because of the highly religious nature of the Catholic schools that were the primary beneficiaries of the program. The teachers who received the salary supplements provided instruction in classrooms and buildings containing religious symbols such as crucifixes. In such an atmosphere, even a person dedicated to remaining religiously neutral probably would allow some religious content to creep into the ostensibly secular instruction. Similar defects were found in the Pennsylvania program. The Court also observed that in order to ensure that the state-funded parochial school teachers did not inject religious dogma into their instruction, the state would be forced to extensively monitor the parochial school classrooms. This would result in excessive state entanglement with religion. Consequently, **the salary supplement programs were held to violate the Establishment Clause of the First Amendment**. *Lemon v. Kurtzman*, 403 U.S. 602, 91 S.Ct. 2105, 29 L.Ed.2d 745 (1971).

◆ *The Supreme Court held that the "secular side" of a college could be distinguished from sectarian programs, making it permissible for a state to provide funding to a religiously affiliated college's secular side.*

The state of Maryland enacted a program that authorized annual, noncategorical grants to religiously affiliated colleges. The program was challenged by taxpayers who alleged that state money was being put to religious uses by the schools, which had wide discretion in spending the funds.

The Supreme Court held that (1) no state aid at all may go to institutions that are so "pervasively sectarian" that secular activities cannot be separated from sectarian ones, and (2) if secular activities can be separated out, they alone may be funded. The colleges involved in this case were not found to be pervasively sectarian even though they were affiliated with the Catholic Church. The Court held that the "secular side" of the colleges could be separated from the sectarian and found that **state aid had only gone to the colleges' secular side**. It was admittedly somewhat difficult to ensure that the colleges and the Maryland Council for Higher Education would take care to avoid spending state funds on religious activities, but the Court expressed its belief that those entities would spend the money in good faith and avoid violating the First Amendment. *Roemer v. Board of Public Works*, 426 U.S. 736, 96 S.Ct. 2337, 49 L.Ed.2d 179 (1976).

◆ *The Supreme Court held that the receipt of Higher Education Facilities Act funds by four religious colleges did not violate the Establishment Clause.*

The Higher Education Facilities Act of 1963 contained an exclusion for any facility used for sectarian instruction or as a place of religious worship or any facility that is used primarily as part of a school divinity department. Federal education officials had powers to enforce the statute for a 20-year time period during which they could seek to recover funds from violators. A group of Connecticut taxpayers filed a federal district court action against government officials and four religious colleges that received Higher Education Facilities Act funds, seeking an order against the release of funds to sectarian institutions that used federal funds to construct libraries and other facilities. The court held the act did not have the effect of promoting religion.

The U.S. Supreme Court reviewed the case and held that the statute had been carefully drafted to ensure that no federal funds were disbursed to support the sectarian aspects of these institutions. **The four colleges named as defendants in this case had not violated any of the restrictions in the statute, as they had placed no religious symbols in facilities constructed with the use of federal funds, and had not used the facilities for any religious purposes.** There was no evidence that any of the colleges maintained a predominantly religious atmosphere, and although each of them was affiliated with the Catholic Church, none excluded non-Catholics from admissions or faculty appointments, and none of them required attendance at religious services. The receipt of funds by the colleges did not violate the Establishment Clause. The Court held, however, that the 20-year limit on federal oversight created the potential for religious use of the facilities after the 20 years expired. Because of the risk of use of the facilities for advancing religion, the court invalidated this portion of the legislation. *Tilton v. Richardson*, 403 U.S. 672, 91 S.Ct. 2091, 29 L.Ed.2d 790 (1971).

◆   *A Tennessee city development board could issue tax-exempt bonds to a sectarian university for a building project without violating the Establishment Clause.*

A Christian university began a renovation project and sought $15 million in low-interest loans from the Industrial Development Board for Nashville, Tennessee. The board approved the loan and issued tax-exempt bonds to the university. A group of taxpayers sued, asserting that the bond issuance impermissibly benefited a religious university in violation of the Establishment Clause. A federal court ruled that the university was so pervasively sectarian that no state aid could go to it. The Sixth Circuit Court of Appeals reversed, noting that **the tax-exempt bonds did not violate the Establishment Clause**. First, public funds were not used to issue the bonds; the university had to arrange for private financing; and bond purchasers only had recourse against the university. Second, the bonds were issued in a neutral manner to nonprofit organizations. Third, the bonds advanced the secular objective of promoting economic development. The university was entitled to receive the tax-exempt bonds. *Steele v. Industrial Development Board of Metropolitan Government of Nashville*, 301 F.3d 401 (6th Cir. 2002).

◆   *A Wisconsin program allowing unrestricted telecommunications access grants to sectarian schools and colleges violated the Establishment Clause.*

A 1997 Wisconsin law created the Technology for Education Achievement (TEACH) Board, which administered the Education Telecommunications Access program. The TEACH board approved access for data lines and video links under a heavily subsidized program in which both public and private schools participated. A taxpayer group objected to the program on constitutional grounds because $58,873 of the program's annual total of over $1.9 million was awarded to nine religiously affiliated Wisconsin schools and private colleges. The taxpayers sued state education officials, including the TEACH board, challenging the program as unconstitutional.

The court held that the program as a whole did not violate the Constitution, but found that unrestricted cash grants to private, sectarian schools violated the Establishment Clause's prohibition on state support of religion.

The parties appealed unfavorable aspects of the decision to the Seventh Circuit. The taxpayers dismissed their appeal concerning the constitutionality of the full program in view of the U.S. Supreme Court's intervening decision in *Mitchell v. Helms*, 530 U.S. 793 (2000). In *Mitchell*, the Supreme Court upheld the constitutionality of a state-aid program that helped parochial schools acquire computers, televisions, and laboratory equipment. The Seventh Circuit proceeded to the question of grants to religious schools, noting that **the Wisconsin law violated the third *Agostini* criteria, because in the absence of any restriction on the expenditure of public funds by the schools, the expenditures had a primary effect that advanced religion**. The subsidies could easily be used for maintenance, chapels, religious instruction, or connection time to view religious Web sites. The law did not bar schools from using the grants for these and other constitutionally impermissible purposes. Because direct aid from the government to a sectarian institution in any form is invalid, the court affirmed the district court's finding that the direct subsidies to religious schools were unconstitutional. *Freedom From Religion Foundation Inc. v. Bugher*, 249 F.3d 606 (7th Cir. 2001).

III. PRIVATE SCHOOL TAXATION

The U.S. Supreme Court has infrequently considered federal income tax cases involving private schools. In Bob Jones Univ. v. U.S., *461 U.S. 574, 103 S.Ct. 2017, 76 L.Ed.2d 157 (1983), it held that private schools must comply with the strong federal interest against race discrimination and that federal tax exempt status can be denied to schools maintaining discriminatory policies. More recently, in* Camps Newfound/Owatonna, Inc. v. Town of Harrison, Maine, *520 U.S. 564, 117 S.Ct. 1590, 137 L.Ed.2d 852 (1997), the Court found no reason why nonprofit status should exempt a private entity from laws regulating commerce, including local property tax laws.*

A. Federal Income Taxation

◆ *A strong public policy against racial discrimination was held sufficient to deny tax-exempt status to an otherwise qualified private college.*

Section 501(c)(3) of the Internal Revenue Code (IRC) provides that "corporations ... organized and operated exclusively for religious, charitable ... or educational purposes" are entitled to tax-exempt status. The Internal Revenue Service routinely granted tax exemption under IRC Section 501(c)(3) to private schools regardless of whether they had racially discriminatory admissions policies. In 1970, however, the IRS concluded it could no longer grant tax-exempt status to racially discriminatory private schools because such schools were not "charitable" within the meaning of Section 501(c)(3). In *Bob Jones Univ. v. U.S.*, two private colleges whose racial admissions policies were allegedly rooted in their interpretations of the Bible sued to prevent the IRS from interpreting the federal tax laws in this manner. The Supreme Court rejected the colleges' challenge and upheld the IRS's interpretation.

The Court's ruling was based on a strong federal public policy against racial discrimination in education. **Because the colleges were operating in violation of that public policy, the colleges could not be considered "charitable" under Section 501(c)(3). Thus, they were ineligible for tax exemption. The Court held that in order to fall under the exemption of Section 501(c)(3) an institution must be in harmony with the public interest.** It also held that the denial of an exemption did not impermissibly burden Bob Jones' alleged religious interest in practicing racial discrimination. *Bob Jones Univ. v. U.S.*, 461 U.S. 574, 103 S.Ct. 2017, 76 L.Ed.2d 157 (1983).

B. State and Local Taxation

◆ *A Maryland local tax on admissions and amusements did not apply to gate receipts from Johns Hopkins University lacrosse games, because the funds were used exclusively for educational purposes.*

Maryland law authorizes counties and municipalities to impose admissions and amusement taxes. But no admissions and amusement taxes may be imposed by a county or municipality on gross receipts that are used exclusively for charitable, educational, or religious purposes. Johns Hopkins University earned substantial revenue from its men's lacrosse program. It paid an admissions and amusement tax to the comptroller of the treasury for several years. The university then sought a refund from Baltimore City, asserting it was entitled to the exception for receipts used exclusively for an educational purpose. The Maryland Tax Court granted the university's request for a refund, and the comptroller appealed to the Court of Special Appeals of Maryland.

The court considered evidence that lacrosse game revenues were used to cover the costs of games and to contribute to the maintenance of the field and surrounding jogging track. The comptroller had already deemed the university field exempt from real property tax, and the university was exempt from federal tax under 26 U.S.C. § 501(c)(3). The court found substantial evidence to support the tax court's conclusion that receipts from the lacrosse games were used exclusively for an educational purpose. **The evidence showed that gross receipts were used to benefit the university, intercollegiate athletes, other non-participating students, and spectators.** About 50% of university students were involved in athletics of some sort. The field was used by all students and their families for commencement exercises, and it was also used by some students for ROTC and intramural games. As intramural athletic contests had always been treated by the Maryland taxing authorities and the Tax Court as "educational" in purpose, the court affirmed the judgment for the university. *Comptroller of Treasury v. Johns Hopkins Univ.*, 186 Md.App. 169, 973 A.2d 256 (Md. Ct. Spec. App. 2009).

◆ *Office space leased by a bank from a university was exempt from property taxation because it was used for a "school purpose."*

The University of Delaware contracted with a bank to develop a student identification card that could also be used as a debit card for services. The university provided office space to the bank for the project. The local land use department discontinued the university's property tax exemption for the space and assessed taxes on it. A county board of assessment review upheld the assessment, but its decision was reversed by a state superior court, which found the space was used for a school purpose under state law.

The Supreme Court of Delaware noted the term "school purpose" was undefined by 9 Del. C. Section 8105. Under that section, college or school property used for educational or school purposes was not subject to taxation. The court rejected the county's argument that Section 8105 must be read narrowly. Statutes exempting educational institutions from taxation are generally "construed more liberally than other tax exempting statutes." The trial court had correctly determined the bank served a "school purpose." The court held "school purposes" included use of school-owned property that contributed to the legitimate welfare, convenience, and/or safety of the school community or its members. The judgment was affirmed. *New Castle County Dep't of Land Use v. Univ. of Delaware*, 842 A.2d 1201 (Del. 2004).

◆ *A university's bus service was not entitled to a credit for fuel taxes for its campus bus service.*

An Ohio public university owned a campus bus service that provided free transportation within the university campus. It also transported disabled students to and from the airport, and serviced the city of Kent and neighboring townships. However, it did not operate under a contract with the city or any other regional transit authority. When it applied for reimbursement of motor vehicle fuel taxes, claiming eligibility for the credits because its buses were transit buses, the tax commissioner and the Board of Tax Appeals ruled that its buses did not meet the statutory definition of "transit buses." The Supreme Court of Ohio upheld that determination. Here, even though the buses benefited non-students as well as students, **the bus service did not meet the requirement that it be operated by or for a municipal corporation**. The bus service was not entitled to the tax reimbursement. *Campus Bus Service v. Zaino*, 786 N.E.2d 889 (Ohio 2003).

◆ *A city was allowed to proceed in its lawsuit against a Catholic university for back taxes.*

The city of Scranton and its school district sued the University of Scranton, a Roman Catholic institution, for payment of back business privilege and/or mercantile taxes since 1995. The city asserted that the university gained income in those years from the sale of books and food, from parking lot revenue and from other sources. Since those income-generating activities took place in the city, the university ought to have to pay mercantile taxes. The university sought to dismiss the suit, **asserting that it was a charitable institution under the state's Purely Public Charity Act**, and the court of common pleas agreed. However, the Pennsylvania Commonwealth Court reversed, finding issues that required the lawsuit to proceed. As a result, the university had to answer the city's complaint. *School Dist. of City of Scranton v. Univ. of Scranton*, No. 2345 C.D. 2001, 2002 WL 876980 (Pa. Commw. Ct. 2002).

◆ *An office building owned by teaching doctors of Midwestern University did not qualify for real estate tax exemptions.*

The primary activities taking place at the property constituted billing, collection, data processing, accounting, administration, management, payroll and related functions for the physician group. When a state court held that the physician group did not qualify for the "charitable purposes" or "school" exemptions under Illinois law, appeal reached the Appellate Court of Illinois. **Under Illinois law, a property entitled to an exemption must be used exclusively for charitable purposes and owned by a charitable organization.** Here, the group failed to meet either requirement. The Appellate Court did not allow the group to use its relationship with the university to cast itself as a charitable organization. No patient care, medical research or instructional classes took place on the property. *Midwest Physician Group, Ltd. v. Dep't of Revenue of Illinois*, 711 N.E.2d 381 (Ill. App. Ct. 1999).

◆ *A university could not claim tax-exempt status for a parking garage or parts of a building leased to for-profit companies.*

A university owned a four-story building with an attached parking garage, and leased space to five tenants. Two tenants were nonprofit organizations, and the other three tenants were for-profit companies. The Board of Tax Appeals found that the building and the land under it were exempt from taxation, but the garage and land under it were not. The Cleveland Board of Education filed a notice of appeal, wanting the whole property to be taxed.

The Supreme Court of Ohio affirmed the Board of Tax Appeals decisions regarding the tax exemption for the space leased by the two nonprofit organizations, and the non-tax-exempt status of the garage and the land under it. It reversed exemptions given to the university for the space held by the for-profit tenants and vacant areas in the building. **The garage did not qualify for tax-exempt status because it was not an essential and integral part of the university's or nonprofit tenants' charitable and/or educational activities.** *Case Western Reserve Univ. v. Tracy*, 84 Ohio St.3d 316, 703 N.E.2d 1240 (Ohio 1999).

◆ *Land used by a seminary for recreational purposes and as a buffer zone was exempt from taxation.*

A North Carolina county reviewed several parcels of land owned by a seminary and determined that they were not eligible for tax exemptions because they were not used for educational or religious purposes. After the state property tax commission held that exemptions applied to three parcels, the county appealed. The North Carolina Court of Appeals affirmed the decision in favor of the seminary. **Although the land was used essentially for recreational purposes, and as a buffer between the campus and commercial development surrounding the campus, it served to provide and maintain a relaxed campus atmosphere.** Further, the seminary's attempt to rezone one of the parcels for commercial development so that it could sell the land for a profit was a planned future use, which did not change the present exempted use of the land. *In the Matter of Southeastern Baptist Theological Seminary*, 135 N.C.App. 247, 520 S.E.2d 302 (N.C. Ct. App. 1999).

◆   *A religious college that paid a non-compulsory development fee could not claim a tax exemption for it.*

A Catholic private college in California acquired an adjacent tract of land in order to build a postgraduate business school and parking structure. The college intended to move its existing business school to the new building, resulting in no increase in students or faculty. Before construction could begin, the college needed a permit that would not be issued unless the college paid a school development fee. Under state statute, any school district can levy a fee against any commercial, industrial or residential development project for the purpose of funding the construction of school facilities. The only exceptions are facilities used exclusively for religious purposes or facilities owned and occupied by agencies of federal, state, or local government. The college paid the fee under protest and then filed a petition for writ of mandamus in state court. The trial court found for the college, and the school district appealed to the California Court of Appeal, Second District. The college argued that the development fee qualified as a tax, which it should not be required to pay as a nonprofit, educational institution. The court agreed that the college was exempt from state taxes because of its status, but found that the development fee was not a tax. It was not compulsory, like a tax, but was imposed only when a property owner decided to develop. Furthermore, **the California Supreme Court has held that exemptions from taxes refer only to property taxes**. The court also found that the development was not going to be used exclusively for religious purposes. The college did not fall into any of the exceptions to the statute and therefore it had to pay the development fee. *Loyola Marymount Univ. v. Los Angeles Unified School Dist.*, 53 Cal.Rptr.2d 424 (Cal. Ct. App. 1996).

◆   *The Commonwealth Court of Pennsylvania held that property owned by the private college in the following two cases was tax exempt because the college was a public charity under state law and the property was regularly used for the purposes of the college.*

A Pennsylvania nonprofit private college owned a house occupied by its grounds crew leader. The college charged the grounds crew leader a discounted rent that averaged about 70% of the fair market value. In exchange for the discount, the grounds crew leader agreed to be available on a 24-hour basis to respond to emergencies and nighttime calls. He was allegedly called to campus after-hours six times in both 1991 and 1992 for snow and ice removal and to remove fallen tree limbs. The Delaware County Board of Assessment Appeals determined that the house was not exempt from property taxes. On appeal by the college, a Pennsylvania trial court reversed, finding the house exempt from taxation. A local public school district appealed the finding to the Commonwealth Court of Pennsylvania.

Article VIII of the **Pennsylvania Constitution provides that the general assembly can exempt real property of public charities "regularly used for the purposes of the institution."** Section 204 of the General County Assessment Law exempts all college property "necessary for the occupancy and enjoyment of the same." The commonwealth court stated that the college need not prove that the property was absolutely necessary to its needs for the exemption to apply. Rather, it was required to show only that it had a reasonable need for the property. Here, emergency personnel were essential to the college community. The grounds crew leader was able to respond much quicker to an emergency than personnel who were living off campus. The college properly chose to forego the additional rental revenues to provide these needed services. Further, the alleged infrequency of emergency situations did not render the house incidental to the college's purposes. **Because emergency services were directly related to the proper functions of the college, the trial court did not err in concluding that the house was tax exempt.** *In re Swarthmore College*, 645 A.2d 470 (Pa. Commw. Ct. 1994).

The college also owned a large house designed for entertaining. The college's vice president for alumni development lived in the house rent-free and was not charged for utilities. The house was used for meetings, special events, receptions and to entertain potential donors from whom one-third of the college's yearly income was derived. The county Board of Assessment Appeals determined that the house was not exempt from property taxes. The Commonwealth Court of Pennsylvania stated that the **college was not required to prove that the property was absolutely necessary to its needs for the exemption to apply. Rather, it was required to show only that it had a reasonable necessity for the property.** Here, the vice president was required to live in the house, use it to cultivate personal relationships with donors, and utilize it for numerous college functions. These uses were directly related to the proper functions of the college. Consequently, the vice president's house was tax-exempt. *In re Swarthmore College*, 643 A.2d 1152 (Pa. Commw. Ct. 1994).

◆ *The Court of Appeal of Louisiana held that state law does not require private colleges to substantiate their tax-exempt status except as set forth by the state legislature.*

A Louisiana church operated a private university that offered a variety of secular undergraduate and graduate programs. The Louisiana Board of Regents notified the university that it had failed to complete and submit the required licensure application and was therefore in violation of state law. Consequently, it sought to close the school. **Although degree-granting institutions were generally required to be registered and licensed by the board, institutions granted a tax exemption under the Internal Revenue Code were exempted from these requirements.** Previously such private universities were required to supply only basic information to obtain a license. The state attorney general filed suit in a Louisiana trial court, seeking to enjoin the church's operation of the university based on its noncompliance with the board's procedural requirements. The trial court found that because the Internal Revenue Code does not require churches to obtain recognition of their exempt status, the board was prohibited from requiring the organization to do so. It denied the state's request for injunctive relief, and the state appealed.

The Court of Appeal of Louisiana affirmed the decision, noting that the state legislature chose to defer to federal law in this procedural area. Federal law, pursuant to the Internal Revenue Code, granted churches automatic exempt status without the necessity of paperwork. Absent a contrary directive from the state legislature, the court refused to read additional requirements into the law. *Ieyoub v. World Christian Church*, 649 So.2d 771 (La. Ct. App. 1994).

IV. PRIVATE ASSISTANCE TO SCHOOLS

Generally, when private parties donate money to schools, they have to be careful to specify how that money will be used or the schools will be able to put the money into their general operating funds.

Colleges and universities often rely on financial boosters to support their athletic programs. But when questions arise as to how money is being raised and spent, relationships between booster organizations and schools can go sour. In the following case, an Iowa court rejected a college's claim that the head of a booster club mishandled funds and engaged in other unauthorized activities.

◆ *Members of nonprofit organizations are not liable for the debts of an organization unless they engage in intentional misconduct.*

Over the course of his long tenure as a benefactor, Charles Talbot personally donated more than $45,000 and helped raise more than $97,000 for Indian Hills Community College. Talbot approached the school to discuss the creation of a more formal tax-exempt booster club in 2001. The school told Talbot it would need to endorse such a move, but he went ahead and formed a nonprofit corporation without asking for approval. The relationship between Talbot and the school began to sour. The president told the group they needed to run the booster club funds through a school-audited account, but the group refused to do so. They also refused to provide the college access to the club's financial records. In April 2004, the college sued Talbot and the booster club in a state court. The suit accused Talbot and the club of conversion, and it claimed he had engaged in unauthorized acts. The trial court held for Talbot, relying on state law immunity for members of nonprofit organizations and corporations. On appeal, the Court of Appeals of Iowa held the trial court had correctly applied state law immunity provisions to block the college's claims.

Members of nonprofit organizations were not liable for debts or obligations of the organization unless they engaged in intentional misconduct, knowingly violated the law, or derived an "improper personal benefit" from a transaction. There was no showing that any actions taken by Talbot were illegal or inappropriate Therefore, he could not be held liable for any of the allegedly improper actions taken on behalf of the booster club. The trial court decision against the college was affirmed. *Indian Hills Community College v. Indian Hills Booster Club*, No. 06-0392, 734 N.W.2d 486 (Table), 2007 WL 911890 (Iowa Ct. App. 3/28/07).

◆ *The departure of a prominent researcher from a university led to a dispute regarding whether donors could authorize a transfer of donated materials.*

A highly respected urologist and researcher had worked at Washington University, a private institution in Missouri, since 1976. His area of specialty was prostate cancer, and he performed thousands of surgeries and spearheaded research activities. The urologist was particularly interested in the genetic basis of prostate cancer, and he focused his research efforts in this area. In 1983, he began collecting samples of biological materials consisting of blood and tissue that was removed during surgery. The storage facility he helped create for biological samples eventually became the largest of its kind in the world. Donors who became research participants by allowing their samples to be used were required to complete an informed consent form, which used the term "donation" to describe the transfer of biological samples from the participant to a university physician or medical technician. The forms also specified that participants agreed to waive any claim to donated body tissues. In early 2003, the urologist accepted a new position at Northwestern University. Soon after he arrived there, he sent a letter to donors, asking them to release their samples to him at his new location. Unwilling to part with the samples, Washington University filed a federal district court lawsuit seeking a declaration that it owned them and was not required to honor any transfer request. The urologist filed a counterclaim, seeking a declaration that the donors had a right to transfer their samples to him. The court held Washington University was the owner of the samples. It also found that neither the urologist nor the donors had an ownership interest in the samples, and that none of the release forms that the urologist prepared transferred ownership of the samples.

The U.S. Court of Appeals for the Eighth Circuit affirmed the district court's ruling, finding the donors did not retain an ownership interest allowing them to transfer the samples to a third party. **All of the donors transferred their samples to the university as gifts.** The university established that a gift was made by showing the donors intended to make a gift. The samples were delivered by the donors, and the university accepted them. The consent form and brochure language supported the conclusion that the sample transfers were gifts, and the university retained "absolute possession" over them. While at Washington, The urologist signed agreements acknowledging the university's ownership of the samples. Although he claimed that the donors retained an ownership interest, he also regularly ordered the destruction of donated samples to create more storage space. This activity was inconsistent with his claim that the donors retained an ownership interest. In addition, both federal and state regulations bar the return of donated body tissue and blood to donors. *Washington Univ. v. Catalona*, 490 F.3d 667 (8th Cir. 2007).

◆ *Vanderbilt University could not change the name of its dormitories in violation of an agreement with a donor organization.*

In 1905, trustees of the Peabody Education Fund voted to direct $1 million to create a permanent endowment for a college of higher education for teachers in the southern states. Trustees of the college voted to buy several properties adjacent to Vanderbilt University. The United Daughters of the Confederacy (UDC) entered into a contract with college trustees to raise $50,000 to construct the women's dorm on the new campus. In return for the gift, the college had to allow female descendants of Confederate soldiers nominated by the UDC to live in the dorm rent-free. In 1927, the college and UDC entered into a second contract specifying that a Confederate Memorial Hall be constructed on the campus. From 1935 until the late 1970s, female descendants of Confederate soldiers nominated by the UDC lived in the dorms rent-free. The college started experiencing financial difficulties. To raise money, college trustees leased two dorms, including Confederate Memorial Hall, to Vanderbilt. When the college's financial situation became worse, it merged with Vanderbilt. A year after the renovation of Confederate Memorial Hall, some Vanderbilt students, faculty and staff expressed dissatisfaction with the building name. They emphasized demographic changes over the years. The chancellor of Vanderbilt decided to change the name to "Memorial Hall" without consulting the UDC. The UDC sued Vanderbilt in a state court for breach of contract. The court awarded summary judgment to Vanderbilt. It found it impractical and unduly burdensome for Vanderbilt to continue to perform the terms of the contract. The UDC appealed to Court of Appeals of Tennessee.

Vanderbilt argued it already had substantially fulfilled its obligations because it had allowed many women to live in the dorms rent-free over the years and had kept the building's original name for almost 70 years. Moreover, the university should no longer be obligated to keep the name because it would be inconsistent with laws prohibiting racial discrimination. **The court held the intent of the UDC was for the funds to be a conditional gift. Generally, if the university failed to comply with the conditions, the donor would recover the gift.** However, since the value of a dollar was different now from when the money was given, returning the gift would be unfair to the UDC. **The court held that as Vanderbilt had refused to abide by the conditions of the gift, the present value of the gift must be returned, or the university would have to agree to abide by the conditions.** The court reversed the judgment and returned the case to the trial court to calculate the gift's present value. *Tennessee Division of United Daughters of the Confederacy v. Vanderbilt Univ.*, 174 S.W.3d 98 (Tenn. Ct. App. 2005).

◆ *A university had to identify donors to its new arena who purchased luxury suites.*

Fresno State University built a new $103 million arena primarily with private donations and created a nonprofit association to operate it. The association leased the arena's luxury suites to interested donors. Prices for the suites ranged from $45,000 to $63,000 per year (with terms of 5, 7 or 10 years). The association promised some of the donors they would remain anonymous. However, when a newspaper sought documents containing the names of the donors who obtained leases, the university and association sought to withhold the information on the grounds that disclosure would cause a decrease in future donations. A state court determined that the documents were public records under the California Public Records Act and thus had to be disclosed. The California Court of Appeal affirmed, noting that **the purchase of luxury suites was more a business transaction than a traditional donation**. People making such a purchase have placed themselves in public view and have a diminished expectation of privacy. Further, because the arena was financed with $8 million in public funds, there was a legitimate public interest in the fairness of the transactions. *California State Univ. v. Superior Court*, 108 Cal.Rptr.2d 870 (Cal. Ct. App. 2001).

◆ *The Court of Appeals of Kentucky denied a claim to property by a college under a property owner's will.*

A Kentucky property owner bequeathed property to a relative. However, the will stated that if the relative died without children, the property was to pass to the relative's younger sister and her heirs. The will also provided Georgetown College would receive the proceeds from the sale of 71 acres of farmland, to be used to fund a permanent endowment at the college. Any additional money would be paid to the college for the endowment fund. Both the relative and her sister died without children. A state court distributed $1.3 million from the estate in three equal shares to the sister's heirs, finding the college was only covered under a specific item in the will. The state appeals court rejected the college's argument that the devises to the sisters were substitutional. **When the property owner died, the court explained, the interest in her property vested in the sister's heirs. The college's reasoning would lead to a finding that the property owner had died without heirs.** As this result was disfavored, the court affirmed the judgment for the heirs. *Georgetown College v. Alexander*, 140 S.W.3d 6 (Ky. Ct. App. 2003).

◆ *A university hospital named as an alternate beneficiary could not get money bequeathed to another institution even though a condition of the will was illegal.*

A doctor associated with the Keswick Home in Baltimore provided for four annuitants in his will and, after the death of the last of them, directed that the remainder of his estate (nearly $29 million) go to the Keswick Home for the acquisition or construction of a new building in his name for "white patients who need[ed] physical rehabilitation." If Keswick found the bequest unacceptable, the money was to pass to the University of Maryland Hospital to be used for physical rehabilitation. A lawsuit developed over the funds, with the university hospital arguing that the illegal racial restriction required the money to be awarded to it. A trial court agreed, but the Maryland Court of Appeals reversed. It excised the illegal condition attached to the will and awarded the money to Keswick. *Home for Incurables of Baltimore City v. Univ. of Maryland Medical System Corp.*, 797 A.2d 746 (Md. 2002).

APPENDIX A

UNITED STATES CONSTITUTION

Provisions of Interest to Higher Educators

ARTICLE I

Section 1. All legislative Powers herein granted shall be vested in a Congress of the United States, which shall consist of a Senate and House of Representatives.

* * *

Section 8. The Congress shall have Power To lay and collect Taxes, Duties, Imposts and Excises, to pay the Debts and provide for the common Defence and general Welfare of the United States; but all Duties, Imposts and Excises shall be uniform throughout the United States;

To borrow money on the credit of the United States;

To regulate Commerce with foreign Nations, and among the several States, and with the Indian Tribes;

To establish an uniform Rule of Naturalization, and uniform Laws on the subject of Bankruptcies throughout the United States;

* * *

To promote the Progress of Science and useful Arts, by securing for limited Times to Authors and Inventors the exclusive Right to their respective Writings and Discoveries;

* * *

To make all Laws which shall be necessary and proper for carrying into Execution for the foregoing Powers, and all other Powers vested by this Constitution in the Government of the United States, or in any Department or Officer thereof.

* * *

Section 9. * * * No Bill of Attainder or ex post facto Law shall be passed.

* * *

Section 10. No State shall * * * pass any Bill of Attainder, ex post facto Law, or Law impairing the Obligation of Contracts, or grant any Title of Nobility.

ARTICLE II

Section 1. The executive Power shall be vested in a President of the United States of America. * * *

ARTICLE III

Section 1. The judicial Power of the United States, shall be vested in one supreme Court, and in such inferior Courts as the Congress may from time to time ordain and establish. The Judges, both of the supreme and inferior courts, shall hold their Offices during good Behaviour, and shall, at stated Times, receive for their Services a Compensation, which shall not be diminished during their Continuance in Office.

Section 2. The judicial Power shall extend to all Cases, in Law and Equity, arising under this Constitution, the Laws of the United States, and Treaties made, or which shall be made, under their Authority; - to all Cases affecting Ambassadors, other public Ministers and Consuls; - to all Cases of admiralty and maritime Jurisdiction, - to Controversies to which the United States shall be a party; - to Controversies between two or more States; - between a State and Citizens of another State; - between Citizens of different States; - between Citizens of the same State claiming Lands under the Grants of different States, and between a State, or the Citizens thereof, and foreign States, Citizens or Subjects.

* * *

ARTICLE IV

Section 1. Full Faith and Credit shall be given in each State to the public Acts, Records and judicial Proceedings of every other State. * * *

Section 2. The Citizens of each State shall be entitled to all Privileges and Immunities of Citizens in the several States.

* * *

Section 4. The United States shall guarantee to every State in this Union a Republican Form of Government, and shall protect each of them against Invasion; and on Application of the Legislature, or of the Executive (when the Legislature cannot be convened) against domestic Violence.

ARTICLE V

The Congress, whenever two thirds of both Houses shall deem it necessary, shall propose Amendments to this Constitution, or, on the Application of the Legislatures of two thirds of the several States, shall call a Convention for proposing Amendments, which, in either Case, shall be valid to all Intents and Purposes, as part of this Constitution, when ratified by the Legislatures of three fourths of the several States, or by Conventions in three fourths thereof, as the one or the other Mode of Ratification may be proposed by the Congress; Provided that no Amendment which may be made prior to the Year One thousand eight hundred and eight shall in any Manner affect the first and fourth Clauses in the Ninth Section of the first Article; and that no State, without its Consent, shall be deprived of its equal Suffrage in the Senate.

ARTICLE VI

* * *

This Constitution, and the Laws of the United States which shall be made in Pursuance thereof; and all Treaties made, or which shall be made, under the Authority of the United States, shall be the supreme Law of the Land; and the Judges in every State shall be bound thereby, any Thing in the Constitution or Laws of any State to the Contrary notwithstanding.

The Senators and Representatives before mentioned, and the Members of the several State Legislatures, and all executive and judicial Officers, both of the United States and of the several States, shall be bound by Oath or Affirmation, to support this Constitution; but no religious Test shall ever be required as a Qualification to any Office or public Trust under the United States.

* * *

AMENDMENT I

Congress shall make no law respecting an establishment of religion, or prohibiting the free exercise thereof; or abridging the freedom of speech, or of the press; or the right of the people peaceably to assemble, and to petition the Government for a redress of grievances.

* * *

AMENDMENT IV

The right of the people to be secure in their persons, houses, papers, and effects, against unreasonable searches and seizures, shall not be violated, and no Warrants shall issue, but upon probable cause, supported by Oath or affirmation, and particularly describing the place to be searched, and the persons or things to be seized.

AMENDMENT V

No person shall be held to answer for a capital, or otherwise infamous crime, unless on a presentment or indictment of a Grand Jury, except in cases arising in the land or naval forces, or in the Militia, when in actual service in time of War or public danger; nor shall any person be subject for the same offence to be twice put in jeopardy of life or limb; nor shall be compelled in any criminal case to be a witness against himself, nor be deprived of life, liberty, or property, without due process of law; nor shall private property be taken for public use, without just compensation.

AMENDMENT VI

In all criminal prosecutions, the accused shall enjoy the right to a speedy and public trial, by an impartial jury of the State and district wherein the crime shall have been committed, which district shall have been previously ascertained by law, and to be informed of the nature and cause of the accusation; to be confronted with the witnesses against him; to have compulsory process for obtaining witnesses in his favor, and to have the Assistance of Counsel for his defense.

AMENDMENT VII

In Suits at common law, where the value in controversy shall exceed twenty dollars, the right of trial by jury shall be preserved, and no fact tried by jury, shall be otherwise re-examined in any Court of the United States, than according to the rules of the common law.

AMENDMENT VIII

Excessive bail shall not be required, nor excessive fines imposed, nor cruel and unusual punishments inflicted.

AMENDMENT IX

The enumeration in the Constitution, of certain rights, shall not be construed to deny or disparage others retained by the people.

AMENDMENT X

The powers not delegated to the United States by the Constitution, nor prohibited by it to the States, are reserved to the States respectively, or to the people.

AMENDMENT XI

The Judicial power of the United States shall not be construed to extend to any suit in law or equity, commenced or prosecuted against one of the United States by Citizens of another State, or by Citizens or Subjects of any Foreign State.

* * *

AMENDMENT XIII

Section 1. Neither slavery nor involuntary servitude, except as a punishment for crime whereof the party shall have been duly convicted, shall exist within the United States, or any place subject to their jurisdiction.

Section 2. Congress shall have power to enforce this article by appropriate legislation.

AMENDMENT XIV

Section 1. All persons born or naturalized in the United States, and subject to the jurisdiction thereof, are citizens of the United States and of the State wherein they reside. No State shall make or enforce any law which shall abridge the privileges or immunities of citizens of the United States; nor shall any State deprive any person of life, liberty, or property, without due process of law; nor deny to any person within its jurisdiction the equal protection of the laws.

* * *

Section 5. The Congress shall have power to enforce, by appropriate legislation, the provisions of this article.

APPENDIX B

Subject Matter Table of United States Supreme Court
Cases Affecting Higher Education

*Note: Please see the Table of Cases (located at the front of this volume)
for Supreme Court cases reported in this volume.*

Academic Freedom
Univ. of Pennsylvania v. EEOC, 493 U.S. 182, 110 S.Ct. 577, 107 L.Ed.2d 571 (1990).
Epperson v. Arkansas, 393 U.S. 97, 89 S.Ct. 266, 21 L.Ed.2d 228 (1968).
Sweezy v. New Hampshire, 354 U.S. 234, 77 S.Ct. 1203, 1 L.Ed.2d 1311 (1957).
Meyer v. Nebraska, 262 U.S. 390, 43 S.Ct. 625, 67 L.Ed.2d 1042 (1923).

Arbitration
Volt Information Sciences v. Board of Trustees of Stanford Univ., 489 U.S. 468, 109 S.Ct. 1248, 103 L.Ed.2d. 488 (1989).

Athletics
NCAA v. Smith, 525 U.S. 459, 119 S.Ct. 924, 142 L.Ed.2d 929 (1999).
NCAA v. Tarkanian, 488 U.S. 179, 109 S.Ct. 454, 102 L.Ed.2d 469 (1988).

Attorneys' Fees
Webb v. Board of Educ., 471 U.S. 234, 105 S.Ct. 1923, 85 L.Ed.2d 233 (1985).
Smith v. Robinson, 468 U.S. 992, 104 S.Ct. 3457, 82 L.Ed.2d 746 (1984).

Civil Rights
Farrar v. Hobby, 506 U.S. 103, 113 S.Ct. 566, 121 L.Ed.2d 494 (1992).
St. Francis College v. Al-Khazraji, 481 U.S. 604, 107 S.Ct. 2022, 97 L.Ed.2d 749 (1987).
Grove City College v. Bell, 465 U.S. 555, 104 S.Ct. 1211, 79 L.Ed.2d 516 (1984).
Rendell-Baker v. Kohn, 457 U.S. 830, 102 S.Ct. 2764, 73 L.Ed.2d 418 (1982).

Collective Bargaining
Davenport v. Washington Educ. Ass'n, 127 S.Ct. 2372 (U.S. 2007).
Cent. State Univ. v. American Ass'n of Univ. Professors, Cent. State Univ. Chapter, 526 U.S. 124, 119 S.Ct. 1162, 143 L.Ed.2d 227 (1999).

Compulsory Attendance
Wisconsin v. Yoder, 406 U.S. 205, 92 S.Ct. 526, 32 L.Ed.2d 15 (1972).
Pierce v. Society of Sisters, 268 U.S. 510, 45 S.Ct. 571, 69 L.Ed. 1070 (1925).

Continuing Education

Austin ISD v. U.S., 443 U.S. 915, 99 S.Ct. 3106, 61 L.Ed.2d 879 (1979).

Harrah ISD v. Martin, 440 U.S. 194, 99 S.Ct. 1062, 59 L.Ed.2d 248 (1979).

Corporal Punishment

Ingraham v. Wright, 430 U.S. 651, 97 S.Ct. 1401, 51 L.Ed.2d 711 (1977).

Court Intervention in School Affairs

Epperson v. Arkansas, 393 U.S. 97, 89 S.Ct. 266, 21 L.Ed.2d 228 (1968).

Criminal Activity

Bates v. U.S., 522 U.S. 23, 118 S.Ct. 285, 139 L.Ed.2d 215 (1997).

Desegregation

U.S. v. Fordice, 505 U.S. 717, 112 S.Ct. 2727, 120 L.Ed.2d 575 (1992).

Freeman v. Pitts, 503 U.S. 467, 112 S.Ct. 1430, 118 L.Ed.2d 108 (1992).

Disabled Students

Florence County School Dist. Four v. Carter, 510 U.S. 7, 114 S.Ct. 361, 126 L.Ed.2d 284 (1993).

Zobrest v. Catalina Foothills School Dist., 509 U.S. 1, 113 S.Ct. 2462, 125 L.Ed.2d 1 (1993).

Dellmuth v. Muth, 491 U.S. 223, 109 S.Ct. 2397, 105 L.Ed.2d 181 (1989).

Honig v. Doe, 484 U.S. 305, 108 S.Ct. 592, 98 L.Ed.2d 686 (1988).

City of Cleburne, Texas v. Cleburne Living Center, 473 U.S. 432, 105 S.Ct. 3249, 87 L.Ed.2d 313 (1985).

Honig v. Students of California School for the Blind, 471 U.S. 148, 105 S.Ct. 1820, 85 L.Ed.2d 114 (1985).

Burlington School Committee v. Dep't of Educ., 471 U.S. 359, 105 S.Ct. 1996, 85 L.Ed.2d 385 (1985).

Smith v. Robinson, 468 U.S. 992, 104 S.Ct. 3457, 82 L.Ed.2d 746 (1984).

Irving Independent School District v. Tatro, 468 U.S. 883, 104 S.Ct. 3371, 82 L.Ed.2d 664 (1984).

Board of Educ. v. Rowley, 458 U.S. 176, 102 S.Ct. 3034, 73 L.Ed.2d 690 (1982).

Univ. of Texas v. Camenisch, 451 U.S. 390, 101 S.Ct. 1830, 68 L.Ed.2d 175 (1981).

Pennhurst State School and Hospital v. Halderman, 451 U.S. 1, 101 S.Ct. 1531, 67 L.Ed.2d 694 (1981).

Southeastern Community College v. Davis, 442 U.S. 397, 99 S.Ct. 2361, 60 L.Ed.2d 980 (1979).

Discrimination, Generally

Edelman v. Lynchburg College, 532 U.S. 106, 122 S.Ct. 1145, 152 L.Ed.2d 188 (2002).

Raygor v. Regents of Univ. of Minnesota, 534 U.S. 533, 122 S.Ct. 999, 152 L.Ed.2d 27 (2002).

Alexander v. Sandoval, 531 U.S. 1049, 121 S.Ct. 1511, 141 L.Ed.2d 517 (2001).

Board of Trustees of the Univ. of Alabama v. Garrett, 531 U.S. 356, 121 S.Ct. 955, 148 L.Ed.2d 866 (2001).

Kimel v. Florida Board of Regents, 528 U.S. 62, 120 S.Ct. 631, 145 L.Ed.2d 522 (2000).

Texas v. Lesage, 528 U.S. 18, 120 S.Ct. 467, 145 L.Ed.2d 347 (1999).

Lane v. Pena, 518 U.S. 187, 116 S.Ct. 2092, 135 L.Ed.2d 486 (1996).

Jett v. Dallas Independent School Dist., 491 U.S. 701, 109 S.Ct. 2702, 105 L.Ed.2d 598 (1989).

Carnegie-Mellon Univ. v. Cohill, 484 U.S. 343, 108 S.Ct. 614, 98 L.Ed.2d 720 (1988).

School Board of Nassau County v. Arline, 480 U.S. 273, 107 S.Ct. 1123, 94 L.Ed.2d 307 (1987).

Hazelwood School Dist. v. U.S., 433 U.S. 299, 97 S.Ct. 2736, 53 L.Ed.2d 768 (1977).

DeFunis v. Odegaard, 416 U.S. 312, 94 S.Ct. 1704, 40 L.Ed.2d 164 (1974).

Due Process

Gilbert v. Homar, 520 U.S. 924, 117 S.Ct. 1807, 138 L.Ed.2d 120 (1997).

Univ. of Tennessee v. Elliot, 478 U.S. 788, 106 S.Ct. 3220, 92 L.Ed.2d 635 (1986).

Memphis Community School Dist. v. Stachura, 477 U.S. 299, 106 S.Ct. 2537, 91 L.Ed.2d 249 (1986).

Cleveland Board of Educ. v. Loudermill, 470 U.S. 532, 105 S.Ct. 1487, 84 L.Ed.2d 494 (1985).

Perry v. Sindermann, 408 U.S. 593, 92 S.Ct. 2694, 33 L.Ed.2d 570 (1972).

Board of Regents v. Roth, 408 U.S. 564, 92 S.Ct. 2701, 33 L.Ed.2d 548 (1972).

Employment

City of Ontario v. Quon, 130 S.Ct. 2619 (U.S. 2010).

Burlington Northern & Santa Fe Railway Co. v. White, 126 S.Ct. 2405 (U.S. 2006).

Smith v. City of Jackson, 125 S.Ct. 1536 (U.S. 2005).

Corporation of the Presiding Bishop of the Church of Jesus Christ of Latter-Day Saints v. Amos, 483 U.S. 327, 107 S.Ct. 2862, 97 L.Ed.2d 273 (1987).

O'Connor v. Ortega, 480 U.S. 709 (1987).

Franklin & Marshall College v. EEOC, 476 U.S. 1163, 106 S.Ct. 2288, 90 L.Ed.2d 729 (1986).

NLRB v. Catholic Bishop of Chicago, 440 U.S. 490, 99 S.Ct. 1313, 59 L.Ed.2d 533 (1979).

Federal Aid

Traynor v. Turnage, 485 U.S. 535, 108 S.Ct. 1372, 99 L.Ed.2d 618 (1988).

Selective Service System v. MPIRG, 468 U.S. 841, 104 S.Ct. 3348, 82 L.Ed.2d 632 (1984).

Bell v. New Jersey and Pennsylvania, 461 U.S. 773, 103 S.Ct. 2187, 76 L.Ed.2d 312 (1984).

Grove City College v. Bell, 465 U.S. 555, 104 S.Ct. 1211, 79 L.Ed.2d 516 (1984).

Valley Forge Christian College v. Americans United for Separation of Church and State, 454 U.S. 464, 102 S.Ct. 752, 70 L.Ed.2d 700 (1982).

Board of Educ. v. Harris, 444 U.S. 130, 100 S.Ct. 363, 62 L.Ed.2d 275 (1979).

Wheeler v. Barrera, 417 U.S. 402, 94 S.Ct. 2274, 41 L.Ed.2d 159 (1974).

Tilton v. Richardson, 403 U.S. 672, 91 S.Ct. 2091, 29 L.Ed.2d 790 (1971).

Freedom of Religion

City of Boerne, Texas v. Flores, 521 U.S. 507, 117 S.Ct. 2157, 138 L.Ed.2d 624 (1997).

Edwards v. Aguillard, 482 U.S. 578, 107 S.Ct. 2573, 96 L.Ed.2d 510 (1987).

Ansonia Board of Educ. v. Philbrook, 499 U.S. 60, 107 S.Ct. 367, 93 L.Ed.2d 305 (1986).

Freedom of Speech

Christian Legal Society Chapter of the University of California, Hastings College of the Law v. Martinez, 130 S.Ct. 2971 (U.S. 2010).

Garcetti v. Ceballos, 126 S.Ct. 1951, 164 L.Ed. 2d 689 (U.S. 2006).

Board of Regents of Univ. of Wisconsin System v. Southworth, 529 U.S. 217, 120 S.Ct. 1346, 146 L.Ed.2d 193 (2000).

Board of Educ. of Westside Community School v. Mergens, 496 U.S. 226, 110 S.Ct. 2356, 110 L.Ed.2d 191 (1990).

Board of Trustees of the State Univ. of New York v. Fox, 492 U.S. 469, 109 S.Ct. 3028, 106 L.Ed.2d 388 (1989).

Hazelwood School Dist. v. Kuhlmeier, 484 U.S. 261, 108 S.Ct. 562, 98 L.Ed.2d 592 (1988).

Rankin v. McPherson, 483 U.S. 378, 107 S.Ct. 2891, 97 L.Ed.2d 315 (1987).

Bethel School Dist. v. Fraser, 478 U.S. 675, 106 S.Ct. 3159, 92 L.Ed.2d 549 (1986).

Wayte v. U.S., 470 U.S. 598, 105 S.Ct. 1524, 84 L.Ed.2d 547 (1985).

Connick v. Myers, 461 U.S. 138, 103 S.Ct. 1684, 75 L.Ed.2d 708 (1983).

Board of Educ. v. Pico, 457 U.S. 853, 102 S.Ct. 2799, 73 L.Ed.2d 435 (1982).

Givhan v. Western Line Consolidated School Dist., 439 U.S. 410, 99 S.Ct. 693, 58 L.Ed.2d 619 (1979).

Mt. Healthy City School v. Doyle, 429 U.S. 274, 97 S.Ct. 568, 50 L.Ed.2d 471 (1977).

Papish v. Board of Curators, 410 U.S. 667, 93 S.Ct. 1197, 35 L.Ed.2d 618 (1973).

Grayned v. City of Rockford, 408 U.S. 104, 92 S.Ct. 2294, 33 L.Ed.2d 222 (1972).

Police Dep't v. Mosley, 408 U.S. 92, 92 S.Ct. 2286, 33 L.Ed.2d 212 (1972).

Tinker v. Des Moines, 393 U.S. 503, 89 S.Ct. 733, 21 L.Ed.2d 733 (1969).

Pickering v. Board of Educ., 391 U.S. 563, 88 S.Ct. 1731, 20 L.Ed.2d 811 (1968).

Whitehill v. Elkins, 389 U.S. 54, 88 S.Ct. 184, 19 L.Ed.2d 228 (1967).

Keyishian v. Board of Regents, 385 U.S. 589, 87 S.Ct. 675, 17 L.Ed.2d 629 (1967).

Elfbrandt v. Russell, 384 U.S. 11, 86 S.Ct. 1238, 16 L.Ed.2d 321 (1965).

Baggett v. Bullitt, 377 U.S. 360, 84 S.Ct. 1316, 12 L.Ed.2d 377 (1963).

Cramp v. Board of Public Instruction of Orange County, 368 U.S. 278, 82 S.Ct. 275, 7 L.Ed.2d 285 (1961).

Shelton v. Tucker, 364 U.S. 479, 81 S.Ct. 247, 5 L.Ed.2d 231 (1960).

Slochower v. Board of Educ., 350 U.S. 551, 76 S.Ct. 637, 100 L.Ed. 692 (1955).

Adler v. Board of Educ., 342 U.S. 485, 72 S.Ct. 380, 96 L.Ed. 517 (1952).

Intellectual Property

New York Times Co. Inc. v. Tasini, 533 U.S. 483, 121 S.Ct. 2381, 150 L.Ed.2d 500 (2001).

Florida Prepaid Postsecondary Educ. Expense Board v. College Savings Bank, 527 U.S. 627, 119 S.Ct. 2199, 144 L.Ed.2d 575 (1999).

College Savings Bank v. Florida Prepaid Postsecondary Educ. Expense Board, 527 U.S. 666, 119 S.Ct. 2219, 144 L.Ed.2d 605 (1999).

Labor Relations

Lehnert v. Ferris Faculty Ass'n, 500 U.S. 507, 111 S.Ct. 1950, 114 L.Ed.2d 572 (1991).

Fort Stewart Schools v. Federal Labor Relations Authority, 495 U.S. 641, 110 S.Ct. 2043, 109 L.Ed.2d 659 (1990).

Minnesota State Board for Community Colleges v. Knight, 465 U.S. 271, 104 S.Ct. 1058, 79 L.Ed.2d 299 (1984).

NLRB v. Yeshiva Univ., 444 U.S. 672, 100 S.Ct. 856, 63 L.Ed.2d 115 (1980).

NLRB v. Catholic Bishop of Chicago, 440 U.S. 490, 99 S.Ct. 1313, 59 L.Ed.2d 533 (1979).

Abood v. Detroit Board of Educ., 431 U.S. 209, 97 S.Ct. 1782, 52 L.Ed.2d 261 (1977).

Maternity Leave

Richmond Unified School Dist. v. Berg, 434 U.S. 158, 98 S.Ct. 623, 54 L.Ed.2d 375 (1977).

Cleveland Board of Educ. v. La Fleur, 414 U.S. 632, 94 S.Ct. 791, 39 L.Ed.2d 52 (1974).

Cohen v. Chesterfield, 414 U.S. 632, 94 S.Ct. 791, 39 L.Ed.2d 52 (1974).

Private School Funding

Agostini v. Felton, 521 U.S. 203, 117 S.Ct. 1997, 138 L.Ed.2d 391 (1997).

Board of Educ. of Kiryas Joel Village School Dist. v. Grumet, 512 U.S. 687, 114 S.Ct. 2481, 129 L.Ed.2d 546 (1994).

Witters v. Washington Dep't of Services for the Blind, 474 U.S. 481, 106 S.Ct. 748, 88 L.Ed.2d 846 (1986).

Aguilar v. Felton, 473 U.S. 402, 105 S.Ct. 3232, 87 L.Ed.2d 290 (1985).

Grand Rapids School District v. Ball, 473 U.S. 373, 105 S.Ct. 3216, 87 L.Ed.2d 267 (1985).

Mueller v. Allen, 463 U.S. 388, 103 S.Ct. 3062, 77 L.Ed.2d 721 (1983).

Valley Forge Christian College v. Americans United for Separation of Church and State, 454 U.S. 464, 102 S.Ct. 752, 70 L.Ed.2d 700 (1982).

Committee for Public Educ. and Religious Liberty v. Regan, 444 U.S. 646, 100 S.Ct. 840, 63 L.Ed.2d 94 (1980).

New York v. Cathedral Academy, 434 U.S. 125, 98 S.Ct. 340, 54 L.Ed.2d 346 (1977).

Wolman v. Walter, 433 U.S. 229, 97 S.Ct. 2593, 53 L.Ed.2d 714 (1977).

Roemer v. Board of Public Works, 426 U.S. 736, 96 S.Ct. 2337, 49 L.Ed.2d 179 (1976).

Meek v. Pittenger, 421 U.S. 349, 95 S.Ct. 1753, 44 L.Ed.2d 217 (1975).

Wheeler v. Barrera, 417 U.S. 402, 94 S.Ct. 2274, 41 L.Ed.2d 159 (1974).

Sloan v. Lemon, 413 U.S. 825, 93 S.Ct. 2982, 37 L.Ed.2d 939 (1973).

Committee for Public Educ. and Religious Liberty v. Nyquist, 413 U.S. 756, 93 S.Ct. 2955, 37 L.Ed.2d 948 (1973).

Hunt v. McNair, 413 U.S. 734, 93 S.Ct. 2868, 37 L.Ed.2d 923 (1973).

Levitt v. Committee for Public Educ. and Religious Liberty, 413 U.S. 472, 93 S.Ct. 2814, 37 L.Ed.2d 736 (1973).

Early v. Di Censo, 403 U.S. 602, 91 S.Ct. 2105, 29 L.Ed.2d 745 (1971).

Lemon v. Kurtzman, 403 U.S. 602, 91 S.Ct. 2105, 29 L.Ed.2d 745 (1971).

Flast v. Cohen, 392 U.S. 83, 88 S.Ct. 1942, 20 L.Ed.2d 947 (1968).

Racial Discrimination

Grutter v. Bollinger, 123 S.Ct. 2325 (2003).

Gratz v. Bollinger, 123 S.Ct. 2411 (2003).

St. Francis College v. Al-Khazraji, 481 U.S. 604, 107 S.Ct. 2022, 97 L.Ed.2d 749 (1987).

City of Pleasant Grove v. United States, 479 U.S. 462, 107 S.Ct. 794, 93 L.Ed.2d 866 (1987).

Wygant v. Jackson Board of Educ., 476 U.S. 267, 106 S.Ct. 1842, 90 L.Ed.2d 260 (1986).

Regents of the Univ. of California v. Bakke, 438 U.S. 265, 98 S.Ct. 2733, 57 L.Ed.2d 750 (1978).

Runyon v. McCrary, 427 U.S. 160, 96 S.Ct. 2586, 49 L.Ed.2d 415 (1976).

Lau v. Nichols, 414 U.S. 563, 94 S.Ct. 786, 39 L.Ed.2d 1 (1974).

Norwood v. Harrison, 413 U.S. 455, 93 S.Ct. 2804, 37 L.Ed.2d 723 (1973).

Recognition of Student Organizations

Bender v. Williamsport Area School Dist., 475 U.S. 534, 106 S.Ct. 1326, 89 L.Ed.2d 501 (1986).

Healy v. James, 408 U.S. 169, 92 S.Ct. 2338, 33 L.Ed.2d 266 (1972).

Release Time

Zorach v. Clauson, 343 U.S. 306, 72 S.Ct. 679, 96 L.Ed. 954 (1952).

McCollum v. Board of Educ., 333 U.S. 203, 68 S.Ct. 461, 92 L.Ed. 649 (1948).

Religious Activities in Public Schools

Rosenberger v. Rector and Visitors of Univ. of Virginia, 515 U.S. 819, 115 S.Ct. 2510, 132 L.Ed.2d 700 (1995).

Lamb's Chapel v. Center Moriches Union Free School District, 508 U.S. 384, 113 S.Ct. 2141, 124 L.Ed.2d 352 (1993).

Lee v. Weisman, 505 U.S. 577, 112 S.Ct. 2649, 120 L.Ed.2d 467 (1992).

Karcher v. May, 484 U.S. 72, 108 S.Ct. 388, 98 L.Ed.2d 327 (1987).

Wallace v. Jaffree, 472 U.S. 38, 105 S.Ct. 2479, 96 L.Ed.2d 29 (1985).

Widmar v. Vincent, 454 U.S. 263, 102 S.Ct. 269, 70 L.Ed.2d 400 (1981).

Stone v. Graham, 449 U.S. 39, 101 S.Ct. 192, 66 L.Ed.2d 199 (1980).

Chamberlin v. Dade County Board of Public Instruction, 377 U.S. 402, 84 S.Ct. 1272, 12 L.Ed.2d 407 (1964).

Abington School Dist. v. Schempp, 374 U.S. 203, 83 S.Ct. 1560, 10 L.Ed.2d 844 (1963).

Residency

Martinez v. Bynum, 461 U.S. 321 103 S.Ct. 1838, 75 L.Ed.2d 879 (1983).

Toll v. Moreno, 458 U.S. 1, 102 S.Ct. 2977, 73 L.Ed.2d 563 (1982).

Elkins v. Moreno, 435 U.S. 647, 98 S.Ct. 1338, 55 L.Ed.2d 614 (1978).

Vlandis v. Kline, 412 U.S. 441, 93 S.Ct. 2230, 37 L.Ed.2d 63 (1973).

School Liability

Gebser v. Lago Vista Independent School Dist., 524 U.S. 274, 118 S.Ct. 1989, 141 L.Ed.2d 277 (1998).

Regents of Univ. of California v. Doe, 519 U.S. 425, 117 S.Ct. 900, 137 L.Ed.2d 55 (1997).

Sex Discrimination and Harassment

Fitzgerald v. Barnstable School Committee, 129 S.Ct. 788 (U.S. 2009).

Jackson v. Birmingham Board of Educ., 125 S.Ct. 1497 (U.S. 2005).

United States (Brzonkala) v. Morrison, 529 U.S. 1062, 120 S.Ct. 1740, 144 L.Ed.2d 658 (2000).

Davis v. Monroe County Board of Educ., 526 U.S. 629, 119 S.Ct. 1661, 143 L.Ed.2d 839 (1999).

U.S. v. Virginia, 518 U.S. 515, 116 S.Ct. 2264, 135 L.Ed.2d 735 (1996).

Franklin v. Gwinnett County Public Schools, 503 U.S. 60, 112 S.Ct. 1028, 117 L.Ed.2d 208 (1992).

Ohio Civil Rights Comm'n v. Dayton Christian Schools, 477 U.S. 619, 106 S.Ct. 2718, 91 L.Ed.2d 512 (1986).

Mississippi Univ. for Women v. Hogan, 458 U.S. 718, 102 S.Ct. 3331, 73 L.Ed.2d 1090 (1982).

Cannon v. Univ. of Chicago, 441 U.S. 677, 99 S.Ct. 1946, 60 L.Ed.2d 560 (1979).

Trustees of Keene State College v. Sweeney, 439 U.S. 24, 99 S.Ct. 295, 58 L.Ed.2d 216 (1978).

Student Loans

Lockhart v. U.S., 126 S.Ct. 699 (U.S. 2005).

Student Privacy

Owasso Independent School Dist. No. I-011 v. Falvo, 534 U.S. 426, 122 S.Ct. 934, 151 L.Ed.2d 896 (2002).

Gonzaga Univ. v. Doe, 536 U.S. 273, 122 S.Ct. 2268, 153 L.Ed.2d 309 (2002).

Student Searches

Vernonia School Dist. 47J v. Acton, 515 U.S. 646, 115 S.Ct. 2386, 132 L.Ed.2d 564 (1995).

New Jersey v. T.L.O., 469 U.S. 325, 105 S.Ct. 733, 83 L.Ed.2d 720 (1985).

Student Suspensions

Regents v. Ewing, 474 U.S. 214, 106 S.Ct. 507, 88 L.Ed.2d 523 (1985).

Board of Educ. v. McCluskey, 458 U.S. 966, 103 S.Ct. 3469, 73 L.Ed.2d 1273 (1982).

Carey v. Piphus, 435 U.S. 247, 98 S.Ct. 1042, 55 L.Ed.2d 252 (1978).

Board of Curators v. Horowitz, 435 U.S. 78, 98 S.Ct. 948, 55 L.Ed.2d 124 (1978).

Wood v. Strickland, 420 U.S. 308, 95 S.Ct. 992, 43 L.Ed.2d 214 (1975).

Goss v. Lopez, 419 U.S. 565, 95 S.Ct. 729, 42 L.Ed.2d 725 (1975).

Taxation

Camps Newfound/Owatonna, Inc. v. Town of Harrison, Maine, 520 U.S. 564, 117 S.Ct. 1590, 137 L.Ed.2d 852 (1997).

Allen v. Wright, 468 U.S. 737, 104 S.Ct. 3315, 82 L.Ed.2d 556 (1984).

Bob Jones Univ. v. United States, 461 U.S. 574, 103 S.Ct. 2017, 76 L.Ed.2d 157 (1983).

Mueller v. Allen, 463 U.S. 388, 103 S.Ct. 3062, 77 L.Ed.2d 721 (1983).

Ramah Navajo School Board v. Bureau of Revenue, 458 U.S. 832, 102 S.Ct. 3394, 73 L.Ed.2d 1174 (1982).

California v. Grace Brethren Church, 457 U.S. 393, 102 S.Ct. 2498, 73 L.Ed.2d 93 (1982).

Gordon v. Lance, 403 U.S. 1, 91 S.Ct. 1889, 29 L.Ed.2d 273 (1971).

Askew v. Hargrave, 401 U.S. 476, 91 S.Ct. 856, 28 L.Ed.2d 196 (1971).

Doremus v. Board of Educ., 342 U.S. 429, 72 S.Ct. 394, 96 L.Ed. 475 (1952).

Teacher Termination

Patsy v. Board of Regents, 457 U.S. 496, 102 S.Ct. 2557, 73 L.Ed.2d 172 (1982).

Chardon v. Fernandez, 454 U.S. 6, 102 S.Ct. 28, 70 L.Ed.2d 6 (1981).

Delaware State College v. Ricks, 449 U.S. 250, 101 S.Ct. 498, 66 L.Ed.2d 431 (1980).

Beilan v. Board of Public Educ., 357 U.S. 399, 78 S.Ct. 1317, 2 L.Ed.2d 1414 (1958).

Textbooks

Norwood v. Harrison, 413 U.S. 455, 93 S.Ct. 2804, 37 L.Ed.2d 723 (1973).

Board of Educ. v. Allen, 392 U.S. 236, 88 S.Ct. 1923, 20 L.Ed.2d 1060 (1968).

Cochran v. Louisiana State Board of Educ., 281 U.S. 370, 50 S.Ct. 335, 74 L.Ed.2d 1929 (1930).

Transportation

Kadrmas v. Dickinson Public Schools, 487 U.S. 450, 108 S.Ct. 2481, 101 L.Ed.2d 399 (1988).

Wolman v. Walter, 433 U.S. 229, 97 S.Ct. 2593, 53 L.Ed.2d 714 (1977).

Everson v. Board of Educ., 330 U.S. 1, 67 S.Ct. 504, 91 L.Ed. 711 (1947).

Weapons

U.S. v. Lopez, 514 U.S. 549, 115 S.Ct. 1624, 131 L.Ed.2d 626 (1995).

The Judicial System

In order to allow you to determine the relative importance of a judicial decision, the cases included in *Higher Education Law in America* identify the particular court from which a decision has been issued. For example, a case decided by a state supreme court generally will be of greater significance than a state circuit court case. Hence a basic knowledge of the structure of our judicial system is important to an understanding of higher education law.

Almost all the reports in this volume are taken from appellate court decisions. Although most education law decisions occur at trial court and administrative levels, appellate court decisions have the effect of binding lower courts and administrators so that appellate court decisions have the effect of law within their court systems.

State and federal court systems generally function independently of each other. Each court system applies its own law according to statutes and the determinations of its highest court. However, judges at all levels often consider opinions from other court systems to settle issues that are new or arise under unique fact situations. Similarly, lawyers look at the opinions of many courts to locate authority that supports their clients' cases.

Once a lawsuit is filed in a particular court system, that system retains the matter until its conclusion. Unsuccessful parties at the administrative or trial court level generally have the right to appeal unfavorable determinations of law to appellate courts within the system. When federal law issues or constitutional grounds are present, lawsuits may be appropriately filed in the federal court system. In those cases, the lawsuit is filed initially in the federal district court for that area.

On rare occasions, the U.S. Supreme Court considers appeals from the highest courts of the states if a distinct federal question exists and at least four justices agree on the question's importance. The federal courts occasionally send cases to state courts for application of state law. These situations are infrequent and, in general, the state and federal court systems should be considered separate from each other.

The most common system, used by nearly all states and also the federal judiciary, is as follows: a legal action is commenced in district court (sometimes called trial court, county court, common pleas court or superior court) where a decision is initially reached. The case may then be appealed to the court of appeals (or appellate court), and in turn this decision may be appealed to the supreme court.

Several states, however, do not have a court of appeals; lower court decisions are appealed directly to the state's supreme court. Additionally, some states have labeled their courts in a nonstandard fashion.

In Maryland, the highest state court is called the Court of Appeals. In the state of New York, the trial court is called the Supreme Court. Decisions of this court may be appealed to the Supreme Court, Appellate Division. The highest court in New York is the Court of Appeals. Pennsylvania has perhaps the most complex court system. The lowest state court is the Court of Common Pleas. Depending on the circumstances of the case, appeals may be taken to either the Commonwealth Court or the Superior Court. In certain instances the Commonwealth Court functions as a trial court as well as an appellate court. The Superior Court, however, is strictly an intermediate appellate court. The highest court in Pennsylvania is the Supreme Court.

While supreme court decisions are generally regarded as the last word in legal matters, it is important to remember that trial and appeals court decisions also create important legal precedents. For the hierarchy of typical state and federal court systems, please see the diagram below.

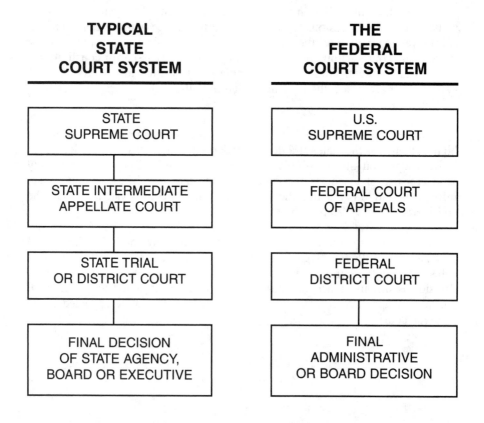

TYPICAL STATE COURT SYSTEM	THE FEDERAL COURT SYSTEM
STATE SUPREME COURT	U.S. SUPREME COURT
STATE INTERMEDIATE APPELLATE COURT	FEDERAL COURT OF APPEALS
STATE TRIAL OR DISTRICT COURT	FEDERAL DISTRICT COURT
FINAL DECISION OF STATE AGENCY, BOARD OR EXECUTIVE	FINAL ADMINISTRATIVE OR BOARD DECISION

Federal courts of appeals hear appeals from the district courts that are located in their circuits. Below is a list of states matched to the federal circuits in which they are located.

First Circuit — Puerto Rico, Maine, New Hampshire, Massachusetts, Rhode Island

Second Circuit — New York, Vermont, Connecticut

Third Circuit — Pennsylvania, New Jersey, Delaware, Virgin Islands

Fourth Circuit — West Virginia, Maryland, Virginia, North Carolina, South Carolina

Fifth Circuit — Texas, Louisiana, Mississippi

Sixth Circuit — Ohio, Kentucky, Tennessee, Michigan

Seventh Circuit — Wisconsin, Indiana, Illinois

Eighth Circuit — North Dakota, South Dakota, Nebraska, Arkansas, Missouri, Iowa, Minnesota

Ninth Circuit — Alaska, Washington, Oregon, California, Hawaii, Arizona, Nevada, Idaho, Montana, Northern Mariana Islands, Guam

Tenth Circuit — Wyoming, Utah, Colorado, Kansas, Oklahoma, New Mexico

Eleventh Circuit — Alabama, Georgia, Florida

District of Columbia — Hears cases from the U.S. District Court for the District of Columbia.

Federal Circuit — Sitting in Washington, D.C., the U.S. Court of Appeals, Federal Circuit hears patent and trade appeals and certain appeals on claims brought against the federal government and its agencies.

How to Read a Case Citation

Generally, court decisions can be located in case reporters at law school or governmental law libraries. Some cases also can be located on the Internet through legal Web sites or official court Web sites.

Each case summary contains the citation, or legal reference, to the full text of the case. The diagram below illustrates how to read a case citation.

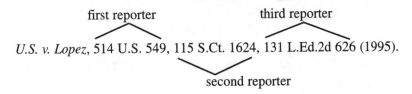

case name (parties)   case reporter name and series   court location

Virginia College v. Moore,   974   So.2d   269   (Miss. Ct. App. 2008).

volume number   first page   year of decision

Some cases may have two or three reporter names, such as U.S. Supreme Court cases and cases reported in regional case reporters as well as state case reporters. For example, a U.S. Supreme Court case usually contains three case reporter citations.

first reporter   third reporter

U.S. v. Lopez, 514 U.S. 549, 115 S.Ct. 1624, 131 L.Ed.2d 626 (1995).

second reporter

The citations are still read in the same manner as if only one citation has been listed.

Occasionally, a case may contain a citation that does not reference a case reporter. For example, a citation may contain a reference such as:

case name   year of decision   first page   date of decision

Maltbia v. Coffie,   No. H-06-834,   2007   WL   43793   (S.D. Tex. 1/5/07).

court file number   WESTLAW[1]   court location

The court file number indicates the specific number assigned to a case by the particular court system deciding the case. In our example, the Texas Court of Appeals has assigned the case of *Maltbia v. Coffie* the case number of "H-06-834," which will

---

[1] WESTLAW® is a computerized database of court cases available for a fee.

serve as the reference number for the case and any matter relating to the case. Locating a case on the Internet generally requires either the case name and date of the decision, and/or the court file number.

Below, we have listed the full names of the regional reporters. As mentioned previously, many states have individual state reporters. The names of those reporters may be obtained from a reference law librarian.

P.	**Pacific Reporter**
	Alaska, Arizona, California, Colorado, Hawaii, Idaho, Kansas, Montana, Nevada, New Mexico, Oklahoma, Oregon, Utah, Washington, Wyoming
A.	**Atlantic Reporter**
	Connecticut, Delaware, District of Columbia, Maine, Maryland, New Hampshire, New Jersey, Pennsylvania, Rhode Island, Vermont
N.E.	**Northeastern Reporter**
	Illinois, Indiana, Massachusetts, New York, Ohio
N.W.	**Northwestern Reporter**
	Iowa, Michigan, Minnesota, Nebraska, North Dakota, South Dakota, Wisconsin
So.	**Southern Reporter**
	Alabama, Florida, Louisiana, Mississippi
S.E.	**Southeastern Reporter**
	Georgia, North Carolina, South Carolina, Virginia, West Virginia
S.W.	**Southwestern Reporter**
	Arkansas, Kentucky, Missouri, Tennessee, Texas
F.	**Federal Reporter**
	The thirteen federal judicial circuits courts of appeals decisions. *See The Judicial System, p. 495* for specific state circuits.
F.Supp.	**Federal Supplement**
	The thirteen federal judicial circuits district court decisions. *See The Judicial System, p. 495* for specific state circuits.
Fed.Appx.	**Federal Appendix**
	Contains unpublished decisions of the U.S. Circuit Courts of Appeal.
U.S.	**United States Reports**
S.Ct.	**Supreme Court Reporter** U.S. Supreme Court Decisions
L.Ed.	**Lawyers' Edition**

GLOSSARY

Ad Valorem Tax - In general usage, a tax on property measured by the property's value.

Age Discrimination in Employment Act (ADEA) - The ADEA, 29 U.S.C. § 621, *et seq.*, is part of the Fair Labor Standards Act. It prohibits discrimination against persons who are at least 40 years old, and applies to employers that have 20 or more employees and that affect interstate commerce.

Americans with Disabilities Act (ADA) - The ADA, 42 U.S.C. § 12101, *et seq.*, was signed into law on July 26, 1990. Among other things, it prohibits discrimination against a qualified individual with a disability because of that person's disability with respect to job application procedures, the hiring, advancement or discharge of employees, employee compensation, job training, and other terms, conditions and privileges of employment. The act also prohibits discrimination against otherwise qualified individuals with respect to the services, programs or activities of a public entity. Further, any entity that operates a place of public accommodation (including private schools) may not discriminate against individuals with disabilities.

Bill of Attainder - A bill of attainder is a law that inflicts punishment on a particular group of individuals without a trial. Such acts are prohibited by Article I, Section 9 of the Constitution.

Bona fide - Latin term meaning "good faith." Generally used to note a party's lack of bad intent or fraudulent purpose.

Claim Preclusion - (see Res Judicata).

Class Action Suit - Federal Rule of Civil Procedure 23 allows members of a class to sue as representatives on behalf of the whole class provided that the class is so large that joinder of all parties is impractical, there are questions of law or fact common to the class, the claims or defenses of the representatives are typical of the claims or defenses of the class, and the representative parties will adequately protect the interests of the class. In addition, there must be some danger of inconsistent verdicts or adjudications if the class action were prosecuted as separate actions. Most states also allow class actions under the same or similar circumstances.

Collateral Estoppel - Also known as issue preclusion. The idea that once an issue has been litigated, it may not be re-tried. Similar to the doctrine of *Res Judicata* (see below).

Due Process Clause - The clauses of the Fifth and Fourteenth Amendments to the Constitution which guarantee the citizens of the United States "due process of law" (see below). The Fifth Amendment's Due Process Clause applies to the federal government, and the Fourteenth Amendment's Due Process Clause applies to the states.

Due Process of Law - The idea of "fair play" in the government's application of law to its citizens, guaranteed by the Fifth and Fourteenth Amendments. Substantive due process is just plain *fairness*, and procedural due process is accorded when the government utilizes adequate procedural safeguards for the protection of an individual's liberty or property interests.

Employee Retirement Income Security Act (ERISA) - Federal legislation that sets uniform standards for employee pension benefit plans and employee welfare benefit plans. It is codified at 29 U.S.C. § 1001, *et seq.*

Enjoin - (see Injunction).

Equal Pay Act - Federal legislation that is part of the Fair Labor Standards Act. It applies to discrimination in wages that is based on gender. For race discrimination, employees paid unequally must utilize Title VII or 42 U.S.C. § 1981. Unlike many labor statutes, there is no minimum number of employees necessary to invoke the act's protection.

Equal Protection Clause - The clause of the Fourteenth Amendment that prohibits a state from denying any person within its jurisdiction equal protection of its laws. Also, the Due Process Clause of the Fifth Amendment that pertains to the federal government. This has been interpreted by the Supreme Court to grant equal protection even though there is no explicit grant in the Constitution.

Establishment Clause - The clause of the First Amendment that prohibits Congress from making "any law respecting an establishment of religion." This clause has been interpreted as creating a "wall of separation" between church and state. The test now used to determine whether government action violates the Establishment Clause, referred to as the *Lemon* test, asks whether the action has a secular purpose, whether its primary effect promotes or inhibits religion, and whether it requires excessive entanglement between church and state.

Ex Post Facto Law - A law that punishes as criminal any action that was not a crime at the time it was performed. Prohibited by Article I, Section 9, of the Constitution.

Exclusionary Rule - Constitutional limitation on the introduction of evidence that states that evidence derived from a constitutional violation must be excluded from trial.

Fair Labor Standards Act (FLSA) - Federal legislation that mandates the payment of minimum wages and overtime compensation to covered employees. The overtime provisions require employers to pay at least time-and-one-half to employees who work more than 40 hours per week.

Federal Tort Claims Act - Federal legislation that determines the circumstances under which the United States waives its sovereign immunity (see below) and agrees to be sued in court for money damages. The government retains its immunity in cases of intentional torts committed by its employees or agents, and where the tort is the result of a "discretionary function" of a federal employee or agency. Many states have similar acts.

42 U.S.C. §§ 1981, 1983 - Section 1983 of the federal Civil Rights Act prohibits any person acting under color of state law from depriving any other person of rights protected by the Constitution or by federal laws. A vast majority of lawsuits claiming constitutional violations are brought under § 1983. Section 1981 provides that all persons enjoy the same right to make and enforce contracts as "white citizens." Section 1981 applies to employment contracts. Further, unlike § 1983, § 1981 applies even to private actors. It is not limited to those acting under color of state law. These sections do not apply to the federal government, though the government may be sued directly under the Constitution for any violations.

Free Exercise Clause - The clause of the First Amendment that prohibits Congress from interfering with citizens' rights to the free exercise of their religion. Through the Fourteenth Amendment, it also has been made applicable to the states and their sub-entities. The Supreme Court has held that laws of general applicability that have an incidental effect on persons' free exercise rights are not violative of the Free Exercise Clause.

Incorporation Doctrine - By its own terms, the Bill of Rights applies only to the federal government. The Incorporation Doctrine states that the Fourteenth Amendment makes the Bill of Rights applicable to the states.

Individuals with Disabilities Education Act (IDEA) - 1990 amendment to the Education of the Handicapped Act (EHA) that renames the act and expands the group of children to whom special education services must be given.

Injunction - An equitable remedy (see Remedies) wherein a court orders a party to do or refrain from doing some particular action.

Issue Preclusion - (see Collateral Estoppel).

Jurisdiction - The power of a court to determine cases and controversies. The Supreme Court's jurisdiction extends to cases arising under the Constitution and under federal law. Federal courts have the power to hear cases where there is diversity of citizenship or where a federal question is involved.

Labor Management Relations Act (LMRA) - Federal labor law that preempts state law with respect to controversies involving collective bargaining agreements. The most important provision of the LMRA is § 301, which is codified at 29 U.S.C. § 185.

Mill - In property tax usage, one-tenth of a cent.

National Labor Relations Act (NLRA) - Federal legislation that guarantees to employees the right to form and participate in labor organizations. It prohibits employers from interfering with employees in the exercise of their rights under the NLRA.

Negligence per se - Negligence on its face. Usually, the violation of an ordinance or statute will be treated as negligence per se because no careful person would have been guilty of it.

Occupational Safety and Health Act (OSHA) - Federal legislation that requires employers to provide a safe workplace. Employers have both general and specific duties under OSHA. The general duty is to provide a workplace that is free from recognized hazards that are likely to result in serious physical harm. The specific duty is to conform to the health and safety standards promulgated by the Secretary of Labor.

Overbroad - A government action is overbroad if, in an attempt to alleviate a specific evil, it impermissibly prohibits or chills a protected action. For example, attempting to deal with street litter by prohibiting the distribution of leaflets or handbills.

Per Curiam - Latin phrase meaning "by the court." Used in court reports to note an opinion written by the court rather than by a single judge or justice.

Preemption Doctrine - Doctrine that states that when federal and state law attempt to regulate the same subject matter, federal law prevents the state law from operating. Based on the Supremacy Clause of Article VI, Clause 2, of the Constitution.

Prior Restraint - Restraining a publication before it is distributed. In general, constitutional law doctrine prohibits government from exercising prior restraint.

Pro Se - A party appearing in court, without the benefit of an attorney, is said to be appearing pro se.

Remand - The act of an appellate court in returning a case to the court from which it came for further action.

Remedies - There are two general categories of remedies, or relief: legal remedies, which consist of money damages, and equitable remedies, which consist of a court mandate that a specific action be prohibited or required. For example, a claim for compensatory and punitive damages seeks a legal remedy; a claim for an injunction seeks an equitable remedy. Equitable remedies are generally unavailable unless legal remedies are inadequate to address the harm.

Res Judicata - The judicial notion that a claim or action may not be tried twice or re-litigated, or that all causes of action arising out of the same set of operative facts should be tried at one time. Also known as claim preclusion.

Section 504 of the Rehabilitation Act of 1973 - Section 504 applies to public or private institutions receiving federal financial assistance. It requires that, in the employment context, an otherwise qualified individual cannot be denied employment based on his or her handicap. An otherwise qualified individual is one who can perform the "essential functions" of the job with "reasonable accommodation."

Section 1981 & Section 1983 - (see 42 U.S.C. §§ 1981, 1983).

Sovereign Immunity - The idea that the government cannot be sued without its consent. It stems from the English notion that the "King could do no wrong." This immunity from suit has been abrogated in most states and by the federal government through legislative acts known as "tort claims acts."

Standing - The judicial doctrine that states that in order to maintain a lawsuit a party must have some real interest at stake in the outcome of the trial.

Statute of Limitations - A statute of limitation provides the time period in which a specific cause of action may be brought.

Summary Judgment - Also referred to as pretrial judgment. Similar to a dismissal. Where there is no genuine issue as to any material fact and all that remains is a question of law, a judge can rule in favor of one party or the other. In general, summary judgment is used to dispose of claims that do not support a legally recognized claim.

Supremacy Clause - Clause in Article VI of the Constitution that states that federal legislation is the supreme law of the land. This clause is used to support the Preemption Doctrine (see above).

Title VI, Civil Rights Act of 1964 (Title VI) - Title VI prohibits racial discrimination in federally funded programs. This extends to admissions, financial aid, and virtually every aspect of the federally assisted programs in which private schools are involved. Codified at 42 U.S.C. § 2000d.

Title VII, Civil Rights Act of 1964 (Title VII) - Title VII prohibits discrimination in employment based upon race, color, sex, national origin, or religion. It applies to any employer having 15 or more employees. Under Title VII, where an employer intentionally discriminates, employees may obtain money damages unless the claim is for race discrimination. For those claims, monetary relief is available under 42 U.S.C. § 1981.

Title IX - Enacted as part of the Education Amendments of 1972, Title IX prohibits sexual discrimination in any private school program or activity receiving federal financial assistance. Codified at 20 U.S.C. § 1981, *et seq.*

U.S. Equal Employment Opportunity Commission (EEOC) - The EEOC is the government entity that is empowered to enforce Title VII (see above) through investigation and/or lawsuits. Private individuals alleging discrimination must pursue administrative remedies within the EEOC before they are allowed to file suit under Title VII.

Vacate - The act of annulling the judgment of a court either by an appellate court or by the court itself. The Supreme Court generally will vacate a lower court's judgment without deciding the case itself, and remand the case to the lower court for further consideration in light of some recent controlling decision.

Void-for-Vagueness Doctrine - A judicial doctrine based on the Fourteenth Amendment's Due Process Clause. In order for a law that regulates speech, or any criminal statute, to pass muster under the doctrine, the law must make clear what actions are prohibited or made criminal. Under the principles of the Due Process Clause, people of average intelligence should not have to guess at the meaning of a law.

Writ of Certiorari - The device used by the Supreme Court to transfer cases from the appellate court's docket to its own. Since the Supreme Court's appellate jurisdiction is largely discretionary, it need only issue such a writ when it desires to rule in the case.

INDEX